Handbook of Families and Aging

Handbook of Families and Aging

Second Edition

Rosemary Blieszner and
Victoria Hilkevitch Bedford, Editors

PRAEGER

AN IMPRINT OF ABC-CLIO, LLC
Santa Barbara, California • Denver, Colorado • Oxford, England

Library of Congress Cataloging-in-Publication Data

Handbook of families and aging / Rosemary Blieszner and Victoria Hilkevitch Bedford,
editors.—2nd ed.
　　　p. cm.
　　Rev. ed. of: Handbook of aging and the family. 1995.
　　Includes index.
　　ISBN 978-0-313-38173-7 (hbk. : alk. paper) — ISBN 978-1-4408-2863-8 (pbk.) —
ISBN 978-0-313-38174-4 (ebook)　1. Aging.　2. Older people—Family relationships.
I. Blieszner, Rosemary.　II. Bedford, Victoria Hilkevitch.　III. Handbook of aging
and the family.
　　HQ1061.H3353　2012
　　305.26—dc23　　　2012022315

ISBN: 978-0-313-38173-7 (hardcover)
ISBN: 978-1-4408-2863-8 (paperback)
EISBN: 978-0-313-38174-4

16　15　14　13　12　　1　2　3　4　5

This book is also available on the World Wide Web as an eBook.
Visit www.abc-clio.com for details.

Praeger
An Imprint of ABC-CLIO, LLC

ABC-CLIO, LLC
130 Cremona Drive, P.O. Box 1911
Santa Barbara, California 93116-1911

This book is printed on acid-free paper ∞

Manufactured in the United States of America

Contents

PART V.   FUTURE RESEARCH

interest in our work and their eagerness to share both their own interpretations of the research and their personal experiences with aging family issues.

We are grateful for the support of our professional endeavors from the Department of Human Development and the Center for Gerontology at Virginia Tech. Blieszner's graduate assistant, Danielle Skurka, provided cheerful help with background research. We acknowledge additional resources from the University of Indianapolis through the awarding of emerita status to Bedford.

Finally, we appreciate our family and friends so much for their encouragement and support. Thank you, dear ones, for your patience and understanding throughout the production process.

—Rosemary Blieszner
Blacksburg, Virginia

—Victoria Hilkevitch Bedford
Bloomington, Indiana

Part I

Background

1

The Family Context of Aging

Rosemary Blieszner and Victoria Hilkevitch Bedford

Lillian Troll began the foreword to the first edition of the *Handbook* by stating, "this handbook heralds the coming-of-age of our field of families and aging. Although we remain rooted in our parent fields of gerontology . . . and family studies . . . we are now declaring our maturity" (1995, p. xi). Indeed, family gerontology has flourished since then, as evidenced by the publication of many hundreds of refereed journal articles on a wide range of family-related topics (see Allen, Blieszner, & Roberto, 2000, for relevant journals and the prevalence of the most common topics), two decade reviews in *Journal of Marriage and Family* (Allen et al., 2000; Silverstein & Giarrusso, 2010), review chapters in *Handbook of Aging and the Social Sciences* (Binstock & George, 2001, 2006, 2011) and other edited volumes (e.g., Cavanaugh & Cavanaugh, 2010; Whitbourne & Sliwinski, 2012), textbooks (Connidis, 2001, 2010; Stoller & Gibson, 1997, 2000; Walker, Manoogian-O'Dell, McGraw, & White, 2001), and scholarly books on specialized topics such as mothers and daughters (Fingerman, 2001), aunts and uncles (Milardo, 2010), grandparents (Szinovacz, 1998), family caregiving (Qualls & Zarit, 2009; Szinovacz & Davey, 2008), and relationships over the life span (Lang & Fingerman, 2004).

Thus, this revision of the original *Handbook* is long overdue and we are pleased to offer a fresh compilation of research reviews and suggestions for future work.

AN INCLUSIVE DEFINITION OF FAMILY
FOR FAMILY GERONTOLOGY RESEARCH

While a political battle rages over what constitutes a legitimate family for the sake of identifying family rights and benefits, scholars are challenged to be clear about those whom they are studying in order to build an accurate and comprehensive body of knowledge in family gerontology. Early in the emergence of family gerontology as a field, we assessed the limitations of common demographic and sociological definitions of family (Bedford & Blieszner, 1997), particularly in light of the dual consideration of family and aging we had highlighted in the first edition of the *Handbook*. In our introductory chapter, we argued for the importance of recognizing that the study of family and aging encompasses viewing old adults both as subjects and objects; that is, as persons *with* various kinds of family relationships and *as* family members of those in other generations (Blieszner & Bedford, 1995).

Thus, we called for new research on both dimensions of family and aging. In keeping with this perspective, we offered an inclusive perspective that accommodated both aspects of the family context of aging by defining *family* as "a set of relationships determined by biology, adoption, marriage, and, in some societies, social designation and existing even in the absence of contact or affective involvement, and, in some cases, even after the death of certain members" (Bedford & Blieszner, 1997, p. 526). In an effort to promote as comprehensive a perspective as possible on family gerontology, we still recommend a definition that directly includes old family members and allows for the influence of distal and even deceased relatives on one's life and well-being.

For the most part, investigators have focused most attention on relationships determined by biological and legal ties, although some work on more informal ties is emerging (Fingerman, 2004, 2009; Fingerman, Brown, & Blieszner, 2011; Voorpostel, chapter 10 this volume). The diversity of family structures that exists in the 21st century, highlighted in all the chapters in this volume, calls for broadening the research focus in family gerontology to study of the less common as well as more common family types and dynamics. We adjusted the wording in the *Handbook* title from *the Family* to *Families* in the new edition to recognize this diversity.

IMPORTANT TRENDS INFLUENCING FAMILY GERONTOLOGY RESEARCH

Most people around the world grow up and grow old in the context of family life, a pattern that has not changed over the centuries, even if a wider range of people is embraced in many family constellations than ever before. Looking at some of the most important family ties, in 2010 in the United States, 95% of women and 96% of men over 65 years of age were or had been married (Greenberg, 2011), and in 2000, 86% of women and 84% of men aged 45 or older had at least one biological child (Halle, 2002). Thus, we consider the study of close relationships of middle-aged and old adults as central to the task of understanding their experiences of aging.

We believe it is important to examine the influence of individual development (both age-related social location and personal maturity) on relationships as well as the influence of relationships (both structural features and interaction dynamics) on personal development (Blieszner, 2006). The current state of family gerontology is probably stronger in examination of the former, the effects of individual characteristics on relationship outcomes (e.g., perceived quality of, satisfaction with, or stability of a relationship), than the latter, the effects of relationships on personal development. Although cross-sectional designs can provide insight into the former, longitudinal data are essential for investigating the latter, particularly for exploring the impact of romantic, parent-child, grandparent-grandchild, or sibling bonds on social, emotional, and even physical dimensions of aging.

At the same time, we acknowledge both that relationships themselves and the family constellations composed of those relationships develop and change over a given lifetime and over historical time. New statistical procedures provide powerful methods of examining change over time, and emerging techniques permit combining data collected on different persons comprising different age groups (Hofer & Piccinin, 2010). These procedures offer promise for achieving a better understanding of the effects of both personal and historical change. Although some national longitudinal data sets contain selected variables pertaining to limited aspects of family and aging, longitudinal studies that intentionally encompass comprehensive sets of family-related variables (e.g., detailed information on both family structures and family interaction processes) are needed, as well as historical data mining to evaluate the extent to which family values and interaction patterns have changed or remain stable across cohorts of old adults.

The influence of historical demographic trends on the field of family gerontology is nowhere more evident than in the press of Baby Boomers on society. The leading edge of this demographic bulge began turning 65 in 2011, bringing aging issues to the forefront of public awareness. Whether Baby Boomers are redefining aging and the family may be less important than the fact that they are pointing to key legal and policy issues that demand attention and intervention from family gerontologists. When Dr. Troll stated in 1995 that the field had come of age, she was referencing research projects and reports of findings. Today, the movement of Baby Boomers toward old age projects individual and family aging issues into the broader public consciousness more forcefully than ever. Family gerontologists are challenged to respond not only by conducting theory-driven investigations bolstered by strong analytic approaches, but also to interpret their findings for gerontology practitioners in many lines of work as well as for policymakers (see examples of applying research results to the design of interventions related to friendship in Adams & Blieszner, 1993). The recent emphasis on translational research evidences this focus on making sure research findings can be used for improving clinical and community practice (e.g., Pillemer, Suitor, & Wethington, 2003). To be as effective as possible, interventions must be

Acknowledgments

This handbook could not have been written if 23 years ago we had not met each other at a professional meeting, and after a long walk that included sharing our research passions and professional goals, began the collaboration that led to the first edition. The success of that volume and the enormous growth of family gerontology since then resulted in many requests for the original handbook to be updated. We have our publisher to thank, especially our editor Debora Carvalko, for encouraging us to accept the challenge of preparing a new edition and for patiently waiting through the lengthy writing and editing process.

No one deserves more appreciation than our heroic authors. They willingly considered our many comments and graciously accepted our requests for multiple revisions. Some wrote in their areas of expertise; others agreed to stretch their talents into new domains. All were prepared to think about the future of the field and help shape it in crafting their recommendations. We thank them for their generosity in applying their expertise and dedication to this enterprise.

We remain eternally grateful to our mentors, Lillian Troll and the late Paul Baltes, our original teachers who introduced us to this field so many years ago. Their writings and friendship have inspired and sustained us throughout our careers, and even, in the case of Paul, after his death.

When it comes to inspiration and sustenance, we are also indebted to our colleagues in the field of family gerontology. Their research and camaraderie make this volume feel in some ways like a joint enterprise across an extended kinship.

Our students, too, have contributed to the new edition of the *Handbook* by participating actively in family gerontology seminars, challenging us to clarify our understanding of the research literature, critiquing the first edition, and offering suggestions for new topics in this one. We appreciate their grounded in relevant theory and in solid findings resulting from use of appropriate research methods.

CATALYZING FAMILY GERONTOLOGY RESEARCH

An important purpose in preparing this new edition of the *Handbook* at this time extends beyond the goal of acknowledging progress in family gerontology research since 1995. Indeed, our intent is to build upon and extend the ensuing knowledge base by triggering creative and innovative work in family gerontology. Toward that end, we asked authors to highlight key developments in their respective domains and point to new research directions as well. Readers will find implications for new research topics and methods within chapters 2 to 22; many of these implications are integrated and synthesized into a useful overview of important emerging research themes in chapter 23.

The chapter topics in this revised edition of the *Handbook* are organized in the same sections as before, because the logic associated with that organization has not changed. The chapters focus on both standard, familiar family gerontology topics and new ones that have gained prominence already or are emerging as important research foci. The authors of the following chapters discuss both traditional and new family structures in their literature reviews, and often they embed their analyses of the literature in national and global trends and perspectives. The introductory chapters on theory and methods set the stage for further elaboration and critique within the content areas of the chapters that follow. All the authors identify and critique gaps in the research findings that warrant filling by further investigation. They also offer ideas for developing or improving interventions, in both professional practice and social policy arenas.

Part I: Background provides foundational essays on demographic trends, theoretical directions, and innovative research methods for the field of family gerontology. Part II: Family Relationships covers all of the most salient family ties for old adults and their relatives at both the peer level (marital and partner, sibling, and stepfamily relationships) and the intergenerational level (parent-child, grandparent-grandchild, and stepfamily relationships). This section also introduces an important type of relationship that is gaining more research attention, namely, discretionary and fictive kin. Part III: Contexts of Family Life reprises and updates research about ethnic and cultural, rural location, policy, and legal influences on late-life families. In addition, this section introduces important new contexts for research on family gerontology—the effects of intersecting social locations (e.g., gender, race, class; elder abuse; and new technologies). The chapters in Part IV: Turning Points in Family Life include classic topics previously addressed (retirement, illness and caregiving, and grief and bereavement) and we have also added specific consideration of divorce along with widowhood. Part V: Future Research presents the chapter on emerging research themes for family gerontology.

Without further ado, we invite readers to taste the fruits of the labor of the outstanding authors who have contributed to the revised *Handbook* and to experience the exciting new developments in the field of family gerontology they have put forth. Although the authors have highlighted the complexities that family life in the 21st century have introduced to adults in middle and old age and to their families, pointing to these complexities can spark a new wave of research designed to explore and comprehend the near-term and long-term effects of those complexities. In turn, that new wave of research could result in more effective interventions designed for these families, inform useful and effective social policies for a society with daunting challenges on the horizon, and inform and enrich the personal journeys of individuals as they traverse the later years of the life course.

REFERENCES

Adams, R. G., & Blieszner, R. (1993). Resources for friendship intervention. *Journal of Sociology and Social Welfare, 4*, 159–175.

Allen, K. R., Blieszner, R., & Roberto, K. A. (2000). Families in the middle and later years: A review and critique of research in the 1990s. *Journal of Marriage and the Family, 62*, 911–926.

Bedford, V. H., & Blieszner, R. (1997). Personal relationships in later life families. In S. Duck (Ed.), *Handbook of personal relationships* (2nd ed., pp. 523–539). New York: Wiley.

Binstock, R. H., & George, L. K. (Eds.). (2001). *Handbook of aging and the social sciences* (5th ed.). San Diego, CA: Academic Press.

Binstock, R. H., & George, L. K. (Eds.). (2006). *Handbook of aging and the social sciences* (6th ed.). San Diego, CA: Academic Press.

Binstock, R. H., & George, L. K. (Eds.). (2011). *Handbook of aging and the social sciences* (7th ed.). San Diego, CA: Academic Press.

Blieszner, R. (2006). A lifetime of caring: Dimensions and dynamics in late-life close relationships. *Personal Relationships, 13*, 1–18.

Blieszner, R., & Bedford, V. H. (1995). The family context of aging: Trends and challenges. In R. Blieszner & V. H. Bedford (Eds.), *Handbook of aging and the family* (pp. 3–12). Westport, CT: Greenwood Press.

Cavanaugh, J. C., & Cavanaugh, C. K. (2010). *Aging in America*. Santa Barbara, CA: Praeger.

Connidis, I. G. (2001). *Family ties & aging*. Thousand Oaks, CA: Pine Forge Press.

Connidis, I. G. (2010). *Family ties & aging* (2nd ed.). Thousand Oaks, CA: Pine Forge Press.

Fingerman, K. L. (2001). *Aging mothers and their adult daughters; A study in mixed emotions*. New York: Springer Publishing Company.

Fingerman, K. L. (2004). The consequential stranger: Peripheral ties across the life span. In F. Lang & K. L. Fingerman (Eds.), *Growing together: Personal relationships across the life span* (pp. 183–209). New York: Cambridge University Press.

Fingerman, K. L. (2009). Consequential strangers and peripheral partners: The importance of unimportant relationships. *Journal of Family Theory Review, 1*, 69–82.

Fingerman, K. L., Brown, B. B., & Blieszner, R. (2011). Informal ties across the life span: Peers, consequential strangers, and people we encounter in daily life. In K. L. Fingerman, C. A. Berg, J. Smith, & T. C. Antonucci (Eds.), *Handbook of life-span development* (pp. 487–511). New York: Springer Publishing Company.

Greenberg, S. (2011). *A profile of older Americans: 2011.* Washington, DC: U.S. Department of Health and Human Development, Administration on Aging.

Halle, T. (2002). *Charting parenthood: A statistical portrait of fathers and mothers in America.* Washington, DC: Child Trends.

Hofer, S. M., & Piccinin, A. M. (2010). Toward an integrative science of life-span development and aging. *Journal of Gerontology: Psychological Sciences, 65B,* 269–278.

Lang, F. R., & Fingerman, K. L. (Eds.). (2004). *Growing together: Personal relationships across the life span.* New York: Cambridge University Press.

Milardo, R. M. (2010). *The forgotten kin: Aunts and uncles.* New York: Cambridge University Press.

Pillemer, K., Suitor, J. J., & Wethington, E. (2003). Integrating theory, basic research, and intervention: Two case studies from caregiving research. *The Gerontologist, 43* (Suppl. 1), 19–28.

Qualls, S. H., & Zarit, S. H. (2009). *Aging families and caregiving.* Hoboken, NJ: John Wiley & Sons.

Silverstein, M., & Giarrusso, R. (2010). Aging and family life: A decade review. *Journal of Marriage and Family, 72,* 1039–1058.

Stoller, E. P., & Gibson, R. C. (Eds.). (1997). *Worlds of difference: Inequality in the aging experience* (2nd ed.). Thousand Oaks, CA: Pine Forge Press.

Stoller, E. P., & Gibson, R. C. (Eds.). (2000). *Worlds of difference: Inequality in the aging experience* (3rd ed.). Thousand Oaks, CA: Pine Forge Press.

Szinovacz, M. E., (Ed.). (1998). *Handbook on grandparenthood.* Westport, CT: Greenwood Press.

Szinovacz, M. E., & Davey, A. (Eds.). (2008). *Caregiving contexts: Cultural, familial and societal implications.* New York: Springer Publishing Company.

Troll, L. E. (1995). Foreword. In R. Blieszner & V. H. Bedford (Eds.), *Handbook of aging and the family* (pp. xi–xx). Westport, CT: Greenwood Press.

Walker, A. J., Manoogian-O'Dell, M., McGraw, L., & White, D. L. (Eds.). (2001). *Families in later life: Connections and transitions.* Thousand Oaks, CA: Pine Forge Press.

Whitbourne, S. K., & Sliwinski, M. J. (Eds.). (2012). *The Wiley-Blackwell handbook of adulthood and aging.* Malden, MA: Wiley-Blackwell.

2

Demographic Trends and Later Life Families in the 21st Century

Emily M. Agree and Mary Elizabeth Hughes

In the decades surrounding the turn of 21st century, the social, economic, and political landscape of the United States was transformed by two powerful forces. First, population aging increased the number of older people relative to the number of younger people, raising fundamental questions about the nature of old age, the future of the U.S. economy, and the allocation of resources among generations. Second, changes in the way families are formed, maintained, and dissolved led to new and more varied family structures and relationships.

Population aging and changes in family life will shape the characteristics of the older population and their families through the first half of the 21st century. However, the way in which these changes unfolded means that much of their impact on the older population is still to come. A key tool for assessing this future impact is the concept of *cohort succession*. Demographers use the term *cohort* to refer to people born in the same year or range of years. At a point in time, a specific age group is composed of members of a particular birth cohort; over time, this cohort is replaced by the subsequent birth cohort. For example, in 2000, members of the age group 65 to 74 were born between 1926 and 1935; in 2010 this age group was born between 1936 and 1945. To the extent that successive cohorts have different characteristics (such as the percentage of cohort members with a college degree or the average number of children born to women in the cohort), cohort succession leads to changes in the characteristics of the older population. As members of younger birth cohorts enter old age and the oldest cohorts die out, the turnover process provides an opportunity for social change to occur (Ryder, 1965).

The implications of cohort succession for growth in the size of the older population have been emphasized, especially with respect to the large Baby Boomer cohorts. The potential consequences of the aging of the Baby Boomers for retirement security and health care have been of academic and policy concern for almost as long as the boomers have lived (e.g., Haber & Cohen, 1961; Lee & Skinner, 1999). Less appreciated is the extent to which the forces of cohort succession will lead to changes in the character of the older population and, in particular, to changes in family structures and relationships. Although all cohorts experienced the family changes of the late 20th century, the effects of these changes on the life courses of individuals differed by the age at which they were experienced. Members of the cohorts that currently constitute the older population experienced many of these changes in midlife or later, which meant that, in general, they were not directly affected, although they were indirectly affected by family change in younger cohorts. In contrast, these trends had a profound effect on the lives of people who are now middle-aged and younger. Men and women in these younger cohorts will carry the legacy of these experiences with them into old age, changing the profile of the older population.

As the chapters in this volume illustrate, families are critical to the well-being of older people. Thus, a clear understanding of the implications of family change is important for aging research, policy, and practice. In this chapter, we describe how family change will shape the profile of the older population in the coming decades. We begin by reviewing the demographic forces underlying population aging. We then outline the changes in family formation that began in the late 1960s, emphasizing how they led to differences in family behavior among 20th-century birth cohorts. Finally, we illustrate how these differences will lead to changes in the family profile of the older population. We conclude by discussing some of the potential implications of changing families for the well-being of the older population.

POPULATION AGING

Aging populations represent a new phase in human demographic history. Significant increases in the median age of national populations first became apparent in Western nations, especially in North America and western Europe, where population aging began in the 19th century. By the latter half of the 20th century, population aging had become widespread, and it is now a global phenomenon. Most nations are experiencing some degree of population aging, although the pace and timing varies across continents and cultures (Hayward & Zhang, 2001; Lutz, Sanderson, & Scherbov, 2008).

Population aging is often assumed to result from increases in longevity, but it can be caused by both declines in fertility and improvements in survival. In fact, reductions in fertility have been the most powerful engine of worldwide population aging in the past century. Declines in the number of children couples desire, combined with greater ability to control the timing and number of children born, led to dramatic reductions in fertility in the 20th century. Within a national population, reductions in births lower the share of the population in the younger ages and raise the share in the older ages, leading to increases in the population's median age and the share of the population that is old. Even when fertility has reached a low level, temporal booms or busts in childbearing can have a strong impact on the age structure of a population (Cornman & Kingson, 1996).

Figure 2.1 presents a set of population pyramids showing the age distribution of the U.S. population from the middle of the last century projected to the near future. The population history of the United States, especially childbearing patterns, is clearly revealed in these pyramids, as is the impact of these patterns on the age structure of the population through cohort succession. In 1960, the bulge of the baby boom, the sudden increase in the number of births that began in 1946 and lasted until 1964 (Hughes & O'Rand, 2004), is shown at the bottom of the pyramid. The baby boom resulted from a combination of higher birthrates, a broad age range of mothers having children at the same time because some of the older women delayed childbearing during World War II, and declines in childlessness. Other demographic events reflected in the 1960 pyramid include the decline in births during the Great Depression of the 1930s and, among males, residual mortality from World Wars I and II. By 1990, we see the full result of the baby boom as a bulge between the ages 26 to 44, with the small cohorts born during the Depression in the older age groups and the relatively small cohorts born in the 1970s in the younger age groups.

In 2010, the baby boom is in the age group 46 to 64 and poised to enter old age. The prospect of the Baby Boom cohort swelling the Medicare and Social Security beneficiary rolls has loomed large in the minds of policymakers as they speculate on the fiscal impact of the increasing size of the elderly population. The 2010 pyramid also shows the small cohorts born in the 1970s and the echo-boom, children of the Baby Boom cohort, advancing to middle age. The median age of the U.S. population is expected to rise to 39 by 2030, reflecting the passage of the Baby Boomers into and through the oldest ages. As the Baby Boom reaches the oldest ages and begins to shrink from old age mortality, the population will continue to age, but more slowly, as consistent, low birthrates yield smaller, more uniformly sized cohorts. The shape of the population pyramid will thus become more rectangular.

In the United States and many other nations, declines in mortality among the aged over the past half century have accelerated the effects of earlier fertility declines, aging the population both proportionately (increasing the share of the population that is old) and absolutely (increasing the size of the older population). These declines are part of dramatic improvements in survival that occurred since the beginning of the 20th century. Figure 2.2 shows life expectancy at birth and at age 65 in the United States from 1900 to the present. Around the turn of the 20th century, life expectancy at birth was estimated to be less than 50 years for both men and women; the average

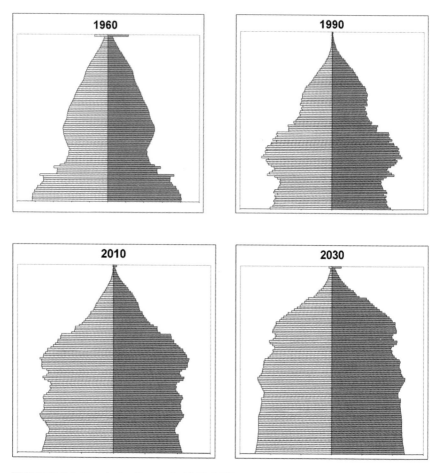

FIGURE 2.1 Population Pyramids 1960–2030

age at death in the population was 46 and 49 years, respectively. Those fortunate enough to survive to age 65 could expect to live another 11 to 12 years, dying on average at age 76. The large gap between these two expectations reflects the very high infant and child mortality of the time. Even though families were on average much larger than they are today, fewer babies could be expected to survive childhood. During the first half of the 20th century, child survival increased dramatically. Thus, by 1950, life expectancy at birth had increased to 65.6 years for men and 71.1 years for women, but later-life survival was relatively unchanged. At the mid-century point, however, we begin to see gains in life expectancy at age 65, whereas infant and child mortality improved more slowly. All else being equal, mortality declines among the aged increase the percentage of older people; thus, for the past 50 years or so improvements in longevity have combined with fewer births to age the population at a steady pace.

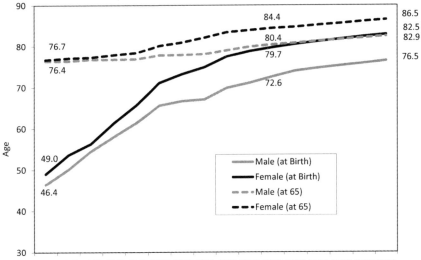

FIGURE 2.2 Changes in Life Expectancy

The median age of the U.S. population as a whole has been rising throughout the past century. Within the United States, however, the pace of aging is not consistent across groups. One notable difference is in the relative age of different racial and ethnic groups. Figure 2.3 shows the current estimates and anticipated changes in the median age of the main racial and ethnic groups in the United States.

The non-Hispanic white population is the oldest, with a median age in 2010 of 38 years, followed by the Asian population (median age 34). The black population and Hispanics (who may be of any race) are far younger at the present time, with median ages of 31 and 27, respectively. However, all of the minority groups are expected to age substantially in the next 40 years, whereas the white population plateaus at a median age of about 39 years. The Hispanic population, which has somewhat higher fertility, is expected to remain younger than other groups in the United States, but the Asian population is anticipated to exceed the non-Hispanic white population, reaching a median age of 41 by 2050. These differences occur at the same time that the relative size of minority groups in the United States is increasing.

As we have described in this section, large-scale demographic changes have made the United States an aging nation. As of 2008 almost one-third of the U.S. population was aged 50 or older and 13% was aged 65 or older. The United States is far from having the oldest population in the world—western and southern Europe are the oldest regions with more than 18% of their populations aged 65 and older, and the countries with the oldest populations are Japan, Germany, and Italy, with 20% of their populations 65 and older (United Nations, 2008).

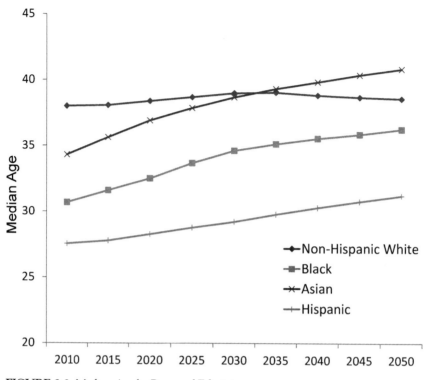

FIGURE 2.3 Median Age by Race and Ethnicity

CHANGING FAMILIES

The long-term demographic forces underlying population aging—lower fertility and improved longevity—also changed the structure of families and the timing of family events in individual lives. Families became smaller, but lengthening life spans increased the duration of family relationships, especially cross-generational relationships (Bengtson, Rosenthal, & Burton, 1990, 1996; Treas & Lawton, 1999). That is, children are more likely to grow up not only with surviving parents but with surviving grandparents and even great-grandparents. As adults, most have living parents and often living grandparents. Thus, Bengtson (2001) argued that intergenerational bonds may become a more important feature of family life than earlier, because the number of surviving generations has increased along with the number of survivors within each generation. At the same time, others have suggested that because older adults will have fewer children to provide support, the importance of same-age peers, especially spouses and siblings, will increase (Agree & Glaser, 2009).

Beginning in the late 1960s, American family life was further transformed by profound changes in the ways people formed, maintained, and dissolved families. These changes were caused by a set of broad social forces that emerged around this time, including the shift from a manufacturing to a service and information-based economy, a revolution in norms surrounding sexuality and gender roles, and an increasing emphasis on expressive individualism as a motivation for personal behavior (Cherlin, 2010). The transformation in family life was thus intertwined with other changes in individuals' lives, such as increases in educational levels, in the economic returns to education, and in women working outside the home (Hughes & O'Rand, 2004).

These changes in family life have been well documented (see, for example, Casper & Bianchi, 2002; Cherlin, 2010). A large research literature considers their causes and consequences, but most of this work is devoted to family experiences early in the life course; we know much less about the implications of family change for persons in midlife and old age. This imbalance is not surprising, because the cohorts at the forefront of family change are only now approaching old age. Given the importance of family relationships to the well-being of older people, considering the potential impact of family change as these cohorts age is of growing importance.

The most central and persistent family relationships in later life are with spouses and with children. They are more likely to coreside and are the primary informal caregivers to elders with disabilities. The most significant transformations in family behavior can thus be seen by comparing marriage, divorce, and childbearing among American women in successive 10-year birth cohorts. The first cohort was born at the turn of the 20th century and the last in the late 1960s and early 1970s (see Table 2.1).

Figure 2.4 shows the percentage of women in each birth cohort who had married by a specific age. For example, the first point on the top line indicates that half the women in the Depression Kids cohort (born between 1926 and 1935) were married by age 20. The timing of marriage varied somewhat among the cohorts born before World War II, with the earliest cohort (Young Progressives) marrying latest and the Depression Kids marrying the earliest. Overall, however, more than 90% of women in these cohorts eventually married. In contrast, women born after World War II delayed marriage, with each

TABLE 2.1 Seven U.S. Birth Cohorts

Cohort name	Birth years
Young Progressives	1906–1915
Jazz Age Babies	1916–1925
Depression Kids	1926–1935
War Babies	1936–1945
Early Boomers	1946–1955
Late Boomers	1956–1965
Generation X	1966–1975

successive cohort marrying later. Among Late Boomers and Generation X, only about two-thirds of women (72% and 69%, respectively) had ever married by age 30, compared with 85% or more of earlier cohorts. Unless the pace at which women in these cohorts marry increases dramatically, by old age a higher percentage of them will have never married compared to cohorts born earlier in the 20th century.

One of the most dramatic changes in American family life has been the rapid increase in the incidence of divorce. The magnitude of its rise can be seen in Figure 2.5, which shows the percentages of women in each cohort who had ever divorced by a specific age. Among women in the Young Progressive cohort, less than 10% had divorced by age 35 and less than 15% by age 50. Divorce is modestly higher in the subsequent two cohorts (Jazz Age Babies and Depression Kids) but rises sharply for the cohorts born during and after World War II. Among Early Boomer women, 24% had divorced by age 35 and more than one-third (35%) by age 50; Late Boomer and Generation X women appear to be on the same trajectory, but with slightly lower percentages divorced at each age. This change in percentage reflects both slightly lower divorce rates and lower percentages marrying. Annual trends show that the divorce revolution had run its course by the time this cohort came of age—divorce rates peaked around 1980 and have declined slightly since then (Cherlin, 1992). This decline in divorce rates is augmented by the fact that

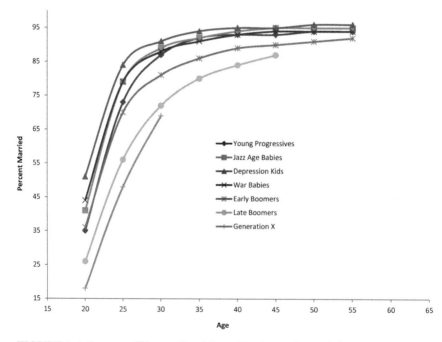

FIGURE 2.4 Percent of Women Ever Married by Age in Seven Cohorts

fewer women in this cohort have married (see Figure 2.4) meaning that fewer were at risk for divorce.

Figure 2.5 also shows that members of various cohorts experienced the divorce revolution at different ages. The revolution began with an abrupt spike in divorce rates in the late 1960s and early 1970s; rates continued to rise before leveling off in the early 1980s. These increases were caused by a constellation of social and economic changes that altered attitudes and beliefs about the institution of marriage. As a result, people became much more likely to end an unsatisfactory marriage than in the past (Cherlin, 1992). At the time of the initial spike, members of the War Babies cohort were in their 20s and 30s; because they had married relatively young (see Figure 2.4), they were in the prime ages for divorce. Their role in the spike can be seen in the relative steepness of their line in Figure 2.5 relative to those of cohorts born earlier; only 6% of War Baby women were divorced at age 25, whereas almost 30% were divorced by age 45. In contrast, the line for the Depression Kids cohort becomes steeper after age 35, because they were older during the divorce revolution, and the lines for both Early and Late Baby Boom cohorts are roughly parallel to that of the War Babies, because these cohorts came of age after the divorce revolution began. The age pattern of divorce in a cohort

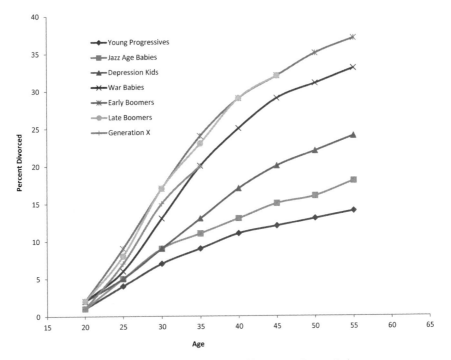

FIGURE 2.5 Percent of Women Ever Divorced by Age in Seven Cohorts

has implications for subsequent family behaviors in that cohort; for example, on average, members of the War Babies cohort had more years of life in which to remarry than the Depression Kids.

Increases in divorce have led some commentators to claim that the institution of marriage is being abandoned, but the relatively high level of remarriage in the United States suggests otherwise. Figure 2.6 shows, for example, that by age by age 35, 14% of women born in the late Baby Boom have been married at least twice. Figure 2.6 also shows that remarriage was not unknown to earlier cohorts; by age 35, 10% of the Jazz Age Babies had been married at least twice. However, most remarriages in earlier cohorts occurred after the death of a spouse, whereas later cohorts experience remarriage more often after divorce. The persistence of remarriage despite the rise in divorce is evidence that marriage remains a desirable state for most adults.

Not shown in these figures is another fundamental change in the organization of American families—the rise of nonmarital cohabitation as a common and accepted form of union. Cohabitation was rare among members of the cohorts born earlier in the century. It emerged among members of the Baby Boom cohorts, with successive cohorts cohabiting at higher rates. For example, among women born 1945 to 1949, only 7% had cohabited prior to age 25.

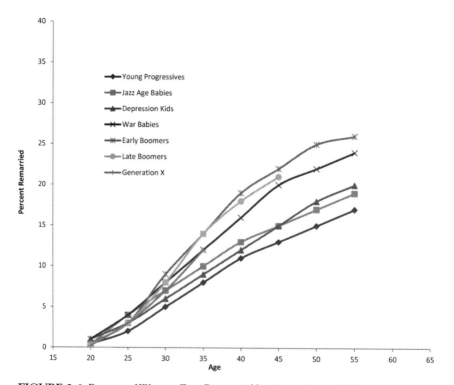

FIGURE 2.6 Percent of Women Ever Remarried by Age in Seven Cohorts

The corresponding figure for women born 1960 to 1964 was 37% (Bumpass & Sweet, 1989)—a dramatic difference among women born on average 15 years apart. High levels of cohabitation are one reason Late Boomer women (born 1956 to 1964) show such low levels of marriage in Figure 2.1; the percentage of these women who have formed any kind of union is much closer to the percentage married among earlier cohorts (Raley, 2000). This equivalence in unions suggests that when both legal marriage and cohabitation are taken into account, there is scant evidence that a commitment to intimate relationships is eroding; instead, the heterogeneity of these ties is growing.

Childbearing also has important implications for quality of life at older ages. Table 2.2 shows selected indicators of fertility for each of our seven cohorts. The Young Progressives and Jazz Age Babies bore, on average, 2.4 and 2.6 children respectively; by the time these cohorts were in their childbearing years, the United States had completed the fertility transition so these numbers are low by historical and contemporary global standards. Women in the Depression Kids cohort bore about 0.5 child more per woman on average than women in the cohorts immediately preceding and following them, reflecting the important role this cohort played in producing the Baby Boom. Further declines in fertility are apparent beginning with the Baby Boom cohorts. Early Boomer women had fewer than 2 children apiece on average, well below what demographers consider replacement level fertility. The Late Boomers and Generation X seem poised to have families about as small, even considering that the women of the Generation X cohort still have a few more years in which to bear children.

Family relations at older ages are vastly different for parents and childless elders, more so than among those with different numbers of children. Thus, cohort differences in childlessness could have important implications for the well-being of future elderly adults. Accordingly, Table 2.2 also shows levels of childlessness for each cohort. About one in five of the women in the Young Progressives cohort had no children and around one in five of the women in the Early Boomers cohort had no children. Levels of childlessness appear similar in the Late Boomers and Generation X cohorts, although the percentage of childless Generation X women may fall slightly as cohort members complete their childbearing. Thus, in contrast to the cohort differences in marriage we described, levels of childlessness among the oldest and youngest cohorts appear similar, whereas the cohort born in between stands out. Women in the Depression Kids cohort were far less likely to remain childless; only 9% had no children. Women in the War Babies cohort fall between the Depression Kids and the other cohorts.

As fertility has declined across cohorts, so has variation in completed family size. Among younger cohorts, those who have children rarely have more than two (O'Connell, 2002). However, this homogeneity in numbers of children masks change in the timing of childbearing. Along with increases in

TABLE 2.2 Fertility Measures for Women in Seven Cohorts

	Young Progressives^	Jazz Age Babies	Depression Kids	War Babies	Early Boomers	Late Boomers*	Generation X**
Mean Number of Children	2.4	2.6	3.1	2.5	2.0	1.9	1.9
Percent Childless	19	16	9	13	17	19	18
Percent with Four or More Children	22	26	37	24	12	11	12
Percent Teenage First Birth			23	29	19	18	19
Percent First Birth Age 30+			8	8	19	25	24
Percent Nonmarital First Birth			12	14	16	20	25

Source: Authors' calculations from the U.S. Census Integrated Public Use Microdata Series 1960 and 1970, and the Survey of Income and Program Participation, 1986, 1996, and 2008.

^Ever married women only.

*Some cohort members have not completed childbearing; cohort members were ages 43–52 when data were collected.

**Cohort members have not completed childbearing; cohort members were ages 33–42 when data were collected.

women's higher education, the women in the Baby Boom cohorts began their childbearing at later ages than their parents (Morgan, 1996). Teen births dropped, and first births past age 30 began a rise that continues today.

These changes in union formation and the context and circumstances of childbearing have led to new and more heterogeneous family structures and relationships. For example, delayed marriage and increases in divorce have led to large increases in the percentage of adults who live alone (Hughes & O'Rand, 2004). Divorce among couples with children and childbearing outside marriage have increased the percentage of single-parent, especially single-mother, families and the percentage of parents, especially fathers, living apart from their children (McLanahan, 2004). Remarriage and cohabitation among people with children have increased the prevalence of complex households and families (Casper & Bianchi, 2002; Ganong & Coleman, chapter 9 this volume). Changes in family structure have led to corresponding changes in family relationships, as family members adjust to new and different types of relations.

Thus, the families of cohorts born after World War II often look different from the families of cohorts born earlier in the century; in addition, they more often look different from each other. The notion of a family life cycle, a relatively predictable order of family events and statuses experienced by the majority of the population, appears less applicable to the cohorts born more recently than it may have been to the cohorts born earlier.

WAVES OF CHANGE

The changes in family formation described above occurred relatively rapidly. For example, divorce rates skyrocketed seemingly overnight in the late 1960s and continued to increase quickly until stabilizing in the 1980s (Cherlin, 1992). Similarly, nonmarital cohabitation, a rare behavior in the early 1970s, had become common by the early 1990s (Raley, 2000). The rapidity of these changes is also illustrated by the differences we showed in family patterns between cohorts of women born on average only 10 years apart.

Despite the swiftness of these changes, they affected mostly those at young ages and the process of cohort succession works slowly. These factors, which are central to understanding the changing demography of older families, have two implications. First, the composition of the older population will be changing for the foreseeable future as cohorts with differing family histories move into old age or die out. Second, family profiles within the older population will be heterogeneous for the foreseeable future, because at any point, the older population will be made up of cohorts with on average very different family histories. Furthermore, as discussed in the previous section, intracohort variability in family histories will be greater in cohorts born later, who are only now beginning to enter later life.

The ways in which cohort succession eventually leads to changes in the family patterns of older people will depend on two additional issues. First, some of the family changes we have discussed that will reduce the number of strong kin ties among older Americans may be offset by improvements in survival. For example, despite increases in the percentage of older people who have experienced divorce, increases in survival mean that those who stay married can expect to share more years with their spouses, so the percentage of older adults who are widows will decline. Improvements in survival also mean that same-aged peers, such as siblings and friends, will be more likely to accompany each other into old age. Second, how family behavior will continue to unfold among the cohorts who are just entering old age (the Early Boomers) or are middle-aged (the Late Boomers) is unknown (Hughes & Waite, 2007). Most likely, these cohorts will continue the trajectories of family behavior that they established at younger ages, which would widen the gaps between their behavior and the behavior of the cohorts preceding them. For example, cohabitation is typically rare among older people, although rates are rising, particularly as an alternative to remarriage (Brown, Lee, & Bulanda, 2006). However, the current older population nearly all came of age when cohabitation was rarer and more stigmatized than it was when the Baby Boom cohorts were forming families. Thus, aging boomers will likely cohabit more than current elderly people do, because cohabitation is part of their established repertoire of family behaviors. Family-related behavior among future older adults is an important uncertainty and an important area for research.

Although the cohorts on the forefront of family changes are only beginning to enter old age, the impact of cohort succession on the family profiles of the older population is visible, if still relatively modest. Table 2.3 shows selected family characteristics of women in the older population, broadly defined as ages 55 and over, in 1998 and 2008. For both years, we show figures for the older female population as a whole and for 10-year age groups, which correspond to the cohorts defined in the preceding section. The figures in this table were estimated from a different national survey (the Health and Retirement Study) than in the previous section (Survey of Income and Program Participation). Differences in study design and sampling error can lead to disparities in point estimates, but our tables show nearly identical patterns in cohort behaviors.

Comparing the older female population as a whole between 1998 and 2008 shows the overall change in family characteristics over the 10-year period. Comparing the characteristics of the same age group in 1998 and 2008 shows how cohort succession changed the family profile of that age group over the 10-year period and the extent to which cohort succession contributed to the overall change.

The first several rows of Table 2.3 focus on marriage. Like the measures in the previous section, these indicators represent the accumulated marital his-

TABLE 2.3 Family Characteristics of the Female Older Population in the United States by Age and Cohort, 1998 and 2008

	1998					2008				
Age	55+	53–62	63–72	73–82	83–92	55+	53–62	63–72	73–82	83–92
Cohort		War Babies	Depression Kids	Jazz Age Babies	Young Progressives		Early Boomers	War Babies	Depression Kids	Jazz Age Babies
		(1936–45)	(1926–35)	(1916–25)	(1906–15)		(1946–55)	(1936–45)	(1926–35)	(1916–25)
Ever Married	96.8%	96.0%	97.0%	97.1%	95.8%	96.1%	95.0%	96.1%	97.2%	98.1%
Ever Divorced*	22.9	39.8	26.0	8.4	2.5	35.8	46.7	40.0	26.8	8.0
Married 2+ times	25.3	29.5	24.5	22.3	23.9	29.3	33.5	29.5	25.7	21.3
Current Marital Status										
Married	51.6	67.7	58.4	40.0	15.3	52.6	65.4	57.7	41.3	18.9
Divorced	11.7	18.7	12.5	6.2	3.6	16.3	21.2	18.1	12.0	5.5
Widowed	33.5	9.9	26.2	50.9	76.8	27.2	8.7	20.6	43.8	73.6
Never Married	3.1	3.7	2.9	2.9	4.4	3.7	4.7	3.6	3.0	2.1
Childless	8.3	6.0	6.6	10.5	16.3	7.1	8.1	6.1	6.3	8.6
Mean # Living Children	3.1	3.2	3.4	2.8	2.4	3.0	2.7	3.2	3.4	2.9
Have Living Parents	18.7	48.7	14.3	1.6	0.0	21.8	45.6	17.0	1.9	0.1
Mean # Living Siblings	2.4	3.0	2.6	2.0	1.4	2.6	3.2	2.7	2.1	1.4

* Percent of ever-married women

Source: Authors' calculations from the Health and Retirement Study, 1998 and 2008.

tory of these cohorts. As shown in the first row of the table, the percentage of the population age 55 and over that had ever married changed little between 1998 and 2008. However, the observed change does correspond to almost a 25% increase in the percentage never married (from 3.2% to 3.9%). Examining changes within age groups, we see a decline between 1998 and 2008 in the percentage ever married in the youngest age group (from 96% to 94%) as the War Babies cohort was replaced by the Early Boomers, who had somewhat lower lifetime marriage rates (see Figure 2.4). The entry of the Late Boomers into the 53 to 62 age group will likely bring a larger change, because the Late Boomers have thus far married at even lower rates than the Early Boomers. As these cohorts with lower lifetime percentages married fill the ranks of the older population, the percentage ever married in the older population as a whole will continue to decrease. At least some of the lower marriage rates in these cohorts are accounted for by higher likelihoods of cohabitation. Thus, the percentage of older people who have ever been in a union may be more similar to earlier cohorts, but the types of unions will be more heterogeneous. The second row shows a large increase between 1998 and 2008 in the percentage of the population over age 55 that had ever divorced (from 22.9% to 35.8%). Examination of the percentages by age group in each year shows clearly that the increase is due to the aging out of the relatively low-divorce Young Progressives and the aging in of the high-divorce Late Boomers. Recall from Figure 2.5 that the lifetime likelihood of divorce increased gradually from the Young Progressives cohort to the Depression Kids cohort and then increased sharply in the War Babies cohort, who along with the Early Boomers, were in the prime ages to have participated in the divorce revolution of the 1960s and 1970s. This trend is visible in the figures for 1998 in the large difference in percent ever-divorced between the 53 to 62 and 63 to 72 age groups (39.8% versus 26.0%). The increase in lifetime divorce was sustained among Late Boomers, which is apparent in the figures for the 53 to 62 age group in 2008 (46.7%). The percentage of older people who have ever been divorced will continue to increase as the Late Boomers and Generation X, who seem poised to match the high rates of divorce among War Babies and Late Boomers, enter old age. We see a similar pattern for the percentage of older people married more than once, although, consistent with Figure 2.6, the overall difference is not as large.

Finally, we present the distribution of marital status in each year. The percentage currently married in the 55+ population increased slightly between 1998 and 2008 (from 51.6% to 52.6%). However, examining changes in the percentage married by age group reveals countervailing trends: increases in the percentage married among the oldest two age groups and decreases in the youngest two age groups. This pattern reflects differences across age groups in the relative impacts of divorce and widowhood. Between 1998 and 2008, the percentage divorced increased in all age groups and the percentage widowed declined. In the two older age groups, declines in widowhood were larger than increases in divorce, whereas in the younger age groups, the reverse was true. This pattern illustrates that overall levels of marriage in the older population are being generated by changes in two countervailing phenomena—the younger cohorts come to old age with slightly lower marriage rates, but greater spousal survival means that widowhood is occurring later.

These data demonstrate how the characteristics of the older population will change due to cohort succession and, in particular, ways in which the older population is an amalgam of cohorts with very different family histories. They also illustrate the capacity of increasing longevity to offset some of the family changes, at least at the population level. However, uncertainty surrounding the family behavior of the Early and Late Baby Boomers and Generation X cohorts as they age means that the picture may look somewhat different than it does now. Cohorts that enter old age with more marital transitions behind them may be more likely to divorce or remarry even at older ages.

The next pair of rows in Table 2.3 focuses on childbearing. As subsequent chapters will show in detail, children have been and remain the linchpin of family support systems in aging families, so cohort differences in childbearing may have important implications for the well-being of older people (Agree & Glaser, 2009). The pattern in Table 2.3 at first appears somewhat contradictory with respect to the fertility trends we described in the previous section: the percentage of childless women declined between 1998 and 2008, but the average number of living children is about the same.

This seeming anomaly is clarified by looking at the cohort composition of the older population in 1998 and 2008. In 1998, the two oldest age groups were filled by members of cohorts born in the first two decades of the 20th century, who had relatively high levels of childlessness, whereas the two younger age slots were filled by members of the Depression Kids and War Babies cohorts, who had historically low levels of childlessness—and the lowest levels of childlessness among cohorts born in the 20th century. In fact, these cohorts produced the baby boom. By 2008, the high-childlessness Young Progressives have disappeared and the Early Boomers who entered old age have levels of childlessness between the Depression Kids and the Young Progressives. Most of today's older population is composed of cohorts who are advantaged in one very specific respect—a wealth of children. However, as the boomer and Generation X cohorts enter the ranks of the older population, the average number of children among older people will decline and childlessness will increase.

As illustrated in Table 2.2, these differences in childbearing are large in magnitude. Moreover, Table 2.2 also shows the increased variation in the circumstances of childbearing in these cohorts. More of the younger cohorts will have had their children later in life and more will have had them out of wedlock—and may or may not have married the father. Thus, changes in fertility have implications for family ties and obligations far beyond the sheer existence of children as a potential source of help. A final lesson from these childbearing figures is that old-age policy will be trying to hit a moving target. The circumstances of the older population will be changing and increasingly variable, making the formation of policies and programs much more difficult.

Thus far, we have examined cohort differences in family formation, which translate into differences in unions and parenthood over the life course and into old age. However, the same trends that we described above will affect other aspects of older people's families. For example, the availability of older family members, especially parents, has been rising in recent years (see Sechrist et al., chapter 7 in this volume, for a discussion of parent-child relationships). Increased longevity, of course, contributes to the survival of these older relatives, just as it has for spouses and partners. Table 2.3 shows that in 1998, 18.7% of those 55 and older had one or more living parents, compared to about 21.83% in 2008. The loss of parents is particularly rapid at older ages, however, and among the oldest-old in both years the percentage with living parents is virtually zero.

Family change and increased survival have also affected configurations of siblings among older people. The average number of living siblings among the older population rose somewhat between 1998 and 2008. Most of the trends we see for siblings in Table 2.3 are driven by increasing longevity, making it more likely siblings will grow old together. However, the high fertility of the cohorts that produced the baby boom endowed members of the Baby Boom cohorts with more siblings than earlier cohorts. Thus, the youngest age group in 2008 has, on average, more living siblings (3.2) than the same age group in 1998 (3.0) because in 2008 the Early Boomers had moved into this age group. The full impact of the Baby Boom cohorts' larger sibships will only be seen when the Late Boomers enter old age (see Bedford & Avioli, chapter 6 in this volume, for a discussion of sibling relationships).

CONCLUSIONS

Large-scale demographic transformations often seem removed from the microcosm of the family, but reductions in fertility and increasing longevity are interwoven with family change. The family is the building block of population change, and future population dynamics will reflect growing variation in the type and timing of family events in individuals' lives. The aging of populations is a global phenomenon, an inevitable result of declining fertility and advancing life expectancy. Demographic trends both reflect and also influence the structure of late-life families. More precisely, the number and type of family relationships that result from population aging, increased diversity, and the successive progression of new cohorts through complex family trajectories created by increasing levels of divorce and remarriage creates a more varied older population with increasingly complex sets of family ties.

The declines in infant and child mortality that resulted from the conquest of infectious disease during and after World War II should have increased the number of surviving children and thus the amount of time spent in childrearing, but declines in fertility and shortened birth intervals had a countervailing effect on the time spent in parenting. At the same time, as years with small numbers of children have declined, increased life expectancy at older ages has led to more years of adult life spent as a son or daughter. In the past, shorter life expectancy meant that the number of years spent in multigenerational families was limited, as many older parents could expect to live a limited amount of time after becoming grandparents (Ruggles, 1987). By the late 20th century, Watkins, Menken, and Bongaarts (1987) estimated that "years with parents over 65 exceeded years with children under 18" (p. 352) These years are not necessarily spent in caretaking, however, because the improved health of the older population, and delayed onset of disability means that older parents and grandparents spend more time enjoying their family, rather than depending on them for help (Agree & Glaser, 2009; see also Pruchno & Gitlin, chapter 21 in this volume, for a discussion of family caregiving).

Demographic change, as discussed above, has changed the membership of families by altering the numbers and kinds of kin both within and across generations. In addition, changes in the timing of demographic events across the life course have led to the development of new family structures. By far the greatest change to affect later-life families is the transformation in marital patterns over the past 50 years. As mortality is pushed back to ever-older ages, new cohorts have a choice between longer marriages, later marriages, or multiple marriages and partnerships over an increasingly long lifetime. At all ages, more widespread acceptance and prevalence of cohabitation as an alternative to marriage, multiple partner childbearing, rising rates of divorce, and patterns of remarriage and stepparenting have radically altered the web of family relationships in which individuals are embedded. Older adults can be expected to spend more years of life not partnered (Sassler, 2010; see also Carr & Pudrovska, chapter 20 in this volume) and the benefits of remarrying later in life, both financial and psychological, also tend to be fewer than in first marriages (Carr, 2004; Hughes & Waite, 2009).

These changes have played out differently across cohorts, in a process dubbed *cohort succession* by demographers. The effect of these waves of change on the characteristics of the older population is of a gradual transition from one dominant or normative pattern of family life to another. In the past decade, elderly adults have been characterized by the beneficial availability of large numbers of children, as well as a greater number of years in long-term marriages, as spouses survive to old age together. Today, we are just beginning to see the effects of the divorce revolution, increases in serial partnerships, and lower fertility, as the large baby boom cohorts enter old age with fewer of the traditional sources of family support (spouses and biological children) available to them, but a greater number of relationships with ex-spouses, stepchildren, and surviving siblings.

Families will thus be in a continuous process of change, and the patterns that we observe at any given point in time will represent ongoing negotiation between generations within families, as cohorts that have different norms and histories move through the roles of child, parent, and grandparent. Matilda White Riley referred to this process as *structural lag* (Riley, 1994)—the ways that individuals adapt differently to changing societal norms and values depending upon the ages at which they encounter these changes. Those in older generations are experiencing new family forms as a result of the increases in cohabitation, divorce, and remarriage among their children and grandchildren. Americans today experience more family transitions than anywhere in the world (Cherlin, 2010). These trends have been difficult to document for the older population, because most surveys were designed to elicit information about more traditional family relationships. However, by examining the progression of changes among younger cohorts today, we can conclude that members of older generations are parents and grandparents to an increasingly mixed lineage of stepchildren and grandchildren, former children-in-law, biological and adopted kin, and biological grandchildren who are the offspring of different partners (see Hayslip & Page, chapter 8 in this volume, for a discussion of grandparent-grandchild relationships). These trends may have profound implications for late-life family support. Some studies have found that perceived obligations to stepparents for care were limited, relative to biological parents, but that greater duration and quality of the relationship with the stepparent could increase a stepchild's role in later life support (Ganong & Coleman, 2006, chapter 9 in this volume; Ganong, Coleman, & Rothrauff, 2009). As younger generations disrupt and reform unions earlier and more often, they will acquire more stepchildren with whom they will spend a greater number of years.

Of course, the structural aspects of the family that arise from demographic trends—such as number of generations and family size—cannot sufficiently capture the behavioral and qualitative aspects of relations among family members in an aging society undergoing such social evolutions in family life. The qualities that make families unique repositories of support in later life cannot be deduced solely from the prevalence and distribution of its members, but stem from the bonds between family members that give meaning to family groups. How these relationships are transformed by the growing diversity of family ties is not yet fully known. Parenthood is generally found to be beneficial to well-being in later life (see Umberson, Pudrovska, & Reczek, 2010, for a review), but the relationship of children to well-being is more nuanced than most studies suggest. For example, poor relationships with children can have more negative effects on mental health than childlessness (Koropeckyj-Cox, 2002).

Serial marriages also have important influences on well-being in later life. Multiple marriages and partnerships may dilute the ties between parents and children as well as within couples. For example, Pezzin, Pollak, and Schone (2009) showed that the presence of stepchildren is associated with lower levels of caregiving between spouses, compared with marriages that have joint biological children. Multiple marriages may have a negative effect on financial transfers to children as well as contact with and support from children, especially for fathers (Kalmijn, 2007; Shapiro & Remle, 2011). These (and other studies in a growing body of literature) postulate that an increasing number of obligatory relationships may diminish the investment in any given child or family member, and thus affect overall levels of support in later life, but the converse may be true as well—the availability of a larger number of kin relations who can step in with instrumental assistance in times of need. More research with better data is needed to elucidate the underlying motivations and mechanisms for these findings.

The interaction and exchange of resources among family members will undoubtedly be influenced by these waves of change as they play out in the older ages in years to come. Most of those who are aging now grew up with ideas about what their families would be like in old age and whom they would rely on in times of need—expectations that increasingly fail to resemble their own family lives. Many of the chapters in this volume delve more deeply into the availability of support and diversity of obligations within the heterogeneous families that have arisen because of the demographic changes we describe here.

The demographic patterns outlined in this chapter point to a number of important areas for new scholarship. We have always known that older persons as a group are heterogeneous. We all bring to later life a myriad of individual experiences that make us unique. In family terms, however, new cohorts will age with more diverse family structures and norms than ever before. This increased variability in family forms and relationships means that policies developed to address economic and long-term care needs in the future will need to accommodate widely different patterns of family support. For example, the rise of alternative forms of union, such as cohabitation, and serial partnerships have not been equally adopted across all socioeconomic strata. How this plethora of current and former relationships will affect well-being in later life among those with fewer personal financial resources (such as pensions) to draw upon is important both for policy and for research.

Among those who do opt for legal marriages, a greater number have been divorced and remarried and enter old age with biological and stepchildren. The extent to which this larger network of looser ties provides and coordinates support to older family members also needs to be better understood.

Research examining the implications of changing families will benefit from integration of qualitative research into motivations and values with quantitative research on the behavior of different types of kin. It will be particularly important to understand how family relationships can be supportive or demanding within different family configurations. We know that siblings share responsibilities for parent care differently, depending on the gender, distance, and economic circumstances of their brothers and sisters. How these negotiations are complicated by different combinations of stepchildren and biological children, as well as the presence of parents and stepparents in need of help, can be informed by research that studies the behavior as well as the motivations for helping.

Scholars of the family are well poised to make important contributions to our understanding of families and aging. We write at a time when some of the largest cohorts in recent history are beginning to enter old age. They bring with them the legacy of social changes that they themselves wrought in their younger years. As the boomers enter early old age, they will be relatively healthy and independent. Attention to the nature of their family lives now can contribute to developing policies and programs that anticipate the needs of these large cohorts so they can age well.

REFERENCES

Agree, E.M., Biddlecom, A.E., & Valente, T.W. (2005). Intergenerational exchanges with extended kin in Taiwan and the Philippines. *Population Studies, 59,* 181–195.

Agree, E.M., & Glaser, K. (2009), Demography of informal caregiving. In P. Uhlenberg (Ed.), *International handbook of population aging* (pp. 647–668). New York: Springer-Verlag.

Bengtson, V.L. (2001). Beyond the nuclear family: The increasing importance of multigenerational bonds. *Journal of Marriage and Family, 63,* 1.

Bengtson, V.L., Rosenthal, C.J., & Burton, L.M. (1990). Families and aging: Diversity and heterogeneity. In R.H. Binstock & L.K. George (Eds.), *Handbook of aging and the social sciences* (3rd ed., pp. 263–287). San Diego, CA: Academic Press.

Bengtson, V.L., Rosenthal, C.J., & Burton, L.M. (1996). Paradoxes of families and aging. In R.H. Binstock & L.K. George (Eds.), *Handbook of aging and the social sciences* (4th ed., pp. 254–282). San Diego, CA: Academic Press.

Brown S.L., Lee, G.R., & Bulanda, J.R. (2006). Cohabitation among older adults: A national portrait. *Journal of Gerontology: Social Sciences, 61B,* S71–S79.

Bumpass, L.L., & Sweet, J.A. (1989). National estimates of cohabitation. *Demography, 26,* 615–625.

Carr, D. (2004). The desire to date and remarry among older widows and widowers. *Journal of Marriage and Family, 66,* 1051–1068.

Casper, L.M., & Bianchi, S.M. (2002). *Continuity and change in the American family.* Thousand Oaks, CA: Sage Publications.

Cherlin A.J. (1992) *Marriage, divorce, remarriage.* Cambridge, MA: Harvard University Press.

Cherlin, A.J. (2010). Demographic trends in the United States: A review of research in the 2000s. *Journal of Marriage and Family, 72,* 403–419.

Cornman J., & Kingson, E. (1996). Trends, issues, perspectives, and values for the aging of the Baby Boom cohorts. *The Gerontologist, 36,*15–26.

Ganong, L.H., & Coleman, M. (2006). Responsibilities to stepparents acquired in later life: Relationship quality and acuity of needs. *Journal of Gerontology: Social Sciences, 61B,* S80–S88.

Ganong, L.H., Coleman, M., & Rothrauff, T. (2009). Patterns of assistance between adult children and their older parents: Resources, responsibilities, and remarriage. *Journal of Social and Personal Relationships, 26,* 161–178.

Haber, W., & Cohen, W.J. (1960). *Social Security: Programs, problems, and policies: Selected readings.* Homewood, IL: R. D. Irwin.

Hayward, M.D., & Zhang, Z. (2001). Demography of aging: A century of global change, 1950–2050. In R.H. Binstock & L.K. George (Eds.), *Handbook of aging and the social sciences* (5th ed., pp. 69–85). New York: Academic Press.

Health and Retirement Study. (2006). *Survey design.* Retrieved from http://hrsonline. isr.umich.edu/intro/sho_uinfo.php?hfyle=design&xtyp=2

Hughes, M.E., & O'Rand, A. M. (2004). *The lives and times of the Baby Boomers.* Washington, DC, and New York: Population Reference Bureau and Russell Sage Foundation.

Hughes, M.E., & Waite, L.J. (2007). The aging of the second demographic transition. In K.W. Schaie & P.R. Uhlenberg (Eds.), *Social structures: The impact of demographic changes on the well-being of older persons* (pp. 179–211). New York: Springer Publishing Company.

Hughes, M.E., & Waite, L.J. (2009). Marital biography and health at mid-life. *Journal of Health and Social Behavior, 50,* 344–358.

Kalmijn, M. (2007). Gender differences in the effects of divorce, widowhood and remarriage on intergenerational support: Does marriage protect fathers? *Social Forces, 85,* 1079–1104.

Koropeckyj-Cox, T. (2002). Beyond parental status: Psychological well-being in middle and old age. *Journal of Marriage and Family, 64,* 957–971.

LaPierre, T.A., & Hughes, M.E. (2009). Population aging in Canada and the United States. In P. Uhlenberg (Ed.), *International handbook of the demography of aging* (pp. 124–145). New York: Springer-Verlag.

Lee, R., & Skinner, J. (1999). Will aging Baby Boomers bust the federal budget? *The Journal of Economic Perspectives, 13,* 117–140.

Lutz, W., Sanderson, W., & Scherbov, S. (2008). The coming acceleration of global population ageing. *Nature, 451,* 716–719.

McLanahan, S.S. (2004). Diverging destinies: How children are faring under the second demographic transition. *Demography, 41*, 607–627.

Morgan, S.P. (1996). Characteristic features of modern American fertility. In J.B. Casterline, R.D. Lee, & K.A. Foote (Eds.), *Fertility in the United States: New patterns, new theories* (pp. 19–67). New York: Population Council.

O'Connell, M. (2002). Childbearing. In L.M. Casper & S.M. Bianchi (Eds.), *Continuity and change in the American family* (pp. 67–94). Thousand Oaks, CA: Sage Publications.

Pezzin, L.E., Pollak, R.A., & Schone, B.S. (2009). Long-term care of the disabled elderly: Do children increase caregiving by spouses? *Review of Economics of the Household, 7*, 323–339.

Raley, R.K. (2000). Recent trends and differentials in marriage and cohabitation: The United States. In L.J. Waite, C.A. Bachrach, M. Hindin, E. Thomson, & A. Thornton (Eds.), *The ties that bind: Perspectives on marriage and cohabitation* (pp. 19–39). New York: Aldine de Gruyter.

Raley, R.K. (2001). Increasing fertility in cohabiting unions: Evidence for the second demographic transition in the United States? *Demography, 38*, 59–66.

Riley, M.W., & Kahn, R. (1994). *Age and structural lag.* New York: John Wiley & Sons.

Ruggles, S. (1987). *Prolonged connections: The rise of the extended family in nineteenth-century England and America.* Madison: University of Wisconsin Press.

Ryder, N.B. (1965). The cohort as a concept in the study of social change. *American Sociological Review, 30*, 843–861.

Sassler, S. (2010). Partnering across the life course: Sex, relationships, and mate selection. *Journal of Marriage and Family, 72*, 557–575.

Shapiro, A., & Cooney, T.M. (2007). Divorce and intergenerational relations across the life course. In T.J. Owens & J.J. Suitor (Eds.), *Advances in the life course research; Volume 12: Interpersonal relations across the life course* (pp. 191–219). Oxford, UK: Elsevier.

Shapiro, A., & Remle, R.C. (2011). Generational jeopardy? Parents' marital transitions and the provision of financial transfers to adult children. *Journal of Gerontology: Social Science 66*, 99–108.

Silverstein, M., & Giarrusso, R. (2010). Aging and family life: A decade review. *Journal of Marriage and Family, 72*, 1039–1058.

Survey of Income and Program Participation. (2011). *Overview of the Survey of Income and Program Participation.* Retrieved from http://www.census.gov/sipp/overview.html

Treas, J., & Lawton, L. (1999). Family relations in adulthood. In M.B. Sussman, S.K. Steinmetz, & G.W. Peterson (Eds.), *Handbook of marriage and the family* (pp. 425–438). New York: Plenum Press.

Umberson, D.A., Pudrovska, T., & Reczek, C. (2010). Parenthood, childlessness, and well-being: A life course perspective. *Journal of Marriage and Family, 72*, 621–629.

United Nations. (2002). *World population ageing 1950–2050*, Department Of Economic And Social Affairs, Population Division, Report No. ST/ESA/SER.A/207. New York: United Nations.

United Nations. (2008). *United Nations demographic yearbook*, Dept. of Economic and Social Affairs, Statistical Office, United Nations, Report No. ST/ESA/STAT/SER.R/2008. New York: United Nations.

U.S. Census Bureau. (2009). *Annual estimates of the resident population* (NC-EST2008) Washington, DC: Government Printing Office.

Watkins, S. C., Menken, J. A., & Bongaarts, J. (1987). Demographic foundations of family change. *American Sociological Review, 52*, 346–358.

3

Theoretical Directions for Studying Family Ties and Aging

Ingrid Arnet Connidis

Some years ago, two Canadian researchers, Victor Marshall and Joseph Tindale (1978–79), called for a radical gerontology. In keeping with developments in sociology at the time, they argued that researchers must desert value-neutrality and recognize their biases; be advocates for the old; value the importance of historical context; consider the reciprocal influences of social, political, and economic factors, and of individual and collective action (and, hence, personal situations are not personally created); appreciate that social processes and interaction involve conflict, negotiation, and compromise; assume and explore variations within age groups; and view individuals as agents of change through their actions. Their rallying cry reflected well the concerns of many sociologists about the entrenched normative approach to studying social life that characterized much of the theory and research in various subject areas, influenced as it was by the strong hold of functionalist theory.

Functionalist thought also permeated—and still permeates—approaches to family and to aging in the United States. With respect to research on family life, threads of functionalism are evident in studies that isolate family relationships from broader social processes; that emphasize women's central role as family nurturers; that treat as a benchmark the assumed virtues of the white, heterosexual, middle-class nuclear family; and that exaggerate agreement and similarity in families (Walker, 2009). The heavily critiqued disengagement perspective that argued for older persons' withdrawal from the usual activities of adulthood (especially work) as functional for both the individual (who could shore up limited reserves) and society (enhancing its smooth functioning) (Cumming & Henry, 1961) lives on in the practice of retirement. Much of today's discourse on successful and productive aging has functionalist underpinnings in the focus on individual responsibility to realize middle-class and capitalist ideas of a good and worthy life in old age.

But sociology has a rich tradition of looking at life from the perspective of the underdog, for appreciating the social construction of reality through negotiated interaction with others, for developing theoretical perspectives that expose the ways in which social arrangements promote inequality, and in promoting change to redress social inequality. For some time now, threads from earlier work in the symbolic interactionist, conflict, and political economy perspectives have made their way into current theoretical frameworks to address various components of the concerns raised by Marshall and Tindale more than 30 years ago. In addition, some scholars in the areas of aging and of family life have been critical of functionalist and normative approaches, encouraging a move toward more critical and interpretive thinking.

In this chapter, I explore a combination of theoretical perspectives that I believe provide useful theoretical directions to appreciating the intersection of aging and family ties. These include the life course, critical, and feminist perspectives and the concept of ambivalence. I draw on these perspectives because combining various facets of each of them encourages us to look at continuity and change in family life and aging over time and in historical context; to take a heterogeneous view of age groups based on the intersecting relations of age, gender, class, race, ethnicity, and sexual orientation; to explore individual agency in the context of social institutions and macrolevel societal forces and relations; to view family relationships as the outcome of negotiations among individuals in the context of socially constructed arrangements and structures that can change; to take an interpretive rather than normative approach to family life and to aging; to consider the interconnections of multiple levels of analysis and multiple facets of social life; and to consider ways of improving the lives of older persons, in part through improving family life and the social process of aging. For the balance of this chapter, I will discuss these core perspectives, the elements of each of them that enhance our understanding of the issues outlined above, and their application to family ties and aging. My goal in doing so is in keeping with Pfohl's view of theoretical frameworks as "ways of naming, ways of conceptually ordering our senses of the world. They are tools with which we decide what it is that we experience, why something is the way it is, and how it is that we might act or react to it" (Pfohl, 1985, p. 9).

Varying disciplinary assumptions and points of focus, including those of sociology, psychology, economics, biology, and political science, pose challenges to theoretical development that takes a multidisciplinary approach. My bias in terms of disciplinary perspective is decidedly sociological. The approaches that I favor represent my attempt over several decades to step back and consider critically the underlying social processes of aging and family life and the ways that individuals attempt to negotiate them. I view taken-for-granted assumptions about current social arrangements, including those related to family life, as social constructions that can be changed (Moen & Coltrane, 2005). My academic training in sociology of deviance sensitized me early on to view the world as socially constructed, imbued with inequality and mechanisms to maintain the status quo that include the use of social categories and institutions. Gender and age relations are two such categories, embedded with variable expectations, responsibilities, advantages, and disadvantages in social life based on social group membership. "The family" stands as a culturally loaded social institution geared toward sustaining established priorities regarding appropriate sexual, age, and gender relations. The ideological viewpoints that permeate family issues are often evident in theoretical approaches to understanding them, despite assumptions of scientific method and objectivity that were the underpinnings of traditional approaches to research.

Theoretical development goes hand in hand with observation, or research, and in some respects, one might say that theoretical perspectives and research methods keep each other honest. For example, research findings may reveal and challenge ideological assumptions that are embedded in theoretical perspectives. At the same time, research findings do not speak for themselves; our interpretation of results is shaped by our theoretical stance. Ideally, theory and method strengthen each other. But, if done uncritically, both theoretical development and research observations can be constrained by unacknowledged or unrecognized biases and weaknesses.

The framework that I outline here reflects a lengthier discussion of theoretical, research, and policy issues related to family ties and aging (Connidis, 2010). In this chapter, I will discuss specific components of the life course perspective, critical and feminist approaches, and the concept of ambivalence that complement one another and provide direction in our theoretical understanding of aging and family life. Symbolic interactionism and social constructionism inform these theoretical orientations. I first select and discuss concepts and themes from each perspective that help forge a useful theoretical framework for studying family ties and aging. I then relate this framework to the concept of ambivalence as a foundational feature of family relationships and as a sensitizing concept that encourages the exploration of the negotiation (action) of family ties in the context of current institutional arrangements (family, work, health, education) and structured social relations (gender, age, class, race, ethnicity, sexual orientation).

Given the range of subject matter subsumed in the areas of family ties, aging, and their intersection, the theoretical directions that I develop here are necessarily broad, but they do provide direction for more focused topics such as caregiving or particular family relationships. In addition, more specific concepts and explanatory models can be incorporated within the broader framework provided here. I will give some examples of this along the way.

DEFINING OUR SUBJECT AREA

Family gerontology merges two distinct areas of study—aging and family life—that have been explored by multiple disciplines. Developing a perspective designed to deal specifically with the intersection of aging and family relations has not been a focal point of theoretical thinking. Yet, one of the benefits of bringing these two areas together is the potential for filling in gaps in one by drawing on strengths from the other. For example, aging researchers draw attention to family ties that fall outside the nuclear household and to their ongoing negotiation in later life. Family researchers who include older persons in their studies discourage the isolation of the old for separate study. Still, both fields continue to focus on traditional topics of study. Commenting on her years as editor of *Journal of Marriage and Family* from 2002 to 2007, Walker (2009) noted the continued emphasis on families with young children and adolescents, the relative absence of research on family ties in middle and later life, and the implicit acceptance of the status quo.

Articulating a theoretical framework that brings together aging and family ties is likely to bolster work in both fields, expanding the horizons and deepening the understanding of both family life and aging. An important starting point in proposing such a framework is defining the key concepts of study. What is meant by family ties and by aging? In addition to clarifying a theoretical focus, clear specification of subject matter later facilitates the link between theory and measurement (how will the concepts in our theoretical perspective be measured?), helping us to understand better what we observe and what we might choose to do about it in research and in recommended policy initiatives.

In my view, a theoretical framework on family life and aging is stronger when centered on the concept of family ties rather than on definitions of families as middle-aged or old (Connidis, 2010). A relatively inclusive definition of family membership defines family ties based on the responsibilities and support that are assumed and exchanged (Scanzoni & Marsiglio, 1993). This view may conflict with official views of who qualifies as family that exclude such family-like ties as those of gay or lesbian couples because they may not marry legally in many jurisdictions. Interest in the processes of negotiating family relationships across the life course places the family lives of older persons in the context of their relationships with other family members of the same and different generations. Taking an inclusive view of family relationships—especially in the case of older persons where both the normative expectations and realities of family life typically involve family ties outside one's home—also demands that we explore a broad range of family ties both within and beyond nuclear units and households. A test of a theoretical perspective's strength includes its relevance to understanding the complex interplay of an array of family relationships, as well as its ability to apply to multiple levels of analysis, and its relevance to practice or action.

Exploring the negotiation of family ties over time emphasizes aging as a process and family relationships as a central social domain throughout life. But there is also a particular interest in the unique situation of older persons and their vantage point on family ties. For convenience, I will consider old persons to be those who are aged 65 and over, recognizing that this is a malleable convention that rests on the relatively recent social designation of 65 as old age, as indicated by typical retirement age and access to state and workplace benefits.

Focusing on family relationships rather than later-life families avoids some of the limits of trying to define middle-aged and old families on the basis of such features as age of children (not all people have children) and highlights the association of the aging process with transitions in family relationships. Is there a place for the concept of family or families in our discussion? Yes. But, I try to confine the terms—*family*, to refer to the family as a social institution. and *families* to reflect multiple ways of performing family life. These terms allow us to distinguish between macrolevel issues of social structure, social trends, globalization, the economy, and actions of the state; the mesolevel of family as a social institution (along with other social institutions such as those of work and education); and the microlevel of family relationships negotiated by individuals in the context of macrolevel and mesolevel processes and forces. Although my focus is on these three levels of analysis, they are all entrenched in cultural views of an ideal family and an ideal old age (Connidis, 2010). Shifting ideals of family life and old age over time intersect and shape assumptions about the place of older persons in families as contributors and dependents and are reflected in the cultural and personal meaning assigned to aging and to family ties.

A LIFE COURSE PERSPECTIVE

The immense popularity of the life course perspective in a range of disciplines (Mayer, 2009) speaks to its strength at the same time that it hints at its major flaw: a somewhat weak theoretical stance. But the life course perspective contains a number of concepts that are both useful and theoretically enriching. Which concepts of the life course perspective are most central to setting important theoretical directions for the intersection of aging and family ties?

Clearly, a life course perspective is compatible with exploring family ties over time. It encourages considering both continuity and change in the family ties of old age, linking the experiences of later life to earlier life and of old family members to younger ones. Placing personal history or biography at the heart of a life course approach creates a context for better understanding current circumstances. Consider the difference in our understanding of family ties and loneliness when marriage is explored in the context of marital history rather than current marital status alone (Peters & Liefbroer, 1997).

The life course perspective has proven resilient in its response to criticisms launched over the years, thus making some earlier critiques of the perspective less applicable to current versions of the approach. The variety of work using the life course perspective has also improved its versatility. For example, a body of European work on the life course, with its greater elaboration of institutions, social structure, and multilevel analysis, complements the emphasis on individual biographies and normative scripts that is more characteristic of theorizing and research in the United States (Hagestad, 2009; Heinz, 2001; Heinz, Huinink, Swader, & Weymann, 2009; Marshall & Mueller, 2003; Marshall, 2009).

The life course approach considers aging a biological, psychological, and social process from birth to death, making it compatible with a range of disciplines. Over their lifetimes, individuals exercise human agency when they choose which paths they will take, making them active participants in building their biographies (Elder & Johnson, 2003; Heinz, 2001). Although we do not necessarily choose our family ties (with some notable exceptions), we regularly make decisions or choices about how we will engage in family relations and about family formation once we are adults.

The life course approach places individual experience into the historical context of social, political, and economic conditions, a link between individual agency and the larger social world that is called the *agency within structure model* (Settersten, 2003). This connection of macrolevel and microlevels of analysis respects the unique circumstances of different age groups, the ever-changing world in which individual life courses are navigated, and the constraints and opportunities in the options available to different groups. At the mesolevel are the social institutions or social spaces in which we live our lives, including institutionalized family life. This is the domain where we experience and negotiate the larger social forces of the macrolevel. By situating family relations in the context of both multiple levels of analysis and of other spheres of social life (Huinink & Feldhaus, 2009), the life course perspective holds considerable promise for studying family ties and aging.

The patterns and arrangements of social life, commonly termed *social structure*, influence but do not completely determine individual action. Variations among individuals in how they respond to very similar circumstances attest to the significance of individual agency, that is, the ability to act on one's own behalf. Yet, our social positions—based on gender, age, class, race, ethnicity, and sexual orientation (Arber, Davidson, & Ginn, 2003; Calasanti & Slevin, 2001; McMullin, 2010)—influence the options available to us. Initial versions of the life course perspective cast social change as preceding individual adaptation, creating an implicit view of individuals as reactive rather than proactive. The concepts of control cycles and situational imperatives (Elder, 1991) suggest a change process in which social change leads individuals to respond with attempts to gain control of a new situation. Developing the concept of human agency as a characteristic of social actors in subsequent work (Settersten, 2003) is compatible with the view that social change can emanate from the combined actions of individuals.

A key challenge in studying how family relationships actually work is to appreciate their connection to macrostructures (Walker, 2009). We do not mindlessly follow prescribed norms, nor do we create family life just as we would like it to be. Rather, we make choices in the face of pressures exerted by social structure to negotiate relationships that we believe constitute a desirable family life. The life course emphasis on constructing our biographies through the exercise of human agency in the context of historical, social, political, and economic conditions emphasizes the link of family relationships to the larger social world. Nonetheless, an ongoing concern about the life course perspective is its weakness in explicating structured social relations and the inequality in resources and power that they create. They are too often treated as given rather than as central processes that must be tackled in both theory and practice. Later I will discuss critical and feminist approaches as ways of addressing this concern.

Trajectories, transitions, and timing are core concepts of the life course approach (Elder & Johnson, 2003). *Trajectories*—the "long-term patterns of stability and change" (George, 2003, p. 672)—are the long view of the life course comprising the sequences of statuses occupied over time. Regarding family ties, these include the long view of the careers that we construct over time in our statuses as parent, partner, child, sibling, and grandparent (Elder, 2009). Because we take part in multiple social domains or institutions—for example, education, family, and work—we negotiate multiple trajectories over time (Settersten, 2003). The multiple statuses that we occupy at any one time, such as mother, sister, daughter, professor, and neighbor, create a *status configuration* (Heinz, 2001). Hence, the *life course* can be defined as a series of status configurations (Heinz, 2001), a definition that captures movement in multiple trajectories across time. The simultaneous negotiation of multiple trajectories underscores the connection of family life to other spheres of life (discouraging the isolated study of family ties) and to process and action over time (discouraging a static view of family relationships).

As we go through life, *transitions* or changes in our situation occur (Elder & Johnson, 2003). In middle and later family life these might include children leaving or returning home, a new partner, acquiring stepchildren, or the death of a partner. Life course trajectories are formed by such transitions in combination with periods of relative stability. Even though some transitions happen to us rather than result from choices that we make (e.g., having grandchildren), their negotiation involves agency as individuals work out how to manage new situations. Consequently, exercising agency applies both to paths taken or not taken—the decisions and choices that we make—and to how we handle a specific chosen or imposed transition.

In addition to historical time, the life course perspective includes the concept of *timing* to refer to expectations about when particular transitions should happen (Marshall & Mueller, 2003). Our involvement in multiple social domains means that there are multiple timetables against which our transitions can be judged as on or off time. There are also cultural views about the ideal *sequencing* (the order in which they should occur) and *duration* (how long one should spend in a particular pattern, for example, attending school) of transitions (Settersten & Mayer, 1997). Establishing normative life course timetables against which our trajectories can be judged as on or off time risks a status quo orientation to social life in general and to family life in particular. To avoid this stance, expectations regarding time can be considered shifting social and cultural constructions, not fixed imperatives for the smooth functioning of society (Hatch, 2000).

Considering the connection of timetables across different social domains and in historical context underscores the connection of family life to other social arenas. For example, shifts in the economy have altered the timing, sequencing, and duration of education and work, which, in turn, have led to delays in the entry to committed relationships or marriage and the birth of first children (Heinz, 2001; Henretta, 2001). These changes in younger generations create shifts in the experience of older family members who experience prolonged responsibilities as parents and delays in becoming grandparents.

The life course principles of life stage and linked lives add dynamism to studies of aging and the family life course by highlighting interconnections between historical time and age and between individuals. The *life stage* principle posits that life transitions and events vary in their impact on individual lives based on the age at which they occur and their place in the order of life events (Elder & Johnson, 2003; Marshall & Mueller, 2003). For example, the Great Recession of the early 21st century had quite different repercussions for young adults in university, graduates trying to enter the workforce, middle-aged parents who had been laid off, and older parents who had planned to retire. Despite sharing this particular historical time, the long-term implications of the recession for personal biographies will vary because of their timing and sequencing.

Especially relevant to studying family ties and aging is the concept of linked lives. *Linked lives* refers to the interdependence of our lives with others and the reciprocal influences of connected lives (Elder, 1991; Elder & Johnson, 2003; Heinz, 2001). In conjunction with our simultaneous involvement in multiple trajectories, the concept of linked lives underscores the link between our ties to family and other social domains, such as paid work. Returning to the example of the recession of the early 21st century, when younger family members could not find stable employment or lost their job, their parents' plans to retire may have been put on hold so that they can offer support to their adult children. When older family members lose their jobs or pensions due to bankruptcies or cutbacks, their children may alter their plans in order to help support them. In the case of younger adults, the timing of the recession was feared to place their job and economic security at risk far into the future. In the case of older adults, plans for a lengthy retirement and greater involvement with grandchildren have become unrealistic for some. These connections between macrolevel phenomena like the global recession and life course trajectories of work and family life negotiated by individuals can also be connected to structured social relations. The life course perspective tends not to elaborate on this connection.

The concepts of *cumulative advantage* and *disadvantage* (Dannefer, 2003) and of *life course risk* (O'Rand, 2006) complement those of life stage and linked lives with their more explicit appreciation for the significance of structured social relations. A life course view of inequality includes the examination of how relative advantage and disadvantage and differential exposure to risk build on themselves over time so that slight disparities early in life become larger ones later in life. This is sometimes referred to as the Matthew effect (Merton, 1968; Settersten, 2003). Despite mixed findings regarding cumulative advantage and disadvantage, in part depending upon the topic of study, and evidence of a leveling off of such differences in old age (Mayer, 2009), the implications of gender, race, and class relations over time for accumulating financial resources in old age are quite clear (Burr & Mutchler, 2007; Schellenberg, Turcotte, & Ram, 2005; Street & Connidis, 2001). White, middle and upper class men are more likely to engage in work histories that result in a financially secure retirement than are those of other race, class, and gender positions. The life stage principle underscores the significance of interruptions such as the recession at particular points in the life course in combination with age, gender, class, race, and ethnic relations. Thoughtful exploration of linked lives connects experiences in work to family life and reveals the ways in which structured social relations permeate family ties, with stronger links both expected of and practiced by women (Heinz, 2001).

The life course perspective provides useful theoretical directions for the study of family ties and aging by fostering multilevel analysis in which individual biographies and the exercise of agency (microlevel) are linked to multiple social domains, including family (mesolevel), that are influenced by social, economic, and political forces in historical time (macrolevel). A key source of dynamism in the life course perspective rests on the juxtaposition of human agency on behalf of social actors, our interdependence with others, and the impact of structured social relations and key economic, political and social forces of a particular time. But assumptions made about these core concepts and their links to one another are often unclear or unspecified. A repeated criticism of the life course approach is its focus on microlevel analysis of individual action and related factors in the immediate environment (Estes, Biggs, & Phillipson, 2003; Hagestad & Dannefer, 2001; Marshall & Mueller, 2003). What are the macrolevel mechanisms through which constraints and opportunities are distributed? How do they influence life course choices? As life course theorists suggest (e.g., Settersten, 2006), the potential for life course concepts to address the interconnections of macro-, meso-, and microlevel phenomena requires the inclusion of other theoretical perspectives. More pointedly, Mayer (2009) argued that the life course perspective requires more theoretical development and far better elaboration of how macro contexts shape the interaction of individual development and social components of the life course.

A CRITICAL PERSPECTIVE

Like many broad theoretical perspectives, the critical perspective contains a range of concepts and views and draws on a number of older theories. Here I highlight the components of a critical approach that elaborate some of the links suggested by the life course perspective. A critical approach incorporates the modernist emphasis on social structure and the postmodernist concern with narrative, personal meaning, individual choice, and subjectivity (Baars, Dannefer, Phillipson, & Walker, 2006). These combined threads underscore the significance of structured social relations in conjunction with an interpretive approach to individual action. Ideally, a critical perspective leads our attention on one hand to the dialectic or tension between the constraints and opportunities of socially constructed institutions and power relations and on the other hand to the subjective experiences and perceptions of individuals. When this delicate balance is maintained, the critical approach can avoid the overdeterminism of perspectives that focus almost exclusively on socially created inequality and the extreme relativism of approaches that focus almost exclusively on subjectivity and individual choice.

When applied to aging, a critical approach considers both the ways that structural inequalities shape everyday life and the unique perspective and interests of old people (Estes et al., 2003). Thus, although socially structured age relations generally put old people at a relative disadvantage in comparison with younger adults, older persons also have the capacity to act on their own behalf in defining and creating their lives. Early formulations of critical theory emphasized class relations as central to social structure, but over time this conception of inequality has expanded to include gender, race, ethnic, and age relations (McMullin, 2010). Because other structured social relations crosscut age relations, the capacity to carry out preferred alternatives in family life varies among old persons. Individuals in less powerful positions do not cease to exercise human agency, however; rather, the range of choices they can make is restricted. The result is varying social circumstances within age groups, including variations in family life.

Reminiscent of earlier work in the symbolic interactionist tradition, the concept of *reflexivity* has emerged as a significant component of a critical perspective. Reflexivity emphasizes the role of human agency in determining the impact that social forces will have on our behavior (Archer, 2007). According to Archer (2007, p. 15), reflexivity is "a personal property of human subjects, which is prior to, relatively autonomous from and possesses causal efficacy in relation to structural or cultural properties." We make decisions about how we will act after considering "ourselves in relation to the social situations that we confront" (p. 15). In turn, the social and cultural milieus in which we act are influenced by the choices we make. This conception of reflexivity counters the implicit treatment in much life course work of the individual as reactive by highlighting our proactive attempts to negotiate the social world and the consequences of these attempts beyond our individual lives.

When enough individuals make unexpected choices, they may alter institutional arrangements, such as those of family, and structured social relations, such as those of gender and sexual orientation (Katz, 2005). For example, regarding family ties, our deliberations about how to negotiate transitions in relationships with intimate partners can both reinforce and challenge the status quo. Multiple individual decisions to marry an opposite-sex partner support the tradition of marriage. Multiple individual decisions to live as married with a same-sex partner or to cohabit with an opposite-sex partner challenge it. Such challenges to traditional family life are not confined to young people. A substantial portion of openly gay and lesbian old persons came out later in life after leading apparently conventional lives in heterosexual marriages, and living apart together (LAT) is an increasingly popular intimate relationship among old couples (see Connidis, 2010). We also make decisions about how to respond to the family-life transitions of those to whom we are linked—such as the divorce or marriage of older parents or adult children, and about ongoing relationships over time.

In sum, the critical perspective complements and strengthens the life course perspective by making explicit links between the dynamic interplay of structured social relations, social institutions such as the family, and individual action by emphasizing the socially constructed nature of power relations and institutions, in tandem with reflexive decision-making and action by individuals. Although there is tension between individual human agency and the structured social relations that are embedded in social institutional arrangements, agency and social structure are not combatants fighting for victory. Instead, according to a critical perspective, the macro-, meso-, and microlevels of social life operate in a reciprocal and recursive model of mutual influence (Estes et al., 2003). A final and significant component of a critical perspective is a concern for praxis: How do we transform theoretical thinking and research into efforts to improve family relationships across the life course and, especially, in old age? How can social arrangements be altered in order improve the prospects of turning desired choices into reality?

A FEMINIST PERSPECTIVE

The gendered nature of family life and of old age makes feminist perspectives particularly relevant to studying family ties and aging (Arber et al., 2003; Calasanti, 2004; Calasanti & Slevin, 2001, 2006; Connidis & Walker, 2009). There are also strong affinities between feminist theorizing and praxis and the key tenets of the critical perspective outlined here (Estes et al., 2003). But family studies, aging studies, and efforts to combine them, have been slow to incorporate a critical, feminist approach to their subject matter. In the area of aging, claims of adopting a feminist approach fell flat when the subsequent focus was in fact on gender differences rather than gender relations (McMullin, 2000). In the case of family studies, for a long time traditional approaches to family research remained immune to feminist influences at the same time that family issues were not seen as central to developing feminist frameworks (Allen, Lloyd, & Few, 2009).

Earlier waves of feminism focused on the links of everyday life to larger social processes, and encouraged social change through individual action (Ray, 2006). Subsequent conceptions of gender in feminist theory moved discussion from sex roles to gender roles to gender relations to intersectionality, which will be defined shortly (Allen et al., 2009). Moving from gender roles to gender relations emphasizes inequality by focusing on the relative advantages and disadvantages of women and men in different social contexts, including family life. A range of work in feminist gerontology makes gender relations explicit in studies of health, family relations, sexuality, and caregiving that explore the relative situations and experiences of men and women (e.g., Calasanti, 2004; Calasanti & Slevin, 2001, 2006).

As early critiques of family life, feminist assessments revealed the gender relations that permeate socially constructed family life as an institution and as experienced by women, men, and children. Feminist gerontology captures both modernist and postmodernist themes. In keeping with the modernist tradition and the life course concept of cumulative disadvantage, feminists spotlight the unrewarded reproductive labor that characterized the lives of many of today's older women, limiting their resources in old age (Powell, 2006). Some feminists highlight the postmodernist tradition in analyses of the personal, social, and cultural significance of the physically aging body

(Powell, 2006). More generally, a postmodern feminist perspective emphasizes the power of language and discourse and the relativity of truth in its focus on how social institutions and social relations are constructed (Baber, 2009). Thus, feminist perspectives encourage an analysis of how structural arrangements and discourse combine to affect the objective and subjective conditions of gender and age relations in family ties across the life course.

In part a response to challenges to consider the concurrent effects of other social locations such as race and ethnicity, feminist theory now emphasizes the concept of *intersectionality*, promoting the view that gender, race, class, and sexuality are not separate systems of power relations but are, instead, "interlocking, overlapping, and mutually constructing one another" (Allen et al., 2009, p. 8; Collins, 1990, 2000). In other words, intersectionality emphasizes the interconnecting or crosscutting socially structured relations that are central to a critical perspective. Age relations have been a latecomer to discussions of intersecting, socially structured power relations, but they are treated as pivotal in some recent work on feminist approaches, on inequality, and on families and aging (Allen & Walker, 2009; Calasanti & Slevin, 2006; Connidis & Walker, 2009; McMullin, 2010).

In some respects, feminist theory has come further than critical theory because of recent efforts not to assume that one system of power relations necessarily trumps the others. This difference in feminist theory is accomplished in part by sensitivity to context. For example, earlier attempts to improve the position of black women included a conception of black feminist consciousness that brings black women and men together to fight racism while encouraging black women to challenge black men in order to combat sexism (Allen et al., 2009). The intersection of aging and family ties reveals gender and age as key power relations within families. Race and class are usually shared by family members but they are important markers of power relations *across* families. Reference to *families* rather than *family* is helpful for exposing variations, for example, between black and white families or between rich and poor families, appreciating that both race and class can and do vary within families. When they do, race and class are played out within as well as across families, as are gender and age relations (Connidis, 2007).

A final note about both the critical and feminist perspectives is their central concern with power relations. A noted risk in the popular call to respect diversity in various disciplines and topics of study is the failure to link difference with inequality (Bell & Hartmann, 2007; Michaels, 2006). Bell and Hartmann (2007, p. 906) described discourse on diversity as "happy talk" and argued that, "In the language of diversity, every American, regardless of background or social standing, is believed to have a place and perhaps even be welcomed. This defining element of the diversity discourse separates discussions about diversity, difference, and multiculturalism from more uncomfortable conversations about inequality, power, and privilege." A focus on structured social relations places relative access to power, privilege, and resources at the heart of analyses of family life across the life course. Thus, while challenging normative assumptions about an ideal family type and respecting diversity in the ways that family life can be done, feminist and critical perspectives focus attention on the need both to understand and to remedy inequalities in social and family life. How do we correct the financial price that women pay for a lifetime of reproductive labor? How do we encourage various social institutions, including health care, to respect a gay or lesbian partner as an old patient's most significant family member?

In sum, critical and feminist perspectives make explicit the links between individual agency and socially constructed relations of gender, age, class, race, ethnicity, and sexuality that are embedded in social institutions, including family, and in social interaction, including that among family members. In turn, a multilevel life course perspective complements the feminist and critical perspectives by emphasizing the context of time (Hatch, 2000).

LINKING THEORETICAL PERSPECTIVES TO FAMILY RELATIONS: THE CONCEPT OF AMBIVALENCE

Despite the compelling reasons for applying life course, critical, and feminist perspectives to studies of family ties and aging, figuring out exactly how to apply them in research on the negotiation of family ties later in life and over time is challenging. How does one move from broad theoretical ideas to conducting research, interpreting findings, and suggesting solutions? Ambivalence is a useful bridging concept for bringing together individual lives, families, the larger social world, and the macrolevel and mesolevel processes that are the context for negotiating family relationships over time and later in life.

The concept of ambivalence has an impressive history in various fields, including some earlier work on family ties (Bedford, 1989). Despite this history, attempts to revive and reformulate ambivalence for the study of family relationships and aging have been quite controversial. The hold of the solidarity perspective on research regarding family ties and aging, particularly intergenerational relations, reflects a long-term tendency to focus largely on the internal workings of family life, isolating the intersection of family ties and aging from the larger social world in which they operate. This isolation created a vacuum regarding critical appraisals of family as an institution and of the reproduction of inequality in family life. Instead, the focus on assessments of solidarity and, possibly, the factors associated with more or less solidarity within families supported an implicit normative approach in which conflict was generally ignored and the existing parameters of family life and structured social relations accepted.

Prompted in part by the dominance of the solidarity model and an undue focus on problems in the study of intergenerational relations (Marshall, Matthews, & Rosenthal, 1993), Lüscher and Pillemer (1998) brought the concept of ambivalence to the attention of family scholars in a pivotal article that outlined its application to intergenerational relations. In their discussion, *intergenerational ambivalence* focuses on contradictions in parent-child ties at the psychological level of mixed feelings and emotions, and at the sociological level of institutional resources and requirements (Lüscher & Pillemer, 1998). In a subsequent article, McMullin and I (2002a) argued for the conception of *sociological ambivalence* that avoided an implicit normative focus by making the dynamic relationship between agency and structured social relations central to understanding how family relationships are worked out. With her usual insight, Alexis Walker, editor of *Journal of Marriage and Family* at the time, suggested an exchange about our ideas on ambivalence that prompted four more articles on the topics of ambivalence and solidarity (Bengtson, Giarrusso, Mabry, & Silverstein, 2002; Connidis & McMullin, 2000b; Curran, 2002; Lüscher, 2004). That exchange, along with the initial article by Lüscher and Pillemer (1998), brought ambivalence to the attention of a variety of family and aging researchers and prompted further development of the concept.

A range of subsequent studies, articles, and books on how best to conceptualize and apply ambivalence to family ties and aging examine intergenerational ties (Pillemer, 2004; Pillemer et al., 2007), including those of in-laws (Peters, Hooker, & Zvonkovic, 2006; Willson, Shuey, & Elder, 2003); gay and lesbian family ties (Connidis, 2003a; Cohler, 2004); nuclear and extended kin ties of single mothers (Sarkisian, 2006); sibling ties (Connidis, 2007), including comparisons with parent-child ties (Fingerman, Hay, & Birditt, 2004); multiple-generation responses to divorce (Connidis, 2003b); and women at midlife (Mandell, Wilson, & Duffy, 2008). The outcome of this body of work is some very innovative treatments of family ties that extend the concept of ambivalence and understanding of the dynamics of family ties in midlife and late life, over time, and in the context of larger mesolevel and macrolevel forces. In addition, the concept of solidarity has been expanded to explicitly include conflict (Bengtson et al., 2002), or revamped so that solidarity is viewed as but one of several ways of characterizing family relations (Van Gaalen & Dykstra, 2006).

A key objective in developing the concept of ambivalence is to avoid dualistic views of family relationships as either running smoothly or conflict-ridden (Pillemer & Lüscher, 2004), a dualism that misses the complexities and contradictions of social and family life. The concept of ambivalence specifies contradiction as characteristic of family relationships and of social life, both in sentiments about family members—psychological ambivalence—and in the negotiations of family ties, influenced as they are by structured social relations—sociological ambivalence (Connidis & McMullin, 2002a, 2002b). A key challenge in reformulating the concept of sociological ambivalence is addressing the contradictions and conflicts that are created by social structure but worked out in interactions among family members (Connidis & McMullin, 2002a). Sociological ambivalence emphasizes the reciprocal links between internal family dynamics and the larger social world in which they occur (Willson et al., 2003).

Ambivalence can be applied at the levels of individuals, relationships, social institutions, and societies (Lettke & Klein, 2004). Measures of mixed feelings may capture psychological ambivalence but they do not capture relational and sociological ambivalence adequately (Katz, Lowenstein, Phillips, & Daatland, 2005). Much of the research on family ties and aging that explores ambivalence focuses on its psychological dimension—the contradictory feelings or sentiments that we have about family members. Such mixed emotions do not necessarily characterize how we experience relationships all of the time. Depending on circumstances and the outcome of attempts to manage the contradictions of social and family life, at any given point in time family ties may be characterized by conflict, mutual contentment, estrangement, or mixed emotions and incompatible demands. Because we work out our relationships in the context of the contradictions created by our multiple positions in structured social relations (e.g., woman, white, immigrant, middle-aged, heterosexual), sociological ambivalence is conceptually prior to solidarity and conflict (Lüscher, 2002). If we are to understand the dynamics and processes of family life, we must determine the conditions that lead solidarity, conflict, or ambivalence to dominate family relationships at specific points in time, in response to specific life transitions, and for particular groups.

Examining the crosscutting impact of age, gender, class, race, ethnicity, and sexual orientation tackles the multiple realities that characterize family life, the varying degrees to which family members will experience ambivalence, and varying capacities of family members and of families to negotiate the contradictions of their lives toward desired outcomes. Motivated to minimize ambivalence, family members exercise agency in the choices they make about how to negotiate particular relationships and circumstances. They do so in the context of institutionalized family practices and structured social relations. The concern with both psychological and sociological ambivalence reflects the influence of critical and symbolic interactionist perspectives (Connidis, 2010; Lüscher, 2004). The contradictions among individual agency, the negotiation of family ties, and structured social relations also have strong roots in postmodern feminist perspectives (Baber, 2009).

Recently, the concept of ambivalence has been extended by incorporating an additional aspect termed *collective ambivalence* (Ward, 2008; Ward,

Deane, & Spitze, 2008). Collective ambivalence refers to "mixed feelings across multiple children," meaning that parents do not feel the same way about all of their children (Ward, 2008, p. S245). The purpose of the concept is to emphasize structural sources of the contradiction or ambivalence that results when older parents have varied feelings about their adult children (Ward et al., 2008). As is true of all ideas that challenge established ways of thinking, the concept of ambivalence has sparked considerable debate, even among those who generally favor and employ it. Pillemer and Suitor (2008) argued that collective ambivalence is not really ambivalence because, in their view, "The most important defining characteristic of ambivalence is a contradictory assessment of or response toward the same object" (p. S395). Using the analogy of a teacher who likes some students and dislikes others, they ask whether this notion can really be considered ambivalence. Regarding both teacher-student and parent-child relations, my answer would be yes, they can be considered ambivalence. Let us consider this view of ambivalence in regard to parent-child ties.

I would argue that the concept of ambivalence, in keeping with life course, critical, and feminist perspectives, encourages a view of individuals as subjects, not objects. In the context of parent-child relations, our experience as parents cannot be reduced to a series of isolated, dyadic relationships with each of our adult children, although our attempts to study families tend to treat family ties this way. Instead, as well as having relationships with and feelings about each of our children, we also experience parenting more generally. Being a parent and our feelings about it are shaped substantially by the relationships that we have with all of our children—a prime example of the whole being greater than the sum of its parts—and by how our experience compares with expectations about what constitutes an ideal family and good parenting. Ward and his colleagues (2008) found that both number of children (network size) and having adult stepchildren are features of family structure that increase collective ambivalence or the prospects of variable feelings about one's children. Collective ambivalence across families, viewed as constellations of relationships, becomes an additional structural feature of family networks for fruitful analysis.

In my view, the concept of collective ambivalence indicates an important dimension of family life in trying to connect ambivalence as experienced by individuals to features of family structure (network size and presence of stepchildren). In viewing families as constellations of relationships, the concept of ambivalence is cast as a feature of relationships as well as of the family as an institution. Collective ambivalence thus serves as a concept that links the multiple sets of relationships comprising a particular family network to the family as an institution, a microlevel-mesolevel link. Network size, in this case the number of children, by definition enhances the potential for collective ambivalence by increasing the number of relationships that can potentially vary from one another. The connections of stepfamily relationships to collective ambivalence and of collective ambivalence to lower well-being among older parents (Ward, 2008) suggest the link between institutionalized expectations of family life (the family as a social institution) and the impact of straying from those expectations.

Despite the reality of divorce, remarriage, cohabiting, single parenthood, and stepchildren, entrenched cultural ideals of family continue to favor the traditional nuclear family, often termed the Standard North American Family (SNAF), and biological ties between parents and children across the life course (Sarkisian, 2006). A strong ethos that one should love and treat one's children equally is also central to institutionalized family life. Ward's finding that violation of these institutionalized practices and expectations heightens ambivalence suggests areas where change in views of family life that are promoted by common research approaches and by policy is needed. Conceptions of family that include the range of real (as opposed to ideal) families, and expectations of good parenting that allow for variable responses to children, are likely to enhance parents' capacity for negotiating variations in their relationships with children without suffering assaults to their well-being. Attempts by parents to resolve such ambivalence are likely to vary according to structured social relations, creating a microlevel-mesolevel-macrolevel link in understanding family ties. For example, a parent or parents with substantial economic resources may be able to mask varying sentiments about their children by offering plentiful support to all of them. Parents with fewer resources may have to make choices that reflect their biases.

Finally, the concept of ambivalence complements the critical and feminist perspectives' views of change. The negotiation of ambivalence may either support established ways of doing family life or challenge them. When enough individuals negotiate ambivalence by creating new ways of relating, or gather support from others for their right to do so, as in the case of same-sex marriage in some jurisdictions, social change will result. But if most individuals negotiate ambivalence in keeping with conventional expectations, either personally or in their views of how others should behave, they will reproduce both traditional family life and the inequalities that it supports.

SUMMARY AND DISCUSSION

Let us go back to where we began and consider how the theoretical directions provided by combining core ideas from the life course, critical, and feminist perspectives along with the concept of ambivalence address the call for a radical gerontology from more than three decades ago. Critical and feminist scholars emphasize the relativity of truth and the use of truth claims as weapons of power. As researchers, we are encouraged to recognize and reveal our biases and to critically evaluate the taken-for-granted.

The emphasis on praxis in the critical and feminist perspectives positions scholars to go beyond claims of being neutral observers to being advocates for old people as well as other groups that are not served well under current social conditions. This includes considering ways in which family life in old age can be improved for those who are now old and for those who will be, a longer-range view advanced by the life course perspective that encourages policy interventions aimed at key life transitions (Cooke, 2006), whenever they may occur. This longer-range view is reflected also in the value of historical context promoted especially by the life course perspective. In addition, the serious treatment of inequality emphasized by critical and feminist approaches includes the call to understand the roots of unequal social relations and attempts to understand them, attending to the past as a route to better understanding the present and anticipating the future.

At the heart of critical and feminist perspectives and central to the concept of ambivalence are the reciprocal influences of social, political, and economic factors, and of individual and collective action. Managing ambivalence in family relationships means dealing with the conflict, negotiation, and compromise that typify interaction and social processes. The intersection of socially constructed relations of gender, class, age, race, ethnicity, and sexuality at the core of critical and feminist approaches emphasize variation and, more importantly, inequality, within age groups. The concept of individual agency in critical perspectives and in the concept of ambivalence makes individuals potential agents of change through their actions. Finally, the perspectives advocated here encourage an interactive framework that stresses the dynamic interplay of individual agency in the negotiation of family ties carried out in the context of established ways of doing family and of structuring social relations that create ambivalence.

Some argue the need for middle-range theories if we are to address the uniqueness of the family group (White & Klein, 2008). Clearly, most research projects and papers would be hard pressed to deal with multiple levels of analysis across multiple life course trajectories simultaneously. There is a risk, however, in isolating families for separate theorizing as opposed to delineating the ways in which family relations can be expected to parallel and differ from other social relations. The risk lies in returning to a focus on internal family dynamics that isolates family life from other social domains and accepts current ways of doing family as the exclusive parameters of family life. The concepts of ambivalence and of linked lives from the life course perspective help to anchor the macrolevel and mesolevel ideas of the life course, critical, and feminist perspectives in relationships and individual action. At the same time, there is value in developing conceptual models designed to deal with more particular family-related issues. The key is to place such efforts in the larger context of the theoretical directions outlined here. Consider the following example.

One of the most popular topics of study related to family ties and aging is the issue of caregiving. How do various approaches to this topic measure up in relation to the core concepts outlined here? A central issue is the growing need for formal care that is associated with aging. Despite the fact that most care received by older persons is provided informally, mostly by family members, government concern and the intergenerational equity debate focus largely on the costs of formal care in later life. But if we view support from the perspective of age relations and across time, we can see that for all ages, informal and formal support are two parallel and interacting continua in which both forms of support are present simultaneously (Connidis, 2010). At younger ages, many public resources go into health care, education, and recreation as complements to the informal support provided by family members. In later life too, informal support continues even when formal support increases. Socially constructed age relations, however, affect our view of this balance. Our tendency to view support offered to youth as an investment and to the old as a cost alters our approach to offering support to each age group. Indeed, we rarely frame the state-funded support that goes to youth as formal support.

Current constructions of age relations fuel the intergenerational equity portrayal of the old as a drain on resources at the expense of the young, failing to take into account the ongoing informal exchanges that occur between generations and typically favor the younger ones. With respect to informal care, only the functional specificity of relationships model allows for the prospect that the same family tie, such as that between siblings, may be negotiated differently. For some, siblings are an important and viable source of support later in late; for others, they are not. This model reflects both the exercise of agency over time and the quite different circumstances that individuals negotiate, based on family structure and on their locations in structured social relations.

The theoretical directions provided here are my attempt to combine ideas that encourage reciprocal links among macrolevel processes including structured social relations (critical and feminist perspectives); mesolevel institutions including family, education, and work (life course perspective, timing; ambivalence); and microlevel family relationships (linked lives; ambivalence). Family relationships are negotiated by individuals across time (life course, life stage, historical events, life transitions) who exercise agency (critical perspective; ambivalence; life course) when interpreting their situation and making decisions in the context of social, cultural, political, economic, and global forces (life course, timing; critical and feminist perspectives; ambivalence). This macrolevel context itself is either sustained or altered by the interpretations and decisions that individuals make.

As noted at the outset, my theoretical preferences are influenced by being a sociologist, and I cannot claim that the perspective outlined in this chapter is exhaustive. I do believe that my theoretical framework is particularly useful for capturing the dynamic nature of family relationships over time and for linking individual experience and efforts to the realities of current social arrangements. These social arrangements include the interdependent institutions of family, work, and education (among others; see Heinz et al., 2009) and the inequality of structured social relations that creates significant ranges in resources and power. The approach encouraged in this chapter is also compatible with concepts from a variety of disciplines that focus on specific components of the framework. This compatibility furthers the interdisciplinary thrust of both aging and family studies (Allen & Walker, 2009). Thoughtfully applied, the theoretical perspective that I propose holds great promise for stronger theoretically based research that addresses current realities along with prospects for improving family life at all ages.

The theoretical framework presented in this chapter encourages insights and clearer thinking about family ties over the life course. As well, this perspective points the way to enhancing family life, not by perfecting one ideal family form, but by creating social conditions that support a variety of family forms capable of meeting the challenges of building strong relationships through personal and historical time.

REFERENCES

Allen, K.R., Lloyd, S.A., & Few, A.L. (2009). Reclaiming feminist theory, method, and praxis for family studies. In S.A. Lloyd, A.L. Few, & K.R. Allen (Eds.), *Handbook of feminist family studies* (pp. 3–17). Los Angeles: Sage.

Allen, K.R., & Walker, A.J. (2009). Theorizing about families and aging from a feminist perspective. In V.L. Bengtson, M. Silverstein, N.M. Putney, & D. Gans (Eds.), *Handbook of theories on aging* (pp. 517–528). New York: Springer.

Arber, S., Davidson, K. & Ginn, J. (2003). Changing approaches to gender and later life. In S. Arber, K. Davidson, & J. Ginn (Eds.), *Gender and ageing: Changing roles and relationships* (pp. 1–14). Philadelphia: Open University Press.

Archer, M.S. (2007). *Making our way through the world.* Cambridge: Cambridge University Press.

Baars, J., Dannefer, D., Phillipson, C., & Walker, A. (2006). Introduction: Critical perspectives in social gerontology. In J. Baars, D. Dannefer, C. Phillipson, & A.Walker (Eds.), *Aging, globalization, and inequality: The new critical gerontology* (pp. 1–14). Amityville, NY: Baywood.

Baber, K.M. (2009). Postmodern feminist perspectives and families. In S.A. Lloyd, A.L. Few, & K.R. Allen (Eds.), *Handbook of feminist family studies* (pp. 56–68). Los Angeles: Sage.

Bedford, V.H. (1989). Sibling ambivalence in adulthood. *Journal of Family Issues, 10,* 211–224.

Bell, J. M., & Hartmann, D. (2007). Diversity in everyday discourse: The cultural ambiguities and consequences of "happy talk." *American Sociological Review, 72*, 895–914.

Bengtson, V., Giarrusso, R., Mabry, J. B., & Silverstein, M. (2002). Solidarity, conflict, and ambivalence: Complementary or competing perspectives on intergenerational relationships? *Journal of Marriage and Family, 64*, 568–576.

Burr, J. A., & Mutchler, J. E. (2007). Employment in later life: A focus on race/ethnicity and gender. *Generations, 31*, 37–44.

Calasanti, T. M. (2004). Feminist gerontology and old men. *Journal of Gerontology: Social Sciences, 59B*, S305–S314.

Calasanti, T. M., & Slevin, K. F. (2001). *Gender, social inequalities, and aging.* Walnut Creek, CA: AltaMira Press.

Calasanti, T. M., & Slevin, K. F. (2006). *Aging matters: Realigning feminist thinking.* New York: Routledge.

Cohler, B. J. (2004). The experience of ambivalence within the family: Young adults 'coming out' gay or lesbian and their parents. In K. Pillemer & K. Lüscher (Eds.), *Intergenerational ambivalences: New perspectives on parent-child relations in later life* (pp. 255–284). New York: Elsevier.

Collins, P. H. (1990). *Black feminist thought: Knowledge, consciousness, and the politics of empowerment.* Boston: Unwin Hyman.

Collins, P. H. (2000). It's all in the family: Intersections of gender, race, and nation. In U. Narayan & S. Harding (Eds.), *Decentering the center: Philosophy for a multicultural, postcolonial, and feminist world* (pp. 156–176). Bloomington: Indiana University Press.

Connidis, I. A. (2003a). Bringing outsiders in: Gay and lesbian family ties over the life course. In S. Arber, K. Davidson, & J. Ginn (Eds.), *Gender and ageing: Changing roles and relationships* (pp. 79–94). Philadelphia: Open University Press.

Connidis, I. A. (2003b). Divorce and union dissolution: Reverberations over three generations. *Canadian Journal on Aging, 22*, 353–368.

Connidis, I. A. (2007). Negotiating inequality among adult siblings: Two case studies. *Journal of Marriage and Family, 69*, 482–499.

Connidis, I. A. (2010). *Family ties & aging* (2nd ed.). Los Angeles: Pine Forge Press.

Connidis, I. A., & McMullin, J. A. (2002a). Sociological ambivalence and family ties: A critical perspective. *Journal of Marriage and Family, 64*, 558–567.

Connidis, I. A., & McMullin, J. A. (2002b). Ambivalence, family ties, and doing sociology. *Journal of Marriage and Family, 64*, 594–601.

Connidis, I. A., & Walker, A. J. (2009). (Re)Visioning gender, age, and aging in families. In S. A. Lloyd, A. L. Few, K. R. Allen (Eds.), *Handbook of feminist family studies* (pp. 147–159). Los Angeles: Sage.

Cooke, M. (2006). Policy changes and the labour force participation of older workers: Evidence from six countries. *Canadian Journal on Aging , 25*, 387–400.

Cumming, E., & Henry, W. E. (1961). *Growing old: The process of disengagement.* New York: Basic Books.

Curran, S. R. (2002). Agency, accountability, and embedded relations: What's love got to do with it? *Journal of Marriage and Family, 64*, 577–584.

Dannefer, D. (2003). Cumulative advantage/disadvantage and the life course: Cross-fertilizing age and social science theory. *Journal of Gerontology: Social Sciences, 58B*, S327–S337.

Elder, G. H., Jr. (1991). Lives and social change. In W. R. Heinz (Ed.), *Theoretical advances in life course research* (pp. 58–85). Weinham: Deutscher Studies Verlag.

Elder, G. H., Jr. (2009). Perspectives on the life course. In W. R. Heinz, J. Huinink, & A. Weymann (Eds.), *The life course reader: Individuals and societies across time* (pp. 91–110). Frankfurt/New York: Campus Verlag.

Elder, G. H., Jr., & Johnson, M. K. (2003). The life course and aging: Challenges, lessons, and new directions. In R. Settersten, Jr. (Ed.), *Invitation to the life course: Toward new understandings of later life* (pp. 49–81). Amityville, NY: Baywood.

Estes, C. L., Biggs, S., & Phillipson, C. (2003). *Social theory, social policy, and ageing: A critical introduction*. Berkshire, England: Open University Press.

Fingerman, K. L., Hay, E. L., & Birditt, K. S. (2004). The best of ties, the worst of ties: Close, problematic, and ambivalent social relationships. *Journal of Marriage and Family, 66*, 792–808.

George, L. K. (2003). Life course research: Achievements and potential. In J. T. Mortimer & M. J. Shanahan (Eds.), *Handbook of the life course* (pp. 671–680). New York: Kluwer Academic/Plenum Publishers.

Hagestad, G. O. (2009). Interdependent lives and relationships in changing times: A life-course view of families and aging. In W. R. Heinz, J. Huinink, & A. Weymann (Eds.), *The life course reader: Individuals and societies across time* (pp. 397–415). Frankfurt and New York: Campus Verlag.

Hagestad, G. O., & Dannefer, D. (2001). Concepts and theories of aging: Beyond microfication in social science approaches. In R. H. Binstock & L. K. George (Eds.), *Handbook of aging and the social sciences*, (5th ed., pp. 3–21). New York: Academic Press.

Hatch, L. R. (2000). *Beyond gender differences: Adaptation to aging in life course perspective*. Amityville, NY: Baywood.

Heinz, W. R. (2001). Work and the life course: A cosmopolitan-local perspective. In V. W. Marshall, W. R. Heinz, H. Kruger, & A. Verma (Eds.), *Restructuring work and the life course* (pp. 3–22). Toronto: University of Toronto Press.

Heinz, W. R., Huinink, J., Swader, C. S., & Weymann, A. (2009). General introduction. In W. R. Heinz, J. Huinink, & A. Weymann (Eds.), *The life course reader: Individuals and societies across time* (pp. 15–30). Frankfurt and New York: Campus Verlag.

Henretta, J. C. (2001). Work and retirement. In R. H. Binstock and L. K. George (Eds.), *Handbook of aging and the social sciences* (5th ed., pp. 255–271). New York: Academic Press.

Huinink, J., & Feldhaus, M. (2009). Family research from the life course perspective. *International Sociology, 24*, 299–324.

Katz, R., Lowenstein, A., Phillips, J., & Daatland, S. O. (2005). Theorizing intergenerational family relations: Solidarity, conflict, and ambivalence in cross-national contexts. In V. L. Bengtson, A. C. Acock, K. R. Allen, P. Dilworth-Anderson, &

D.M. Klein (Eds.), *Sourcebook of family theory and research* (pp. 393–407). Thousand Oaks, CA: Sage.

Katz, S. (2005). *Cultural aging: Life course, life style, and senior worlds*. Peterborough, Ontario: Broadview Press.

Lettke, F., & Klein, D.M. (2004). Methodological issues in assessing ambivalences in intergenerational relations. In K. Pillemer & K. Lüscher (Eds.), *Intergenerational ambivalences: New perspectives on parent-child relations in later life* (pp. 85–113). New York: Elsevier.

Lüscher, K. (2002). Intergenerational ambivalence: Further steps in theory and research. *Journal of Marriage and Family, 64*, 585–593.

Lüscher, K. (2004). Conceptualizing and uncovering intergenerational ambivalence. In K. Pillemer & K. Lüscher (Eds.), *Intergenerational ambivalences: New perspectives on parent-child relations in later life* (pp. 23–62). New York: Elsevier.

Lüscher, K., & Pillemer, K. (1998). Intergenerational ambivalence: A new approach to the study of parent-child relations in later life. *Journal of Marriage and Family, 60*, 413–425.

Mandell, N., Wilson, S., & Duffy, A. *Connection, compromise, and control: Canadian women discuss midlife*. Don Mills, Ontario: Oxford University Press.

Marshall, V.W. (2009). Theory informing public policy: The life course perspective as a policy tool. In V.L. Bengtson, M. Silverstein, N.M. Putney, & D. Gans (Eds.), *Handbook of theories on aging* (pp. 573–593). New York: Springer.

Marshall, V.W., & Mueller, M.M. (2003). Theoretical roots of the life course perspective. In W.R. Heinz & V.W. Marshall (Eds.), *Social dynamics of the life course* (pp. 3–32). New York: Aldine de Gruyter.

Marshall, V. W., Matthews, S.H., & Rosenthal, C.R. (1993). Elusiveness of family life: A challenge for the sociology of aging. In G.L. Maddox & M. Powell Lawton (Eds.), *Annual Review of Gerontology and Geriatrics, 13*, 37–92. New York: Springer.

Marshall, V. W., & Tindale, J. (1978–79). Notes for a radical gerontology. *International Journal of Aging and Human Development, 9*, 163–175.

Mayer, K.U. (2009). New directions in life course research. *American Review of Sociology, 35*, 413–433.

McMullin, J.A. (2000). Diversity and the state of sociological aging theory. *The Gerontologist, 40*, 517–530.

McMullin, J.A. (2010). *Understanding social inequality* (2nd ed.). Don Mills, Ontario: Oxford University Press.

Merton, R.K. (1968). The Matthew effect in science: The reward and communications systems of science. *Science, 199*, 55–63.

Michaels, W.B. (2006). *The trouble with diversity: How we learned to love identity and ignore inequality*. New York: Metropolitan Books.

Moen, P., & Coltrane, S. (2005). Families, theories, and social policy. In V.L. Bengtson, A.C. Acock, K.R. Allen, P. Dilworth-Anderson, & D.M. Klein (Eds.), *Sourcebook of family theory and research* (pp. 543–556). Thousand Oaks: Sage.

O'Rand, A. M. (2006). Stratification and the life course: Life course capital, life course risks, and social inequality. In R.H. Binstock & L.K. George (Eds.),

Handbook of aging and the social sciences (6th ed., pp. 145–162). San Diego: Elsevier.

Peters, A., & Liefbroer, A. C. (1997). Beyond marital status: Partner history and well-being in old age. *Journal of Marriage and Family, 59,* 687–699.

Peters, C. L., Hooker, K., &. Zvonkovic, A. M. (2006). Older parents' perceptions of ambivalence in relationships with their children. *Family Relations, 55,* 539–551.

Pfohl, S. J. (1985). *Images of deviance and social control: A sociological history.* New York: McGraw-Hill.

Pillemer, K. (2004). Can't live with 'em, can't live without 'em: Older mothers' ambivalence toward their adult children. In K. Pillemer & K. Lüscher (Eds.), *Intergenerational ambivalences: New perspectives on parent-child relations in later life* (pp. 115–132). New York: Elsevier.

Pillemer, K., & Lüscher, K. (Eds.). (2004). *Intergenerational ambivalences: New perspectives on parent-child relations in later life.* New York: Elsevier.

Pillemer, K., & Suitor, J. J. (2008). Collective ambivalence: Considering new approaches to the complexity of intergenerational relations. *Journal of Gerontology: Social Sciences, 63B,* S394–S396.

Pillemer, K., Suitor, J. J., Mock, S. E., Sabir, M., Pardo, T., & Sechrist, J. (2007). Capturing the complexity of intergenerational relations: Exploring ambivalence within later-life families. *Journal of Social Issues, 63,* 1–16.

Powell, J. L. (2006). *Social theory and aging.* Lanham, MD: Rowman & Littlefield.

Ray, R. E. (2006). The personal as political: The legacy of Betty Friedan. In T. M. Calasanti & K. F. Slevin (Eds.), *Aging matters: Realigning feminist thinking* (pp. 21–45). New York: Routledge.

Sarkisian, N. (2006). "Doing family ambivalence": Nuclear and extended families in single mothers' lives. *Journal of Marriage and Family, 68,* 804–811.

Scanzoni, J., & Marsiglio, W. (1993). New action theory and contemporary families. *Journal of Family Issues, 1,* 105–132.

Schellenberg, G., Turcotte, M., & Ram, B. (2005). Post-retirement employment. *Perspectives, 6,* 14–17. Ottawa, Ontario: Statistics Canada.

Settersten, R. A., Jr. (2003). Propositions and controversies in life-course scholarship. In R. A. Settersten Jr. (Ed.), *Invitation to the life course: Toward new understandings of later life* (pp. 15–45). Amityville, NY: Baywood.

Settersten, R. A., Jr. (2006). Aging and the life course. In R. H. Binstock & L. K. George (Eds.), *Handbook of aging and the social sciences* (pp. 3–19). Burlington, MA: Elsevier.

Settersten, R. A., Jr., & Mayer, K. U. (1997). The measurement of age, age structuring, and the life course. *Annual Review of Sociology, 23,* 233–61.

Street, D., & Connidis, I. A. (2001). Creeping selectivity in women's pensions. In J. Ginn, D. Street, & S. Arber (Eds.), *Women, work and pensions: International issues and prospects* (pp. 158–178). Philadelphia: Open University Press.

Van Gaalen, R. I., & Dykstra, P. A. (2006). Solidarity and conflict between adult children and parents: A latent class analysis. *Journal of Marriage and Family, 68,* 947–960.

Walker, A. J. (2009). A feminist critique of family studies. In S. A. Lloyd, A. L. Few, & K. R. Allen (Eds.), *Handbook of feminist family studies* (pp. 18–27). Los Angeles: Sage.

Ward, R. A. (2008). Multiple parent-adult child relations and well-being in middle and later life. *Journal of Gerontology: Social Sciences, 61B,* S239–S247.

Ward, R. A., Deane, G., & Spitze, G. (2008). Ambivalence about ambivalence: Reply to Pillemer and Suitor. *Journal of Gerontology: Social Sciences, 63B,* S397–S398.

White, J. M., & Klein, D. M. (2008). *Family theories* (3rd ed.). Los Angeles: Sage.

Willson, A. E., Shuey, K. M., & Elder, G. H., Jr. (2003). Ambivalence in the relationship of adult children to aging parents and in-laws. *Journal of Marriage and Family, 65,* 1055–1072.

4

Innovative Research Methods
for Family Gerontology

Aloen L. Townsend

The two goals of this chapter are to provide an overview of methodological innovations in study design, sampling, measurement, and analysis that have blossomed in the 17 years since the first *Handbook of Aging and the Family* was published and to provide examples of how these innovations have been applied in family gerontology. Methods were deemed innovative if they met one or more of the following criteria: (1) they were infrequently used in the past but are increasingly used in recent years, (2) important or cutting-edge methodological advances have occurred, and (3) they are being applied in novel ways or generating new knowledge. Coverage is not exhaustive; rather, it is intended to give a flavor of state-of-the-science methodological developments and their potential to expand knowledge about families and aging in novel directions.

To gather examples, electronic searches were conducted in the PsycInfo, CINAHL, and Medline databases and tables of contents were reviewed for journals that have traditionally published articles on aging families: *Journal of Marriage and Family, Family Relations, The Gerontologist, Journals of Gerontology: Psychological Sciences and Social Sciences, Psychology and Aging, Research on Aging, Journal of Aging Studies,* and *Health Psychology.* Family was conceptualized broadly to include ties defined by blood, law, custom, affection, or choice in order to represent the diversity of contemporary family structures and ties, nontraditional and traditional definitions of family, and less visible family types (Carter & McGoldrick, 2005). Similarly, aging was conceptualized broadly to capture relationships across longer life expectancies and the greater number of family generations alive today (Carter & McGoldrick, 2005). Database searches and reviews of journals were restricted to 1995 to the present.

INNOVATIONS IN STUDY DESIGN

Life Span and Life Course Designs

More frequent use of life span or life course designs is one notable innovation in family gerontology. These designs help us understand the myriad ways in which both aging and families are shaped by time, place, and history (Settersten & Mayer, 1997). Recent life span studies have compared similarities and differences in family relations across various points in the adult years—for example, sibling relationships from infancy to old age (Bedford & Volling, 2004), positive and negative social interactions reported by people aged 13 to 96 (Akiyama, Antonucci, Takahashi, & Langfahl, 2003), and spousal support and strain among married grandparents aged 35 to 74 years (Matzek & Cooney, 2009). Life span approaches illuminate features such as historical embeddedness and the influence of other contextual variables; the dynamic interplay between gains and losses; life-long processes of development, growth, and change; and plasticity (Blieszner, 2006; Hofer & Piccinin, 2010). Life span designs are not restricted to research on individuals; Berg and Upchurch (2007) offered a conceptual model for studying couples coping with chronic illness across the life span.

Examples of life course designs are Burton's (1996) investigation of age norms, intergenerational caregiving, and the timing of transitions in family roles among African American women in three-generational families; Chesley and Moen's (2006) examination of the impact of husbands' and wives' changing family caregiving responsibilities on well-being in dual-earner couples; Stephens and Townsend's (1997) research on stresses and rewards experienced by midlife women juggling the roles of caregiver to an aging parent or parent-in-law, mother, wife, and employee; and Schafer's (2009) study of the impact of death of a parent during childhood on subjective age in middle adulthood. Settersten and Mayer (1997) reviewed a number of innovative designs for collecting life course information. Life course designs illuminate features such as interdependent lives; social stratification forces related to gender, race, ethnicity, age, and socioeconomic status; socialization; social institutions; cultural norms; and social roles and role transitions (Blieszner, 2006; MacMillan & Copher, 2005).

Given increased use of life span and life course designs, it is surprising that attention to family history or past relationships remains uncommon. There are some noteworthy exceptions: for example, a history of strained or estranged family relationships and long-standing family rules for suppression of emotion negatively influenced social support from grandparents when adult children experienced an infant's death (White, Walker, & Richards, 2008), and retrospective family histories collected from aging mothers revealed that mothers were most likely to favor adult children who had experienced illness that was perceived as not within the child's control (Suitor & Pillemer,

2000). Both of these examples employed qualitative designs; quantitative research has been even less likely to incorporate measures of family history.

Longitudinal Designs

Exploration of life span and life course issues do not require longitudinal designs, but longitudinal designs offer many advantages (Hofer & Piccinin, 2010; Schaie, 2005). Large panel surveys that include prospective (and sometimes retrospective) information are increasingly available—such as the Longitudinal Study of Generations (LSOG), Wisconsin Longitudinal Survey (WLS), Cardiovascular Health Study (CHS), Study of Midlife in the United States (MIDUS), Health and Retirement Study (HRS, which includes the Assets and Health Dynamics Among the Oldest Old Survey), National Survey of Families and Households (NSFH), National Survey of Black Americans (NSBA), National Survey of American Life (NSAL), and National Social Life, Health, and Aging Project (NSHAP)—and offer family gerontologists an array of opportunities. A growing number of panel surveys from other countries—such as the Longitudinal Aging Study Amsterdam; Netherlands Kinship Panel Study; the five-country Study of Old Age and Autonomy: The Role of Service Systems and Intergenerational Family Solidarity; German Life History Study; Berlin Aging Study; and the Survey of Health, Ageing, and Retirement in Europe—are providing new international insights.

Longitudinal designs are increasingly used to investigate a wide variety of topics related to families and aging, such as marital discord in middle-aged and older couples (Whisman & Uebelacker, 2009); adjustment to widowhood after caregiving (Aneshensel, Boticello, & Yamamoto-Mitani, 2004); relationship quality and intergenerational support (Merz, Schengel, & Schulze, 2009) or caregiving (Li & Seltzer, 2003); and grandparents' perceived affection toward and contact with grandchildren (Silverstein & Long, 1998). The move toward more longitudinal designs has many scientific motivations: growing interest in understanding development across the life span, including how earlier life experiences and circumstances influence later experiences and circumstances, and growing curiosity about long-term and short-term dynamics and outcomes (Hofer & Piccinin, 2010); growing recognition that individuals (and relationships) are dynamic entities (Boker, Molenaar, & Nesselroade, 2009); and growing attention to when, how, why, and how fast change occurs with age (Schaie, 2005).

One novel use of panel surveys is to construct individual life histories or profiles that can capture diverse and complex pathways to outcomes (Gruenewald, Mroczek, Ryff, & Singer, 2008). Ethnographic life histories are another method for capturing dynamic processes (Valsiner, Molenaar,

Lyra, & Chaudhary, 2009). Life histories can be a particularly insightful method for uncovering life course diversity (Giele, 2009). Life history methods have not yet been widely applied to later-life families, and they are labor intensive, but they would seem to hold particular promise for family gerontologists.

Longitudinal designs vary widely in the duration, number, and spacing of measurement occasions and in their breadth of coverage of the life span. The examples above are panel surveys that typically spanned a number of years. More intensive designs are considered next.

Data-Intensive Designs

Data-intensive designs with daily interview bursts, daily diaries, or momentary experience sampling are a third innovation. As Laurenceau and Bolger (2005) noted, these methods can capture marital and family processes at a more microlevel (e.g., multiple times per day or daily) and in ways that are not possible with traditional methods (e.g., in their natural habitat and spontaneous context). One example, which investigated dynamic links between daily intimacy and disclosure in married couples, is a study by Boker and Laurenceau (2006). Although most often applied to dyads, these methods could be extended to larger family units.

Data-intensive methods have not yet been widely applied with older adults. One notable exception, Bisconti, Bergeman, and Boker (2004), used daily questionnaires and two interviews over a three-month period to study adjustment to recent bereavement. Another is research by Savla, Roberto, Blieszner, Cox, and Gwazdauskas (2011) in which daily cortisol levels were compared to daily interview data on stressful events to ascertain the effects of living with a spouse exhibiting mild cognitive impairment. There also are studies of aging and interpersonal tensions (not limited to family) that used daily interviews or daily diaries. For example, Charles, Piazza, Luong, and Almeida (2009) investigated emotional reactivity to interpersonal tensions, based on eight daily telephone interviews with older adults (aged 60 to 74), middle-aged adults (aged 40 to 59), and younger adults (aged 25 to 39), and Birditt, Fingerman, and Almeida (2005) investigated daily interpersonal tensions and their perceived stressfulness, as reported by adults aged 25 to 74. Given sufficient frequency of interaction, there is nothing intrinsic preventing these data-intensive methods from being applied specifically to family relations in later life. Although not without challenges (see Boker et al., 2009; Laurenceau & Bolger, 2005), it seems likely that data-intensive methods will be increasingly used by family gerontologists.

Designs with Multiple Family Members

A fourth notable innovation over the past 15 years is the increase in designs that collect data from multiple family members. The majority of these designs are dyadic, although a few involve triads or varying numbers. This design development has been spurred by advances in quantitative methods for analyzing nested and nonindependent data (discussed in a later section of this chapter) and a desire to move away from the atomistic consideration of individuals to focus on social context, interdependence, mutual influence, social networks, and family systems (Eichelsheim, Dekovic, Buist, & Cook, 2009; Kenny, Kashy, & Cook, 2006).

Gerontologists interested in the marital context of depression, interpersonal conflict, or illness have contributed disproportionately to the surge in multiple-member designs. For example, recent dyadic studies have contributed new knowledge about physical health and psychological distress in couples facing end-stage renal disease (Pruchno, Wilson-Genderson, & Cartwright, 2009); predictors of depressive symptomatology in middle-aged and older couples (Townsend, Miller, & Guo, 2001); well-being in dual-earner couples engaged in family caregiving (Chesley & Moen, 2006); well-being of older couples when one partner has osteoarthritis (Monin, Schulz, Martire, Jennings, Lingler, & Greenberg, 2010); health-related support and control when a spouse is in cardiac rehabilitation (Franks, Stephens, Rook, Franklin, Keteyian, & Artinian, 2006); and marital strain and cardiovascular reactivity during collaborative problem-solving among middle-aged and older couples (Smith, Uchino, Berg, Florsheim, Pearce, Hawkins, Henry, Beveridge, Skinner, Ko, & Olsen-Cerny, 2009).

Some dyadic studies have investigated relationships other than marriage—for example, parents and adult children (Birditt, Rott, & Fingerman, 2009; van Gaalen, Dykstra, & Komter, 2010); middle-aged parents and adult children who had a young child (Barnett, Scaramella, Neppl, Ontai, & Conger, 2010); adult siblings (de Vries, Kalmijn, & Liefbroer, 2009); aging mothers and daughters (Fingerman, 1996; Nauk & Suckow, 2006); and immigrant mothers from Japan and their adult daughters in the United States (Usita & Blieszner, 2002). The majority of nonmarital dyadic studies have focused on an adult child (most often a daughter) and an older parent (most often the mother). Many other family relationships are ripe for exploration.

Designs with more than two family members are still rare. Notable exceptions are studies of midlife sibling relationships that included multiple siblings per family (Suitor, Pardo, Gilligan, & Pillemer, 2009); intergenerational solidarity and support that included triads of two adult siblings and a parent (Voorpostel & Blieszner, 2008); interpersonal tensions that included triads of an adult child and two parents (Birditt et al., 2009); negotiation of intergenerational caregiving responsibilities among members of three-generation families (Connidis & Kemp, 2008); and family triad responses when a relative is diagnosed with early memory impairment (Roberto, Blieszner, McCann, & McPherson, 2011). A variation on multiple member designs is to ask individuals to report on relationships with several other family members. Examples of this are Davey, Savla, Janke, and Anderson

(2009), who interviewed grandchildren about their relationships with multiple grandparents, and Pillemer, Suitor, Mock, Sabir, Pardo, and Sechrist (2007), who interviewed mothers about their relationships with multiple adult children. Social network data have been collected from older adults (Fiori, Smith, & Antonucci, 2007), adult children (Merz et al., 2009), and samples spanning young adulthood to old age (Akiyama et al., 2003; de Vries et al., 2009).

Multiple-member designs provide many opportunities for family gerontologists to assess potential bias in theories, results, and conclusions if only one person per family is studied; investigate variability within and between family units; examine properties of relationships such as reciprocity, agreement, interdependence, discrepancy, mutual influence, and joint problem solving; and observe family members' interactions with each other. Innovations in data analysis, discussed in a later section, have facilitated the growth in multiple-member designs.

International and Cross-National Designs

A fifth notable design innovation is the increase in international or cross-national studies. Gerontologists outside the United States have actively contributed to innovative research on aging families, using the growing number of international data sets relevant to aging and families (see earlier section on longitudinal designs for examples). Voorpostel and Blieszner's (2008) study of adult sibling solidarity; Geurts, Poortman, van Tilburg and Dykstra's (2009) study of contact between young-adult grandchildren and grandparents; and van Gaalen, Dykstra, and Komter's (2010) study of solidarity and conflict between adult children and parents all used data from the Netherlands. Fiori and colleagues' (2007) study of older adults' social networks used German data. Nauk and Suckow (2006) used data from aging mother-daughter dyads in seven countries to investigate intergenerational networks. A study of exchanges between adult children and parents (Lowenstein, Katz, & Gur-Yaish, 2007), drew its data from four European countries and Israel.

Two examples of a cross-national design with the United States and another country are the Social Relations and Mental Health Over the Life Course Study, which collected data in the United States and Japan (Akiyama et al., 2003), and a study of intergenerational coresidence that compared data from the United States and China (Logan & Bian, 2004). Insightful discussion of advantages and challenges of cross-national or cross-cultural designs is provided by Blossfeld (2009), Harkness, Van de Vijver, and Mohler (2003) and Tesch-Romer and von Kondratowitz (2006).

These international and cross-national studies offer important insights into the many ways that aging and families are influenced by culture, politics, economic forces, geography, social norms and customs, social institutions, and history. They allow unique opportunities to learn about international similarities and differences. Although growing in number, these designs remain a small proportion of the research published in American journals, research from more developed countries is better represented than that from developing countries, and there are many areas around the globe from which little is known about family life of older adults. Gerontological research in Asian countries, for example, is just becoming accessible to most American gerontologists.

Qualitative and Mixed Qualitative-Quantitative Designs

A final design innovation since the first *Handbook of Aging and the Family* was published is the growth in qualitative research and greater appreciation for its unique contributions (Matthews, 2005). Attention to strategies for strengthening the quality and rigor of qualitative research also has grown (Creswell, 2009; Patton, 1999). Examples of qualitative designs include Allen, Blieszner, Roberto, Farnsworth, and Wilcox's (1999) in-depth interviews with older adults about their families; Kopera-Fry's (2009) in-depth interviews with custodial grandparents; Fingerman's (1996) joint interviews with aging mothers and their adult daughters regarding the last tense situation in their relationship; and Roberto, Allen, and Blieszner's (2001) use of in-depth interviews to explore grandfathers' expectations for relationships with their adult grandchildren.

Appreciation for mixed qualitative-quantitative designs also is growing (Creswell, 2009; Curry, Shield, & Wetle, 2006), although they have been infrequently used in research on aging and families. The research mentioned above by Fingerman (1996) was embedded within a larger mixed-methods design, although the 1996 publication only reported qualitative findings. Corsentino, Molinari, Gum, Roscoe, and Mills (2008) collected both quantitative and qualitative information from family caregivers to younger or older adults with severe mental illness; Turner, Young, and Black (2006) combined focus groups and semistructured interviews with unrelated daughters-in-law and mothers-in-law to study that kin relationship; Goodman (2007) used both closed-ended and open-ended questions to elicit information about family dynamics involving grandparents in three-generation families; and Roberto, Gold, and Yorgason (2004) combined closed-ended questions and open-ended guided interviews to measure older couples' perceptions of the influence of osteoporosis on their marital relationship. As these examples illustrate, there are many variations on mixed-methods designs. There also are many challenges in successfully integrating mixed-method results, a point returned to later under innovations in analysis.

INNOVATIONS IN SAMPLING

Age and Cohort

Over the past 15 years, a surge of attention to midlife, a previously understudied part of the life span, has emerged. The Study of Midlife in the United States (MIDUS) is one indicator of this trend. Other indicators are the large number of recent studies on the interface between work and family life, dual-earner couples, midlife women's multiple roles, and middle-aged children's relationships with aging parents.

While attention to midlife is welcome, another innovation is that recent studies have begun to include broader coverage of the adult life span, either including a wider range of adult years (e.g., Akiyama et al., 2003; Charles et al., 2009) or focusing more on older adults (e.g., August, Rook, & Newsom, 2007; Bisconti et al., 2004). For example, Burton (1996) studied three-generation African American families that included young mothers who were aged 21 to 26 and their mothers who were aged 42 to 57, and Barnett, Scaramella, Neppl, Ontai, and Conger (2010) studied middle-aged grandparents (mean age = 51) with young grandchildren (aged 3–4). Recent studies of parent-child relations have sampled a broader range of adult children's ages (e.g., 18 to 79 in van Gaalen et al., 2010; 20 to 61 in Pillemer et al., 2007; and 22 to 49 in Fingerman, Pitzer, Lefkowitz, Birditt, & Mroczek, 2008). Relationships between young adults (or adolescents) and aging family members remain less frequently studied. At the other end of the adult span, research on families and their oldest-old members remains less common than research on young-old relatives, despite increasing longevity. Notable exceptions are Fiori and colleagues (2007), who compared social networks of young-old adults (aged 70 to 84) with those of oldest-old adults (aged 85 to 103), and August and colleagues (2007), who investigated social exchanges reported by adults aged 65 to 91.

Cohort is a less prominent feature of most studies on families than age, although a historical or demographic perspective has much to contribute to understanding of aging and families (Settersten & Mayer, 1997). Current research in family gerontology, however, more often focuses on what Alwin and McCammon (2007) call family lineage generations than on birth cohort generations or cohorts defined by their participation in some historical event. More research that places aging and families in a larger demographic or historical context is needed, like Almeida, Serido, and McDonald's (2006) comparison of exposure and reactivity to daily stressors between Early and Late Baby Boomers, and Bedford and Avioli's (2006) comparison of intimacy between brothers in World War II and baby boomer generations.

Gender and Sexual Orientation

Research remains dominated by studies of daughters, mothers, wives, and grandmothers. Sons, fathers, husbands, and grandfathers remain understudied. Caregiving literature has devoted more attention to males in recent years (e.g., Pinquart & Sörenson, 2006), but studies of male caregivers are still not common. In literature on aging and families, gender is more often a covariate than a subject of investigation. Notable exceptions are Pudrovska's (2009) study of gender differences in parenthood experiences during late midlife and early old age and Roberto and colleagues' (2001) study of grandfathers' experiences and expectations. Studies such as these go beyond merely documenting whether gender differences exist to illuminating ways in which later-life family experiences are shaped by gender. (See Bedford & Avioli, chapter 6 in this volume, for studies on gender differences in sibling relationships in middle adulthood and old age, especially in relation to caring for parents, and Calasanti & Kiecolt, chapter 11 in this volume, for research on the intersection of gender and other social locations.)

Research on families and aging also continues to favor heterosexual relationships. Aging individuals who are lesbian, gay, bisexual, or transgendered (LGBT) remain underrepresented (Connidis, 2010). A recent review of literature on the health, social, and housing needs of older adults from LGBT groups (Addis, Davies, Greene, MacBride-Stewart, & Shepherd, 2009) concluded that research on these populations (especially bisexual and transgendered older adults) is very limited, focused on a narrow range of topics, and often based on small samples of questionable generalizability. There are relatively few studies of social relations or networks of older adults from LGBT groups (including studies of relationships between partners). Two noteworthy exceptions are research by Grossman, D'Augelli, & Hershberger (2000) on the social support networks of lesbian, gay, and bisexual adults aged 60 and older and Cohen and Murray (2007) on caregiving to families of choice and families of origin by lesbian and gay older adults. Studies such as these can illuminate less-visible family ties, counteract stereotypes, and allow consideration of whether, when, and how sexual orientation, gender identity, or gender orientation influence later-life family relationships.

Kin Relationships

Literature on aging families remains dominated by relationships between adult children and parents (most often daughters and mothers) and marital relationships. Innovative studies are expanding the relationships under consideration, however. More attention is being given to sibling relationships (e.g., Bedford & Volling, 2004; Suitor et al., 2009). Some studies focused on in-law relationships are appearing (e.g., Turner et al., 2006). Custodial grandparenting (and grandparenting in general) has received wider attention (e.g., Kopera-Fry, 2009; Smith & Hancock, 2010). Some investigators are studying partnered as well as married adults (e.g., Windsor & Butterworth, 2010), although partnerships or unions other than marriage are still rarely the focus of investigation (see Bookwala, chapter 5 in this volume, for a review of both marital and other partnered relationships). Some attention is being given to relationships between older parents and stepchildren versus biological children (van der Pas & van Tilburg, 2010; see Ganong & Coleman, chapter 9 in this volume).

Many kin (or kinlike) relationships are understudied, including cousins, nieces and nephews, aunts and uncles, stepchildren, and other blended family relationships, adopted and foster children, fictive or chosen kin, great-grandparents. Connidis (2010) noted that kin relationships of older adults who remain single, are childless, or have divorced are understudied. Research on kin relationships of cohabiting older adults is rare, although that is a growing population of elders (Brown, Lee, & Bulanda, 2006). Relationships where there are special needs that alter the traditional family life cycle also are less-often studied; one important exception is Smith, Greenberg, and Seltzer's (2007) study of sibling expectations for future caregiving when there is an aging parent and a brother or sister with mental illness.

Race and Ethnicity

The majority of studies on aging and families continue to have predominantly U.S.-born non-Hispanic white samples. Consequently, there are large gaps in knowledge about aging and African American families, Latino families, Asian American families, Arab American families, or other racial and ethnic minority families (see Silverstein, Lendon, & Giarrusso, chapter 12 in this volume, for a review of studies on intergenerational caregiving in minority families). Because of the predominant focus on U.S.-born samples, limited attention has been paid to immigration, acculturation, immigration status, or family separation (Boyce & Fuligni, 2007), especially in later life (see Usita & Shakya, chapter 14 in this volume, for a review of family immigration studies). Knowledge about multiracial and multiethnic families and aging also is sorely lacking.

Some innovative efforts have occurred during the past 15 years to broaden the racial and ethnic composition of our knowledge base. Some of these have been designs that compare two or more ethnoracial groups within the United States, and others have been focused on a single underrepresented group. Examples of single-group designs include Ajrouch's (2005) study of immigrant and U.S.-born Arab American elders' social integration and networks; research on kin and other support networks among older black Americans by Chatters, Taylor, Lincoln, and Schroepfer (2002) and Taylor, Chatters, and Jackson (1997); Burton's (1996) examination of intergenerational caregiving among three-generation African American families; Gonzales's (2007) investigation of determinants of parent-child coresidence in Hispanic families; a study of depressive symptomatology in older Mexican American couples by Peek, Stimpson, Townsend, and Markides (2006); and research on family relations and well-being in Caribbean blacks by Jackson, Forsythe-Brown, and

Govia (2007). Studies such as these are contributing innovative knowledge not only about differences in family life across underrepresented groups but also about variability within these groups.

Some noteworthy comparative designs include Coleman, Ganong, and Rothrauff's (2006) study of beliefs about intergenerational assistance to older adults among Latinos, African Americans, Asian Americans, and white European Americans; Kim, Knight, and Longmire's (2007) study of familism, stress, and coping in African American and white caregivers of persons with dementia; Sarkisian, Gerena, and Gerstel's (2007) comparison of family contact, proximity, and support among Mexican American and white European American families; Kopera-Fry's (2009) study of Latino and Native American custodial grandparents; Pillemer and colleagues' (2007) study of intergenerational ambivalence among black and white older mothers; and Mui's (1996) study of correlates of psychological distress (including family conflict and caregiving duty) among Mexican, Cuban, and Puerto Rican elders residing in the United States. Literature reviews have been done on African American, Hispanic, white, and Asian American family caregivers to older adults (Pinquart & Sörenson, 2005) and antecedents of intergenerational support among black, white, and Hispanic families (Davey, Janke, & Savla, 2004). Comparative studies such as these are contributing important new knowledge about ethnoracial similarities and differences, the importance of culture, and the generalizability of prior theories, results, and conclusions.

Asian American elders are one of the fastest growing groups of older adults (Choi, 2001), but research on Asian American families and aging has only recently begun to appear. For example, Wong, Yoo, and Stewart (2006) investigated changes in the meaning of family support among older Chinese and Korean immigrants, and Yoon (2005) studied needs and characteristics of Chinese American and Korean American grandparents. Research on aging Asian American families is currently sparse and limited to only a few Asian groups.

As more studies make race or ethnicity a focus, greater attention is being given to the special methodological challenges that arise during recruiting, retaining, and studying members of underrepresented groups and the special strategies needed to address those challenges (Cauce, Coronado, & Watson, 1998; Knight, Roosa, & Umaña-Taylor, 2009). For example, Boyce and Fuligni (2007) discussed issues for developmental research among racial and ethnic minority populations and immigrant families, and Choi (2001) discussed research issues related to studying aging Asian American families.

Large Population-Based Studies

More large-scale, national or multisite population-based panel surveys both in the United States and abroad (see the sections above on longitudinal designs and international or cross-national designs) are providing family gerontologists with a wealth of new opportunities. These large population-based panel surveys typically rely on sophisticated sampling frames (or, in the case of some international studies and a few U.S. studies, comprehensive enumerations of the population) that provide an important antidote to the small, convenience samples of questionable generalizability that formerly dominated research on aging and families.

Data from surveys on specific ethnoracial groups—such as the National Survey of Hispanic Elderly People in the U.S.A. (used by Mui, 1996), the Hispanic Established Populations for the Epidemiologic Studies of the Elderly (used by Peek et al., 2006), the National Survey of Black Americans (used by Taylor et al., 1997), or the National Survey of American Life (African American and Caribbean black adults, used by Jackson et al., 2007)—provide unique opportunities to examine social and cultural influences on aging and families. Large national surveys that oversample from, but are not restricted to, specific racial and ethnic groups—such as the Health and Retirement Study (used by Townsend et al., 2001), and the National Survey of Families and Households (used by Sarkisian et al., 2007)—also permit researchers to study ethnoracial variability in aging and family relationships.

INNOVATIONS IN MEASUREMENT

Quality of Family Relationships

One very noticeable trend in the past 15 years has been a proliferation of studies that take a more complex approach to measuring the quality of family relationships. This trend has not been restricted to research on aging families, but it has been particularly evident there. It has been especially prominent in research on relationships between children and aging parents. This trend started with research examining negative aspects of social relations, research designed to counter the previous focus on primarily positive aspects. Concurrently, research on caregiving to older adults began to move in the opposite direction, as studies began to redress the predominant focus on caregiving burden or stress with a focus on caregiving rewards or benefits. What these developments share is the desire to capture a more complex, nuanced, and balanced picture of family relationships.

In family gerontology, some examples of innovative research that investigated both positive and negative social relations include Akiyama and colleagues' (2003) study of positive and negative interactions across the adult life course; Ingersoll-Dayton, Morgan, and Antonucci's (1997) research on aging adults' positive and negative social exchanges; van Gaalen and colleagues' (2010) examination of solidarity and conflict between adult children and parents; and Mavandadi, Rook, and Newsom's (2007) investigation of older adults' reports of positive and negative social exchanges.

Studies focused solely on negative relationships also have increased: for example, Suitor and colleagues' (2009) investigation of adult children's perceptions of maternal favoritism; Krause and Rook's (2003) study on older adults' negative social exchanges (not just family); Heffner, Kiecolt-Glaser, Loving, Glaser, and Malarkey's (2004) study of marital conflict; and Birditt and colleagues' (2009) study of tensions between adult children and parents.

An even more recent innovation in measurement of the quality of family relationships is attention to the concept of ambivalence. Previously, researchers treated positive and negative social relations as separate dimensions and devoted limited attention to their possible coexistence or interaction. In reaction, research arose that focused on relationships that were both positive and negative. Pillemer and Suitor (2004), for example, argued for the value of studying intergenerational ambivalence and its sources, highlighted methodological strengths and limitations in prior approaches to measuring ambivalence, and presented empirical evidence on ambivalence in relationships between aging mothers and adult children. Other researchers who have investigated ambivalence include Fingerman and colleagues (2008) and van Gaalen and colleagues (2010), who studied adult children and parents; Willson, Shuey, and Elder (2003), who studied adult children and parents or parents-in-law; and Windsor and Butterworth (2010), who studied ambivalence (and indifference) in marital and partner relationships. It is worth noting that most research on ambivalence has centered on the adult child-parent relationship and, even more specifically, adult children and aging mothers.

Much still remains to be learned about how best to conceptualize and measure the quality of family relationships, what the antecedents and consequences are, similarities and differences in the quality of relationships across different family ties, and within-family variability. Some facets of the quality of later-life family relationships, such as indifference, are rarely studied (for a noteworthy exception, see Cicirelli, 1995).

Physiological or Biological Measures

A second measurement innovation is the introduction of physiological or biological measures to the study of aging families. The majority of family gerontology measures remain closed-ended, self-report survey measures, responses to in-depth interviews, or a combination of closed-ended and open-ended questionnaire responses. A few studies, however, have begun to include physiological measures. Heffner and colleagues (2004), for example, have collected physiological responses to marital conflict in younger and older married couples; Levenson, Carstensen, and Gottman (1994) collected measures of physiological arousal, as well as self-reports of affect, in middle-aged and older married couples; Smith and colleagues (2009) collected measures of cardiovascular reactivity during stressful marital interactions with middle-aged and older couples; and Savla and colleagues (2011) measured cortisol levels in spouses of individuals with mild cognitive impairment. As these examples illustrate, physiological or biological measures have most often been collected in studies of the marital relationship. Availability of biomarker and physiological measures in several large, panel surveys (e.g., HRS, WLS, MIDUS) will allow family gerontologists to incorporate more biological or physiological measures in future research. Integration of biological and social science measures has been encouraged by the National Research Council (Finch, Vaupel, & Kinsella, 2001).

Culturally Sensitive Measures

A third innovation is of greater concern for culturally sensitive measures (Boyce & Fuligni, 2007; Cauce et al., 1998; Knight et al., 2009). Researchers increasingly question the universal applicability of measures across cultures. These concerns have quickened as the U.S. population becomes more diverse (Hobbs & Stoops, 2002). Reciprocity or familial obligation, for example, may have different meaning, manifestations, or relevance across cultures. Qualitative or mixed quantitative-qualitative methods, as well as cognitive interviewing (Willis, 2005), have been suggested as sensitive means to uncover cultural variability in meaning, reveal missing elements from current measures, and develop more culturally valid measures (Curry et al., 2006; Knight et al., 2009).

Although not in the vanguard of this cultural critique and search for more culturally appropriate ways of measuring key constructs, family gerontology has begun to contribute to this cultural critique. Notable family gerontology contributions include Burton's (1996) exploration of African American intergenerational caregiving and family role transitions; Coleman and colleagues' (2006) investigation of similarities and differences in beliefs among Latinos, African Americans, Asian Americans, and white European Americans about intergenerational assistance to elders after divorce and remarriage; Kim and colleagues' (2007) study of the role of familism in African American and white families caring for an elder with dementia; Lowenstein and colleagues' (2007) and Nauk and Suckow's (2006) studies of intergenerational relations across multiple countries; Akiyama and colleagues' (2003) comparison of social interactions of adults in the United States. and Japan; and Kopera-Fry's (2009) investigation of custodial grandparenting in Latino and Native American communities.

INNOVATIONS IN QUANTITATIVE ANALYSIS

Testing Measurement Models and Measurement Equivalence

Comparisons between or among groups assume that the measure used is conceptually and psychometrically equivalent (Horn & McArdle, 1992). Methodological innovations for assessing this assumption have relevance not just for efforts to assess measures' comparability across racial, ethnic, linguistic, or international cultures, but also across stages of the life course, chronological age groups, birth cohorts, multiple family members or generations, and time. As mentioned in the prior section on culturally sensitive measures, qualitative and mixed methods, as well as cognitive interviewing, have been proposed as useful methods for exploring measurement equivalence. For quantitative designs, multiple-group confirmatory factor analysis (CFA) is a major innovation for testing measurement equivalence. Application to later-life family relations is rare, although CFA has been widely applied to family relations in earlier parts of the life span. Thus, CFA is an innovation yet to be adopted by many family gerontologists. One exception is a study that tested equivalence of measures of support satisfaction (among others) between dyads of custodial grandmothers and grandfathers (Smith & Hancock, 2010).

CFA can also be used to test cross-sectional measurement models within a single group. This use of CFA is very relevant to research on aging and families, where many scales have been used with limited investigation of their underlying structure. CFA can be conducted as an end in itself or embedded within a larger structural equation model (SEM) testing relationships between or among constructs. Other new approaches to testing measurement models have emerged—notably item response theory (IRT), Rasch models, or differential item functioning (DIF) (Bergeman & Wallace, 2006; Bingenheimer, Raudenbush, Leventhal, & Brooks-Gunn, 2005)—but these alternatives have been even less frequently adopted by family gerontologists.

Examples of testing measurement models in aging families are surprisingly uncommon, although increasing in recent years. Some exceptions are research by Krause and Rook (2003), who presented results from a CFA of items measuring negative interactions with spouse, other family, and friends (analyzed both globally and separately by relationship) as part of a larger SEM of the stability and generalizability of older adults' negative interactions; Newsom, Mahan, Rook, and Krause (2008), who conducted a CFA of older adults' reports of negative social exchanges (including but not limited to family), as part of a larger SEM of negative exchanges and health; de Vries and colleagues (2009), who conducted a CFA of kinship, filial, and parental norms in a SEM of family solidarity in adult sibling dyads; and Li and Seltzer (2003), who presented a measurement model of items assessing relationship quality as part of a SEM of predictors of mental health among adult daughters providing parent care.

Analyses of Multiple Family Members

As described earlier, designs with multiple family members (mainly dyads to date) are increasingly used in research on aging families. In part, this explosion has been driven by recent statistical innovations that permit the simultaneous analysis of multiple parties who are related. The Actor-Partner Interaction Model (APIM) is one such statistical innovation (Kenny et al., 2006). The APIM and related models allow testing of novel research hypotheses about actor and partner effects (e.g., the effect of an actor's behavior on her or his own outcome versus the effect on a partner's outcome), mutual influence (e.g., reciprocally related behavior between partners), and common fate (e.g., when both partners' outcome is due to a shared environment).

Two major approaches are being used to analyze data from related individuals: SEM (Kenny et al., 2006) and multilevel modeling (MLM; Laurenceau & Bolger, 2005; Sayer & Klute, 2005). In SEM, multiple family members' data can be modeled either as repeated measures of a single family-level latent construct or each family member's data can be modeled with his or her own latent construct. In family gerontology, the SEM approach was used by de Vries and colleagues (2009) in their study of family norms among adult sibling dyads; Barnett, Scaramella, Neppl, Ontai, and Conger's (2010) in their study of quality of family relationships and involvement among married grandparent dyads; and Peek and colleagues (2006) in their study of older Mexican American couples.

MLM was used by Voorpostel and Blieszner (2008) in their study of intergenerational solidarity and support among family triads (two adult siblings and a parent), Birditt and colleagues (2009) in their study of relationship quality among family triads (an adult child and two parents), Townsend and colleagues (2001) in their study of depressive symptoms among middle-aged and older married couples, and Roberts, Smith, Jackson, and Edmonds (2009) in their study of health among older married couples.

Unlike traditional methods of analyzing data from multiple family members (e.g., OLS regression) that ignore the fact that family data violate the assumption of independent observations, both MLM and SEM take nonindependence into account (indeed, the degree of nonindependence is of scientific interest). Consequently, SEM and MLM estimate more accurate standard errors, leading to more valid conclusions about statistical significance. Both SEM and MLM can test hypotheses about interdependence, mutual influence, or common fate, and both allow incorporation of individual-level and family-level covariates.

SEM has the advantage of testing both measurement and structural models and, because of the measurement modeling capability, SEM also has the advantage of being able to estimate and model measurement error. SEM can test the equivalence of measurement models or structural models across time, family members, or groups. MLM, on the other hand, has some advantage when there are covariates that are numerous or time-varying. MLM also offers greater flexibility when data are collected from more than two or three family members; indeed, one advantage of MLM over SEM is that it can handle varying numbers of family members across families. Suitor and colleagues (2009), for example, used MLM to study adult children's perceptions of maternal favoritism where the number of adult children per family varied.

MLM has been widely used in studies that collect daily diary data from couples. An example is Almeida, Wethington, and Chandler's (1999) study of daily tensions between spouses and between parents and children, as reported by middle-aged married couples. Data-intensive analyses are well suited to test questions about daily transmission of emotions within families, spillover of stress between work and family, and interdependence of daily stressors and reactivity within and between family members.

Another innovative technique for analyzing intensive data from dyads is dynamical systems modeling (Bergeman & Wallace, 2006). Valsiner and colleagues (2009) argued that such methods for analyzing dynamic social processes are essential for understanding complex family contexts. This approach conceptualizes individuals in shared environments as coupled dynamic systems with potential for mutual regulation, and it uses coupled simultaneous differential equations to model these dynamic systems. An application of this approach (not specific to aging) is provided by Boker and Laurenceau's (2006) research on the regulation of intimacy and disclosure in marriage. Given the unique research questions this technique can address, it is likely to see greater use by family gerontologists in the future.

Analyses of Intensive Data from Unrelated Individuals

The intensive and nested design of data-intensive studies (i.e., many repeated measures per individual) also makes MLM an analytic technique of choice for data-intensive designs with unrelated individuals (Laurenceau & Bolger, 2005). Examples of this type of MLM analysis are Almeida and colleagues' (2006) comparison of daily stressors among Early and Late Baby Boomers; Charles and colleagues' (2009) comparison of daily emotional reactivity to social tensions in young, middle-aged, and older adults; and Birditt and colleagues' (2005) investigation of interpersonal tensions among adults aged 25 to 74. MLM combined with data-intensive designs is well-suited to investigate research questions related to intraindividual variability and its predictors, while simultaneously investigating interindividual variability and its predictors (Bergeman & Wallace, 2006).

Dynamical systems modeling, mentioned previously under innovations related to analyzing intensive data from dyads, is also leading to novel insights about dynamic processes in unrelated individuals. These dynamic systems models are uniquely suited to investigate individual variability in dynamic patterns of stability, change, and equilibrium across a more microlevel of time than are traditional methods (Boker et al., 2009). Two examples that applied a dynamic systems approach to aging and families are Bisconti and colleagues' (2004) study of adjustment to widowhood over a three-month period after the death and Bedford and Volling's (2004) model of emotion regulation within sibling relations across the life span.

Other Longitudinal Analyses

Many of the techniques described in the preceding sections represent innovative approaches to analyzing longitudinal designs other than data-intensive designs. CFA and IRT can be applied to test measurement invariance over time (Horn & McArdle, 1992). SEM and MLM (whether with multiple family members or unrelated individuals) are applicable to longitudinal as well as cross-sectional data. MLM, in particular, has the advantage that it can handle designs where there are varying numbers of measurement occasions and assessment intervals (Sayer & Klute, 2005).

Examples of SEM applied to longitudinal data on aging and family relationships include Whisman and Uebelacker (2009), who investigated marital discord and depressive symptoms in middle-aged and older adults over time, and Newsom and colleagues (2008), who studied the stability of negative social exchanges and their longitudinal effects on health in older adults. Examples of MLM applied to longitudinal data on aging and family relationships include Amirkhanyan and Wolf's (2006) study of parent care and adult children's mental health and Windsor and Butterworth's (2010) investigation of the quality of partner relationships in midlife and young-old adults who were married or partnered.

Another innovative technique over the past 15 years for analyzing longitudinal data is latent growth analysis (LGA). LGA analyzes trajectories of intraindividual stability and change and their predictors (Bergeman & Wallace, 2006; George, 2009). LGA has become increasingly popular as panel studies have accumulated more measurement occasions. A minimum of three measurement occasions is required, and more if nonlinear rates of change are of interest (George, 2009). Created to investigate developmental growth in earlier stages of the life span, LGA is increasingly applied across the life span and to patterns of change other than growth. Application of LGA has been criticized for often outpacing development of theoretical frameworks for conceptualizing and interpreting the change that is seen (George, 2009). Examples of LGA applied to aging families are Walker, Acock, Bowman, and Li's (1996) test of the wear-and-tear hypothesis of adult child caregivers' strain and Silverstein and Long's (1998) study of trajectories of grandparents' perceived solidarity and contact with grandchildren.

A second statistical technique called latent class growth analysis (LCGA) or growth mixture modeling (GMM) also has arisen to derive trajectories (George, 2009). This approach is not without critics (e.g., Bauer, 2007). Unlike LGA, which analyzes individual trajectories, GMM is a group-based approach to modeling development or change over time that seeks to identify how many latent classes can be used to represent the individual growth curves. Two gerontological GMM examples are Mavandadi and colleagues' (2007) typology of trajectories of positive and negative social exchanges and disability among older adults and Aneshensel, Boticello, and Yamamoto-Mitani's (2004) study of the relationship between dementia caregiving experiences and trajectories of postbereavement depressive symptoms among older spouses and adult children. GMM has been used in studies of aging and families even less often than LGA.

Multilevel Analyses

MLM has already been mentioned as an innovative approach to analyze data collected over time or multiple family members. It is worth noting that MLM also is suited for studies that collect information (either cross-sectionally or longitudinally) from individuals (or multiple family members) and from larger environments within which those individuals (or families) are embedded. Extended family units, service agencies, employment settings, religious institutions, residential settings (e.g., assisted living facilities), neighborhoods, cities, and countries are only some of the possible ecological contexts within which aging individuals and their families may be situated. Designs that collect information from multiple individuals within an environment and from multiple levels (e.g., from multiple custodial grandparents per neighborhood and multiple neighborhoods) lend themselves to MLM. Multilevel designs also can be tested in SEM, but may be more easily tested in MLM. No examples, however, of these sorts of multilevel analyses related to aging and families were identified.

INNOVATIONS IN INTEGRATING QUALITATIVE AND QUANTITATIVE DATA

Although examples of integrated qualitative and quantitative results are hard to find in research on aging and families, there are a growing number of models of ways to integrate, combine, or synthesize mixed methods (Creswell, 2009; Curry et al., 2006). In practice, results from the two methods often are presented separately and do not even address the same constructs (e.g., Corsentino et al., 2008; Roberto et al., 2004). In contrast, in Goodman's

(2007) study of family dynamics in grandmother-headed families, quantitative results were used to place families into groups, and similarities and differences in qualitative themes were then explored across these groups. Thus, examples of integrating mixed quantitative and qualitative methods are rare in research on aging and families and have used a very limited range of strategies to bring the two methods into conversation with each other. Mixed methods have great potential, however, for enriching understanding of aging families, uncovering neglected areas for research, improving our measures, elucidating the meaning of quantitative findings, and generating novel hypotheses or research questions.

CONCLUSIONS

In the 17 years since the first edition of the *Handbook* appeared, research on aging and families has made use of a variety of methodological innovations related to study designs, sampling, measurement, and analysis. Quantitative, qualitative, and mixed designs have all benefited from new methodological innovations. Nevertheless, family gerontologists have been slow to adopt some innovative designs, samples, measurement approaches, and analytic techniques, even though these innovations offer substantial promise for moving research on aging and families forward in novel directions.

REFERENCES

Addis, S., Davies, M., Greene, G., MacBride-Stewart, S., & Shepherd, M. (2009). The health, social care, and housing needs of lesbian, gay, bisexual and transgender older people: A review of the literature. *Health and Social Care in the Community, 17,* 647–658.

Ajrouch, K. (2005). Arab American elders: Network structure, perceptions of relationship quality, and discrimination. *Research in Human Development, 2,* 213–228.

Akiyama, H., Antonucci, T., Takahashi, K., & Langfahl, E. (2003). Negative interactions in close relationships across the life span. *Journal of Gerontology: Psychological Sciences, 58B,* P70–P79.

Allen, K., Blieszner, R., Roberto, K., Farnsworth, E., & Wilcox, K. (1999). Older adults and their children: Family patterns of structural diversity. *Family Relations, 48,* 151–157.

Almeida, D., Serido, J., & McDonald, D. (2006). Daily life stressors of early and late baby boomers. In S. Whitbourne & S. Willis (Eds.), *The baby boomers grow up: Contemporary perspectives on midlife* (pp. 165–183). Mahwah, NJ: Lawrence Erlbaum & Associates.

Almeida, D., Wethington, E., & Chandler, A. (1999). Daily transmission of tensions between marital dyads and parent-child dyads. *Journal of Marriage and the Family, 61,* 49–61.

Alwin, D., & McCammon, R. (2007). Rethinking generations. *Research in Human Development, 4*, 219–237.

Amirkhanyan, A. A., & Wolf, D. A. (2006). Parent care and the stress process: Findings from panel data. *Journal of Gerontology: Social Sciences, 61B*, S248–S255.

Aneshensel, C., Boticello, A., & Yamamoto-Mitani, N. (2004). When caregiving ends: The course of depressive symptoms after bereavement. *Journal of Health and Social Behavior, 45*, 422–440.

August, K., Rook, K., & Newsom, J. (2007). The joint effects of life stress and negative social exchanges on emotional distress. *Journal of Gerontology: Social Sciences, 62B*, S304–S314.

Barnett, M., Scaramella, L., Neppl, T., Ontai, L., & Conger, R. (2010). Intergenerational relationship quality, gender, and grandparent involvement. *Family Relations, 59*, 28–44.

Bauer, D. (2007). Observations on the use of growth mixture models in psychological research (2004 Cattell Award Address). *Multivariate Behavioral Research, 42*, 757–786.

Bedford, V.H., & Avioli, P.S. (2006). "Shooting the bull": Cohort comparisons of fraternal intimacy in mid-life and old age. In V.H. Bedford & B.F. Turner (Eds.), *Men in relationships: A new look from a life course perspective* (pp. 81–101). New York: Springer.

Bedford, V.H., & Volling, B. (2004). A dynamic ecological systems perspective on emotion regulation development within the sibling relationship context. In F. Lang & K. Fingerman (Eds.), *Growing together: Personal relationships across the lifespan* (pp. 76–102). New York: Cambridge University Press.

Berg, C., & Upchurch, R. (2007). A developmental-contextual model of couples coping with chronic illness across adult the life span. *Psychological Bulletin, 133*, 920–954.

Bergeman, C., & Wallace, K. (2006). The theory-methods interface. In C. Bergeman & S. Boker (Eds.), *Methodological issues in aging research* (pp. 19–42). Mahwah, NJ: Lawrence Erlbaum & Associates.

Bingenheimer, J., Raudenbush, S., Leventhal, T., & Brooks-Gunn, J. (2005). Measurement equivalence and differential item functioning in family psychology. *Journal of Family Psychology, 19*, 441–455.

Birditt, K., Fingerman, K., & Almeida, D. (2005). Age differences in exposure and reactions to interpersonal tensions: A daily diary study. *Psychology and Aging, 20*, 330–340.

Birditt, K., Rott, L., & Fingerman, K. (2009). "If you can't say something nice, don't say anything at all": Coping with interpersonal tensions in the parent-child relationship during adulthood. *Journal of Family Psychology, 23*, 769–778.

Bisconti, T., Bergeman, C., & Boker, S. (2004). Emotional well-being in recently bereaved widows: A dynamical systems approach. *Journal of Gerontology: Psychological Sciences, 59B*, P158–P167.

Blieszner, R. (2006). A lifetime of caring: Dimensions and dynamics in late-life close relationships. *Personal Relationships, 13*, 1–18.

Blossfeld, H-P. (2009). Comparative life course research: A cross-national and longitudinal perspective. In G. Elder, Jr., & J. Giele (Eds.), *The craft of life course research* (pp. 280–306). New York: Guilford Press.

Boker, S., & Laurenceau, J-P. (2006). Dynamical systems modeling: An application to the regulation of intimacy and disclosure in marriage. In T. Walls & J. Schafer (Eds.), *Models for intensive longitudinal data* (pp. 195–218). New York: Oxford University Press.

Boker S., Molenaar, P., & Nesselroade, J. (2009). Issues in intraindividual variability: Individual differences in equilibria and dynamics over multiple time scales. *Psychology and Aging, 24*, 858–862.

Boyce, C., & Fuligni, A. (2007). Issues for developmental research among racial/ethnic minority and immigrant families. *Research in Human Development, 4*, 1–17.

Brown, S.L., Lee, G.R., & Bulanda, J.R. (2006). Cohabitation among older adults: A national portrait. *Journals of Gerontology: Psychological Sciences and Social Sciences, 61B*, S71–S79.

Burton, L. (1996). Age norms, the timing of family role transitions, and integernerational caregiving among aging African American women. *The Gerontologist, 36*, 199–208.

Carter, B., & McGoldrick, M. (2005). *The expanded family life cycle: Individual, family, and social perspectives* (3rd ed.). Boston: Allyn & Bacon.

Cauce, A. M., Coronado, N., & Watson, J. (1998). Conceptual, methodological, and statistical issues in culturally competent research. In M. Hernandez & M. Isaacs (Eds.), *Promoting cultural competence in children's mental health services* (pp. 305–329). Baltimore: Brookes Publishing.

Charles, S., Piazza, J., Luong, G., & Almeida, D. (2009). Now you see it, now you don't: Age differences in affective reactivity to social tensions. *Psychology and Aging, 24*, 645–653.

Chatters, L., Taylor, R., Lincoln, K., & Schroepfer, T. (2002). Patterns of informal support from family and church members among African Americans. *Journal of Black Studies, 33*, 66–85.

Chesley, N., & Moen, P. (2006). When workers care: Dual-earner couples' caregiving strategies, benefit use, and psychological well-being. *American Behavioral Scientist, 49*, 1248–1269.

Choi, N. (2001). Diversity within diversity: Research and social work practice issues with Asian American elders. In N. Choi (Ed.), *Psychosocial aspects of the Asian-American experience: Diversity within diversity* (pp. 301–319). Binghampton, NY: Haworth Press.

Cicirelli, V. G. (1995). A measure of caregiving daughters' attachment to elderly mothers. *Journal of Family Psychology, 9*, 89–94.

Cohen, H., & Murray, Y. (2007). Older lesbian and gay caregivers: Caring for families of choice and caring for families of origin. *Journal of Human Behavior in the Social Sciences, 14*, 275–298.

Coleman, M., Ganong, L., & Rothrauff, T. (2006). Racial and ethnic similarities and differences in beliefs about intergenerational assistance to older adults after divorce and remarriage. *Family Relations, 55*, 576–587.

Connidis, I. (2010). *Family ties and aging.* Thousand Oaks, CA: Pine Forge Press/Sage.

Connidis, I., & Kemp, C. (2008). Negotiating actual and anticipated parental support: Multiple sibling voices in three-generation families. *Journal of Aging Studies, 22*, 229–238.

Corsentino, E., Molinari, V., Gum, A., Roscoe, L., & Mills, W. (2008). Family care-givers' future planning for younger and older adults with serious mental illness (SMI). *Journal of Applied Gerontology, 27*, 466–485.

Creswell, J. (2009). *Research design: Qualitative, quantitative, and mixed methods approaches* (3rd ed.). Thousand Oaks, CA: Sage.

Curry, L., Shield, R., & Wetle, T. (2006). *Improving aging and public health research: Qualitative and mixed methods.* Washington, DC: American Public Health Association.

Davey, A., Janke, M., & Savla, J. (2004). Antecedents of intergenerational support: Families in context and families as context. *Annual Review of Gerontology and Geriatrics, 24*, 29–54.

Davey, A., Savla, J., Janke, M., & Anderson, S. (2009). Grandparent-grandchild rela-tionships: From families in contexts to families as contexts. *International Journal of Aging and Human Development, 69*, 311–325.

de Vries, J., Kalmijn, M., & Liefbroer, A. (2009). Intergenerational transmission of kinship norms? Evidence from siblings in a multi-actor survey. *Social Science Research, 38*, 188–200.

Eichelsheim, V., Dekovic, M., Buist, K., & Cook, W. (2009). The social relations model in family studies: A systematic review. *Journal of Marriage and Family, 71*, 1052–1069.

Finch, C., Vaupel, J., & Kinsella, K. (2001). *Cells and surveys: Should biological mea-sures be included in social science research?* Washington, DC: National Acad-emies Press.

Fingerman, K. (1996). Sources of tension in the aging mother and adult daughter relationship. *Psychology and Aging, 11*, 591–606.

Fingerman, K., Pitzer, L., Lefkowitz, E., Birditt, K., & Mroczek, D. (2008). Ambiva-lent relationship qualities between adults and their parents: Implications for the well-being of both parties. *Journal of Gerontology: Psychological Sciences, 63B*, P362–P371.

Fiori, K., Smith, J., & Antonucci, T. (2007). Social network types among older adults: A multidimensional approach. *Journal of Gerontology: Psychological Sciences, 62B*, P322–P330.

Franks, M., Stephens, M.A.P., Rook, K., Franklin, B., Keteyian, S., & Artinian, N. (2006). Spouses' provision of health-related support and control to patients participating in cardiac rehabilitation. *Journal of Family Psychology, 20*, 311–318.

George, L. (2009). Conceptualizing and measuring trajectories. In G. Elder, Jr., & J. Giele (Eds.), *The craft of life course research* (pp. 163–186). New York: Guilford Press.

Geurts, T., Poortman, A-R., van Tilburg, T., & Dykstra, P. (2009). Contact between grandchildren and their grandparents in early adulthood. *Journal of Family Is-sues, 30*, 1698–1713.

Giele, J. (2009). Life stories to understand diversity: Variations by class, race, and gender. In G. Elder, Jr., & J. Giele (Eds.), *The craft of life course research* (pp. 236–257). New York: Guilford Press.

Gonzales, A. (2007). Determinants of parent-child coresidence among older Mexican parents: The salience of cultural values. *Sociological Perspectives, 50*, 561–577.

Goodman, C. (2007). Family dynamics in three-generation grandfamilies. *Journal of Family Issues, 28,* 355–379.

Grossman, A., D'Augelli, A., & Hershberger, S. (2000). Social support networks of lesbian, gay, and bisexual adults 60 years of age and older. *Journal of Gerontology: Psychological Sciences, 55B,* P171–P179.

Gruenewald, T., Mroczek, D., Ryff, C., & Singer, B. (2008). Diverse pathways to positive and negative affect in adulthood and later life: An integrative approach using recursive partitioning. *Developmental Psychology, 44,* 330–343.

Harkness, J. A., Van de Vijver, F. J. R., & Mohler, P. Ph. (2003). *Cross-cultural survey methods.* Hoboken, NJ: John Wiley & Sons.

Heffner, K., Kiecolt-Glaser, J., Loving, T., Glaser, R., & Malarkey, W. (2004). Spousal support satisfaction as a modifier of physiological responses to marital conflict in younger and older couples. *Journal of Behavioral Medicine, 27,* 233–254.

Hobbs, F., & Stoops, N. (2002). *Demographic trends in the 20th century: Census 2000 special reports* (Series CENSR-4). Washington, DC: Government Printing Office.

Hofer, S., & Piccinin, A. (2010). Toward an integrative science of life-span development and aging. *Journal of Gerontology: Psychological Sciences, 65B,* 269–278.

Horn, J. L., & McArdle, J. J. (1992). A practical and theoretical guide to measurement invariance in aging research. *Experimental Aging Research, 18,* 117–144.

Ingersoll-Dayton, B., Morgan, D., & Antonucci, T. (1997). The effects of positive and negative exchanges on aging adults. *Journal of Gerontology: Social Sciences, 52B,* S190–S199.

Jackson, J., Forsythe-Brown, I., & Govia, I. (2007). Age cohort, ancestry, and immigrant generation influences in family relations and psychological well-being among Black Caribbean family members. *Journal of Social Issues, 63,* 729–743.

Kenny, D., Kashy, D., & Cook, W. (2006). *Dyadic data analysis.* New York: Guilford Press.

Kim, J-H., Knight, B., & Longmire, C. (2007). The role of familism in stress and coping processes among African American and White dementia caregivers: Effects on mental and physical health. *Health Psychology, 26,* 564–576.

Knight, G. P., Roosa, M. W., & Umaña-Taylor, A. J. (2009). *Studying ethnic minority and/or economically disadvantaged populations: Methodological challenges and best practices.* Washington, DC: American Psychological Association.

Kopera-Fry, K. (2009). Needs and issues of Latino and Native American nonparental relative caregivers: Strengths and challenges within a cultural context. *Family and Consumer Sciences Research Journal, 37,* 394–410.

Krause, N., & Rook, K. (2003). Negative interaction in late life: Issues in the stability and generalizability of conflict across relationships. *Journal of Gerontology: Psychological Sciences, 58B,* P88–P99.

Laurenceau, J-P., & Bolger, N. (2005). Using diary methods to study marital and family processes. *Journal of Family Psychology, 19,* 86–97.

Levenson, R., Carstensen, L., & Gottman, J. (1994). The influence of age and gender on affect, physiology, and their interrelations: A study of long-term marriages. *Journal of Personality and Social Psychology, 67,* 56–68.

Li, L., & Seltzer, M. (2003). Parent care, intergenerational relationship quality, and mental health of adult daughters. *Research on Aging, 25,* 484–504.

Logan, J., & Bian, F. (2004). Intergenerational family relations in the United States and China. *Annual Review of Gerontology & Geriatrics, 24,* 249–265.

Lowenstein, A., Katz, R., & Gur-Yaish, N. (2007). Reciprocity in parent-child exchanges and life satisfaction among the elderly: A cross-national perspective. *Journal of Social Issues, 63,* 865–883.

MacMillan, R., & Copher, R. (2005). Families in the life course: Interdependency of roles, role configurations, and pathways. *Journal of Marriage and Family, 67,* 858–879.

Matthews, S. (2005). Crafting qualitative research articles on marriages and families. *Journal of Marriage and Family, 67,* 799–808.

Matzek, A., & Cooney, T. (2009). Spousal perceptions of marital stress and support among grandparent caregivers: Variations by life stage. *International Journal of Aging and Human Development, 68,* 109–126.

Mavandadi, S., Rook, K., & Newsom, J. (2007). Positive and negative social exchanges and disability in later life: An investigation of trajectories of change. *Journal of Gerontology: Social Sciences, 62B,* S361–S370.

Merz, E-M., Schengel, C., & Schulze, H-J. (2009). Intergenerational relations across 4 years: Well-being is affected by quality, not by support exchange. *The Gerontologist, 49,* 536–548.

Monin, J., Schulz, R., Martire, L., Jennings, J. R., Lingler, J., & Greenberg, M. (2010). Spouses' cardiovascular reactivity to their partners' suffering. *Journal of Gerontology: Psychological Sciences, 65B,* 195–201.

Mui, A. (1996). Correlates of psychological distress among Mexican, Cuban, and Puerto Rican elders living in the USA. *Journal of Cross-Cultural Gerontology, 11,* 131–147.

Nauk, B., & Suckow, J. (2006). Intergenerational relationships in cross-cultural context: How social networks frame intergenerational relations between mothers and grandmothers in Japan, Korea, China, Indonesia, Israel, Germany, and Turkey. *Journal of Family Issues, 27,* 1159–1185.

Newsom, J., Mahan, T., Rook, K., & Krause, N. (2008). Stable negative social exchanges and health. *Health Psychology, 27,* 78–86.

Patton, M. (1999). Enhancing the quality and credibility of qualitative analysis. *Health Services Research, 34,* 1189–1208.

Peek, M. K., Stimpson, J., Townsend, A., & Markides, K. (2006). Well-being in older Mexican American spouses. *The Gerontologist, 46,* 258–265.

Pillemer, K., & Suitor, J. (2004). Ambivalence and the study of intergenerational relations. *Annual Review of Gerontology and Geriatrics, 24,* 3–28.

Pillemer, K., Suitor, J., Mock, S., Sabir, M., Pardo, T., & Sechrist, J. (2007). Capturing the complexity of intergenerational relations: Exploring ambivalence within later-life families. *Journal of Social Issues, 63,* 775–791.

Pinquart, M., & Sörenson, S. (2005). Ethnic differences in stressors, resources, and psychological outcomes of family caregiving: A meta-analysis. *The Gerontologist, 45,* 90–106.

Pinquart, M., & Sörenson, S. (2006). Gender differences in caregiver stressors, social resources, and health: An updated meta-analysis. *Journal of Gerontology: Psychological Sciences, 61B,* P33–P45.

Pruchno, R., Wilson-Genderson, M., & Cartwright, F. (2009). Self-rated health and depressive symptoms in patients with end-stage renal disease and their spouses: A longitudinal dyadic analysis of late-life marriages. *Journal of Gerontology: Psychological Sciences, 64B,* 212–221.

Pudrovska, T. (2009). Parenthood, stress, and mental health in late midlife and early old age. *International Journal of Aging and Human Development, 68,* 127–147.

Roberto, K. A., Allen, K., & Blieszner, R. (2001). Grandfathers' perceptions and expectations of relationships with their adult grandchildren. *Journal of Family Issues, 22,* 407–426.

Roberto, K. A., Blieszner, R., McCann, B., & McPherson, M. (2011). Family triad perceptions of mild cognitive impairment. *Journal of Gerontology: Social Sciences, 66,* 756–768.

Roberto, K. A., Gold, D., & Yorgason, J. (2004). The influence of osteoporosis on the marital relationship of older couples. *Journal of Applied Gerontology, 23,* 443–456.

Roberts, B., Smith, J., Jackson, J., & Edmonds, G. (2009). Compensatory conscientiousness and health in older couples. *Psychological Science, 20,* 553–559.

Sarkisian, N., Gerena, M., & Gerstel, N. (2007). Extended family integration among Euro and Mexican Americans: Ethnicity, gender, and class. *Journal of Marriage and Family, 69,* 40–54.

Savla, J., Roberto, K. A., Blieszner, R., Cox, M., & Gwazdauskas, F. (2011). Effects of daily stressors on the psychological and biological well-being of spouses of persons with mild cognitive impairment. *Journal of Gerontology: Psychological Sciences, 66,* 653–664.

Sayer, A., & Klute, M. (2005). In V. Bengtson, A. Acock, K. Allen, P. Dilworth-Anderson, & D. Klein (Eds.), *Sourcebook of family theory & research* (pp. 289–313). Thousand Oaks, CA: Sage.

Schafer, M. (2009). Parental death and subjective age: Indelible imprints from early in the life course? *Sociological Inquiry, 79,* 75–97.

Schaie, K.W. (2005). What can we learn from longitudinal studies of adult development? *Research in Adult Development, 2,* 133–158.

Settersten, R., & Mayer, K. (1997). The measurement of age, age structuring, and the life course. *Annual Review of Sociology, 23,* 233–261.

Silverstein, M., & Long, J. (1998). Trajectories of grandparents' perceived solidarity with adult grandchildren: A growth curve analysis over 23 years. *Journal of Marriage and Family, 60,* 912–923.

Smith, G., & Hancock, G. (2010). Custodial grandmother-grandfather dyads: Pathways among marital distress, grandparent dysphoria, parenting practice, and grandchild adjustment. *Family Relations, 59,* 45–59.

Smith, M., Greenberg, J., & Seltzer, M. (2007). Siblings of adults with schizophrenia: Expectations about future caregiving roles. *American Journal of Orthopsychiatry, 77,* 29–37.

Smith, T., Uchino, B., Berg, C., Florsheim, P., Pearce, G., Hawkins, M., Henry, N., Beveridge, R., Skinner, M., Ko, K., & Olsen-Cerny, C. (2009). Conflict and collaboration in middle-aged and older couples: II. Cardiovascular reactivity during marital interaction. *Psychology and Aging, 24*, 274–286.

Stephens, M.A.P., & Townsend, A. (1997). Stress of parent care: Positive and negative effects of women's other roles. *Psychology and Aging, 12*, 376–386.

Suitor, J., Pardo, S., Gilligan, M., & Pillemer, K. (2009). The role of perceived maternal favoritism in sibling relations in midlife. *Journal of Marriage and Family, 71*, 1026–1038.

Suitor, J., & Pillemer, K. (2000). Did mom really love you best? Developmental histories, status transitions, and parental favoritism in later life families. *Motivation and Emotion, 24*, 105–120.

Taylor, R., Chatters, L., & Jackson, J. (1997). Changes over time in support network involvement among Black Americans. In R. Taylor, J. Jackson, & L. Chatters (Eds.), *Family life in black America* (pp. 293–316). Thousand Oaks, CA: Sage.

Tesch-Romer, C., & von Kondratowitz, H-J. (2006). Comparative ageing research: A flourishing field in need of theoretical cultivation. *European Journal of Ageing, 3*(3), 155–167.

Townsend, A., Miller, B., & Guo, S. (2001). Depressive symptomatology in middle-aged and older married couples: A dyadic analysis. *Journal of Gerontology: Social Sciences, 56B*, S352–S364.

Turner, M.J., Young, C., & Black, K. (2006). Daughters-in-law and mothers-in-law seeking their place within the family: A qualitative study of differing viewpoints. *Family Relations, 55*, 588–600.

Usita, P., & Blieszner, R. (2002). Immigrant family strengths: Meeting communication challenges. *Journal of Family Issues, 23*, 266–286.

Valsiner, J., Molenaar, P., Lyra, M., & Chaudhary, N. (2009). *Dynamic process methodology in the social and developmental sciences.* New York: Springer.

van der Pas, S., & van Tilburg, T. (2010). The influence of family structure on the contact between older parents and their adult biological children and stepchildren in the Netherlands. *The Journals of Gerontology: Psychological Sciences and Social Sciences, 65B*, 236–245.

van Gaalen, R., Dykstra, P., & Komter, A. (2010). Where is the exit? Intergenerational ambivalence and relationship quality in high contact ties. *Journal of Aging Studies, 24*, 105–114.

Voorpostel, M., & Blieszner, R. (2008). Intergenerational solidarity and support between adult siblings. *Journal of Marriage and Family, 70*, 157–167.

Walker, A., Acock, A., Bowman, S., & Li, F. (1996). Amount of care given and caregiving satisfaction: A latent growth curve analysis. *Journal of Gerontology: Psychological Sciences, 51B*, P130–P142.

Whisman, M., & Uebelacker, L. (2009). Prospective associations between marital discord and depressive symptoms in middle-aged and older adults. *Psychology and Aging, 24*, 184–189.

White, D., Walker, A., & Richards, L. (2008). Intergenerational family support following infant death. *International Journal of Aging and Human Development, 67*, 187–208.

Willis, G. (2005). *Cognitive interviewing: A tool for improving questionnaire design.* Thousand Oaks, CA: Sage.

Willson, A., Shuey, K., & Elder, G., Jr. (2003). Ambivalence in the relationship of adult children to aging parents and in-laws. *Journal of Marriage and Family, 65,* 1055–1072.

Windsor, T., & Butterworth, P. (2010). Supportive, aversive, ambivalent, and indifferent partner evaluations in midlife and young-old adulthood. *Journal of Gerontology: Psychological Sciences, 65B,* 287–295.

Wong, S., Yoo, G., & Stewart, A. (2006). The changing meaning of family support among older Chinese and Korean immigrants. *Journal of Gerontology: Social Sciences, 61B,* S4–S9.

Yoon, S. (2005). The characteristics and needs of Asian-American grandparent caregivers: A study of Chinese-American and Korean-American grandparents. *Journal of Gerontological Social Work, 44,* 75–94.

Part II

Family Relationships

5

Marriage and Other Partnered Relationships in Middle and Late Adulthood

Jamila Bookwala

Marriage and similar partnered relationships—such as heterosexual or same-sex intimate relationships with or without cohabitation—are among the most significant interpersonal relationships in which individuals engage during the adulthood years. Views held by young adults about marriage are largely positive, and demographers project that most young adults will eventually marry; however, more accepting social attitudes that prevail today regarding single lifestyles and unions outside of marriage have resulted in increasing numbers of individuals opting for intimate relationships other than traditional marriage (Amato, Booth, Johnson, & Rogers, 2007). This chapter reviews empirical developments published after 1995 (when the first edition of this handbook was published) on (a) the nature and quality of marriage and similar partnered unions during the middle and late adulthood years, (b) factors that play a role in shaping these relationships, and (c) the role of such relationships in health during this life stage. Contemporary theoretical explanations for trends in findings also are discussed. Although the vast majority of the research on midlife and late life partnered relationships has focused specifically on marriage between heterosexual adults, evidence on other marriagelike intimate relationships is reviewed where available.

With its social and legal recognition as a distinctive relationship characterized by specific benefits, protections, rights, and obligations, marriage between heterosexual individuals remains the most common intimate relationship of its kind during the middle and later adulthood years, especially for men. According to the 2000 U.S. Census (U.S. Census Bureau, 2003), upward of 75% of men between the ages of 55 and 74 were married and more than 70% of those aged 45 to 54 years and 75 to 84 years were married. In contrast, a much smaller percentage of men 85 years and older was married

(56.3%). The proportions of married women by age group were substantially lower relative to the statistics for men. Approximately two-thirds of women aged 45 to 64, slightly more than one-half of those aged 65 to 74, and about one-third of women 75 to 84 years of age were married. Of women who were more than 85 years of age, only 19.4% were married; moreover, more than half of these women's husbands did not reside with them in the same home, presumably due to serious health conditions requiring institutionalization. (In comparison, only one-fifth of men's wives in the same age category did not reside with them.)

Despite the widespread prevalence of marriage as a social institution, other forms of partnered relationships are gaining in popularity and societal acceptance (Amato et al., 2007). Legal recognition of civil unions between same-sex partners is widespread (Kennedy, 2005), and gay and lesbian families reside in 99.3% of all counties in the United States (Human Rights Campaign Foundation, 2001). Cohabiting relationships, those wherein couples elect to live together sans marriage, also are becoming common among middle-aged and older adults in the United States and other Western societies. Based on 2000 U.S. census data, Brown, Lee, and Bulanda (2006) found that 4% of the nonmarried older adult population cohabited with a partner and the vast majority of these cohabiting elders had been previously married. Beckman, Waern, Gustafson, and Skoog (2008) found that among Swedish 70-year-olds, 6% of men and 5% of women were involved in cohabitational relationships in 2000 compared with 1% and 3%, respectively, in 1992. Likewise, Moustgaard and Martikainen (2009) reported that cohabiting relationships among Finnish older men and women nearly doubled between 1990 and 2003 (to 3.4% and 2.1%, respectively).

An emerging form of noncohabiting intimate relationships in Western societies includes living apart together or LAT relationships (Levin, 2004). An LAT relationship is one in which a couple does not share the same household but the two individuals define themselves and are defined by their social network as a couple (Levin & Trost, 1999). Levin and Trost reported that more than 4% of the Swedish population aged 18 to 74 participated in LAT relationships, with even larger proportions reported in other Western European countries such as France and Germany. Using national data from the 1996 and 1998 General Social Surveys, Strohm, Seltzer, Cochran, and Mays (2009) reported that 6% of men and 7% of women aged 23 to 70 were in LAT relationships. Using data from California in 2004–2005, they reported that the prevalence rates of LAT relationships were even higher for those in both heterosexual relationships (13% of men, 12% of women) and same-sex relationships (17% of gay men, 15% of lesbians) in that state. Although a focus on LAT relationships specifically among middle-aged and older adults in the United States is lacking (Casalanti & Kiecolt, 2007), researchers in Western Europe have recognized them as a growing phenomenon in these age groups. For example, De Jong Gierveld and Peeters (2003) reported that 32% of Dutch elders who started a new partnered relationship after experiencing the dissolution of a marriage later embarked on a LAT relationship.

Ghazanfareeon Karlsson, Johansson, Gerdner, and Borell (2007) described LAT relationships as primarily serving as a vehicle for giving and receiving emotional support without the duties and obligations associated with marriage. As such, LAT relationships offer the opportunity to combine intimacy with autonomy. Some common reasons uncovered by Levin and Trost (1999) for establishing an LAT relationship included one or both individuals having minor children living with them in the home, providing care to another person (especially a parent), being employed or pursuing education in different places, and personal reasons such as not wanting to repeat a mistake and wanting to maintain their own household after retirement. Gender differences appear to underlie motives for involvement in LAT relationships. Ghazanfareeon Karlsson and Borell (2002) found that women offered less ambiguous reasons than men for being in LAT relationships and were often the driving force behind the establishment of such a union. Women were especially likely to endorse reasons such as the desire for and privilege of maintaining one's own household and of being freed from household and partner-related duties that occur in marriage.

RELATIONSHIP QUALITY AND SATISFACTION

Research on relationship quality across the adult life span, especially within marriage, has seen considerable growth in the past decade or so. Cross-sectional studies comparing positive dimensions of marital quality (e.g., marital satisfaction, marital happiness) across young, middle-aged, and older adults have found support for a U-shaped trend with marital satisfaction and happiness lower among middle-aged adults compared to those who are younger or older (e.g., Henry, Berg, Smith, & Florsheim, 2007; Van Laningham, Johnson, & Amato, 2001). However, longitudinal studies spanning extended periods of time have found that marital satisfaction and happiness typically decline after the newlywed years and into middle adulthood and then either stabilize or continue to decline after midlife (Umberson, Williams, Powers, Liu, & Needham, 2006; Van Laningham et al., 2001). Methodological artifacts are likely to be responsible for the U-shaped marital quality curve over the adult lifespan that is evident in cross-sectional research. Marriages of especially poor quality are most likely to be terminated prior to entry into the late adulthood years resulting in the uptick observed in marital quality in older samples. Cohort effects also may operate whereby different age groups have different expectations for their marriage that, in turn, influence their ratings of marital quality.

In contrast to marital research, longitudinal research on changes in relationship quality within cohabiting relationships or stable gay and lesbian relationships is scarce. One exception is a study conducted by Willetts (2006) who compared the relationship quality of long-term cohabiting relationships and marriages. Using a probability-based sample with an average age in the early to mid-40s, Willetts found that long-term cohabiting relationships are likely to share similar characteristics as marital unions in terms of relationship quality with only small differences between these two groups of couples on relationship satisfaction, frequency of interaction with the partner, or frequency of conflict. In a study comparing relationship quality across heterosexual marriages and stable same-sex relationships, Kurdek (2008b) found that relative to the declining trend evident in marital quality, stable gay and lesbian relationships showed no significant change in relationship quality over a 10-year period following relationship initiation. In addition, he reported that overall relationship quality was fairly high in these stable gay and lesbian relationships. It should be noted, however, that Kurdek's study only speaks to temporal trends in relationship quality among gay and lesbian couples until they are in their mid-40s, and thus, we cannot draw conclusions about changes in the quality of these relationships in late adulthood. Moreover, the gay and lesbian respondents were considerably older (in their mid-30s) at the start of Kurdek's study than were the heterosexual respondents (late-20s), thereby confounding age with group membership.

The experience of love within partnered relationships is theorized by some researchers to undergo a transformation over time, in which a predominance of passionate love during the young adulthood years is replaced by the experience of higher levels of companionate love during the midlife and later years (Bierhoff & Schmohr, 2004). Passionate love is characterized by intense emotional, psychological, and physiological longing for the partner, whereas companionate love comprises affection, intimacy, and commitment (Hatfield & Rapson, 1993). Using existing theories of love (e.g., Hatfield, 1985; Hatfield & Rapson, 1993; Lee, 1973) and the lifespan theory of control (Heckhausen & Schulz, 1995), Bierhoff and Schmohr posited that, in general, the opportunities for forming and sustaining passionate love relationships decline starting in middle adulthood because the formation of partnered relationships is characterized by age-graded opportunity structures and age-graded goals in partnered relationships. Starting at midlife, unpartnered individuals may find fewer age-peers with whom they can initiate new intimate relationships because by this life stage most of them are already involved in long-term relationships. According to Bierhoff and Schmohr, the gain in importance of companionate love over passionate love within long-term relationships as people age represents a type of compensatory secondary control strategy in the face of diminished availability of romantic experiences.

Bierhoff and Schmohr's model is consistent with other models that describe life course changes in the experience of love within long-term relationships. For example, Hatfield and Rapson (1993) also pointed out that, in general, passionate love relationships between older individuals are less likely to develop because such relationships more closely coincide with the developmental tasks of young adulthood that include forming a sexual union, entering marriage, and starting a family. Bierhoff and Schmohr also blamed prevailing negative age stereotypes for the lower likelihood of forming a new relationship marked by passionate love during or after middle adulthood. Resulting from these negative age stereotypes, older individuals are more likely to engage in the deactivation of passionate love goals as a compensatory mechanism to avoid the negative consequences associated with failure to attain such goals. Drawing further on the lifespan theory of control, Bierhoff and Schmohr proposed that older individuals are motivated to substitute goals more in line with companionate love in forming and sustaining partnered relationships. It is plausible that this strategy serves as a means to protect elders' emotional and motivational resources and may be more successful because later life offers a more favorable opportunity structure for companionate love relationships with age-peers. Factors associated with the formation and maintenance of partnered relationships in late life and how these may be moderated by contextual factors such as gender, ethnicity, and sexual orientation are important areas for future research.

When evaluating the fit of their lifespan model of love using findings obtained by their team and others, Bierhoff and Schmohr (2004) found some support for their hypotheses. Romantic love (a component of passionate love) was lower in respondents who were middle-aged, whereas the pragmatic form of love (a component of companionate love) was more common among middle-aged and older individuals. However, other components of passionate love (e.g., love styles marked by possessiveness and manipulation) did not show the expected negative trend over increasing age, nor did some elements of companionate love (e.g., altruistic love and friendship-based love) show the expected positive linear relationship with age. Bierhoff and Schmohr's results indicate that, despite theoretical explanations for hypothesized differences in the experience of love with aging, the data do not necessarily conform to such expectations. Moreover, it is important to note that these theoretical models for the development and experience of love over the life course appear to be most relevant to partnered relationships with age-peers or life stage–peers. They do not account for individual differences that may prompt older individuals to engage in passionate love relationships with considerably younger partners. Moreover, Bierhoff and Schmohr's (2004) model primarily addresses lifespan-related changes in the experience of love within heterosexual relationships. They speculated, however, that the age-related change in opportunity structures associated with intimate relationships and the use of compensatory control strategies to deal with such change are, in general, likely to characterize same-sex relationships as well. Kurdek's work (2008a) supports this view, showing that processes that regulate relationships are similar across both heterosexual and cohabiting same-sex intimate partnerships.

MARITAL DISAGREEMENT AND CONFLICT

Marital and other partnered relationships are not characterized exclusively by positive dimensions during the middle and late adulthood years. Indeed, marital relationships can be marked by ambivalence, with criticism and other hurtful emotional behaviors co-occurring with positive feelings and behaviors (Akiyama, Antonucci, Takahashi, & Langfahl, 2003; Birditt, Fingerman, & Almeida, 2005; Fingerman, Hay, & Birditt, 2004). Marital conflict also occurs in midlife and late-life marriages. For example, in a qualitative study with 105 late-life married couples, Henry, Miller, and Giarrusso (2005) found that the most common conflict issue was related to leisure activities (in 23% of the responses) followed by issues related to emotional and physical intimacy, finances, personality, relationships with children and grandchildren, household concerns, personal habits, health issues, and work or retirement.

Several early studies found inequities in marital role allocation or division of household labor to be significant areas of disagreement and conflict, especially during the child-rearing middle-adulthood years, and that such marital role inequities typically favor husbands over wives (e.g., Feeney, Peterson, & Noller, 1994; Peterson, 1990). In addition, Bookwala (2009) found that middle-aged married women caregivers were more likely to report inequities in the allocation of marital roles than their married male counterparts. Studies with individuals in late life (rather than midlife), however, tend to report more role equity in marriage. Kulik (2002a, 2002b), for example, found no differences between husbands and wives among Israeli late-life couples in the performance of domestic tasks, maintenance tasks, and outdoor tasks. Hagedoorn, van Yperen, Coyne, van Jaarsveld, Ranchor, van Sonderen, and Sanderman (2006) likewise found that marital inequity was more the exception than the rule in the later years. In their longitudinal population-based study of Dutch older adults, 84% of married persons described their marriage to be equitable compared to less than 10% each reporting that they were underbenefited in their marriage or overbenefited.

In a probability-based sample of long-term heterosexual cohabiters and married adults with an average age of early to mid-40s, Willetts (2006) found no differences between the groups on perceived relationship equity at baseline or follow-up five to seven years later. In fact, Willetts found age to play a role in perceptions of relationship equity such that as the age of the couple increased, perceptions of equity increased; however, older cohabiters showed a larger gain in perceptions of equity over time relative to their married counterparts.

Disagreement and conflict are not unique to heterosexual couples. They occur in same-sex couples as well, with some relationships showing a spiraling cycle of escalating abuse (Peplau & Fingerhut, 2007). Research on same-sex intimate relationships indicates, however, that role equity is more typical of gay and lesbian relationships (see Kurdek, 2006; Peplau & Fingerhut, 2007) with greater equity in same-sex couples with no children (and heterosexual couples with no children) compared to heterosexual couples with children (Kurdek, 2006), and greater equity in lesbian relationships than in gay partnerships (Kurdek, 2007). It is important to note, however, that these studies have typically focused on lesbian and gay partnerships between young rather than older persons and little is known about equity in same-sex relationships during the middle and late adulthood years.

Although marriages are not free from conflict in midlife and late life, cross-sectional data show a downward age-related trend for negative marital processes, with marital disagreement and conflict being reported less often by older respondents than younger respondents. Bookwala, Sobin, and Zdaniuk (2005) found an age-graded decline in the frequency of heated arguments and aggressive acts within marriage (namely, hitting or throwing things at each other) in a national probability-based sample of adults. Henry et al. (2005) found age differences in the types of difficulties and disagreements that were reported in married older adults. Older respondents (65+ years) were more likely to mention difficulties or disagreements related to leisure activities, intergenerational relationships, and household concerns, whereas younger respondents (<65 years) were more likely to face challenges in the realms of emotional and physical intimacy and personality. Henry et al. also reported that respondents who were 65+ years were more likely to report no problems in their relationship relative to those who were younger than 65.

Findings about the lower likelihood of marital disagreement or conflict in late-life marriage relative to earlier life stages should be treated with caution because alternative explanations may exist for the age-related trend. Possible explanations include the operation of cohort effects in cross-sectional samples or selection effects wherein the most seriously conflictual and abusive marriages do not endure into middle and late adulthood. Moreover, some longitudinal evidence supporting the reverse age-trend has been reported recently. Using multiwave data from a national sample, Umberson and Williams (2005) found that marital strain in the form of feeling upset about the marriage or feeling upset about disagreements in the marriage tends to increase linearly over time after age 40. They found, however, that this upward trend was more characteristic of women than men; men were more likely to experience an increase in marital strain until age 60, after which their marital strain showed a plateauing trend. In addition, Umberson and Williams found that women after age 40 report higher levels of baseline marital strain relative to men, and this gender difference widens further at older ages.

Regardless of the frequency of marital disagreement in midlife and late life, how spouses behave during disagreement can undermine marital satisfaction. Henry et al. (2007) examined the relationship between marital satisfaction and couples' positive and negative spouse behaviors during an observation task in which they discussed a topic of disagreement. Henry et al. found that positive spouse behaviors were associated with higher marital satisfaction and negative behaviors with lower marital satisfaction in middle-aged and late-life couples, with no distinction in the strength of these associations between the two age groups. Smith et al. (2009) instructed couples to discuss a topic representing an unresolved issue for them. They found that although older couples reported less anger and rated their spouses as less hostile than did middle-aged couples, these age differences disappeared when couples' marital satisfaction was controlled.

Inequity in role allocations within intimate relationships also has consequences for relationship quality and well-being. Role inequities in long-term marriages are associated with lower marital quality (Kulik, 2002b) and greater psychological distress (Hagedoorn et al., 2006). Likewise, Kurdek (2007) found that satisfaction with the division of labor within gay and lesbian couples was related to higher relationship satisfaction and relationship stability. Moreover, he found that the association between satisfaction with the division of labor and relationship satisfaction was fully mediated via perceived equality in the relationship. These findings linking role allocation inequities and relationship satisfaction are consistent in general with equity theory (Walster, Walster, & Berscheid, 1978), which posits that individuals seek fairness in their intimate relationships, and unfairness is likely to be associated with relationship and more general distress.

SEXUAL ACTIVITY AND SEXUAL SATISFACTION

Despite pervasive negative stereotypes and conventional wisdom regarding the sexuality of older individuals, sexual intimacy and satisfaction are prevalent in marriage and similar relationships during the later years and are important to older adults. For example, on examining the attitudes regarding the role and value of sex in later life in a small sample, Gott and Hinchcliff found that partnered elders rated sex as at least somewhat important and several respondents rated it to be very or extremely important; only unpartnered elders rated sex to be of no importance at all. In a large national study of premenopausal and early perimenopausal women conducted at multiple sites in the United States, Cain et al. (2003) also found that 76% of the sample reported that sex was of moderate or greater importance. Upward of 86% of those who had engaged in sexual activity in the preceding six-month period, regardless of menopause status, reported feeling moderate or greater emotional satisfaction. An even greater proportion of women reported feeling similarly high levels of physical satisfaction. Indeed, sexual intimacy and satisfaction play an important role in positive relationship evaluations in the later years. DeLamater and Moorman (2007) found that more frequent sexual activity was associated with more positive evaluations of the relationship in a large representative sample of elders 45 to 94 years of age. In a longitudinal study using five waves of data from 283 middle-aged married couples, Yeh, Lorenz, Wickrama, Conger, and Elder (2006) found that higher sexual satisfaction was related to greater marital satisfaction that, in turn, was related to lower marital instability among both husbands and wives.

The importance of sexual behavior and satisfaction in middle and late life notwithstanding, large-scale studies with heterosexual elders typically have found that age is negatively related with sexual activity. For example, in a probability-based sample of men and women between the ages of 57 and 85 years Lindau et al. (2007) found that sexual activity declined from a fairly high level of 73% of respondents aged 57 to 64 years to 53% of those aged 65 to 74 years to 26% among those aged 75+ years. From her review of research findings related to sexual behavior among middle-aged and older adults, Burgess (2004) also concluded that the frequency of sexual activity was lower in older than younger age groups; however, she noted that there was considerable variability in their sexual activity. This variability was strongly linked to relationship status; partnered elders were more likely to report sexual engagement than their single counterparts.

Some recent evidence suggests, however, that rates of sexual activity in older samples appear to be rising overall. A recent time-series cohort analysis of trends in self-reported sexual activity among 70-year-old Swedes revealed increases over time (Beckman et al., 2008). This study used data on sexual activity and satisfaction from four cohorts (*N* = 249–500) during the time period spanning 1971–2001. Findings indicated that the proportion of respondents who reported engaging in sexual intercourse increased over time among both married and unmarried cohorts with a much greater proportional increase among unmarried elders. More recent cohorts also reported higher satisfaction with their sexual activity, fewer sexual dysfunctions, and more positive attitudes toward sexuality in later life than earlier-born cohorts. Although a similar analysis has not been undertaken in the United States and similar cultures, it is likely that Beckman et al.'s findings would be replicated given the changing social and sexual norms in most Western societies.

As with heterosexual relationships, age is negatively related to sexual activity in same-sex relationships (Peplau, Fingerhut, & Beals, 2004). In their review of research on gay and lesbian sexuality, Peplau and her colleagues noted that being older was significantly associated with lower frequency of sexual activity in a number of studies; however, this association was weaker than the one between length of relationship and frequency of sexual activity. Consistent with findings on heterosexual relationships, Peplau et al. also noted that higher sexual frequency was associated with higher sexual satisfaction and with higher levels of relationship satisfaction in same-sex relationships. Note, however, that Peplau et al. did not focus their review specifically on research done with gay and lesbian older adults. The studies they reviewed often included samples with a wide age range (e.g., 20 to 77 years); however, these studies typically controlled for age and relationship length in their statistical analyses rather than focusing on the effects of these variables.

Although increasing age is widely viewed as a broad-based explanation for decline in sexual interest and activity during the late life years, this link may be far more complex. For example, DeLamater and Moorman (2007) proposed that declines in sexual activity over the life span can be better understood by applying the broad biopsychosocial model that has been used effectively to understand declining health over the life span. They studied sexuality in late life using secondary data from nearly 1,400 individuals aged 45+ years (mean age approximately 60 years). As hypothesized, DeLamater and Moorman found that age was negatively associated with frequency of partnered and unpartnered sexual behavior but that this relationship was significantly attenuated when biological and psychosocial factors were controlled. Thus, age may serve as a proxy for poorer health and declines in psychosocial resources as underlying factors responsible for the decrease observed in sexual behavior as people age.

Gender and Sexuality

In studies that compared the sexual activity of older women and men, significantly more men than women reported engaging in sexual activity (DeLamater & Moorman, 2007; Lindau et al., 2007). For example, DeLamater and Moorman found that 71% of men aged 60 to 69 years and 64% of men aged 70 to 79 years reported sexual activity at least once in the preceding month; for women, the corresponding percentages were considerably lower at 47% and 26%, respectively. It is important to note that these studies typically defined sexual behavior broadly to include behaviors ranging from masturbation to coital sexual intercourse. The higher levels of sexual activity reported in studies of more recent cohorts of middle-aged and older men also may be partially explained by the male sexual performance-enhancing drugs that have become available to this age group and the availability of more options for them to partner with younger women than available for older women to partner with young men. These studies, however, did not qualify their results based on these factors. Moreover, individuals vary in their levels of sexual responsiveness over the life span and studies show that gender-based differences exist in sexual response (e.g., see Bancroft, Graham, Janssen, & Sanders, 2009). With age, sexual excitation decreases for both women and men while sexual inhibition is largely unrelated to age among women but can increase among men and may be related to the occurrence of erectile problems. These studies have generally found that women score lower on sexual excitation and higher on sexual inhibition than men.

Women's sexuality during the middle adulthood years, when menopause and its accompanying hormonal changes typically occur, has received considerable research attention. Based on their review of studies on menopause and sexuality that used population-based samples, Dennerstein, Alexander, and Kotz (2003) concluded that the postmenopausal phase is characterized by declines in sexual arousal and interest and that the proportion of women experiencing sexual dysfunction during this phase increases. Mansfield, Koch, and Voda (1998) found that 40% of their sample experienced a change; these changes were more often in terms of a decline in some aspect of sexual responsiveness (that is, decline in desire, arousal, ease of orgasm, enjoyment, and frequency), although a proportion of this group reported an increase in these aspects of sexual responsiveness. Several investigators have examined the links between both age and postmenopausal status and found that postmenopausal status remains significantly linked with declines in sexual function and sexual interest (e.g., see Dennerstein et al., 2003). Other researchers, however, have found that the changes in sexual activity and interest that are seen in middle-aged postmenopausal women may be influenced by other changes such as those related to sexual intimacy in the relationship (Birnbaum, Cohen, & Wertheimer, 2007) and women's desire for change in their own and their partner's sexual qualities (Mansfield et al., 1998).

Early menopausal status (relative to postmenopausal) appears to be less influential in women's sexual interest and activity. Using data from a large national survey of premenopausal and early perimenopausal women, Cain et al. (2003) found that 79% of middle-aged women (who were neither hysterectomized nor using hormone replacement therapy) reported high levels of sexual engagement with a partner during the preceding six-month period. In addition, they found that early menopausal status was not associated with either the importance of or engagement in sex for women. Instead, the most common reason the women provided for not engaging in sex during the preceding six months was the unavailability of a partner (cited by 67%). Lack of interest and the women or their partners being too tired or too busy for sex also were mentioned but less frequently. The most common reasons offered by the women for engaging in sex were the expression of love or the experience of pleasure and enjoyment (cited by 90% of women who had engaged in sex) and because their partner wanted them to engage in sex (cited by 75%).

MARRIAGE AND LIFE TRANSITIONS

Life transitions can play a powerful role in defining the nature and quality of marriage in midlife and late life (Van Laningham et al., 2001). Some common life transitions include children leaving the home (i.e., the emptying of the nest), retirement, and taking on the caregiver role for an ill parent, parent-in-law, or spouse. Contrary to popular belief regarding the negative marital impact of the empty-nest syndrome, early and more recent studies have shown that the empty nest is associated with significant increases in marital happiness. Gorchoff, John, and Helson (2008), using data from an 18-year study of middle-aged women (spanning the ages of 43 to 61 years), found that marital satisfaction increased in middle adulthood and that this increase was associated with the empty-nest transition. This trend was further explained by an increase in the women's enjoyment of time with their partners (but not an increase in the quantity of time spent with the partner).

Mackey and O'Brien (1999) conducted retrospective semistructured interviews with a small sample of Caucasian, African American, and Mexican American older couples regarding marital adjustment at different life stages including the empty-nest years. They found that couples in all three groups reported less marital conflict and the use of more face-to-face discussions to resolve marital conflict during the empty-nest years relative to the early marriage years and the child-rearing years. The quality of sexual relations declined during the empty-nest years for all three groups of elders, but more than 75% of the sample indicated that sexual relations were important to marital quality. Psychological intimacy, however, remained high during the empty-nest years, with 77% of the husbands and 70% of the wives describing their relationships as psychologically intimate. Marital satisfaction also was high, with 87% and 85% for husbands and wives, respectively. No differences were recorded on psychological intimacy or marital satisfaction across the three ethnic groups.

Rather than the departure of children from the home compromising parental satisfaction with the marriage during the empty-nest years, Mitchell and Gee (1996) found that the return of adult children to their parents' home can compromise their parents' marital satisfaction. They examined the impact on parents' marital satisfaction of *boomerang kids* (adult children who had returned home for at least six months). Mitchell and Gee found that having a boomerang kid return home three or more times and having an adult child who returned home after leaving to pursue work or school (as opposed to leaving home to experience independence) significantly increased the odds of low parental marital satisfaction. Qualitative responses indicated that boomerang effects may be due to the loss of intimacy and privacy for the parental couple on the child's return, an increase in incurred expenses in providing a home and care for the adult child, and the loss of freedom to pursue their own interests that the parental couple may have enjoyed after launching the children.

Despite support for an increase in marital satisfaction during the empty-nest years, the empty-nest transition can in some cases play a role in marital disruption. Using longitudinal data from a sample of middle-aged women who were in their first marriages at baseline, Hiedemann, Suhomlinova, and O'Rand (1998) found that the empty nest is associated with an increased risk of marital disruption and that this risk is qualified by the duration of the marriage. The transition to the empty nest dramatically increased the odds of divorce or separation for respondents who reached the empty-nest experience relatively early in their marriages but decreased the odds of marital disruption for those who arrived at this life stage relatively late in their marriages. Heidemann et al. also found that women who were employed during the empty-nest transition were at greater risk for marital disruption presumably because employed women were favored with economic independence that permitted them to end poor marriages after the children had been launched. Other reasons for midlife divorce after long-term marriages that were mentioned in a large-scale survey commissioned by the American Association of Retired Persons (AARP; 2004) include some form of abuse (verbal, emotional, or physical), differences between spouses in terms of values or lifestyles, and infidelity. The AARP survey also found that midlife divorce is often initiated by women, with more men being caught by surprise by their divorce.

The transition to retirement from one's primary employment also can bring the marital relationship into central focus (Trudel, Turgeon, & Piche, 2000). Decisions to transition into retirement among older married couples are typically influenced by both spouses (Pienta & Hayward, 2002; Smith & Moen, 1998), and studies show a link between retirement and marital quality at the couple level. For example, Moen, Kim, and Hofmeister (2001) longitudinally studied the link between marital quality and various phases of retirement using a random sample of individuals residing in upstate New York. They found that for older adults who retired between the two study waves marital quality was lower and marital conflict higher relative to those who remained employed over the course of the study or who were already retired at baseline. These findings were characteristic of both women and men in the sample. Interestingly, Moen et al. also found that the level of marital conflict was contingent on the retirement status of both members of the couple.

Marital conflict was greater for women and men who transitioned into retirement but whose spouse remained employed versus for those who transitioned into retirement and whose spouse was not employed. In addition, older women who had not yet retired reported greater marital conflict if their husbands were no longer employed.

Research conducted by Szinovacz and her team (Szinovacz, 1996; Szinovacz & Schaffer, 2000) shows that the retirement status of both husbands and wives influences marital satisfaction and marital conflict. Using data from married couples participating in a national probability-based sample, Szinovacz (1996) found that when couples were characterized by traditional gender roles, marital quality was lower if the husband was retired but the wife worked. Marital quality also was lower in cases where both spouses were retired and the wife had recently entered retirement compared to those where both spouses were still employed. Using the same national sample of older couples, Szinovacz and Schaffer (2000) found that husbands reported a decline in heated arguments upon their wives' retirement but wives did not; moreover, if either spouse reported strong attachment to the marriage, husbands reported greater engagement in calm discussions upon their own retirement. Although research on retirement in same-sex couples is scarce, a recent study on a small convenience sample indicates that relationship satisfaction is typically high among retirees in same-sex relationships and that those who reported engagement in financial planning and life planning were likely to report higher relationship satisfaction (Mock, Taylor, & Savin-Williams, 2006).

Transitioning into the role of caregiver to a family member or friend is a widely prevalent experience during the middle or late adulthood years (e.g., Bookwala, 2009; Marks, Lambert, & Choi, 2002). According to recent national estimates, 19% of all adults occupy the role of informal caregiver to an individual aged 50+ years (National Alliance for Caregiving, 2009). Although little research has examined caregiving issues in couple relationships other than marriage in the midlife and later years, preliminary evidence suggests that care expectations and experiences are common in other types of partnered relationships as well. Ghazanfareeon Karlsson et al. (2007) examined care-related attitudes and experiences in a sample of older Swedish adults engaged in LAT relationships. They found that both women and men rated their LAT partner as providing more support than any other network member and expected more care from their partner than from other relatives. Men in LAT relationships reported more willingness to provide future care to their LAT partner relative to women in such relationships, and they were less likely to consider ending the LAT relationship in the event that their partner became seriously ill.

Studies show that occupation of the informal caregiver role is related to lower marital quality among adult-child caregivers and spouse caregivers alike. For example, Bookwala (2009) conducted a prospective study using data from a national probability sample to examine differences in marital quality as a function of transitions into and out of the parent care role. She found that sustained occupation of the parent care role is related to poorer marital quality. Adult sons and daughters who transitioned into the parent care role and occupied this role across two subsequent waves of data collection over a 15-year period reported less marital happiness and more marital role inequity than those who were more recent occupants of the parent care role (i.e., the transition occurred later in the study period).

A study with a community-based sample of individuals providing care to a spouse or coresiding partner also examined the relationship between caregiving and relationship quality (Svetlik, Dooley, Weiner, Williamson, & Walters, 2005). Svetlik et al. found that greater care provision emerged as the only significant predictor of decline in caregivers' satisfaction with physical intimacy in the relationship, which, in turn, was related to a greater sense of relationship loss experienced by the caregiving spouse or partner. When examining discrepancies between spouses' evaluations of marital quality in a sample of elderly couples, Carr and Boerner (2009) found that spouse caregivers provided more negative appraisals of their marriage than did their partners. Spouse caregivers were only half as likely as noncaregivers to rate their marriage more positively than did their spouse.

MARRIAGE, MARITAL QUALITY, AND HEALTH

Marital Status and Health

Numerous studies point to the health protective role of married status in middle and late adulthood. Pienta, Hayward, and Jenkins (2000) found that being married during the retirement years has a wide array of health benefits including lower prevalence of fatal and nonfatal chronic diseases, higher functional levels, and lower disability. In a large study of long-term illness rates in Great Britain, Murphy, Glaser, and Grundy (1997) found that until about the age of 70 years, long-term illness rates are lowest among individuals in first marriages compared with all other marital status categories (widowed, remarried, divorced, and never married). Likewise, Prigerson, Maciejewski, and Rosenheck (2000) found that married individuals aged 50 years and older reported fewer chronic illnesses, better functional health, fewer nursing home days, and fewer physician visits than widowed individuals in the same age group.

Zhang and Hayward (2006) used longitudinal data from a national probability-based sample to show that the prevalence of cardiovascular disease is higher among middle-aged and older women and men who have experienced some form of marital loss (in the form of widowhood or divorce) relative to continuously married individuals. Gender differences in the incidence of cardiovascular disease, however, were observed by Zhang and Hayward. They found that women who experienced marital loss were at higher risk of developing cardiovascular disease over the course of the eight-year study whereas the onset of cardiovascular disease in male participants during this same period was largely unrelated to marital loss. Cohabiting elders do not necessarily enjoy the same health privileges as their married counterparts. Brown and colleagues (2006) compared cohabiting elders with other marital status groups on functional disability and alcohol use using national-level data. They found that although cohabiters did not vary from married or remarried individuals on functional disability, they reported greater alcohol use than both married groups.

Remarriage and Health

Even remarriage may not offer the same health protections as stable marriages; studies have shown that marital disruptions in the form of divorce and widowhood are linked to greater morbidity. Zhang and Hayward (2006) found that the prevalence of cardiovascular disease was higher among remarried women and men relative to their continuously married peers. Using data from a national longitudinal study of middle-aged adults, Hughes and Waite (2009) found that marital disruptions in the form of divorce and widowhood had adverse health consequences in the form of more chronic conditions, greater mobility limitations, poorer self-rated health, and more depressive symptoms. Furthermore, even among individuals who had remarried after marital disruption, health was worse than among those who were continuously married. The negative impact of early marital disruptions also was greater for slower-to-develop and more chronic health conditions.

Gender differences exist, however, in the link between marital transitions and health. In their study with middle-aged and older adults, Zhang and Hayward (2006) found that remarried men had a lower incidence of cardiovascular disease than continuously married men whereas remarried women had a higher incidence of the disease than continuously married women. Although they did not examine explanatory factors for this gender difference, a comparison of remarried men and women in the sample indicated that remarried women had lower incomes, more depressive symptoms and emotional problems, and higher cholesterol than remarried men, which, in turn, may make them more vulnerable to cardiovascular disease.

Dupre and Meadows (2007) found that failure to remarry following divorce or widowhood for both women and men is associated with higher risk of disease (diabetes, cancer, heart attack, or stroke). They further found that the negative effects of divorce transitions are greater for women and those of widowhood are greater for men and that having more (re)married years attenuated the negative health effects of divorce for women but not of widowhood for men. Although they did not test possible explanations for these gender differences, Dupre and Meadows suggested that women may more effectively adjust to divorce over time, especially because marital dissolution tends to occur earlier in the life course relative to widowhood; widowhood tends to occur at a later age for men, making it more difficult for them to recover from its negative health effects.

Marriage and Mortality

The link between married status and survival across the adult life span is similar to that seen with other health indicators. The risk of mortality is lower for married elders relative to their nonmarried counterparts (see Kaplan & Kronick, 2006). Cohabitation with a partner once again does not appear to have the same protective benefits for survival as seen with married persons. Moustgaard and Martikainen (2009) found that cohabiting elders had a somewhat higher mortality risk compared to their married counterparts: 27% of cohabiting men and 15% of cohabiting women had died over a five-year period compared with 22% and 11% of married men and women, respectively. That cohabitation is not as protective for survival as being married may be due to the higher risk of separation and resulting loss of partner support and care that can be associated with cohabitation.

To gain a better understanding of the relative risk of mortality by marital status among older adults, Manzoli, Villari, Pirone, and Boccia (2007) performed a meta-analysis in which they pooled the findings of 53 studies conducted on European or American samples. Pooling comparisons that drew data from more than 250,000 elders, their meta-analysis confirmed that the relative odds for survival was significantly greater for married than widowed, divorced, and never married elders. This risk differential remained significant after controlling for gender and study quality characteristics. As with the link between marital history and health, the occurrence of marital disruptions also is linked to higher risk of mortality. Tucker, Friedman, Wingard, and Schwartz (1996) used longitudinal data from a sample of highly educated and intelligent women and men to examine the relationship between marital history at midlife and mortality. They found that continuously married individuals survived longer than those who had experienced a marital disruption even if the latter had remarried.

Unlike Kaplan and Kronick's (2006) findings that never-married individuals have a higher mortality risk relative to their ever-married peers, Tucker et al. (1996) reported that in their privileged sample, those who had never married were at no higher mortality risk relative to those who were continuously married. Recent research shows that adults who remain single after age 40 are not at higher risk for poor emotional well-being relative to their married counterparts if they are high in personal mastery and self-sufficiency (Bookwala & Fekete, 2009). Tucker et al.'s privileged sample may comprise a group with such personal resources that, in turn, may partially explain why never-married participants' survival in their study matched that of the continuously married. Another explanation for the resilience of older never-married individuals may be that they have less stressful life experiences than elders who are single for other reasons such as widowhood, separation or divorce, or institutionalization of the spouse. Some support for this explanation comes from research showing that the strains associated with being single in later life are higher among widowed and divorced individuals than among never-married elders (Pudrovska, Schieman, & Carr, 2006). These findings also may explain why never-married middle-aged and older adults were comparable to their continuously married peers on the prevalence and incidence of cardiovascular disease (Zhang & Hayward, 2006).

Marital Quality and Health

Among married elders, the quality of the marital relationship plays a significant role in health and well-being. Numerous empirical studies have documented that marriages of better relationship quality are associated with higher psychological and physical well-being among older adults. For example, Bookwala and Jacobs (2004) found that greater marital happiness and less marital disagreement was associated with lower depressive symptomatology among older adults participating in a national study and that negative aspects of marriage are less salient and positive aspects of marriage are more salient to depressed affect with increasing age maturity. These findings are consistent with socioemotional selectivity theory (Carstensen, Isaacowitz, & Charles, 1999), which predicts that as individuals become older and view their time as becoming more limited, they are more likely to regulate their emotions to maximize the experience of positive emotions. Thus, married older adults are more likely to focus on positive emotional experiences within their spousal relationship relative to their younger counterparts and, in turn, why positive marital processes rather than negative ones are more salient to their well-being. Mancini and Bonanno (2006) found that greater marital closeness in late life was associated with lower levels of depressive symptoms, less anxiety, and greater self-esteem in a national probability sample of married older adults.

In a probability-based sample of older adults in the Netherlands, Hagedoorn et al. (2006) observed a curvilinear relationship between marital inequity and psychological distress such that psychological distress was higher among respondents who reported feeling either underbenefited or overbenefited in their marriage relative to those who perceived their marriages as equitable. Miller, Townsend, and Ishler (2004) found that greater marital dissatisfaction at baseline and increments in marital dissatisfaction over time predicted more negative mood symptoms at follow-up among wives (but not husbands) using data from a probability sample of older couples. A recent literature review on the relationship between characteristics of the marital relationship and health in studies that focused on both members of late-life couples confirmed a link between marital quality and psychological well-being. Walker and Luszcz (2009) found that, in general, psychological well-being in one or both partners in the marriage was higher when the marital relationship was marked by support and closeness, whereas psychological well-being was lower when the marital relationship was marked by dissatisfaction or conflict.

In terms of physical health, Bookwala (2005) found that from among a range of marital quality indicators, negative exchanges with the spouse singly and consistently were related to multiple physical health indicators in a probability-based sample of middle-aged and older adults. More negative spouse exchanges were associated with more physical disability, higher physical symptomatology, more chronic health conditions, and poorer self-rated health. Using panel data obtained from a national sample of older adults, Umberson and colleagues (2006) also found that marital strain was associated with poorer physical health over time and that this association was strengthened with increasing age for both older women and older men. However, Umberson and Williams (2005) found that older women reported greater marital strain in midlife and later relative to older men and that this gender difference only increases with age. They attributed this gender difference to the trend for women typically to marry older men combined with the likelihood for men to experience serious illnesses that could be chronic or terminal earlier than do women.

For these reasons, in late life married women may be more likely to be involved in providing care to an ill spouse than their male counterparts, which, in turn, may contribute to the higher levels of marital strain they experience. Umberson and Williams concluded that this gender difference in marital strain in old age may provide men with a clear advantage over women during the very life stage when marital strain is most strongly related to poor physical health.

Clearly, sufficient evidence exists to document the importance of a good quality marriage to better health and well-being. These findings are further strengthened by studies that have examined the interplay of marital status and marital quality in contributing to well-being. These studies show that poor quality marriages in late life are associated with compromised health and well-being and may be at levels that are lower than those associated with nonmarried elders. For example, Hagedoorn et al. (2006) found that older adults who were in an inequitable marital relationship were more distressed than their counterparts who had always been single. Gallo, Troxel,

Matthews, and Kuller (2003) examined the interplay of marital status and marital quality in cardiovascular health using longitudinal data from middle-aged women who were in the perimenopausal or postmenopausal phase. They found that women in less satisfying marriages showed levels of cardiovascular risk factors over time that were parallel to those found among non-married women; both groups had cardiovascular profiles over time that were less healthy relative to women in more satisfying marriages.

In addition to the direct benefits associated with a good quality marriage, such a marriage can act as a buffer in the face of stress during the middle-aged and subsequent years. These buffering effects are especially clear in the link between functional disability and psychological well-being. Bookwala and Franks (2005) found that older adults who were more functionally disabled and in better quality marriages (i.e., they reported fewer disagreements) had lower levels of depressive symptoms than those with similar levels of functional disability and high levels of marital disagreement. Likewise, Mancini and Bonanno (2006) found that older adults who were more functionally disabled and reported high marital closeness had lower levels of depressive and anxiety symptoms and higher self-esteem than their functionally disabled counterparts who were in marriages marked by low levels of closeness. More recently, Bookwala (2011) found that higher marital satisfaction mitigates the adverse effects of poor vision on depressive symptoms and functional loss in a national sample of older adults.

These findings demonstrate that the negative impact of stressors can be buffered by a good quality marriage. As such, these findings are consistent with the stress-buffering hypothesis of social support delineated in social support theory (see Cohen & Wills, 1985), which posits that the availability of supportive social relationships can serve as an effective buffer against stressors that individuals encounter. In addition, Mancini and Bonanno used socio-emotional selectivity theory (Carstensen et al., 1999) to explain the stress-buffering nature of a good marriage in late life. According to them, functional disability in late life serves as a proxy for the perception that one's time is constrained and, as a result, older adults derive especially significant benefits from the positive emotional characteristics of their marital relationships.

Couples Coping with Illness

The health benefits of a good marriage notwithstanding, it is important to note that marital relationships themselves may be vulnerable to the stress associated with health problems that may occur in late life. For example, Roberto, Gold, and Yorgason (2004) examined the impact of pain associated with osteoporosis on the marital relationship among elderly couples. They found that discrepancies within dyads about the pain experienced by the wife were related to marital adjustment. Specifically, wives who reported experiencing greater pain than they were perceived to experience by their husband reported lower marital adjustment than their counterparts whose husbands perceived the wife to be experiencing greater pain than she herself reported experiencing.

Pruchno, Wilson-Genderson, and Cartwright (2009) found varying patterns of change in marital satisfaction in a community-based sample of older couples where one spouse was diagnosed with end-stage renal disease. Marital satisfaction for the patient remained relatively stable over time but declined significantly for the spouse. Pruchno et al. interpreted the downward linear trend in marital satisfaction for the undiagnosed spouse as a self-preservation strategy of emotional withdrawal employed in the face of a terminally ill spouse who may have limited time to live.

Research also has shown domain-specific concordance between spouses on indicators of well-being. Using data from a probability-based sample of older couples, Bookwala and Schulz (1996) found that more depressive symptoms and poorer self-rated health in one spouse predicted more depressive symptoms and poorer self-rated health, respectively, in the other. Siegel, Bradley, Gallo, and Kasl (2004), who used longitudinal data from a national sample of older couples, also found evidence for spousal concordance in depressive symptomatology. In their study, participants who had a spouse with more depressive symptoms at baseline and whose spouse experienced an increase in depressive symptomatology across time reported more depressive symptoms at follow-up. More recently, Pruchno et al. (2009) found that depressive symptoms of both the person with end-stage renal disease and the spouse increased over time. Both patients and spouses had similar initial levels of depressive symptoms and similar growth patterns over time in these symptoms.

The findings on spousal similarity or concordance of well-being are consistent with Berg and Upchurch's (2007) developmental-contextual model of couples coping with chronic illness. Berg and Upchurch posited that illness experienced by one spouse makes coping and adjustment demands on both the patient and the spouse. As a result, how patient and spouse react to and cope with the illness is of import to their own and each other's adjustment. Further, Berg and Upchurch noted that how couples cope with chronic illness varies as a function of individuals' life stages, the day-to-day demands associated with the illness, and the unfolding stages of the chronic illness. The broader (sociocultural factors, gender) and more proximal (the quality of the couple relationship, the type of illness) contexts within which the couple operates also play a role in shaping the dyad's responses and adjustment to the illness condition. The concordance of emotion between spouses in the context of illness also is consistent with Larson and Almeida's (1999) model of emotional transmission. According to this model, emotions are transmitted from one spouse to another on a day-to-day basis and these, in turn, can influence the health and well-being of both members of the dyad.

SUPPORT FUNCTIONS IN PARTNERED RELATIONSHIPS

Throughout adulthood, intimate relationships serve as a significant source of support (Antonucci, Lansford, & Akiyama, 2001), especially in times of stress. Cutrona (1996) explained that in the context of marriage and similar relationships, support is conceptualized as responsiveness to a loved one's needs and involves acts that communicate caring and facilitate adaptive coping with stressors. Franks, Wendorf, Gonzalez, and Ketterer (2004), for example, examined the frequency of health-promoting support exchanges in older couples. They found that 100% of wives and husbands reported initiating some form of health-promoting spousal support at least once or twice in the previous month and upward of 93% of wives and a full 100% of husbands reported receiving as much support from their spouse. Hong and colleagues (2005) also examined the support of exercise behavior in older married couples wherein one member was a cardiac rehabilitation patient. They found that among couples in which both spouses engaged in similar exercise behavior, dyadic exchanges of exercise support were likely to be reported independently, demonstrating that intended exercise support given by one spouse was perceived as such by the other.

When older adults are coping with chronic illness, the types of support offered by the spouse can play a significant role in psychological well-being. Fekete, Stephens, Mickelson, and Druley (2007) studied the role of emotional (positive) and problematic (negative) support from the husband in the psychological well-being of older women experiencing a lupus flare-up. They found that more lupus-related emotional support from the husband was interpreted as greater emotional responsiveness from him, which, in turn, was associated with higher well-being in the wife. In contrast, more problematic support from the husband that was related specifically to the wife's lupus was perceived by the wife as him being less emotionally responsive and this, in turn, was associated with lower well-being in the wife. In a subsequent study with the same sample, Khan, Masumi, Stephens, Fekete, Druley, and Greene (2009) found that patients' self-efficacy rather than perceived emotional responsiveness mediated the link between spousal support and patients' psychological and physical well-being. These studies demonstrate that support by the spouse plays an integral role in coping with illness in the later years but that the specific mechanisms through which support may shape patient adjustment to illness require further clarification.

Social control theory has been used to explain the mechanisms and strategies through which spouses can play a positive or negative role in managing their partners' health-related behaviors during times of illness. Social control refers to tactics used by an individual to effect change in another person's behavior. Typically, such tactics are intended to promote health-protective and health-maintenance behaviors but can do so with the accompanying costs of frustrating the recipient of social control especially when more coercive strategies are employed (Lewis & Rook, 1999; Tucker, Orlando, Elliott, & Klein, 2006).

Within marriage and similar partnered relationships, the spouse often serves as a powerful source of control, notably so later in life when health-related problems become more common. Stephens, Fekete, Franks, Rook, Druley, and Greene (2009) examined the role of the spouse as an agent of control in promoting medical adherence pursuant to orthopedic knee surgery among older adults diagnosed with osteoarthritis. Comparing two forms of social control strategies, they found that both persuasive and pressure strategies were associated with greater medical adherence even though they were differentially associated with positive and negative emotional reactions in the patient with osteoarthritis. Positive emotional responses in the patient were associated with the use of persuasion strategies by the spouse whereas negative emotional responses in the patient were associated with the use of pressure tactics by the spouse. Moreover, Stephens et al. found that the association between the spouse's involvement early in the recovery period and health benefits experienced by the patient in the long-term following the surgery was indirectly explained by the experience of positive reactions in the patient to the control strategies used by the spouse. These findings suggest that persuasion strategies (which result in positive emotional reactions in the recovering spouse) may be the most beneficial form of social control in the context of couples coping with illness.

In addition to being a resource during times of illness, particularly during the middle and late adulthood years when illness becomes more normative (Siegler, Bosworth, & Poon, 2003), spouses also can be supportive as collaborators in the domain of cognitive function, serving to enhance cognitive performance in the later years. Partnered relationships in late life may offer older individuals the opportunity to optimize their cognitive performance and compensate for losses they may experience in the cognitive domain (Meegan & Berg, 2002; Strough & Margrett, 2002). In general, working with a social partner on cognitive tasks in experimental conditions, commonly referred to as collaborative cognition, increases performance outcomes among older adults (Cheng & Strough, 2004; Dixon & Gould, 1998).

These gains can be especially marked when working collaboratively with one's spouse (Dixon & Gould, 1998). For example, Kimbler and Margrett (2009) conducted a study in which older adults were required to perform both individually and collaboratively on an everyday problem-solving task. They manipulated the familiarity of the collaborative partner across older adults such that participants worked either with a stranger or their spouse. Performance was superior in the collaborative engagement condition than when the participant worked alone. Moreover, the familiarity of the partner influenced cognitive performance with older adults who worked with their spouse showing better outcomes than those who worked with a stranger.

The benefits of collaboration are not limited to the domain of cognition, however. In a daily diary study, Berg and her colleagues (2008) showed that among older couples dealing with the husband's prostate cancer, perceiving the spouse to be a collaborative partner in day-to-day decision-making was related to more same-day positive mood in both the men dealing with prostate cancer and their wives and less same-day negative mood in the men. In addition, these associations were mediated by greater perceived effectiveness of dealing with the stressor such that both husbands and wives reported more coping effectiveness on days in which they perceived their spouses to be more collaborative partners in coping efforts. Results from both studies are generally consistent with social support theory (Cohen & Wills, 1985) that explains the direct benefit of interpersonal support on well being. In addition, these findings are consistent with the developmental-contextual model of couples coping with illness (Berg & Upchurch, 2007) that views individual members of couples as interdependent in their appraisal of stressors and the way they cope with these stressors.

CONCLUSIONS AND IMPLICATIONS

The literature reviewed in this chapter indicates that partnered relationships are diverse in nature, and while research on marriage remains the most widely prevalent, other types of intimate relationships, such as same-sex relationships, LAT relationships, and cohabiting relationships, also are emerging as important foci of research. In general, partnered relationships in late life are marked by higher levels of companionate love and longitudinal research shows that relationship satisfaction at least within marriage may decline over the life span. It also is common for partnered relationships to be marked by role inequities, disagreement, and conflict but such negative relationship processes typically are less salient to well-being as individuals age. Sexual intimacy remains significant to relationship satisfaction in middle and late adulthood although sexual interest and activity decline during this period. Relationship satisfaction in the later years also is responsive to the experience of life transitions, such as transitions into the empty-nest years, retirement, and the caregiving role.

A major theoretical and empirical focus has been on the effects of marital or partnered relationship status and quality on health. Research continues to document the health-protective role of married status in the middle and later years and the importance of a good quality relationship in enhancing health and well-being and protecting partners from the adverse consequences of health-related stressors. It also is clear that couples cope collectively with such stressors and partners offer support in health-protective behaviors and serve as valuable allies in enhancing cognitive function as individuals age.

The findings reviewed in this chapter have important clinical implications for gerontological practitioners. Sexual concerns of middle-aged and older individuals are important elements of partnered relationships and it is important to assess the extent to which declines in sexual interest or activity are caused by health or psychosocial factors that may be amenable to clinical intervention. Likewise, clinicians working with middle-aged women should consider seeking broader explanations than menopausal status alone for changes in their clients' sexuality. Such alternatives may better enable them to assist with women's sexuality concerns during the later years.

The quality of marital and similar relationships clearly plays a role in health and well-being and thus, a comprehensive assessment of the latter should include obtaining information about the quality of older adults' partnered relationships. By doing so, practitioners will be better able to determine the extent to which difficulties in such relationships underlie their clients' psychological and physical well-being. To the extent that these relationship difficulties are amenable to modification, effective intervention efforts may result in a substantial gain in health and well-being for elderly clients. Moreover, given that better relationship quality buffers the health impact of age-related stressors, couple-focused workshops via the use of role-playing and a focus on improving communication strategies could augment the resources available in midlife and late life for effectively dealing with stressors. When a client has an ill partner or spouse, gerontological practitioners also must assess the impact of the illness on both members of the dyad and offer strategies that can enhance the couple's efficacy in coping with the illness.

Finally, it is important that clinicians address the importance of stressful life transitions in the lives of their clients. These transitions often can have an impact on the quality of the partnered relationship of the individual, which, in turn, can negatively affect the spouse's well-being. Creating an awareness in older adults of the impact of life transitions on their relationship and offering strategies to maintain relationship quality may be valuable in maintaining health and well-being in the midlife and late life years.

Despite the considerable gains in current knowledge about marriage and similar partnerships in middle and late adulthood, significant gaps exist in the literature. First, research must expand its focus to incorporate the diversity of intimate relationships that exist in this life stage, directing attention to the processes, correlates, and consequences of nonmarital cohabiting and noncohabiting intimate relationships among heterosexual and same-sex couples. For example, studies on the impact of life transitions such as retirement and caregiving have focused almost exclusively on married individuals; the study of these same variables within the context of same-sex, cohabiting, and LAT couples is an important need in the field. Second, cross-sectional studies remain the norm in much of relationship research; more longitudinal studies are required that examine the nature, causes, and consequences of relationship quality change during the later years in marriage and other partnered relationships. Third, more studies are necessary that use the couple as the unit of analysis. Using data gathered from both members of the dyad will provide a more comprehensive understanding about the nature of partnered relationships at the couple level, the process by which relevant factors influence relationship quality for both members, and the interplay of health and relationship quality for each of them. Fourth, further clarity is necessary on the links between menopause and sexuality for older women. Existing studies have typically included women in their 50s or early 60s and are quite diverse in terms of the phases of menopausal transition they examine, the outcomes they assess (e.g., sexual interest, desire, responsiveness, or activity), and the sampling strategy they use (ranging from convenience sampling to the use of probability-based samples). These factors underscore the need for both more methodologically consistent studies on the effects of age versus menopause on women's sexuality and studies that use prospective longitudinal designs spanning several years. Research also is needed on the extent to which menopausal status may serve as a proxy for other health-related and psychosocial changes that also occur during menopause in explaining changes in women's sexuality. Finally, a focus on diversity in terms of cultural and ethnic differences in the nature and structure of intimate relationships also is largely missing in the field.

Studies are needed on couple relationships in the later years that specifically focus on cultural and ethnic similarities and differences in relationship quality, including causes and consequences of differences. Future studies must be grounded in existing life course and life span theoretical frameworks related to social support, control strategies, socioemotional selectivity, collaborative coping and cognition, and developmental-contextual models of relationships and health and use their findings to further inform and refine these models. Such a generation of new studies will result in significant advancement of relationship research over the life span, building knowledge about establishing and maintaining these intimate partnerships and enhancing their effects on well-being in the middle and late adulthood years.

REFERENCES

Akiyama, H., Antonucci, T., Takahashi, K., & Langfahl, E. S. (2003). Negative interactions in close relationships across the life span. *Journal of Gerontology: Psychological Sciences, 53B,* P70–P79.

Amato, P. R., Booth, A., Johnson, D. R., & Rogers, S. J. (2007). *Alone together: How marriage in America is changing.* Cambridge, MA: Harvard University Press.

American Association of Retired Persons (2004). *The divorce experience: A study of divorce at midlife and beyond*. Washington, DC: AARP.

Antonucci, T.C., Lansford, J.E., & Akiyama, H. (2001). Impact of positive and negative aspects of marital relationships and friendships on well-being of older adults. *Applied Developmental Science, 5*, 68–75.

Bancroft, J., Graham, C.A., Janssen, E., & Sanders, S.A. (2009). The dual control model: Current status and future directions. *Journal of Sex Research, 46*, 121–142.

Beckman, N., Waern, M., Gustafson, D., & Skoog, I. (2008). Secular trends in self-reported sexual activity and satisfaction in Swedish 70-year-olds: Cross-sectional survey of four populations, 1971–2001. *BMJ, 337*, a279.

Berg, C.A., & Upchurch, R. (2007). A developmental-contextual model of couples coping with chronic illness across the adult life span. *Psychological Bulletin, 133*, 920–954.

Berg, C.A., Wiebe, D.J., Butner, J., Bloor, L., Bradstreet, C., Upchurch, R., . . . Patton, G. (2008). Collaborative coping and daily mood in couples dealing with prostate cancer. *Psychology and Aging, 23*, 505–516.

Bierhoff, H-W., & Schmohr, M. (2004). Romantic and marital relationships. In F.R. Lang & K.L. Fingerman (Eds.), *Growing together: Personal relationships across the life span* (pp. 103–129). New York: Cambridge University Press.

Birditt, K.S., Fingerman, K.L., & Almeida, D.M. (2005). Age differences in exposure and reactions to interpersonal tensions: A daily diary study. *Psychology and Aging, 20*, 330–340.

Birnbaum, G.E., Cohen, O., & Wertheimer, V. (2007). Is it all about sexual intimacy? Age, menopausal status, and women's sexuality. *Personal Relationships, 14*, 167–185.

Bookwala, J. (2005). The role of marital quality in physical health during the mature years. *Journal of Aging and Health, 17*, 85–104.

Bookwala, J. (2009). The impact of parent care on marital quality and well-being in adult daughters and sons. *Journal of Gerontology: Psychological Sciences, 64B*, 339–347.

Bookwala, J. (2011). Marital quality as a moderator of the effects of poor vision on quality of life among older adults. *Journal of Gerontology: Social Sciences, 66*, 605–616.

Bookwala, J., & Fekete, E. (2009). The role of psychological resources in the affective well-being of never-married adults. *Journal of Social and Personal Relationships, 26*, 411–428.

Bookwala, J., & Franks, M.M. (2005). The moderating role of marital quality in older adults' depressed affect: Beyond the main-effects model. *Journal of Gerontology: Psychological Sciences, 60*, 338–341.

Bookwala, J., & Jacobs, J. (2004). Age, marital processes, and depressed affect. *The Gerontologist, 44*, 328–338.

Bookwala, J., & Schulz, R. (1996). Spousal similarity in well-being: The Cardiovascular Health Study. *Psychology & Aging, 11*, 582–590.

Bookwala, J., Sobin, J., & Zdaniuk, B. (2005). Gender and aggression in marital relationships: A life span perspective. *Sex Roles, 52*, 797–807.

Brown, S. L., Lee, G. R., & Bulanda, J. R. (2006). Cohabitation among older adults: A national portrait. *Journal of Gerontology: Social Sciences, 61B,* S71–S79.

Burgess, E. (2004). Sexuality in midlife and later life couples. In J. H. Harvey, A. Wenzel, & S. Sprecher (Eds.), *The handbook of sexuality in close relationships* (pp. 437–454). Mahwah, NJ: Lawrence Erlbaum Associates.

Cain, V. S., Johannes, C. B., Avis, N. E., Mohr, B., Schocken, M., Skurnick, J., & Ory, M. (2003). Sexual functioning and practices in a multi-ethnic study of midlife women: Baseline results from SWAN. *The Journal of Sex Research, 40,* 266–276.

Carr, D., & Boerner, K. (2009). Do spousal discrepancies in marital quality assessments affect psychological adjustment to widowhood? *Journal of Marriage and Family, 71,* 495–509.

Carstensen, L. L., Isaacowitz, D. M., & Charles, S. T. (1999). Taking time seriously: A theory of socioemotional selectivity. *American Psychologist, 54,* 165–181.

Casalanti, T., & Kiecolt, K. J. (2007). Diversity among late-life couples. *Generations, 31,* 10–17.

Cheng, S., & Strough, J. (2004). A comparison of collaborative and individual everyday problem-solving in younger and older adults. *International Journal of Aging and Human Development, 58,* 167–195.

Cohen, S., & Wills, T. A. (1985). Stress, social support, and the buffering hypothesis. *Psychological Bulletin, 98,* 310–357.

Cutrona, C. E. (1996). *Social support in couples: Marriage as a resource in times of stress.* Thousand Oaks, CA: Sage.

De Jong Gierveld, J., & Peeters, A. (2003). The interweaving of repartnered older adults' lives with their children and siblings. *Ageing & Society, 23,* 187–203.

DeLamater, J., & Moorman, S. M. (2007). Sexual behavior in later life. *Journal of Aging and Health, 19,* 921–945.

Dennerstein, L., Alexander, J. L., & Kotz, K. (2003). The menopause and sexual functioning: A review of the population-based studies. *Annual Review of Sex Research, 14,* 64–82.

Dixon, R. A., & Gould, O. N. (1998). Younger and older adults collaborating on retelling everyday stories. *Applied Developmental Science, 2,* 160–171.

Dupre, M. E., & Meadows, S. O. (2007). Disaggregating the effects of marital trajectories on health. *Journal of Family Issues, 28,* 623–652.

Feeney, J., Peterson, C., & Noller, P. (1994). Equity and marital satisfaction over the family life cycle. *Personal Relationships, 1,* 83–99.

Fekete, E., Stephens, M. A. P., Mickelson, K. D., & Druley, J. A. (2007). Couples' support provision during illness: The role of perceived emotional responsiveness. *Families, Systems, and Health, 25,* 204–217.

Fingerman, K. L., Hay, E. L., & Birditt, K. S. (2004). The best of ties, the worst of ties: Close, problematic, and ambivalent social relationships. *Journal of Marriage and Family, 66,* 792–808.

Franks, M. M., Wendorf, C. A., Gonzalez, R., & Ketterer, M. (2004). Aid and influence: Health-promoting exchanges of older married partners. *Journal of Social and Personal Relationships, 21,* 431–445.

Gallo, L. C., Troxel, W. M., Matthews, K. A., & Kuller, L. H. (2003). Marital status and quality in middle-aged women: Associations with levels and trajectories of cardiovascular risk factors. *Health Psychology, 22,* 453–463.

Ghazanfareeon Karlsson, S., & Borell, K. (2002). Intimacy and autonomy, gender and ageing: Living apart together. *Ageing International, 27,* 11–26.

Ghazanfareeon Karlsson, S., Johansson, S., Gerdner, A., & Borell, K. (2007). Caring while living apart. *Journal of Gerontological Social Work, 49,* 3–27.

Gorchoff, S. M., John, O. P., & Helson, R. (2008). Contextualizing change in marital satisfaction during middle age: An 18-year longitudinal study. *Psychological Science, 19,* 1194–1200.

Gott, M., & Hinchcliff, S. (2003). How important is sex in later life? The views of older people. *Social Science and Medicine, 56,* 1617–1628.

Hagedoorn, M., van Yperen, N. W., Coyne, J. C., van Jaarsveld, C. H. M., Ranchor, A. V., van Sonderen, E., & Sanderman, R. (2006). Does marriage protect older people from distress? The role of equity and recency of bereavement. *Psychology and Aging, 21,* 611–620.

Hatfield, E. (1985). Passionate and companionate love. In R. J. Sternberg & M. L. Barnes (Eds.), *The psychology of love* (pp. 191–217). Cambridge, MA: Yale University Press.

Hatfield, E., & Rapson, R. L. (1993). Love, sex, and intimacy: Their psychology, biology, and history. New York: Harper Collins.

Heckhausen, J., & Schulz, R. (1995). A life span theory of control. *Psychological Review, 102,* 284–304.

Henry, N. J. M., Berg, C. A., Smith, T. W., & Florsheim, P. (2007). Positive and negative characteristics of marital interaction and their association with marital satisfaction in middle-aged and older couples. *Psychology and Aging, 22,* 428–441.

Henry, R. G., Miller, R. B., & Giarrusso, R. (2005). Difficulties, disagreements, and disappointments in late-life marriages. *International Journal of Aging and Human Development, 61,* 243–264.

Hiedemann, B., Suhomlinova, O., & O'Rand, A. M. (1998). Economic independence, economic status, and empty nest in midlife marital disruption. *Journal of Marriage and Family, 60,* 219–231.

Hong, T. B., Franks, M. M., Gonzalez, R., Keteyian, S. J., Franklin, B. A., & Artinian, N. T. (2005). A dyadic investigation of exercise support between cardiac patients and their spouses. *Health Psychology, 24,* 430–434.

Hughes, M. E., & Waite, L. J. (2009). Marital biography and health at midlife. *Journal of Health and Social Behavior, 50,* 344–358.

Human Rights Campaign Foundation (2001). Gay and lesbian families in the United States: Same-sex unmarried partner households. Available online at www.hrc.org/familynet/documents/1%20.census.pdf

Kaplan, R. M., & Kronick, R. G. (2006). Marital status and longevity in the United States population. *Journal of Epidemiology and Community Health, 60,* 760–765.

Kennedy, R. (2005). Lesbian and gay families: The changing and unsteady legal and social environment. In F. K. O. Yuen (Ed.), *Social work practice with children and families* (pp. 165–182). New York: Haworth Press.

Khan, C.M., Masumi, I., Stephens, M.A.P., Fekete, E.M., Druley, J., & Greene, K.A. (2009). Spousal support following knee surgery: Roles of self-efficacy and perceived emotional responsiveness. *Rehabilitation Psychology, 54*, 28–32.

Kimbler, K.J., & Margrett, J.A. (2009). Older adults' interactive behaviors during collaboration on everyday problems: Linking process and outcome. *International Journal of Behavioral Development, 33*, 531–542.

Kulik, L. (2002a). His and her marriage: Differences in spousal perceptions of marital life in late adulthood. In S.P. Shohov (Ed.), *Advances in psychology research* (pp. 21–32). Huntington, NY: Nova Science Publishers.

Kulik, L. (2002b). Marital equality and the quality of long-term marriage in later life. *Ageing and Society, 22*, 459–481.

Kurdek, L.A. (2006). Differences between partners from heterosexual, gay, and cohabiting couples. *Journal of Marriage and Family, 68*, 509–528.

Kurdek, L.A. (2007). The allocation of household labor by partners in gay and lesbian couples. *Journal of Family Issues, 28*, 132–148.

Kurdek, L.A. (2008a). A general model of relationship commitment: Evidence from same-sex partners. Personal Relationships, 15, 391–405.

Kurdek, L.A. (2008b). Change in relationship quality for partners from lesbian, gay male, and heterosexual couples. *Journal of Family Psychology, 22*, 701–711.

Larson, R.W., & Almeida, D.M. (1999). Emotional transmission in the daily lives of families: A new paradigm for studying family process. *Journal of Marriage and Family, 61*, 5–20.

Lee, J.H. (1973). *The colors of love*. Englewood Cliffs, NJ: Prentice Hall.

Levin, I. (2004). Living apart together: A new family forum. *Current Sociology, 52*, 223–230.

Levin, I., & Trost, J. (1999). Living apart together. *Community, Work, & Family, 2*, 279–294.

Lewis, M.A., & Rook, K.S. (1999). Social control in personal relationships: Impact on health behaviors and psychological distress. *Health Psychology, 18*, 63–71.

Lindau, S.T., Schumm, L.P., Laumann, E.O., Levinson, W., O'Muircheartaigh, C.A., & Waite, L.J. (2007). A study of sexuality and health among older adults in the United States. *New England Journal of Medicine, 357*, 762–775.

Mackey, R.A., & O'Brien, B.A. (1999). Adaptation in lasting marriages. *Families in Society, 80*, 587–596.

Mancini, A.D., & Bonanno, G.A. (2006). Marital closeness, functional disability, and adjustment in late life. *Psychology and Aging, 21*, 600–610.

Mansfield, P.K., Voda, A., & Koch, P.B. (1998). Predictors of sexual response changes in heterosexual midlife women. *Health Values, 19*, 10–20.

Manzoli, L., Villari, P., Pirone, G.M., & Boccia, A. (2007). Marital status and mortality in the elderly: A systematic review and meta-analysis. *Social Science and Medicine, 64*, 77–94.

Marks, N.F., Lambert, J.D., & Choi, H. (2002). Transitions to caregiving, gender, and psychological well-being: A prospective U.S. national study. *Journal of Marriage and Family, 64*, 657–667.

Meegan, S.P., & Berg, C.A. (2002). Contexts, functions, forms, and processes of collaborative everyday problem solving in older adulthood. *International Journal of Behavioral Development, 26*, 6–15.

Miller, B., Townsend, A. L., & Ishler, K. J. (2004). Change in marital dissatisfaction, health, and depression in married couples. *Journal of Mental Health and Aging, 10,* 65–77.

Mitchell, B. A., & Gee, E. M. (1996). "Boomerang kids" and midlife parental marital satisfaction. *Family Relations, 45,* 442–448.

Mock, S. E., Taylor, C. J., & Savin-Williams, R. C. (2006). Aging together: The retirement plans of same-sex couples. In D. Kimmel, T. Rose, & S. David (Eds.), *Lesbian, gay, bisexual, and transgender aging: Research and clinical perspectives* (pp. 152–174). New York: Columbia University Press.

Moen, P., Kim, J. E., & Hofmeister, H. (2001). Couples' work/retirement transitions, gender, and marital quality. *Social Psychology Quarterly, 64,* 55–71.

Moustgaard, H., & Martikainen, P. (2009). Nonmarital cohabitation among older Finnish men and women: Socioeconomic characteristics and forms of union dissolution. *Journal of Gerontology: Social Sciences, 64B,* 507–516.

Murphy, M., Glaser, K., & Grundy, E. (1997). Marital status and long-term illness in Great Britain. *Journal of Marriage and Family, 59,* 156–164.

National Alliance for Caregiving. (2009). *Caregiving in the U.S.: A focused look at those caring for someone age 50 or older.* Bethesda, MD: National Alliance for Caregiving.

Peplau, L. A., & Fingerhut, A. W. (2007). The close relationships of lesbians and gay men. *Annual Review of Psychology, 58,* 405–424.

Peplau, L. A., Fingerhut, A. W., & Beals, K. P. (2004). Sexuality in the relationships of lesbians and gay men. In J. H. Harvey, A. Wenzel, & S. Sprecher (Eds.), *The handbook of sexuality in close relationships* (pp. 349–369). Mahwah, NJ: Lawrence Erlbaum Associates.

Peterson, C. (1990). Husbands' and wives' perceptions of marital fairness across the family life cycle. *International Journal of Aging and Human Development, 39,* 179–188.

Pienta, A. M., & Hayward, M. D. (2002). Who expects to continue working after age 62? The retirement plans of couples. *Journal of Gerontology: Social Sciences, 57B,* S199–S208.

Pienta, A. M., Hayward, M. D., & Jenkins, K. R. (2000). Health consequences of marriage for the retirement years. *Journal of Family Issues, 21,* 559–586.

Prigerson, H. G., Maciejewski, P. K., & Rosenheck, R. A. (2000). Preliminary explorations of the harmful interactive effects of widowhood and marital harmony on health, health service use, and health care costs. *The Gerontologist, 40,* 349–357.

Pruchno, R., Wilson-Genderson, M., & Cartwright, F. P. (2009). Depressive symptoms and marital satisfaction in the context of chronic disease: A longitudinal data analysis. *Journal of Family Psychology, 23,* 573–584.

Pudrovska, T., Schieman, S., & Carr, D. (2006). Strains of singlehood in later life: Do race and gender matter? *Journal of Gerontology: Social Sciences, 61B,* S315–S322.

Roberto, K. A., Gold, D. T., & Yorgason, J. B. (2004). The influence of osteoporosis on the marital relationship of older couples. *Journal of Applied Gerontology, 23,* 443–456.

Siegel, M. J., Bradley, E. H., Gallo, W. T., & Kasl, S. V. (2004). The effect of spousal mental and physical health on husbands' and wives' depressive symptoms among older adults: Longitudinal evidence from the Health and Retirement Study. *Journal of Aging and Health, 16,* 398–425.

Siegler, I. C., Bosworth, H. B., & Poon, L. W. (2003). Disease, health, and aging. In R. Lerner & A. Easterbrooks (Eds.), *Handbook of psychology: Developmental psychology,* (Vol. 6, pp. 423–442). New York: Wiley.

Smith, D. B., & Moen, P. (1998). Spousal influence on retirement: His, her, and their perceptions. *Journal of Marriage and Family, 60,* 734–744.

Smith, T. W., Berg, C. A., Florsheim, P., Uchino, B. N., Pearce, G., Hawkins, M. . . . Olsen-Cerny, C. (2009). Conflict and collaboration in middle-aged and older couples: I. Age differences in agency and communion during marital interaction. *Psychology and Aging, 24,* 259–273.

Stephens, M. A. P., Fekete, E. M., Franks, M. M., Rook, K. S., Druley, J. A., & Greene, K. (2009). Spouses' use of pressure and persuasion to promote osteoarthritis patients' medical adherence after orthopedic surgery. *Health Psychology, 28,* 48–55.

Strohm, C. Q., Seltzer, J. A., Cochran, S. D., & Mays, V. M. (2009). "Living apart together" relationships in the United States. *Demographic Research, 21,* 177–214.

Strough, J., & Margrett, J. (2002). Overview of the special section on collaborative cognition in later adulthood. *International Journal of Behavioral Development, 26,* 2–5.

Svetlik, D., Dooley, W. K., Weiner, M. F., Williamson, G. M., & Walters, A. S. (2005). Declines in satisfaction with physical intimacy predict caregiver perceptions of overall relationship loss: A study of elderly caregiving spousal dyads. *Sexuality and Disability, 23,* 65–79.

Szinovacz, M. E. (1996). Couples' employment/retirement patterns and perceptions of marital quality. *Research on Aging, 18,* 243–268.

Szinovacz, M. E., & Schaffer, A. M. (2000). Effects of retirement on marital conflict tactics. *Journal of Family Issues, 21,* 367–389.

Trudel, G., Turgeon, L., & Piche, L. (2000). Marital and sexual aspects of old age. *Sexual and Relationship Therapy, 15,* 381–406.

Tucker, J. S., Friedman, H. S., Wingard, D. L., & Schwartz, J. E. (1996). Marital history at midlife as a predictor of longevity: Alternative explanations to the protective effect of marriage. *Health Psychology, 15,* 94–101.

Tucker, J. S., Orlando, M., Elliott, M. N., & Klein, D. J. (2006). Affective and behavioral responses to health-related social control. *Health Psychology, 25,* 715–722.

Umberson, D., & Williams, K. (2005). Marital quality, health, and aging: Gender equity? *Journals of Gerontology (Special Issue II), 60B,* 109–112.

Umberson, D., Williams, K., Powers, D. A., Liu, H., & Needham, B. (2006). You make me sick: Marital quality and health over the life course. *Journal of Health and Social Behavior, 47,* 1–16.

U.S. Census Bureau. (2003). *Marital status: 2000.* Washington, DC: U.S. Department of Commerce.

Van Laningham, J., Johnson, D. R., & Amato, P. (2001). Marital happiness, marital duration, and the U-shaped curve: Evidence from a five-wave panel study. *Social Forces, 79,* 1313–1323.

Walker, R. B., & Luszcz, M. A. (2009). The health and relationship dynamics of late-life couples: A systematic review of the literature. *Ageing & Society, 29,* 455–480.

Walster, E., Walster G. W., & Berscheid, E. (1978). *Equity: Theory and research.* Boston: Allyn & Bacon.

Willetts, M. C. (2006). Union quality comparisons between long-term heterosexual cohabitation and legal marriage. *Journal of Family Issues, 27,* 110–127.

Yeh, H-C., Lorenz, F. O., Wickrama, K. A. S., Conger, R. D., & Elder, G. H., Jr. (2006). Relationships among sexual satisfaction, marital quality, and marital instability at midlife. *Journal of Family Psychology, 20,* 339–343.

Zhang, Z., & Hayward, M. D. (2006). Gender, the marital life course, and cardiovascular disease in late midlife. *Journal of Marriage and the Family, 68,* 639–657.

6

Sibling Relationships from Midlife to Old Age

Victoria Hilkevitch Bedford and
Paula Smith Avioli

This chapter updates the chapter on siblings in middle and old age in the first edition of this handbook. Of note is the increasing visibility of the adult sibling bond in recent decades reflecting a much greater interest in the topic. As a result of this increased interest, several current literature reviews are available (e.g., Connidis, 2005, 2010; van Volkom, 2006) as well as encyclopedia entries (e.g., Bedford, 2002, 2008; Bedford & Diderich, 2009; Cicirelli, 2008). The present chapter will focus on changes in emphasis and the acquisition of new understandings of sibling relationships in middle through old age. We will begin with consideration as to why interest in siblings has burgeoned, followed by an examination of the breadth of what constitutes a sibling, some theoretical approaches to the subject, and some methodological trends in sibling research. We will then review the findings of old topics that have been revisited in new ways, as well as promising new topics. Last, we will use these new topics as a springboard to delineate intriguing questions for future research.

CONTEMPORARY SIBLING RESEARCH

Broadly Defining Siblings

Generally, siblings constitute the closest degree of family relatedness within a single generation of the family. They are usually peers, although wide age spacing may modify this definition. Many relationships are designated as siblings: biological and adopted offspring of the same parents, those who share one biological or adopted parent (half-siblings), and those who share neither parent biologically (stepsiblings) nor legally (quasi-siblings and fictive siblings). A useful classification system comes from anthropology. Consanguinal siblings are the siblings related by blood, whether they share one or two biological parents. Affinal siblings are related by adoption or marriage (siblings-in-law). Quasi-siblings have separate parents who live together or they fall into the foster sibling category.

Other kinds of quasi-siblings are more commonly found within specific minority or developing world cultures. Milk brothers or sisters are children who are wet-nursed by the same woman, meaning they are breast-fed by a woman other than their biological mother. In Islam, children who are younger than two years old when they were wet-nursed become siblings to the biological children of their wet nurse, and the same rules apply to them that apply to biological siblings (e.g., they are not allowed to marry each other as adults, and the rules of modesty known as *hijab* are relaxed). Unlike milk siblings, godsiblings are common in Western European culture, but they are not typically recognized in any formal way. A godsibling relationship occurs when one child is a godchild of another child's parents. Godsiblings may or may not be related to one another. Finally, foster siblings are raised in the same foster home; the term applies to the foster children's relationship to one another as well as their relationship to the foster parents' biological children (http://en.wikipedia.org/wiki/Sibling).

Increasingly common are stepsiblings and half-siblings who are acquired in childhood or adulthood after parents' unions are dissolved and new ones are formed. Parents' remarriage frequently ends in divorce, which results in the status of former siblings (Bedford & Diderich, 2009).

Most studies are limited to full siblings (often without specifying whether this includes adopted siblings), but it is important to recognize the diversity of sibling relationships as a context for viewing the narrow range of sibling relationships typically targeted in the sibling literature. This limitation in the literature ignores important potential sources of social support and stress across the life span. Exceptions are recent studies that include or focus on siblings-in-law (Fingerman, Hay, & Birditt, 2004; Guiaux, van Tilburg, & van Groenou, 2007), stepsiblings, half-siblings (Diderich, 2008), and fictive siblings (Allen, Roberto, & Blieszner, 2011).

The Importance of Siblings in Family Research

In 1989, the sibling relationship in adulthood was described as "forgotten" in the title of a special issue of a journal on the topic (Bedford & Gold, 1989). Soon after this publication appeared, the number of works published on the topic increased dramatically and has remained relatively high. For example, our review of the literature (not including behavioral genetic studies) shows there were 10 publications in the 1960s and 65 in the first decade of the 21st century. Various reasons for this striking rise in sibling publications have been suggested. Changes in family structure and demographics may bring siblings more to the attention of researchers. For example, increased life expectancy (Neyer, 2002) coupled with loss and changes of partners in subsequent decades may result in a smaller pool of potential social relations in later life, putting more emphasis on the sibling relationship (Connidis, 2005).

Further, when sibling relationships are valued, they may elicit more research interest, which is more likely to be the case of Baby Boomers due to their larger sibships. Compared to adults with small sibships, adults with large sibships are more likely to feel closer to a selected closest sibling than to others, as well as to confide in and contact this sibling most often given the wider choice a larger sibship offers (Connidis & Campbell, 1995).

Finally, increased longevity of parents results in more families that have parents with chronic illness and dementia (see Teaster, Wangmo, & Vorsky, chapter 17 in this volume), which translates into the normative experience of caring for one's frail parents (Brody, 1985). Typically, parent care brings siblings into active contact, often reactivating a dormant or more symbolic relationship. A large body of sibling research addresses this phenomenon, which Brian de Vries reviews in chapter 22 of this volume (see also a review by Davey & Szinovacz, 2008).

Theoretical Approaches in Sibling Research

Sibling research has been criticized for its lack of theoretical grounding (Walker, Allen, & Connidis, 2005). This observation, however, overlooks some early theorizing about siblings. For example, psychological theories were applied by Cicirelli (1989) using attachment theory (Bowlby, 1987) and by Bedford (1989) using the psychoanalytic theory of Karen Horney (1945). The problem with such approaches, however, is that they are limited to the subjective experience or microlevel of sibling relationships and cannot tap implications of sibling structure and interaction processes or societal influences. Other trends have been to contextualize this subjective experience. One such approach views sibling relationships within the broader family perspective by applying family systems theory (e.g., Campbell, Connidis, & Davies, 1999).

Cicirelli (2005) described the sibling relationship as a partial system in which the various components are interdependent. A disturbance in one component reverberates throughout the system. This reverberation is due to a chain reaction whereby the effect of the disturbance on one component (family member) in turn affects another, and so on. These interactions can be direct or indirect (i.e., as feedback). The systems can be open or closed based on the strength of their boundaries, which determines whether input from other systems can penetrate. Applied to sibling relations, family systems theory can describe interactions among siblings, how individual siblings influence one another, and how a set of siblings influences an individual member and vice versa. These family system properties can also be applied to a larger family unit by including parents as well as other relatives. A parent's needs, for instance, may dominate within the family unit such that the sibling group becomes dysfunctional. For example, when the demands of dementia care for parents overwhelm the resources of even close siblings, their relationship quality can be seriously compromised (Bedford, 2005). Qualls and Noecker's (2009) family treatment strategies illustrate the application of systems principles to sibling as well as other family relationships for solving problems related to caring for frail old parents.

Nonetheless, family systems theory has both methodological and theoretical limitations. One methodological issue is obtaining data from multiple members within families in order to investigate mutual influences. One potential source of such data has been qualitative case studies of family networks (e.g., Connidis, 2007). Some recent studies have questioned parents about all of their adult children (e.g., Fingerman, Cheng, Birditt, & Zarit, 2011), and, a few large-scale studies have successfully obtained data from more than one sibling directly, such as the Netherlands Kinship Panel Study (Dykstra et al., 2005).

In terms of the theory itself, family systems does not directly address the more macro influences that inform interpersonal behaviors and responses, in particular, the influences of family members' locations in various social structures (i.e., the way in which society orders relationships in the absence of autonomy). Accordingly, relationships can be ordered depending on one's status with respect to race, gender, social class, sexual orientation, age, and ethnicity (e.g., Connidis, 2005).

Recent theorizing on sibling relationships has primarily championed the insights offered by the life course perspective and the concept of ambivalence (Connidis, 2005; Walker et al., 2005; also see Connidis, chapter 3 in this volume, for its history and its relation to other theories). Most of the recent theorizing on ambivalence has fallen within the realm of sociology and, therefore, is not readily accessible to nonsociologists. Further, there are few empirical applications to sibling relationships. The following discussion, therefore, is a preliminary deconstruction of the meaning of the ambivalence concept, a discussion of its appropriateness to siblings, and descriptions of two empirical studies of sibling ambivalence.

A popular dictionary definition of ambivalence is "simultaneous or contradictory attitudes or feelings (such as attraction and repulsion) toward an object, person, or action" (*Merriam-Webster Online Dictionary*. Retrieved from http://www.merriam-webster.com/dictionary/ambivalence). Applied to family relationships, a distinction is made between psychological and sociological ambivalence. Psychological ambivalence typically refers to sustaining these simultaneous or contradictory attitudes or feelings toward a family member or, collectively, to a group of family members. Sociological ambivalence involves contradictions in social structures that lead to ambivalent feelings and attitudes (Connidis, 2007). An example of sociological ambivalence is the traditional view of marriage and divorce. Contradictions in the structures are apparent in the belief that marriage should last until death separates the partners, whereas divorce legally terminates marriage (Connidis, 2003), even without cause if one partner so wishes in the case of no-fault divorce. The ambivalent feelings and attitudes are apparent when one believes in the permanence of marriage while having to accept the fact of one's own divorce or that of a loved one.

Sociological ambivalence also involves interpersonal behaviors, specifically, negotiations between family members when experiencing contradictions of social structures such as power differentials based on age, race, gender, social class, and ethnicity. Negotiations also contain autonomous acts, namely, agency on behalf of one's own interests despite the pressures of social structures (Connidis, 2003). Collective ambivalence refers to views on family relationships when several individuals occupy the same position, such as the siblingship as a whole (see Connidis, chapter 3 in this volume).

Ambivalence theory's contribution to understanding family relationships is that it provides a model for understanding their enormous complexity, rejecting a positivist or reductionist approach to family science. The notion that feelings and structures related to family can contain contradictions opens the possibility that understandings of families can violate expectations more generally. For instance, relationships with family members are not variations on any one standard, such as solidarity (Connidis, 2010), nor do historical visions of family necessarily apply to the present or future.

In evaluating the appropriateness of the ambivalence concept to siblings, it is important to consider the causes of ambivalence and whether they also apply to siblings, because these causes were originally proposed in a literature targeting intergenerational relationships. They are interdependence, the emotional intensity which occurs in the case of frequent contact, coresidence, and close proximity (van Gaalen, Dykstra, & Komter, 2010); health issues resulting in the inability of one family member to help another, having unequal resources, childhood relationship quality, femaleness of dyads (on a continuum from 0 to 2) (Willson, Shuey, & Elder, 2003); status transitions, conflicting norms, nonvoluntary ties, and length of the relationship (Fingerman et al., 2004).

A few studies have identified similar factors related to sibling ambivalence as well as unique ones. Fingerman et al. (2004) compared a variety of network members, including family, and, specifically, siblings, on both the prevalence of ambivalence and the factors associated with it. Closeness was confirmed: Close family ties, including siblings, were viewed with greater ambivalence than more distal family ties, as well as friendships and acquaintances even though the proportion of individuals who felt ambivalence toward their siblings was the lowest within the category of close kin. Age was a factor: When broken down by age a large proportion of oldest-old adults felt more ambivalent toward their siblings than toward their sons and daughters, but spousal ambivalence exceeded by far both sibling and offspring ambivalence. Connidis (2005) identified unique sources of sibling ambivalence based on the inherent contradictions of the bond: the relationship is assigned by birth or adoption usually, but sibling roles are voluntary in dominant Western cultures; siblings live separate lives yet share life course events; despite having ambivalent feelings toward one another they must cooperate to solve shared family tasks; their lifelong relationship presents continuity even as the individuals change; they share obligations to each other yet look after their own interests.

Two empirical studies that include the ambivalence concept have targeted sibling relationships exclusively. One examined the influence of a life transition on sibling ambivalence, specifically, the case of divorce and union dissolutions (Connidis, 2003). Connidis examined how divorce reverberates beyond the couple to other family ties, including siblings. She examined how individuals negotiate ambivalence due to divorce, whether they reproduce the "existing structural arrangements" or produce "a break with status quo" (Connidis, 2003, p. 355). In fact, both outcomes were illustrated. In the cases of parents' divorces the existing structured arrangements remained; strong bonds between the siblings did not change, despite siblings' conflicting views of their parents' roles in fomenting divorce. In the case of one sibling's divorce, however, there was a break with the status quo; the divorce resulted in an initial period of intense closeness between the siblings. Although this level of closeness did not last, the relationship sustained a greater level of closeness than before the divorce.

The second study addressed the contribution of power differentials to ambivalence in sibling relationships (Connidis, 2007). Constraints on agency can create ambivalence, and those with less power have fewer resources to exercise the agency needed to resolve ambivalence. Connidis's study of sibling socioeconomic inequality showed how this power differential was negotiated in two families. In this qualitative study, ambivalence was one of many outcomes. It was expected that ambivalence for siblings is due to the contradictions to the assumption that the relationship is based on equality, while at the same time there is considerable material inequality between the siblings. However, some siblings were able to negotiate closer relationships than others, despite this contradiction. What accounted for the closer relationships were the ordinal position of the privileged siblings and the source of their wealth. Younger, wealthier siblings elicited parentlike pride in their accomplishment; wealth earned by the spouse rather than the sibling made it more acceptable, because the wealthy siblings were no more successful than their less wealthy siblings, a fact that resonates with the expectations for equality in the relationship. A source of ambivalence was likely to linger, however, in the case of ordinal position; the sibling who had to sustain a parenting quality with a younger yet mature adult sibling who is loved would rather be on equal footing at this time of life.

Clearly, ambivalence theory represents a new approach to conceptualizing sibling relationships and, in turn, has the potential of not only fortifying sibling research with a theoretical foundation, but also ushering in a richer orientation to empirical sibling studies in the future.

Innovative Methods in Sibling Research

Sibling research is found in the fields of psychology, sociology, human development, anthropology, and communication. Having the perspective of multiple disciplines results not only in a wide variety of questions being asked but also different methodologies being employed in sibling studies. Research on siblings in the past 15 years encompasses many more and oftentimes innovative methodological approaches, some of which are reviewed in this section.

Large-scale surveys have been used for some time but the convenience of computer-assisted questionnaires (e.g., Tancredy & Fraley, 2006) and online services such as Qualtrics have made it easier to collect larger and more representative samples (Qualtrics Labs, Inc., Provo, UT. http://www.qualtrics.com). Face-to-face and telephone interviews have long been used to collect sibling data, including semistructured formats (e.g., Connidis & Kemp, 2008), but joint interviews with multiple siblings participating have noticeably increased with the invaluable advantage of obtaining several perspectives within each family (e.g., Connidis, 2003; Connidis & Kemp, 2008; Mize & Pinjala, 2002). One study creatively used several methodologies within the same investigation; Bras and van Tilburg (2007) used a mixed methods research strategy, combining ethnographies and qualitative historical materials with quantitative survey data. They found that for rural Dutch elderly adults, inheritance patterns significantly influenced sibling solidarity operationalized as contact frequency. Specifically, sibling contact was greater in northern areas that practiced impartible inheritance. Accordingly, the caregiving child, who stayed on the parent's farm to do so, was the sole inheritor, although other siblings could live on the farm if they desired to work there. Sibling contact was lower in families living in the south, where partible inheritance (equal distribution among offspring) was practiced.

Generalizability of findings in sibling research is often limited due to shortcomings in sampling. The majority of investigators still collect data from a single respondent with the researchers often designating or randomly selecting the target sibling relationship the respondent is to consider. Only rarely are all siblings discussed or interviewed (see Connidis, 2007, for an exception). For example, Spitze and Trent (2006) noted that in the National Survey of Families and Households (NSFH), questionnaire items ask about all siblings as a group. The experience of siblings as a group, however, though valuable in its own right, does not address the multiplicity of sibling relationships and perspectives within the family, nor the contextual contribution of the larger sibling group on the sibling dyadic experience.

Moving beyond the dyad creates methodological problems, challenging the application of statistical techniques that require all respondents to have equivalent and independent data (Matthews, 2005). To get around this problem, some researchers average the participant's response across all siblings. For example, Cicirelli (2009) calculated average closeness to siblings in his study of sibling death. A limitation to this approach is that we are unable to capture variability in the participants' relationships to their various siblings. Only recently have some sibling researchers used multilevel modeling (e.g., Poortman & Voorpostel, 2009; Suitor et al., 2009) to take into account nested, thus nonindependent, data (e.g., techniques that can control for the fact that siblings belong to the same family). In some studies where data are collected from the respondents and their siblings, the respondents are interviewed and the sibling data are collected via a questionnaire. This design raises concerns, as noted by Floyd (1997) about whether these methodological differences affect the findings.

There is still a dearth of longitudinal analyses of sibling relationships in current research (see Bedford & Avioli, 2006, Waldinger, Valliant, & Orav, 2007, and White, 2001, for the exceptions). Most analyses are cross-sectional (e.g., Suitor et al., 2009; Tancredy & Fraley, 2006; Voorpostel & Blieszner, 2008), which obfuscates continuity and change in sibling relations (Bedford, 1995).

Analyses are also limited in those sibling studies based on secondary data analyses (as noted by Eriksen & Gerstel, 2002), because the studies were designed for other purposes. Studies designed to focus specifically on sibling relationships typically have employed qualitative methods and relatively small samples, partly because of the advantages of qualitative methods, (such as allowing for unanticipated information to emerge on this relatively unexplored topic), and, perhaps, due to the relatively marginal status of the topic until recently, resulting in difficulty in obtaining sufficient funding to finance large-scale studies of siblings. Recent applications of qualitative methods include focus groups (e.g., Ingersoll-Dayton, Neal, Ha, & Hammer, 2003a), open-ended interviews of brother pairs (e.g., Matthews & Heidorn, 1998), and in-depth joint and individual interviews (e.g., Mauthner, 2005).

Future studies on siblings should build on the advances mentioned above. It is important that researchers consider the unique characteristics of sibling relationships, such as their highly variable and complex structure (size of siblingship, gender composition, birth order of participant and target), and their strength even in the absence of contact. Kalmijn, Liefbroer, van Poppel, and van Solinge (2006) used a novel approach to the analysis of multilevel data. They used a restrictive iterative generalized least squares approach to estimate simultaneously the differences among families and differences among individual siblings with the dichotomous dependent variable of intermarriage. Researchers would do well to consider multiple perspectives in the examination of family life in the context of the social world (Connidis, 2007; Voorpostel & Blieszner, 2008) by investigating individual, dyadic, and multilevel perspectives (Walker et al. 2005). Furthermore, social scientists should take advantage of the new Internet technologies such as Skype and computer conferencing, which would permit the live observation of siblings and their interactions. Moreover, collaborative efforts that reach across disciplines are likely to enhance investigations and understanding of the dynamic relations between diverse siblings and their contexts.

OLD TOPICS REVISITED

Attachment Studies

A central question asked about the sibling relationship is what role siblings play in adults' lives. Often siblings appear to be of marginal status compared to parents, children, and spouses. Recent studies grounded in attachment theory provide some answers by examining how siblings compare to others in meeting the criteria of an attachment object. For example, Doherty and Feeney (2004) investigated whether siblings qualify as complete (full-blown) attachment figures. To do so they needed to rank at least second (compared to friends, family, romantic partner) on two of the three functions of attachment figures, namely, safe haven, separation protest, and secure base. The researchers also asked whether siblings qualify as the primary attachment figure, a place occupied by only one person; this person had to score highest on all the attachment functions listed above plus one more, proximity-seeking. The results indicated that of the six relationships targeted, siblings ranked fifth as the primary attachment figure (followed only by fathers). However, siblings did function as a complete attachment figure for 22% of the participants; friends were somewhat ahead at 30%, and fathers were somewhat behind siblings at 16%. Attachment was stronger for respondents who were older and childfree, older and without a partner, and without a partner or children. Similarly, one-fifth of the participants without a romantic partner named a sibling or child as the primary attachment figure. Thus, individuals vary considerably in their attachment choice or choices. The primacy of sibling relationships, like other social relationships, is influenced by life circumstances.

In contrast to Doherty and Feeney's (2004) findings that siblings were rarely identified as primary attachment figures and only about one in five respondents rated siblings as complete attachment figures, twins are different. Both monozygotic and dizygotic twins are more likely to regard their twin as an attachment figure than are nontwins and monozygotic twins more so than dizygotic (Tancredy & Fraley, 2006). This pattern increases with age. In this way, twins differ from nontwin siblings, but there is no difference in their placement of other relationships in the attachment hierarchy (i.e., partner and friends are at the top followed by mother then father); twins include cotwin at the top; siblings are at the bottom with father for nontwins. Importantly, the twin relationship is not unique with regard to attachment; it simply resembles that of romantic partners as an attachment relationship, unlike siblings of nontwins. This finding expands the range of sibling experiences, given that twins fully qualify as biological siblings. It suggests a way that sibling research may enrich understandings of romantic relationships. For example, it appears that zygosity (degree of genetic similarity) is a significant contributor to the attachment function; perhaps this signals the importance of similarities for successful romantic relationships. This finding also illustrates the diversity of sibling relationships and what is ignored when sibling samples are restricted to nontwins.

Social Network Studies

The bulk of the recent sibling literature continues to ask where siblings figure in older adults' social networks, a topic reviewed in the first edition of this handbook. What social support functions do siblings perform, how balanced are the exchanges of support, what factors predict the quality and quantity of support? The newer research has gone into greater depth, has incorporated theory more, and has provided new and broader social network contexts. A few have begun to include siblings-in-law, stepsiblings, halfsiblings, and adopted siblings, as well as siblings with varied sexual orientations.

One way to interpret sibling functions in the social support network is to determine what pattern it models. The three traditional support models are hierarchical-compensatory (Cantor, 1979), task-specificity (Litvak, 1985), and functional-specificity (Weiss, 1974). Campbell et al. (1999) found in their study of four social support networks (confidants, companions, emotional support, and instrumental support) that siblings did not simply substitute or compensate for missing relationships (i.e., child, parent, spouse) as designated in the hierarchical-compensatory model, even though childfree persons (Mollen, 2006), single women, and widowed adults were most involved with their siblings. Rather, the strength of their sibling relationships in certain networks was likely to have evolved from the history of the relationship. For example, in the case of childfree women with a sibling living nearby, the sibling was particularly pronounced in the companion and instrumental support networks. Given the volitional nature of the sibling relationship, it is likely that these active roles had been negotiated over a lifetime, a process that characterizes the functional-specificity model. Notably, Miner and Uhlenberg's (1997) results also reject a hierarchical or substitution model.

Of great importance, given demographic changes in family structure, is research that contributes to understanding factors that increase the likelihood that siblings will be a source of support, especially instrumental support, in later life. These demographic changes include increased life expectancy in that more adults will survive acute illness and will be more likely to have several chronic illnesses, for which they may need assistance (Elias, Elias, & Elias, 1990). At the same time, these long-lived adults will have fewer children to rely on, and those they have are less bound by social norms regarding obligation than are earlier cohorts.

Instrumental Support

Because most adults have at least one living sibling well into old age, siblings are becoming a potential source of instrumental aid, even though earlier cohorts rarely relied upon their siblings in this capacity (Spitze & Trent, 2006). Some studies have found that adults assume they will receive instrumental support from their siblings if needed, but only those who have maintained a high quality relationship actually receive it (Voorpostel & Van Der Lippe, 2007). Those factors that predict the degree to which siblings engage in instrumental support exchanges are described in the following section on gender.

Gender

Using data from the National Survey of Families and Households (NSFH), Miner and Uhlenberg (1997) found that women are more likely to receive instrumental support from their siblings than are men, but there was no gender difference in the giving of instrumental support to siblings (albeit women gave more expressive support). These data contain a representative sample of black and white adults over age 55 with full siblings, but informants refer to siblings as a group (Spitze & Trent, 2006). By limiting their analysis of these data to siblings with only one sibling, Spitze and Trent (2006) were able to compare whether the sex commonality principle (same gender exchanges more support) or the femaleness principle (the more females, the more exchange) applied to siblings.

When it came to giving help, results varied by the type of help rendered. Men and women were equally likely to provide transportation to a sibling.

Men were much more likely to report doing repairs for their sibling, but more so for a brother than a sister. There were no gender differences in the receipt of any of these forms of support. Giving advice was most frequent by far, but especially among sister pairs, followed by men with a brother and women with a brother. When it came to receiving advice, women with a sister received advice the most, followed by women with a brother. Few men with sisters or brothers reported receiving advice. In general, it appears that women with sisters are most involved in exchanges, which is corroborated by many other recent studies (e.g., Voorpostel, Van der Lippe, Dykstra, & Flap, 2007). No other patterns were found for the receiving of support; rather, the particular task determined which gender dyad was most likely to engage in the exchange. In a study limited to the giving of support to siblings (care work), there were no tasks that brothers were more likely to provide than sisters, but there were numerous tasks that sisters provided that brothers did not (Eriksen & Gerstel, 2002).

It appears that sibling relationships are no different from others in conforming to gender stereotypes in the giving and receiving of support. Whether greater gender equality in society will result in less time for working women to engage in support to siblings and for men to step up to the plate in greater numbers has not yet been studied.

Other Predictors of Instrumental Support

Many other variables have been investigated and some implicated in the exchange of aid to siblings. Campbell et al. (1999) detailed the influence of marital status, parent status, sibling proximity, as well as gender, on the role siblings play in providing instrumental support to one another, compared to exchanging support with a child, friend, spouse, and other relative. They also examined the influence of these variables on the probability of including the sibling in one's instrumental support network. Women more than men, those never married more than those who married, and those with a sibling nearby rather than farther away reported a greater likelihood of including one's sibling in the exchange of instrumental support. As for the relative importance of siblings in instrumental exchanges, adult children and friends are central to men and women, except that siblings trump friends for women when they live nearby. Also, for most never married men and women, nearby siblings rank number one as targets and sources of support. Siblings also dominate in the instrumental network of those who are childfree. For married women, siblings follow spouse and children as likely to give and receive support. For widowed, divorced, and separated persons, children are named first.

Other potential predictors of sibling support have been examined. Some investigators found that race did not affect instrumental exchange (Eriksen &

Gerstel, 2002; Miner & Uhlenberg, 1997), but others did find racial differences. Riedmann and White (1996) found that blacks had fewer exchanges with siblings than did non-Hispanic whites. Most researchers have found that blacks have more sibling contact than whites (Riedmann & White, 1996) and are more likely to live in close proximity to their siblings (Miner & Uhlenberg, 1997). Income is consistently related to instrumental exchange; those with more money give more to siblings (Miner & Uhlenberg, 1997). Having living parents also increases sibling giving (Eriksen & Gerstel, 2002), and having a poor relationship with parents and little contact with them result in even more sibling support, including practical support, as demonstrated in a large Dutch study (Voorpostel & Blieszner, 2008). Some characteristics of the siblings have also been found to play a role. Although, in general, homogamy is thought to cement relationships, Voorpostel et al. (2007) found that it rarely predicts instrumental support between siblings with two exceptions, namely, gender in the case of women and childlessness.

Whereas quality of relationships sometimes subsumes contact and exchange of support (Bras & van Tilburg, 2007), in this review, quality is limited to the affective aspect of the relationship. Most studies of adult sibling relationships have focused on positive feelings such as affectional closeness (see Bedford, 1995), although some have targeted negative feelings, and some have examined both. More recently, ambivalence toward siblings has been studied as discussed in the theory section above. We will review recent results on positive feelings toward siblings in relation to instrumental support exchanges.

Feelings appear to play an important part in the frequency of contact between siblings (Connidis & Campbell, 1995), confirming that help exchanges between siblings have a voluntary component rather than being driven by a sense of obligation. Voorpostel and Blieszner (2008) also demonstrated that feelings (i.e., how positively participants rated the relationship) influence the exchange of practical support between siblings. In another analysis using the same Dutch database (Voorpostel & Van Der Lippe, 2007), siblings were compared to friendship in this regard, because friendship is volitional and thus assumed to be based on positive feelings, whereas siblings are usually assigned. Surprisingly, support exchanges depended on the quality of the relationship even more for siblings than for friends, despite beliefs to the contrary. Sibling relationships thus require more, not less, maintenance than friends as an instrumental support resource.

SIBLING RELATIONSHIP QUALITY

If the quality of the sibling relationship is so important in relation to instrumental support exchanges, it is essential to determine what contributes to the quality of sibling relationships in adulthood. Many researchers have examined structural variables such as socioeconomic status (SES), race and ethnicity, marital status, parent status, age, and gender as potential predictors of the quality of sibling relationships. Connidis and Campbell (1995) found that working class per se is not associated with sibling closeness, but, rather, lower educational level is. Moreover, this finding only applied to one's closest sibling, not to the entire sibling network. In terms of gender, in a study of German adults, Buhl (2009) found that both men and women preferred their sister.

Other recent findings on sibling closeness indicate that family size influences closeness; those in larger families feel closer to their emotionally closest sibling than those from smaller families (Connidis & Campbell, 1995), perhaps because larger families provide more choices in selecting that closest sibling. In larger families, geographic proximity also supports closeness, but only to the sibling network, not to one's closest sibling. This level of intimacy, it appears, can be sustained in the absence of face-to-face contact (Wilson, Calsyn, & Orlofsky, 1994). In terms of the effect of marital status, the most emotionally close siblings tend to be those who are widowed (Connidis & Campbell, 1995). Those who are single and childfree are also closer to their siblings compared to those who are married and parents (see Connidis, 2010, for a more complete review of the sibling closeness literature).

Conversely, Buhl (2009) found that sibling conflict was influenced by birth order. Adults felt more conflict toward their younger than their older siblings. Compared with other network members, they reported more conflict among family members than friends, but within the family, sibling conflict level was the lowest. Fuller-Thomson (1999–2000) examined correlates of conflict, not in sibling pairs, but in the whole sibship. Results indicated that siblingships had more conflict as reported by younger respondents (mean age of 38.5 years), for those not black or Hispanic, for those whose parents were dead, especially when both were dead, and when siblings or parents were in poor health. It appears, then, that conflict is greater among siblings in times of stress (specifically, health issues), in the absence of their kinkeeper(s) (mother usually), in more competitive, individualistic cultures, and, perhaps, when complications arise surrounding parental health care needs or death. An early experience related to adult sibling conflict is parental divorce (Poortman & Voorpostel, 2009), but it turns out that the conflict between the parents, not the actual divorce, led to more sibling conflict. Divorce in high-conflict families actually reduces sibling conflict. Notably, parental divorce that occurred during siblings' childhood had no influence on the positive feelings adult siblings have for each other.

Of particular interest is the influence of parents on the quality of adult sibling relationships. A source of sibling rivalry and jealousy in childhood (Ross & Milgram, 1982) as well as in literary and biblical writings is parental favoritism, sometimes referred to as differential parental treatment. Investigators have examined this parental influence on sibling relationships in later life recently. Boll, Ferring, and Filipp (2003) found that for middle-aged German men and women with at least one living parent, differential parental treatment had a curvilinear relation to the sibling relationship quality. When both siblings were treated equally, the sibling relationship was experienced most positively and least negatively. If the adult child perceived favoritism or disfavoritism, then the sibling relationship was experienced as less positive and more negative. Whereas Boll et al. compared adults' perceptions of parental favoritism in the present, Suitor et al. (2009) compared middle-aged adults' perceptions of both childhood and present favoritism by mother. They found that perceptions of favoritism recalled in childhood adversely affected closeness and increased conflict among adult siblings, whereas current favoritism only adversely affected closeness. Concurring with Boll et al.'s findings, the effect of favoritism was independent of who was favored.

The impact of parental death on adult sibling relationships has also been studied and the impact appears to be negative (see de Vries, chapter 22 in this volume, for a review of this literature). If parents think they can prevent this consequence by leaving a living will or assigning a durable power of attorney for health care (DPAHC), a recent study found otherwise. Khodyakov and Carr (2009), using data from the Wisconsin Longitudinal Study, found that health directives only affect the quality of the sibling relationship adversely when the adult children see the directives as having been problematic. In most cases, however, the directives had no effect on sibling closeness. In the rare case when they increased sibling affection significantly, the person appointed as DPAHC was not a member of the immediate family.

Another potential source of poorer sibling relationship quality after the death of a parent is the problems that arose between siblings over caregiving toward the end of the parent's life. Siblings may feel resentment toward one another if they perceive that their brothers or sisters have not contributed their fair share to parent care (Ingersoll-Dayton, Neal, Ha, & Hammer, 2003b). Some evidence indicates that these feelings continue to cause strain among siblings after a parent's death (Hequembourg & Brailler, 2005). Filial caregiving, however, does not have only negative effects on sibling relationships. Ingersoll-Dayton et al. (2003a) investigated factors that promoted collaboration in caregiving among siblings and, in turn, improved sibling relationships in middle and later life. Judging from their findings from focus groups, equity played an important role in achieving a successful collaborative process. Equity was promoted by means of siblings alternating roles and working in teams, in order to protect each other from overworking. Parents also contributed to their children's equity by providing the same information and instructions to each child.

LIFE COURSE INFLUENCES

The life course perspective adds the dimensions of time and life transitions to an understanding of sibling relationships, as well as interconnected lives, which overlaps with other perspectives. A few recent studies have focused on the sibling relationship with respect to its trajectory or career. Connidis (2005) attributed the shape of sibling relationship trajectories to a combination of factors: significant changes in one's life (transitions), the social structuring of relationships from a societal perspective, and the exercising of agency whereby siblings negotiate the ambivalent feelings (e.g., rivalry versus cooperation) and expectations of their relationships.

Trajectories

The sibling career has been studied in terms of continuity and change in the relationship with respect to age. Neyer (2002) traced the sibling career, comparing the genetic relatedness of siblings: dizygotic twins (DZ), monozygotic twins (MZ) and the nontwin of the twins, or an aggregated score in the case of multiple nontwins. Using retrospective data generated from adults in their 70s, Neyer reported a U-shaped developmental trend for degree of emotional closeness and contact frequency, which is found in Western cultures for other close relationships as well. Genetic relatedness varied systematically within this trend, whereby MZ twins' relationships were more intense with respect to contact, intimacy, conflict, and support, followed by those of DZ twins and then those with their nontwin(s). Neyer attributed these differences to genetic and environmental factors as well as to societal trends related to increased life expectancies, such that higher life expectancies "require the reconstruction and stabilization of social resources, of which siblings may constitute an important part" (p. 175).

Not all studies agree with the U-curve trajectory of adult sibling relationships. Buhl (2009) found that with respect to received support, the trajectory was quadratic; after a U-shape, there was a shift downward in late life. Also, conflict decreased in late life as did relative power differential (which also occurred with partners and friends). White (2001) found a slight rise after age 70 in sibling exchange. In contrast, Connidis and Campbell (1995) found that with age, attachment to the sibling network grew, but not to the closest sibling.

Another sibling relationship trajectory was found with respect to contact frequency. In a 12-year longitudinal study, rural women, initially aged 65 and older, showed no decrease in contact frequency with the sibling group when controlling for geographic proximity (Scott, 1996). Because some siblings died, this finding shows that contact with each individual surviving sibling must have increased in order for the total amount of sibling contact to remain constant. Although women had more sisters than brothers, more brothers lived nearby and were in more frequent contact with the women than sisters were. Moreover, these very old rural women showed no preference for sisters. Although sibling contact and proximity were not related to well-being in this study, other studies demonstrate that sibling relationships often have consequences for the well-being of middle-aged and old adults (e.g., De Jong Gierveld & Dykstra, 2008; McCamish-Svensson, Samuelsson, Hagberg, Svensson, & Dehlin, 1999). Scott attributed her findings to the rural (non-Hispanic white) culture.

Cohort

The question remains as to why there are contradictions in the sibling trajectories that are not explained by social structural factors or methodological differences in the studies. Because most of these studies rely on retrospective, cross-sectional data and single cohort prospective data, it is necessary to consider what role cohort differences may play in these inconsistencies. Bedford and Avioli (2006), in one of the few longitudinal studies including several cohorts, were able to analyze potential cohort effects on the trajectory of sibling intimacy between brothers over a 20-year period. Comparing sibling stories told by men with age-near brothers every four years (six waves), they found that men were less adept at demonstrating intimacy with their age-near brother in late life than in middle age. Because data on three cohorts at identical ages could be compared, Bedford and Avioli found that the World War II generation's stories (i.e., reflecting the historical period at which the men had come of age) displayed fewer intimate affective skills with brothers, such as supportive listening, but better intimate problem-solving skills than in the Baby Boomer cohort. Thus, it was cohort rather than development that accounted for the observed differences.

Life Transitions

The decrease in sibling involvement in early adulthood is typically attributed to generativity (such as childrearing) (Connidis, 2005; Neyer, 2002) and career-building (Bedford, 1989). Childfree adults appear to have a different sibling relationship trajectory with respect to certain aspects of helping siblings compared to their parenting siblings. Voorpostel et al. (2007) found that childfree siblings assist their parenting siblings who are raising young children with odd jobs in early adulthood (ages 18–35 years) and, in their middle to later years (ages 55–80), the childfree siblings tend to play an advisory role to their siblings, whether the siblings are parents or not.

Another important transition addressed in a recent study is repartnering. A growing number of divorces after age 55 as well as the increased likelihood of widowhood, especially for women (Cooney, 1993), have led many middle-aged and late life adults to repartner. Repartnering not only includes remarrying, but also consensual unions. In fact, the remarriage rate is declining and more older adults are preferring more flexible partner arrangements such as cohabitation (Chevan, 1996) and living apart together (De Jong Gierveld, 2002). De Jong Gierveld and Peeters (2003) investigated how repartnering affects the number of siblings and siblings-in-law in one's network and the probability of being in touch regularly with these siblings. Those in their first marriages were compared with widows and divorcees living alone with various categories of being repartnered. Findings indicated that Dutch 55–89-year-old adults in original marriages and those who lived alone after widowhood or divorce had larger partial networks of siblings and siblings-in-law than those who repartnered. The authors credited this difference to the stress and uncertainty that repartnered older adults experience. It seems likely that the siblings of those who are repartnered also experience stress and uncertainty in having to incorporate a new person into their relationship with their repartnered sibling.

Guiaux et al. (2007) focused on the transition to widowhood of adults (mean age of 70 years). They tracked contact and both emotional and instrumental support exchanges with social network members including siblings. Sibling contact and support were low until just before widowhood, after which they began increasing, no doubt related to intense caregiving for the soon-to-be deceased spouse. These activities peaked at 2.5 years after the spouse's death, at which point they gradually decreased to their original low level. During this period, support functions were higher in frequency than those given to married adults, but ordinarily there was no difference by marital status. Thus, widowhood influenced the sibling relationship trajectory for only about three years, suggesting that such transitional events may only have temporary effects on the relationship.

SIBLING RELATIONSHIPS AND PERSONAL WELL-BEING

A fundamental question in the sibling literature is whether having siblings in midlife and late life influences one's level of well-being. This question has been posed in terms of the effect of the number of living siblings (Falbo, Kim, & Chen, 2009; Tucker, Schwartz, Clark, & Friedman, 1999), one's birth order relative to a particular sibling (Falbo et al., 2009), support exchanges with siblings (De Jong Gierveld & Dykstra, 2008), contact with siblings and satisfaction with sibling contact (McCamish-Svensson et al., 1999), filial caregiving (Amirkhanyan & Wolf, 2003), marital status (Pinquart, 2003), conflict or trouble in sibling relationships (Bedford, 1998; Bedford & Volling, 2004; Bedford, Volling, & Avioli, 2000), differential parental treatment (Davey, Tucker, Fingerman, & Savla, 2009), and death of a sibling

(Cicirelli, 2009). The concept of well-being is operationalized as loneliness (De Jong Gierveld & Dykstra, 2008; Pinquart, 2003), depression (Amirkhanyan & Wolf, 2003; Cicirelli, 2009; Hays, Gold, & Pieper, 1997; Scott, 1996; Waldinger et al, 2007), functional and cognitive impairment (Hays et al., 1997), life satisfaction, including mood, and objective health (morbidity) (McCamish-Svensson et al., 1999), mortality risk (Tucker et al., 1999), emotion regulation (Bedford & Volling, 2004), stress (Ingersoll-Dayton et al., 2003b), affect (Davey et al., 2009), morale (Scott, 1996; Wilson et al., 1994), and participant-generated benefits (Bedford, 1998; Bedford et al., 2000).

Given the fact that older adults are likely to live alone and to experience losses due to death, geographic relocation, and, occasionally but increasingly, divorce, loneliness is an important well-being outcome to consider. In fact, relationships with siblings appear to reduce levels of loneliness in later life. De Jong Gierveld and Dykstra (2008) found that among 45–79-year-old participants in the Netherlands Kinship Panel Study (NKPS), those who engaged in balanced (i.e., equitable) exchanges of social support with siblings (as well as parents and children) were the least lonely. The direction of giving also made a difference; giving to siblings but not to parents or children was related to less loneliness. Nonreciprocated support to siblings was also related to lower levels of loneliness.

Notably, it appears that with siblings, it is better to be on the giving than the receiving end of social support. Pinquart (2003) considered how marital status and parent status affected whether contact with siblings reduced loneliness. In contrast to the social support findings above, siblings were not unique compared to several other relationships in this regard, even though the perceived quality of the sibling relationship was highest for never married compared to widowed and divorced persons. Contact with siblings reduced loneliness for unmarried more than married adults, as did contact with children, friends, and neighbors. It also reduced loneliness for childless unmarried people as did contact with friends (but not contact with unmarried parents). As for gender differences, lower levels of loneliness in never-married and divorced women compared to never-married and divorced men was attributed to more contact with siblings, as well as more contact with children and friends.

Whereas the provision of social support by spouses and children impacted mortality, provision of social support by siblings had no demonstrated effect on mortality according to Tucker et al. (1999). They believe, however, that due to strong feelings of rivalry, attachment, or both, sibling relationships are likely to have consequences for health. Yet Falbo et al. (2009) found that sibling status (birth order and family size) had no effect on health at age 65. Their analysis showed that the apparent effect of family size on health was actually due to educational attainment and to parents' SES (coincidently, lower SES parents have larger families). Others, however, have confirmed

Tucker et al.'s suspicion. For example, in their longitudinal study of oldest-old adults in Sweden, McCamish-Svensson et al. (1999) not only found a strong correlation between sibling support and health, but this finding was unique compared to research on friends and children. At age 80, satisfaction with frequency of sibling contact had robust correlations with self-reported health, doctor-reported health, and positive mood. In addition, contact frequency with sibling was positively correlated with mood. In contrast, friends' and children's support had no effect on the health or mood of these late life adults. Three years later, these correlations with health measures were no longer found, but satisfaction with sibling contact frequency was correlated with overall life satisfaction, a result not found for any other relationship.

SUMMARY AND RECOMMENDATIONS

Despite the contradictions in this literature, findings from both early and most current studies appear to support a few generalizations. Early studies show that siblings, having the oldest and most enduring relationships, are especially suited to be a source of coreminiscence in late life and are uniquely valued as such (Scott, 1996). Further, although siblings provide little instrumental support, they at least provide a sense of security based on the belief that one's sibling will come through in a crisis (Connidis, 1994). New research findings show that siblings do not always give assistance when the need arrives. Aid is more likely to be proffered when the relationship has been nurtured to be a positive one (Voorpostel & Van Der Lippe, 2007).

Another generalization is that the sibling relationship is most valued when it is egalitarian. Being treated equally (or at least fairly) by others, particularly by parents, having equal exchanges of social support (Bedford & Avioli, 2001), or underbenefitting in the exchanges are the preferred and most beneficial arrangements, both for the quality of the relationship and the well-being of the individuals (De Jong Gierveld & Dykstra, 2008). Also, the composition of one's social network and societal norms are likely to set the parameters for siblings' location in each other's networks. Specifically, these conditions determine the functions siblings provide, the degree to which they are provided, and whether siblings perform these functions directly to one another or indirectly through mutual relationships, such as giving care to their parents. Within these constraints, but sometimes overriding them, individual agency and negotiation, not a hierarchy of relationship importance, determine the nature of the sibling relationship and its trajectory over time. Thus, a functional-specificity model of social support usually applies to sibling relationships and social support.

Perhaps the most dramatic shift in adult sibling research is its inclusion in so many studies that target social networks, social support, kinship, and human processes that address relationship identities in their designs. This inclusion indicates that siblings are no longer invisible or marginalized. By removing the limitations on family studies imposed by targeting households, nuclear families, dependent children, marriage, age, sexual orientation (see Grossman, D'Augelli, & Hershberger, 2000), and biological connections, the centrality of siblings to family and social life indeed emerges (Walker et al., 2005; White, 2001).

Given the plethora of new research, we take our lead from the new directions initiated by these studies. By holding a less restricted view of families, new studies should begin to bring other relations into view, such as one's siblings' personal relations (e.g., with close friends, children, in-laws, grandchildren) and one's parents' sibling relations (great-aunts and great-uncles, cousins, close friends) (Matthews, 2005). If, indeed, loneliness is a hazard in later adulthood, considering the potential relationship resources siblings offer, more research should target effective strategies for maintaining and nurturing the sibling tie, beginning in childhood.

New research is increasingly acknowledging historical changes in families, the broader family network, and a greater understanding of men's family relationships in later life particularly with brothers. New research has begun to address sibling relationships as they develop and end when families are reconstituted and dissolved, sometimes multiple times, and at all ages (e.g., Diderich, 2008). A few studies have targeted the sibling relationships of gay, lesbian, bisexual, and transsexual adults in the case of sisters (e.g., Mize, Turell, & Meier, 2004) and within a larger network (Grossman et al., 2000). More investigators need to pursue these topics, using larger and more representative samples. Finally, the notion that women's family ties are the closest may neglect the sibling relationships of very old persons as well as those of rural adults where ties with brothers are stronger (Scott, 1996). It is also possible that men's ties are measured by criteria that apply more to women (Fingerman et al., 2004). Further, studies are needed to understand and take into account cohort changes, such as how increasing gender equity may be impacting traditional views about the differences in sibling relationships of men and women.

A neglected methodological issue unique to the sibling relationship is the appropriate unit of analysis. It behooves researchers to choose the unit most appropriate to the research goal, whether it be the dyad, the siblingship, or the average of the sibling group. Further, given the complexity and structural variability of sibling groups (size, gender composition, and its interaction with ordinal position), the influence of the sibling context as well as units of analysis should be considered.

CONCLUSION

In response to the historical events, social movements, and technological innovations that have taken place in the past 15 years, sibling researchers are beginning to change the questions they ask as well as the way they conduct investigations and analyses. Clearly the "forgotten relationship" has not only come of age but may be moving to front and center stage based on innovations in family theory, changing demographics, and recognition of the importance of siblings in middle and old age. The extensive variety of topics discussed even in this limited review is evidence of this shift. As a result, a growing literature is helping to delineate the many ways in which adult siblings impact each other's lives and the predictors of these influences. Recent inroads in family therapy (e.g., Qualls & Noecker, 2009) and the lay media (e.g., Russo, 2010) will expand and ultimately support strategies for nurturing these valuable relationships and for reaping their potential rewards.

REFERENCES

Allen, K. R., Roberto, K., & Blieszner, R. (2011). Perspectives on extended family and fictive kin in the later years: Strategies and meanings of kin reinterpretation. *Journal of Family Issues, 32,* 1156–1177.

Amirkhanyan, A. A., & Wolf, D. A. (2003). Caregiver stress and noncaregiver stress: Exploring the pathways of psychiatric morbidity. *The Gerontologist, 43,* 817–827.

Bedford, V. H. (1989). A comparison of thematic apperceptions of sibling affiliation, conflict, and separation at two periods of adulthood. *International Journal of Aging and Human Development, 28,* 53–65.

Bedford, V. H. (1995). Sibling relationships in middle adulthood and old age. In R. Blieszner & V. H. Bedford (Eds.), *Handbook of aging and the family* (pp. 201–222). Westport, CT: Greenwood.

Bedford, V. H. (1998). Sibling relationships troubles and well-being in middle and old age. *Family Relations, 47,* 369–376.

Bedford, V. H. (2002). Sibling relationships. In D. J. Ekerdt, R. A. Applebaum, K. C. Holden, S. G. Post, K. Rockwood, R. Schulz, R. L. Sprott, & P. Uhlenberg, (Eds.), *Encyclopedia of aging* (pp. 1270–1274). New York: Macmillan Reference USA.

Bedford, V. H. (2005). Theorizing about sibling relationships when parents become frail. In V. Bengtson, A. Acock, K. Allen, P. Dilworth-Anderson, & D. Klein (Eds.), *Sourcebook of family theory and research* (pp. 173–174). Thousand Oaks, CA: Sage.

Bedford, V. H. (2008). Sibling relations, adulthood. sibling relations: Later life. In D. Carr (Ed.), *Encyclopedia of the life course and human development* (pp. 407–410). Framingham Hills, MI: Macmillan.

Bedford, V. H., & Avioli, P. S. (2001). Variations on sibling intimacy in old age. *Generations, 25,* 34–40.

Bedford, V. H., & Avioli, P. S. (2006). "Shooting the bull": Cohort comparisons of fraternal intimacy in mid-life and old age. In V. H. Bedford & B. F. Turner (Eds.), *Men in relationships: A new look from a life course perspective* (pp. 81–101). New York: Springer.

Bedford, V. H., & Diderich, M. (2009). Adulthood, sibling relationships in. In H. Reis & S. Sprecher (Eds.), *Encyclopedia of human relationships, Vol. 1* (pp. 41–44). Newbury Park, CA: Sage.

Bedford, V. H., & Gold, D. (Eds.). (1989). Siblings in later life: A neglected family relationship. *American Behavioral Scientist, 33*(1) Special Issue.

Bedford, V. H., & Volling, B. (2004). A dynamic ecological systems perspective on emotion regulation development within the sibling relationship context. In F. R. Lang & K. L. Fingerman (Eds.), *Growing together: Personal relationships across the lifespan* (pp. 76–101). Cambridge, UK: Cambridge University Press.

Bedford, V. H., Volling, B. L., & Avioli, P. S. (2000). Positive consequences of sibling conflict in childhood and adulthood. *International Journal of Aging and Human Development, 51*, 53–69 Special Issue.

Boll, T., Ferring, D., & Filipp, S. H. (2003). Perceived parental differential treatment in middle adulthood: Curvilinear relations with individuals' experienced relationship quality to sibling and parents. *Journal of Family Psychology, 17*, 472–487.

Bowlby, J. (1987). Growing points of attachment theory and research. *Journal of Family Therapy, 9*, 89–90.

Bras, H., & van Tilburg, T. (2007). Kinship and social networks: A regional analysis of sibling relations in twentieth-century Netherlands. *Journal of Family History, 32*, 296–322.

Brody, E. M. (1985). Parent care as a normative family stress, *The Gerontologist, 25*, 19–29.

Buhl, H. (2009). My mother: My best friend? Adults' relationships with significant others across the lifespan. *Journal of Adult Development, 16*, 239–249.

Campbell, L. D., Connidis, I. A., & Davies, L. (1999). Sibling ties in later life. *Journal of Family Issues, 20*, 114–148.

Cantor, M. (1979). Neighbors and friends: An overlooked resource in the informal support system. *Research on Aging, 1*, 434–463.

Chevan, A. (1996). As cheaply as one: Cohabitation in the older population. *Journal of Marriage and Family, 58*, 656–667.

Cicirelli, V. G. (1989). Feelings of attachment to siblings and well-being in later life. *Psychology and Aging, 4*, 211–216.

Cicirelli, V. G. (2005). *Sibling relationships across the life span.* New York: Plenum Press.

Cicirelli, V. G. (2008). Sibling relations: Later life. In D. Carr (Ed.), *Encyclopedia of the life course and human development* (p. 370). Framingham Hills, MI: Macmillan.

Cicirelli, V. G. (2009). Sibling death and death fear in relation to depressive symptomatology in older adults. *Journal of Gerontology: Psychological Sciences, 64*, 24–32.

Connidis, I. A. (1994). Sibling support in older age. *Journal of Gerontology: Social Sciences, 49*, S309–S317.

Connidis, I. A. (2003). Divorce and union dissolution: Reverberations over three generations. *Canadian Journal on Aging, 22*, 353–368.

Connidis, I. A. (2005). Sibling ties across time: The middle and later years. In M. Johnson, V. L. Bengtson, P. G. Coleman, & T. B. L. Kirkwood (Eds.), *The*

Cambridge handbook of age and ageing (pp. 429–436). Cambridge, UK: Cambridge University Press.

Connidis, I. A. (2007). Negotiating inequality among adult siblings: Two case studies. *Journal of Marriage and Family*, 69, 482–499.

Connidis, I. A. (2010). *Family ties and aging* (2nd ed.). Thousand Oaks, CA: Pine Forge Press.

Connidis, I. A., & Campbell, L. (1995). Closeness, confiding, and contact among siblings in middle and late adulthood. *Journal of Family Issues*, 16, 722–745.

Connidis, I. A., & Kemp, C. L. (2008). Negotiating actual and anticipated parental support: Multiple sibling voices in three-generation families. *Journal of Aging Studies*, 22, 229–238.

Cooney, T. M. (1993). Recent demographic change: Implications for families planning for the future. *Marriage and Family Review*, 18, 677–688.

Davey, A., & Szinovacz, M. E. (2008). Division of care among adult children. In M. E. Szinovacz & A. Davey (Eds.), *Caregiving contexts: Cultural, familial, and societal implications* (pp. 115–132). New York: Springer.

Davey, A., Tucker, C., Fingerman, K., & Savla, J. (2009). Within-family variability in representations of past relationships with parents. *Journals of Gerontology: Series B: Psychological Sciences and Social Sciences*, 64B, 125–136.

De Jong Gierveld, J. (2002). The dilemma of repartnering: Considerations of older men and women entering new intimate relationships in later life. *Ageing International*, 27, 61–79.

De Jong Gierveld, J., & Dykstra, P. A. (2008). Virtue is its own reward? Support-giving in the family and loneliness in middle and old age. *Ageing & Society*, 28, 271–287.

De Jong Gierveld, J., & Peeters, A. (2003). The interweaving of repartnered older adults' lives with their children and siblings. *Ageing & Society*, 23, 187–205.

Diderich, M. (2008). *Sibling relationships in step-families: A sociological study*. Lewiston, NY: Edwin Mellen.

Doherty, N., & Feeney, J. (2004). The composition of attachment networks throughout the adult years. *Personal Relationships*, 11, 469–488.

Dykstra, P. A., Kalmijn, M., Knijn, G. C. M., Komter, A. E., Liefbroer, A. C., & Mulder, C. H. (2005). *Codebook of the Netherlands Kinship Panel Study, a multi-actor, multi-method panel study on solidarity in family relationships. Wave 1. NKPS working Paper No. 4*. The Hague, Netherlands: Netherlands Interdisciplinary Demographic Institute.

Elias, M. P., Elias, J. W., & Elias, P. K. (1990). Biological and health influences on behavior. *Handbook of the psychology of aging* (3rd ed., pp. 80–102). New York: Academic.

Eriksen, S., & Gerstel, N. (2002). A labor of love or labor itself: Care work among adult brothers and sisters. *Journal of Family Issues*, 23, 836–856.

Falbo, T., Kim, S., & Chen, K. (2009). Alternate models of sibling status effects on health in later life. *Developmental Psychology*, 45, 677–687.

Fingerman, K. L., Cheng, Y.-P., Birditt, K., & Zarit, S. (2011). Only as happy as the least happy child: Multiple grown children's problems and successes and middle-aged parents' well-being. *Journals of Gerontology, Series B: Psychological Sciences and Social Sciences*, 66, 1–10.

Fingerman, K. L., Hay, E. L., & Birditt, K. S. (2004). The best of ties, the worst of ties: Close, problematic, and ambivalent social relationships. *Journal of Marriage and Family, 66,* 792–808.

Floyd, K. (1997). Brotherly love II: A developmental perspective on liking, love, and closeness in the fraternal dyad. *Journal of Family Psychology, 11,* 196–209.

Fuller-Thomson, E. (1999–2000). Loss of the kin-keeper?: Sibling conflict following parental death. *Omega, 40,* 547–559.

Grossman, A., D'Augelli, A., & Hershberger, S. (2000). Social support networks of lesbian, gay, and bisexual adults 60 years and older. *Journals of Gerontology: Series B: Psychological Sciences and Social Sciences, 55B,* P171–P179.

Guiaux, M., van Tilburg, T., & van Groenou, M. B. (2007). Changes in contact and support exchange in personal networks after widowhood. *Personal Relationships, 13,* 457–473.

Hays, J. C., Gold, D. T., & Pieper, C. E. (1997). Sibling bereavement in late life. *Omega, 35,* 25–42.

Hequembourg, A., & Brailler, S. (2005). Gendered stories of parental caregiving among siblings. *Journal of Aging Studies, 19,* 53–71.

Horney, K. (1945). *Our inner conflicts.* New York: Norton.

Ingersoll-Dayton, B., Neal, M. B., Ha, J., & Hammer, L. B. (2003a). Collaboration among siblings providing care for older parents. *Journal of Gerontological Social Work, 40,* 51–66.

Ingersoll-Dayton, B., Neal, M. B., Ha, J., & Hammer, L. B. (2003b). Redressing inequity in parent care among siblings. *Journal of Marriage and Family, 65,* 201–212.

Kalmijn, M., Liefbroer, A. C., van Poppel, F., & van Solinge, H. (2006). The family factor in Jewish-Gentile intermarriage: A sibling analysis of The Netherlands. *Social Forces, 84,* 1347–1358.

Khodyakov, D., & Carr, D. (2009). The impact of late-life parental death on adult sibling relationships: Do parents' advance directives help or hurt? *Research on Aging, 31,* 495–519.

Litvak, E. (1985). *Helping the elderly: The complementary roles of informal networks and formal systems.* New York: Guilford.

Matthews, S. H. (2005). Reaching beyond the dyad: Research on adult siblings. In V. L. Bengtson, A. C. Acock, K. A. Allen, P. Dilworth-Anderson, & D. M. Klein (Eds.), *Sourcebook of family theory and research* (pp. 181–184). Thousand Oaks, CA: Sage.

Matthews, S. H., & Heidorn, J. (1998). Meeting filial responsibilities in brothers-only sibling groups. *Journal of Gerontology: Social Sciences, 42B,* S278–S286.

Mauthner, M. (2005). Distant lives, still voice: Sistering in family sociology. *Sociology, 39,* 623–642.

McCamish-Svensson, C., Samuelsson, G., Hagberg, B., Svensson, T., & Dehlin, O. (1999). Social relationships and health as predictors of life satisfaction in advanced old age: Results from a Swedish longitudinal study. *The International Journal of Aging & Human Development, 48,* 301–324.

Miner, S., & Uhlenberg, P. (1997). Intragenerational proximity and the social role of sibling neighbors after midlife. *Family Relations, 46,* 145–154.

Mize, L. K., & Pinjala, A. (2002). Sisterhood narratives: Opportunities in connections. *Journal of Feminist Family Therapy, 14,* 21–51.

Mize, L.K., Turell, S., & Meier, J. (2004). Sexual orientation and the sister relationship: Conversations and opportunities. *Journal of Feminist Family Therapy, 16*, 1–19.

Mollen, D. (2006). Voluntarily childfree women: Experiences and counseling considerations. *Journal of Mental Health Counseling, 28*, 269–284.

Neyer, F.J. (2002). Twin relationships in old age: A developmental perspective. *Journal of Social and Personal Relationships, 19*, 155–177.

Pinquart, M. (2003). Loneliness in married, widowed, divorced, and never-married older adults. *Journal of Social and Personal Relationships, 20*, 31–53.

Poortman, A., & Voorpostel, M. (2009). Parental divorce and sibling relationships: A research note. *Journal of Family Issues, 30*, 74–91.

Qualls, S.H., & Noecker, T.L. (2009). Caregiver family therapy for conflicted families. In S.H. Qualls & S.H. Zarit (Eds.), *Aging families and caregiving* (pp. 155–188). Hoboken, NJ: Wiley.

Qualtrics Labs, Inc. Survey Research Suite software (2005). Qualtrics Labs, Inc., Provo, UT: http://www.qualtrics.com

Riedmann, A., & White, L. (1996). Adult sibling relationships: Racial and ethnic comparisons. In G.H. Brody (Ed.), *Sibling relationships: Their causes and consequences* (pp. 105–126). Norwood, NJ: Ablex Publishing.

Ross, H.G., & Milgram, J.I. (1982). Important variables in adult sibling relationships: A qualitative study. In M.E. Lamb & B. Sutton-Smith (Eds.), *Sibling relationships: Their nature and significance across the lifespan* (pp. 225–249). Hillsdale, NJ: Lawrence Erlbaum.

Russo, F. (2010). *They're your parents, too: How siblings can survive their parents' aging without driving each other crazy.* New York: Bantam.

Scott, J.P. (1996). Sisters in later life: Changes in contact and availability. *Journal of Women and Aging, 8*, 41–53.

Spitze, G., & Trent, K. (2006). Gender differences in adult sibling relations in two-child families. *Journal of Marriage and Family, 68*, 977–992.

Suitor, J.J., Sechrist, J., Plikuhn, M., Pardo, S.T., Gilligan, M., & Pillemer, K. (2009). The role of perceived maternal favoritism in sibling relations in midlife. *Journal of Marriage and Family, 71*, 1026–1038.

Tancredy, C.M., & Fraley, R.C. (2006). The nature of adult twin relationships: An attachment-theoretical perspective. *Journal of Personality and Social Psychology, 90*, 78–93.

Tucker, J., Schwartz, J., Clark, K., & Friedman, H. (1999). Age-related changes in the associations of social network ties with mortality risk. *Psychology and Aging, 14*, 564–571.

van Gaalen, R., Dykstra, P.A., & Komter, A. (2010). Where is the exit? Intergenerational ambivalence and relationship quality in high contact ties. *Journal of Aging Studies, 24*, 105–114.

van Volkom, M. (2006). Sibling relationships in middle and older adulthood: A review of the literature. *Marriage and Family Review, 40*, 151–170.

Voorpostel, M., & Blieszner, R. (2008). Intergenerational solidarity and support between adult siblings. *Journal of Marriage and Family, 70*, 157–167.

Voorpostel, M., & Van der Lippe, T. (2007). Support between siblings and between friends: Two worlds apart? *Journal of Marriage and Family, 69*, 1271–1282.

Voorpostel, M., Van der Lippe, T., Dykstra, P. A., & Flap, H. (2007). Similar or different? The importance of similarities and differences for support between siblings. *Journal of Family Issues, 28,* 1026–1053.

Waldinger, R. J., Vaillant, G. E., & Orav, E. J. (2007). Childhood sibling relationships as a predictor of major depression in adulthood: A 30-year prospective study. *American Journal of Psychiatry, 164,* 949–954.

Walker, A. J., Allen, K. R., & Connidis, I. A. (2005). Theorizing and studying sibling ties in adulthood. In V. L. Bengtson, A. C. Acock, K. A. Allen, P. Dilworth-Anderson, & D. M. Klein (Eds.), *Sourcebook of family theory & research* (pp. 181–184). Thousand Oaks, CA: Sage.

Weiss, R. S. (1974). *Loneliness: The experience of emotional and social isolation.* Cambridge, MA: MIT Press.

White, L. (2001). Sibling relationships over the life course: A panel analysis. *Journal of Marriage and the Family, 63,* 555–568.

Willson, A. E., Shuey, K. M., & Elder Jr., G. H. (2003). Ambivalence in the relationship of adult children to aging parents and in-laws. *Journal of Marriage and Family, 65,* 1055–1072.

Wilson, J. G., Calsyn, R. J., & Orlofsky, J. L. (1994). Impact of sibling relationships on social support and morale in the elderly. *Journal of Gerontological Social Work, 22,* 157–170.

7

Aging Parents and Adult Children: Determinants of Relationship Quality

Jori Sechrist, J. Jill Suitor, Karl Pillemer, Megan Gilligan, Abigail R. Howard, and Shirley A. Keeton

·When we revisited the chapter on parent–adult child relations that we contributed to the first edition of this volume more than 15 years ago, we were struck by how dated the title appeared to us. The title of our 1995 chapter was "Aged Parents and Aging Children," but the new chapter is "Aging Parents and Adult Children." In part, we made this change because the term *aged* has been replaced by *older* in the literature on later-life families. However, we believe that there is meaning to the change in terms that has important bearing on parent–adult child relations. Perhaps the best way to characterize the new perspective on aging can be found in a recent cartoon in *The New Yorker* magazine, which shows a wife saying to her husband with great enthusiasm, "70 is the new 50." Although an oversimplification, this piece of popular culture illustrates a trend in attitudes held both toward and by individuals in what used to be called "old age."

First, individuals in their 60s and 70s currently enjoy far better health and much more active lives than did their counterparts as recently as two decades ago. By 2007, only 3% of persons ages 65 to 74 and slightly more than 10% of those 75 and older in the United States had limitations in their activities of daily living (ADLs), whereas only 6% of those 65 to 74 and less than 20% of those 75 or older had limitations in their instrumental activities of daily living (IADLs) (U.S. Bureau of the Census, 2010). Second, as a consequence of better health, individuals aged 65 and over have become increasingly likely to remain active and independent, often continuing to be employed (U.S. Census, 2010) or engaging extensively in volunteer activities reflecting careers they pursued in earlier decades (Mutchler, Burr, & Caro, 2003). As a result of these changes, we currently see a greater focus on the study of parent–adult child relations when the older generation is living independently in the community than in past decades, as well as increased attention to intergenerational exchange, as opposed to focusing primarily on support from the younger to the older generation (Suitor, Sechrist, Gilligan, & Pillemer, 2011). This trend does not reflect a decreased interest in family caregiving to older parents; in fact, that literature continues to grow at a rapid pace. However, scholars have begun to question when children's support to parents should be characterized as caregiving, as opposed to part of an exchange relationship (Suitor et al., 2011).

Over the same period, several exciting theoretical and methodological developments have been influential in shaping the study of parent–adult child relations. Thus, the recent changes in the meaning and experience of aging, combined with the focus on new theories and methodologies, necessitate taking a comparative approach in some aspects of this chapter.

We begin with recent theoretical and methodological approaches in scholarship on parent–adult child relations, followed by a framework for studying this central intergenerational relationship. We then discuss the ways in which parents and children affect one another's well-being, and conclude with a brief outline of the directions in which we believe that the study of parent-child relations will move in the coming years.

NEW PERSPECTIVES IN THE STUDY OF PARENT–ADULT CHILD RELATIONSHIPS

Theoretical Perspectives

Throughout the 20th century, two fundamental themes emerged in the study of parent–adult child relations. The first of these themes highlights family solidarity and views adult children and older parents as primary sources of both emotional and instrumental support for one another. In contrast, the second theme focuses on the potential for conflict with, and abandonment of, older parents, perhaps reflecting generalized societal fears about the welfare of older adults. At different historical points, one of the themes tended to be particularly dominant, whereas the other receded into the background. As the century drew to a close, greater consideration was given to including these two aspects of family relations in the same studies, exploring whether they shared similar predictors and consequences for well-being (Aquilino, 1999; Parrott & Bengtson, 1999; Townsend & Franks, 1995).

A new theoretical development in this period was bringing positive and negative dimensions of parent–adult child relations together in the concept of intergenerational ambivalence (Lüscher & Pillemer, 1998). The ambivalence framework is based on the assumption that family relationships are characterized by simultaneous positive and negative feelings or attitudes, in great part because family roles are often contradictory (Pillemer & Suitor,

2005; 2008). Empirical studies have shown that ambivalence is very common in later-life families, regardless of whether the reports are provided by parents or adult children (Fingerman, Hay, & Birditt, 2004; Pillemer, Suitor, Mock, Sabir, & Sechrist, 2007; Willson, Shuey, Elder, & Wickrama, 2006).

Methodological Advances: Individual versus Multiple-Respondent Designs

Although as early as the 1970s research had demonstrated that members of the same intergenerational dyad often hold different perspectives on their relationship (Bengtson & Kuypers, 1971), only recently has substantial attention been directed toward collecting data from multiple respondents in the same family regarding the same relationships (Davey, Eggebeen, & Salva, 2007; Fingerman, Pitzer, Lefkowitz, Birditt, & Mroczek, 2008; Fingerman, Miller, Birditt, & Zarit, 2009; Suitor, Sechrist, Steinhour, & Pillemer, 2006). This line of research has shown that there is often substantial variation in the quality of parent-child relationships within the same family as well as in the patterns of intergenerational exchange (Lin, 2008; Suitor, Pillemer, & Sechrist, 2006; Shapiro, 2004). For example, when parents report about relationships with each of their adult children, both mothers and fathers tend to favor some adult children over others in terms of emotional closeness and the provision of emotional and instrumental support (Suitor & Pillemer, 2012; Suitor, Sechrist, & Pillemer, 2007). Further, such differentiation in the family, both in adulthood and childhood, has detrimental consequences for adult children's psychological well-being (Pillemer, Suitor, Pardo, & Henderson, 2010) and their relationships with their siblings (Suitor et al., 2009).

A FRAMEWORK FOR UNDERSTANDING THE QUALITY OF PARENT-CHILD RELATIONS IN LATER LIFE

If we had been writing this chapter several decades ago, the essential factors to include in a framework for studying parent–adult child relations would have been markedly different from those that are essential when considering contemporary Western industrial societies. First, research has increasingly shown that contemporary family processes greatly mirror those of other small groups, such as friendship networks. This similarity probably reflects the increasingly voluntary nature of parent-child relations in later life. That is, parents' relationships with grown children are characterized by choice, rather than by an obligation to remain together (Suitor et al., 2011). In the past, the control of family resources was a major method of ensuring contact with, and care by, children. In contemporary society, most young adults are dependent on the labor market for their livelihood, rather than on their parents (Myles, 1989). Further, norms of filial responsibility were more clearly articulated in the past. At present, the amount and nature of parent-child contact and the degree of mutual aid between the generations tend to be individually negotiated, with only limited guidance from society. Further, research has shown that particularly for daughters, who are the primary sources of support to parents, assistance is fueled by feelings of affection (Silverstein, Parrott, & Bengtson, 1995). Thus, it is increasingly important to understand the factors that shape the quality of parent–adult child relations because they hold a central key to understanding all aspects of interaction and intergenerational exchange in contemporary later-life families.

In developing a framework of determinants of parent–adult child relationship quality, we follow House (1989) in our view that it is important to examine both social structural and psychosocial determinants of relationship quality. In examining multiple factors including both parents' and adult children's social positions and characteristics unique to each parent–adult child dyad, this perspective can help to reduce the overemphasis on problems of family caregiving in discussions of intergenerational relations. For example, discussions of parent-child relationships in later life are often framed around parental dependency, role reversal, parents moving in with children because of illness, and the psychological well-being of adult child caregivers. As we have discussed elsewhere (Suitor et al., 2011), until quite recently, this view had become such a dominant paradigm in the field that there had been relatively little attention to relationships in which parents are in good health—a state that characterizes a majority of the population over 65 years of age. It also failed to recognize that adult children are likely to affect their *parents*, as well as the reverse.

For this reason, we treat parental dependency as only one among several factors that are important in explaining parent-child relationships. This multifactor approach allows for the construction of a more exhaustive conceptual framework to understand determinants of relationship quality. We organize the framework into three general sets of factors: social structural positions, status transitions, and stressful life events and resulting changes in dependency.

Social Structure and Intergenerational Relations

The past two decades have seen the development of a greater focus on the effects of social structural factors in explaining family relationships. It has been demonstrated that the social structural positions of both parents and children are crucial to an understanding of intergenerational relations. In this section, we begin by focusing on two social structural positions that play a particularly important role in determining the quality of parent-child relations in later life. These are age and birth order, and gender.

Age and Birth Order

Theories of adult development and intergenerational relations suggest that the age of the adult child affects the quality of parent-child relations. This literature argues that as adult children become older, less conflict and greater closeness occur in the parent-child relationship. Specifically, these theories maintain that maturational changes are likely to reduce differences between parents and adult children, thus minimizing the bases for conflict between them. For example, Bengtson (1979) suggested that as children mature, their orientations become more similar to those of their parents, whereas Blenkner (1965) proposed that adult children's identification with their parents increases as part of the process of developing *filial maturity*. Similarly, Hagestad (1987) posited both that differences between parents and children become muted across time and that there is greater tolerance for differences that remain.

Based on these theories we might expect a consistent association between children's ages and the quality of parent–adult child relationship, with greater closeness and less conflict as children become older, but this association does not appear to be the case. Studies have found that relations are less conflictual when adult children are older (Birditt, Jackey, & Antonucci, 2009), and that parents are more likely to rely on their eldest children as sources of various dimensions on instrumental support (Suitor & Pillemer, 2007). However, parents, particularly mothers, are more likely to report that they are most emotionally close to their youngest children (Suitor & Pillemer, 2007).

These patterns can be explained by theory and research on birth order and family relations. Firstborns are most likely to be identified as mature, conscientious, and responsible (Eckstein, 2000; Paulhus, Trapnell, & Chen, 1999; Sulloway, 1996). Further, because parents tend to attribute these personality characteristics to their firstborns and act accordingly in terms of granting them greater autonomy and independence, these children may actually become more mature and responsive to responsibilities (Bumpass, Crouter, & McHale, 2001; Hertwig, Davis, & Sulloway, 2002; Sulloway, 1996). In contrast, scholars studying birth order have suggested that lastborns develop more sensitive social skills in an attempt to create a special position in families, enabling them to compensate for resource advantages their eldest siblings accrue (Paulhus et al., 1999; Sulloway, 1996), and resulting in their carving out a unique niche in childhood that appears to continue through adulthood (Suitor & Pillemer, 2007). The importance of birth order is also evident when examining what is often referred to as the *middle child disadvantage*, which appears to begin in childhood and can be found throughout the life course in terms of parents' distribution of instrumental and expressive resources (Jenkins, Rasbash, & O'Connor, 2003; Salmon, 1999; Suitor & Pillemer, 2007).

Gender

A review of the literature suggests that the gender of both parent and child affects intergenerational relations. Studies of the effects of gender consistently demonstrate stronger affectional ties between mothers and daughters than any other combination. For example, mothers report more positive affect with adult daughters than with sons (Angres, 1975; Rossi & Rossi, 1990), are more likely to rely on daughters than sons as confidants and comforters (Aldous, Klaus, & Klein, 1985; Lopata, 1979), and are less likely to become angry (Lopata, 1979) or disappointed (Aldous et al., 1985) with daughters. In turn, adult daughters report greater feelings of closeness to mothers than to fathers (Adams, 1968; Cicirelli, 1981; Rossi & Rossi, 1990) and are more likely to rely on mothers as confidants (Suitor, 1984).

The literature on other parent-child gender combinations suggests greater closeness and less conflict in both mother-son and father-daughter pairs than in father-son pairs. The preponderance of studies of intergenerational relations has found that adult sons report greater closeness to mothers than to fathers (Adams, 1968; Lowenthal, Thurnher, & Chiriboga, 1975; see Rossi & Rossi, 1990, for an exception), whereas fathers report greater closeness in their relationships with their daughters than with their sons (Aldous et al., 1985; Miller, Bengtson, & Richards, 1987; Rossi & Rossi, 1990).

Status Transitions, Similarity, and Parent-Child Relations

Adult Children's Social Statuses

Readers might be surprised that we did not include a larger number of social structural positions in the previous section. This is because research on the effects of other social structural characteristics of children on parent-child relations has yielded much less consistent results. Classic theories of similarity and interpersonal relationships (Homans, 1950; Lazarsfeld & Merton, 1954) would lead to the expectation that parents and children would be closer when they share structural characteristics, such as education, parental status, marital status, and religion. Further, sharing parents' sociodemographic characteristics often indicates that adult children have achieved normative benchmarks in development that are highly valued by parents. However, the empirical literature has not supported this hypothesis as consistently as theory would predict.

For example, some studies have found greater closeness and harmony when adult children become parents themselves (Spitze, Logan, Deane, & Zerger, 1994; Umberson, 1992); however, other studies found either no positive effects of parenthood (Suitor & Pillemer, 2006) or effects specific only to particular parent-child combinations (Kaufman & Uhlenberg, 1998; Rossi &

Rossi, 1990), some of which were negative (Aquilino, 1999; Kaufman & Uhlenberg,1998). Findings regarding the effects of other dimensions of status similarity, such as marital status, occupational status, and educational attainment, provide an equally inconsistent picture.

We believe there are two reasons for this inconsistent pattern, for which the transition to parenting provides one of the clearest examples. Becoming parents increases adult children's structural similarity to their parents, yet also creates responsibilities that make adult children less available to their parents. Second, as Suitor and colleagues' (Suitor, Pillemer, & Keeton, 1995) research has shown, the reason that status similarity leads to better relationship quality is because such similarity increases the likelihood that associates will have similar experiences, leading to shared values and perspectives. Such similarity of values and experiences is associated with greater closeness and less conflict and ambivalence between the generations (Pillemer et al., 2007; Rossi & Rossi, 1990; Suitor & Pillemer, 2006). In the case of becoming parents, the status transition may heighten value similarity between adult children and their parents, thus increasing closeness; however, if the two generations do not share expectations regarding childrearing, the transition to parenthood may result in perceptions of lower value similarity, leading to tension and conflict (Fischer, 1983; Merrill, 2007).

In sum, parent-child relations may become more harmonious when offspring share a larger number of social statuses with their parents, but such increased harmony is unlikely unless these transitions result in greater value congruence while not producing substantial barriers to interaction or disrupting the flow of exchange.

Children's Nonnormative Transitions

Up to this point, we have been discussing only normative transitions, which, as we have noted, may or may not intensify affectional bonds. In contrast, children's nonnormative transitions have almost uniformly negative effects on relations with their parents. In part, these effects can be attributed to decreases in similarity between adult children and parents. For example, Suitor's study of married women who entered college while raising families revealed that the return to school often created stress in the mother-daughter relationship when the transition created value differences between the generations (Plikuhn, Suitor, & Powers, 2009; Suitor, 1987).

Nonnormative transitions may also have detrimental effects on parent-child relations because they increase children's demands on parents. For example, Newman (1988) found that relations between middle-class sons and their parents often became strained when the sons lost their jobs, and Aquilino and Supple (1991) found that adult children's unemployment was one of the best predictors of conflict with parents when the generations shared a home.

Serious violations of normative expectations may also have detrimental effects on parent–adult child relations through embarrassment and disappointment. For example, even though deviant behaviors committed in adulthood do not always increase dependence, these nonnormative events often reduce parents' closeness and willingness to exchange emotional support with those children (Suitor & Pillemer, 2007) as well as increase parents' ambivalence toward them (Pillemer et al., 2007). This distancing may occur because parents evaluate themselves on the basis of their ability to help their children succeed in life; voluntary deviant behaviors lead them to question their parenting competence (Ryff, Schmutte, & Lee, 1996)

Nonnormative transitions that neither create value dissimilarities nor challenge the parents' values appear to have little or no impact on parent–adult child relations. For example, at the point when adult children began returning to their parents' homes, some scholars argued that such coresidence would have detrimental effects on parents' marital quality and well-being (Clemens & Axelson, 1985); however, findings from most large-scale surveys reported that such negative effects appeared only when coupled with high levels of conflict between parents and coresident children (Pillemer & Suitor, 1991; Suitor & Pillemer, 1988) and when children's coresidence resulted from problems in their own lives (Aquilino & Supple, 1991; Pudrovska, 2009). However, it remains to be seen whether the current economic crisis, involving the highest level of unemployment and home loss in nearly three decades and resulting in increased coresidence (Fleck, 2009), may lead to difficulties when multiple generations coreside.

Finally, the preponderance of the literature suggests that divorce also has little or no deleterious effect on the quality of parent-child relations (Glaser, Tomassini, & Stuchbury, 2008; see Umberson, 1992, for an exception), even when the divorce precipitates a return to the parents' home (Aquilino, 1996; Aquilino & Supple, 1991; Choi, 2003; White & Peterson, 1995). In fact, some findings suggest a possible increase in parent–adult child closeness following the child's divorce (Bengtson, 2001; Dykstra, 1997; Sarkisian & Gerstel, 2008; Suitor & Pillemer, 2006), particularly when daughters maintain custody of their children (Sarkisian & Gerstel, 2007; Sprey & Matthews, 1982). Parents' support to children—particularly daughters—appears to increase during the period immediately following the divorce (Aquilino, 1996; Hamon, 1995; Kaufman & Uhlenberg, 1998; Swartz, 2009); however, in most cases, this support does not affect the quality of the parent-child relationship (Sarkisian & Gerstel, 2008; Swartz, 2009).

Parents' Transitions

Both retirement and widowhood are normative transitions that have potential for affecting relationships between parents and adult children

(Remnet, 1987). However, there is no consensus on the type or extent of these effects.

In the past two decades, numerous studies have shed light on the transition of retirement (Reitzes & Mutran, 2004); most have focused on the effects of retirement on the retiree and his or her social, psychological, and physical health (Herzog, House, & Morgan, 1991; Kim & Moen, 2001; 2002; Marshall, Clarke, & Ballantyne, 2001; Reitzes, Mutran, & Fernandez, 1996), and for women, on marital quality (Moen, Kim, & Hofmeister, 2001). Considerably less is known regarding the effects of retirement on the parent–adult child relationship. The few studies that have addressed this question have found that the loss of the work role can pose a crisis for both the retiree and his or her family (Moen, Fields, Quick, & Hofmeister, 2000; Ragan, 1979), but even when this occurs, seldom does it translate into either changes in the quality of parent-child relations or high levels of burden on offspring (McCallum, 1986; Moen et al., 2000).

Not surprisingly, most studies show that retirement increases activity with adult children (Broese van Groenou & van Tilburg, 1993; Moen et al., 2000), but the findings of one study suggest that the effects of retirement on parent-child interaction appears to vary by parents' gender, proximity of children, and the presence of grandchildren (Szinovacz & Davey, 2001). Szinovacz and Davey found that mothers' retirement decreased visits with adult children who lived nearby, particularly those without children, whereas fathers' retirement increased such visits. These findings mirror those of Moen and colleagues (2001) in suggesting that husbands' and wives' retirement have different effects on family relations.

In contrast to retirement, the widowhood of a parent involves a direct change in the lives of both the surviving spouse and the couple's adult children. Although the loss of a spouse or parent has the potential to alter the parent-child relationship considerably, empirical evidence has shown a general pattern of stability and continuity in parent-child relationships following widowhood (Anderson, 1984; Dean, Matt, & Wood, 1992; Ferraro, 1984; Umberson, 1992). For example, studies have shown that widowhood improves parent-child relations (Ha & Ingersoll-Dayton, 2008) and increases contact with (Roan & Raley, 1996) and support from adult children (Ha, 2008; Ha, Carr, Utz, & Nesse, 2006; Stuifbergen, van Delden & Dykstra, 2008). These increases often occur soon after the death of a spouse-parent and return to earlier levels after a year or so (Ha, 2008; Ha & Ingersoll-Dayton, 2008; Ha et al., 2006). Evidence also suggests that close proximity to, frequent contact with, and support from adult children improves the well-being of widowed adults (Ha & Carr, 2005; Pinquart, 2003; Silverstein & Bengtson, 1994).

Taken together, these lines of research suggest that although the most common life course transitions experienced by parents—retirement and widowhood—greatly alter the lives of those individuals, they have surprisingly muted effects on parent-child relations. Further, when these transitions do affect relations with adult children, the effects appear to be disproportionately positive.

Effects of Parents' Nonnormative Transitions

Divorce is the parental nonnormative transition most likely to affect parent–adult child relations. The present generation of older parents was unlikely to experience their own parents' divorces because prior to the 1970s almost all marriages ended with the death of one partner; however, the skyrocketing divorce rate of that decade created a notable population of older divorced parents. The consequences of parental divorce fall far more heavily on fathers' relationships with their adult children than those of mothers. Most studies find little difference in support to older mothers (Lye, 1996; Pezzin & Schone, 1999), but divorced fathers are far less likely to receive support than are their counterparts who remain married to their children's mothers (Kalmijn, 2007; Pezzin & Schone, 1999; Silverstein, Bengtson, & Lawton, 1997), a pattern that remains consistent despite the age of the children when parental divorce occurs (Kalmijn, 2007; Pezzin & Schone, 1999). Further, even if these divorced fathers remarry, their children are less likely to provide them with support (Davey et al., 2007; Lin, 2008; Pezzin & Schone, 1999). Equally important, parental divorce greatly decreases the likelihood that fathers will have close relationships with their children in adulthood (Bulcroft & Bulcroft, 1991; Cooney & Uhlenberg, 1990; Seltzer & Bianchi, 1998; Shapiro, 2003), mirroring a pattern of less closeness and contact begun in the early years following parents' marital disruption (Aquilino, 2006; Scott, Booth, King, & Johnson, 2007). Although divorced mothers are at a slightly increased risk of having strained relationships with their children than are mothers who did not divorce (Umberson, 1992), most mothers continue to have close relationships with their children in the face of divorce (Amato & Booth, 1996; Aquilino, 1994).

STRESSFUL LIFE EVENTS AND DEPENDENCY

Early research on infancy, childhood, and adolescence presumed the unidirectional influence of parents on children (Bell, 1979; Steinberg, 1988). In recent decades, however, researchers have moved toward a more bidirectional view of family influence in studying the early stages of the family life cycle. Such a perspective is greatly needed in the study of parent-child relations in later life as well. As noted earlier, the predominance of the view that highlights parental dependency and resulting stress for caregivers has limited our understanding of parent-child relations in later life. However, recent research indicates that adult children and parents have strong reciprocal effects on one another. In particular, negative events in the lives of *either* children or parents affect their relationship and, in turn, affect psychological well-being. In this section, we first examine the impact of stressful life events and adult children's dependency on the parent-child relationship. We then explore the impact of declining health of parents and resulting dependency on caregiving children.

Effects of Children on Parents

It is surprising that the effect of adult children's problems on parents' well-being did not begin to attract attention among scholars until the past two decades. The impact of the child's problems did not escape notice by practitioners who work with adults facing mental illness or engaged in substance abuse or unlawful behaviors that led to incarceration (Clark, 1998; Dressel & Barnhill, 1994; Seltzer, Greenberg, Krauss, & Hong, 1997). The burden placed on parents faced with helping adult children with these problems becomes obvious when noting practitioners' emphasis on the role of strong family ties in recovery and rehabilitation (Knight & Simpson, 1996). Parents are also expected to assist adult children who experience substantial financial problems due to employment or home ownership difficulties, both of which have risen in the past two years to levels not seen in several decades (Berry, 2008).

Research on the effects of such problems on parents' well-being began appearing in the early 1990s and has become more prominent across the past two decades. Consistent with research on the negative effects of social interaction, problems experienced by adult children and contact with children during these periods typically affect parents' well-being. In one of the earliest studies, Pillemer and Suitor (1991) found that parents whose adult children had mental, physical, substance abuse, or stress-related problems experienced greater depression than did parents whose children did not have these problems. In fact, children's problems were the second strongest predictor of mothers' depression, only after their own physical health, and the third best predictor for father's depression after physical health and children's marital status. More recent studies have found the same pattern. Problems that adult children experience negatively influence parents in terms of affect and self-acceptance (Greenfield & Marks, 2006), whereas children's successes and normative transitions positively influence parents' well-being and feelings of mastery (Ryff, Lee, Essex, & Schmutte, 1994; Ryff et al., 1996).

The effects of children's problems on parents' well-being stem not only from worries about the way these problems affect the children's lives, but also from the direct effect on the parents' lives. For example, adult children who experience serious physical and mental health problems receive greater support from parents (Seltzer, Greenberg, Orsmond, Lounds, & Smith, 2008; Suitor et al., 2006a), as do children who are divorced (Spitze et al., 1994), unemployed (Suitor et al., 2007), or who have engaged in deviant behaviors as adults (Suitor et al., 2006a). Support given to children in need is, in a sense, more costly to parents because the children's needs often render them unable to reciprocate in either the short-term or the long-term (Greenfield & Marks, 2006; Pillemer & Suitor, 1991; Suitor & Pillemer, 2007), which becomes more problematic as parents age and their needs increase while their ability to provide support to needy children declines (Seltzer et al., 2008). Further, parents of mentally ill adults experience both substantial psychological distress and reduced marital quality resulting from problems associated with their children's bizarre and threatening behaviors (Baronet, 2003; Cook, Cohler, Pickette, & Beeler, 1997; Cook, Hoffschmidt, Cohler, & Pickett, 1992; Rogers & Hogan, 2003). Violence and abuse by adult children are particularly distressing to older parents (Lachs & Pillemer, 2004; Pillemer & Prescott, 1989; Pillemer & Suitor, 1988; Wolf, 2001). Finally, as noted earlier, parents also often experience feelings of shame and disappointment in themselves when their adult children voluntarily engage in deviant behaviors (Carr, 2004).

Effects of Parents on Children: Family Caregiving

Patterns of Support to Older Parents

As noted at several points thus far, the study of aging families has emphasized the flow of support from adult children to their parents. Interest in this subject has been so great that family caregiving has become one of the most rapidly growing bodies of literature in the social sciences since the early 1980s. One reason for this interest is the increasing number of adult children in their 40s, 50s, and 60s who have living parents (U.S. Bureau of the Census, 2010), relative to earlier decades. However, as already noted, not all of these parents need care. In fact, the flow of support is disproportionately from parents to children typically until parents are in their 70s, at which point it typically begins to reverse. However, recent data on the health and activity of adults suggests that studies may soon find either that the flow continues toward children for a longer period than in earlier decades, or that there is an interlude in which there is little flow in either direction.

Such changes in older individuals' health and activity raise an important question: When should children's support to parents be characterized as caregiving as opposed to part of an exchange relationship? The difficulty scholars face when drawing these distinctions can best be illustrated by the age distributions of subsamples used in some of the investigations of intergenerational exchange and caregiving. In many studies, the adult children range well into their 60s (e.g., Cooney & Uhlenberg, 1992), in fact, sometimes up to age 70 (Wakabayashi & Donato, 2005). In other studies, however, the age range of older parent care recipients begins in the 50s (Davey & Eggebeen, 1998). Thus, confusion continues about when parents become care recipients as opposed to exchange partners.

Although these issues are now being considered in the scholarly literature (cf. Suitor et al., 2011), studies of support to parents beyond their mid-50s continue to emphasize the flow of support from the younger to the older generation. This line of research has revealed several consistent patterns that are likely to continue playing an important role in studying caregiving, regardless of the age of the parents being provided support.

First, gender of both parents and children continues to play the greatest role in the study of support to the older generation. Mothers receive more emotional and instrumental support from their adult children than do fathers (Ikkink, van Tilburg, & Knipscher, 1999; Lee, Dwyer, & Coward, 1993; Silverstein, Conroy, Wang, Giarrusso, & Bengtson, 2002), and daughters are more likely than sons to be the source of that support (Horowitz, 1985; Spitze & Logan, 1990). We might have expected that this gendered pattern of support would become less prominent in the face of changing gender-role attitudes in recent decades (Powers et al., 2003), but this expected shift does not appear to be the case. Recent studies mirror earlier ones in showing that both mothers and daughters are more likely to provide and receive support than are fathers and sons (Ingersoll-Dayton, Starrels, & Dowler, 1996; Suitor et al., 2006a). Further, not only do daughters provide more support than do sons, daughters are typically both mothers' and fathers' preferred source of emotional support and help during illness (Suitor & Pillemer, 2006; in press).

Due to daughters' prominent role in providing support to parents, two areas of concern have been whether women's increasing labor force participation or marital instability would reduce their ability to provide care. However, studies across the past three decades have shown that these fears were unsubstantiated (Pavalko, 2011; Pavalko & Artis, 1997; Spitze et al., 1994). For instance, Pavalko and Artis (1997) found that employment did not affect whether daughters began caregiving; rather, employed women who took on this role were more likely to reduce their hours or quit their jobs because of the demands of caring. Further, Spitze and her colleagues (1994) found that although divorce increased daughters' need of support themselves, it did not decrease their support of parents compared to their married counterparts.

Costs of Caring on Adult Children's Well-Being

Regardless of the point where caregiving begins, the literature has shown that it has some costs to adult children in most cases, even while sometimes also providing a source of satisfaction. Both theoretical and empirical scholarship on caregiving suggest that becoming a caregiver is a life course transition that often intensifies preexisting strains while also bringing older problems to the forefront (Pearlin, 1989; Pearlin, Lieberman, Menaghan, & Mullen, 1981). Caregiving requires adhering to the norms of providing physical and emotional support to the care recipient (Silverstein, Gans, & Yang, 2006; Suitor & Pillemer, 1990); however, the ability to do so is likely to involve some role renegotiation with the parent (Brody, 1990; Doronfino & Kellet, 2003; Walker, Shin, & Bird, 1990). Further, the transition to caregiver for a parent also involves changes in role relationships with siblings, spouses, other kin, and even friends.

New caregivers must negotiate the expectations of their new role with all of these role partners, typically leading to changes in their relationships with members of their preexisting social support networks (Litvin, Albert, Brody, & Hoffman, 1995; Stevens & Townsend, 1997; Suitor & Pillemer, 1987; 1992), a process that often rekindles conflict and ambivalence from earlier points in the relationship. For example, married adult children may find that the responsibilities of caregiving interfere with the performance of marital and parenting roles, often resulting in conflict with partners in these roles (Bookwala, 2009; Stevens & Townsend, 1997), particularly if spouses have no experience with caregiving to their own parents (Suitor & Pillemer, 1994). Changes in the relationship with the care recipient may also prove to be stressful. Parents may actually serve as sources of emotional support to their adult children early in the caregiving career (Walker, Pratt, & Oppy, 1992); however, as the parent's physical or cognitive health declines, the relationship with the parent may become a source of stress rather than comfort (Aquilino, 1998; Kramer, 1997), particularly in the case of dementia.

Given the potential for interpersonal stress, combined with the physical demands of caregiving, it is not surprising that research has found that many caregivers experience substantial burden (Szinovacz & Davey, 2007), and are at greater risk for depression and physical ailments than are their noncaregiving peers (Bookwala, 2009; Pinquart & Sörensen, 2004; 2007; Schulz, Alison, & O'Brien, 1995; Schulz, Visintainer, & Williamson,1990). In fact, the difficulties faced by many caregivers helps to explain why, in families with a larger number of offspring, particularly daughters, individuals are sometimes replaced as caregivers by their siblings (Szinovacz & Davey, 2007).

It is interesting to note that despite these costs, some research has found positive consequences of providing care to older parents. For example, Walker, Shin, and Bird (1990) found that half of daughters reported positive effects of caregiving on their relationships with their mothers and only 5% reported negative effects. Almost half of the mothers also reported positive effects of caregiving whereas only two reported negative effects. Similarly, Cohen and colleagues (Cohen, Colantonio, & Vernich, 2003) found that more than 70% of caregivers in their study held positive feelings toward caregiving. Studies have shown that caregivers reported greater closeness as the result of the increased dependency of their parents (see Kramer, 1997, for a review). See Pruchno and Gitlin (chapter 21 in this volume) for a comprehensive examination of family caregiving.

The Role of Race and Ethnicity in Parent–Adult Child Relations

Up to this point, we have been discussing parent–adult child relations without taking race and ethnicity into account. However, interest in the support networks of older individuals and families from minority groups has grown considerably over the past several decades. Many early studies showed stronger ties and larger kin support networks among minority than nonminority families (Jayakody, Chatters, & Taylor, 1993; Kim & McKenry, 1998; Stack, 1974; Taylor, 1986), often implying that minority individuals had stronger kin ties and kin support systems than non-Hispanic white individuals. However, neither relationship quality nor exchanges between parents and adult children are consistently *greater* in minority parent-child relations compared to those of whites.

Despite the cultural norms of high familism in minority families, findings regarding race and ethnic variations in parent–adult child relationship quality have been inconclusive. Whereas some studies have reported that black families have more positive relationships (Aquilino, 1997; 1999; Lawton, Silverstein, & Bengtson, 1994a; 1994b), others have found no difference (Caldwell, Antonucci, & Jackson, 1998). Very few studies have compared white parent-child dyads to Hispanic or Asian American dyads directly; those that have done so have not found consistent ethnic differences. Some studies find more positive relations between parents and adult children among Hispanic and Asian than non-Hispanic white dyads (Rastogi & Wampler, 1999), but others find no difference or, in some cases, more conflictual relations in Hispanic dyads (Aquilino, 1997; 1999).

Similar patterns emerge when comparing white and minority parent-child support exchanges. When considering all forms of support, white, black, and Hispanic parents and children report similar levels of exchanges (Hogan, Eggebeen, & Clogg, 1993; Laditka & Laditka, 2001; Peek, Coward, & Peek, 2000). However, differences are found when type of support and respondent's generational status are considered. For example, black and Hispanic children provide more financial assistance to parents (Shuey & Hardy, 2003), whereas non-Hispanic white parents are more likely than both black and Hispanic parents to give financial assistance to their adult children and to provide greater amounts of financial transfers (Berry, 2006; Jayakody, 1998; Lee & Aytac, 1998; Wong, Kitayama, & Soldo, 1999), even when controlling on economic factors (Jayakody, 1998; Lee & Aytac, 1998; Shuey & Hardy, 2003).

Larger and more consistent differences are found when considering coresidence by race and ethnicity. Black, Hispanic, and Asian parents and children are substantially more likely to coreside than those in non-Hispanic white families (Burr & Mutchler, 1999; Choi, 2003; Cohen & Casper, 2002; Lubben & Becerra, 1987; Roan & Raley, 1996), even when taking into account socioeconomic status (Choi, 1995; Roan & Raley, 1996). When coresidence does occur in non-Hispanic white families and in black families, it is more often for the benefit of both parents and children or because the child needs such support.(Choi, 2003; Cohen & Casper, 2002; Glick & van Hook, 2002; Hill, 2003; Kamo, 2000). In contrast, among Hispanic and Asian families, coresidence is more often due to dependency of the older parent (Cohen & Casper, 2002; Glick & van Hook, 2002).

Despite the race and ethnic variations in *patterns* of relationship quality and support in the parent–adult child relationship, the *predictors* of relationship quality and support in these relations vary surprisingly little by race and ethnicity. In particular, both gender and proximity play a prominent role in explaining intergenerational relations in black and white families (cf. Spitze & Miner, 1992 and Suitor et al., 2007, regarding gender; and Spitze & Miner, 1992 and Taylor & Chatters, 1991, regarding proximity). Further, both black and white mothers tend to provide support to those children who are in greater need (Suitor et al., 2007).

In sum, despite early arguments that substantial differences by race and ethnicity existed in both expressive and instrumental dimensions of parent–adult child relations, the empirical literature has revealed far more overlap than divergence in these intergenerational relations. In fact, the only area in which clear differences emerge is intergenerational coresidence. Although these differences occur when controlling on SES, they are most marked in families with fewer resources. This raises the question of whether these patterns will continue as minority families become more economically stable.

CONCLUSION

Over the past century, much scholarship on the family has focused on minor children and their families, most likely because parent-child relations in this period are more intense and the direct influence of parents on children is undoubtedly greater. In the early stages of childrearing, family members cannot easily escape one another's influence. In later life, by contrast, relations between parents and children assume a more voluntary character. This difference is best reflected in the fact that young children almost always live with their parents, whereas in contemporary society adult offspring most often do not.

Nevertheless, during the past three decades covered in this review, increasing numbers of scholars have come to focus on the period when children have reached adulthood and parents are in middle or old age. As we have indicated, a vast body of research indicates the enduring importance of children in the lives of parents until the end of life. Both high levels of contact and mutually supportive exchanges are reported by parents and by their adult children. Toward the end of the life course, adult children often provide needed care and support to their parents. Indeed, given high rates of divorce and geographical mobility, intergenerational relationships may well be the most stable ones that people in contemporary society experience. Therefore, we believe it is highly appropriate that the relationship between adult children and older parents is represented in the present volume.

One conclusion of our review is a very positive one. Almost four decades ago, Troll (1971) pointed to the dearth of knowledge about midlife and later-life parent–adult child relations: "Studies of older parent-child relations have thus far attended to the launching stage, when the parents are in early middle age, and then focused on aged parents and their adult children" (p. 276). Further, research on parent-child relations in later life emphasized problems of parental dependency and family caregiving, almost to the exclusion of other themes in the period when Troll made this statement. In contrast, over the past three decades, scholarship has greatly expanded, bringing sophisticated theoretical approaches combined with new empirical strategies to shed light on a wider array of issues regarding relations with children after they become adults.

As we look to the future, many opportunities exist that will continue to make this field a vibrant and interesting one. One clear need is for close collaboration among disciplines to advance the study of intergenerational relations. It is likely that many important scientific discoveries in this area will increasingly result from transdisciplinary efforts. For example, sociological approaches highlighting social structural factors in intergenerational relationships can benefit from individual- and relationship-level psychological scholarship on attachment and family systems (Cicirelli, 1991; Fingerman & Bermann, 2000). Collaboration among sociologists and economists has already enhanced understanding of family caregiving issues (Booth, Crouter, Bianchi, & Seltzer, 2008). In general, scholars will need to take into account the interplay of complex social, economic, and demographic trends with psychological factors in parent-child relationships; such efforts will require stepping beyond disciplinary boundaries.

Second, in this chapter we have proposed a conceptual framework for understanding parent-child relations that included structural positions, status transitions, and life events and resulting dependency. One particularly useful approach would be to consider parent–adult child relationship quality as an intervening variable. For example, researchers frequently investigate the effects of status transitions, such as becoming divorced or widowed, on physical and psychological well-being in the middle and later years without considering the possible mediating effects of intergenerational relationship quality. How-ever, evidence from the broader literature on support networks suggests that this factor might serve as a critical mediator between stressors and well-being outcomes. We believe that such an approach would greatly enhance under-standing of the role of parent-child relations for both generations.

A third important priority is to address the question: To what degree will demographic trends affect intergenerational relationships of older persons? To answer this question, it is important to analyze in detail the dynamics of the current generation of middle-aged adults (the baby-boom generation). This article has necessarily dealt with the older population as it is today. However, current older cohorts appear to have large resources for family sup-port, including relatively large numbers of living children and greater likeli-hood of an intact marriage Both scholarship and societal preparations for the baby-boom generation as it enters old age must take a different set of cir-cumstances into account: larger numbers of persons living alone, without the benefits conferred by a spouse, and with fewer offspring. Given the projected increase in the older population overall, a shortage of caregiving resources in both the formal and the informal sectors is likely to result. The outcomes of these demographic changes are likely to present fertile grounds for scholar-ship over the coming three decades.

REFERENCES

Adams, B. N. (1968). *Kinship in an urban setting*. Chicago: Markham.

Aldous, J., Klaus, E., & Klein, D.M. (1985). The understanding heart: Aging parents and their favorite child. *Child Development, 56,* 303–316.

Amato, P. R., & Booth, A. (1996). A prospective study of divorce and parent-child relationships. *Journal of Marriage and Family, 58,* 356–365.

Anderson, T. B. (1984). Widowhood as a life transition: Its impact on kinship ties. *Journal of Marriage and Family, 46,* 105–114.

Angres, S. (1975). *Intergenerational relations and value congruence between young adults and their mothers*. Unpublished Ph.D. dissertation, University of Chicago.

Aquilino, W. S. (1994). Impact of childhood family disruption young adults' relation-ships with parents. *Journal of Marriage and Family, 56,* 295–313.

Aquilino, W. S. (1996). The life course of children born to unmarried mothers: Childhood living arrangements and young adult outcomes. *Journal of Marriage and Family, 58,* 293–310.

Aquilino, W. S. (1997). From adolescent to young adult: A prospective study of parent-child relations during the transition to adulthood. *Journal of Marriage and Family, 59,* 670–686.

Aquilino, W. S. (1998). Effects of interview mode on measuring depression in younger adults. *Journal of Official Statistics, 14,* 15–29.

Aquilino, W. S. (1999). Two views of one relationship: Comparing parents' and young adult children's reports of the quality of intergenerational relations. *Journal of Marriage and Family, 61,* 858–870.

Aquilino, W. S. (2006). Family relationships and support systems in emerging adulthood. In J.J. Arnett & J. L. Tanner (Eds.), *Emerging adults in America: Coming of age in the 21st century* (pp. 193–217). Washington, DC: American Psychological Association.

Aquilino, W. S., & Supple, K. (1991). Parent-child relations and parents' satisfaction with living arrangements when adult children live at home. *Journal of Marriage and Family, 53,* 13–27.

Baronet, A. M. (2003). The impact of childhood family relations on caregivers' positive and the negative appraisal of their caretaking activities. *Family Relations, 52,* 137–142.

Bell, R. Q. (1979). Parent, child, and reciprocal influences. *American Psychologist, 34,* 821–826.

Bengtson, V. L. (1979). Research perspectives on intergenerational interaction. In P. K. Ragan (Ed.), *Aging parents* (pp. 37–57). Los Angeles: University of Southern California Press.

Bengtson, V. L. (2001). Beyond the nuclear family: The increasing importance of multigenerational bonds. *Journal of Marriage and Family, 64,* 558–567.

Bengtson, V. L., & Kuypers, J. A. (1971). Generational differences and the developmental stake hypothesis. *Aging and Human Development, 2,* 249–260.

Berry, B. (2006). What accounts for race and ethnic differences in parental financial transfers to adult children in the United States? *Journal of Family Issues, 27,* 1583–1604.

Berry, B. (2008). Financial transfers from living parents to adult children: Who is helped and why? *American Journal of Economics and Sociology, 67,* 207–239.

Birditt, K., Jackey, L., & Antonucci, T. (2009). Longitudinal patterns of negative relationship quality across adulthood. *Journals of Gerontology Series B: Psychological Sciences and Social Sciences, 64B,* 55–64.

Blenkner, M. (1965). Social work and family in later life, with some thoughts on filial maturity. In E. Shinas & G. Streib (Eds.), *Social structure and the family: Generational relations* (pp. 46–59). Englewood Cliffs, NJ: Prentice Hall.

Bookwala, J. (2009). The impact of parent care on marital quality and well-being in adult daughters and sons. *Journals of Gerontology Series B: Psychological Sciences and Social Sciences, 64B,* 339–347.

Booth, A., Crouter, A. C., Bianchi, S. M., & Seltzer, J. A. (2008). *Intergenerational caregiving.* Washington, DC: Urban Institute Press.

Brody, E. M. (1990). *Women in the middle: Their parent-care years.* New York: Springer Publishing.

Broese van Groenou, M. I., & van Tilburg, T. G. (1993, February). *Mapping changes in the network following retirement: A comparison of two identification methods.* Paper presented at the International Sunbelt Social Network Conferences, Tampa.

Bulcroft, K. A., & Bulcroft, R. A. (1991). The timing of divorce: Effects on parent-child relationships in later life. *Research on Aging, 13,* 226–243.

Bumpass, M. F., Crouter, A. C., & McHale, S. M. (2001). Parental autonomy granting during adolescence: Exploring gender differences in context. *Developmental Psychology, 37,* 163–173.

Burr, J. A., & Mutchler, J. E. (1999). Race and ethnic variation in norms of filial responsibility among older persons. *Journal of Marriage and Family, 61,* 674–687.

Caldwell, C. H., Antonucci, T. C., & Jackson, J. S. (1998). Supportive/conflictual family relations and depressive symptomology: Teenage mother and grandmother perspectives. *Family Relations, 47,* 395–402.

Carr, D. (2004). My daughter has a career; I just raised babies: The psychological consequences of women's intergenerational social comparisons. *Social Psychology Quarterly, 67,* 132–154.

Choi, N. G. (1995). Racial differences in the determinants of the coresidence of and contacts between elderly parents and their adult children. *Journal of Gerontological Social Work, 24,* 77–95.

Choi, N. G. (2003). Coresidence between unmarried aging parents and their adult children: Who moved in with whom and why. *Research on Aging, 25,* 384–404.

Cicirelli, V. G. (1981). *Helping elderly parents: Role of adult children.* Boston: Auburn House.

Cicirelli, V. G. (1991). Attachment theory in old age: Protection of the attachment figure. In K. Pillemer & K. McCartney (Eds.), *Parent-child relations throughout life* (pp. 25–42). Hillsdale, NY: Lawrence Erlbaum Associates, Inc.

Clark, R. E. (1998). Family costs associated with severe mental illness and substance abuse. In *Families and mental health treatment: A compendium of articles from psychiatric services and hospital and community psychiatry* (pp. 58–63). Washington, DC: American Psychiatric Association.

Clemens, A., &. Axelson, L. J. (1985). The not-so-empty-nest: The return of the fledging adult. *Family Relations, 34,* 259–264.

Cohen, C. A., Colantonio, A., & Vernich, L. (2003). Positive aspects of caregiving: Rounding out the caregiver experience. *International Journal of Geriatric Psychiatry, 17*(2), 184–188.

Cohen, P. N., & Casper, L. M. (2002). In whose home? Multigenerational families in the United States, 1998–2000. *Sociological Perspectives, 45,* 1–20.

Cook, J., Cohler, B. J., Pickett, S. A., & Beeler, J. A. (1997). Life-course and severe mental illness: Implications for caregiving within the family of later life. *Family Relations, 46,* 427–436.

Cook, J., Hoffschmidt, S., Cohler, B. J., & Pickett, S. (1992). Marital satisfaction among parents of the severely mentally ill living in the community. *American Journal of Orthopsychiatry, 62,* 552–563.

Cooney, T. M., & Uhlenberg, P. (1990). The role of divorce in men's relations with their adult children after mid-life. *Journal of Marriage and Family, 52,* 677–688.

Cooney, T. M., & Uhlenberg, P. (1992). Support from parents over the life course: The adult child's perspective. *Social Forces, 71,* 63–84.

Davey, A., & Eggebeen, D. (1998). Patterns of intergenerational exchange and mental health. *Journal of Gerontology, 53B,* 86–95.

Davey, A., Eggebeen, D., & Savla, J. (2007). Parental marital transitions and assistance between generations: A within-family longitudinal analysis. *Advances in Life Course Research, 12,* 221–242.

Dean, A., Matt, G. E., & Wood, P. (1992). The effects of widowhood on social support from significant others. *Journal of Community Psychology, 20,* 309–325.

Doronfino, L.K.M., & Kellet, K. (2006). Filial responsibility and transitions involved: A qualitative exploration of caregiving daughters and frail mothers. *Journal of Adult Development, 13*(3–4), 158–167.

Dressel, P. L., & Barnhill, S. K. (1994). Reframing gerontological thought and practice: The case of grandmothers with daughters in prison. *The Gerontologist, 34,* 685–691.

Dykstra, P. A. (1997). The effects of divorce on intergenerational exchanges in families. *Netherlands Journal of Social Sciences, 33,* 77–93.

Eckstein, D. (2000). Empirical studies indicating significant birth-order-related personality differences. *Journal of Individual Psychology, 56,* 481–494.

Ferraro, K. F. (1984). Widowhood and social participation in later life. *Research on Aging, 6,* 451–468.

Fingerman, K. L., & Bermann, E. (2000). Applications of family systems theory to the study of adulthood. *International Journal of Aging and Human Development, 51,* 5–29.

Fingerman, K. L., Hay, E. L., & Birditt, K. S. (2004). The best of ties, the worst of ties: Close, problematic, and ambivalent social relationships. *Journal of Marriage and Family, 66,* 792–808.

Fingerman, K. L., Miller, L. M., Birditt, K. S., & Zarit, S. (2009). Giving to the good and the needy: Parental support of grown children. *Journal of Marriage and Family, 71,* 1220–1233.

Fingerman, K. L., Pitzer, L., Lefkowitz. E. S., Birditt, K. S., & Mroczek, D. (2008). Ambivalent relationship qualities between adults and their parents: Implications for both parties' well-being. *Journal of Gerontology: Psychological Sciences, 63B,* P362–P371.

Fischer, L. R. (1983). Mothers and mothers-in-law. *Journal of Marriage and Family, 45,* 187–192.

Fleck, C. (2009). All under one roof. *AARP Bulletin, 50,* 24–25.

Glaser, K., Tomassini, C., & Stuchbury, R. (2008). Differences over time in the relationship between partnership disruptions and support in early old age in Britain. *Journals of Gerontology Series B: Psychological Sciences and Social Sciences, 63B,* S359–S368.

Glick, J.E., & van Hook, J. (2002). Parents' coresidence with adult children: Can immigration explain racial and ethnic variation? *Journal of Marriage and Family, 64,* 240–253.

Greenfield, E. A., & Marks, N. F. (2006). Linked lives: Adult children's problems and their parents' psychological and relational well-being. *Journal of Marriage and Family, 68,* 442–454.

Ha, J. H. (2008). Changes in support from confidants, children, and friends following widowhood. *Journal of Marriage and Family, 70,* 306–318.

Ha, J. H., & Carr, D. (2005). The effect of parent-child geographic proximity on widowed parents' psychological adjustment and social integration. *Research on Aging, 27,* 578–610.

Ha, J. H., Carr, D., Utz, R. L., & Nesse, R. (2006). Older adults' perceptions of intergenerational support after widowhood: How do men and women differ? *Journal of Family Issues, 27,* 3–30.

Ha, J. H., & Ingersoll-Dayton, B. (2008). The effect of widowhood on intergenerational ambivalence. *Journals of Gerontology Series B: Psychological Sciences and Social Sciences, 63B*, S49–S58.

Hagestad, G. O. (1987). Able elderly in the family contact: Changes, chances, and challenges. *The Gerontologist, 27*, 417–428.

Hamon, R. R. (1995). Parents as resources when adult children divorce. *Journal of Divorce and Remarriage, 23*, 171–184.

Hertwig, R., Davis, J. N., & Sulloway, F. J. (2002). Parental investment: How an equity motive can produce inequality. *Psychological Bulletin, 128*, 728–745.

Herzog, A.R., House, J.S., & Morgan, J.N. (1991). Relation of work and retirement to health and well-being in older age. *Psychology and Aging, 6*, 201–211.

Hill, R. B. (2003). *The strengths of black families* (2nd ed). Lanham, MD: University Press of America.

Hogan, D. P., Eggebeen, D. J., & Clogg, C. C. (1993). The structure of intergenerational exchanges in American families. *American Journal of Sociology, 98*, 1428–1458.

Homans, G. C. (1950). *Social behavior: Its elementary forms*. New York: Harcourt Brace Jovanovich.

Horowitz, A. (1985). Sons and daughters as caregivers to older parents: Differences in role performance and consequences. *The Gerontologist, 25*, 612–617.

House, J. S. (1989). Social structure and interpersonal relations: A discussion of Alice Rossi's chapter. In K. W. Schaie & C. Schooler (Eds.), *Social structure and aging: Psychological processes* (pp. 237–243). Hillsdale, NJ: Erlbaum.

Ikkink, K. K., van Tilburg, T., & Knipscher, K.C.P.M. (1999). Perceived instrumental support exchanges in relationships between elderly parents and their adult children: Normative and structural explanations. *Journal of Marriage and the Family, 61*, 831–844.

Ingersoll-Dayton, B., Starrels, M. E., & Dowler, D. (1996). Caregiving for parents and parents-in-law: Is gender important? *The Gerontologist, 36*, 483–491.

Jayakody, R. (1998). Race differences in intergenerational financial assistance: The needs of children and the resources of parents. *Journal of Family Issues, 19*, 508–533.

Jayakody, R., Chatters, L. M., & Taylor, R. J. (1993). Family support to single and married African American mothers: The provision of financial, emotional and child care assistance. *Journal of Marriage and Family, 55*, 261–276.

Jenkins, J. M., Rasbash, J., & O'Connor, T.G. (2003). The role of the shared family context in differential parenting. *Developmental Psychology, 39*, 99–113.

Kalmijn, M. (2007). Gender differences in the effects of divorce, widowhood and remarriage on intergenerational support: Does marriage protect fathers? *Social Forces, 85*, 1079–1104.

Kamo, Y. (2000). 'He said, she said': Assessing discrepancies in husbands' and wives' reports on the division of household labor. *Social Science Research, 29*, 459–476.

Kaufman, G., & Uhlenberg, P. (1998). Effects of life course transitions on the quality of relationships between adult children and their parents. *Journal of Marriage and Family, 60*, 924–938.

Kim, H. K., & McKenry, P. C. (1998). Social networks and support: A comparison of African Americans, Asian Americans, Caucasians, and Hispanics. *Journal of Comparative Family Studies, 29*, 313–336.

Kim, J. E., & Moen, P. (2001). Is retirement good or bad for subjective well-being? *Current Directions in Psychological Science, 10*, 83–86.

Kim, J. E., & Moen, P. (2002). Retirement transitions, gender, and psychological well-being: A life-course, ecological model. *Journal of Gerontology: Psychological Sciences, 57*, P212–P222.

Knight, D. K., & Simpson, D. (1996). Influences of family and friends on client progress during drug abuse treatment. *Journal of Substance Abuse, 9*, 417–429.

Kramer, B. J. (1997). Gain in the caregiving experience: Where are we? *The Gerontologist, 37*, 218–232.

Lachs, M. S., & Pillemer, K. (2004). Elder abuse. *The Lancet, 364*, 1263–1272.

Laditka, J. N., & Laditka, S. B. (2001). Adult children helping older parents: Variations in the likelihood and hours by gender, race, and family role. *Research on Aging, 23*, 429–456.

Lawton, L., Silverstein, M., & Bengtson, V. L. (1994a). Affection, social contact, and geographic distance between adult children and their parents. *Journal of Marriage and the Family, 56*, 57–68.

Lawton, L., Silverstein, M., & Bengtson, V. L. (1994b). Solidarity between generations in families. In V.L. Bengtson and R.A. Harootyan (Eds.), *Intergenerational linkages: Hidden connections in American society* (pp. 19–42). New York: Springer Publishing.

Lazarsfeld, P. F., & Merton, R. K. (1954). Friendship as a social process: A substantive and methodological analysis. In M. Berger et al. (Eds.), *Freedom and control in modern society* (pp. 18–66). New York: Litton.

Lee, G. R., Dwyer, J. W., & Coward, R. T. (1993). Gender differences in parent care: Demographic factors and same-gender preferences. *Journals of Gerontology: Social Sciences, 48*, S9–S16.

Lee, Y.J., & Aytac, I.A. (1998). Intergenerational financial support among whites, African Americans, and Latinos. *Journal of Marriage and the Family, 60*, 426–441.

Lin, I. F. (2008). Consequences of parental divorce for adult children's support of their frail parents. *Journal of Marriage and Family, 70*, 113–128.

Litvin, S. J., Albert, S. M., Brody, E. M., & Hoffman, C. (1995). Marital status, competing demands, and role priorities of parent-caring daughters. *Journal of Applied Gerontology, 14*, 372–390.

Lopata, H. Z. (1979). *Woman as widows: Support systems*. New York: Elsevier.

Lowenthal, M. F., Thurnher, M., & Chiriboga, D. (1975). *Four stages of life*. San Francisco: Jossey-Bass.

Lubben, J. E., & Becerra, R. M. (1987). Social support among black, Mexican, and Chinese elderly. In D. E. Gelfand & C. M. Barresi (Eds.), *Ethnic dimensions of aging* (pp. 130–144). New York: Springer Publishing.

Lüscher, K., & Pillemer, K. (1998). Intergenerational ambivalence: A new approach to the study of parent-child relations in later-life. *Journal of Marriage and Family, 60*, 413–425.

Lye, D. N. (1996). Adult child-parent relationships. *Annual Review of Sociology, 22,* 79–102.

Marshall, V., Clarke, P., & Ballantyne, P. (2001). Instability in the retirement transition: Effects on health and well-being. *Research on Aging, 23,* 379–409.

McCallum, J. (1986). Retirement and widowhood transitions. In H. L Kendig (Ed.), *Ageing and families* (pp. 129–148). Sydney: Allen & Unwin.

Merrill, D. M. (2007). *Mothers-in-law and daughters-in-law: Understanding the relationship and what makes them friends or foe.* Westport, CT: Praeger Publishers.

Miller, R. B., Bengtson, V. L., & Richards, L. (1987, Aug). *Patterns and predictors of parent-child relationships in aging families.* Paper presented at the Annual Meeting of the American Sociological Association, Chicago.

Moen, P., Fields, V., Quick, H. E., & Hofmeister, H. (2000). A life-course approach to retirement and social integration. In K. Pillemer, P. Moen, E. Wethington, & N. Glasgow (Eds.), *Social integration in the second half of life* (pp. 75–104). Baltimore, MD: Johns Hopkins University Press.

Moen, P., Kim, J. E., & Hofmeister, H. (2001). Couples' work/retirement transitions, gender, and marital quality. *Social Psychology Quarterly, 64,* 55–71.

Mutchler, J. E., Burr, J. A., & Caro, F. G. (2003). From paid worker to volunteer: Leaving the paid workforce and volunteering in later life. *Social Forces, 81,* 1267–1293.

Myles, J. (1989). *Old age in the welfare state.* Lawrence: University Press of Kansas.

Newman, K. S. (1988). *Falling from grace: The experience of downward mobility in the American middle class.* New York: Free Press.

Parrott, T. M., & Bengtson, V. L. (1999). The effects of intergenerational affection, normative expectations, and family conflict on contemporary exchanges of help and support. *Research on Aging, 21,* 73–105.

Paulhus, D. L., Trapnell, P. D., & Chen, D. (1999). Birth order effects on personality and achievements within families. *Psychological Sciences, 10,* 482–488.

Pavalko, E. K. (2011). Caregiving and the life course. In R. Settersten & J. Angel (Eds.), *Handbook of sociology of aging* (pp. 603–616). New York: Springer Publishing.

Pavalko, E. K., & Artis, J. E. (1997). Women's caregiving and paid work: Causal relationships in late midlife. *Journals of Gerontology: Social Sciences, 52B,* S170–S179.

Pearlin, L. I. (1989). The sociological study of stress. *Journal of Health and Social Behavior, 30,* 241–256.

Pearlin, L. I., Lieberman, M. A., Menaghan, E. G., & Mullen, J. T. (1981). The stress process. *Journal of Health and Social Behavior, 22,* 337–356.

Peek, M. K., Coward, R. T., & Peek, C. W. (2000). Race, aging, and care: Can differences in family and household in informal care? *Research on Aging, 22,* 117–142.

Pezzin, L. E., & Schone, B. S. (1999). Parental marital disruption and intergenerational transfers: An analysis of lone elderly parents and their children. *Demography, 36,* 287–297.

Pillemer, K., & Prescott, D. (1989). Psychological effects of elder abuse: A research note. *Journal of Elder Abuse and Neglect, 1,* 65–73.

Pillemer, K., & Suitor, J. J. (1988). Elder abuse. In V. van Hasselt, H. Bellack, R. Morrison, & M. Hersen (Eds.), *Handbook of family violence* (pp. 247–270). New York: Plenum Press.

Pillemer, K., & Suitor, J. J. (1991). "Will I ever escape my child's problems?" Effects of adult children's problems on elderly parents. *Journal of Marriage and Family, 53*, 585–594.

Pillemer, K., & Suitor, J. J. (2005). Ambivalence in intergenerational relations over the life-course. In M. Silverstein (Ed.), *Annual review of gerontology and geriatrics, volume 2: Intergenerational relations across time and place* (pp. 3–28). New York: Springer Publishing.

Pillemer, K., & Suitor, J. J. (2008). Collective ambivalence: Considering new approaches to the complexity of intergenerational relations. *Journals of Gerontology: Social Sciences, 63*, 394–396.

Pillemer, K., Suitor, J. J., Mock, S., Sabir, M., & Sechrist, J. (2007). Capturing the complexity of intergenerational relations: Exploring ambivalence within later-life families. *Journal of Social Issues, 63*, 775–791.

Pillemer, K., Suitor, J. J., Pardo, S., & Henderson, C., Jr. (2010). Mothers' differentiation and depressive symptoms among adult children. *Journal of Marriage and Family, 72*, 333–345.

Pinquart, M. (2003). Loneliness in married, widowed, divorced, and never-married older adults. *Journal of Social and Personal Relationships, 20*, 31–53.

Pinquart, M., & Sörensen, S. (2004). Associations of caregiver stressors and uplifts with subjective well-being and depressive mood: A meta-analytic comparison. *Aging and Mental Health, 8*, 438–449.

Pinquart, M., & Sörensen, S. (2007). Correlates of physical health of informal caregivers: A meta-analysis. *Journals of Gerontology: Series B Psychological Sciences and Social Sciences, 62*, P126–P137.

Plikuhn, M., Suitor, J. J., & Powers, R. S. (2009). *Mother's support for education: Intergenerational socialization after daughters' return to school.* Paper presented at the Annual Meeting of the Gerontological Society of America, Atlanta, Georgia.

Powers, R., Suitor, J., Guerra, S., Shackelford, M., Mecom, D., & Gusman, K. (2003). Regional differences in gender-role attitudes: Variations by gender and race. *Gender Issues, 21*, 40–54.

Pudrovska, T. (2009). Parenthood, stress, and mental health in late midlife and early old age. *International Journal of Aging and Human Development, 68*, 127–147.

Ragan, P. K. (1979). *Aging parents.* Los Angeles: University of Southern California Press.

Rastogi, M., & Wampler, K. S. (1999). Adult daughters' perceptions of the mother-daughter relationship: A cross-cultural comparison. *Family Relations, 48*, 327–336.

Reitzes, D. C., & Mutran, E. J. (2004). The transition to retirement: Stages and factors that influence retirement adjustment. *International Journal of Aging and Human Development, 59*, 63–84.

Reitzes, V. L., Mutran, E. J., & Fernandez, M. E. (1996). Does retirement hurt well-being? Factors influencing self-esteem and depression among retires and workers. *The Gerontologist, 36*, 649–656.

Remnet, V. L. (1987). How adult children respond to role transitions in the lives of their aging parents. *Educational Gerontology, 13*, 341–355.

Roan, C. L., & Raley, R. K. (1996). Intergenerational coresidence and contact: A longitudinal analysis of adult children's response to their mother's widowhood. *Journal of Marriage and Family, 58*, 708–717.

Rogers, M. L., & Hogan, D. P. (2003). Family life with children with disabilities: The key role of rehabilitation. *Journal of Marriage and Family, 65*, 818–833.

Rossi, A. S., & Rossi, P. H. (1990). *Of human bonding: Parent-child relations across the life course.* New York: Aldine de Gruyter.

Ryff, C. D., Lee, Y. H., Essex, M. J., & Schmutte, P. S. (1994). My children and me—Midlife evaluations of grown children and of self. *Psychology and Aging, 9*, 195–205.

Ryff, C. D., Schmutte, P. S., & Lee, H. Y. (1996). How children turn out: Implications for parental self-evaluation. In C. D. Ryff & M. Mailick (Eds.), *The parental experience in midlife* (pp. 383–422). Chicago: University of Chicago Press.

Salmon, C. A. (1999). On the impact of sex and birth order on contact with kin. *Human Nature, 10*, 183–197.

Sarkisian, N., & Gerstel, N. (2007). Race, class, and extended family involvement. *Family Focus, 52*(1), 14–15.

Sarkisian, N., & Gerstel, N. (2008). Till marriage do us part: Adult children's relationships with their parents. *Journal of Marriage and Family, 70*(2), 360–376.

Schulz, R., Alison, T., & O'Brien, A. T. (1995). Psychiatric and physical morbidity effects of dementia care. *The Gerontologist, 35*(6), 771.

Schulz, R., Visintainer, P., & Williamson, C. M. (1990). Psychiatric and physical morbidity effects of caregiving. *Journals of Gerontology: Psychological Sciences, 45*, P181–191.

Scott, M. E., Booth, A., King, V., & Johnson, D. R. (2007). Post divorce father-adolescent closeness. *Journal of Marriage and Family, 69*, 1194–1209.

Seltzer, J. A., & Bianchi, S. M. (1998). Children's contact with absent parents. *Journal of Marriage and the Family, 50*, 663–677.

Seltzer, M. M., Greenberg, J. S., Krauss, M. W., & Hong, J. (1997). Predictors and outcomes of the end of coresident caregiving in aging families of adults with mental retardation or mental illness. *Family Relations, 46*, 13–22.

Seltzer, M. M., Greenberg, J. S., Orsmond, G. I., Lounds, J., & Smith, M. J. (2008). Unanticipated lives: Inter- and intra-generational relationships in families with children with disabilities. In A. Booth, A. Crouter, S. Bianchi, & J. A. Seltzer (Eds.), *Intergenerational caregiving* (pp. 233–242). Washington, DC: Urban Institute Press.

Shapiro, A. (2003). Later-life divorce and parent-adult child contact and proximity: A longitudinal analysis. *Journal of Family Issues, 24*, 264–285.

Shapiro, A. (2004). Revisiting the generation gap: Exploring the relationships of parent/adult-child dyads. *International Journal of Aging and Human Development, 58*(2), 127–146.

Shuey, K., & Hardy, M. A. (2003). Assistance to aging parents and parents-in-law: Does lineage affect family allocation decisions? *Journal of Marriage and Family, 65*, 418–431.

Silverstein, M., & Bengtson, V. L. (1994). Does intergenerational social support influence the psychological well-being of older parents? The contingencies of declining health and widowhood. *Social Science & Medicine, 38,* 943–957.

Silverstein, M., Bengtson, V. L., & Lawton, L. (1997). Intergenerational solidarity and the structure of adult child-parent relationships in American families. *American Journal of Sociology, 103,* 429–460.

Silverstein, M., Conroy, S. J., Wang, H., Giarrusso, R., & Bengtson, V. L. (2002). Reciprocity in parent-child relations over the adult life course. *Journals of Gerontology: Social Sciences, 57B,* S3–S13.

Silverstein, M., Gans, D., & Yang, F. M. (2006). Intergenerational support to aging parents. *Journal of Family Issues, 27,* 1068–1084.

Silverstein, M., Parrott, T. M., & Bengtson, V. L. (1995). Factors that predispose middle-aged sons and daughters to provide social support to older parents. *Journal of Marriage and Family, 57,* 465–475.

Spitze, G., & Logan, J. (1990). More evidence on women (and men) in the middle. *Research on Aging, 12,* 182–198.

Spitze, G., Logan, J., Deane, G., & Zerger, S. (1994). Adult children's divorce and intergenerational relationships. *Journal of Marriage and the Family, 56,* 279–293.

Spitze, G., & Miner, S. (1992). Gender differences in adult child contact among black elderly parents. *The Gerontologist, 32,* 213–218.

Sprey, J. S., & Matthews, S. H. (1982). Contemporary grandparenthood: A systematic transition. *Annals of the American Academy of Political and Social Sciences, 464,* 91–103.

Stack, C. (1974). *All our kin: Strategies for survival in black communities.* New York: Harper and Row.

Steinberg, L. (1988). Reciprocal relations between parent-child and pubertal maturation. *Developmental Psychology, 24,* 122–128.

Stevens, M. A. P., & Townsend, A. L. (1997). Stress of parent care: Positive and negative effects of women's other roles. *Psychology and Aging, 12,* 376–386.

Stuifbergen, M. C., van Delden, J. J. M., & Dykstra, P. A. (2008). The implications of today's family structures for support giving to older parents. *Aging and Society, 28,* 413–434.

Suitor, J. J. (1984). *Family members' support for married mothers' return to school.* Paper presented at the Annual Meeting of the New York State Council on Family Relations, Ithaca.

Suitor, J. J. (1987). Mother-daughter relations when married daughters return to school: Effects of status similarity. *Journal of Marriage and Family, 49,* 435–444.

Suitor, J. J., & Pillemer, K. (1987). The presence of adult children: A source of stress for elderly couples' marriages? *Journal of Marriage and Family, 49,* 717–725.

Suitor, J. J., & Pillemer, K. (1988). Explaining conflict when adult children and their elderly parents live together. *Journal of Marriage and Family, 50,* 1037–1047.

Suitor, J. J., & Pillemer, K. (1990). Transition to the status of family caregiver: A new framework for studying social support and well-being. In S. M. Stahl (Ed.), *The legacy of longevity: Health, illness, and long-term care in later life* (pp. 310–320). Beverly Hills: Sage.

Suitor, J. J., & Pillemer, K. (1992). Status transitions and marital satisfaction: The case of adult children caring for elderly parents suffering from dementia. *Journal of Social and Personal Relationships, 9,* 549–562.

Suitor, J. J. & Pillemer, K. (1994). Family caregiving and marital satisfaction: Findings from a one-year panel study of women caring for parents with dementia. *Journal of Marriage and Family, 56,* 681–690.

Suitor, J. J., & Pillemer, K. (2006). Choosing daughters: Exploring why mothers favor adult daughters over sons. *Sociological Perspectives, 49,* 139–160.

Suitor, J. J., & Pillemer, K. (2007). Mothers' favoritism in later life—The role of children's birth order. *Research on Aging, 29,* 32–55.

Suitor, J. J., & Pillemer, K. (in press). Differences in mothers' and fathers' parental favoritism in later-life: A within-family analysis. In M. Silverstein & R. Giarrusso (Eds.), *From generation to generation: Continuity and discontinuity in aging families.* Baltimore, MD: Johns Hopkins University Press.

Suitor, J. J., Pillemer, K., & Keeton, S. (1995). When experience counts: The effects of experiential and structural similarity on patterns of support and interpersonal stress. *Social Forces, 73,* 1573–1588.

Suitor, J. J., Pillemer, K., & Sechrist, J. (2006). Within-family differences in mothers' support to adult children. *Journals of Gerontology Series B: Psychological Sciences and Social Sciences, 61B,* S10–S17.

Suitor, J. J., Sechrist, J., Gilligan, M., & Pillemer, K. (2011). Intergenerational relations in later life families: A three decade review. In R. Settersten & J. Angel (Eds.), *Handbook of sociology of aging* (pp. 161–178). New York: Springer Publishing.

Suitor, J. J., Sechrist, J., & Pillemer, K. (2007). Within-family differences in mothers' support to adult children in black and white families. *Research on Aging, 29,* 410–435.

Suitor, J. J., Sechrist, J., Plikuhn, M., Pardo, S. T., Gilligan, M., & Pillemer, K. (2009). The role of perceived maternal favoritism in sibling relations in midlife. *Journal of Marriage and Family, 71,* 1026–1038.

Suitor, J. J., Sechrist, J., Steinhour, M., & Pillemer, K. (2006). "I'm sure she chose me!" Consistency in intergenerational reports of mothers' favoritism in later-life families. *Family Relations, 55,* 526–538.

Sulloway, F. J. (1996). *Born to rebel: Family conflict and radical genius.* New York: Pantheon.

Swartz, T. T. (2009). Intergenerational family relations in adulthood: Patterns, variations, and implications in the contemporary United States. *Annual Review of Sociology, 35,* 191–212.

Szinovacz, M. E., & Davey, A. (2001). Retirement effects of parent-adult child contacts. *The Gerontologist, 41,* 191–200.

Szinovacz, M. E., & Davey, A. (2007). Changes in adult child caregiver networks. *The Gerontologist, 47,* 280–295.

Taylor, R. J. (1986). Receipt of support from family among black Americans: Demographic and familial differences. *Journal of Marriage and the Family, 48,* 67–77.

Taylor, R. J., & Chatters, L. M. (1991). Extended family networks of older black adults. *Journals of Gerontology: Social Sciences, 46,* 210–217.

Townsend, A. L., & Franks, M. M. (1995). Binding ties: Closeness and conflict in adult children's caregiving relationships. *Psychology and Aging, 10*, 343–351.

Troll, L. E. (1971). A decade review. *Journal of Marriage and Family, 33*, 263–290.

Umberson, D. (1992). Relationships between adult children and their parents: Psychological consequences for both generations. *Journal of Marriage and the Family, 54*, 664–674.

U.S. Bureau of the Census. (2010). *2010 Census*. Washington, DC: Government Printing Office.

Walker, A. J., Pratt, C. C., & Oppy, N. C. (1992). Perceived reciprocity in family caregiving. *Family Relations, 41*, 82–85.

Walker, A. J., Shin, H., & Bird, D. N. (1990). Perceptions of relationship change and caregiver satisfaction. *Family Relations, 39*, 147–152.

Wakabayashi, C., & Donato, K. M. (2005). Does caregiving increase poverty among women in later life? Evidence from the health and retirement survey. *Journal of Health and Social Behavior, 47*, 258–274.

White, L., & Peterson, D. (1995). The retreat from marriage: Its effect on unmarried children's exchange with parents. *Journal of Marriage and Family, 57*, 428.

Willson, A. E., Shuey, K. M., Elder, G. H., Jr., & Wickrama, K.,A.,S. (2006). Ambivalence in mother-adult child relations: A dyadic analysis. *Social Psychology Quarterly, 69*, 235–252.

Wolf, R. S. (2001). Understanding elder abuse and neglect. In A. J. Walker and M. Manoogian-O'Dell (Eds.), *Families in later life: Connections and transitions* (pp. 258–261). Thousand Oaks, CA: Pine Forge Press.

Wong, R., Kitayama, K. E., & Soldo, B. J. (1999). Ethnic differences in time transfers from adult children to elderly parents. *Research on Aging, 21*, 144–175.

8

Grandparenthood: Grandchild and Great-Grandchild Relationships

Bert Hayslip Jr. and Kyle S. Page

CONCEPTUAL FRAMEWORK

This chapter discusses grandparents and their relationships to their grandchildren and great-grandchildren. In doing so, we will for the most part concentrate on literature published since the previous (1995) *Handbook* chapter on grandparenting written by Joan Robertson. Within the framework of life span development as it applies to grandparenting (see Hayslip & Hicks Patrick, 2003), we emphasize the developmental and the cultural-historical aspects of grandparenthood, as well as both the normative and nonnormative aspects of grandparenting. An emphasis on each dimension of grandparenting is consistent with the life span perspective in describing and understanding the impact of life events on individuals in adulthood.

One of the perspectives that guides our discussion of grandparenting and great-grandparenting embeds grandparenting in the context of *cultural-historical change*. Such changes embrace the ecological-contextual model of Bronfenbrenner (2004), wherein the macrosystem (the cultural-historical context) influences grandparents and, by implication, grandparents' relationships to their (great-) grandchildren. In addition, grandparents help define the microsystem (the familial and immediate environment) and in some cases, the child's exosystem (e.g., extended familial influences).

The other perspective framing our discussion emphasizes *developmental life course change* (MacMillan & Copher, 2005), which stresses the changing family system. It centralizes the embeddedness of the grandparent in the larger context of a multigenerational family system, which itself changes as grandparents' and grandchildren's lives change (Hayslip & White, 2008). A developmental systemic framework is important because grandparents often not only serve as role models for their grandchildren and great-grandchildren, but also in many cases exert considerable influence on such children's lives in shaping their moral and vocational development over time.

HISTORICAL CHANGE AND GRANDPARENTING

Clearly, in a cultural-historical sense, families have changed over the past two decades, as evidenced by the growth of the aging population and the greater longevity that persons now enjoy and will continue to experience in the near future (Olshansky, Goldman, Zheng, & Rowe, 2009). These demographic realities suggest that the nature of grandparenthood will change in concert with the increasing numbers of persons living into their 80s and beyond. This increase in longevity, in concert with the flattening out of the birth rate in recent years (Statistical Abstract of the United States, 2008), will lead to increasing numbers of *verticalized* family structures (where the number of generations in a multigenerational family system is greater, and the number of persons within a generation is smaller) (Hagestad, 1988), increasing the likelihood of persons having grandchildren and great-grandchildren.

Future cohorts of grandparents will differ from their predecessors in several respects: today's grandparents are likely to live longer (and therefore be more likely to retain their roles as grandparents well into their 80s), be more highly educated, be in better health, have fewer grandchildren (decreasing competition between grandchildren for a grandparent's time), and be more likely to have retired (Uhlenberg, 2004, 2009; Uhlenberg & Kirby, 1998). Thus, grandparents will have more opportunities to make meaningful investments of time, effort, and resources in their grandchildren's lives, due to the greater longevity of and availability of programs and services for older adults (Uhlenberg, 2009). Children who are economically disadvantaged, have single parents, have grandparents who are in poorer health, and have many siblings may not realize these same advantages (Uhlenberg, 2009).

CULTURE AND GRANDPARENTING

Related to cultural change as a factor in understanding grandparenting is the influence of culture per se. Culture reflects internalized shared norms and mores as well as intergenerationally transmitted values (Cole, 1999). This perspective reflects views of grandparents as mentors for younger parents, as transmitters of cultural values and heritage, or as agents of socialization and influence for their grandchildren. Whether one's cultural or ethnic background uniquely defines grandparenting depends upon whether this role is a valued one. In this respect, Sandel, Cho, Miller, and Wang (2006) reported differences in the meaning of the grandparent role between Taiwanese and Euro American grandmothers, where the latter emphasized their roles as companions to their grandchildren and the former saw themselves as temporary caregivers, disciplining grandchildren when necessary.

Studying the cultural context in which grandparenting occurs also stresses race and ethnicity as influences on grandparenting, where some grandparents may be more involved with their grandchildren, and therefore have a greater opportunity to serve as the family historian or living ancestor who can teach the grandchild ethnic traditions, culture, and history (Strom, Carter, & Schmidt, 2004; Szinovacz, 1998). For example, African American grandparents have almost twice the degree of involvement with their grandchildren than non-Hispanic whites (see Szinovacz, 1998), though the greater likelihood of coresidence among the former likely influences the roles that such grandparents may play in their grandchildren's lives, making it more likely that they can hand down family traditions to their grandchildren. Likewise, Mexican Americans have larger, more multigenerational families, report higher satisfaction from relating to their grandchildren, and have more intergenerational contact (Toledo, Hayslip, Emick, Toledo, & Henderson, 2000). Underscoring cultural influences on grandparenting, among Asian Indian immigrant grandchildren, having more contact with their grandparents, being more acculturated, and assigning more importance to their grandparents' influence on them all contributed to better relationship quality, which increases grandparents' likely influence in their lives (Saxena & Sanders, 2009).

The literature on culture and grandparenting is quite limited and, for the most part, dated (see Smith & Drew, 2002). However, central to understanding the influence of culture on grandparental meaning is whether familism is a valued attribute in persons' lives, the degree of intergenerational support, the extent of acculturation and immigration status, whether the grandparent speaks English, and the coresidence of grandparents and grandchildren. All of these factors influence the grandparent's relationship to the grandchild, the nature of help and support that is provided to the latter, and the socialization of the grandchild into the dominant culture. It is important to point out that though there is little empirical work addressing the influence of grandchildren on their grandparents in the context of culture, it is likely that at least some grandchildren might help socialize grandparents in terms of new matters in contemporary culture (e.g., educating them about technology) or make them aware of the challenges they face as younger persons (e.g., violence in the schools, drug use, sexuality).

DEVELOPMENTAL ASPECTS OF GRANDPARENTING

Whereas the transition of parent to grandparent is commonplace and often begins in middle age, grandparent-grandchild ties are stronger when the ties between parent and grandparent are strong (Mueller & Elder, 2003).

In some cases, relationships between older adults and their children-in-law might be even more important as influences on grandparent-grandchild relationship quality than relationships with their own children (Fingerman, 2004). Often, the adult child's needs for instrumental and emotional support are central and are what activate the grandparent support system in times of family stress, where maternal grandmothers are the most likely to be involved in this respect (Hayslip & White, 2008).

When all is well with their adult children and their relationships with their own children, grandparents typically do not interfere and do not play an authoritative role with their grandchildren (Connidis, 2010; Smith & Drew, 2002). This norm of noninterference may, however, put grandparents in a double bind, in that they are caught between the expectation that they be available to help their children with a child and the clear limits set by their adult children regarding matters of childrearing (Mason, May, & Clarke, 2007). Nevertheless, grandparents may provide many types of support to a single, divorced, widowed, or never-married child. For example, how grandparents respond to a grandchild's disability or illness affects the ability of parents to adjust; in such cases, previously established relationships and the perception by family members that they are "that kind of family," one in which members help one another in times of need, are quite important (Mirfin-Veitch, Bray, & Watson, 1997). Although intergenerational support from family members in times of crisis is common, it may not be a universal experience for remote or distant grandparents. Such grandparents may not be helpful and indeed may cause additional stress to parents in time of need in bringing up longstanding family conflicts or insisting on being involved in decision-making (Silverstein & Bengtson, 1997).

A developmental life course perspective suggests that grandparent-grandchild relationships are systemic in nature. One's influence on the other is dynamic and bidirectional, and often mediated by the changing nature of the grandparent's relationship to the grandchild's parent (see Connidis, 2010), other family members' expectations of a grandparent's behavior, as well as the health of the grandparent. In this context, the grandparent-grandchild relationship is likely to be different when grandchildren are little and grandparents are in good health versus when grandchildren are adults and grandparents are older or frail (Boon, Shaw, & McKinnon, 2008). In this respect, Johnson and Barer (1997) noted that despite their attachment to very old grandparents (those over age 85), grandchildren's instrumental support to them is diminished.

If the grandparent's health deteriorates significantly or the grandparent is diagnosed with dementia, the likelihood of that person's eventual death becomes a loss with which the adult child and the grandchild must cope. Grandparents with dementia present many socioemotional difficulties for grandchildren (Howard & Jerome, 2001), and demented grandparents and their grandchildren attribute less attitudinal and behavioral importance, but no less symbolic and emotional salience, to the grandparent role as compared to nondemented grandparents and their grandchildren (Werner & Lowenstein, 2001). Yet, grandchildren may learn new ways of coping, develop patience, and gain insight about the meaning of life in caring for a physically ill or cognitively impaired grandparent (Celdran, Tirado, & Villar, 2009; Fruhauf & Orel, 2008).

As grandparents age, many are less likely to be involved in active, physical interactions with grandchildren, most likely due to the former's declining health. Health can also influence one's emotional readiness to be a grandparent. Fujiwara and Lee (2008) found that grandparents' mental health was affected by the extent to which their grandchildren provided instrumental support in view of the grandparent's declining physical health. The need for such support was especially evident for grandfathers, who were often older and likely had experienced more chronic health difficulties than grandmothers, who tended to be younger. Generally speaking, with increasing age however, grandparents are available to provide more emotional support and advice to grandchildren than in the past, and sometimes support their grandchildren financially (Connidis, 2010).

Whereas grandparents' impact does not necessarily diminish as grandchildren reach adulthood, recent literature has largely ignored this aspect of grandparent-grandchild relationships (however, see Attar-Schwartz, Tan, & Buchanan, 2009; Hayslip, Glover et al., 2009). Indeed, with few exceptions, most work to date has focused upon younger grandchildren. Adult grandchildren do, however, list knowing their grandparents and feeling close to them as important relationship qualities. They also expect grandparents to buffer parental relationships and be a role model and a financial advisor (see Robertson, 1995; Smith & Drew, 2002 for reviews). Whereas parents are perceived as mediators and indeed function as such regarding grandparent-grandchild relationships, to the extent that children and parents are close, the grandchild's relationship with the grandparent will also be so (Monserud, 2008).

Given that the cultural-historical and developmental life course frameworks interact, consistent with historical shifts in demographics, the salience of developmental changes in grandparent-grandchild relationships also changes. Simply put, being an older grandparent will take on new meaning as persons live longer. In this respect, King, Russell, and Elder (1998) noted that an ecologically relevant family systems approach, that is, defining the family in a cultural or historical context (Mueller & Elder, 2003), is necessary to understanding grandparents' family relationships. Thus, views about families in later life are historically bound. For example, the odds of living with a grandparent will likely co-vary with economic crises (e.g., the Great Depression) because an economic downturn increases the incidence of coresidence with a grandparent. Likewise, extended dependence on older persons in the family in the event of joblessness increases the likelihood of adult children and the grandchildren coresiding with grandparents (Generations United, 2009). In addition, family systems have now become more verticalized than in the past (see Hagestad, 1988) in response to the slowing of the birth rate and greater longevity, resulting in greater caregiving burden experienced by younger generations. Thus, different cohorts of grandparents may hold different attitudes toward the grandparent role, born of historical influences on multigenerational family systems. How historical change will affect future generations of grandparents and grandchildren has yet to be explored, though the analysis by Uhlenberg (2009) suggests that future generations of grandchildren are likely to be positively influenced by grandparents who are healthier and more highly educated than their predecessors.

THE MEANING ATTRIBUTED TO AND STYLES OF GRANDPARENTING

Having examined the historical and developmental frameworks defining this chapter, we now discuss grandparental *meaning* and the behavioral manifestations of this meaning (i.e., grandparenting *styles*), both of which are central to grandparents' well-being, their identity as grandparents, and whether they find their roles satisfying or not. Both meaning and its manifestation in behavior also influence the frequency and nature of adults' contact with grandchildren and great-grandchildren. As grandparent-grandchild relationships must be viewed systemically, the meaning and consequently the style one adopts in relating to grandchildren must be understood at the following interdependent levels (see Connidis, 2010; Kulik, 2007): (a) intrapsychically, how grandparents emotionally process their role-specific experiences; (b) socially, via expectations for role performance by family or society; and (c) historically, because of the shifting demographics of grandparents and grandchildren. In this respect, King et al. (1998) suggested that the degree of interdependence of generations within the family and the nature and patterning of life course events for each member of the family affect the transition to grandparenthood as well as the enactment of the role once persons have become grandparents. In addition, the meaning attributed to grandparenting reflects the substantial variability among grandparents along a number of dimensions (i.e., race, ethnicity, SES, religion, recency of immigration, etc.). Grandparents also vary in age and health and may still be raising children at home when they first become grandparents (Paul, 2002). This variability contributes to the *tenuousness* of the grandparent role as defined by grandparents themselves, wherein grandparents frequently have no clear criteria for what constitutes appropriate behavior (Rosow, 1985). For this reason, grandparenting and the meaning attributed to it are largely individual experiences, despite the normative nature of grandparenthood.

Grandparental meaning must also be understood in a developmental context in terms of the life course trajectories of each generation, which are superimposed upon one another (Combrinck-Graham, 1985). In the context of family dynamics, such developmental influences reflect the grandparent's reciprocal relationships with a spouse, adult children, grandchildren, and siblings (Williams & Harwood, 2004).

The meaning one assigns to being a grandparent must be actively constructed, evolving out of interactions with adult children, grandchildren, and other grandparents. As persons can anticipate the role of grandparent, the process of constructing a meaning and creating a satisfying style of grandparenting may begin long before the birth of the grandchild, wherein grandparents in varying degrees seem to be able to accurately anticipate the rewards of grandparenting. In this respect, maternal grandparents are more satisfied with their grandparent role than they anticipated earlier (prior to the child's birth), versus paternal grandparents (Somary & Stricker, 1998).

Key to understanding the meaning persons assign to grandparenting is the *centrality* of the role; grandparents clearly vary in this respect. The centrality of grandparenthood reflects dimensions that define it, dimensions that are symbolic (reflecting the meaning one assigns to it), attitudinal (beliefs about one's activities as a grandparent), emotional (one's feelings about being a grandparent), and, relevant to grandparental style, behavioral (activities involved in one's interactions with grandchildren as well as their quality). These aspects of the centrality of the grandparent role need not complement one another; grandparents may or may not centralize the role or behave in ways that are expected of them by others.

More recent cohorts of grandparents may construct a role, which is either meaningful or not in global terms (i.e., the grandparent role is or is not central to them), rather than thinking about their roles as grandparents in many ways (e.g., in terms of the opportunity to parent again, living on through one's grandchildren, being able to indulge a grandchild; see Hayslip, Henderson, & Shore, 2003). Indeed, grandparental meaning has historically been viewed as multidimensional in nature, as has grandparental style (see Connidis, 2010, and Szinovacz, 1998, for reviews). That the centrality of the role and one's satisfaction with it are important dimensions of grandparenting is supported by recent work highlighting the *process* by which women come to redefine their roles, that is, from wife and mother to caregiver (Montgomery, Rowe, & Kosloski, 2007). At present, virtually nothing is known about this aspect of grandparenting, wherein one's identity as a grandparent is likely acquired gradually, given the fact that the grandparent role is imposed upon persons by virtue of the birth of a grandchild. Moreover, what is known regarding this aspect of the grandparent role is limited to women.

Grandparenting meaning-style relationships likely vary over time and with one's unique life situation (e.g., one's health, how far away one lives from one's grandchildren), but there is virtually no longitudinal work to support this assertion empirically. Nor is there any guarantee that existing grandparental meaning or style typologies would apply to more recently born cohorts of grandparents, that grandchildren's perceptions of their grandparents would parallel the latter's self-defined meaning and style of grandparenting, or that one's memories of a grandparent might influence grandparental meaning and style later on in life. Given the idiosyncratic nature of grandparenting, each of these scenarios is possible. However, they do require empirical confirmation, incorporating both grandparent and grandchild perspectives.

NORMATIVE AND NONNORMATIVE ASPECTS OF GRANDPARENTING

We now discuss both normative and nonnormative forms and dimensions of grandparenting as well as great-grandparenting. For example, whereas most persons eventually become grandparents, emphasizing the normative aspects of the role, nonnormative aspects are caring for one's grandchild in the event of the death or incarceration of one's child, being a great-grandparent, or coping with the death of a grandchild—they do not apply to most grandparents. Both the normative and nonnormative forms of grandparenting can alter the quality of intergenerational connections as well as impact grandparent well-being and role satisfaction.

Normative Aspects of Grandparenting

Benefits for Grandparents and Grandchildren

Being a grandparent is often viewed as a developmental task of middle or late adulthood. Because people do not choose to be grandparents, becoming a grandparent is *countertransitional* (Hagestad, 1985); it depends upon the actions of others (i.e., one's son or daughter). Thus, it is not a role whose assumption individuals can control. Seventy-five percent of those born in 2000 can expect to have at least one grandparent still living when they reach age 30 (Uhlenberg & Kirby, 1998); nearly 70% of older adults are grandparents, and 60% of all grandparents have more than one grandchild. If persons younger than 50 who are grandparents are included, estimates approach 80% (American Association of Retired Persons [AARP], 2002). Most persons become grandparents in their late 40s, and this does not seem to vary by gender, race, or ethnicity (AARP, 2002).

The onset of the grandparenthood role can be either on time (between the ages of 40 and 60) or off time (before age 40 or after age 60). For off-timers, grandparenting may disrupt life or work plans, and such persons may fear that they may not live long enough to fully enjoy the fruits of a relationship with a grandchild, or that poor health may undermine the quality of their interactions with their grandchildren. Assuming that young adulthood itself becomes more elongated (Arnett, 2000), what, age-wise, is considered on time or off time will likely need to be redefined in the future. In addition, if couples delay having children, this delay will necessarily redefine the onset of grandparenthood as an off-time role.

In discussing the timing of grandparenthood, acknowledging the fact that grandparents themselves are quite heterogeneous is important, in that this variability mediates the impact of the role, depending upon the health of the grandparent, his or her financial resources, and the quality of the relationship with one's adult child or grandchild. Thus, the notion that grandparenting may or may not be normatively beneficial to grandparents and grandchildren must be tempered by the diversity (see above) among grandparents (Kornhaber, 1996; Kulik, 2007), reflecting the variety of factors influencing grandparent-grandchild contact (see Uhlenberg & Hammill, 1998) as well as variation in the quality of such relationships (e.g., loving and supportive versus neglectful and abusing). This diversity creates distinct subgroups of grandparents, who are, in varying degrees, close to their grandchildren or affected to a greater or lesser extent by ill health or the divorce or remarriage of their children (Kemp, 2007). Thus, values about and norms for interacting with children and grandchildren are likely to vary across subgroups of grandparents.

Normatively, grandparenting may have adaptive consequences for middle-aged and older persons. In this respect, Strom, Strom, and Collinsworth (1991) posited that grandparents underestimated their contribution to the socialization and guidance of their grandchildren. Whether grandparents feel they are important influences in the lives of their grandchildren thus influences how grandparents define their roles (as either central or peripheral to the children's and grandchildren's lives) and lays the groundwork for how (and if) they will aid in the grandchild's development as well as influence the family as a whole. In this respect, the responsibility for child discipline, financial assistance, patterns of visitation, giving advice to the parent, sharing religious faith, and supporting the parents in decision-making are salient dimensions of the grandparent role. An awareness of these dimensions may be useful for grandparents coping with a child's divorce or in meeting a step-grandchild after this adult child remarries.

Becoming a grandparent can help one compensate for other losses and help persons gain a new purpose in life. It can buffer fears about isolation, loneliness, dying, or simply not feeling valued as a person for many older adults. In this respect, Friedman, Hechter, and Kreager (2008) reported that grandparents who invested themselves more fully into the role reduced uncertainty about the end of life. Indeed, Fung, Siu, Choy, and McBride-Chang (2005) found that grandparents who felt they had less time to live and who were more aware of their mortality reported more positive grandparental meaning. Kaufman and Elder (2003) concluded that grandparents who found their roles satisfying saw more benefits in growing older and reported feeling younger. Thiele and Whelan (2006) have underscored the *generative* nature of grandparenting, reflecting the purposeful investment of oneself in the lives of one's grandchildren. Generative grandparents know that the "family theme" is being carried on by their grandchildren; they may even see characteristics of their parents in their grandchildren, even if contact with the latter is minimal. Thus, there are many potential advantages to those who centralize the role and who see themselves as *self-efficacious* grandparents (those who feel that they can exert a significant positive influence on the lives of their grandchildren) (King & Elder, 1998; Reitzes & Mutran, 2004a).

Reciprocally, grandchildren benefit from having grandparents when they recognize the positive impact grandparents have on their lives (Connidis, 2010; Hayslip, Shore, & Henderson, 2000). The work of McGuinn and Mosher-Ashley (2002) suggested that children and adolescents who reported closer relationships with their grandparents also reported more positive characteristics associated with the latter's eventually growing older. Indeed, the more positive terms in which such younger persons see aging grandparents likely influences their own expectations about growing older. Reflecting this positive view of grandparents, Seibert and Kerns (2009) reported that, at times, children used grandparents as attachment figures, providing stability and security in their lives. Wood and Liossis (2007) observed increased closeness with grandparents among young adults who had experienced an impactful life event. Collectively, these studies indicate that feeling emotionally connected to a grandparent seems to have benefits for grandchildren.

Through the transmission of values (Pratt, Norris, Hebblethwaite, & Arnold, 2008) and in serving as a support system in times of crisis, grandparents can also positively influence grandchildren (Ruiz, 2004). In this respect, having meaningful frequent contact with a grandparent can buffer the effect of a parent's divorce, mental illness, or death (see Henderson, Hayslip, Sanders, & Louden, 2009).

Grandparents' roles in the family system can be seen in both positive and negative terms. For example, grandparents may report greater closeness in the relationship than do their grandchildren, a situation termed the *generational stake* (Harwood, 2001). This perception reflects grandparents' investment in their roles as influential figures in their grandchildren's lives, in spite of the fact that their grandchildren may not necessarily share this view about their grandparents. In contrast, the potential for grandparents to foster maladaptive behavior in their grandchildren is also present (Bailey, Hill, Oesterle, & Hawkins, 2009; Silverstein & Ruiz, 2006). Grandparents can contribute to marital discord or model pathological behaviors, which grandchildren may internalize, reflecting the latter's response to family conflict.

Influences on Grandparents' Contact with Their Grandchildren

Central to thinking about grandparenting as a normative experience is information on grandparent-grandchild contact. As noted above, contact with grandchildren is a dimension of grandparental style and is therefore influenced by the meaning one assigns to being a grandparent, wherein more positive intergenerational perceptions of grandparenting likely enhance such contact.

Race and ethnicity co-vary with contact with grandchildren, favoring African American grandmothers (see Szinovacz, 1998; Uhlenberg & Hammill, 1998) as does kinship position (Roberto & Stroes, 1992), with grandchildren reporting stronger relationships with maternal grandmothers than with other grandparents. Whereas maternal grandmothers and paternal grandfathers tend to display the greatest closeness and warmth toward their grandchildren, maternal grandfathers and paternal grandmothers manifest more negative attitudes toward their grandchildren (see Connidis, 2010). This pattern may be explained by adult fathers' greater closeness to their own fathers and adult mothers' greater closeness to their own mothers. Gender also affects contact with grandchildren, where grandmothers anticipate the role earlier in life and get involved sooner after the birth of a grandchild (Smith & Drew, 2002). This gender difference in grandparental involvement may be due to grandmothers having been principally responsible for raising their own children. Indeed, children tend to favor grandmothers over grandfathers (see Connidis, 2010).

Men who express more satisfaction with the grandparent role tend to be older, have had more active relationships with their young grandchildren, and are happier with their involvement in the tasks of child rearing. Reitzes and Mutran (2004b) found that grandparent identity, meaning, and centrality all influenced contact with grandchildren for grandfathers, whereas these variables influenced role satisfaction for both grandfathers and grandmothers.

Grandchild age influences contact with grandparents. When grandchildren are young, grandparents focus primarily on direct child care and involvement. During adolescence, grandparents listen, support, and serve as the family historian. As grandchildren become older and more independent, contact with grandparents likely lessens, although this change in contact frequency may not necessarily translate into less meaningful contact or less perceived grandparental influence. Of course, as adults, children can indeed initiate contact with grandparents, and thus, it may not be that contact with grandparents necessarily lessens with age. Such contact is, however, likely mediated by geographical closeness between the adult grandchild and his or her grandparents.

Marital status, gender, geographic proximity, and the number of grandchildren one has also influence contact with them. For example, having more grandchildren tends to decrease the frequency of contact with a given grandchild (Uhlenberg & Hammill, 1998). Marital status also affects contact with grandchildren, especially for grandfathers (Uhlenberg & Hammill, 1998), wherein divorced older men have far less contact versus married ones. Further, widowed grandfathers may have less contact with their grandchildren than married ones because they lack a wife to facilitate the maintenance of family ties. While grandmothers generally interact with their grandchildren more often than grandfathers, if grandmothers are widowed or divorced, the lack of a spouse may weaken ties to grandchildren or reduce resources needed for traveling to visit them, should the grandmother live far away.

Despite the above influences, understandably, geographic distance is by far the strongest predictor of grandparent-grandchild contact (Uhlenberg & Hammill, 1998). With less geographic distance comes more opportunities for interaction, although electronic forms of communication may ultimately mitigate the effects of living far from one's grandparent. Equally important in reducing the effects of geographic distance is the quality of the grandparent-adult child relationship, where the adult child serves as a *gatekeeper* in influencing the degree and nature of contact between grandchild and grandparent. Thus, positive relationships between grandparents and their adult children (as well as the spouses of these children) tend to enhance grandparent-grandchild relationship and contact, whereas conflictual grandparent-adult child relationships discourage contact between grandparents and grandchildren (Connidis, 2010; Smith & Drew, 2002; Uhlenberg & Hammill, 1998).

Grandfathering

A last normative aspect of grandparenting is grandfathering, about which we know considerably less, relative to research with grandmothers. Given the influence of gender on grandchild contact, it is not surprising to find that grandfathers are viewed as less central than are grandmothers. This gender difference likely reflects the little published research on this topic; this lack of research is especially true for rural grandfathers (White, 2008). Despite the perception that grandfathers are less influential in grandchildren's lives (Hayslip, Shore, et al., 2000), grandfathers can be sources of wisdom and role models for those not regularly exposed to male family members. Roberto, Allen, and Blieszner (2001) found that, whereas geographic proximity to grandchildren affected grandfathers' involvement and role satisfaction, in crisis situations they became more actively involved and were quite amenable to transcending a male-oriented remote style of grandparenting to form close and loving grandchild relationships. In this respect, the construct of *generative grandfathering* underscores the active involvement and contributions that grandfathers can make in the lives of their grandchildren (Bates, 2009).

Nonnormative Dimensions of Grandparent-Grandchild Relationships

Grandparents and Grief

Although death of a grandchild is unusual, when it does occur, its impact on grandparents is substantial. Likewise, the loss of contact with a grandchild via the divorce of an adult son or daughter can be traumatic (Hayslip & White, 2008). Whereas little is known about grief as it relates to grandparenting, the death or divorce of an adult child or grandchild may symbolize the latest in a series of losses to which the grandparent has yet to adjust, complicating everyday functioning and impairing mental and physical health (Hayslip & White, 2008). See a discussion of child and grandchild grief as experienced by grandparents by de Vries, chapter 22 in this volume.

Grandparents' grief may coexist with the loss of their own physical vitality, the death of a spouse, the loss of a salient work role via retirement or job loss, changes in a relationship with a spouse via the latter's mental or physical incapacitation, or the loss of a relationship with the youngest child via the empty nest (Crowley, Hayslip, & Hobdy, 2003). Such life changes may overlap, leading to *bereavement overload*, undermining one's adaptive response to any single loss (Kastenbaum, 2009). Such losses are therefore not independent of one another in their impact on grandparents. Complementarily, grandparents who are ill, impaired, retired, or widowed may be viewed differently by grandchildren who expect grandparents to be physically active and have the resources to travel, or expect to have both grandparents still living. Thus, changes in the perception of the grandchild-grandparent relationship by both older and younger persons may be a source of grief to both.

Disagreements between adult children and their parents about child rearing can undermine opportunities for and the quality of relationships with living grandchildren, emotionally isolating grandparents (Kornhaber, 1996). If a grandchild has died, such disagreements can undermine relationships with surviving grandchildren, or with an adult child (in the event of a divorce or the death of a grandchild). Grandparents' responses to such losses are analogous to *acute grief*, commonly believed to be more problematic than grief that is *anticipatory* in nature (see Corr, Nabe, & Corr, 2009). Indeed, the grief that grandparents experience can best be understood as *disenfranchised* (Doka, 2002; Moss & Moss, 1995). Such grief is deemed unimportant by others, and thus, survivors are "not accorded a right to grieve" (Doka, 2002, p. 5), resulting in a lack of support from others. This disenfranchised grief may lead to diminished opportunities for the grandparent to reach out emotionally to others who may not understand or empathize with the grandparent's feelings. Grandfathers, for example, may be especially handicapped in this respect, in that they are more likely to express their grief *instrumentally*, by means of working, taking on tasks around the house, or offering financial assistance (Doka & Martin, 2002).

Whereas the scientific literature is just emerging as it relates to grandparents' emotional needs when a grandchild dies, grandparents' grief appears to be twofold; they grieve for their adult child as well as for themselves (Reed, 2000). Family customs and rituals may not meet a grandparent's needs, and grandparents are put in the delicate position of attempting to support their adult child as well as meet their own needs for support from others. Indeed, published empirical research specific to grandparent bereavement following death of a child supports the perception that grandparents' grief is indeed disenfranchised (Hayslip & Glover, 2008–2009; Lemon, 2002). Although parents and grandparents have different role relationships with the child who died and parents may express feelings more often and exhibit greater distress, grandparents share many of the same responses as do parents to a child's death (see Hayslip & White, 2008). Support offered by grandparents may therefore be at the cost of putting aside their own grief to attend to the needs of their children and their surviving grandchildren.

While little is known about whether an older or a younger grandchild's death is more impactful, one might predict that older grandchildren's deaths would be seen as more unlikely and therefore of greater impact when they do happen, based upon what is known about the impact of child loss on parents (see Murphy, 2008), although the quality of the grandchild-grandparent relationship and degree of contact likely mitigate the influence of grandchild age in this respect. Grandfathers, more than grandmothers, offer instrumental support to their children, and engaging in work as a means to help with their recovery is more common among grandfathers than grandmothers (Hayslip & White, 2008). Important for grandparents are continuing bonds with the child who died, that is, funerals, memorial services, sharing memories of the child, rituals associated with holidays, birth and death dates, spiritual connections, and symbolic representations (photographs and objects representing the child) (White, Walker, & Richards, 2008). Not surprisingly, grandparents identify being included by their adult children and being able to express their own feelings and emotions as evidence of personal support from a bereaved child (White et al., 2008).

Grandparents also grieve when they lose contact with their grandchildren because of their adult child's divorce, though this depends on physical proximity, grandchild age, and the gender and lineage of the grandparent. A parent's divorce, separation, or remarriage can be seen as an opportunity for a granddaughter to reconnect with a grandmother (Holladay, Lackovich, Lee,

Coleman, Harding, & Dento, 1998). Not surprisingly however, when the mother has custody and moves away, both maternal and paternal grandparents' contact with a grandchild is limited (Drew & Smith, 1999). Moreover, less post-divorce contact with grandchildren is associated with a grandparent's poorer physical health and well-being (Drew & Smith, 1999).

The impact of divorce on the grandparent depends upon whether the grandparent is viewed as an *agent* in the life of a grandchild (by providing support and serving as a role model), or whether the grandparent is viewed as a *victim* (grandparenting is viewed as a compensation for the lack of other sources of life satisfaction; Drew & Smith, 1999). In the context of women being more likely to assume custody in the event of a divorce, relationships with grandchildren are most satisfying when visits are maintained with both the daughter and the grandchildren (Ehrenberg & Smith, 2003). Also, closer grandparental relationships in the event of divorce can positively affect a grandchild's adjustment (Henderson et al., 2009). The benefits for a grandchild may vary by race in that white children are more likely to benefit from coresidence with both a grandparent and a single parent than are black children (Dunifon & Kowaleski-Jones, 2007).

For grandmothers, closer geographic proximity predicts greater involvement, especially for the children of single fathers (Hilton & Macari, 1997). To the extent that children's relationships with their fathers deteriorate after divorce, relationships with their grandparents become more distant, consistent with the father's remarriage being seen as more stressful by children (Ahrons, 2007). When grandparents themselves divorce, they report feeling less close to their grandchildren, are less likely to play a friend role, and have more conflicts with grandchildren, although such effects are moderated by the quality of the relationship with the adult child (King, 2003).

Underscoring the emotional dilemma for grandparents when their children divorce and thus influencing grandparents' reactions to an adult child's divorce is the fact that many states have enacted laws to guarantee grandparents' visitation rights (Giles-Sims & Lockart, 2006). In the event of divorce, some grandparents are able to acquire court-ordered visitation successfully if it is in the best interests of the child and does not intrude on the relationship of the newly remarried parent to the child (Henderson, 2005), allowing grandparents to maintain contact with their grandchildren.

Stepgrandparenting

Via the divorce and remarriage of an adult child, one becomes by definition a stepgrandparent; this role's incidence fluctuates with historical shifts in the rates of divorce. A limited, but emerging literature on stepgrandparenting suggests being a stepgrandparent is a particularly ambiguous experience (Ganong, 2008). However, positive stepgrandchild relationships can be facilitated by parental and stepparental support and authentic communication (Soliz, 2007). The quality of these relationships often have much to do with the age of the stepgrandchild, when the remarriage occurred, and the quality of that child's relationship to the stepparent. Christensen and Smith (2002) reported that relative to grandparents, stepgrandparents enjoyed less positive relationships with their stepgrandchildren and experienced more conflict in interacting with them, perhaps because of less positive relationships with a son's or daughter's new spouse. The topic is covered in depth by Ganong and Coleman in chapter 9 in this volume.

Great-Grandparenting

Regarding great-grandparents, who are more numerous because persons live well into their 80s, the small amount of available evidence suggests this role can have positive consequences in contributing to the older adult's self-esteem if the great-grandparent role in the extended family is well defined and internalized as important by the great-grandparent (Roberto & Skoglund, 1996), despite the great-grandparent's greater lineage distance from the parent (Drew & Silverstein, 2004). Moreover, some great-grandparents raise their great-grandchildren, giving them great satisfaction. In general though, the great-grandparent role is limited largely to infrequent events (e.g., holiday and birthday celebrations) as well as being limited by the great-grandparent's health (Roberto & Skoglund, 1996). Despite their presumed limited influence, many children identify great-grandparents when asked to draw a grandparent (Mietkiewicz & Jolliot, 2004). Having a great-grandparent can enable young children to learn about the realities of aging, especially from great-grandfathers, who are likely to be older than great-grandmothers (Mietkiewicz & Venditti, 2004).

Custodial Grandparenting

Custodial grandparents, who are caring for their grandchildren on a full-time basis, are quite prevalent in the United States. In 2006, 6.1 million grandparents lived with their grandchildren, and approximately 2.4 million of such persons were raising their grandchildren (Statistical Abstract of the United States, 2006). Although the absolute incidence of grandparent caregiving is greater for whites, the odds of assuming a caregiver role are greater for Hispanic and African American grandparents (U.S. Bureau of the Census, 2000). Normatively, custodial grandparents tend to be younger, the mother's parents, in worse health, more isolated, poorer, less highly educated, and raising boys, all relative to traditional, noncaregiving grandparents (Generations United, 2009; Shore & Hayslip, 1994).

In some cases, grandparent caregiving exists in a skipped generation household, where the adult parent is absent. Even in a coparenting household, where the grandparent and adult child coreside, the grandparent may have primary responsibility for caring for the grandchild. Coparenting is more common, relative to Caucasians, among Hispanics and African Americans (Fuller-Thomson & Minkler, 2001). Generally speaking, grandparents in skipped generation households tend to fare worse physically and emotionally (Fuller-Thomson & Minkler, 2001; Generations United, 2009; Hayslip & Kaminski, 2005).

Unfortunately, grandparent caregiving is usually linked to the divorce, drug use, incarceration, job loss, or death of the adult child, as well as to the abandonment or abuse of the latter's child. These circumstances stigmatize and isolate grandparents from needed social and emotional support as well as make it difficult for them to be treated equitably, relative to other clients, by social service providers (see Hayslip & Kaminski, 2005). Indeed, ambivalence and contradiction define grandparent caregivers' experiences, contributing to the distress many report (Ebert & Aleman, 2008). Not surprisingly, if the relationship with the adult child is ambivalent or the nature of contact between the grandparent and either the grandchild or the adult child is poorly structured, the demands on the grandparent caregiver are more debilitating (Hayslip, Glover et al., 2009).

Raising a grandchild often disrupts one's life plans (Jendrek, 1993). This disruption is likely linked to the difficulties often reported by custodial grandparents: poor physical or emotional health, less satisfaction with grandparenting, impaired or strained relationships with spouses and their grandchildren, and isolation from other grandchildren and friends because of their parental responsibilities (Hayslip & Kaminski, 2005). Such persons often feel overloaded and confused about their roles as parents and grandparents. Some grandchildren, particularly grandsons, may have behavioral or school difficulties for which grandparents are less likely to seek help than are parents (Hayslip & Shore, 2000; Hayslip, Shore, Henderson, & Lambert, 1998). Importantly, the impact of grandmothers' distress on grandchildren's adjustment is mediated by dysfunctional parenting (Smith, Palmieri, Hancock, & Richardson, 2008), and may be exacerbated by the grandparent's attitudes toward child rearing as well as the tendency of some grandparents to rely on their grandchildren for emotional support (Kaminski, Hayslip, Wilson, & Casto, 2008). Interestingly, but consistent with the lack of focus on grandfathers, virtually nothing is known about the impact of raising grandchildren on grandfathers. Health concerns, depression, and feelings of powerlessness in child rearing sometimes, but not always, characterize men's responses to parenting a grandchild (Hayslip, Kaminski, & Earnheart, 2006; McCallion & Kolomer, 2006).

Children who are raised by their grandparents suffer as well; relative to children who live with their parents, more of those being raised by grandparents live in poverty (U.S. Bureau of the Census, 2000). Many such children have difficulty registering for school (Silverstein & Vehvilainen, 2000) and are more likely than those living with their parents not to have health insurance (Kirby & Kaneda, 2002). Such difficulties are greatest for grandchildren cared for informally, wherein grandparents lack a formal legal basis (e.g., adoption, legal custody, guardianship) for securing services (Generations United, 2002). Many custodial grandparents come to resent their children for creating the situation leading to the care of the grandchild, and yet they may feel guilty over having failed as parents in raising such a child (Shore & Hayslip, 1994).

Custodial grandparents often have little time to prepare for parenting, assume the obligation of caring for their grandchildren under socially stigmatizing, negative family circumstances, and have had little direct or ongoing responsibility for raising children for many years. Thus, social support (i.e., having access to support groups or being able to rely on other family members) is important to their well-being (Generations United, 2002; Gerard, Landry-Meyer, & Roe, 2006). Importantly, many grandparent caregivers display resilience in response to the many challenges they face (Hayslip, Davis, Goodman, Smith, & Green, 2009). Their task is indeed a generative one, and most carry out this obligation with love and a passionate commitment to their grandchildren.

IMPLICATIONS FOR GRANDPARENTING RESEARCH

Clearly, there is much more to learn about grandparenting. Based upon what is (and is not) known at present, greater attention needs to be paid to theory (Roberto, Blieszner, & Allen, 2006; Smith & Drew, 2002). For example, expanding upon the life-span perspective taken here (see Hayslip & Hicks-Patrick, 2003), embedding grandparenting in an antecedent-consequent framework and stressing its multidimensional, systemic nature might be fruitful in providing insight into the process by which grandparents define their roles or adopt a particular behavioral style in response to this role. Adapting a developmental focus derived from Eriksonian theory (e.g., to further explore generativity among grandparents) or attachment theory (e.g., to better understand grandchildren's relationships to their grandparents and vice versa) holds much promise in understanding grandparent-grandchild relationships (see Poehlmann, 2003).

Prospective longitudinal work targeting grandparenting at multiple levels (i.e., the grandparent-grandchild dyad, the grandparent marital or partnered dyad, the family system incorporating grandparents, adult children, and grandchildren) is sorely needed. Likewise, at a cultural or interpersonal level, targeting attitudes and biases about grandparenting may also aid in understanding the antecedents of the meaning and style of grandparenting as well as the impact of historical change on grandparent-grandchild relationships.

A stronger emphasis upon the family context will also expand the knowledge base about grandparenting. For example, contexts such as grandparents' romantic relationship, relationships with all of one's grandchildren versus the typical approach of reporting on one focal grandchild where contact is most extensive or relationship quality is most positive, relationships with one's children-in-law after divorce or death of offspring, and relationships with custodial grandchildren all require more attention. Moreover, little effort has been devoted to understanding grandparents' relationships with other members of the intergenerational family system (e.g., siblings, cousins) whose influence on grandparents can be supportive or conflictual in nature.

Of particular importance is attention to the dynamic nature of grandparenting, given that individuals actively construct and modify the role. Which variables influence this process? What factors explain changes in perceptions and enactment of this role? What are the consequences of such changes for the grandparent and grandchild? Is the dynamic nature of grandparenting comparable across stepgrandparents, custodial grandparents, great-grandparents, grandmothers, and grandfathers? What indeed is the association between grandparental meaning and style and does it change over time? What are the long-term consequences of grieving for grandparents? What grandparents are at risk for difficulties in grieving?

More needs to be known about understudied subpopulations of grandparents (e.g., grandfathers and great-grandparents), including how the grandparent role is defined for each. Is it meaningful or not, from the perspectives of both the older and the younger generations? Some information exists regarding culture and grandparenting, but little is known about the *process* of acculturation as it bears on immigrant grandparent-grandchild relationships. Greater effort is still necessary in the development of reliable and valid means by which data are gathered regarding grandparent-grandchild relationships (Collinsworth, Strom, Strom, & Young, 1991; Hayslip, Shore et al., 2000; Rempusheski & O'Hara, 2005; Smith & Drew, 2002), wherein self-report or interview methods may unfairly bias or inaccurately paint the picture of grandparenting that we have. Incorporating the method of triangulation via multiple informants (e.g., grandparent, adult child, grandchild, and grandchild's teacher), might hold promise in this regard. Also reflecting a triangulated approach would be the use of expressive, unstructured techniques (e.g., drawings, open-ended questions) in gathering data. Expansion of research methods beyond the typically used survey techniques would permit a greater understanding of the idiosyncratic nature of grandparenting as well as allow for the influence of response bias that some grandparents may display in reporting about emotionally difficult issues (e.g., their adult children's drug abuse or divorce, topics pertinent to sexuality as they apply to their grand-children).

IMPLICATIONS FOR PRACTITIONERS

For practitioners, theory-guided research can form the basis for the design and evaluation of interventions to enhance grandparental communication and relational skills and improve grandparent-grandchild relationship quality (see Strom et al., 1991). Clinicians can employ a family systems perspective, which can be useful in understanding the family dynamics of both traditional and custodial grandparents (Kaminski & Murrell, 2008; Maiden & Zuckerman, 2008). As grandparent and grandchild mental health are reciprocally influential (Goodman & Hayslip, 2008), working with just one individual may do the other (and consequently the family unit) a disservice. When practitioners take a family systems perspective in designing and carrying out interventions with grandparents and their grandchildren and great-grandchildren, professionals become advocates for intergenerational family units (Maiden & Zuckerman, 2008).

From a systems perspective, understanding grandchildren's views of grand-parents can shed light on their world. What roles do they see their grandparents playing in the family? Adapting a systems approach requires that one consider the personal growth of the grandparent as well. For example, being a grandparent does not always mean being able to carry out this role in an adaptive, meaningful manner. Divorce, geographic distance, and physical limitations can hinder the relationship building process. In this light, Roberto, Dolbin-MacNab, and Finney (2008) found, particular to custodial grand-mothers, an association between length of parenting grandchildren and the use of preventative health practices, wherein the longer the care, the fewer preventative measures taken. This problem becomes increasingly important for both generations as grandparents (both traditional and custodial) grow older. In addition, as grandparents' mental health suffers if they are raising grandchildren with behavioral problems (Roberto et al., 2008), grandparents may not be able to be fully "present" in the relationship.

The advantages of a systemic approach are illustrated by Strong, Bean, and Feinauer (2010) who presented a model of family therapy that incorporated an understanding of attachment and trauma in grandchildren raised by custodial grandparents. Their model suggested placing importance on fostering the attachment between grandchildren and grandparents in concert with an understanding of children's emotional and intellectual development.

Individuals working with grandchildren and grandparents will also greatly benefit from understanding the unique developmental trajectories of each generation in the family. For example, Knight (2004) presented a model for understanding older adult mental health that incorporated the older adult's social context, generational group influences, developmental processes, and unique challenges. Knight's model can guide practitioners by emphasizing the multifaceted context in which grandparent-grandchild relationships can be understood. Has the family experienced a divorce? Has the grandchild been under the care of the grandparent since birth? What mental or physical health issues require remediation? To what extent have relationships with adult children, other grandchildren, friends, or coworkers deteriorated? Does grandparenting or grandparent caregiving exacerbate or reflect existing marital difficulties? If a divorce has occurred (see Soliz, 2007), are there relational difficulties between grandchildren and their biological grandparents? How are such difficulties experienced by grandparents? What of the grandchild's relationship to his or her stepgrandparents? If the grandparent is raising the grandchild, what boundaries have been established to define the relationship with the adult child? What barriers exist in defining such boundaries? Understanding the pattern and nature of communication among members of the intergenerational family can guide practitioners in adjusting their interventions accordingly.

In order to be most effective in working with grandparents, professionals must be knowledgeable about the developmental and cultural influences on grandparents' definition of their roles, influences on contact with their grandchildren, and the normative and nonnormative aspects of grandparenting. Besides accessing research reports for ideas about applied implications, other valuable sources of information and tips are Grandparents.com, as well as the AARP, the National Institute on Aging, and Generations United. Online resources (www.grandfamilies.org) for state laws and resources concerning grandfamilies also exist (Butts, 2009; Cox, 2009). Area Agencies on Aging can also provide information about needed services. Such knowledge, as well as networking with local service providers and educators, can better enable practitioners to make timely and effective referrals for custodial grandparents who need support. Indeed, at present, a lack of expertise, training, or knowledge about resources may explain the negative interactions of grandparent caregivers with service providers, contributing to such persons rejecting help from outsiders. Grandparents ask for help for themselves only as a last resort, putting their grandchildren's needs first (Baker & Silverstein, 2008). This pattern suggests that practitioners who are sensitive to grandparents' unique life situations and cultural traditions may be effective in facilitating custodial grandparents' access to needed resources and services.

Grandparents and grandchildren who are not living under the same roof can also benefit from supportive services (e.g., community programs, volunteer organizations, mentoring programs). For example, a program on many college campuses, Grandparent University, offers joint learning opportunities for grandchildren and grandparents in an exciting and intellectually stimulating atmosphere.

Clinicians working with grandparents and great-grandparents would be wise to heed the advice of Strom and Strom (1991a, 1991b) in helping grandparents take an active role in their grandchildren's and great-grandchildren's lives. Strom and Strom recommend keeping in touch regularly, communicating directly with grandchildren, taking time to know each grandchild individually, and having reasonable expectations for grandchildren's growth and development. Online resources (such as http://www.aarp.org/relationships/friends-family/info-08-2011/grandfamlies-guide-resources.html) are quite helpful in this respect.

We wish to emphasize that many, if not most grandparents' relationships with their children and grandchildren are fulfilling, beneficial, and productive. However, in cases where relationships have become conflictual or distant, being systemically proactive in dealing with a strained relationship with the grandchild's parent can avoid family conflicts that could interfere with grandchild and great-grandchild relationships. Helping professionals must be nonjudgmental, utilize active listening, and be empathic. These approaches allow the needs of each member of the intergenerational family system to become evident and enable professionals to assist them in meeting those needs.

REFERENCES

Ahrons, C.R. (2007). Family ties after divorce: Long-term implications for children. *Family Process, 46,* 53–65.

American Association for Retired Persons (AARP). (2002). *The grandparent study 2002 report.* Washington, DC: Author.

Arnett, J. (2000). Emerging adulthood: A theory of development from the late teens through the twenties. *American Psychologist, 55,* 469–480.

Attar-Schwartz, S., Tan, J., & Buchanan, A. (2009). Adolescents' perspectives on relationships with grandparents: The contribution of adolescent, grandparent, and parent-grandparent relationship variables. *Children and Youth Services Review, 31,* 1057–1066.

Bailey, J., Hill, K., Oesterle, S., & Hawkins, D. (2009). Parenting practices and problem behavior across three generations: Monitoring, harsh discipline, and drug use in the intergenerational transmission of externalizing behavior. *Developmental Psychology, 45,* 1214–1226.

Baker, L., & Silverstein, M. (2008). Preventative health behaviors among grandmothers raising grandchildren. *Journals of Gerontology: Social Sciences, 63B,* S304–S311.

Bates, J.S. (2009). Generative grandfathering: A conceptual framework for nurturing grandchildren. *Marriage and Family Review, 45,* 331–352.

Boon, S.D., Shaw, M., & MacKinnon, S. (2008). Grandparent health and young adults' judgments of their grandparent-grandchild relationships. *Journal of Intergenerational Relationships, 6,* 155–173.

Bronfenbrenner, U. (2004). *Making human beings human: Bioecological perspectives on human development.* Thousand Oaks, CA: Sage.

Butts, D. M. (2009). Generations United for grandfamilies. *Journal of Intergenerational Relationships, 7*, 322–324.

Celdran, M., Tirado, C., & Villar, F. (2009). Learning from the disease: Lessons drawn from adolescents having a grandparent suffering from dementia. *International Journal of Aging and Human Development, 68*, 243–259.

Christensen, F., & Smith, T. (2002). What is happening to satisfaction and quality of relationships between step/grandparents and step/grandchildren? *Journal of Divorce and Remarriage, 37*, 117–133.

Cole, M. (1999). Culture in development. In M. Bornstein & M. Lamb (Eds.), *Developmental psychology: An advanced textbook* (pp. 73–124). Mahwah, NJ: Lawrence Erlbaum.

Collinsworth, P., Strom, R., Strom, S., & Young, D. (1991). The grandparent strengths and needs inventory: Development and factorial validation. *Educational and Psychological Measurement, 51*, 785–792.

Combrinck-Graham, L. (1985). A developmental model for family systems. *Family Process, 24*, 139–150.

Connidis, I. A. (2010). *Family ties and aging.* Thousand Oaks, CA: Pine Forge Press.

Corr, C. A., Nabe, C. M., & Corr, D. M. (2009). *Death and dying, life and living.* Belmont, CA: Wadsworth.

Cox, C. (2009). Custodial grandparents: Policies affecting care. *Journal of Intergenerational Relationships, 7*, 177–190.

Crowley, B., Hayslip, B., & Hobdy, J. (2003). Psychological hardiness and adjustment to life events in adulthood. *Journal of Adult Development, 10*, 237–248.

Doka, K. J. (Ed.). (2002). *Disenfranchised grief: New directions, challenges, and strategies for practice.* Champaign, IL: Research Press.

Doka, K. J., & Martin, T. (2002). How we grieve: Culture, class, and gender. In K. J. Doka (Ed.), *Disenfranchised grief: New directions, challenges, and strategies for practice* (pp. 337–348). Champaign, IL: Research Press.

Drew, L., & Silverstein, M. (2004). Inter-generational role investments for great-grandparents: Consequences of psychological well-being. *Ageing and Society, 24*, 95–111.

Drew, L., & Smith, P. (1999). The impact of parental separation/divorce on grandparent-grandchild relationships. *International Journal of Aging and Human Development, 48*, 191–216.

Dunifon, R., & Kowalski-Jones, L. (2007). The influence of grandparents in single-mother families. *Journal of Marriage and Family, 69*, 465–481.

Ebert, L., & Aleman, M. (2008). Taking the grand out of grandparent: Dialectical tensions in grandparent perceptions of surrogate parenting. *Journal of Social and Personal Relationships, 25*, 671–695.

Ehrenberg, M. F., & Smith, S. T. L. (2003). Grandmother-grandchild contacts before and after an adult daughter's divorce. *Journal of Divorce and Remarriage, 39*, 27–43.

Fingerman, K. L. (2004). The role of offspring and in-laws in grandparents' ties to their grandchildren. *Journal of Family Issues, 25*, 1026–1049.

Friedman, D., Hechter, M., & Kreager, D. (2008). A theory of the value of grandchildren. *Rationality and Society, 20*, 31–63.

Fruhauf, C. A., & Orel, N. (2008). Developmental issues of grandchildren who provide care to grandparents. *International Journal of Aging and Human Development, 67*, 209–230.

Fujiwara, T., & Lee, C. (2008). The impact of altruistic behaviors for children and grandchildren on major depression among parents and grandparents in the United States: A prospective study. *Journal of Affective Disorders, 107*, 29–36.

Fuller-Thomson, E., & Minkler, M. (2001). American grandparents providing extensive child care to their grandchildren: Prevalence and profile. *The Gerontologist, 41*, 201–209.

Fung. H., Siu, C., Choy, W., & McBride-Chang, C. (2005). Meaning of grandparenthood: Do concerns about time and mortality matter? *Ageing International, 30*, 122–146.

Ganong, L. (2008). Intergenerational relationships in stepfamilies. In J. Pryor (Ed.), *International handbook of stepfamilies: Policy and practice in legal, research, and clinical environments* (pp. 394–420). Hoboken, NJ: Wiley.

Generations United. (2002). *Fact sheet grandparents and other relatives raising children: Caregiver support groups.* Retrieved from http://www.gu.org/documents/A0/Caregiver_Support_Groups.pdf

Generations United. (2009). *Grandfacts: Data, interpretation, and implications for caregivers.* Washington, DC: Author.

Gerard, J. M., Landry-Meyer, L., & Roe, J. G. (2006). Grandparents raising grandchildren: The role of social support. *International Journal of Aging and Human Development, 62*, 359–384.

Giles-Sims, J., & Lockart, C. (2006). Grandparents' visitation rights: Using culture to explain cross-state variation. *Journal of Divorce and Remarriage, 44*, 1–16.

Goodman, C. C., & Hayslip, B., Jr. (2008). Mentally healthy grandparents' impact on their grandchildren's behavior. In B. Hayslip Jr. & P. Kaminski (Eds.), *Parenting the custodial grandchild: Implications for clinical practice* (pp. 41–52). New York: Springer.

Hagestad, G. O. (1985). Continuity and connectedness. In V. L. Bengtson & J. F. Robertson (Eds.), *Grandparenthood* (pp. 31–48). Beverly Hills, CA: Sage.

Hagestad, G. O. (1988). Demographic change and the life course: Some emerging trends in the family realm. *Family Relations, 37*, 405–410.

Harwood, J. (2001). Comparing grandchildren's and grandparents' stake in their relationship. *International Journal of Aging and Human development, 53*, 195–210.

Hayslip, B., Davis, S., Goodman, C., Smith, G., & Green, Y. (2009, November). *Resilience among custodial grandparents.* Paper presented at the 62nd Annual Scientific Meeting of the Gerontological Society of America, Atlanta, GA.

Hayslip, B., & Glover, R. (2008–2009). Custodial grandparenting: Perceptions of loss by traditional grandparent peers. *Omega: Journal of Death and Dying, 58*, 165–177.

Hayslip, B., Glover, R., Harris, B., Miltenberger, P., Baird, A., & Kaminski, P. (2009). Perceptions of custodial grandparents among young adults. *Journal of Intergenerational Relationships, 7*, 209–224.

Hayslip, B., Henderson, C., & Shore, J. (2003). The structure of grandparental role meaning. *Journal of Adult Development, 10*, 1–11.

Hayslip, B., & Hicks-Patrick, J. (2003). *Working with custodial grandparents*. New York: Springer.

Hayslip, B., & Kaminski, P. (2005). Grandparents raising their grandchildren: A review of the literature and suggestions for practice. *The Gerontologist, 45*, 262–269.

Hayslip, B., Kaminski, P., & Earnheart, K. (2006). Gender differences among custodial grandparents. In B. Hayslip & J. Hicks-Patrick (Eds.), *Custodial grandparents: Individual, cultural, and ethnic diversity* (pp. 151–168). New York: Springer.

Hayslip, B., & Shore, R. J. (2000). Custodial grandparenting and mental health services. *Journal of Mental Health and Aging, 6*, 367–384.

Hayslip, B., Shore, R. J., & Henderson, C. (2000). Perceptions of grandparents' influence in the lives of their grandchildren. In B. Hayslip & R. Goldberg-Glen (Eds.), *Grandparents raising grandchildren: Theoretical, empirical, and clinical perspectives* (pp. 35–46). New York: Springer.

Hayslip, B., Shore, R. J., Henderson, C. E., & Lambert, P. L. (1998). Custodial grandparenting and grandchildren with problems: Their impact on role satisfaction and role meaning, *Journal of Gerontology: Social Sciences, 53B*, S164–S174.

Hayslip, B., & White, D. (2008). Grandparents as grievers. In M. S. Stroebe, R. O. Hansson, W. Stroebe, & H. Schut (Eds.), *Handbook of bereavement research* (3rd ed., pp. 441–460). Washington, DC: American Psychological Association.

Henderson, C., Hayslip, B., Sanders, L., & Louden, L. (2009). Grandmother-grandchild relationship quality predicts psychological adjustment among youth from divorced families. *Journal of Family Issues, 30*, 1245–1264.

Henderson, T. (2005). Grandparent visitation rights: Successful acquisition of court ordered visitation. *Journal of Family Issues, 26*, 107–137.

Hilton, J. M., & Macari, D. (1997). Grandparent involvement following divorce: A comparison of single-mother and single-father families. *Journal of Divorce and Remarriage, 28*, 203–224.

Holladay, S., Lackovich, R., Lee, M., Coleman, M., Harding, D., & Dento, D. (1998). (Re)constructing relationships with grandparents: A turning point analysis of granddaughters' relational development with maternal grandmothers. *International Journal of Aging and Human Development, 46*, 287–303.

Howard, K., & Jerome, F. (2001). The forgotten generation: The impact a grandmother with Alzheimer's disease has on a granddaughter. *Activities, Adaptation, and Aging, 25*, 45–57.

Jendrek, M. (1993). Grandparents who parent their grandchildren: Effects on lifestyle. *Journal of Marriage and Family, 55*, 609–621.

Johnson, C. L., & Barer, B. M. (1997). *Life beyond 85 years: The aura of survivorship*. New York: Springer.

Kaminski, P., Hayslip, B., Wilson, J., & Casto, L. (2008). Parenting attitudes and adjustment among custodial grandparents. *Journal of Intergenerational Relationships, 6*, 263–284.

Kaminski, P. L., & Murrell, A. R. (2008). Counseling custodial grandchildren. In B. Hayslip Jr. & P. Kaminski (Eds.), *Parenting the custodial grandchild: Implications for clinical practice* (pp. 215–236). New York: Springer.

Kastenbaum, R. (2009). *Death, society, and human existence* (10th ed.). Boston: Allyn & Bacon.

Kaufman, G., & Elder, G. H. (2003). Grandparenting and age identity. *Journal of Aging Studies, 17,* 269–282.

Kemp, C. L. (2007). Grandparent-grandchild ties: Reflections on continuity and change across three generations. *Journal of Family Issues, 28,* 855–881.

King, V. (2003). The legacy of a grandparent's divorce: Consequences for grandparents and grandchildren. *Journal of Marriage and Family, 65,* 170–183.

King, V., & Elder, G. H. (1998). Perceived self efficacy and grandparenting. *Journal of Gerontology: Social Sciences, 53B,* S249–S257.

King, V., Russell, S. T., & Elder, G. H. (1998). Grandparenting in family systems: An ecological perspective. In M. E. Szinovacz (Ed.), *Handbook of grandparenthood* (pp. 53–69). Westport, CT: Greenwood.

Kirby, J., & Kaneda, T. (2002). Health insurance and family structure: The case of adolescents in skipped generation families. *Medical Care Research and Review, 59,* 146–165.

Knight, B. G. (2004). *Psychotherapy with older adults* (3rd ed.). Thousand Oaks, CA: Sage.

Kornhaber, A. (1996). *Contemporary grandparenting.* Thousand Oaks, CA: Sage.

Kulik, L. (2007). Contemporary midlife grandparenthood. In V. Muhlbauer & J. C. Chrisler (Eds.), *Women over 50: Psychological perspectives* (pp. 131–146). New York: Springer.

Lemon, B. S. (2002). Experiencing grandparent grief: 'A piece of my heart died twice.' *AWHONN Lifelines, 6,* 470–472.

MacMillan, R., & Copher, R. (2005). Families in the life course: Interdependency of roles, role configurations, and pathways. *Journal of Marriage and the Family, 67,* 858–879.

Maiden, R. J., & Zuckerman, C. (2008). Counseling grandparents parenting their children's children: Case studies. In B. Hayslip Jr. & P. Kaminski (Eds.), *Parenting the custodial grandchild: Implications for clinical practice* (pp. 197–214). New York: Springer.

Mason, J., May, V., & Clarke, L. (2007). Ambivalence and the paradoxes of grandparenting. *The Sociological Review, 55,* 687–706.

McCallion, P., & Kolomer, S. (2006). Depression and caregiver mastery in grandfathers caring for their grandchildren. In B. Hayslip & J. Patrick (Eds.), *Custodial grandparenting: Individual, cultural, and ethnic diversity* (pp. 105–114). New York: Springer.

McGuinn, K., & Mosher-Ashley, P. (2002). Children's fears about personal aging. *Educational Gerontology, 28,* 561–575.

Mietkiewicz, M., & Joilliot, C. (2004). Grandparents, greatgrandparents, and stepgrandparents: Young children's representations. *Neuropsychiatrie de l'Enfance et de l'Adolescence, 52,* 330–336.

Mietkiewicz, M., & Venditti, L. (2004). Great-grandfathers from their greatgrandchildrens' point of view. *Psychologie & Neuropsychiatrie du Viellissement, 2,* 275–283.

Mirfin-Veitch, B., Bray, A., & Watson, M. (1997). "We're just that sort of family:" Intergenerational relationships in families including children with disabilities. *Family Relations*, *46*, 305–311.

Monserud, M.A. (2008). Intergenerational relationships and affectional solidarity between grandparents and young adults. *Journal of Marriage and Family*, *70*, 182–195.

Montgomery, R., Rowe, J., & Kosloski, K. (2007). Family caregiving. In J. Blackburn & C. Dulmus (Eds.), *Handbook of gerontology: Evidence-based approaches to theory, practice, and policy* (pp. 426–454). New York: Wiley.

Moss, M.S., & Moss, S.Z. (1995). Death and bereavement. In R. Blieszner & V.H. Bedford (Eds.), *Handbook of aging and the family* (pp. 422–439). Westport, CT: Greenwood Publishing.

Mueller, M., & Elder, G.H. (2003). Family contingencies across the generations: Grandparent-grandchild relationships in a holistic perspective. *Journal of Marriage and Family*, *65*, 404–417.

Murphy, S.A. (2008). The loss of a child: Sudden death and illness perspectives. In M.S. Stroebe, R.O. Hansson, W. Stroebe, & H. Schut (Eds.), *Handbook of bereavement research* (3rd ed., pp. 375–395). Washington, DC: American Psychological Association.

Olshansky, S., Goldman, D., Zheng, Y., & Rowe, J. (2009). Aging in America in the twenty-first century: Demographic forecasts from the MacArthur Foundation Network on an Aging Society. *The Milbank Quarterly*, *84*, 842–862.

Paul, P. (2002).Make room for granddaddy. *American Demographics*. Retrieved from http://findarticles.com/p/articles/mi_m4201/is_2002_April_1/ai_87109767

Poehlmann, J. (2003). An attachment perspective on grandparents raising their very young grandchildren: Implications for intervention and research. *Infant Mental Health Journal*, *24*, 149–173.

Pratt, N., Norris, J.E., Hebblethwaite, S., & Arnold, M. (2008). Intergenerational transmission of values: Family generativity and adolescents' narratives of parent and grandparent value teaching. *Journal of Personality*, *76*, 171–198.

Reed, M.L. (2000). *Grandparents cry twice: Help for bereaved grandparents*. Amityville, NY: Baywood Publishing Company.

Reitzes, D. C., & Mutran, E.J. (2004a). Grandparent identity, intergenerational family identity, and well-being. *Journal of Gerontology: Social Sciences*, *59B*, S213–S219.

Reitzes, D. C., & Mutran, E.J. (2004b). Grandparenthood: Factors influencing frequency of grandparent-grandchild contact and grandparent role satisfaction. *Journal of Gerontology: Social Sciences*, *59B*, S9–S16.

Rempusheski, V., & O'Hara, C. (2005). Psychometric properties of the Grandparent Perceptions of Family Scale (GPFS). *Nursing Research*, *54*, 363–371.

Roberto, K.A., Allen, K., & Blieszner, R. (2001). Grandfathers' perceptions and expectations of relationships with their adult grandchildren. *Journal of Family Issues*, *22*, 407–426.

Roberto, K. A., Blieszner, R., & Allen, K. R. (2006). Theorizing in family gerontology: New opportunities for research and practice. *Family Relations, 55,* 513–525.

Roberto, K. A., Dolbin-MacNab, M. L., & Finney, J. W. (2008). Promoting health for grandmothers parenting young children. In B. Hayslip Jr. & P. Kaminski (Eds.), *Parenting the custodial grandchild: Implications for clinical practice* (pp. 75–89). New York: Springer.

Roberto, K. A., & Skoglund, R. (1996). Interactions with grandparents and great-grandparents: A comparison of activities, influences, and relationships. *International Journal of Aging and Human Development, 43,* 107–118.

Roberto, K. A., & Stroes, J. (1992). Grandchildren and grandparents: Roles, influences, and relationships. *International Journal of Aging and Human Development, 34, 227–239.*

Robertson, J. (1995). Grandparenting in an era of rapid change. In R. Blieszner & V. H. Bedford (Eds.), *Handbook of aging and the family* (pp. 243–260). Westport, CT: Greenwood Press.

Rosow, I. (1985). Status role change through the life cycle. In R. Binstock & E. Shanas (Eds.), *Handbook of aging and the social sciences* (2nd ed., pp. 62–93). New York: Academic Press.

Ruiz, D. S. (2004). *Amazing grace: African American grandmothers as caregivers and conveyors of traditional values.* Westport, CT: Praeger.

Sandel, T., Cho, G., Miller, P., & Wang, S. (2006). What it means to be a grandmother: A cross-cultural study of Taiwanese and Euro-American grandmothers' beliefs. *Journal of Family Communication, 64,* 255–278.

Saxena, D., & Sanders, G. F. (2009). Quality of grandparent-grandchild relationships in Asian-Indian immigrant families. *International Journal of Aging and Human Development, 68,* 321–338.

Seibert, A., & Kerns, K. (2009). Attachment figures in middle childhood. *International Journal of Behavioral Development, 33,* 347–355.

Shore, R. J., & Hayslip, B. (1994). Custodial grandparenting: Implications for children's development. In A. E. Gottfried & A. W. Gottfried (Eds.), *Redefining families: Implications for children's development* (pp. 171–218). New York: Plenum.

Silverstein, M., & Bengtson, V. L. (1997). Intergenerational solidarity and the structure of adult child-parent relationships in American families. *American Journal of Sociology, 103,* 429–460.

Silverstein, M., & Ruiz, S. (2006). Breaking the chain: How grandparents moderate the transmission of maternal depression to their children. *Family Relations, 55,* 601–612.

Silverstein, N., & Vehvilainen, L. (2000). Grandparents and schools: Issues and potential challenges. In C. Cox (Ed.), *To grandmother's house we go and stay: Perspectives on custodial grandparents* (pp. 268–282). New York: Springer.

Smith, G. C., Palmieri, P., Hancock, G., & Richardson, R. (2008). Custodial grandmothers' psychological distress, dysfunctional parenting, and grandchildren's adjustment. *International Journal of Aging and Human Development, 67,* 327–358.

Smith, P. K., & Drew, L. M. (2002). Grandparenthood. In M. Bornstein (Ed.), *Handbook of parenting* (Vol. 3, pp. 141–172). Mahwah, NJ: Lawrence Erlbaum.

Soliz, J. (2007). Communicative predictors of a shared family identity: Comparison of grandchildren's perceptions of family of origin grandparents and stepgrandparents. *Journal of Family Communication, 7*, 177–194.

Somary, K., & Stricker, G. (1998). Becoming a grandparent: A longitudinal study of expectations and early experiences as a function of age and lineage. *The Gerontologist, 38*, 53–61.

Statistical Abstract of the United States. (2006). *Grandparents living with grandchildren by race and sex: 2006* (Subject table S1002). Washington, DC: U.S. Census Bureau, American Community Survey.

Statistical Abstract of the United States. (2008). *Births and birth rates.* Washington, DC: U.S. Census Bureau, American Community Survey.

Strom, R. D., Carter, T., & Schmidt, K. (2004). African-Americans in senior settings: On the need for educating grandparents. *Educational Gerontology, 30*, 287–304.

Strom, R. D., & Strom, S. K. (1991a). *Achieving grandparent potential: Viewpoints on building intergenerational relationships.* Newbury Park, CA: Sage.

Strom, R. D., & Strom, S. K. (1991b). *Becoming a better grandparent: Viewpoints on strengthening the family.* Newbury Park, CA: Sage.

Strom, R. D., Strom, S. K., & Collinsworth, P. (1991). Improving grandparent success. *Journal of Applied Gerontology, 9*, 480–491.

Strong, D. D., Bean, R. A., & Feinauer, L. L. (2010). Trauma, attachment, and family therapy with grandfamilies: A model for treatment. *Children and Youth Services Review, 32*, 44–50.

Szinovacz, M. E. (1998). Grandparent research: Past, present, and future. In M. Szinovacz (Ed.), *Handbook of grandparenthood* (pp. 1–22). Westport, CT: Greenwood.

Thiele, D. M., & Whelan, T. (2006). The nature and dimensions of the grandparent role. *Marriage and Family Review, 40*, 93–108.

Toledo, R., Hayslip, B., Emick, M., Toledo, C., & Henderson, C. (2000). Cross-cultural differences in custodial grandparenting. In B. Hayslip & R. Goldberg-Glen (Eds.), *Grandparents raising grandchildren: Theoretical, empirical, and clinical perspectives* (pp. 107–124). New York: Springer.

Uhlenberg, P. (2004). Historical forces shaping grandparent-grandchild relationships: Demography and beyond. *Annual Review of Gerontology and Geriatrics, 26*, 77–97.

Uhlenberg, P. (2009). Children in an aging society. *Journal of Gerontology: Social Sciences, 64B*, S489–S496.

Uhlenberg, P., & Hammill, B. (1998). Frequency of grandparent contact with grandchild sets: Six factors that make a difference. *The Gerontologist, 38*, 276–285.

Uhlenberg, P., & Kirby, J. (1998). Grandparenthood over time: Historical and demographic trends. In M. Szinovacz (Ed.), *Handbook on grandparenthood* (pp. 23–39). Westport, CT: Greenwood Press.

U.S. Bureau of the Census. (2000). *Current population survey.* Washington, DC: Government Printing Office.

Werner, P., & Lowenstein, A. (2001). Grandparenthood and dementia. *Clinical Gerontologist, 23*, 115–129.

White, D., Walker, A., & Richards, L. (2008). Intergenerational family support following infant death. *International Journal of Aging and Human Development, 67,* 187–208.

White, J. (2008). A phenomenological approach to understanding rural grandfather roles. *Dissertation Abstracts International Section A: Humanities and Social Sciences, 68,* 4426.

Williams, A., & Harwood, J. (2004). Intergenerational communication: Intergroup, accommodation, and family perspectives. In J. F. Nussbaum & J. Coupland (Eds.), *Handbook of aging and communication research* (2nd ed., pp. 115–137). New York: Lawrence Erlbaum.

Wood, S., & Liossis, P. (2007). Potentially stressful events and emotional closeness between grandparents and adult grandchildren. *Journal of Family Issues, 28,* 380–398.

9

Relationships in Older Stepfamilies

Lawrence Ganong and Marilyn Coleman

A stepfamily is a family in which at least one of the adults has a child or children from one or more previous unions (Ganong & Coleman, 2004). The members of a stepfamily may live in more than one household or they may share one residence—what all stepfamilies *must* have is a stepparent and a stepchild. A *stepparent* is an adult whose partner has at least one child from a previous union. A *stepchild* is a person of any age whose parent has partnered with someone who is not the stepchild's biological or adoptive parent. Stepchildren may have two stepparents if both parents repartner. Stepfamilies may be formed following divorce, separation of a cohabiting union, or the death of a parent. A stepfamily is also formed when a never-married mother marries a man who is not the father of her child. Over the life course, an individual may be a member of several stepfamilies, particularly if a parent or the individual has a series of intimate relationships.

A *multigenerational stepfamily* is an extended family system of three or more generations that contain one or more intergenerational steprelationships. A *stepgrandparent* is an adult who either (a) has a partner who has offspring from one or more prior unions and those offspring have children or (b) has offspring who have remarried or repartnered with someone who has at least one child from a previous union. A *stepgrandchild* is an individual who either (a) has a stepparent with living parents (i.e., the stepgrandparents) or (b) has a grandparent who has remarried or repartnered with someone who is not related genetically or legally to the individual.

The definitions in the previous paragraphs are broad definitions of stepfamilies and stepfamily positions that include stepfamilies formed after remarriages as well as those formed after cohabitation. These definitions include homosexual as well as heterosexual relationships and allow for the possibility that adults in each generation may have experienced multiple intimate unions in which they may or may not have reproduced or adopted children. These inclusive conceptualizations of stepfamily relationships reflect the complexity and diversity of stepfamily systems; such broad definitions make it imperative that those who study stepfamilies think carefully about which groups of stepfamilies or which specific steprelationships they are studying.

REMARRIAGES AND REPARTNERING

Stepfamilies are formed when an adult remarries or cohabits, or in the case of multigenerational stepfamilies, they also may be formed when a son or daughter remarries or cohabits. Therefore, steprelationships are involuntary—they are created because other family members have joined together in an intimate union. It makes sense to consider the effects of remarriages and repartnerships on stepfamily relationships in later life, and to do that it is important to understand the contexts and processes involving these involuntary stepfamily relationships.

Remarriage and Repartnering in Later Life

"Romance begins in the cradle and extends to the grave" (Huyck, 2001, p. 1). This quotation highlights the fact that seeking and maintaining intimate attachments are normal activities at any age, although older adults often experience barriers to romantic relationships. Alemán (2009) reported that initial research examining long-term marriages and later-life dating and remarriage uncovered some ambivalence regarding romantic relationships among older adults. For example, many residents in a retirement community felt tension between wanting a physical relationship yet perceiving such a relationship as inappropriate (Alemán, 2009). Gibson (1993) found that many older adults viewed their sexuality shamefully and likened romance among the elderly to public drunkenness.

Cultural ideologies support older adult's feelings of shame and inappropriateness considering romantic relationships. For one, there is a cultural myth that older adults are essentially asexual and not interested in romantic relationships (Alemán, 2003). No doubt that is true of some older adults, but it certainly is not the case for all. This myth, however, likely affects how older persons think about themselves as well as how others think about them.

A second disincentive, particularly for older adults who are single, is the fact that family members often do not approve of their elderly relatives engaging in romantic relationships (De Jong Gierveld & Peeters, 2003; Sherman & Boss, 2007), and children often treat their elderly parent's romantic partner as an unwelcome interloper. Some adult children may be unwilling to accept a replacement of their dead parent, and others may be concerned about their inheritance should their widowed parent become romantically involved (Brown, Lee, & Bulanda, 2006). When an older adult lives with an adult child, that child may discourage the parent from seeking romantic ties. Staff in nursing homes and assisted living facilities also seldom support romantic relationships between unmarried adults and may provide disincentives for them, although if the older adults are not cognitively impaired, such relationships should not be discouraged (M. Rantz, personal communication, October 27, 2010).

In other cases, older widows and widowers may ignore the possibility of romance out of loyalty to the deceased partner. Men may avoid romantic relationships for fear of sexual dysfunction, and women may feel that they are no longer sexually attractive (Gibson, 1993). Cultural myths (e.g., older people are asexual), combined with other social barriers (e.g., romantic partnerships are not supported by family, friends, or caregivers in elder care facilities) probably repress romantic relationships, remarriage, and cohabiting among elderly adults in the United States, although there are demographic factors that suggest that romantic repartnerships in later life could increase in the next few decades despite barriers.

The romantic partnership status of older adults is challenging to study, and it is difficult to draw conclusions from the limited research that exists. One reason for this difficulty is that numerous paths can lead to later-life remarriage and cohabitation, and these pathways represent substantively different life courses (see Figure 9.1). For example, some older adults have been remarried for years, even decades, whereas other older adults did not remarry until they were middle aged, and still others met new partners in a nursing home or senior center at quite advanced ages. Factors related to later life repartnering include prior marital statuses (i.e., death of a spouse or divorce), gender, health, age, the number of children, and financial status (Bulcroft, Bulcroft, Hatch, & Borgatta, 1989). It is also likely that the number of prior intimate unions, race and ethnicity, and perhaps other variables predict whether or not older adults will remarry in later life. Unfortunately, many studies of remarried adults examine only a few of these variables, and samples of older remarried couples seldom distinguish between those in long-term remarriages and those who more recently repartnered.

The marital status of older persons differs by gender. The majority of men remain married until death, which is not true of women (De Jong Gierveld, 2002). For example, in the United States unmarried women outnumber unmarried men by 1.5:1 among those 55 and older, and that ratio becomes even less balanced with advancing age (U.S. Bureau of the Census, 2003). Consequently, older women who are divorced or widowed are more likely to be unpartnered (73%) than men are (41%), and men are twice as likely as women to cohabit (6% vs. 3%) or remarry (53% vs. 24%), in part because of a greater availability of partners for men (Chevan, 1996).

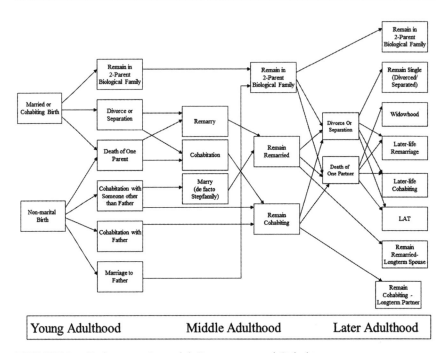

FIGURE 9.1 Pathways to Later-life Remarriage and Cohabitation

Remarriage Statistics

In recent years, approximately one-half million persons over the age of 65 have remarried each year in the United States (U.S. Bureau of the Census, 1995). Older adults who had remarried at least once and who remained remarried in 2000 included 23.3% of men and 19.4% of women in the 50–59-year-old cohort, 22.1% of men and 13.7% of women in the 60–69-year-old cohort, and 15.7% of men and 7.2% of women in the 70+ cohort (Kreider, 2005).

Approximately 4% to 10% of widows over the age of 65 (Schoen & Standish, 2001) and 20% of older widowers (Smith, Zick, & Duncan, 1991) have been remarried. Widowed men have higher rates of remarriage shortly after a spouse dies, but these rates are lower with age. This reduction in likelihood of remarriage may indicate that men's interest in remarrying wanes over time, despite the increasing pool of eligible women (Smith et al., 1991). Men's reduced financial resources and poorer health as they age also may contribute to their lowered rate of remarriage as they get older—they become less desirable to eligible women. Women who have financial resources are less apt than men to remarry after divorce or widowhood (Elman & London, 2002).

In England, divorced women between the ages of 55 and 64 are three times more likely than widowed women to remarry (12.5% compared to 4.4%), but this discrepancy disappears with age (U.K. Marriage, Divorce, and Adoptions Statistics, 2002). Divorced women over the age of 75 are only slightly more likely than widows to remarry (0.5% versus 0.3%). Divorced men over the age of 75, however, are 12 times more likely to remarry than divorced women. Although there is a low probability of remarriage, divorced women between the ages of 65 and 74 are more likely to remarry than are widowed men over the age of 74 (3.3% compared to 2%).

Cohabitation Statistics

The number of persons over age 50 who cohabit was approximately 2.2 million in 2008 (Brown & Kawamura, 2010), an increase from 1.2 million in 2000 (U.S. Bureau of the Census, 2000). Although men comprise only 25% of the elderly unmarried population, they account for nearly 60% of older cohabitors (Chevan, 1996).

There are many things we do not know about older cohabitors, but we do know that nearly all have had prior marital experience and that cohabiting is more common among blacks and Hispanics than among non-Hispanic whites (Brown et al., 2006). Because blacks and Hispanics are increasing as a proportion of the U.S. older population (Wherry & Finegold, 2004), it is likely that the number of older cohabitors will continue to increase. To provide perspective on the cohabitation trend, Chevan (1996) estimated that fewer than 10,000 older people cohabited in the United States in 1960. That figure had increased to 500,000 older couples in 1970, and today there are nearly 6.8 million older cohabiting couples (Brown & Kawamura, 2010). Despite this increase, however, only about 2% of persons over the age of 51 cohabit (Brown et al., 2006).

It is perhaps not surprising that older individuals in the younger cohort (those older than 50 but younger than 70—the young old) cohabit in greater numbers than those in the older cohort. Cohabiting became more common as these young old people reached adulthood, so a large percentage of this cohort likely experienced cohabiting when younger, and they generally are not morally opposed to it. The fact that the current younger cohort of older persons is more likely to cohabit is another factor indicating that the number of older adults cohabiting will likely increase in the future, as more Baby Boomers reach 50. Although little is known about the dynamics of cohabiting among older adults, evidence shows that the motivations to cohabit are different for them than for younger adults (Brown et al., 2006; King & Scott, 2005). For example, there are greater incentives for older adults to cohabit and fewer to remarry, especially if they have substantial economic resources.

Motivations for Repartnering in Later Life

Davidson (2002) found that the chances of repartnering after age 65 depended on three factors: (1) availability of partners (sex ratio), (2) feasibility (determined by variables such as age, health, and financial assets), and (3) desirability (motivation to repartner, which is governed by desire but also by societal and familial expectations). Some researchers found that men, who have a favorable sex ratio (many more older women than men), are interested in repartnerships: "I'd say to anyone who has been left on his own, go out and find yourself a nice lady friend to live with as quickly as you can" (quote from a 73-year-old cohabiting man, De Jong Gierveld, 2002, p. 65). But older men's interest in repartnering may have been overstated. Carr (2004), in an analysis of the Changing Lives of Older Couples Study, found that less than half of the men in the study were interested in dating or remarriage, and other studies have reported that older (55–69) single men and women had less desire to marry than younger single adults (Mahay & Lewis, 2007) and that older cohabitors plan to marry their partners less often than young cohabitors do (King & Scott, 2005).

The women in Davidson's (2002) study had little desire to remarry or, in some cases, to even establish cross-gender friendships. Mrs. J. B., aged 75, said, "No, I wouldn't want to marry again. You know if you get 'life' you only do 25 years [in prison]. I did 50!" (Davidson, 2002, p, 311). The low motivation to repartner appeared to be due primarily to avoid becoming obligated to take care of someone else. Some women had been in marriages with traditionally gendered divisions of household labor and did not want to repeat that experience. Other women had experienced the stress of caring for a dying spouse and were unwilling to relive those events.

Women who remarry and end up caring for an elderly partner may live to regret the decision to remarry. Although spousal caregiving research has focused almost totally on couples in first-married families, a study of late-life remarried caregivers of husbands suffering dementia found that several women regretted that their remarriage did not result in a shared sense of belonging to a stepfamily (Sherman & Boss, 2007). These women were both surprised and dismayed by the lack of help with caregiving tasks offered by both their own children and the children of their remarried husbands. In addition to failing to provide caregiving support, the women's adult stepchildren often challenged their decisions regarding the care of their husbands. Because health policies in the United States primarily rely on family members to provide care for older adults, including those with dementia, the authors concluded that there is a need for research on spousal caregiving in later-life remarriages: "Research on late-life remarried couples facing chronic illness and caregiving is practically nonexistent" (Sherman & Boss, 2007, p. 249).

It may be that in addition to wanting to avoid burdensome end-of-life caregiving, older unmarried women do not wish to remarry for fear of losing the personal control and independence they have. Pyke (1994) found that young and middle-aged women who remarried wanted to establish more decision-making power in their second marriages than they had in first marriages. Older women also may be uninterested in remarriage if they think it will require assuming a subordinate role, and losing some of their autonomy. However, repartnering may be appealing to some older adults because they are lonely (Peters & Liefbroer, 1997; Vinick, 1978) or because they find it financially challenging to maintain a household alone.

Examining remarriage and cohabitation among older adults is important because the well-being of older persons is at least partially determined by their living arrangements—those who live alone do less well unless they create living arrangements that involve social integration (Harper, 2003). Cross-sectional and longitudinal evidence suggests that divorced elders tend to have the highest mortality rate, followed by widowed persons, those who never married, and finally those who are married, a comparative marital status advantage that is greater for men than women (Harper, 2003). There is limited evidence that later-life remarriage has a health benefit for older adults (Burks, Lund, Gregg, & Bluhm, 1988), but the extent to which this holds true for remarried older couples (Carr & Springer, 2010) or those in other kinds of romantic relationships (e.g., cohabiting), is unknown.

How people cope with romantic relationships and their living arrangements in old age depends on a number of things, including whether they choose to cohabit or remarry. For example, religious beliefs and social disapproval by family and social networks are barriers to cohabiting; the more religious people are, the less likely they are to cohabit (Clarksberg, Stolzenberg, & Waite, 1995). Older cohabitors, especially men, also are more likely than remarriers to have been previously divorced rather than widowed and to have more physical problems. Brown and colleagues (2006) speculated that older men with poorer health seek new partners to help care for them, and they can find women willing to cohabit but not to marry them. Cohabiting is probably easier than marriage for women to leave when relationships are unsatisfying or when support for the relationship from adult children and stepchildren is not forthcoming.

To put the romantic relationships of older adults and the subsequent effects of those relationships on later life stepfamilies into perspective, Sheehy (1995) described five different cohorts (three of them are described below) and the factors that have influenced how they moved through the life course. The Depression Kids cohort (called the Greatest Generation by some, see Chapter 2) were ages 16 to 19 from 1937 to 1944. They entered young adulthood when gender roles were strictly differentiated and marriage was the bedrock of society. For this religiously oriented cohort, the only acceptable forms of sexual gratification were heterosexual, within a legal marriage. Few in this age group divorced, and when they were widowed, few looked to remarry and even fewer to cohabit. Stepfamilies would be seen as unusual by this cohort, who reached later adulthood in the last two decades of the 20th century. This cohort likely would be uncomfortable with stepfamily status, even to the extent of hiding it by presenting steprelationships as nuclear family ties.

The next cohort, the War Babies, which has been termed the Silent Generation, was born between 1936 and 1945. Members of this group married early, and almost all married and had children. Their relationships were bound to a great extent by differentiated gender roles, but much less so than the Greatest Generation. It was this generation that began the trend of divorcing at higher levels than previous generations. Women entered the workforce and male-female relationships were undergoing changes as these adults reached middle age. Those who remarried created incompletely institutionalized families— stepfamilies lacked norms to follow, laws and policies did not include their distinct configurations and relationships, and people even lacked labels with which to describe their stepfamily roles and relationships (Cherlin, 1978).

Those born from 1946 to 1955 were called the Vietnam Generation (Early Boomers cohort) and were the leading edge of the Baby Boomers. Cohabiting became more acceptable when they were young adults, and because of the advent of the birth control pill, they were the first cohort able to separate sexual activity from marriage without fear of pregnancy. Many of this generation espoused egalitarian romantic relationships, and religious affiliation is generally lower in this cohort although there is great within-group diversity. This cohort likely will be the first set of older adults to cohabit in significant numbers. Many of them have been divorced, so they are much more likely to have been a member of a stepfamily prior to age 65. They also may be more likely than earlier cohorts to enter into later-life unions and become stepgrandparents. This cohort also contains a substantial proportion of adults who have had serial intimate partnerships, and who may have been involved in a series of stepfamilies as adults. Each of these cohorts will have had different experiences with remarriage, cohabiting, raising stepchildren, and becoming stepgrandparents.

In northern Europe, changes in partnering among elderly couples have followed changes that have taken place over the last several decades among younger couples. There has been a marked increase in older couples who cohabit and an even greater increase in older couples who engage in what is termed living apart together or LAT (see Bookwala, chapter 5 in this volume, for a discussion of LAT caregiving in later life). In the Netherlands, researchers found that adults 50 and older who repartnered later in life chose cohabiting or living apart together more often than remarriage (De Jong Gierveld & Peeters, 2003). Reasons given for not remarrying included: (a) wanting to remain independent; (b) wanting to continue living in their own home, and (c) not wanting to lose or reduce financial benefits from a previous marriage. LAT relationships allow older adults to avoid loneliness yet remain independent, continue living in their home, and not lose their previous spouse's Social Security and pension benefits. An advantage that LAT couples in the

Netherlands have over couples in the United States, however, is that in the Netherlands government-provided pensions are large enough that elderly persons can afford to live alone in their own homes. As is true of much of northern Europe, the Netherlands is increasingly becoming a secular society, so there are fewer religious and moral imperatives inhibiting LAT relationships than is true in the United States.

A recent mixed-method investigation in Sweden of 116 elderly men and women living in LAT relationships found that women may be choosing LAT relationships to escape gendered distribution of household labor (Karlsson & Borell, 2005). More women than men were in LAT relationships, which provides some support for this notion. Four women who were interviewed in depth shared that having their own home represented freedom to them and allowed them control over how much cleaning and cooking they wanted to do for their partner. LAT partners kept their finances separate, and some argued over whether or not they should have keys to each other's homes. The amount of contact between LAT partners varied considerably—36% met one another almost every day, 51% one or more times per week, and 12% twice a month or less. More than half the sample (66%) had integrated the LAT partner into their network of friends and kin at some level. The LAT relationships were characterized by a primary focus on the satisfaction that emotional closeness with another person can provide, but focus was also on autonomy. The absence of established cultural rules seemed to make establishing boundaries for LAT couples a deliberate, strategic, and often untried process.

Older persons in Western cultures who remarry probably do so, at least partly, because of traditional values they and their friends and family hold. LAT couples cite maintaining independence as well as not having to adjust to incompatibilities in personality and routines that might make the person a good partner for some purposes but not to marry or share a household (Karlsson & Borell, 2005; Davidson, 2001). Individualism and secularism appear to be factors influencing the number of older adults who cohabit or choose LAT relationships, but it is difficult to speculate about how these trends might play out in the United States over the next few decades. Americans are highly individualistic but rather mixed on secularism.

Regardless of how it is done, repartnering in old age has significant psychological and physical benefits (Moorman, Booth, & Fingerman, 2006). Marriage is a protective factor associated with longer life, a finding that appears to be true across developed countries and across time periods (Carr & Springer, 2010), although a few studies have found this to be true only of men (Tower, Kasl, & Darefsky, 2002). Older people with partners, whether in first marriages or remarriages, take fewer health risks than those who do not have partners, and partners also take care of each other's health needs (Franks, Wendorf, Gonzalez, & Ketterer, 2004). When older adults are alone it means that companionship, solidarity, assistance, and care have to come from outside the household. Some older adults living alone seem to be able to expand their networks in other ways, but most do this by repartnering. Older divorced persons, particularly men who live alone, tend to be socially isolated, even more so than widowed men who live alone (Kaufman & Uhlenberg, 1998). Women who are widowed or divorced may gain confidence from learning the tasks that their husbands performed, but rather than learning the tasks their wives performed for them, men tend to become depressed. Therefore, men stand to gain more psychological and physical benefits from repartnering than do women (see Bookwala, chapter 5 in this volume, for an extensive literature review on differences in morbidity and mortality related to different partner and repartnered statuses).

Partner Satisfaction in Old Age

Bograd and Spilka (1996) compared adults who remarried between the ages of 60 and 75 with adults who remarried in midlife (30–45), and, as is typical of most studies of marriage, the women were slightly but not significantly less satisfied with their marriages than were the men. There was less disclosure in later-life remarriages than in midlife remarriages, yet the men in late-life remarriages were significantly more satisfied than men in midlife remarriage. One possible reason for the differences is that men in midlife remarriages likely had stepchildren living with them, which tends to be a stressor for stepfamily members (Ganong & Coleman, 2004).

Using the naming of the spouse as a confidant as a measure of marital satisfaction, Tower and colleagues (2002) concluded that adults in both first marriages and remarriages named their spouses as a confidant and were named by their spouses as a confidant in similar proportions, and this was independent of the number of years married. Although not a direct measure of marital satisfaction, perceptions of sexual relationships may be a related factor. Clarke (2006) interviewed 24 women aged 52 to 90 who had remarried after age 50 and asked them to recount and compare their sexual relationships (defined as sexual intercourse) with their first, second, and in a few cases, third husbands. Most reported satisfying sexual chemistry with their later-life spouses, but they also reported that their own and their spouse's health often interfered with the ability to have intercourse, an inability, however, that was not related to their overall marital satisfaction. Although sexual intercourse rates declined over time, most reported that they established strong emotional bonds with their husbands and found other ways to express affection. Most of these women reported that they had remarried for companionship, and the most important things they and their remarried spouses shared were companionship, closeness, and emotional warmth; sexual intercourse was not a priority in their remarried relationships.

Not all remarriages, however, are satisfying. Adapting to remarriage in old age is more difficult than is true for younger persons, and in some cases the inability to adapt results in extreme dissatisfaction and even spousal abuse. Lowenstein and Ron (1999) studied a group of 12 older remarried Israelis who were identified by welfare and health professionals as victims of abuse by family members. They found that causes of conflict, unhappiness, and abuse were unrealistic expectations, difficulties dealing with the emotions associated with combining households, a sense of being financially exploited, issues of power and control, and issues of jealousy related to a sense of competition with the deceased spouse. They also determined that older adults who remarried for pragmatic reasons, such as a desire for the positive financial and social aspects of being married rather than the selection of an appropriate partner, fared poorly. These older persons seemed to have ignored personal-psychological reasons for remarriage such as emotional and social closeness. The authors suggested that older people considering remarriage should talk about issues related to their living arrangement and finances, their expectations for the remarriage, how decisions will be made, and how they will handle problems with each other's children and grandchildren.

Although most studies of relationship quality have been of remarried older couples, King and Scott (2005) reported that older cohabiting couples experienced higher levels of relationship satisfaction and stability than did younger cohabitors. Older cohabitors were more likely to see their relationships as an alternative to marriage, whereas younger cohabitors were more likely to plan to marry their partner.

ADULT CHILDREN AND STEPCHILDREN

Although most of the studies on the relationships among stepparents, parents, and children in stepfamilies have focused on younger stepfamilies, there are a few longitudinal investigations in which children or adolescents in stepfamilies have been followed into adulthood. There are even a few studies on middle-aged adults and their elderly parents and stepparents. The research on parents' and stepparents' relationships with adult stepchildren in older stepfamilies generally has examined two dimensions of these relationships—closeness and resources exchanged among family members.

Virtually all of the research on the relationships between adult children and their aging remarried parents and stepparents has been predicated on the assumption that parental divorce and subsequent remarriages negatively affect relationships, with researchers hypothesizing that these marital transitions (a) reduce parental investments in children across the life course, even into later life (e.g., Kalmijn, 2007), (b) increase stress and conflict within families (De Jong Gierveld & Peeters, 2003), and (c) reduce family solidarity (e.g., Soliz, 2007). Differences in remarried mothers' and fathers' closeness to children are largely explained by mothers' greater kinkeeping proclivities compared to fathers (e.g., Kalmijn, 2007), and differences in adult children's closeness to parents and stepparents have been explained by differential investments in children, greater conflicts between stepparents and stepchildren, and greater solidarity and identification with biological parents (Kalmijn, 2007).

Closeness

Frequency of contact between adult children and their remarried parents and stepparents is a commonly used measure of relationship closeness. Older parents who remarried when their children were young have less contact with their adult children than do continuously married parents (Aquilino, 1994; Kalmijn, 2007; Lawton, Silverstein, & Bengtson, 1994), as do parents whose remarriages started later in life (De Jong Gierveld & Peeters, 2003; Kalmijn, 2007). In addition, parents in cohabiting and LAT relationships formed later in life have less contact with adult children than do remarried parents (De Jong Gierveld & Peeters, 2003).

Comparisons of remarried mothers' and fathers' contacts with children have mixed findings. For instance, remarried noncustodial fathers had significantly less contact with adult children than did remarried mothers (Aquilino, 1994; Kalmijn, 2007). Aquilino (1994) found that remarried custodial mothers had only slightly lower relationship quality with adult children, compared to continuously married mothers, but that these remarried mothers' contacts with their adult children were significantly fewer than for married mothers and their adult children. The remarriage of custodial fathers had small but nonsignificant effects on their frequency of contacts with adult children and relationship quality, compared to married fathers. Aquilino (1994) also reported that when mothers remarried and adult children acquired a stepfather, the adult children's contacts with nonresidential fathers were lower than contacts between divorced mothers and their adult children, although relationship quality was not. Custodial fathers' remarriages had large negative effects on adult children's contact frequency and relationship quality with nonresidential mothers. Sons and daughters did not react differently to parental remarriages (Aquilino, 1994).

Adult offspring and their older parents live together for many reasons (e.g., financial, health-related). Some researchers have defined the coresidence of adult children and their parents as an indicator of relationship quality. Findings about adult children sharing a residence with older parents and stepparents have been mixed, however, with some researchers reporting that adult children were less likely to live in a remarried parent's home than were children whose parents had remained married when they were young (Aquilino, 1991; Pezzin, Pollak, & Schone, 2008), whereas others found that coresidence was less likely with remarried fathers and more likely with remarried mothers (Szinovacz, 1997). Still other studies reported no differences in residence sharing of adult stepchildren and individuals from first-marriage families (White & Rogers, 1997).

Vinick (1998), in a qualitative study of 36 long-term remarried couples, reported that both mothers and fathers felt they had worked hard to rectify difficult relationships with children over the years. She referred to stepmothers as carpenters because they helped rebuild and repair disengaged relationships between their husbands and the husbands' adult children (Vinick & Lanspery, 2000). Stepmothers also worked hard at maintaining good relationships with their stepchildren. Men felt that they were closer to the stepchildren they had reared than they were to their nonresidential children, whereas women felt they had closer ties with their children (most of whom had lived with them growing up) than with their stepchildren, irrespective of whether the stepchildren lived with them while growing up (Vinick, 1998).

Women generally are involved in what is called *kinkeeping*—maintaining relationships with extended family members, smoothing disagreements among kin, and making sure that relationships are amicable. Because of these kinkeeping activities, remarried mothers and stepmothers develop different relationships than fathers and stepfathers do, and their relationships with adult children differ from those of fathers and stepfathers as a result (Schmeekle, 2007). For example, Schmeekle (2007) reported that older stepmothers' kinkeeping was instrumental in children maintaining ties with nonresidential fathers when they were young, whereas stepfathers primarily were sources of financial support for children. These gendered practices continued into the children's adulthood and affected relationship closeness, not only among stepfamily household members but also with children's nonresidential parents. Although stepmothers were kinkeepers, parents and stepparents, regardless of sex, served as relationship gatekeepers for their own kin and invested more energy and resources into their own children than stepchildren.

Exchanging Resources

Support for Older Adults

Wachter (1997) argued that older adults who had stepchildren had an expanded pool of potential caregivers compared to older adults without children and those with a small number of genetic or adopted offspring. Whether or not this is the case may depend primarily on the quality of the stepkin relationship, which likely depends mainly on how much the older stepparent

helped raise the adult stepchild and provided support to the stepchild financially, emotionally, physically, and in other ways over the years (Coleman,
Ganong, Hans, Sharp, & Rothrauff, 2005; Ganong & Coleman, 1998, 2006a;
Ganong, Coleman, & Rothrauff, 2009). In several studies, Ganong,
Coleman, and colleagues found that having helped raise a stepchild was
important because it elicited a belief that the older stepparent was a family
member to whom the adult stepchild owed a debt that should be repaid.

Although other factors such as the availability of resources for both generations may be relevant in making judgments about a stepchild providing
assistance to an older stepparent in need (Ganong & Coleman, 2006b), relationship closeness or relationship quality was the primary consideration
of whether or not there is an intergenerational obligation to assist an older
family member (Coleman et al., 2005; Ganong & Coleman, 1998, 2006a;
Ganong at al., 2009). If steprelationships are emotionally close, they are seen
as family bonds, and therefore normative beliefs about family obligations to
assist kin in need and norms about intergenerational reciprocity were applied (Coleman et al., 2005; Ganong & Coleman, 1998, 2006a; Ganong et al.,
2009). Consequently, it is unlikely that a stepparent acquired in later life will
receive much aid from adult stepchildren because the stepparent would not
have had time to build a close relationship or share resources with adult stepchildren. Steprelationships acquired in later life are not typically seen as family ties by either older stepparents or adult stepchildren, and therefore there
is no feeling of family obligation to assist the older stepparent (Ganong &
Coleman, 2006a). In addition, the presence of adult children of the stepparent further reduces any sense of obligation ascribed to stepchildren
(Ganong & Coleman, 2006a).

Wachter (1997) may have been right about more help being available
to long-term stepparents who helped raise their stepchildren and who created and maintained emotionally close bonds with them, but it is doubtful
that stepparents with distant or hostile relationships with stepchildren, or
stepparents who are not seen as kin to the stepchild, would receive much
support later in life. In a related finding, Pezzin, Pollack, and Schone (2009)
reported that stepchildren have weaker incentives to provide care for elderly
stepparents because attachment is weaker in steprelationships than in genetic
parent-child bonds.

In general, adult children who lived in stepfamilies provide less support on
average to older parents and stepparents than do adult children from nuclear
families (Aquilino, 2005; De Jong Gierveld & Peeters, 2003; Kalmijn, 2007;
Pezzin & Schone, 1999; Pezzin et al., 2008; White, 1994b, but see Aquilino,
1994). The lesser support of stepparents than parents is true even when older
parents have supported children in the past. Amato, Rezac, and Booth (1995)
found that even though remarried mothers gave as much to their adult children as did married mothers, they received less support from children than

did first marriage mothers. Fathers generally receive less support of various kinds than do mothers, regardless of age and family structure.

Resources Given to Younger Adults

Although not all studies report differences between first-marriage and re-marriage families in the amount of resources exchanged between adult children and parents and stepparents (e.g., Aquilino, 1994; Eggebeen, 1992), most researchers have reported, on average, that remarried parents provide less financial and instrumental support to adult children and stepchildren than parents in first marriages provide support to children (White, 1992, 1994b). Remarried mothers may give some types of support to adult children as much as do married mothers (Amato et al., 1995; Marks, 1995; Spitze & Logan, 1992), however, and they exchange more resources with adult children than do remarried fathers (Amato et al., 1995; White, 1994a). Remarried parents and stepparents are less likely to perceive that they have obligations to provide financial support to adult children than are married mothers and fathers (Aquilino, 2005; Killian, 2004).

Most studies of resource exchanges between adult children and parents and stepparents have ignored the possibility that adult stepchildren may receive and give resources to adults living in two households. The differences in intergenerational exchanges found between adult children in stepfamilies and those in nuclear families are often relatively small. For example, White (1994b) found that 47% of adult children from first-marriage families received help from parents compared to 41% from stepfather households and 38% from stepmother households. Given the small differences in intergenerational exchanges between adult stepchildren and adult children in nuclear families, it is likely that adult stepchildren may receive almost as much support as adult children from continuously married parents, if both of their biological parents' households are examined. The fact is, some adult stepchildren have three or four older adults living in two households for whom they might need to provide support, so researchers must be careful when studying intergenerational exchanges in stepfamilies to accurately assess the demands and resources available.

SIBLINGS, HALF-SIBLINGS, AND STEPSIBLINGS IN OLDER STEPFAMILIES

Sibling relationships are generally the longest close relationships that individuals have over their lives. In stepfamilies, in addition to sibling relationships, there are also half-siblings and stepsiblings. Half-siblings share a genetic connection through one parent, sharing either a mother or a father.

Stepsiblings are not related, but are brought together in a stepfamily when the parent of one stepsibling marries or repartners with the parent of another.

Half-siblings and stepsiblings are less likely to have shared a residence full-time while growing up than are full siblings (White & Reidman, 1992). Perhaps as a result, sibling solidarity and relational closeness are greater among middle-aged siblings in stepfamilies than among half-siblings and stepsiblings (White & Reidman, 1992). Contact with siblings as middle aged adults is greater for siblings than for half-siblings and stepsiblings

Studies of children and adolescents indicate that sibling attachment is stronger than stepsibling attachment (Jankowiak & Diderich, 2000). Some researchers also have reported closer emotional bonds between full siblings than half-siblings (Jankowiak & Diderich, 2000). In qualitative studies, however, researchers have reported that half-siblings are generally indistinguishable in emotional closeness from siblings when the half-siblings live together all or most of the time during their childhoods (Bernstein, 1997; Ganong & Coleman, 2004). Younger half-siblings who share a residence generally consider themselves to be brothers and sisters, and rarely do children and adolescents who live with half-siblings use the "half" label to designate these relationships or to differentiate them from full sibling ties (Ganong & Coleman, 2004). It is primarily when children and adolescents who are half-siblings live in separate households, see each other rarely, and have relatively large age differences between them that they consider themselves to be half-siblings. Adult half-siblings and stepsiblings are likely not as close as full siblings because the opportunities to develop bonds are less frequent for them.

Stepsiblings and half-siblings are more likely than siblings to have large age differences between them, primarily because there are larger age differences between remarried partners than between first-marriage couples. When there are 10 or more years difference in age between remarried partners, and they both have children from prior unions, it would not be terribly unusual for there to be large age gaps between the stepsiblings.

What implications do these findings from younger stepfamilies have for stepsibling relationships in later life? It may be conjectured that relationships between middle-aged adult stepsibling are distant. Contact is likely to be infrequent, and would likely center around holidays or birthday celebrations of the older parent or stepparent. If the remarriage or repartnering of the older generation adults did not take place until later in their lives when adult children have grown and established their own homes, it is probable that adult stepsiblings may not have met each other, or have seen each other rarely. It also is probable that they do not recognize each other as kin, and it is unlikely that they would use labels such as stepbrother or stepsister to describe each other to outsiders. Stepsiblings who grew up together probably would regard each other with more affection than stepsiblings who entered the relationship later in life as adults, but even long-term stepsiblings are unlikely to be as close as siblings unless they had spent substantial time together growing up. The same factors would hold for half-siblings in older stepfamilies—contact growing up would be important. Half-siblings with little contact as youth would likely not relate closely as middle-aged adults in older stepfamilies.

Some evidence shows that stepsiblings are seen as sources of aid when older stepparents become frail and in need of daily care or when other chronic health problems might require adult stepchildren to function as caregivers (Pezzin et al., 2009). When an older stepparent needs aid, then stepchildren turn to their stepsiblings, the offspring of the stepparent, for help in caregiving—in fact, they usually expect the stepsiblings to assume responsibility for their own parent (Ganong & Coleman, 2006a; Pezzin et al., 2009). In other words, stepsiblings generally expect biological children to take care of their biological parents.

Few researchers have studied half-siblings, stepsiblings, and full siblings as adults in older stepfamilies. Nearly all of the studies have focused on younger stepfamilies, so much more needs to be investigated about how half-siblings and stepsiblings relate to each other as middle-aged or older adults.

The social network consequences of remarrying or repartnering on sibling relationships have rarely been studied, but the evidence suggests that reunions in later life have little effect on contact with siblings (De Jong Gierveld & Peeters, 2003). It is not known if remarriages or repartnering affect half-sibling and stepsibling relationships of older adults.

STEPGRANDPARENTS AND STEPGRANDCHILDREN IN STEPFAMILIES

Among older cohorts of adults, greater percentages are stepgrandparents and stepgreat-grandparents than ever before. Several demographic trends have led to an unparalleled number of multigenerational stepfamilies in the United States and other Western industrialized nations. These demographic trends are increased longevity; relatively high rates of both marital and nonmarital transitions (i.e., divorce, remarriage, cohabitation, and nonmarital repartnering); and increased multipartner fertility, both within and outside of marriage. For example, over a decade ago, nearly 40% of U.S. families had a stepgrandparent (Szinovacz, 1998). By 2030, estimates show that American grandparents will have almost as many stepgrandchildren as they do biological grandchildren (Wachter, 1997).

The multigenerational families that contain stepgrandparents and stepgrandchildren are structurally complex and heterogeneous. It is meaningless to discuss stepgrandparents without paying attention to issues such as when in the life course of all stepfamily members these relationships began, the type of relationships (biological or stepkin) that exist among older adults and middle-generation adults, and how long stepfamily members' lives have been linked together (Ganong & Coleman, 2004).

For example, stepgrandparent-stepgrandchild relationships are formed in three basic ways that occur within fundamentally different familial contexts. Long-term stepgrandparent-stepgrandchild relationships are created when an adult stepchild who grew up with a stepparent gives birth to or adopts children. Other stepgrandparent-stepgrandchild relationships are formed as a result of later-life marriages or nonmarital unions of a grandparent or when an older individual's adult child marries or forms a nonmarital union with a person who has children. Each of these ways of coming together is likely to yield distinct patterns of intergenerational interactions in these steprelationships.

STEPFAMILIES FORMED LATER IN LIFE

Stepgrandparent–Stepgrandchild Relationships

Children and grandchildren often do not welcome a grandparents' new partner into the family (Sherman & Boss, 2007). New partners are frequently perceived by children and grandchildren as a threat to family wealth, and they worry about the loss of inheritance to a grandparent's new partner and his or her children (Bornat, Dimmock, Jones, & Peace, 1999). People hold strong feelings about the inheritance of property and financial resources staying within genetic family lines (Coleman & Ganong, 1998). Children and grandchildren also express concern about who will take care of grandparents' new partners if they become frail (Kuhn, Morhardt, & Monbrod-Framburg, 1993; Sherman & Boss, 2007) and who will pay the costs involved with long-term care (Sherman & Bauer, 2008). These are difficult issues in all families, and the absence of long-term emotional attachments to stepkin acquired later in life may mean that stepfamilies often split along genetic family lines when caregiving crises occur (Ganong & Coleman, 2006a; Ganong et al., 2009). In general, individuals believe that genetic kin are responsible for taking care of their own elderly kin and that stepkin are responsible for taking care of their biological relatives (Ganong & Coleman, 2006a; Sherman & Boss, 2007).

It is probable, therefore, that stepgrandparent relationships formed via later-life marriages or cohabiting unions rarely become emotionally close; they may not even be perceived as kinship bonds (Bornat et al., 1999; Ganong & Coleman, 2006a; Ganong et al., 2009). If middle-generation adults whose parents remarry later in life do not think of themselves as being related to the new partner (Bornat et al., 1999), they would be disinclined to encourage their children to think of the stepgrandparent as kin, and would not encourage them to bond. Instead, it is more likely that a new spouse or cohabiting partner of a grandparent will be seen at best as a family friend or acquaintance rather than as a family member (Ganong & Coleman, 2006a). The reason that new partners of grandparents are not accepted as kin is relatively straightforward—members of intergenerational stepfamily relationships formed later in life generally have less contact than long-term stepfamily members because they have fewer years with which to build intergenerational relationships.

Moreover, members of intergenerational stepfamilies formed later in life may have little motivation to develop close ties. For example, because grandchildren are often adolescents or young adults when grandparents' later-life remarriages or repartnerings occur, developmental reasons may explain why they are less interested in establishing a relationship with the grandparent's new partner than if they were younger. One reason may be that adolescent or emerging adult grandchildren are typically withdrawing from family connections and exploring opportunities to develop pair bonds for themselves. Cherlin and Furstenberg (1986) found that the older the grandchildren were at the grandparent's remarriage, the less likely they were to regard stepgrandparents to be as important to them as genetic grandparents. Stepgrandparents in a union formed later in life also may be disinterested in developing relationships with stepgrandchildren, particularly if they have grandchildren of their own.

OFFSPRING REMARRIAGES OR REPARTNERSHIPS

Grandparent–Grandchild Relationships

Divorced and separated mothers with minor-aged children frequently turn to their parents for financial support, child care, emotional support, advice, and even a place to live (Johnson, 1992). Divorced fathers also seek support from their parents—particularly help with child care (Troilo & Coleman, in press). Support and grandparents' involvement with grandchildren often is reduced when the middle-generation parent remarries (Cherlin & Furstenberg, 1986; Clingempeel, Colyar, Brand, & Hetherington, 1992). Henry, Ceglian, and Ostrander (1993) postulated that grandparents' roles may need to be renegotiated when an adult child remarries or cohabits with a new partner because grandparents' access to grandchildren and their involvement with them may be mediated by the remarried couple.

After remarriage, it appears that the couple draws a boundary around their new stepfamily household, creating distance between themselves and others, including grandparents (Clingempeel et al., 1992). Because most stepfamily households are headed by mothers and stepfathers (Kreider, 2005), maternal grandparents probably see grandchildren after remarriage more often than paternal grandparents do. Moreover, mothers are more active than fathers in encouraging the parents of their new partners to develop grandparentlike relationships with their children. Consequently, paternal grandparents may lose more time with grandchildren after middle-generation remarriage than do maternal grandparents. In addition, some remarried fathers emotionally and psychologically replace their nonresidential biological children with the stepchildren with whom they live (Manning & Smock, 2000), and, if this is the case, there may be pressure on paternal grandparents to substitute one set of children for the other as well. On the other hand, it might be possible that kinkeeping custodial mothers are more likely than fathers to help paternal grandparents remain connected to their grandchildren, even after the mother remarries or cohabits with a new partner. Nonresidential stepmothers also may be kinkeepers and serve this function for stepchildren (Schmeekle, 2007), which should help paternal grandparents remain involved with grandchildren. Of course, adult grandchildren are able to maintain ties with grandparents with less interference from parents than younger grandchildren experience, although they still may be affected by the quality of their parents' relationships with their grandparents.

Despite the potential importance of the middle generation as a gatekeeper, evidence shows that long-term stepgrandparents can function as grandparents and are seen by stepgrandchildren as grandparents even when stepparent-stepchild relationships have been affectively neutral or even emotionally distant (Clawson & Ganong, 2002). In a grounded theory study of adult stepchild–older stepparent relationships, Clawson and Ganong found that adult stepchildren reconsidered their negative judgments about older stepparents when they saw how close their children felt toward the older stepgrandparents. Observing their stepparents reach out to their children with love, tangible resources, and emotional support changed how they felt about their stepparents. Close and loving relationships between long-term stepgrandparents and stepgrandchildren helped facilitate the development of closer relationships between stepgrandparents and their adult stepchildren.

Although grandparent involvement may be reduced after remarriage or repartnering of the middle generation, grandparents continue to be actively involved in their grandchildren's lives and their support and involvement benefit grandchildren in multiple ways (Attar-Schwartz, Tan, Buchanan, Flouri, & Griggs, 2009; Bornat et al., 1999; Lussier, Deater-Deckard, Dunn, & Davies, 2002; Mills, Wakeman, & Fea, 2001; Soliz, 2007). Unfortunately, we do not know much about how grandparents manage to remain involved with grandchildren after the remarriage of a child or former in-law, other than in communicating support to grandchildren (Soliz, 2007), nor do we know why their involvement benefits grandchildren in stepfamilies. Researchers speculate that grandparents provide stability when grandchildren are stressed by their parents' remarriages and the changes that accompany remarriage, such as moving, adjusting to a new stepparent and possibly stepsiblings, adapting to changes in household rules, and trying to maintain relationships with parents amidst these changes (Soliz, 2007).

Clinicians have asserted that grandparents can be either helpful or harmful to new stepfamilies (Visher & Visher, 1996). Grandparents can support the new stepfamily by accepting the remarried spouse, offering assistance when requested, and attempting to develop positive relationships with stepgrandchildren while maintaining good attachments with grandchildren, or they can try to undermine the stepfamily by criticizing the new stepparent's treatment of their grandchildren, refusing to accept new stepgrandchildren or a new son- or daughter-in law, using money and inheritance to punish or to divide younger generations, and favoring grandchildren over stepgrandchildren. Clinicians' assertions about how grandparents can affect stepfamilies are credible, but researchers have not conducted studies that examine them. Even less is known about grandparents in cohabiting stepfamilies.

AN AGENDA FOR RESEARCHERS

Remarriage and Repartnering in Cohabiting Relationships

Much of the focus on remarriage among older adults has been on who remarries later in life and who does not. Clearly, more research is needed on cohabitation and living apart together (LAT) relationships, not only who chooses such arrangements, but how the dynamics of cohabiting and LAT relationships differ from those of remarried couples in later life. Knowing about dynamics in these relationships formed later in life would help practitioners and even policymakers better understand how these couple bonds affect multigenerational family dynamics as well.

Researchers of younger stepfamily dynamics often contend that stepfamilies differ from first-marriage families in multiple ways (Ganong & Coleman, 2004); does this assertion hold for older stepfamilies as well? Do long-term remarriages, for instance, resemble long-term marriages in couple interactions, or are they more like remarriages formed later in life? Much of the literature on stepfamilies has focused on stepfamilies with minor-aged children, with a particular emphasis on the early years of stepfamily living. Very few studies of long-term steprelationships exist; consequently, little is known about the most durable and in some cases the most effective stepfamilies. More research on long-term remarriages and the stepfamilies created would yield valuable insights for researchers, practitioners, and policymakers.

Older adults are pressured by children and grandchildren not to remarry (Alemán, 2002), and individuals in later-life remarriages are not well supported by younger kin and stepkin (Sherman & Boss, 2007). Are these dynamics different when the older couple has made decisions prior to re-marriage on issues of inheritance, financial distributions, and even future caregiving? How do older couples prepare for remarriage or for cohabiting later in life? Are adult children and grandchildren included in remarriage or repartnering preparations?

How do family members perceive cohabiting unions formed in later life? Do older adults who have had a series of marriages or intimate cohabiting unions have different relationships with children and grandchildren than older adults who have had only one remarriage or repartnership? Serial unions over the life course create more complex stepfamily situations because they are more likely to include half-siblings born from multiple parental dyads and a greater likelihood of fictive kinship with ex-steprelationship partners. There is very little research on serial partnerships among older adults, yet some evidence shows that the stepfamilies formed following multiple part-nerships may be different from second unions (Ganong & Coleman, 2004). As the Baby Boomers reach old age, the number of older adults who have had multiple partners before their remarriages or repartnerships in their later years is likely to increase.

In addition, data indicate that women who have the financial resources to live alone are increasingly choosing to do so. They are opting out of remar-riage and cohabiting after divorce and widowhood, despite feeling somewhat guilty about their reluctance to become involved again in gendered care-giving. Caregiving in the United States is considered a family obligation, so how will spousal care be substituted among those who do not recouple after divorce and widowhood? Evidence of more gender neutral distribution of household labor among younger couples has emerged recently. Will older women be more amenable to partnering with men who are more egalitarian? Will LAT relationships spread in the United States as they have in north-ern and central Europe, and what will that mean for the well-being of older adults and their families? What effect does the economy have on the for-mation and maintenance of LAT unions? Economic downturns conceivably may either make LAT relationships more attractive (e.g., homes cannot be sold) or less attractive (e.g., two households are more expensive to maintain than one).

Finally, research about processes in older adult cohabiting and remarried families is absent from the literature. What do these couples do during an average day? Many are retired so they have large blocks of time they could spend together. Do they spend as much time together as older continuously married couples? How do they divide household labor? How do they make decisions about finances and other issues that have the potential to be con-tentious? How do older adults make decisions about dating, LAT, cohabit-ing, and remarriage? What societal factors do they view as supportive of their wishes to repartner? How do they locate suitable partners? Will social media and social networking play an increasing role in older adults finding new partners?

Older Stepparent and Adult Stepchild Relationships

Why do remarried parents and stepparents exchange fewer resources with stepchildren and biological children than married couples do with their children? Do differences in intergenerational support disappear when stepfamily complexity (two parental households) is taken into account? How does serial repartnering affect resource exchanges in older stepfamilies?

Wachter's (1997) speculation that older stepparents potentially widen the pool of younger kin and stepkin that can provide resources for them in later life has received some research attention, but questions still remain. Under what conditions is this speculation true, and when is it not the case? Ganong and Coleman (1999) hypothesized that relationship quality and a history of mutual intergenerational helping contribute to stepfamily members defining stepkin relationships as kinship bonds, and defining stepparents and stepchildren as family members results in greater perceived and felt obligations to assist. How robust is this complex hypothesis? Under what conditions and contexts, if any, is this hypothesis supported?

Grandparents and Stepgrandparents in Older Stepfamilies

In examinations of stepgrandparent-stepgrandchild relationships, researchers need to carefully disaggregate long-term stepgrandparents from those who acquire stepgrandchildren as middle-aged adults and from those who become stepgrandparents due to a later-life union. It is rarely clear in studies how long stepgrandchildren have known their stepgrandparents, and sometimes it is not clear how much contact they have had (e.g., daily, never met them). The early studies on intergenerational steprelationships were largely exploratory, and there is little research on relational processes (i.e., the development of relationships, how stepgrandparent-stepchild relationships are maintained). Qualitative research in which in-depth data are collected and observational studies would help address these gaps.

Some studies have found that some stepgrandparents play an important part in the lives of their stepgrandchildren (Henry et al., 1993; Sanders & Trygstad, 1989; Soliz, 2007). What do stepgrandparents do that enhances the lives of their stepgrandchildren? Are stepgrandparents perceived as kin by stepgrandchildren, and, if so, under what conditions? How do long-term stepfamilies decide that they will construct stepgrandparenthood as grandparenthood? How do the long-term stepfamilies who do this construction differ from those who do not? Does redefining these steprelationships as kinship bonds change the nature of the relationships? How does adding stepgrandparents as kin affect relations with biological grandparents?

Although later-life remarriages and repartnerings are still relatively rare, improved health into the later years and a growing number of older adults suggest that these unions may soon become more common as the Baby Boomers age. Thus far, however, researchers have conducted few studies on the effects of later-life unions on grandparents and grandchildren. Perhaps a grandparent's new partner's prior marital history (i.e., number, type of prior relationships), the number of children and grandchildren, physical health status, income, age, race and ethnicity, and other factors are relevant in predicting the nature of stepgrandparent-stepgrandchild relationships after later-life remarriage or cohabitation. In addition, it may be hypothesized that the ways in which grandchildren and adult children respond to the new union are likely to be related to whether the grandparent was widowed, divorced, or separated from the other grandparent, how long the grandparent had been single before remarriage or repartnering, and the number of prior relational transitions the grandparent had experienced. Much remains to be known about grandparent-grandchild relationships after a later-life reunion.

Stepsiblings, Half-siblings, and Siblings in Older Stepfamilies

Even though horizontal ties such as sibling relationships are often more important in the lives of older adults than intergenerational ties, there have been few investigations about any of the possible sibling bonds among stepchildren in later life. How relevant are sibling relationships in later life? Under what conditions are relationships with half-siblings and stepsiblings perceived to be as close as full sibling relationships? Are resources exchanged among half-siblings and stepsiblings in later life? Does parental remarriage at any time during the life course affect sibling support and contact in later life? Given the probability that an increasing number of older adults will have stepsiblings and half-siblings, understanding the dynamics of these relationships will be imperative.

INTERGENERATIONAL BRIDGES OR WALLS?

Curran, McLanahan, and Knab (2003) sampled remarried people aged 65 and older in the United States and concluded that marital diversity and diverse kin networks (stepkin, in-laws) are greater among current and future elderly people than was true in the past (see Figure 9.1). Wachter (1997) speculated that diversification may have positive effects on the financial resources of old persons, which may help offset potential cuts in Social Security or Medicare. In contrast, social exchange theory suggests that more diverse kin networks may not necessarily translate into greater social support. Social exchange theory assumes that dense, homogeneous networks are more likely to provide social support than diverse networks. Our research on intergenerational obligations supports the dense network perspective. It remains to be seen how these increasingly diverse later-life repartnerships, and the multigenerational family members of such partnerships, will fare in the future. As we have indicated, there are substantial gaps in what is known about older stepfamilies.

Future studies could examine the development of steprelationships, or they could investigate patterns of how bridges and walls are constructed by stepfamily members. A number of questions are pertinent: What resources are exchanged between stepkin? How are responsibilities to stepkin negotiated? What are stepchildren's concerns about aging stepparents? How does the death of a parent affect intergenerational relationships between stepkin? How are inheritance issues resolved in stepfamilies? How do cohabiting stepfamilies in later life differ from remarried intergenerational stepfamilies? What are the effects of serial parental relationships on parent-child bonds? What roles do gender expectations play in the development and maintenance of intergenerational relationships in stepfamilies? The list of unaddressed and underaddressed questions could go on and on. Much remains to be known about the dynamics of relationships in stepfamilies.

REFERENCES

Alemán, M. (2002). Enabling romantic relationships in later life: Discarding cultural myths and facilitating dialogue. *Oates Journal, 5,* 1098–1446.

Alemán, M. (2003). "You should get yourself a boyfriend" but "let's not get serious": Communicating a code of romance in a retirement community. *Qualitative Research Reports in Communication, 4,* 31–37.

Alemán, M. (2009). Managing dialectical tensions in later life marriage and families. *Oates Journal, 9.* Retrieved from http://journal.oats.org/current/tipoc-aging/223-aleman-2009

Amato, P.R., Rezac, S.J., & Booth, A. (1995). Helping between parents and young adult offspring: The role of parental marital quality, divorce, and remarriage. *Journal of Marriage and the Family, 57,* 363–374.

Aquilino, W.S. (1991). Predicting parents' experiences with coresident adult children. *Journal of Family Issues, 12,* 323–342.

Aquilino, W.S. (1994). Impact of childhood family disruption on young adults' relationships with parents. *Journal of Marriage and Family, 56,* 295–313.

Aquilino, W.S. (2005). Impact of family structure on parental attitudes toward the economic support of adult children over the transition to adulthood. *Journal of Family Issues, 26,* 143–167.

Attar-Schwartz, S., Tan, J., Buchanan, A., Flouri, E., & Griggs, J. (2009). Grandparenting and adolescent adjustment in two-parent biological, lone-parent, and step-families. *Journal of Family Psychology, 23*, 67–75.

Bernstein, A. C. (1997). Stepfamilies from siblings' perspective. *Marriage & Family Review, 26*, 153–175.

Bograd, R., & Spilka, B. (1996). Self-disclosure and marital satisfaction in mid-life and late-life remarriages. *International Journal of Aging and Human Development, 42*, 161–172.

Bornat, J., Dimmock, B., Jones, D., & Peace, S. (1999). Stepfamilies and older people: Evaluating the implications of family change for an aging population. *Aging and Society, 19*, 239–261.

Brown, S., & Kawamura, S. (2010). Relationship quality among cohabitors and marrieds in older adulthood. *Working Paper Series WP-10-01*. National Center for Family & Marriage Research, Bowling Green State University.

Brown, S. L., Lee, G. R., & Bulanda, J. R. (2006). Cohabitation among older adults: A national portrait. *Journal of Gerontology: Social Sciences, 61B*, S71–S79.

Bulcroft, K., Bulcroft, R., Hatch, L., & Borgatta, E. (1989). Antecedents and consequences of remarriage in later life. *Research on Aging, 11*, 82–106.

Burks, V., Lund, D., Gregg, C., & Bluhm, H. (1988). Bereavement and remarriage for older adults. *Death Studies, 12*, 51–60.

Carr, D. (2004). The desire to date and remarry among older widows and widowers. *Journal of Marriage and Family, 66*, 1051–1068.

Carr, D., & Springer, K. (2010). Advances in families and health research in the 21st century. *Journal of Marriage and Family, 72*, 743–761.

Cherlin, A. (1978). Remarriage as an incomplete institution. *American Journal of Sociology, 84*, 634–650.

Cherlin, A., & Furstenberg, F. (1986). *American grandparenthood*. New York: Basic Books.

Chevan, A. (1996). As cheaply as one: Cohabitation in the older population. *Journal of Marriage and Family, 58*, 656–667.

Clarke, L. (2006). Older women and sexuality: Experiences in marital relationships across the life course. *Canadian Journal on Aging, 25*, 129–140.

Clarksberg, M, Stolzenberg, R. M., & Waite, L. (1995). Attitudes, values, and entrance into cohabitational versus marital unions. *Social Forces, 74*, 609–632.

Clawson, J., & Ganong, L. (2002). Adult stepchildren's obligations to older stepparents. *Journal of Family Nursing, 8*, 50–73.

Clingempeel, W. G., Colyar, J. J., Brand, E., & Hetherington, E. M. (1992). Children's relationships with maternal grandparents: A longitudinal study of family structure and pubertal status effects. *Child Development, 63*, 1404–1422.

Coleman, M., & Ganong, L. (1998). Attitudes toward inheritance following divorce and remarriage. *Journal of Family and Economic Issues, 19*, 289–314.

Coleman, M., Ganong, L., Hans, J., Sharp, E. A., & Rothrauff, T. (2005). Filial obligations in post-divorce stepfamilies. *Journal of Divorce and Remarriage, 43*(3/4), 1–27.

Curran, S. R., McLanahan, S., & Knab, J. (2003). Does remarriage expand perceptions of kinship support among the elderly? *Social Science Research, 32*, 171–190.

Davidson, K. (2001). Late life widowhood, selfishness and new partnership choices: A gendered perspective. *Ageing and Society, 21*, 297–317.

Davidson, K. (2002). Gender differences in new partnership choices and constraints for older widows and widowers. *Ageing International, 27*, 43–60.

De Jong Gierveld, J. (2002). The dilemma of repartnering: Considerations of older men and women entering new intimate relationships in later life. *Ageing International, 27*, 61–78.

De Jong Gierveld, J. (2004). Remarriage, unmarried cohabitation, living apart together: Partner relationships following bereavement or divorce. *Journal of Marriage and Family, 66*, 236–243.

De Jong Gierveld, J., & Peeters, A. (2003). The interweaving of repartnered older adults' lives with their children and siblings. *Ageing and Society, 23*, 187–205.

Eggebeen, D. J. (1992). From generation unto generation: Parent-child support in aging American families. *Generations, 16*, 45–69.

Elman, C., & London, A. S. (2002). Sociohistorical and demographic perspectives on U.S. remarriage in 1910. *Social Science History, 26*, 199–241.

Franks, M. M., Wendorf, C. A., Gonzalez, R., & Ketterer, M. (2004). Aid and influence: Health promoting exchange of older married partners. *Journal of Social and Personal Relationships, 21*, 431–45.

Ganong, L., & Coleman, M. (1998). Attitudes regarding filial responsibilities to help elderly divorced parents and stepparents. *Journal of Aging Studies, 12*, 271–290.

Ganong, L., & Coleman, M. (1999). *Changing families, changing responsibilities: Family obligations following divorce and remarriage.* Hillsdale, NJ: Erlbaum.

Ganong, L., & Coleman, M. (2004). *Stepfamily relationships: Development, dynamics, and intervention.* New York: Springer.

Ganong, L., & Coleman, M. (2006a). Responsibilities to stepparents acquired in later life: Relationship quality and acuity of needs. *Journal of Gerontology: Social Sciences, 61B*, S80–S88.

Ganong, L., & Coleman, M. (2006b). Patterns of exchanges and intergenerational obligations after divorce and remarriage. *Journal of Aging Studies, 20*, 265–278.

Ganong, L., Coleman, M., & Rothrauff, T. (2009). Patterns of assistance between adult children and their older parents: Resources, responsibilities, and remarriage. *Journal of Social and Personal Relationships, 26*, 161–178.

Gibson, H. B. (1993). Emotional and sexual adjustment in later life. In S. Arber & M. Evandrou (Eds.). *Ageing, independence, and the life course* (pp. 104–118). London: Jessica Kingley Publishers.

Harper, S. (2003). Understanding the implications of population ageing for mid-life women. *Journal of British Menopause Society, 30*, 147–150.

Henry, C. S., Ceglian, C. P., & Ostrander, D. L. (1993). The transition to stepgrandparenthood. *Journal of Divorce and Remarriage, 19*, 25–44.

Huyk, M. (2001). Romantic relationships in later life. *Generations, 25*, 9–17.

Jankowiak, W., & Diderich, M. (2000). Sibling solidarity in a polygamous community in the USA: Unpacking inclusive fitness. *Evolution and Human Behavior, 21*, 125–139.

Johnson, C. L. (1992). Divorced and reconstituted families: Effects on the older generation. *Generations, 16*, 17–20.

Kalmijn, M. (2007). Gender differences in the effects of divorce, widowhood and remarriage on intergenerational support: Does marriage protect fathers? *Social Forces, 85*, 1079–1085.

Karlsson, S. G., & Borell, K. (2005). A home of their own: Women's boundary work in LAT-relationships. *Journal of Aging Studies, 19*, 73–84.

Kaufman, G., & Uhlenberg, P. (1998). Effects of life course transitions on the quality of relationships between adult children and their parents. *Journal of Marriage and Family, 60*, 924–938.

Killian, T. S. (2004). Intergenerational monetary transfers to adult children and stepchildren: A household level analysis. *Journal of Divorce & Remarriage, 42*, 105–130.

King, V., & Scott, M. (2005). A comparison of cohabiting relationships among older and younger adults. *Journal of Marriage and Family, 67*, 271–285.

Kreider, R. M. (2005). *Number, timing, and duration of marriages and divorces: 2001.* Current Population Reports, P70–97. U.S. Bureau of the Census, Washington, DC: Government Printing Office.

Kuhn, D. R., Morhardt, D. J., & Monbrod-Framburg, G. (1993). Late-life marriage, older stepfamilies, and Alzheimer's disease. *Families in Society, 74*, 154–162.

Lawton, L., Silverstein, M., & Bengtson, V. (1994). Affection, social contact, and geographic distance between adult children and their parents. *Journal of Marriage and Family, 56*, 57–68.

Lowenstein, A., & Ron, P. (1999). Adult children of elderly parents who remarry: Etiology of domestic abuse. *The Journal of Adult Protection, 2*, 22–32.

Lussier, G., Deater-Deckard, K., Dunn, J., & Davies, L. (2002). Support across two generations: Children. *Journal of Family Psychology, 16*, 363–376.

Mahay, J., & Lewin, A. (2007). Age and the desire to marry. *Journal of Family Issues, 28*, 706–723.

Manning, W. D., & Smock, P. J. (2000). "Swapping families": Serial parenting and economic support for children. *Journal of Marriage and Family, 62*, 111–122.

Marks, N. (1995). Midlife marital status differences in special support relationships with adult children and psychological well-being. *Journal of Family Issues, 16*, 5–28.

Mills, T. L., Wakeman, M. A., & Fea, C. B. (2001). Adult grandchildren's perceptions of emotional closeness and consensus with their maternal and paternal grandparents. *Journal of Family Issues, 22*, 427–455.

Moorman, S. M., Booth, A., & Fingerman, K. L. (2006). Women's romantic relationships after widowhood. *Journal of Family Issues, 27*, 1281–1304.

Peters, A. & Liefbroer, A. (1997). Beyond marital status: Partner history and well-being in old age. *Journal of Marriage and Family, 59*, 687–699.

Pezzin, L. E., Pollak, R. A., & Schone, B. S. (2008). Parental marital disruption, family type, and transfers to disabled elderly parents. *Journal of Gerontology: Social Sciences, 63B*, S349–S358.

Pezzin, L. E., Pollak, R. A., & Schone, B. S. (2009). Long-term care of the disabled elderly: Do children increase caregiving by spouses? *Review of Economics of the Household, 7*, 323–339.

Pezzin, L. E., & Schone, B. S. (1999). Parental marital disruption and intergenerational transfers: An analysis of lone elderly parents and children. *Demography, 36*, 287–297.

Pyke, K. D. (1994). Women's employment as gift or burden? Marital power across marriage, divorce, and remarriage. *Gender & Society, 8* (1), 73–91.

Sanders, G. F., & Trygstad, D. W. (1989). Stepgrandparents and grandparents: The view from young adults. *Family Relations, 38*, 71–75.

Schmeekle, M. (2007). Gender dynamics in stepfamilies: Adult stepchildren's views. *Journal of Marriage and Family, 69*, 174–189.

Schoen, R., & Standish, N. (2001). The retrenchment of marriage: Results from Marital Status Life Tables for the United States 1995. *Population and Development Review, 27*, 553–563.

Sheehy, G. (1995). *New passages: Mapping our life across time.* New York. Ballantine Books.

Sherman, C. W., & Bauer, J. M. (2008). Financial conflicts facing late-life remarried Alzheimer's disease caregivers. *Family Relations, 57*, 492–503.

Sherman, C. W., & Boss, P. (2007). Spousal dementia caregiving in the context of late-life remarriage. *Dementia, 6*, 245–270.

Smith, K. R., Zick, C. D., & Duncan, G. J. (1991). Remarriage partners among recent widows and widowers. *Demography, 28*, 361–374.

Soliz, J. (2007). Communicative predictors of a shared family identity: Comparison of grandchildren's perceptions of family-of-origin grandparents and stepgrandparents. *Journal of Family Communication, 7*, 177–194.

Spitze, G., & Logan, J. R. (1992). Helping as a component of parent-adult child relations. *Research on Aging, 14*, 291–312.

Szinovacz, M. (1997). Adult children taking parents into their homes: Effects of childhood living arrangements. *Journal of Marriage and Family, 59*, 700–717.

Szinovacz, M. (1998). Grandparents today: A demographic profile. *The Gerontologist, 38*, 37–52.

Tower, R. B., Kasl, S. V., & Darefsky, A. S. (2002). Types of marital closeness and mortality risk in older couples. *Psychosomatic Medicine, 64*, 644–659.

Troilo, J., & Coleman, M. (in press). "I know it looks like I'm leaving you, but I'm not.": Divorced nonresidential fathers' identities. *Family Relations.*

U.K. Marriage, Divorce, and Adoption Statistics. (2000). *Marriage, divorce, and adoption statistics* (ONS, Series FM2. No. 26). London: HMSO.

U.S. Bureau of the Census. (1995). *Statistical abstract of the United States: 1995* (115th ed.). Washington, DC: Author.

U.S. Bureau of the Census. (2003). *The older population in the United States: March 2002.* (Current Population Reports, P20-546). Washington, DC: Author.

Vinick, B. (1978). Remarriage in old age. *The Family Coordinator, 27*, 359–363.

Vinick, B. (1998, December). *Older stepfamilies: Views from the parental generation.* Report to the AARP-Andrus Foundation.

Vinick, B. H., & Lanspery, S. (2000). Cinderella's sequel: Stepmothers' long-term relationships with adult stepchildren. *Journal of Comparative Family Studies, 31*, 377–384.

Visher, E. B., & Visher, J. S. (1996). *Therapy with stepfamilies.* New York: Brunner/Mazel.

Wachter, K. W. (1997). Kinship resources for the elderly. *Philosophical Transactions of the Royal Society of London Biological Sciences, 352*(13631), 1811–1817.

Wherry, L., & Finegold, K. (2004). Marriage promotion and the living arrangements of black, Hispanic, and white children. In *New federalism: National survey of America's families* (Publication No. B-61). Washington, DC: The Urban Institute.

White, L. (1992). The effects of parental divorce and remarriage on parental support for adult children. *Journal of Family Issues, 13,* 234–250.

White, L. (1994a). Growing up with single parents and stepparents: Long-term effects on family solidarity. *Journal of Marriage and Family, 56,* 935–948.

White, L. (1994b). Stepfamilies over the life course: Social support. In A. Booth & J. Dunn (Eds.), *Stepfamilies: Who benefits? Who does not?* (pp. 109–138). Hillsdale, NJ: Erlbaum.

White, L., & Reidman, A. (1992). Ties among adult siblings. *Social Forces, 71,* 85–102.

White, L., & Rogers, S. J. (1997). Strong support but uneasy relationships: Coresidence and adult children's relationships with their parents. *Journal of Marriage and Family, 59,* 62–76.

10

The Importance of Discretionary and Fictive Kin Relationships for Older Adults

Marieke Voorpostel

INTRODUCTION

What makes someone family? While this seems an easy enough question to answer at first glance—family members are related by blood or marriage—the complicating factor is that *family* comes with all sorts of connotations. People expect family members to feel a sense of obligation toward each other, continue the relationship in times of conflict or when there is no contact, and provide support. Real family members may not always meet these conditions, and certain nonkin relationships may come with familylike obligations and sentiments. With increasing diversity in families and with the blurring of boundaries between what constitutes kin and what does not, some have proposed people are making a shift from families of fate to families of choice (Pahl & Spencer, 2004).

Among older adults, the most researched ties are those to family (Mac Rae, 1992). But, as aging families are also becoming more and more diverse (Allen, Blieszner, & Roberto, 2000), whom people include in their family is becoming increasingly flexible. Bedford and Blieszner (2000) provided a definition of family that fits better the current lived experience of older adults: "a set of relationships determined by biology, adoption, marriage, and, in some societies, social designation, and existing even in the absence of contact or affective involvement, and, in some cases, even after the death of certain members" (p. 160). Thus, this chapter examines those family relationships that fall outside the more conventional definition of family, yet in the experience of many people are part of one's family, namely, fictive kin.

Several changes in families and in society in general might lead to less availability of conventional kin and give way to an increasing importance of fictive kin ties. First of all, while people's life spans continue to grow, more and more people will outlive their helping networks (Johnson, 1999). Second, demographic trends toward smaller families—fewer children and hence fewer siblings—will result in future generations of older adults with, on average, fewer traditional family ties. Also, geographical mobility rates have increased, which has led to an increasing prevalence of older adults without children or siblings living nearby (Jordan-Marsh & Harden, 2005; Mac Rae, 1992). Third, increasing divorce rates will leave a growing number of older adults without the social support of a spouse later in life (Wu & Penning, 1997). Finally, a growing number of individuals are rejecting the ideal of the nuclear family, for varying reasons such as sexual preference or unwed motherhood (Johnson, 1999). In the absence of close kin, more remote kin or nonkin ties can gain in importance, and may even come to be considered close family.

Given these trends in society, older adults may have to rely more and more on nontraditional forms of support and caregiving. This includes turning to *fictive kin*, individuals one considers close family, but who are not related legally or by blood (Johnson, 1999). Family ties on the periphery of the family system that are upgraded to a more prominent spot (*discretionary kin*) are here also included as fictive kin. As we will see in this chapter, although these definitions give an idea of which relationships fall within which category, the reality as experienced by older adults provides a wide range of relationships, some close, some less close, and some ambivalent, that fall within these groups.

Expanding family boundaries is an adaptive strategy in meeting the needs of older people. Studying the extent to which people make use of this strategy, how these fictive ties come into being, and how they are experienced and deepened sheds light on how personal choices and restrictions on people's social networks lead to alternative solutions to who provides care when no family is available. This phenomenon has not received sufficient attention in the literature, although one could expect the importance of these kinds of ties to increase.

This chapter first addresses different definitions and prevalence of fictive kin in the lives of older adults, characteristics of older adults that are associated with the development of such ties, and the nature of those ties. The next section takes a closer look at fictive kin ties that develop between older adults and their formal and informal caregivers. Then I discuss what makes fictive kin ties so special and what theories help explain the development of these ties and the differences in occurrence and roles these relationships play. Concluding, I assess the strengths and weaknesses of fictive kin ties for an aging population with smaller families in an ever more mobile society.

DISCRETIONARY AND FICTIVE KIN: DEFINITIONS AND PREVALENCE

Discretionary Kin

Two kinds of chosen family relationships can be distinguished: fictive kin and discretionary kin. These two types were already mentioned as distinct categories of kinship some 40 years ago (Ballweg, 1969; Ball, 1972). According to Ball (1972) discretionary kin are kin relationships that differ from conventional kin (those family members who are directly connected to each other legally or by blood) by being part of the family constellation, but being more distant. The spouses of two siblings, for example, may or may not regard each other as related to each other, often depending on the quality of the relationship. For these relationships, whether or not members see each other as close kin, with all the obligations that are involved, is subject to a certain level of personal choice.

Research evidence shows that for many people there exists a hierarchy of family relations. This hierarchy is determined on the one hand by a distinction between primary and secondary ties, in which partner, parents, and children are seen as closest and most supportive, invoking the strongest feelings of obligation. These primary kin relationships are followed by other family relationships, usually in the order of decreasing levels of genetic relatedness (Cantor, 1979; Hoyt & Babchuk, 1983; Rossi & Rossi, 1990). On the other hand, this hierarchy is by no means universal, because the content of relationships is negotiated over time. For example, never-married individuals develop more supportive relationships with their siblings over time compared to divorced individuals, although for both groups a partner is lacking (Campbell, Connidis, & Davies, 1999; Connidis & Davies, 1990). Many examples of more remote kin taking a prominent place in the social networks of older adults exist (Johnson & Barer, 1990; Rook & Schuster, 1996). In sum, where one draws the line between primary and secondary kin is not the same for everyone, meaning that the distinction between discretionary kin and conventional kin might differ depending on individual circumstances.

The place extended kin takes in peoples' networks varies for different groups. Studies often show that blacks have larger extended families than whites, although results on differences in the exchange of support are mixed (Erikson & Gerstel, 2002; Hays & Mindel, 1973; Johnson, 1999; Johnson & Barer, 1990; Miner & Uhlenberg, 1997; Taylor & Chatters, 1991). Older adults in general have smaller networks than younger individuals, which in large part are made up of kin. The dominance of kin in older adults' social networks is even stronger in the case of blacks, although racial differences decrease with increasing age (Ajrouch, Antonucci, & Janevic, 2001). Older blacks are also more likely than whites to live with other relatives in extended family households and are more likely to give more prominence to relationships with collateral relatives, such as nieces, nephews, and cousins (Johnson, 1999). Johnson and Barer (1990) found in the case of their San Francisco sample of 200 older adults aged 65 and older, that although support from primary relationships such as partners and children may not vary between elderly whites and blacks, blacks receive more support and have more contact with relatives in general. Relatives on the periphery of the kinship system were, however, found to provide emotional rather than instrumental support.

In her study drawn from the oldest-old African Americans living in San Francisco (122 participants aged 85 years and older), Johnson (1999) found that 8% expanded their number of close kin by upgrading distant relatives, mostly by redefining a *collateral* relative (ties such as those to aunts, uncles, nephews, and nieces) as a *lineal* one, like ties between (grand)parents and (grand)children, but also by defining an in-law as a blood relative. Allen, Blieszner, and Roberto (2011) explored perspectives on the roles of extended and fictive kin in a sample of 34 women and 11 men aged 56 to 88 (84% white and 16% African American), and found five strategies of *kin reinterpretation: kin promotion*, where a distant relative is redefined as a close one; *kin exchange*, where roles of close kin are switched, for example redefining a parent-child tie as a sibling tie; *kin retention*, where former in-laws remain in the extended family network; *kin loss*, where a family member was dropped from the network; and *nonkin conversion*, where friends and others are deemed close kin. Among these five types, kin promotion and kin retention are ways of creating discretionary kin, whereas nonkin conversion is a mechanism to create fictive kin. They found that both the creation of fictive kin and discretionary kin was a common practice in their diverse sample of older adults in Virginia, and this form of kin reinterpretation was not limited to persons without close kin available.

Fictive Kin

A general definition of fictive kin is "people to whom one considers to be related but who are not related by blood or marriage" (Johnson, p. S369). Although Johnson did not explicitly mention them, *legal kin* (i.e., in-laws and kin by adoption) should be added to the definition of conventional family. Fictive kin ties can hence be described as "non-kin kin" (Ball, 1972, p. 300). Fictive kinship is different from conventional kin in the sense that it is not reinforced by the social structure and not shared by others, but rather is personal and consists of using kinship terms, often to indicate a degree of closeness, for unrelated persons.

The use of kin terms for specific relationships represents a reinforcement and institutionalization of the relationship (Ballweg, 1969). Addressing people using kin terms expresses familiarity and closeness within a personal relationship and is a public validation and institutionalization of a special kind of association (Ballweg, 1969; Ibsen & Klobus, 1972; Rubinstein, Alexander, Goodman, & Luborsky, 1991). It is a means to claim legitimacy of the relationship in the eyes of loved ones and of society (Barker, 2002).

Several approaches to and definitions of fictive kin exist. This chapter focuses on family-based fictive kin. *Family-based fictive kin* refers to the inclusion of a nonfamily member in the extended family network (Chatters, Taylor, & Jayakody, 1994). In contrast, another form of fictive kin involves the peer group. *Peer group-based fictive kin* ties consist of groups of nonrelated people who develop kinlike relationships with each other or use family terms for each other, such as street families (McCarthy, Hagan, & Martin, 2002) or the street corner men in the classic study by Liebow (1967). These latter ties fall outside the scope of this chapter.

Related to the content of fictive kin relationships Ebaugh and Curry (2000) point out the similarities with conventional kin ties: "A relationship, based not on blood or marriage but rather on religious rituals or close friend-ships ties, that replicates many of the rights and obligations usually associated with family ties" (p. 189). Chatters, Taylor, and Jayakody (1994) referred in this respect to bonds of mutual obligation that blend respect, responsibility, and duties. Generally, definitions focus on the designation of someone who is not related as family and sometimes also include a description of what char-acterizes family relationships: mutual obligations.

Fictive kin relationships typically involve frequent contact, subjective closeness, and support (Barker, 2002; Mac Rae, 1992; Rubinstein et al., 1991). Johnson (1999) demonstrated nicely the several degrees of fictive kin in her sample of older African Americans and showed that prevalence of this type of tie and its similarity to family ties is related to which of the following definitions is chosen, ordered by decreasing similarity to family ties: nonkin ties that are regarded as part of the family and are characterized by diffuse enduring solidarity ("They are my family"); ties that are not quite family, but are close friendships with whom intimate problems and feelings are shared ("They are like my family"); relationships that provide support ("She is my daughter, because she helps me"); context-specific relationships that entail using kinship terminology ("Some call me mom at church"); and group-based connections ("Everyone at church is family"). This array of bonds demon-strates the wide variety of fictive kin relationships, which complicates the study of this type of tie (Mac Rae, 1992).

Studies that examined fictive kin relationships reveal a wide variety in the prevalence of these ties. This variety results from the different popula-tions studied and the different approaches to fictive kinship employed. Some studies looked at only the use of kinship terms for nonfamily relationships (Ballweg, 1969; Gubrium & Buckholdt, 1982; Ibsen & Klobus, 1972) and found this to be quite common: 64% in a student sample (Ballweg, 1969) and 61% in a sample of wives of faculty members (Ibsen & Klobus, 1972). But also when the content of the relationship is included, prevalence is quite high. In a large sample of black Americans (the National Survey of Black Americans), 66% reported someone who was not related but was treated as a relative (Chatters et al., 1994). Mac Rae's study (1992) of 142 older women (65 to 98 years old) in a small town in Nova Scotia, Canada, asked respon-dents to identify "people who are not related to you, who are longtime friends of your family, but whom you think of in a sense as members of your family"

(p. 231). In this sample, 40% reported that they had at least one fictive family member. Typically, these relationships had existed since childhood and were very close. In Johnson's (1999) study, 45% of the respondents mentioned unrelated individuals whom they considered family. In a study of 114 caregivers and care recipients focused on nonkin caregivers of community-living dependent elders (Barker, 2002), more than half of the older adults used kin terms to characterize their relationship with their nonkin caregivers, whereas 10% of the caregivers claimed they were family. In Allen and colleagues' (2011) study, 22 of the 45 older adults had converted nonkin into kin.

For Whom Are Fictive Kin Ties Most Common?

Fictive kin relationships are not uncommon, especially among older adults (Piercy, 2001), and are found across all cultural groups (Jordan-Marsh & Harden, 2005). Yet certain groups in society are more likely to include fictive kin ties than others. As mentioned previously, African Americans often have more flexible definitions of family, including fictive kin, and are more likely to upgrade distant kin to the status of primary kin (Johnson, 1999; Johnson & Barer, 1990) in the San Francisco Bay area. Both studies showed that blacks had more active support networks than whites, despite the low incidence of support from spouses and children in this group. They had more active ties with extended family members as well as a higher prevalence of fictive kin relationships. Additional research shows that several ethnic minority groups have developed various forms of fictive kin, such as the *compadrazgo* among Hispanic immigrants and godparenthood among Asians and practitioners of Yoruba, a religion with roots in western Africa (Ebaugh & Curry, 2000).

Further, women are more likely than men to include fictive kin in their family networks (Chatters et al., 1994; Johnson, 1999), a finding that is not limited to older adults but is also found in other populations, such as college students (Ballweg, 1969). Other characteristics positively related to the mention of fictive kin are geographic proximity (Ballweg, 1969; Mac Rae, 1992), a longer shared history (Ballweg, 1969; Barker & King, 2001; Karner, 1998; Mac Rae, 1992; Rubinstein et al., 1991), unavailability of a spouse (Johnson, 1999; Mac Rae, 1992; White-Means, 1993), and childlessness, or no children living in the vicinity (Johnson, 1999; Mac Rae, 1992; Rubinstein et al., 1991).

Whether age is related to the occurrence of fictive kin varies according to the particular focus of the studies. When the focus is on use of kinship terms for unrelated others, researchers report a decrease in occurrence of fictive kin ties from childhood to adulthood, mainly because parents often initiate that children address family friends with "aunt" or "uncle," rather than the child initiating such terminology, and such parental influence is likely to decrease as children grow older. Fictive kin identified this way are assumed to be less close than those assigned primary kinship terms (Ibsen & Klobus, 1972). When the focus is on actually considering someone as family and not just using family terminology, no research covers the whole life course. Looking specifically at older adults, the occurrence of fictive kin ties is rather common (Mac Rae, 1992). For aging African Americans, however, there is a negative association between age and seeing someone as family, which is in line with other research demonstrating a negative association of age with the receipt of support from extended family members (Chatters et al., 1994).

The association between fictive kin and socioeconomic status is unclear. Whereas the creation of fictive kinship out of need would lead to fictive kin ties being more important for people from lower socioeconomic strata, Chatters et al. (1994) found a positive relationship between socioeconomic status and the inclusion of fictive kin in a sample of older African American adults. They interpreted this finding in light of their proposal that a certain amount of social and economic resources are needed to be able to create and maintain fictive kin. Although fictive kin relations are important for the informal support network, the life circumstances of persons of lower socioeconomic status families may limit the resources available to create such ties. Some other studies found no effect of social status or education on mentioning fictive kin relationships (Ibsen & Klobus, 1972).

Other personal characteristics are also related to the creation of fictive kin. For the creation of fictive kin in the context of the church, being active in the church community and being embedded in active friendship networks are important (Johnson, 1999). Also, the care recipient's level of disability is related to the fundamental role of nonimmediate family members in the care of black elderly persons, with nonimmediate family caregivers providing more help when need was higher (White-Means, 1993).

Who Are These Fictive Kin?

Relationships to which family terminology are assigned tend to be close and involved in terms of geographical proximity and frequent contact (Ballweg, 1969). Use of kinship terms for nonkin usually develops slowly over an extended period of time (Ballweg, 1969; Barker & King, 2001; Piercy, 2000; Rubinstein et al., 1991; Schmeeckle, Giarrusso, Feng, & Bengtson, 2006).

Fictive kin relationships can be horizontal (i.e., between age peers, resembling sibling ties) as well as vertical (i.e., resembling intergenerational ties). Studies of older adults show that their most common type of fictive tie is a vertical one, resembling the parent-child relationship (Johnson, 1999; Piercy, 2000), but also fictive siblings are not uncommon (Allen et al., 2011). Barker's study on nonkin caregivers (Barker, 2002) showed that whereas many of the nonkin caregivers were themselves older adults, most of the nonkin caregivers who resembled family relationships were younger, had been involved with the older adult for a relatively long time, and were providing personal care. Rubinstein et al. (1991) investigated key relationships of 31 never-married, childless older women and found that respondents likened some of the key nonfamily ties to family ties. These familylike ties could have a quasi-parental status, as, for instance, in the case of the children of friends. When these familylike ties concerned same-generation, same-gender companionate relationships, they sometimes resembled marital ties, in the sense that they could offer extensive caregiving activities.

Another characteristic of fictive kin relationships is that women receive the label more often than men (Ballweg, 1969; Ibsen & Klobus, 1972). Partly contributing to this trend is the fact that informal caregivers as well as home care workers—who sometimes are labeled as fictive kin by the care recipient— are usually female.

HOME CARE WORKERS AND INFORMAL CAREGIVERS AS FICTIVE KIN

This chapter includes special attention on home care workers and informal caregivers because the sparse research on fictive kin is found predominantly in this area. Among volunteer or paid caregivers, friendships and fictive kinships are likely to develop (Piercy, 2001).

Home Care Workers

Some relationships develop from friendship to fictive family relationship over a long period of time, where the long shared history and exchange of support have slowly changed how people view this relationship. But fictive kin ties can also develop over a shorter period of time. When tasks performed are of a very intimate nature and people see each other frequently—which is the case for home care workers—people can come to see each other as family, not because of a long shared history, but because it normalizes a stranger performing intimate tasks.

A study by Karner (1998) deals with this process explicitly. Drawing from intensive interviews with 39 home care workers and their supervisors, she studied the "collaboration of the care recipient and caregivers to negotiate the social expectation of the appropriateness of family with the economic and situational realities of formal assistance" (p. 70). Home care workers usually perform those tasks that used to be the domain of the family, such as housekeeping, meal preparation, and personal care such as bathing, dressing, and eating. Care recipients have to come to terms with allowing a stranger in the house to perform these tasks of an intimate nature. Accepting the care worker as kin is a way to redefine the relationship, making these intimate tasks suitable for a relatively newly established relationship.

Although relationships between home care workers and their clients have not been in existence as long as friends who are converted to kin, it still takes some time for them to move from worker-client to familylike relationships. Karner (1998) distinguished three phases: the introductory stage, the sharing of selves phase, and the familial adoption phase. Going through these phases, the client and the care worker develop from two strangers who cooperate to perform specific tasks, via the deepening of the relationship to friendship, to further increasing expectations and seeing the care worker "friend" as a member of the family. Familial adoption is associated with caregiving as an emotional obligation similar to family responsibilities. This emotional obligation often goes hand in hand with ambivalence mostly on the part of the care worker, who as a professional is not supposed to get too involved with the clients, but at the same time is more satisfied with her job when it includes the development of a close relationship with the client.

The likelihood of a home care worker to go through all of these three phases and become a fictive kin tie becomes greater when actual family is not available or not much involved in the care for the older adult. Also, family might limit the sort of care they are willing to provide, outsourcing additional tasks to a home care worker, which allows the family members to maintain their previous roles. Together with the fact that care recipients spend most of their time with the home care worker—usually more than with their family—the extensive provision of care might place the care worker in a position where she is more trusted than the actual family.

Other studies on the relationship between home care workers and their care recipients refer to the development of a friendship or a familylike relationship (Aronson & Neysmith, 1996; Piercy, 2000). Aronson and Neysmith (1996) showed in their study of 30 home care workers in southern Ontario that for the home care workers the practical and emotional labor is inseparable and that there is some blurring between their identities as formal service providers and informal caregivers. As the nature of the job is highly personalized it comes as no surprise that often significant relationships develop between the care workers and their clients. Home care workers often describe the relationships with their clients in terms of friendshiplike or familylike, where both care giver and care recipient feel they can talk to each other about their lives and their problems. Work is often not limited to the tasks described.

Piercy (2000) examined the relation between home care workers and their clients in a study of families with positive experiences with home health care. The study included perspectives of the dyad (care recipient and home health aide) and the family caregivers in a sample of members of 16 families. She found that most relationships between aides and older adults were described as friendship or like part of the family. Several contextual aspects contributed to the development of the relationship between client and aide, and as such may be related to the development of fictive ties. Ties were more likely to become close when there was time to develop such a relationship and when the care from the same aide was continuous. When an aide was described as one of the family, the duration of the care was at least a year. Again, the availability of the family to provide support stands out as an important determinant. When the older adults were more socially isolated, the aides had a more prominent place in their lives. Aides who developed kinlike relationships with their clients sometimes had trouble in maintaining boundaries and in finding the right degree of closeness considered appropriate. This ambivalence was, however, not only experienced on the part of the care worker, but could also be felt by the care recipient.

Informal Caregivers

Familylike relationships can also develop between informal nonkin caregivers and older adults. Unavailability of family may lead older adults to depend on support from nonkin. Barker (2002) described four styles of relationships in the context of nonkin caregiving: casual, bounded, committed, and incorporative, with an increase in involvement, multidimensionality, and emotional intimacy from the casual to the incorporative type. One-fifth of the relationships between nonkin caregivers and older adults were characterized as incorporative. In this type of relationship, either the care provider or the older adult, or both, is seen as a member of the other person's family. Remarkably, a large proportion of the nonkin care providers served as the primary or sole caregiver (38%). The use of kinship terms in relationships like these signaled closeness. In 56% of these relationships, the care recipients or care providers used family terminology to describe the quality of the relationship. In 10% of the cases, the caregivers claimed they were family. This difference between the use of family terminology and the claim of being family suggests that using kinship terminology and actually perceiving someone as part of the family is not the same thing.

Especially for older black adults, who tend to have more involved extended family and have a cultural tradition of fictive kin, fictive kin and remote kin step in to provide care when relatives are not available (White-Means, 1993). In fact, White-Means's study of 1,929 caregivers for black old adults found no significant differences in the caregiving hours of immediate family, nonimmediate family, and nonkin, showing that family support in this group encompassed extended family, including fictive kin, all with similar responsibilities. Care provided by remote relatives and nonkin came third and fourth in line after daughters and spouses.

SPECIAL ASPECTS OF FICTIVE KIN RELATIONSHIPS

Deserving special mention are a few aspects in which fictive kin ties differ from other family ties. First of all, unlike other family relationships, fictive kin ties are personal. As a consequence, fictive kin designation is not always mutual. For example, an older adult may consider a home care worker as part of the family, given the tasks she performs and her centrality in the older adult's life, but this does not necessarily mean that this feeling is mutual. Aides may be aware they are seen in a familylike way, but they do not necessarily reciprocate this feeling (Piercy, 2000). The home care worker usually has more than one client and a social life outside of her work, making the older adult less central in her life than the other way around. This, however, does not mean that home care workers would never see their clients as "just like grandparents" (Karner, 1998). Other categories of fictive kin ties are not likely to be unidirectional, as in the case of fictive kin in African American families, whether in the context of the church ("play mothers" and "play children") or informal adoption (Chatters et al., 1994; Johnson, 1999).

A second consequence of a fictive kin tie being personal is that fictive kin ties are usually not part of the family as a whole; for example, someone's fictive sister does not automatically become a fictive child of that person's mother (Chatters et al., 1994). Also in the case of home care workers, the development of a fictive kin relationship between the aide and the care recipient usually does not extend to the care recipient's family. For example, a home care worker who is "like a daughter" to the care recipient usually does not become "like a sister" to the care recipient's children (Karner, 1998).

In contrast, some of the never-married, childless older women in the study by Rubinstein et al. (1991) felt they were adopted into an entire family to which they were not biologically related. Although these relationships were characterized by support and affection, they were voluntary, with a wide range of involvement, and were not seen as morally binding. Ballweg's study of students' use of kinship terms for unrelated others revealed that in two-third of the cases, use of kinship terms was unique to the individual, and only in one-third of the cases did others in the family use the same term. Furthermore, when ties were less close, it was more likely that others in the family used kin terms for this person as well, often because in these cases use of kinship terms was initiated by the parents (Ballweg, 1969).

Another aspect in which fictive kin ties are different from other kin ties is that they are less permanent. Being like family is an acquired status that can be dissolved. As Chatters, Taylor, and Jayakody (1994) put it: "Unlike kinship, the fictive kin relationship is maintained by a consensus between the individuals involved and can be relinquished at any time. In some instances fictive kinships can last a lifetime" (p. 303).

A final aspect of fictive kin relationships that deserves attention, especially in the case of nonkin caregivers and home care workers, is the existence of ambivalence in such ties, mostly on the part of the person providing care. Ambivalence is a well known characteristic of family relationships (e.g., Bedford, 1989; Fingerman, Hay, & Birditt, 2004; Lüscher & Pillemer, 1998; Willson, Shuey, & Elder, 2003). When people find themselves confronted with a choice between two contradicting courses of action result-ing from conflicting roles—for example the combination of a paid job and taking care of a family member—they experience ambivalence (Connidis & McMullin, 2002). Nonkin caregivers and home care workers can also face conflicting roles. On the one hand, home care workers have to follow pro-fessional guidelines in their work, which explicitly mention not getting too involved with clients on the one hand, but on the other hand, many factors conflict with this guideline. For example, personal aides find themselves in situations where it is easy to get more involved than they should, where it is hard to maintain boundaries, and where pride and satisfaction with the job actually come from the bond they develop with their clients.

Being regarded as part of the client's family implies additional expectations, obligations, and duties (Karner, 1998). Aronson and Neysmith's (1996) study also showed that home care workers' practical and emotional support were inseparable and that there often was a blurring of identities as formal service providers and informal caregivers. Nonkin caregivers faced ambivalence as well when relationships developed into familylike bonds, where sentiments of getting too involved and not being able to maintain boundaries coincided with feeling rewarded by being considered family and feeling a moral obliga-tion to provide support (Barker, 2002). On the part of the care recipient, defining a relative stranger who provides intimate care as part of the family can be regarded as a way to resolve ambivalent feelings and to reinstate ap-propriateness of the tasks performed (Karner, 1998).

THEORETICAL EXPLANATIONS FOR THE DEVELOPMENT OF FICTIVE KIN TIES

The literature mentions three somewhat related explanations for the for-mation of fictive kin. First, fictive kin ties are more likely to develop when primary family relationships are absent or unavailable. An assumption of this theory is that everybody feels a need to be surrounded by close family. In this desire for family, or close personal relationships, absence of family might lead older adults to find replacements for these ties. Absence of family may be interpreted widely; there may be no family left, there may be no family living nearby, or the family might simply be relatively uninvolved, unconcerned, or overburdened. In these cases home care workers, nonkin caregivers, or friendships can fill the void between family and need, and can develop into fictive kin (Karner, 1998; Piercy, 2000; Rubinstein, 1991). Mac Rae's (1992) study of fictive kin in older adults' networks found evidence for the *substitu-tion principle*, where older adults without kin were found to substitute miss-ing family members by means of the creation of fictive kin ties. Also, Piercy (2000) found that aides felt that when a family support system was in place, the aide's role was not supposed to be familylike. The concept of *replacement family* is also found in other groups with less access to family. For example, lesbians and gay men who face rejection by family and are excluded from cultural definitions of family also create fictive kin ties out of friendships as a way to legitimize and reinforce these relationships, increasing their resilience (Muraco, 2006; Oswald, 2002).

A second, related explanation for development of fictive kin ties is that they are an important source of social capital. Social capital provides benefits for members of social networks (Coleman, 1990). It is related to the aforementioned explanation of the unavailability of primary kin, because in these situations the need for support from nonkin network members is greater. Fictive kin serve a purpose; they are a resource to meet specific needs (Mac Rae, 1992). The family is an influential, if not the most influential, relationship network. This social network often comes with extensive mutual obligations and responsibilities. As such, it is a major source of social capital (Jordan-Marsh & Harden, 2005). To designate a relationship as fictive kin stresses the important status of this relationship for providing support, care, closeness, and a sense of belonging. Thus, fictive kin expand the social network to provide social, economic, and emotional capital (Jordan-Marsh & Harden, 2005). People create fictive kin ties to secure these resources and embed them in a relationship or network characterized by responsibilities and obligations. The personal choice in the creation and designation of fictive kin and expanding family boundaries is a way of meeting needs of older adults (Johnson, 1999) as well as younger persons. Similarly, Gubrium and Buckholdt (1982) viewed fictive kin, or the use of kin terminology for unrelated individuals, as "a means of dealing with the ongoing challenges of particular settings, not as a type of social organization in its own right, distinguished from formal kinship" (p. 879). Fictive kin as social capital is also found in literature on migration among members of ethnic minority groups, where they form a resource for immigrants as they confront the challenges of finding their way in a new and strange society (Ebaugh & Curry, 2000). Another group in society where fictive kin ties are used as a way to create social capital is among homeless youth, who form street families. These street family members look out for each other and provide protection from violent victimization among other valued outcomes (McCarthy et al., 2002).

A third explanation as to why especially older adults form fictive kin ties comes from socioemotional selectivity theory. This approach goes against the perception of aging as a process involving loss and disengagement from society, but rather sees people as active agents who construct their social environment to match their goals (Carstensen, Isaacowitz, & Charles, 1999). Socioemotional selectivity theory states that with time left to live becoming increasingly limited, emotional goals become more important than knowledge-oriented goals. This limitation of time means that older adults place increasing importance on close personal relationships at the cost of network size.

Hence, a decreasing network size and a larger proportion of kin represent successful adaptation rather than loss. The increasing likelihood of upgrading distant kin to primary kin and of converting nonkin to kin resulting from increasing investments in close relationships fits well in this view of increased centrality of emotionally close, meaningful, and supportive relationships (Jordan-Marsh & Harden, 2005).

STRENGTHS AND WEAKNESSES OF FICTIVE KIN RELATIONSHIPS

Fictive kin relationships are important ties in the lives of many older adults. Fictive kin expand people's social networks and provide a sense of belonging. They are important sources of support, sociability, and joy. As such, they are meaningful ties that help older adults to meet their needs. When people get older, opportunities for contacts and social transactions decrease, but if older adults focus on relationships they find most beneficial, this enhances successful aging (Ajrouch et al., 2001). Nonkin relationships can develop into fictive kin ties, and as such they can contribute to people's well-being (Dykstra, 1990) and health (Bosworth & Schaie, 1997; Uchino, Cacioppo, & Kiecolt-Glaser, 1996), which for older adults is associated with aging well (Allen et al., 2000).

Conversion of nonkin to kin relationships is based on individual choice and effort. Older adults who have flexible definitions of family membership feel more at ease with their current life circumstances and allow for a potentially larger kin network to provide support (Allen et al., 2011). At the same time, because fictive kin ties are less permanent and are based on individual choice, they may be relatively fragile and also characterized by ambiguity with respect to obligations (Chatters et al., 1994). Furthermore, like other family relationships, fictive kin ties may also be a source of stress (Jordan-Marsh & Harden, 2005).

Nonetheless, understanding the potential of an expanded view of the family and of fictive kin ties as significant personal familylike relationships of older adults may provide valuable insights into social network processes that contribute to successful aging in the 21st century. Fictive kin relationships have so far been studied almost exclusively among particular subpopulations, such as African Americans (Johnson, 1999) and migrant groups (Ebaugh & Curry, 2000), often focusing on particular fictive kin ties, and are almost exclusively based on in-depth interviews with relatively small sample sizes (for an exception, see White-Means, 1993). Although these studies form a rich source of information on the nature of fictive kin ties, more research is needed to get insight into the extent to which this phenomenon is of a truly general nature and into the place fictive kin relationships take in people's social networks. Research so far indicates fictive kin ties are common to many groups in society, yet only little is known about the prevalence and content of fictive kin ties among older adults in general or among other age groups.

REFERENCES

Ajrouch, K. J., Antonucci, T. C., & Janevic, M. R. (2001). Social networks among blacks and whites: The interaction between race and age. *Journal of Gerontology: Social Sciences, 56B*, S112–S118.

Allen, K. R., Blieszner, R., & Roberto, K. A. (2000). Families in the middle and later years: A review and critique of research on the 1990s. *Journal of Marriage and Family, 62*, 911–926.

Allen, K. R., Blieszner, R., & Roberto, K. A. (2011). Perspectives on extended family and fictive kin in the later years: Strategies and meanings of kin reinterpretation. *Journal of Family Issues, 32*, 1156–1177.

Aronson, J., & Neysmith, S. M. (1996). "You're not just in there to do the work": Depersonalizing policies and the exploitation of home care workers' labor. *Gender and Society, 10*, 59–77.

Ball, D. W. (1972). The "family" as a sociological problem: Conceptualization of the taken-for-granted as prologue to social problems analysis. *Social Problems, 19*, 295–307.

Ballweg, J. A. (1969). Extensions of meaning and use for kinship terms. *American Anthropologist, 71*, 84–87.

Barker, J. C. (2002). Neighbors, friends, and other nonkin caregivers of community-living dependent elders. *Journal of Gerontology: Social Sciences, 57B*, S158–S167.

Barker, J. C., & King, D. (2001). Taking care of my parents' friends: Non-kin guardians and their older female wards. *Journal of Elder Abuse and Neglect, 13*, 45–69.

Bedford, V. H. (1989). Ambivalence in adult sibling relationships. *Journal of Family Issues, 10*, 211–224.

Bedford, V. H., & Blieszner, R. (2000). Personal relationships in later life families. In R. M. Milardo & S. Duck (Eds.), *Families as relationships*. Chichester/New York: Wiley.

Bosworth, H. B., & Schaie, K. W. (1997). The relationship of social environment, social networks, and health outcomes in the Seattle Longitudinal Study: Two analytical approaches. *Journal of Gerontology: Psychological Sciences, 52B*, P197–P205.

Campbell, L. D., Connidis, I. A., & Davies, L. (1999). Sibling ties in later life: A social network analysis. *Journal of Family Issues, 20*, 114–148.

Cantor, M. H. (1979). Neighbors and friends: An overlooked resource in the informal support system. *Research on Aging, 1*, 434–463.

Carstensen, L. L., Isaacowitz, D. M., & Charles, S. T. (1999). Taking time seriously: A theory of socioemotional selectivity. *American Psychologist, 54*, 165–181.

Chatters, L. M., Taylor, R. J., & Jayakody, R. (1994). Fictive kinship relations in black extended families. *Journal of Comparative Family Studies, 25*, 297–312.

Coleman, J. S. (1990). *Foundations of social theory*. Cambridge, MA: Harvard University Press.

Connidis, I. A., & Davies, L. D. (1990). Confidents and companions in later life: The place of family and friends. *Journal of Gerontology: Social Sciences, 45,* S141–S149.

Connidis, I. A., & McMullin, J. A. (2002). Sociological ambivalence and family ties: A critical perspective. *Journal of Marriage and Family, 64,* 558–567.

Dykstra, P. A. (1990). *Next of (non)kin: The importance of primary relationships for older adults' well-being.* Amsterdam: Swets & Zeitlinger.

Ebaugh, H. R., & Curry, M. (2000). Fictive kin as social capital in new immigrant communities. *Sociological Perspectives, 43,* 189–209.

Erikson, S., & Gerstel, N. (2002). A labor of love or labor itself: Care work among adult brothers and sisters. *Journal of Family Issues, 23,* 836–856.

Fingerman, K. L., Hay, E. L., & Birditt, K. S. (2004). The best of ties, the worst of ties: Close, problematic, and ambivalent social relationships. *Journal of Marriage and Family, 66,* 792–808.

Gubrium, J. F., & Buckholdt, D. R. (1982). Fictive family: Everyday usage, analytic, and human service considerations. *American Anthropologist, 84,* 878–885.

Hays, W. C., & Mindel, C. H. (1973). Extended kinship relations in black and white families. *Journal of Marriage and the Family, 35,* 51–57.

Hoyt, D. R., & Babchuk, N. (1983). Adult kinship networks: The selective formation of intimate ties with kin. *Social Forces, 62,* 84–101.

Ibsen, C. A. I., & Klobus, P. (1972). Fictive kin term use and social relationships: Alternative interpretations. *Journal of Marriage and Family, 34,* 615–620.

Johnson, C. L. (1999). Fictive kin among oldest old African Americans in the San Francisco Bay area. *Journal of Gerontology: Social Sciences, 54B,* S368–S375.

Johnson, C. L., & Barer, B. M. (1990). Families and networks among older inner-city blacks. *The Gerontologist, 30,* 726–733.

Jordan-Marsh, M., & Harden, T. (2005). Fictive kin: Friends as family supporting older adults as they age. *Journal of Gerontological Nursing, 31,* 24–31.

Karner, T. X. (1998). Professional caring: Homecare workers as fictive kin. *Journal of Aging Studies, 12,* 69–82.

Liebow, E. (1967). *Tally's Corner: A study of Negro streetcorner men.* Boston: Little, Brown and Company.

Lüscher, K., & Pillemer, K. (1998). Intergenerational ambivalence: A new approach to the study of parent-child relations in later life. *Journal of Marriage and the Family, 60,* 413–425.

Mac Rae, H. (1992). Fictive kin as a component of the social networks of older people. *Research on Aging, 14,* 226–247.

McCarthy, B., Hagan, J., & Martin, M. J. (2002). In and out of harm's way: Violent victimization and the social capital of fictive street families. *Criminology, 40,* 831–866.

Miner, S., & Uhlenberg, P. (1997). Intragenerational proximity and the social role of sibling neighbors after midlife. *Family Relations, 46,* 145–153.

Muraco, A. (2006). Intentional families: Fictive kin ties between cross-gender, different sexual orientation friends. *Journal of Marriage and Family, 68,* 1313–1325.

Oswald, R. F. (2002). Resilience within the family networks of lesbians and gay men: Intentionality and redefinition. *Journal of Marriage and Family, 64,* 374–383.

Pahl, R., & Spencer, L. (2004). Personal communities: Not simply families of 'fate' or 'choice'. *Current Sociology, 52,* 199–221.

Piercy, K. W. (2000). When it is more than a job: Close relationships between home health aides and older clients. *Journal of Aging and Health, 12,* 362–387.

Piercy, K. W. (2001). "We couldn't do without them": The value of close relationships between older adults and their nonfamily caregivers. *Generations, 25,* 41–47.

Rook, K. S., & Schuster, T. L. (1996). Compensatory processes in the social networks of older adults. In G. R. Pierce, B. R. Sarason, & I. G. Sarason (Eds.), *Handbook of social support and the family.* New York: Plenum Press.

Rossi, A. S., & Rossi, P. H. (1990). *Of human bonding: Parent-child relations across the life-course.* New York: Aldine de Gruyter.

Rubinstein, R. L., Alexander, B. B., Goodman, M., & Luborsky, M. (1991). Key relationships of never married, childless older women: A cultural analysis. *Journal of Gerontology: Social Sciences, 46,* S270–S277.

Schmeeckle, M., Giarrusso, R., Feng, D., & Bengtson, V. L. (2006). What makes someone family? Adult children's perceptions of current and former stepparents. *Journal of Marriage and Family, 68,* 595–610.

Taylor, R. J., & Chatters, L. M. (1991). Extended family networks of older black adults. *Journal of Gerontology: Social Sciences, 46,* S210–S217.

Uchino, B. U., Cacioppo, J. T., & Kiecolt-Glaser, J. K. (1996). The relationship between social support and physiological processes: A review with emphasis on underlying mechanisms and implications for health. *Psychological Bulletin, 119,* 488–531.

White-Means, S. I. (1993). Informal home care for frail black elderly. *Journal of Applied Gerontology, 12,* 18–33.

Willson, A. E., Shuey, K. M., & Elder, G. H. (2003). Ambivalence in the relationship of adult children to aging parents and in-laws. *Journal of Marriage and Family, 65,* 1055–1072.

Wu, Z., & Penning, M. J. 1997. Marital instability after midlife. *Journal of Family Issues, 18,* 459–478.

Part III

Contexts of Family Life

11

Intersectionality and Aging Families

Toni Calasanti and K. Jill Kiecolt

In the past two decades, research on families that takes a gender relations approach has grown dramatically. More recently, advances in gender theory, which posits the importance of intersections with other inequalities, have also appeared in the literature on marriage and families (Ferree, 2010). In research on aging families, however, a gender-relations perspective has been far less influential, and intersectional approaches used even less frequently (Silverstein & Giarrusso, 2010).

Intersectionality is both a theoretical and methodological approach to understanding inequalities (Choo & Ferree, 2010; McCall, 2005). Despite its limited use in work on aging families, contemporary scholars can now survey some 20 years of intersectional scholarship in the social sciences. In this chapter we use extant research to discuss intersectionality in relation to family support, care work, and spousal care work, and then briefly discuss where scholars and practitioners can go from here. We discuss intersectionality as a theoretical lens and then briefly consider methodological approaches to intersectionality, although in practice these are interrelated.

SYSTEMS OF INEQUALITY

As a theoretical lens, intersectionality refers to the interactions among systems of inequality—power-based differences in life chances that accrue to group members. Such hierarchies vary with time and place. In the contemporary United States, the main systems of inequality are based on gender, race and ethnicity, class, sexuality, and age. We briefly discuss each of these below, but first, we clarify our conceptualization of inequality.

To begin, a system of inequality describes a *relationship of privilege and oppression* based on group membership—ascribed status that is usually seen to be "natural"—and not on achievement, individual skills, personality, and the like. This assertion has two corollaries. One, privilege and oppression exist *in relation to* one another. Without a disadvantaged position, there is no privilege. This means that studying privilege is necessary for understanding disadvantage, and vice versa (Choo & Ferree, 2010; McCall, 2005). Second, privilege is unearned advantage, just as oppression is unearned. Even though those with privilege may work hard to achieve in life, they nevertheless begin from an advantaged position.

Second, the idea of *systems* of inequalities means that privileges and disadvantages are *embedded in social institutions*. Often normal ways of doing things—in the workplace, the family, and the like—privilege some groups while disadvantaging others. Because these patterned behaviors are buttressed by taken-for-granted ideas about what is right and desirable (When should we have children? What counts as a "family"? How do we obtain money, or food, or shelter?), group members usually engage in these behaviors, even if it is against the interests of some based on their social locations.

Third, inequalities tend to be invisible, especially to those in dominant groups. They seem natural, even though people continuously recreate them in interaction. For example, in contemporary U.S. society, we view women as naturally more nurturing than men, usually without recognizing that we cultivate such gender differences via socialization and divisions of labor. These assumed differences reinforce and legitimate men's greater power and resources.

The embeddedness of such inequalities and their impacts on life chances in later life can be seen in relation to the Social Security program. The division of domestic labor in families influences men and women throughout their lives, through workplace experiences, level of remuneration, and retirement income. Because Social Security was designed principally to benefit (white, middle-class, heterosexual) men, it assumes careers in the public realm and reliance on others to do reproductive labor—the work involved in social reproduction, which includes domestic labor. Benefits are calculated on that basis. The social construction of men's privilege within families often is invisible; and it results in a polarization of retirement privileges (e.g., "of course people are only rewarded for *paid* labor").

Finally, the fact that power relations are embedded in social institutions means that inequalities do not depend on individual intentions. The example of Social Security makes clear that basing benefit levels on paid work—which discriminates against families whose members are systematically paid less or not at all for their work—need not be based upon deliberate intent. Still, Social Security rests on and reinforces the privileges that white, heterosexual, and middle-class men have.

INTERSECTING INEQUALITIES

The concept of intersectionality has its roots in the scholarship and activism by feminists of color, who objected to the essentialism that defined women as a homogeneous group. Coined by Kimberle Crenshaw to "refer to the interdefining structures of racism and sexism" (Crenshaw, 1989), intersectionality was born of "a critique of gender-based and race-based research for failing to account for lives experienced at neglected points of intersection—ones that tended to reflect multiple subordinate locations as opposed to dominant or mixed locations" (McCall, 2005, p. 1780). Since then, the concept has widened to include class, sexual inequality, nationality, and other relevant social locations, which are often subjects of debate (e.g., Daniels, 2008). Thus, social institutions not only sustain inequality on the bases of gender and race and ethnicity but also such statuses as class, sexual orientation, and age. Each of these systems of inequality intersect with one another to create experiences that are far more nuanced than simply "privileged" or "disadvantaged." People may be privileged on one status but not another. As a result, privilege sometimes can be invisible. For example, many men who struggle with having subordinate positions in other systems of inequality fail to recognize that they are privileged in some respects.

The concept of intersectionality does not refer to additive or multiplicative dimensions of inequalities; "it describes a more fluid, mutually constructive process" than the more static notion of multiple jeopardy (Luft & Ward, 2009, p. 14). Positions along each axis of inequality are experienced simultaneously. Certainly, one or two status characteristics may be most salient in a given context and thus influence experiences therein, but other statuses do not disappear. The intersection of inequalities means that social scientists cannot just add up privileged and disadvantaged statuses to compute an index that would describe all groups with equal validity. For example, if we added together their statuses, we might equate the experiences of a white, middle-class, heterosexual woman and a black, middle-class heterosexual man—an equation that is clearly inaccurate. Similarly, a Hispanic, middle-class, heterosexual woman and a black, middle-class, heterosexual woman may both experience sexism and racism, in both similar and different ways. An intersectional approach recognizes these important distinctions.

Using an Intersectional Approach

McCall (2005) described three approaches to exploring intersectionality, only two of which we use here. (The anticategorical approach, which we do not discuss here, considers social life to be too complex to be reduced to categories and thus rejects them altogether.) Both approaches acknowledge that categories are social constructions. At the same time, they also "acknowledge the stable and even durable relationships that social categories represent at any given point in time. . ." (p. 1774).

The first, the *intracategorical* approach, focuses "on particular social groups at neglected points of intersection . . . in order to reveal the complexity of . . . experience within such groups" (McCall, 2005, p. 1774). In this approach, researchers explore "a single social group at a neglected point of intersection of multiple master categories" (McCall, 2005, p. 1780). It is not a descriptive approach, or at least not merely so. That is, researchers analyze a single group's experiences, but in the context of multiple systems of inequality, in relation to both privilege and disadvantage. This analysis thus goes beyond description to focus on processes of inequality. It represents Choo and Ferree's (2010) process-centered model of intersectionality (which Glenn, 1999, terms "relational"), and it "places primary attention on context and comparison at the intersections as revealing structural processes organizing power" (Choo & Ferree, 2010, p. 134).

The second approach, *intercategorical*, compares groups defined by multiple intersecting dimensions in order to chart measurable inequalities. But rather than reifying social categories such as gender and race, this approach views them as dynamic "anchor points" (Glenn, 2002, p. 14) and uses them strategically (McCall, 2005, p. 1785) in order to discover how they jointly affect life chances and outcomes.

The intercategorical approach, which is not frequently undertaken in part because of the lack of data on many different groups, tends to be quantitative. Ideally in such analyses, scholars view intersectionality as a complex system in which, methodologically, all dimensions interact and no one "main effect" of inequality has priority in theory or analysis. Instead, "each relationship of inequality works on and through the others . . ." (Choo & Ferree, 2010, p. 136).

Whether scholars take an intracategorical approach, an intercategorical approach, or an in-between approach (comparing just two groups) to intersectional analysis, they should be just as attuned to theorizing the consequences of occupying privileged statuses (being "unmarked," Choo & Ferree, 2010) as of occupying marginal statuses. Even in an intracategorical analysis that explores one group, scholars need to attend to sources of power as well as disadvantages for group members. For example, looking only at gender and age, researchers might attend to the voices of old people to reveal how men and women "do (hetero) sex" in later life in similar and different ways, and to dispel myths that old people are not sexual. Their voices might even be used to try to broaden what counts as sex, beyond penile penetration. But an intersectional analysis goes further, challenging, for example, why it is that what younger people do counts as sex, or better sex. As procreation is not the (usual) reason that people engage in sex, why privilege certain acts in the first place?

In the next section, we briefly outline some systems of inequality to which researchers should attend in looking at intersections. We then turn to two topics in relation to aging families and discuss how an intersectional approach might proceed.

Structural Bases of Intersecting Inequalities

The status characteristics that help structure societies define systems of oppression and privilege to the extent that they result in inequalities in distributions of authority, status, and wealth, and are seen to be based on nature and thus indisputable. Such bases for inequality vary by time and place; in contemporary U.S. society, such hierarchies include those based on gender, race and ethnicity, class, sexuality, and age. Much has been written already on how the social organization of gender, race, and class influences identity, power, and life chances. Thus, we discuss these only briefly, and instead focus on their intersections in relation to families. We then discuss sexual and age inequalities before applying all these intersections to aging families.

Gender, Class, and Race

Gender relations refer to the fact that men and women gain identities and power in relation to one another. Societies organize on the basis of gender such that popular ideals of manhood and womanhood both stem from and affirm gendered divisions of labor, authority, and status. Gender identities, like those of other inequalities, are internalized, naturalized ideals of behavior formed and reshaped in interaction between people held accountable to gender ideals. "Doing gender" by appearing competently to conform to the dictates of biological givens influences life chances, that is, access to social and material resources (West & Fenstermaker, 1995). In enacting gender identities, people behave in ways that tend to privilege men—give them an unearned advantage—and to disadvantage women, even as people resist and reformulate seemingly "natural" gender differences and gender meanings. Thus, gender relations are "characterized by power inequalities that hierarchically produce, organize, and evaluate masculinities and femininities through the contested but controlling practices of individuals, organizations, and societies" (Ferree, 2010, p. 424). West and Fenstermaker (1995) showed that intersecting inequalities such as class and race operate in the same way, by categorizing people and holding them accountable to naturalized ideals of behavior. Groups distribute resources, including routine deference, responsibility for labor, title to property, and positions of formal authority, in ways that maintain systemic inequality.

Class has been conceived in multiple ways. Two theoretical perspectives, Marxist and Weberian, provide useful analytic directions (Wright, 2009). From a Marxist perspective, class is defined in relation to ownership of the means of production, amount of authority in the workplace, and the performance of manual or mental labor. Domination—"the ability to control the activities of others" and exploitation—the ability to reap "economic benefits from the labour of those who are dominated" are key to designating class membership (Wright, 2009, p. 107). From this perspective, the middle class falls between labor and capital. Middle-class workers do the "mental labor necessary to control the labor and lives of the working class." They plan, manage, and monitor others' work, and they have greater incomes, prestige, and education than other workers (Higginbotham, 1994, pp. 114–115). A Weberian approach sees classes as "defined by access to and exclusion from certain economic opportunities" (Wright, 2009, p. 104). Higher status groups maintain their advantaged positions by obtaining expensive credentials, displaying cultural capital through dress and behaviors, and including or excluding others in their networks. From this standpoint, lifestyles are more than shared understandings among group members; they are manifestations of cultural capital that rest on and reinforce power relations.

Similar to gender, race relations structure identities and power among groups defined by members' physical features. These routine, naturalized categorizations bestow advantages and disadvantages. Racial categories are dynamic; what counts as race and what race means are shaped by socioeconomic and historical context. In the United States, races have been redefined (sometimes by the Supreme Court, as in the early 20th century when Japanese people were ruled to be nonwhite and thus noncitizens), with implications for citizenship and life chances. While racial domination and class domination are intimately linked (Amott & Matthaei, 1996), these systems also have independent impacts, and neither is reducible to the other.

Understanding how contemporary race relations intersect with gender and class gives insights into families in later life. For example, present gender relations in black and white families are rooted in 19th-century contexts of slavery, racial segregation, and class relations. A relatively small group of landowning white men performed paid managerial work and owned family members and servants, whose labor supported them. Similarly, a relatively small group of white women occupied prestigious but powerless positions as spousal property, providing legitimate sexual access and heirs. Most whites labored in agriculture, paid service, or manufacturing. Most nonwhites slaved at more menial versions of the same supporting tasks: labor-intensive farm work, construction, and domestic work. Slave women were treated as genderless in the fields, where they were judged to be as capable as men of performing physical labor. At the same time, as women, they were singled out for more intimate forms of exploitation as childbearers or sexual objects. In response, in their own families (which were not recognized by whites) and communities, slaves had clear gender divisions of labor.

As slaves gained emancipation, they mostly retained occupational niches in manual labor and menial service. Within the domestic sphere, they sought a gender division of labor that restored women's status as wives and mothers. But most could not emulate white, middle-class family forms and gender relations. Blacks faced continued labor market discrimination, which prevented most black men from securing well-paid jobs. Consequently, both black men and women were employed, and black women (unlike white women) aspired to economic independence, not just marriage (Jones, 1985; Glenn, 1992; Amott & Matthaei, 1996).

More recently, partly due to affirmative action, black women's occupational distribution has broadened to include employment in civil service and managerial positions (Higginbotham, 1994). These historical and contemporary factors have led to a more egalitarian gender division of labor in black, middle-class families (Szinovacz & Davey, 2008), which may extend into later life. Family relations may differ for the many black women and men who are unemployed or poor. Understanding the ways that gender, race, and class relations play out among blacks illuminates the experiences and behaviors of members of aging families.

Such socioeconomic histories form a backdrop for intersectional analyses of aging families (see Amott & Matthaei, 1996, for gender, race, and class intersections for a variety of groups). For example, in the 1800s, male Asian immigrants (from China, then Japan, and finally, the Philippines) were recruited to fill low-waged positions in the United States. However, because of limits on women's immigration, many men had no wife or had a wife who remained in China (Amott & Matthaei, 1996). In old age, that cohort of single Chinese men lacked social support (Lockery, 1991). Recent immigration laws and patterns have resulted in other family forms that may run counter to cultural preferences and shape older families. Among recent Southeast Asian immigrants to the United States, regardless of ideals of care for extended family, immigration can create or decimate supportive networks. Korean elders, for example, may follow their children to the United States, but sometimes they cannot live with their children and thus do not find the kinds of social supports they expected. In other instances, older immigrant men may go out into the community and become more accustomed to their host countries, whereas older immigrant women who come to help with child care may stay within the household, learn little English, and end up isolated. Immigrant elders' well-being and intergenerational relationships depend on their gender, level of acculturation, language skills, and their children's ability to find well-paid work (Yee, 1997; Lockery, 1991).

Sexual Inequality

Most research assumes heterosexual family forms, ignoring relations of sexuality. As a system of privilege and oppression, sexuality structures inequalities in wealth and authority via heteronormativity—ideals and practices that treat heterosexuality as natural. As a key organizing principle of society, heteronormativity shapes the experiences of people of *all* sexual preferences (Stein, 2008). Heterosexuals are "policed"—held accountable for doing sexuality correctly. By doing so, they gain inclusion into privileged networks and receive systemic advantages. Nonheterosexuals are stigmatized and subject to various methods of control, including violence and employment discrimination. Gay men earn less than their heterosexual peers. Despite discrimination, lesbians earn more than comparable heterosexual women (Badgett, 2001; Baumle, Compton, & Poston, 2009; Heaphy, 2007). Even so, wealth disparities based on sexuality accrue. Federal laws in the United States typically grant married couples more benefits, rights, and privileges, including Social Security and Medicare, access to affordable housing, employee benefits, death benefits, and tax breaks (Herek, 2006, p. 614; see Harrington Meyer & Frazier, chapter 15 in this volume).

Contemporary arguments against same-sex marriage are based in ideals that naturalize only sex between women and men. Historically, sexual activity between persons of the same sex was neither seen as sexual nor marked as same sex. Not until the end of the 19th century did the terms heterosexual and homosexual come to be used and sexual identity emerge as an issue. The concept of *sexuality* emerged with 19th-century industrialization. Moral reformers concerned with disciplining labor and consumption created labels for and condemned seemingly reckless, unproductive activity (e.g., prostitution and homosexuality) as threats to social order (Greenberg, 1988; Laqueur, 1992). As a social organizing principle, sexuality was distinct from gender relations, which denied women professional and citizen status (Rubin, 1984).

Sexuality relates to labor in another way, which intersects with other relations of oppression. Ideals of sexuality include opposite-sex couples engaged in marital, reproductive activity; people who do not conform to this ideal are denied occupational and family-based privileges. *Compulsory heterosexuality* refers to institutionalized pressures on all women to form sexual relationships with men, or to risk social exclusion or even violence (Rich, 1986). Single, unmarried women remain suspect, although today censure for singlehood varies by class (for example, middle-class women are expected to complete higher education before marrying) and race (for example, black women face a shortage of marriageable men).

We can see the importance of compulsory heterosexuality as an organizing principle by thinking of the economy as a system of *provisioning*— providing what is socially recognized as needed for individual and community survival—whether the work is paid or unpaid (Acker, 2008). Provisioning involves production, social reproduction, and distribution. Provisioning takes a particular form within capitalism, wherein reproductive labor supports production in the public (traditionally, men's) realm. The gender division of labor assures that women are chiefly responsible for this unpaid reproductive work. This system rests on compulsory heterosexuality. Thus, heteronormativity undergirds a social order in which women perform unpaid, reproductive labor that benefits men and bolsters their status in the public realm.

This analysis reveals a system of sexual oppression—appropriation and control of labor—that is further shaped by intersections with race, class, and gender. How many contemporary elders are oppressed by this inequality is hard to estimate, given measurement and sampling difficulties, an unwillingness to self-identify (Fredriksen-Goldsen & Muraco, 2010), and failure to measure sexual orientation. About 2% to 8% of the U.S. population is estimated to be lesbian, gay, or bisexual (LGB), translating to 1–3 million gay elders now and 2–6 million by 2030 (Fredriksen-Goldsen & Muraco, 2010).

More studies on lesbian and gay (and to a lesser degree, bisexual and transgender) families have appeared in recent years, though few have examined intersections by race and class (Biblarz & Savci, 2010). For example, the greater gender egalitarianism found among nonheterosexual than heterosexual couples may vary by race. White, middle-class lesbian comother families typically share paid labor, housework, and child care. In contrast, black comothers tend to emphasize financial independence, so sharing paid labor takes precedence over sharing unpaid work. The sparse research on gay cofathers also has focused on white, middle-class gay men, whose parenting resembles that of their lesbian counterparts (Biblarz & Savci, 2010). Divisions of labor in later life are unknown, as almost no research has studied aging LGBT families.

Age

Ironically, scholars who study families in later life often overlook the importance of old age as a political location. Age as a system of inequality encompasses more than the cumulative impact of other social locations such as gender, race, class, and sexuality over the life course; it also represents more than the physical changes that accompany aging. Responses to later life physical changes are shaped as much or more by ageism as by the impact of age on functional and cognitive abilities (Calasanti, 2003, 2005).

All societies organize tasks, responsibilities, and behaviors based on age. What makes age-based organization a system of inequality is that different age groups not only gain identities but also power in relation to one another. Membership in age categories shapes self-concepts and interactions in ways that have material consequences and thus influence life chances. In concrete terms, some age groups—those who are "not old"—benefit from ageism at the expense of those defined as "old," by monopolizing valuable resources. They stigmatize the oppressed group and entitle themselves to own or manage resources that might otherwise go to the latter. By contrast, people who are old lose power, even if they are advantaged by their positions on other hierarchies. Old people lose autonomy and authority; they find it more difficult to be heard and to influence decisions made about their bodies. They are marginalized in the labor market and in the workplace. When they become dependent on the state, they are seen as less than full citizens (Wilson, 2000, p. 161). Being old is to be avoided at all costs. It is "socially contagious;" even associating with old people can reduce one's status (Hurd, 1999).

In the rest of this chapter, we apply an intersectional lens to families in later life. Two important notes shape our discussion. First, the kinds of intersectional approaches outlined above are rare, but studies that have looked at one or two intersections offer insights. Second, given the lack of intersectional analyses available, we do not claim to report findings only from intersectional analyses per se. Instead, we draw on available quantitative and qualitative research on one or more groups to consider how intersections might shape family relations in older families and suggest directions and possibilities for future research.

FAMILY SUPPORT

Families are primary sites of provisioning, including caring and nurturing (Acker, 2008, p. 105). Family members provide each other with emotional, instrumental, and material support (Swartz, 2009). As families also are sites in which members reproduce social inequalities, we might expect that elders who belong to more privileged groups would receive more support. But the situation is not so simple. Support has benefits and costs, whether one receives it or provides it. Perceiving that support is available and receiving support are generally beneficial (Silverstein, Chen, & Heller, 1996). At the same time, needing or receiving support implies greater dependence, hence, less power in a relationship (Pyke, 1999), which means that intersections of class and age relations will complicate life for old people financially secure enough to demand lots of care. Receiving excessive support decreases older parents' psychological well-being (Silverstein et al., 1996).

An intersectional approach to studying provisioning by family members involves examining how exchanges of support among family members vary by intersecting social categories—of age, gender, race, ethnicity, social class, and sexuality—which describe relationships of privilege and oppression. We point out several studies that have elements of or use an intersectional approach, drawing selectively from the literature on network ties and emotional and instrumental support among family members.

Women give and receive more support than men do (Swartz, 2009). In addition, they have larger networks. A study of respondents aged 40–93 years found that older women, but not older men, had smaller networks and less contact with network members than their younger counterparts. This difference suggested that women's networks shrank with age. The oldest women (aged 75–93 years) had somewhat larger networks but less contact with network members than the oldest men did (Ajrouch, Blandon, & Antonucci, 2005).

In the context of race relations in the United States, African Americans have smaller social networks than whites regardless of age. At the same time, African Americans have more frequent contact with network members than whites. The gap narrows, but remains, at older ages (Ajrouch, Antonucci, & Janevic, 2001). Researchers on support given and received have long debated whether African Americans and members of other racial and ethnic minority groups have more or less family support than whites. Early studies of low-income black families found high levels of supportive exchanges. Later quantitative studies using representative samples found complex and mixed results that depended on types of support given, received, and exchanged. In general, though, the findings challenge earlier assumptions that racial and ethnic minority families inevitably engage in more supportive exchanges than whites (Roschelle, 1997).

To the extent that racial and ethnic differences in family support exist, scholars can seek to explain why and can use intersectional theory for that purpose. Two mediating factors may help explain any observed differences—social structural location and culture (Roschelle, 1997; Sarkisian & Gerstel, 2004). Specifically, the lower average socioeconomic status of racial and ethnic minorities decreases some of the resources family members have to exchange with kin, while increasing family members' need to participate in exchanges. Culture, which also is shaped by intersecting relations of inequality, typically enters as adherence to values or norms such as familism or filial norms, or more broadly as collectivistic or individualistic orientations. African Americans and people in other racial and ethnic minority groups often are assumed to have more familistic values than whites (Sarkisian & Gerstel, 2004).

A series of studies has examined how and why race or ethnicity and gender together influence exchanges of emotional and instrumental support with extended kin. One study examined exchanges of kin support among African Americans and whites by gender (Sarkisian & Gerstel, 2004). Not surprisingly, both African American and white men exchanged less emotional and instrumental support with kin than women did, and the men did not differ from each other. Racial differences in exchanges were found among women, however. White women exchanged more emotional support with kin; African American women, more instrumental support. African Americans scored higher on measures of culture (scales of extended familism and altruism) than whites, and lower on measures of economic position. Neither class nor cultural variables explained the differential exchange of emotional support, whereas economic position explained the difference in instrumental support: The higher average socioeconomic standing of white women reduced their instrumental exchanges with kin. Sarkisian (2007) later compared emotional and instrumental support given to extended kin among African American and white men. As in the earlier study, no racial differences between the two groups emerged. The reason was that socioeconomic status and culture had opposite effects: African American men's lower socioeconomic status discouraged their providing kin support, whereas their more familistic and altruistic values boosted their kin support. Other work suggests that class may interact with race and ethnicity to influence exchanges of support. Higher income was positively related to exchanges of instrumental support with kin among African Americans, but not whites (Fiori, Consedine, & Magai, 2008).

Researchers of another study investigated whether Mexican American men and women provide more or less support to extended kin than their white peers, and whether socioeconomic status and culture (familistic values, traditional gender ideology) explained any differences (Sarkisian, Gerena, & Gerstel, 2007). The authors found that Mexican American and white women provided equal emotional support, whereas Mexican American women provided more instrumental support. The differences in instrumental support were partly explained by Mexican Americans' lower socioeconomic status, but not by indicators of culture. Mexican American and white men did not differ in the amount of emotional and instrumental support they provided.

Research on race and ethnicity and support using an intracategorical perspective most commonly has examined the experiences of elders in particular racial-ethnic minority groups. These studies reveal how historical time and life course histories influence support in later life. For example, intracategorical studies of elderly urban African Americans reveal how gender and class influence their access to social support. Barker, Morrow, and Mitteness (1998) found that married men had less access than married women to informal social support in later life. Social barriers had kept these black men from fulfilling their provider role, and the resulting financial hardships often had led to a previous divorce. Divorce, along with such historical factors as northward migration, severed family ties and left many black men without supportive networks in old age. In contrast, men who had remained married to their children's mother had larger networks that included their children and other kin.

A qualitative study of African American and Puerto Rican elders in New York City revealed a similar shortage of family support, but for different reasons. Through widowhood or divorce, these elders had become single parents early in life. The time when their children (or a nephew they were rearing) became adolescents coincided with the crack epidemic, and their children succumbed. Two mothers helped their children financially until doing so undermined their own financial security, and then cut ties. Perhaps indicating a gender difference, an uncle cut ties to a drug-using nephew immediately. In all cases, the lack of support from the younger generation attenuated the older members' support networks (Newman, 2003).

Intracategorical studies of elders in racial and ethnic minority groups can also reveal differences in how elders view familial support. In particular, immigrant elders often must negotiate tensions between cultural ideals and the material constraints they and their children face. For example, Arabic-speaking Arab American elders hold strong filial beliefs in children's obligations to care for them—to show compassion. At the same time, elders dread being a burden on their children (Ajrouch, 2005).

A small but growing body of research has explored support among elders from sexual minority groups, mostly lesbians and gay men. Samples typically have only a small number of bisexuals and no transgendered people. Contrary to earlier stereotypes, research on older gays and lesbians has consistently demonstrated that most have ties with families of origin and the majority have strong social networks composed of partners and close friends—families of choice (Cantor, Brennan, & Shippy, 2004; Grossman, D'Augelli, & Hirschberger, 2000; Metlife Mature Market Institute, 2006). Just as heterosexual men and women turn first to spouses, gay men and lesbians turn to their partners; but beyond this, the former rely more on other family members and the latter receive more support from friends (Cantor et al., 2004). Regardless of kin ties, older gays and lesbians usually perceive and receive more emotional support from friends and chosen families than from extended kin (Carrington, 1999; Heaphy, 2007; Masini & Barrett, 2008).

Sexuality intersects with other dimensions of inequality as well. Older gays and lesbians may confront ageism in their communities, a reality that can limit the support they can expect to receive from younger people. Brotman, Ryan, & Cormier (2003, p. 198) reported that these "communities have spent a lot of energy articulating and responding to the needs of its [sic] younger members, but have done much less in an effort to develop services for its [sic] senior members." In addition, many noted the "ageist attitudes that dominate gay and lesbian communities and culture" (p. 198). Ageism may be more acute for men than women. In one study, older lesbians anticipated mutual instrumental support to and from their LGB community. Older gay men wanted to receive such support, but some felt excluded from their communities because they were older (Heaphy, 2007). Class also may influence older LGB people's support as well. One study of younger LGB persons found that class was positively associated with network size and social support. Gay men and lesbians of lower class tended to have smaller social networks, partly because they could not afford to live in higher-cost, urban LGB enclaves. Instead, they lived in less expensive suburban areas with smaller LGB populations. They also seemed less inclined to maintain extensive network ties with friends (Carrington, 1999). Almost nothing is known about how race or ethnicity influence network ties and support among older LGB people.

CARE WORK

Women predominate as family caregivers, serving more hours and providing more personal assistance than do men (Silverstein & Giarrusso, 2010). A

2009 national study confirmed that women comprise two-thirds of reported caregivers for persons over the age of 50. This proportion did not vary by race and ethnicity, except among Asian Americans, where men represented nearly half (48%) of caregivers. Perhaps this high rate of caregiving among Asian men occurred because a larger proportion of those in this sample were single, never married (29%), about twice the national average for all caregivers (National Alliance for Caregiving, 2009a). Asian American respondents, whether male or female, differed from the rest of the sample in other significant ways as well. First, Asian American respondents were less likely to be primary caregivers (43%) than were African Americans (57%) or Hispanics (61%). Second, they also provided fewer hours of care per week (13 hours, versus 24 hours among African Americans and 25 hours among Hispanics) and reported less burden. Thus, it is unclear from these data whether or not Asian American men are simply more likely to provide care, were overrepresented in the sample, performed care work that was less demanding or less needed, or share care work with others in the family more frequently than do men in other groups.

Unpaid care work tends to be coordinated among family (and perhaps nonfamily) members (Silverstein & Giarrusso, 2010). Two-thirds of respondents in the National Alliance for Caregiving study (2009b) reported receiving help from others, whereas one-third reported using paid help. Larger networks that share more tasks lower burdens (Tolkacheva, Van Gorenou, DeBoer, & Van Tilburg, 2011), but the ease of constructing such networks varies by age, gender, race, ethnicity, class, and sexual orientation. For example, nonwhite caregivers tend to have more diverse informal support networks than their white counterparts, who tend to rely only on immediate family (Dilworth-Anderson, Williams, & Gibson, 2002). Of course, having more diverse networks does not necessarily mean greater sharing among group members.

Among couples who care for parents, gender and race, along with kinship ties and cross-gender taboos, shape participation in care work (Szinovacz & Davey, 2008). Husbands provide the majority of care (more than 50%) for their fathers. In contrast, wives provide the majority of care to both their mothers and fathers, and they give at least as much care to their husbands' mothers. In addition, black husbands provide more care for their own and their wives' parents than white husbands do, a finding that reflects the intersection of race and gender on family organization—the division of domestic labor between spouses.

In the National Alliance for Caregiving data, men, whites, Asian Americans, and caregivers under age 65 share caregiving with others more than do women, African Americans, and people aged 65 and older. In addition, class influences care work; caregivers with higher household incomes are more likely to pay for help with caregiving (National Alliance for Caregiving, 2009b).

Experiences of Care Work

Across all relationships, men generally report lower levels of caregiver stress than do women (e.g., Yee & Schulz, 2000). Researchers, however, tend to ignore both gender relations and their intersections with other systems of inequality as they develop theories to explain these findings. Taking intersections into account complicates what these self-reports might mean.

To begin, men certainly experience distress, and why they report so little has been discussed in both caregiver and health literatures (e.g., Calasanti & King, 2007; Courtenay, 2000). Gender-relations theory posits that men and women apply situational ideals of behavior based on their respective structural locations, so caregiving should differ by gender. Skills and resources gained over life courses affirm gender identities and influence stressors, coping strategies, and the rewards that caregiving offers (Calasanti & King, 2007; Russell, 2001), but caregiving experiences are further shaped by their intersections with race and ethnicity. For example, Aranda and Knight (1997) reported that both Latino and African American caregivers seemed more bothered than whites by performing personal care tasks such as feeding or toileting, whereas whites were more burdened by instrumental care tasks such as shopping or money management. Yet Latinos and whites reacted similarly to dealing with dangerous behaviors. Blacks reported less stress than whites did in caring for those with Alzheimer's disease; they also reported less depression than white or Latino caregivers. In fact, black caregivers did not differ from noncaregiving blacks or whites, whereas white caregivers were more depressed than noncaregivers or black caregivers. Complicating this picture further, research finds intragroup variation by economic status. Higher-income whites reported more burden than did their lower-income counterparts, whereas the reverse relationship appeared among blacks. Such results led Aranda and Knight (1997) to call for more research on both intergroup and intragroup differences.

An intersectional analysis goes further, not just documenting differences but also relating them to power relations. Calderon and Tennstedt (1998) posited that "reported ethnic differences in caregiver burden are a result of measurement" (p. 161), which they noted does not capture racial-ethnic differences (p. 162). To explore this possibility, they studied a small sample of Puerto Rican, black, and white care workers, and found that, whereas all of these respondents described positive aspects of their care work and reported sources of strain and negative outcomes, members of different racial and gender groups explained these answers differently and in response to different questions. Thus, despite caring for elders who were less impaired, whites reported more feelings of burden. Puerto Rican women reported feeling isolated, and black men and women described their care work as extremely demanding and time-consuming. Men from all groups and white women more often reported feeling angrier than women belonging to minority groups; Puerto Rican and black men expressed frustration with care work. Women, regardless of race and ethnicity, expressed burden more indirectly, through somatic complaints such as exhaustion, weight loss, anxiety, and weakness. Women from racial-ethnic minority groups, especially Puerto Rican women, expressed burden and found coping resources related to the self-sacrificing aspects of mother-hood. That is, women's engagement of domestic labor in Puerto Rican cul-ture is naturalized as a part of motherhood, as is the expectation that their less "assertive role" means that they will be "less vocal about their feelings and opinions" (p. 174). Thus, Puerto Rican women's performance of caregiving tasks that represent nurturing and motherhood both produces particular (in-direct) expressions of burden and provides an ideological resource for coping.

The emphasis on informal caregiving among aging families can lead re-searchers to overlook the ways that sexual inequality influences late-life fam-ily forms and caregiving. One study found that older gays and lesbians often were called on to provide care not only for a partner but also for members of their family of choice (Shippy, 2007). As a result, they are more likely to engage in care work than their heterosexual peers are. For example, one-fourth of a national sample of middle-aged LGBT adults provided care in the last six months, as compared with 20% of the general population. In addi-tion, approximately equal numbers of gay and bisexual men and women gave care (Metlife Mature Market Institute, 2006). Nonheterosexual men may be more involved in caregiving than their heterosexual counterparts because their families of choice contain more men, and same-sex groups lack natural-ized gender divisions of labor. But, among a sample of 155 LGBT caregivers (average age 60) in the New York City area, two times as many lesbian and bisexual women provided care to family of origin members, usually parents, than gay men (Shippy, 2007). This finding indicates continued importance of gender in providing care when a spouse or partner is not available.

Although gender did not influence how much strain caregivers reported in this study, women reported feeling more burdened, regardless of their rela-tionships to care receivers. Women were more likely than men to take time off work, conceal their sexuality, and find their social life limited. In addition, women who cared for family of origin members reported more strained rela-tions with partners than caregiving men did. Shippy (2007) concluded that lesbians' experiences of care work bear more similarities to than differences from those of heterosexual women. In both groups, women are more often called on to care for family members and to juggle family and work respon-sibilities, and, as a result, they feel more burdened by care work than men.

Still, sexual inequality adds to caregiving strain. Lesbians' families of origin assumed that they had fewer traditional family obligations, so they expected them to do more care; this expectation led lesbians to feel burdened. In addition, 26% of men and women caregivers for family of choice members had problems with formal care providers, and fear of discrimination shaped their experiences with medical personnel (Shippy, 2007; see also Brotman et al., 2003).

Spousal Care Work

Spousal caregiving provides a case for intersectional analysis, in that inequalities correlate with the provision of such care. Spouses are preferred caregivers, and perform 25% of informal care in later life; but only about half of old people have spouses available to provide care for them (Silverstein & Giarrusso, 2010). Nevertheless, people over age 65—who are likely to be spouses—are also the most likely group to be sole unpaid caregivers, receiving no help from others (National Alliance for Caregiving, 2009b, p. 7).

Gender intersects with age and sexuality to shape experiences of caregiving situations. Given age relations, caring for old people, even one's spouse, is even less valued than caring for children (Calasanti, 2006). And unlike other caregiving situations, husbands and wives perform similar kinds and amounts of care (Arber & Ginn, 1995). At the same time, occupying positions of privilege—being heterosexual men, in this case—influences care work.

Husbands and wives both view care work as a marital duty—a demonstration of love and commitment—and they believe that their spouses would do the same for them (Calasanti, 2006; Hayes, Boylstein, & Zimmerman, 2009). Perhaps this is why gender differences in reported burdens are smaller among spousal caregivers than others (Silverstein & Giarrusso, 2010). Still, gender relations influence how husbands and wives approach and experience care work.

Husbands' greater investments in the public realm of paid labor as markers of gender status lead them to approach care work as a set of challenges—tasks to master, problems to solve, and tests of their organizational skills. They liken it to learning trades or to military service (Calasanti, 2006; Ribiero, Paul, & Noguiera, 2007; Russell, 2007). This orientation can afford a greater sense of control, and it may help men manage their emotions and take respite when needed (Calasanti & King, 2007; Russell, 2007). Although men express concern for and emotional commitment to their spouses (Calasanti & King, 2007; Russell, 2007), they do not see themselves as natural caregivers (e.g., Ribiero et al., 2007), but as problem-solvers. Thus, they tend to evaluate their care work based on successful task performance rather than on their ability to nurture or to make their wives happy when conflicts arise (a common challenge in caring for a spouse with dementia) (Calasanti & King, 2007).

The gender division of labor, governed by relations of sexuality that presume women's natural commitments to men, assigns women primary responsibility for care work and emphasizes naturalized ideals of nurturing. Their previous care work leads wives to expect to care easily for spouses both physically *and* emotionally (Calasanti, 2006). Wives' (and others') expectations that they can handle all the difficulties of caregiving (especially for cognitively impaired spouses) may leave them more vulnerable to stressors than husbands are (Calasanti, 2006; Calasanti & King, 2007).

Care working husbands struggle with the fact that their work goes largely unseen after lifetimes of recognition for work in public realms (Russell, 2007). By contrast, women's care work throughout their marriages has prepared them for its lack of visibility. Instead, caregiving wives struggle with their spouses' demands (and controlling behavior), unreasonable requests, and the increased relationship strain (e.g., Davidson, Arber, & Ginn, 2000).

Husbands and wives also respond differently to some similar aspects of care work. Two studies (Hayes et al., 2009; Calasanti, 2006) found that wives are more bothered by aspects of physical care, such as poor toileting behaviors, than are husbands, because of the ways in which gender relations structure marriages. Specifically, care-receiving wives "often had less status and power relative to their husbands throughout their marriage, and this changed little after wives' diagnosis" (Hayes et al., 2009, p. 55). By contrast, cognitively impaired husbands lost status (Hayes et al., 2009). Toileting issues signal a loss of power far more for husbands than for wives.

Finally, Calasanti and King (2007) found that husbands reported distress, but in ways consistent with ideals of manhood and on dimensions generally not captured by survey questions on depression or anxiety. Often they blocked or controlled their emotions by focusing on tasks or pursuing distractions. Expressing emotions that signaled distress was not a valid option. If negative emotions did surface, some caregiving husbands (but no caregiving wives) used prescription drugs and alcohol to cope.

Research on spousal care work takes for granted the ways that heterosexuality shapes gender repertoires by dictating husbands' and wives' roles. In contrast, same-sex couples do not have the same cultural legitimacy to assume such naturalized roles and must negotiate them. Indeed, gay and lesbian couples tend to be relatively egalitarian (Heaphy, 2007). Gay men, for example, may develop workplace skills and identities, and they also perform domestic labor that, unlike husbands, they cannot assign to wives. How such gender repertoires influence care work in old age remains unknown but is an important area for future research.

DISCUSSION

Our aim in this chapter was to explicate an intersectional approach to aging families. Few studies live up to the gold standard of examining multiple intersections simultaneously; more common are those that examine two inequalities or three.

The theory of intersecting systems of inequality and their effects on aging families provides a valuable lens through which policymakers can look at diverse experiences and thus improve outcomes. For example, interventions that might work for one group—old, white, middle-class caregiving husbands—might be ineffective for similarly situated gay men or for their female, working-class, or black counterparts. Among spousal caregivers, recommending that wives should act more like their male counterparts would create more problems than it solves, as wives could not enact gender appropriately. Similarly, husbands would not attend support groups where they were encouraged to talk about feelings (Calasanti & King, 2007).

Any discussion of intersections in research on aging families is tentative, as little is known about the specific situations of particular groups. For example, we do not know how being disadvantaged by relations of race and gender influences the situations of African American versus Puerto Rican women. Still, researchers and practitioners must be sensitive to differences as well as similarities among women from differing racial and ethnic minority groups.

Whereas our overview only touched on a few areas, it suggests a wide range of research questions to be addressed in looking at aging families. The discussion of gender and spousal care was based on research generally limited to white, middle-class, heterosexual couples. How the more egalitarian division of domestic labor reported by African American couples or how African American women's longer labor-force histories influence spousal care work are important questions. Predictions are not straightforward because, for example, African American men and women typically hold occupations with lower autonomy, pay, and benefits; such work may not have the same impact as that performed by middle-class, white men.

Similarly, whereas scholars have acknowledged that adults in LGB relationships may develop families of choice, little is known about their intergenerational relationships—a question that gains significance as cohorts of LGB elders age and lose members of their support networks. From this standpoint, the ageism within LGB communities presents real problems for care. And whereas some LGB elders have children, the extent to which children would provide care to them and their partners is unknown. So, too, are the ways in which these supports might vary by gender, class, race, and ethnicity, or the reasons why.

In like manner, the assumption that families of racial and ethnic minority groups will provide care merely assumes cultural practices that are divorced from structural roots. The ability and desire to care for or be cared for by one's own depend on availability of and access to other forms of care, such as long-term care facilities or community-based services (Blieszner, Roberto, & Singh, 2002), or migration patterns that are influenced by economic opportunities (Magilvy, Congdon, Martinez, Davis, & Averill, 2000). Indeed, even as international migration patterns are increasing the number of transnational families, the effects on aging family members are not yet understood (Calasanti, 2010). In all such cases, understanding the challenges that face aging families begins with data and theory on the intersections of relations of inequality.

REFERENCES

Acker, J. (2008). Feminist theory's unfinished business: Comment on Andersen. *Gender & Society, 22*, 105–108.

Ajrouch, K. J. (2005). Arab-American immigrant elders' views about social support. *Ageing & Society, 25*, 655–673.

Ajrouch, K. J., Antonucci, T. C., & Janevic, M. R. (2001). Social networks among blacks and whites: The interaction between race and age. *Journals of Gerontology Series B: Psychological Sciences and Social Sciences, 56B*, S112–S118.

Ajrouch, K. J., Blandon, A. Y., & Antonucci, T. C. (2005). Social networks among men and women: The effects of age and socioeconomic status. *Journals of Gerontology Series B: Psychological Sciences and Social Sciences, 60B*, S311–S317.

Amott, T., & Matthaei, J. (1996). *Race, gender, and work: A multicultural economic history of women in the United States* (rev. ed.). Boston: South End Press.

Aranda, M. P., & Knight, B. G. (1997). The influence of ethnicity and culture on the caregiver stress and coping process: A sociocultural review and analysis. *The Gerontologist, 37*, 342–354.

Arber, S., & Ginn, J. (1995). Gender differences in informal caring. *Health and Social Care in the Community, 3*, 19–31.

Badgett, M.V.L. (2001). *Money, myths, and change: The economic lives of lesbians and gay men*. Chicago: University of Chicago Press.

Barker, J. C., Morrow, J., & Mitteness, L. S. (1998). Gender, informal social support networks, and elderly urban African Americans. *Journal of Aging Studies, 12*, 199–222.

Baumle, A. K., Compton, D. R., & Poston, D. L., Jr. (2009). *Same-sex partners: The demography of sexual orientation*. Albany, NY: SUNY Press.

Biblarz, T. J., & Savci, E. (2010). Lesbian, gay, bisexual, and transgender families. *Journal of Marriage and Family, 72*, 480–497.

Blieszner, R., Roberto, K., & Singh, K. (2002). The helping networks of rural elders: Demographic and social psychological influences on services use. *Ageing International, 27*, 89–119.

Brotman, S., Ryan, B., & Cormier, R. (2003). The health and social service needs of gay and lesbian elders and their families in Canada. *The Gerontologist, 43*, 192–202.

Calasanti, T. (2003). Theorizing age relations. In S. Biggs, A. Lowenstein, & J. Hendricks (Eds.), *The need for theory: Critical approaches to social gerontology for the 21st century* (pp. 199–218). Amityville, NY: Baywood.

Calasanti, T. (2005). Ageism, gravity, and gender: Experiences of aging bodies. *Generations, 29*, 8–12.

Calasanti, T. (2006). Gender and old age: Lessons from spousal caregivers. In T. Calasanti & K. Slevin (Eds.), *Age matters: Re-aligning feminist thinking* (pp. 269–294). New York: Routledge.

Calasanti, T. (2010). Gender and ageing in the context of globalization. In D. Dannefer & C. Phillipson (Eds.), *The Sage handbook of social gerontology* (pp. 137–149). London: Sage.

Calasanti, T., & King, N. (2007). Taking "women's work" "like a man": Husbands' experiences of care work. *The Gerontologist, 47,* 516–527.

Calderon, V., & Tennstedt, S.L. (1998). Ethnic differences in the expression of caregiver burden: Results of a qualitative study. *Journal of Gerontological Social Work, 30,* 159–178.

Cantor, M.H., Brennan, M., & Shippy, R.A. (2004). *Caregiving among older lesbian, gay, bisexual and transgender New Yorkers.* New York: National Gay and Lesbian Task Force Policy Institute.

Carrington, C. (1999). *No place like home: Relationships and family life among lesbians and gay men.* Chicago: University of Chicago Press.

Choo, H.Y., & Ferree, M.M. (2010). Practicing intersectionality in sociological research: A critical analysis of inclusions, interactions, and institutions in the study of inequalities. *Sociological Theory, 28,* 129–149.

Courtenay, W.H. (2000). Constructions of masculinity and their influence on men's well-being: A theory of gender and health. Social Science & Medicine, *50,* 1385–1401.

Crenshaw, K. (1989). Demarginalizing the intersection of race and sex: A black feminist critique of antidiscrimination doctrine, feminist theory, and antiracist politics. *University of Chicago Legal Forum, 1989,* 139–168.

Daniels, J. (Guest Ed.). (2008). Symposium. *Gender & Society, 22,* 83–125.

Davidson, K., Arber, S., & Ginn, J. (2000). Gendered meanings of care work within late life marital relationships. *Canadian Journal of Aging, 19,* 536–53.

Delgado, M., & Tennstedt, S. (1997). Puerto Rican sons as primary caregivers of elderly persons. *Social Work, 42,* 125–134.

Dilworth-Anderson, P., Williams, I.C., & Gibson, B.E. (2002). Issues of race, ethnicity, and culture in caregiving research: A 20-year review (1980–2000). *The Gerontologist, 42,* 237–272.

Ferree, M.M. (2010). Filling the glass: Gender perspectives on families. *Journal of Marriage and Family, 72,* 420–439.

Fiori, K.L., Consedine, N.S., & Magai, C. (2008). Ethnic differences in patterns of social exchange among older adults: The role of resource context. *Ageing & Society, 28,* 495–524.

Fredriksen-Goldsen, K.I., & Muraco, A. (2010). Aging and sexual orientation: A 25-year review of the literature. Research on Aging, *32,* 372–413.

Glenn, E.N. (1992). From servitude to service work: Historical continuities in the racial division of paid reproductive labor. Signs, 18, 1–43.

Glenn, E.N. (1999). The social construction and institutionalization of gender and race: An integrative framework. In M.M. Ferree, J. Lorber, & B. Hess (Eds.), *Revisioning gender* (pp. 3–43). Thousand Oaks, CA: Sage.

Glenn, E.N. (2002). *Unequal freedom: How race and gender shaped American freedom and labor.* Cambridge, MA: Harvard University Press.

Greenberg, D.F. (1988). *The construction of homosexuality.* Chicago: University of Chicago Press.

Grossman, A.H., D'Augelli, A.R., & Hirschberger, S.L. (2000). Social support networks of lesbian, gay, and bisexual adults 60 years of age and older. *Journals of Gerontology Series B: Psychological Sciences and Social Sciences, 55B*, P151–P179.

Hayes, J., Boylstein, C., & Zimmerman, M. K. (2009). Living and loving with dementia: Negotiating spousal and caregiver identity through narrative. *Journal of Aging Studies, 23*, 48–59.

Heaphy, B. (2007). Sexualities, gender and ageing: Resources and social change. *Current Sociology, 55*, 193–210.

Herek, G. M. (2006). Legal recognition of same-sex relationships in the United States. *American Psychologist, 61*, 607–621.

Higginbotham, E. (1994). Black professional women: Job ceilings and employment sectors. In M. Baca Zinn & B. Thornton Dill (Eds.), *Women of color in U.S. society* (pp. 113–131). Philadelphia: Temple University Press.

Hurd, L. (1999). "We're not old!": Older women's negotiation of aging and oldness. *Journal of Aging Studies, 13*, 419–439.

Jones, J. (1985). Labor of love, labor of sorrow: Black women, work, and the family from slavery to the present. New York: Basic Books.

Laqueur, T.W. (1992). Sexual desire and the market economy during the industrial revolution. In D. C. Stanton (Ed.), *Discourses of sexuality: From Aristotle to AIDS* (pp. 185–215). Ann Arbor: University of Michigan Press.

Lockery, S. (1991). Caregiving among racial and ethnic minority elders. *Generations, 15*, 58–62.

Luft, R.E., & Ward, J. (2009). Toward an intersectionality just out of reach. In V. Demos & M.T. Segal (Eds.), *Advances in Gender Research* (Vol. 1, pp. 9–37). Bingley, UK: Emerald Jai.

Magilvy, J. K., Congdon, J.G., Martinez, R.J., Davis, R., & Averill, J. (2000). Caring for our own: Health care experiences of rural Hispanic elders. *Journal of Aging Studies, 14*, 171–90.

Masini, B.E., & Barrett, H.A. (2008). Social support as a predictor of psychological and physical well-being and lifestyle in lesbian, gay, and bisexual adults aged 50 and over. *Journal of Gay & Lesbian Social Services, 20*, 91–110.

McCall, L. (2005). The complexity of intersectionality. *Signs: Journal of Women in Culture and Society, 30*, 1771–1800.

Metlife Mature Market Institute (2006). Out and aging: The Metlife study of gay and lesbian baby boomers. Retrieved from http://www.asaging.org/networks/lgain/OutandAging.pdf

National Alliance for Caregiving in Collaboration with AARP. (2009a). *Caregiving in the U.S.: A focused look at the ethnicity of those caring for someone age 50 or older: Executive summary.* Retrieved from http://www.caregiving.org/data/FINAL_EthnicExSum_formatted_w_toc.pdf

National Alliance for Caregiving in Collaboration with AARP. (2009b). *Caregiving in the U.S.* Retrieved from http://www.caregiving.org/data/Caregiving_in_the_US_2009_full_report.pdf

Newman, K.S. (2003). *A different shade of gray: Midlife and beyond in the inner city.* New York: The New Press.

Pyke, K. (1999). The micropolitics of care in relationships between aging parents and adult children: Individualism, collectivism, and power. *Journal of Marriage and Family, 61,* 661–672.

Ribiero, O., Paul, C., & Nogueira, C. (2007). Real men, real husbands: Caregiving and masculinities in later life. *Journal of Aging Studies, 21,* 302–313.

Rich, A. (1986). Compulsory heterosexuality and lesbian existence. In A. Rich, *Blood, bread, and poetry: Selected prose, 1979–1985* (pp. 23–75). New York: Norton.

Roschelle, A. R. (1997). *No more kin: Exploring race, class, and gender in family networks.* Thousand Oaks, CA: Sage Publications.

Rubin, G. S. (1984). Thinking sex: Notes for a radical theory of the politics of sexuality. In C. Vance (Ed.), *Pleasure and danger: Exploring female sexuality* (pp. 267–293). Boston: Routledge.

Russell, R. (2007). The work of elderly men caregivers: From public careers to an unseen world. *Men and Masculinities, 9,* 298–331.

Sarkisian, N. (2007). Street men, family men: Race and men's extended family integration. *Social Forces, 86,* 763–794.

Sarkisian, N., Gerena, M., & Gerstel, N. (2007). Extended family integration among Euro and Mexican Americans: Ethnicity, gender, and class. *Journal of Marriage and Family, 69,* 40–54.

Sarkisian, N., & Gerstel, N. (2004). Kin support among blacks and whites: Race and family organization. *American Sociological Review, 69,* 812–837.

Shippy, R. A. (2007). We cannot go it alone: The impact of informal support and stressors in older gay, lesbian, and bisexual caregivers. *Journal of Gay & Lesbian Social Services, 18,* 39–51.

Silverstein, M., Chen, X., & Heller, K. (1996). Too much of a good thing? Intergenerational social support and the psychological well-being of older parents. *Journal of Marriage and Family, 58,* 970–982.

Silverstein, M., & Giarrusso, R. (2010). Aging and family life: A decade review. *Journal of Marriage and Family, 72,* 1039–1058.

Stein, A. (2008). Feminism's sexual problem: Comment on Andersen. *Gender & Society, 22,* 115–119.

Swartz, T. T. (2009). Intergenerational family relations in adulthood: Patterns, variations, and implications in the contemporary United States. *Annual Review of Sociology, 35,* 191–212.

Szinovacz, M. E., & Davey, A. (2008). The division of parent care between spouses. *Ageing & Society, 28,* 571–597.

Tolkacheva, N., Van Groenou, M. B., De Boer, A., & Van Tilburg, T. (2011). The impact of informal care-giving networks on adult children's care-giver burden. *Ageing & Society, 31,* 34–51.

West, C., & Fenstermaker, S. (1995). Doing difference. *Gender & Society, 9,* 8–37.

Wilson, G. (2000). *Understanding old age.* London: Sage.

Wright, E. O. (2009). Understanding class: Towards an integrated analytical approach. *New Left Review, 60,* 101–116.

Yee, B.W.K. (1997). The social and cultural context of adaptive aging by Southeast Asian elders. In J. Sokolovsky (Ed.), *The cultural context of aging: Worldwide perspectives* (2nd ed., pp. 293–303). Westport, CT: Bergin & Garvey.

Yee, J.L., & Schulz, R. (2000). Gender differences in psychiatric morbidity among family caregivers: A review and analysis. *The Gerontologist, 40,* 147–164.

12

Ethnic and Cultural Diversity in Aging Families: Implications for Resource Allocation and Well-Being across Generations

Merril Silverstein, Jessica Lendon,
and Roseann Giarrusso

INTRODUCTION

In this chapter we discuss how ethnic and cultural contexts shape the inter-generational experiences of families that contain older adults and trace their implications for the well-being of members of such families. Ethnic culture is broadly defined as a multidimensional construct represented by values, iden-tity, race, religious orientation, immigrant status, and nationality. We focus our substantive discussion on several areas in which the intergenerational literature on this topic has primarily concentrated: caregiving to impaired older adults, grandparents as caregivers to dependent grandchildren, and provisions of financial support and housing. We discuss the literature in the context of trends in the United States (and many European nations) toward greater representation of minority, multiethnic, and immigrant families and the swelling number of grandparents raising grandchildren, where ethnic cul-ture is considered both a risk factor and a resource. Unlike most treatments of culture, we also discuss the nation-state as implicitly representing a set of values that form preferences for government policies that intersect with the family lives of older people.

Our review primarily relies on peer-reviewed journal articles in the fam-ily and gerontological literatures that were published since 1995, when the first edition of this volume was published, and that are principally concerned with the role of ethnicity, race, and culture in aging families. In order to limit the scope of the scholarly material covered, we intentionally omit from our review the many studies that treat ethnicity and culture tangentially, often as control variables in a quantitative analysis, and almost exclusively consider cultural subgroups that predominate in the United States (with the notable exception of several cross-national studies). In Figure 12.1, we present a heuristic model that summarizes how the literature incorporates cultural elements into the study of aging families. Specifically, the elements of ethnicity, race, nativity, and nationality contribute to time (caregiving), financial, and space resource allocations across generations through their association with mechanisms of exigent need and filial norms that then have consequences for individual and family well-being. Our review is organized by the three types of resource allocations as they are connected to culturally determined pathways and well-being outcomes.

We begin by addressing how ethnic culture forms a basis for family caregiving to and by older adults. Family caregiving is inarguably the topic on which the majority of research on aging families has focused, and this is no less true for the specialty area focusing on ethnicity and culture. The provision of family care to impaired older adults and by older adults to their dependent grandchildren, though not perfect mirror images of each other, rest on common notions that the value of familism—as a form of cultural capital—represents a resource that families draw on to manage emergent needs of their members. However, as we will see, explanations for why minority families tend have strong commitment to serving dependent members also rest on social inequalities and material conditions that both necessitate and challenge ethnic minority caregivers.

We then turn to the exchange of tangible resources of housing and money. As with caregiving, ethnic differences in rates of extended-family coresidence and transfers of economic resources are considered products of both norms of filial responsibility and the need for filial support. The interplay between

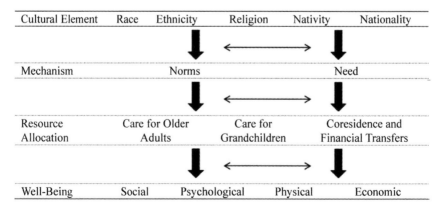

FIGURE 12.1 Culture and Intergenerational Resource Transfers in Aging Families

norms and need in minority immigrant populations is given closer inspection for their impact on acculturation and the well-being of older family members.

CAREGIVING AND SUPPORT TO OLDER ADULTS

That ethnic groups differ in their caregiving styles is widely accepted as a truism in gerontological scholarship. This conclusion was reified in a meta-analysis performed by Pinquart and Sörensen (2005) that examined 116 empirical studies published over more than a decade that allowed comparisons among white non-Hispanic caregivers and African American, Hispanic, and Asian caregivers. Their findings showed that caregivers in these three minority groups were younger, less likely to be a spouse, and had lower education and income than white non-Hispanic caregivers. African Americans provided the most intensive care to their recipients, but despite having a wider set of coping resources at their disposal, they experienced more health and cognitive problems than white non-Hispanics. Asian caregivers had worse relationships with their care recipients than white non-Hispanic caregivers, possibly because they were also less likely to rely on formal services. Ethnic differences observed across this wide variety of investigations on caregiving practices and outcomes suggest that a cultural lens is indispensable in coming to a better understanding of the risks, rewards, and resources in caregiving to older adults.

Caregiving in African American families has been studied in some depth with the general conclusion that family care is much preferred over institutional and other formal care alternatives and is a more reliable and diversified resource than it is in white families. Roth, Haley, Wadley, Clay, and Howard (2007), for example, found that middle-aged and older African Americans were more likely than comparable whites to perceive that a caregiver would be available to them in the event of a serious illness or disability, and were also more likely to choose daughters than spouses, a likely compensation for their greater risk of being unmarried. African Americans tend to rely on a more diversified set of providers than do whites, as a result of a more inclusive definition of family that includes fictive kin; spousal caregiving in African American families is more likely to be supplemented with care from other family members (Feld, Dunkle, & Schroepfer, 2004). In general, African American caregivers have a wider set of culturally relevant resources at their disposal including internal (coping) and external (support) resources. Older African Americans tend to have kin-focused support networks compared to older whites, although this differential attenuates with age as family members of both races become more important as care providers (Ajrouch, Antonucci, & Janevic, 2001).

With a preference for family care often comes a corresponding disinclination to use institutional care. However, whether reliance on family reflects strong filial preferences or the unavailability of formal alternatives has been the subject of some study. Wallace, Levy-Storms, Kington, and Andersen, (1998) found that African American elders were less likely to use institutional care than similarly situated whites, a difference the authors attributed to some combination of culture, class, and lack of access to residential care settings that leaves African American elders reliant on family members. African American caregivers in providing a higher intensity of care than whites also report greater unmet need because their efforts are not supplemented by formal services (Navaie-Waliser, Feldman, Gould, Levine, Kuerbis, & Donelan, 2001). This finding is mirrored in research by Miner (1995) who found that formal services did not compensate when informal family care was unavailable to older African Americans in need of care; the resulting support deficit was attributed to their difficulty in obtaining public and private services.

Despite making greater investments in providing care and experiencing more acute needs, African American caregivers tend to experience less stress and burden, as well as to receive greater subjective rewards in their caregiver roles, than do white caregivers (White, Townsend, & Stephens, 2000; Martin, 2000). Explanations for this seeming advantage revolve around the benefits of their own support networks, adherence to a strong religious tradition, and the fulfillment of familistic expectations. Resources of caregivers are mobilized in different ways across ethnic groups and with unique consequences. Overall, nonfinancial caregiving assets tend to be more abundant in minority caregivers in terms of informal support received, finding positive rewards in caregiving, and endorsing beliefs in filial obligation (Pinquart & Sörensen, 2005). African American caregivers for persons with dementia tend to receive more support from their own networks than do their white counterparts, reducing their sense of burden as a result of caregiving (Shurgot & Knight, 2005).

More positive appraisal of caregiving by African American caregivers is also partially explained by a greater reliance on religiosity to frame their caregiving experiences (Roff, Burgio, Gitlin, Nicholas, Chaplin, & Hardin 2004). African Americans tend to receive a variety of kinlike benefits from church involvement that include enhanced social integration, formation of emotionally close relationships, and access to practical support (Taylor, Lincoln, & Chatters, 2005; Williams & Dilworth-Anderson, 2002).

A strong familistic orientation is sometimes taken as a cognitive resource that compensates for the lower material resources of African American caregivers. Filial obligation—the belief that younger adults are obligated to help older kin—tends to be stronger among African Americans than whites (Coleman, Ganong, & Rothrauff, 2006). That time commitment to caregiving is greater among African American caregivers when a host of sociodemographic and economic factors are controlled is typically taken as implicit evidence for racial differences in the cultural value ascribed to family caregiving (Lee, Peek, & Coward, 1998; Laditka & Laditka, 2001). Explicit tests of this ethnocultural framework using validated measures have found that cultural justifications for caregiving are stronger among African American caregivers than among white caregivers (Dilworth-Anderson, Brummet, Goodwin, Williams, Williams, & Siegler, 2005; Jackson, Antonucci, & Brown, 2004). Given this evidence, it is not surprising that filial responsibility expressed by caregivers is more strongly associated with the intrinsic rewards of caregiving among African Americans than it is among whites (Foley, Tung, & Mutran, 2002). Ethnicity forms a cultural frame of professed values and norms that informs individuals how to evaluate their caregiving actions.

However, a familistic orientation may also function as a liability if it results in African American caregivers shouldering more of the effort to the exclusion of alternative support resources (Rozario & DeRienzis, 2008; Shurgot & Knight, 2005). Sudha and Mutran (1999) found that whereas preferences for family care were predictably stronger among African American elders, dislike of institutional care was surprisingly weaker than it was for whites, suggesting that the tendency of African American elders to prefer family care may have as much to do with the actual or perceived lack of alternatives as it does with cultural norms. Native American culture also emphasizes norms that elder care primarily be provided by family members, yet the burdens of caregiving—including role conflict, negative feelings, lack of efficacy, and guilt—are substantial when formal services are infrequently used (John, Hennessy, Dyeson, & Garrett, 2001). Thus, it is likely that having a strained informal support system in the absence of formal support services is problematic for many minority caregivers.

Many of the patterns found among African American caregivers hold for Hispanic caregivers as well. When asked to whom they would turn when faced with severe care needs, a greater proportion of Mexican Americans than non-Latino whites stated a preference for informal caregivers (Min & Barrio, 2009). Enactment of valued cultural scripts guided by the norms of *familismo* provides benefits by easing the sense of burden that Hispanic caregivers experience (John, Resendiz, & De Vargas, 1997). Mexican American caregivers who are more familistic tend to express their caregiving decisions as implicitly derived, that is, without formal negotiation (Radina, Gibbons, & Lim, 2009), supporting the view that cultural assumptions about the allocation of roles—who does what for whom—in immigrant Latino caregiving families may suppress intrafamilial conflict (Pyke, 1999). Yet these unstated cultural assumptions also tend to assign primary caregiver roles to female family members, thereby exacerbating the burden they experience as care providers (Pyke, 2004).

Although research demonstrates that heightened norms of filial obligation—as well as intergenerational support and interaction—persist among the descendants of immigrants, they are preserved in a somewhat weakened form (Aranda & Miranda, 1997; John, Resendiz, & DeVargas, 1997). In their multigenerational study of Mexican American families in Los Angeles and San Antonio, Telles and Ortiz (2008) found that the rate of acculturation across generations operated inconsistently depending on the cultural measure considered. Some cultural content exhibited wide differences between grandparents, parents, and children. Adult children had substantially higher rates of intermarriage, less use and understanding of Spanish, fewer Hispanic friends, and weaker identification as Catholics than their parents. However, there was also evidence of stability, and in some cases a resurgence of other cultural dimensions such as identifying as Mexican American, celebrating Mexican American holidays, and reporting the importance of Mexican American values. But the extent to which divergences in cultural beliefs and practices undermine caregiving in these cross-generation relationships is not well understood. Some evidence suggests that a culture gap across generations may produce invidious effects on the quality of intergenerational relationships (Silverstein & Chen, 1999; Treas & Mazumdar, 2004). Intergenerational relations in immigrant families represent a prime arena within which conflict between cultural expectations of older and younger family members play out.

Complex and sometimes contradictory filial expectations are characteristic of upwardly striving ethnic families. For example, Asian American elders—Chinese, Japanese, Korean, and Vietnamese—while emphasizing filial piety also express a desire for their children to be successful, which may come at the cost of their caregiving commitment (Pang, Jordan-Marsh, Silverstein, & Cody, 2003; Pyke, 2000; Young, McCormick, & Vitaliano, 2002). Thus, a more nuanced perspective on cultural norms and caregiving points to the possibility that filial duty may be tempered by conflicting preferences, laying the groundwork for ambivalent feelings on the part of care receivers and care providers.

Caregiving and support preferences have their bases in national cultures as well. How care responsibilities are allocated reflects to a large degree societal values concerning the appropriate allocation of care among three key institutions: the state, the market, and the family. Several multinational comparative studies have found that older parents have greater interaction with, live closer to, and are more likely to live with and receive more intensive care from their adult children the more southerly their location on the European continent (Brandt, Haberkern, & Szydlik, 2009; Broese van Groenou, Glaser, Tomassini, & Jacobs, 2006; Glaser, Tomassini, & Grundy, 2004; Daatland & Herlofson, 2003; Silverstein, Gans, Lowenstein, Giarrusso, & Bengtson, 2010). These differences map well onto the structure of welfare states that tend to be less generous in the southern nations than in the northern nations of the continent. The cultural underpinnings of these patterns are often underappreciated as support for public services is inversely correlated with values of exclusive familism (Lowenstein & Daatland, 2006).

GRANDPARENTS AS CAREGIVERS

Race and ethnic differences in styles of grandparenting have been long observed. For instance, African American grandparents tend to be more involved with their grandchildren than white grandparents and are more apt than other grandparents to provide discipline, guidance, support, and surrogate care to their grandchildren (Hunter & Taylor, 1998). African American grandparents also closely identify with their role as grandparents and derive a great sense of meaning and accomplishment from contributing to the development of their grandchildren (Silverstein & Marenco, 2001; Timberlake & Chipungu, 1992). The stronger, more authoritative role taken by black grandmothers has deep cultural roots reflecting a tradition of surrogate parenting and extended familism going back to the time of slavery (Hunter & Taylor, 1998; Jimenez, 2002). This role of black grandparents is in stark relief to earlier literature on grandparenting.

Earlier literature on grandparenting tended to emphasize grandparents as fun-loving companions to their grandchildren, primarily ruled by a norm of noninterference with their grandchild's family (see Cherlin & Furstenberg, 1986). This image has since given way to the important functional roles of grandparents, treating them more as guardians of family stability than as peripheral companions (Hagestad & Oppelaar, 2004). This model of grandparenting was brought into sharp relief when the percentage of children living in grandparent-headed households rose sharply in the 1980s and 1990s (Bryson & Casper, 1999). Whereas this phenomenon touched all socioeconomic and ethnic groups, it was most dramatically seen in African American families that were particularly hard hit by the crack-cocaine epidemic, HIV-AIDS, lack of employment, and high rates of incarceration (Fuller-Thomson & Minkler, 2001).

Of the 2.4 million grandparents in 2000 who claimed primary responsibility for at least one coresident grandchild (Simmons & Lawler Dye, 2003), about one-quarter were African American, the most vulnerable ethnic group in this population (Minkler & Fuller-Thompson, 2005). There are also strong incentives for grandparents to provide care for their grandchildren in single-parent families, a household type that is disproportionately headed by African American mothers (Baydar and Brooks-Gunn, 1998). Among single-mother families, the presence of grandparents in the household substantially reduces economic hardship (Mutchler & Baker, 2009). Research suggests that children being cared for full-time by grandparents are at elevated risk for behavioral and emotional problems (Billing, Ehrle, & Kortenkamp, 2002), often assumed to be the consequence of the dire home environments that created the need for grandparents' care in the first place (Fuller-Thomson, Minkler, & Driver, 1997).

While stress levels are typically high among grandparent caregivers—particularly for those with the fewest resources such as African Americans (Ross & Aday, 2006) and Native Americans (Letiecq, Bailey, & Kurtz, 2008)—culturally relevant resources tend to moderate the effects of caregiving stress. Grandparents from cultures with strong expectations to care for at-risk grandchildren adapt more successfully to their custodial role. For example, a study comparing African American, Latina, and white grandmothers raising their grandchildren found that African American custodial grandmothers had the best psychological outcomes once the reason for adopting the role was controlled (Goodman & Silverstein, 2006). African American grandmothers are more apt to know others raising grandchildren and to have themselves been raised by grandparents, further legitimating this family form (Pruchno, 1999).

Both Latina and African American grandparents caring for grandchildren tend to rely on secondary caregivers, most often other family member (Burnette, 1999; Gibson, 2005). However, the role played by secondary caregivers tends to vary by ethnic group. Hispanic grandparent caregivers are more likely than their white and black counterparts to provide care for a grandchild in conjunction with the child's mother, and this arrangement tends to produce less distress than in ethnic groups without a strong tradition of coparenting (Goodman & Silverstein, 2002).

Grandparent-grandchild relations in Hispanic families are typically viewed as being stronger and more durable than those in non-Hispanic white families (Strom, Buki, & Strom, 1997). However, there is variation depending on immigrant status and level of acculturation across generations. In a study of Mexican American immigrant families findings indicated that young adult grandchildren who moved away from their native language and traditional customs tended to feel emotionally and socially detached from their more traditional grandparents; grandparents did not view the culture gap as detrimental to the relationship (Silverstein & Chen, 1999).

Regional and national conditions also influence relations between grandparents and grandchildren. For example, King and Elder (1995) in their study of rural Iowa farm families found that grandchildren tended to have stronger relations with their paternal grandparents than with their maternal grandparents, a reversal of the pattern found in urban families of Los Angeles (King, Silverstein, Elder, Bengtson, & Conger, 2003). The strength of paternal ties is the cultural legacy of patrilineal inheritance patterns in agricultural communities where land ownership was traditionally passed from father to son. While maternal grandparents tend to be more active than paternal grandparents in most Western nations (Uhlenberg & Hammill, 1998), the opposite lineage preferences tend to be realized in more traditional countries (Pashos,

2000). This discrepancy challenges the essentialist bioevolutionary view of grandparenting and suggests a cultural basis for how grandparent roles are enacted.

The type and level of grandparent involvement has a basis in the national characteristics that may enable or substitute for family functions that grandparents are apt to perform. For instance, grandparents in Norway care for their grandchildren at nearly twice the rate of grandparents in other European nations, ostensibly because women in that country have achieved such high rates of labor force participation (Hagestad & Oppelaar, 2004). Grandparents in economically precarious immigrant families are key contributors to child care, thereby allowing mothers to work for pay (Ralitza & Wolff, 2007; Treas & Mazumdar, 2004).

High levels of need and strong familistic values are in alignment within less developed nations, resulting in highly active grandparenting. Many grandparents in Saharan Africa have been thrust into caregiving roles due to the AIDS epidemic such that households consisting of older adults and grandchildren of deceased parents are quite common (Oppong, 2006; Zimmer & Dayton, 2005). In China and other developing nations, it is not unusual for rural grandparents to serve as surrogate parents so that their adult children can seek employment in urban areas (Agree, Biddlecom, Chang, & Perez, 2002; Chen, Short & Entwisle, 2000; Silverstein, Cong & Li, 2006; see also Keating & Fletcher, chapter 13 in this volume).

Grandparents are not only influenced by cultural forces, they embody them as well. In fact, grandparents are said to excel at the transmission of culture from one generation to another. They play an important symbolic role with respect to their grandchildren by conveying core values and providing a cultural window to family history and traditions (King, 2003; King & Elder, 1999; Pratt & Fiese, 2004). Religious orientation, a cultural thread that spans the generations, is transmitted by grandparents to their grandchildren net of parental influences (Copen & Silverstein, 2007). Grandchildren with greater exposure to grandparents earlier in life also tend to hold more positive attitudes toward older people (McGuinn & Mosher-Ashley, 2002), express stronger support for entitlement programs targeting aged adults (Silverstein & Parrott, 1997), and are more willing to live with their aging parents (Szinovacz, 1997).

CORESIDENT LIVING ARRANGEMENTS

Much research has documented that extended-family households are more common among elders in ethnic minority populations (Chatters & Jayakody, 1995; Himes, Hogan & Eggebeen, 1996). Coresidence affords greater opportunities to exchange family support across generations and provides a strategy to deal with economic scarcity in low income ethnic groups (Ajrouch et al., 2001; Angel & Angel, 2006), but coresidence is also a manifestation of cultural values of familism (Lum, 2005; Peek, Coward, & Peek, 2000). When presented as a hypothetical question, blacks and Hispanics tend more than their white counterparts to endorse the norm that adult children should coreside with their frail older parents (Burr & Mutchler, 1999), suggesting a cultural basis for coresidence patterns.

Among ethnic minorities, immigrants represent a subgroup that is particularly likely to live in multigenerational households (Kritz, Gurak, & Chen, 2000). This pattern is characteristic of immigrants worldwide (see Lowenstein, 2002, concerning Russian immigrants to Israel, and Attias-Donfut, Ogg, & Wolff, 2005, concerning North African immigrants to France). Coresidence between older immigrants and their adult children confers benefits to both generations in terms of pooling economic and space resources, and grants young parents trustworthy and low-cost child care assistance (Kritz, Gurak, & Chen, 2000; Treas & Chen, 2000; Treas & Torrecilha, 1995). Relying on resources embedded in their intergenerational relationships is a way for older immigrants to compensate for their poor economic conditions and linguistic and cultural isolation from the mainstream culture.

Cultural forces also play a role in coresidence decisions, although the interplay of culture with economic need can be complex. For instance, Kamo and Zhou (1994) found that coresidence of Chinese and Japanese older adults with their married children was common even when their attributes were matched to a similar group of older non-Hispanic whites, indicating the persistence of cultural values when objective conditions of social circumstances and birthplace are held constant. Wilmoth (2001) similarly found that older Hispanic and Asian immigrants were more likely to live with family members after controlling for resources, needs, and demographic characteristics. However, multigenerational coresidence declines as income rises in all ethnic minority groups, leading to the conclusion that coresidence may be based on need as well as ethnic preferences (Cohen & Casper, 2002). In a study of older adults consisting of multiple ethnic backgrounds—Mexican, Puerto Rican, Japanese, Chinese, Filipino, and Korean—the tendency to live in complex households diminished as income increased (Burr & Mutchler, 1993a; 1993b), supporting the idea that cultural tendencies to coreside with other generations are rendered less powerful when the ability to purchase privacy is strengthened.

Another way to assess culture as a guiding force has been to examine the consequences of different living arrangements on the well-being of household members based on race and ethnicity. For example, Waite and Hughes (1999) found that among late-middle aged individuals both blacks and Hispanics living in vertically extended multigenerational households had better mental and physical health than their white non-Hispanic counterparts, concluding that cultural values in minority groups favoring coresidence and intergenerational cohesion were likely behind such patterns. In a similar vein, Russell and Taylor (2009) found that living with others reduced depression more among older Hispanic adults than it did among older non-Hispanics by fulfilling a cultural ideal.

There is also evidence, however, that multigenerational coresidence may come at a cost to older individuals as well as to the younger generations in their households. Older Hispanic immigrant parents who live with their adult children are likely to be financially and socially dependent on them (Glick &Van Hook, 2002; Wilmoth, 2001). Such dependence may isolate older migrants from the wider social environment (Wilmoth & Chen, 2003) and create conflict with their children regarding household decisions and practices (Treas & Mazumdar, 2002). Among those immigrants who are less acculturated to their new environments, this may produce strains in their intergenerational relationships (Angel, Angel, & Markides, 2000; Wilmoth, 2001). Indeed, older immigrants with the least English proficiency tend to have more depressive symptoms than their native counterparts (Wilmoth & Chen, 2003), and, contrary to expectations, the quality of family relations does little to mitigate these symptoms (Angel, Buckley, & Finch, 2001). Treas and Mazumdar (2004) pointed out several challenges faced by older Hispanic immigrants who live with their adult children. Older immigrants are at elevated risk of social isolation as a result of their limited English proficiency and may tend to subordinate their own needs to those of their families, particularly in taking care of their grandchildren at an age when they are also likely to experience the need for care themselves. They are also often called upon to perform the difficult task of sustaining the cultural integrity of their native land while their children and grandchildren are rapidly acculturating into the host society. Finally, older and younger generations in immigrant Hispanic families may be separated by national borders, producing challenges in negotiating geographic distance and introducing risks associated with multiple border crossings.

Older African Americans tend to experience greater fluidity in their household composition than whites, most of which is related to the circulation of household members consisting of various children, grandchildren, and nonrelatives (Peek, Koropeckyj-Cox, Zsembik, & Coward, 2004). Persistent family stress, a likely consequence of household instability, is associated with poor physical functioning in older African American women (Kasper, Ensminger, Green, Fothergill, Juon, Robertson, & Thorpe, 2008).

Thus, the popular image of immigrant elders contentedly embedded in family-rich households is likely an oversimplification. Divergent views on the role of ethnicity—whether considered a resource or a source of jeopardy—call into question some of the broad assumptions made about support networks in minority and immigrant families, and demand more detailed research on preferences and opportunities for coresidence for different generations in these families. Taken together, these findings suggest that culturally embedded role expectations as well as resources shape the experience of multigenerational living arrangements and govern the contexts under which such arrangements are deemed appropriate or desirable.

FINANCIAL TRANSFERS

While exigent need is greater among older adults in ethnic minority families, intergenerational financial transfers occur at relatively low rates due to economic insufficiency of younger family members who tend to compensate by providing care, support, and housing (Berry, 2006). That middle-aged Hispanics and African Americans are less likely than comparable whites to provide financial assistance to extended family members, but more likely to live in close proximity and provide instrumental support to them (Sarkisian, Gerena, & Gerstel, 2006; Wong, Capoferro, & Soldo, 1999), may be viewed within the context of a time-for-money tradeoff. Yet economic need does tend to be greatest in the very families that have the fewest options for economic support. For example, the relative loss of income due to widowhood tends to be greater for African American and Hispanic widows than for white widows (Angel, Jimenez, & Angel, 2007).

When financial transfers do occur across generations within ethnic minority families, they tend to be of great significance. Older blacks may delay their retirement if they need to economically support another family member or accelerate their retirement if needed economic support from family members is forthcoming (Szinovacz, DeViney, & Davey, 2001). Members of ethnic minorities are also less likely to receive bequests and when they do receive them, such bequests are of lesser value than they are for white non-Hispanics. This disadvantage is expected to grow as cross-ethnic disparities in wealth available to bequeath appear to be widening (Avery & Rendall, 2002).

Whereas provisions of financial support to older parents in African American and Latino families is strongly based on need, such provisions from older parents to adult children tend to go to more advantaged children based on their education and income, suggesting that downward transfers are intended more as investments in children with the most promising endowments than as a means to redistribute resources to more needy children (Lee & Aytac, 1998), a pattern opposite to that seen with respect to social support (Suitor, Sechrist, & Pillemer, 2007).

CONCLUSION

In this chapter we reviewed research from the past 15 years on the role of ethnic culture in shaping the allocation of resources across generations in aging families and its consequences for the well-being of family members. As noted by two authors of this chapter in a decade review of research on aging families, ethnic culture is noticeable in the literature by its relative absence (Silverstein & Giarrusso, 2010). This finding is somewhat surprising given recent growth in the representation of minority and multiethnic families in the population. We do, however, note that the literature has responded to several social changes affecting older families, such as the growing number of African American grandparents who are raising their grandchildren and the rapid increase in the Hispanic elderly population that is expected to triple in the next 50 years (U.S. Bureau of the Census, 2002). The steep rise in custodial grandparenting is viewed by many as a response to breakdown in low income African American families but also as a signal of great resilience with cultural-historical precedents. Growth in the immigrant population together with the uneven acculturation of older immigrants and their descendants presents opportunities for developing new paradigms to understand culture as a transformative social force in aging families. Ethnic diversity due to immigration from Latin America, as well as from Asia, may portend a change in the normative context and functions of intergenerational families in relation to older adults.

Divergent views on the role of ethnicity—whether considered a resource or a source of jeopardy—demand more detailed research on preferences and opportunities for informal and formal support in aging families. Across several ethnic groups it can be observed that arrangements consistent with cultural traditions and expectations are associated with more successful adaptation and better outcomes. Greater attention has been paid to the cultural meaning of caregiving and examining the psychic rewards it provides the caregiver. We have also reviewed evidence that strong norms of familism that are characteristic of many ethnic minorities might isolate family caregivers and be associated with receiving less outside help. Acting according to cultural scripts may suppress conflict among caregivers, but may also lead to inequalities and excess burden. When and under what conditions ethnic norms are helpful or harmful is an empirical question that remains unresolved.

It is a well established fact that African American, Hispanic, and Asian families are more likely to care for their impaired elderly members and do so at higher intensities and within family-dense care networks. However, a more inclusive cognitive map of who is considered family may be needed in ethnic groups that are more fluid in their composition (Dilworth-Anderson, Burton, & Turner, 1993). How boundary ambiguity is negotiated in minority families and where extended and nuclear familism is more or less distinct would shed light on ethnic differences in the very interpretation of who counts as kin.

With the availability of multinational data sets, growing attention is being paid to the role of the nation-states as embodying value preferences for government policies that intersect with the family lives of older people. The welfare state acts as a moral agent, a sociocultural ideal that variously frees or obligates helping behaviors in late-life families. Few discussions consider how moral political-economies at the macrolevel (i.e., whether the state is redistributive or residualist) intersect with family life (i.e., preferences and enactment of care roles) at the microlevel.

A central debate in the study of ethnicity surrounds the question of whether cultural values or economic deprivation drives the familistic attitudes and behaviors that are associated with minority families. Highly energized support systems in aging minority families are either considered the realization of cultural capital embedded in ethnic norms or an adaptation to sheer necessity, but this may be a false dichotomy. We suggest that these are explanations and it is likely that each reinforces the other. Because the response to need may be a cultural resource in its own right, the two mechanisms are not mutually exclusive and they are likely to be inextricably entwined. However, care must be taken not to overstate the role of ethnic culture in family life when economic and structural conditions are also at play. As research has shown with respect to African American caregiving to older adults, reliance on family members may have as much to do with blocked access to formal services as the preference for family care.

At its core, ethnic culture is a collective cognitive scheme with the power to structure social and family arrangements. The following theorem derived from a study of the cultural life of Polish immigrants in the early 20th century is revealing for its treatment of ethnic culture as a distinctive phenomenon, not reducible to other social forces: "If men define situations as real, they are real in their consequences" (Thomas & Thomas 1928, p. 572). It is in the space between an intersubjective consensus about how the world should work and the objective conditions of the world where ethnic culture continues to be a potent force in mature families. As such, ethnic culture has real consequences for the well-being of older individuals and the family members with whom they are connected.

REFERENCES

Agree, E. M., Biddlecom, A. E., Chang, M. C., & Perez, A. E. (2002). Transfers from older parents to their children in Taiwan and the Philippines. *Journal of Cross-Cultural Gerontology, 17*, 269–294.

Ajrouch, K. J., Antonucci, T. C., & Janevic, M. R. (2001). Social networks among blacks and whites: The interaction between race and age. *Journal of Gerontology: Social Sciences, 56B*, S112–S118.

Angel, J. L., & Angel, R. J. (2006). Minority group status and healthful aging: Social structure still matters. *American Journal of Public Health, 96*, 1152–1159.

Angel, J. L., Angel, R. J., & Markides, K. S. (2000). Late life immigration: Changes in living arrangements and headship status among older Mexican-origin individuals. *Social Science Quarterly 81*, 389–403.

Angel, J. L., Buckley, C. J., & Finch, B. K. (2001). Nativity and self-assessed health among pre-retirement age Hispanics and non-Hispanic whites. *International Migration Review 35*, 784–804.

Angel, J. L., Jimenez, M. A., & Angel, R. J. (2007). The economic consequences of widowhood for older minority women. *The Gerontologist, 47*, 224–234.

Aranda, M. P., & Miranda, M. R. (1997). Hispanic aging, social support and health: Does acculturation make a difference? In K. S. Markides & M. R. Miranda (Eds.), *Minorities, aging and health* (pp. 271–294). Thousand Oaks, CA: Sage.

Attias-Donfut, C., Ogg, J., & Wolff, F. C. (2005). European patterns of intergenerational financial and time transfers. *European Journal of Aging, 2*, 161–173.

Avery, R. B., & Rendall, M. S. (2002). Lifetime inheritance of three generations of whites and blacks. *American Journal of Sociology, 107*, 1300–1346.

Baydar, N., & Brooks-Gunn, J. (1998). Profiles of grandmothers who help care for their grandchildren in the United States. *Family Relations, 47*, 385–393.

Berry, B. (2006). What accounts for race and ethnic differences in parental financial transfers to adult children in the United States? *Journal of Family Issues, 27*, 1583–1604.

Billing, A., Ehrle, J., & Kortenkamp, K. (2002). *Children cared for by relatives: What do we know about their well-being?* (Series B, No. B-46). Washington, DC: Urban Institute. Retrieved from http://www.urban.org/Uploaded PDF/310486.pdf

Brandt, M., Haberkern, K., & Szydlik, M. (2009). Intergenerational help and care in Europe. *European Sociological Review, 25*, 585–601.

Broese van Groenou, M., Glaser, K., Tomassini, C., & Jacobs, T. (2006). Socioeconomic status differences in older people's use of informal and formal help: A comparison of four European countries. *Ageing & Society, 26*, 745–766.

Bryson, K., & Casper, L. M. (1999). *Co-resident grandparents and grandchildren.* (Publication No. P23–198). Washington, DC: U.S. Census Bureau. Retrieved from www.census.gov/prod/99pubs/p23-198.pdf

Burnette, D. (1999). Social relationships of Latino grandparent caregivers: A role theory perspective. *The Gerontologist, 39*, 49–58.

Burr, J. A., & Mutchler, J. E. (1993a). Ethnic living arrangements: Cultural convergence or cultural manifestation? *Social Forces, 72*, 169–180.

Burr, J. A., & Mutchler, J. E. (1993b). Nativity, acculturation, and economic status: Explanations of Asian American living arrangements in later life. *Journal of Gerontology: Social Sciences 4*, S55–S63.

Burr, J. A., & Mutchler, J. E. (1999). Race and ethnic variation in norms of filial responsibility among older persons. *Journal of Marriage and Family, 61*, 674–687.

Chatters, L. M., & Jayakody, R. (1995). Intergenerational support within African American families: Concepts and methods. In V. L. Bengtson, K. W. Schaie, & L. M. Burton (Eds.), *Intergenerational Issues in Aging.* New York: Springer.

Chen, F., Short, S. E., & Entwisle, B. (2000). The impact of grandparental proximity on maternal child care in China. *Population Research and Policy Review, 19*, 571–590.

Cherlin, A. J., & Furstenberg, F. F. (1986). *The new American grandparent: A place in the family, a life apart.* New York: Basic Books.

Cohen, P. N., & Casper, L. M. (2002). In whose home? Multigenerational families in the United States, 1998–2000. *Sociological Perspectives*, 45, 1–20.

Coleman, M., Ganong, L. H., & Rothrauff, T. C. (2006). Racial and ethnic similarities and differences in beliefs about intergenerational assistance to older adults after divorce and remarriage. *Family Relations*, 55, 576–587.

Copen, C., & Silverstein, M. (2007). The transmission of religious beliefs across generations: Do grandparents matter? *Journal of Comparative Family Studies*, 38, 497–510.

Daatland, S. O., & Herlofson, K. (2003). "Lost solidarity" or "changed solidarity": A comparative European view of normative family solidarity. *Ageing and Society*, 23, 537–560.

Dilworth-Anderson, P., Brummett, B. H., Goodwin, P., Williams, S. W., Williams, R. B., & Siegler, I. C. (2005). Effect of race on cultural justifications for caregiving. *Journal of Gerontology*, 60B, 257–262.

Dilworth-Anderson, P., Burton, L. M., & Turner, W. L. (1993). The importance of values in the study of culturally diverse families. *Family Relations*, 42, 238–242.

Feld, S., Dunkle, R. E., & Schroepfer, T. (2004). Race/ethnicity and marital status in IADL caregiver networks. *Research on Aging*, 26, 531–558.

Foley, K. L., Tung, H. J., & Mutran, E. J. (2002). Self-gain and self-loss among African American and white caregivers. *Journal of Gerontology: Social Sciences*, 57B, S14–S22.

Fuller-Thomson, E., & Minkler, M. (2001). American grandparents providing extensive child care to their grandchildren. *The Gerontologist*, 41, 201–209.

Fuller-Thomson, E., Minkler, M., & Driver, D. (1997). A profile of grandparents raising grandchildren in the United States. *The Gerontologist*, 37, 406–411.

Gibson, P. A. (2005). Intergenerational parenting from the perspective of African American grandmothers. *Family Relations*, 54, 280–297.

Glaser, K., Tomassini, C., & Grundy, E. (2004). Revisiting convergence and divergence: Support for older people in Europe. *European Journal of Ageing*, 1, 64–72.

Glick, J. E., & Van Hook, J. (2002). Parents' coresidence with adult children: Can immigration explain racial and ethnic variation? *Journal of Marriage and Family*, 64, 240–253.

Goodman, C. C., & Silverstein, M. (2002). Grandmothers raising grandchildren: Family structure and well-being in culturally diverse families. *The Gerontologist*, 42, 676–689.

Goodman, C. C., & Silverstein, M. (2006). Grandmothers raising grandchildren: Ethnic and racial differences in well-being among custodial and coparenting families. *Journal of Family Issues*, 27, 1605–1626.

Hagestad, G. O., & Oppelaar, J. A. (2004, November). *Grandparenthood and intergenerational context*. Paper presented at the annual meeting of the Gerontological Society of America, Washington, DC.

Himes, C. L., Hogan, D. P., & Eggebeen, D. J. (1996). Living arrangements of minority elders. *Journal of Gerontology: Social Sciences*, 51B, S42–S48.

Hunter, A. G. (1997). Counting on grandmothers: Black mothers' and fathers' reliance on grandmothers for parenting support. *Journal of Family Issues*, 18, 251–269.

Hunter, A. G., & Taylor, R. J. (1998). Grandparenthood in African American families. In M. E. Szinovacz (Ed.), *Handbook on grandparenthood* (pp. 70–86). Westport, CT: Greenwood Press.

Jackson, J. S., Antonucci, T. C., & Brown, E. (2004). Cultural lens on biopsychosocial model. In P. T. Costa & I. C. Siegler (Eds.), *Advances in cell aging and gerontology, Vol. 15* (pp. 221–241). New York: Elsevier.

Jimenez, J. (2002). The history of grandmothers in the African American community. *Social Service Review, 76,* 523–551.

John, R., Hennessy, C. H., Dyeson, T. B., & Garrett, M. D. (2001). Toward the conceptualization and measurement of caregiver burden among Pueblo Indian family caregivers. *The Gerontologist, 41,* 210–219.

John, R., Resendiz, R., & De Vargas, L. W. (1997). Beyond familism? Familism as explicit motive for eldercare among Mexican American caregivers. *Journal of Cross-Cultural Gerontology, 12,* 145–162.

Kamo, Y., & Zhou, M. (1994). Living arrangements of elderly Chinese and Japanese in the United States. *Journal of Marriage and Family, 56,* 544–558.

Kasper, J. D., Ensminger, M. E., Green, K. M., Fothergill, K. E., Juon, H. S., Robertson, J., & Thorpe, R. J. (2008). Effects of poverty and family stress over three decades on the functional status of older African American women. *Journal of Gerontology: Social Sciences, 63B,* S201–S210.

King, V. (2003). The legacy of a grandparent's divorce: Consequences for ties between grandparents and grandchildren. *Journal of Marriage and Family, 65,* 170–183.

King, V., & Elder, G. H., Jr. (1995). American children view their grandparents: Linked lives across three rural generations. *Journal of Marriage and Family 57,* 165–178.

King, V., & Elder, G. H., Jr. (1999). Are religious grandparents more involved grandparents? *Journal of Gerontology: Social Sciences, 54B,* S317–S328.

King, V., Silverstein, M., Elder, G. H., Jr., Bengtson, V. L., & Conger, R. D. (2003). Relations with grandparents: Rural Midwest versus urban southern California. *Journal of Family Issues, 24,* 1044–1069.

Kritz, M., Gurak, D. T., & Chen, L. (2000). Elderly immigrants: Their composition and living arrangements. *Journal of Sociology and Social Welfare, 27,* 85–114.

Laditka, J. N., & Laditka, S. B. (2001). Adult children helping older parents. *Research on Aging, 23,* 429–456.

Lee, G. R., Peek, C. W., & Coward, R. T. (1998). Race differences in filial responsibility expectations among older parents. *Journal of Marriage and Family, 60,* 404–412.

Lee, S. M., & Edmonston, B. (2005), New marriages, new families: U.S. racial and Hispanic intermarriage, *Population Bulletin 60, no. 2.* Washington, DC: Population Reference Bureau.

Lee, Y. J., & Aytac, I. A. (1998). Intergenerational financial support among whites, African Americans, and Latinos. *Journal of Marriage and Family, 60,* 426–441.

Letiecq, B. L., Bailey, S. J., & Kurtz, M. A. (2008). Depression among rural Native American and European American grandparents rearing their grandchildren. *Journal of Family Issues, 29,* 334–356.

Lowenstein, A. (2002). Solidarity and conflicts in coresidence of three-generational immigrant families from the former Soviet Union. *Journal of Aging Studies, 16*, 221–241.

Lowenstein, A., & Daatland, S.O. (2006). Filial norms and family support in a comparative cross-national context: Evidence from the OASIS study. *Ageing & Society 26*, 203–223.

Lum, T.Y. (2005). Understanding the racial and ethnic differences in caregiving arrangements. *Journal of Gerontological Social Work, 45*, 3–21.

Martin, C.D. (2000). More than the work: Race and gender differences in caregiving burden. *Journal of Family Issues, 21*, 986–1005.

McGuinn, K., & Mosher-Ashley, P.M. (2002). Children's fears about personal aging. *Educational Gerontology, 28*, 561–575.

Min, J.W., & Barrio C. (2009) Cultural values and caregiver preference for Mexican-American and non-Latino white elders. *Journal of Cross-Cultural Gerontology, 24*, 225–239.

Miner, S. (1995). Racial differences in family support and formal service utilization among older persons: A nonrecursive model. *Journal of Gerontology: Social Sciences, 50B*, S143–S153.

Minkler, M., & Fuller-Thomson, E. (2005). African American grandparents raising grandchildren: A national study using the Census 2000 American Community Survey. *Journal of Gerontology: Social Sciences, 60B*, S82–S92.

Mutchler, J.E., & Baker, L.A. (2009). The implications of grandparent coresidence for economic hardship among children in mother-only families. *Journal of Family Issues, 30*, 1576–1597.

Navaie-Waliser, M., Felderman, P.H., Gould, D.A., Levine, C., Kuerbis, A.N., & Donelan, K. (2001). The experiences and challenges of informal caregivers: Common themes and differences among whites, blacks, and Hispanics. *The Gerontologist, 41*, 733–741.

Oppong, C. (2006). Familial roles and social transformations: Older men and women in sub-Saharan Africa. *Research on Aging, 28*, 654–668.

Pang, E.C., Jordan-Marsh, M., Silverstein, M., & Cody, M. (2003). Health-seeking behaviors of elderly Chinese Americans: Shifts in expectations. *The Gerontologist, 43*, 864–874.

Pashos, A. (2000). Does paternal uncertainty explain discriminative grandparental solicitude? A cross-cultural study in Greece and Germany. *Evolution and Human Behavior, 21*, 97–109.

Peek, M.K., Coward, R.T., & Peek, C.W. (2000). Race, aging, and care. *Research on Aging, 22*, 117–142.

Peek, M.K., Koropeckyj-Cox, T., Zsembik, B.A., & Coward, R.T. (2004). Race comparisons of the household dynamics of older adults. *Research on Aging, 26*, 179–201.

Pinquart, M., & Sörensen, S. (2005). Ethnic differences in stressors, resources, and psychological outcomes of family caregiving: A meta-analysis. *The Gerontologist, 45*, 90–106.

Pratt, M.W., & Fiese, B.H. (Eds.). (2004). *Family stories and the life course: Across time and generations*. Mahwah, NJ: Lawrence Erlbaum Associates.

Pruchno, R. (1999). Raising grandchildren: The experiences of black and white grandmothers. *The Gerontologist, 39,* 209–221.

Pyke, K. D. (1999). The micropolitics of care in relationships between aging parents and adult children: Individualism, collectivism, and power. *Journal of Marriage and Family, 61,* 661–672.

Pyke, K. D. (2000). "The normal American family" as an interpretive structure of family life among grown children of Korean and Vietnamese immigrants. *Journal of Marriage and Family, 62,* 240–255.

Pyke, K. D. (2004). Becoming Asian American: Second-generation Chinese and Korean American identities. *Contemporary Sociology, 33,* 47.

Radina, M. E., Gibbons, H. M., & Lim, J. Y. (2009). Explicit versus implicit family decision-making strategies among Mexican American caregiving adult children. *Marriage & Family Review, 45,* 392–411.

Ralitza, D., & Wolff, F-C. (2007). Grandchild care transfers by ageing immigrants in France: Intra-household allocation and labour market implications. *European Journal of Population, 24,* 315–340.

Roff, L. L., Burgio, L. D., Gitlin, L., Nicholas, L., Chaplin, W., & Hardin, J. M. (2004). Positive aspects of Alzheimer's caregiving: The role of race. *Journal of Gerontology: Psychological Sciences, 59B,* P185–P190.

Ross, M.E.T., & Aday, L. A. (2006). Stress and coping in African American grandparents who are raising their grandchildren. *Journal of Family Issues, 27,* 912–932.

Roth, D. L., Haley, W. E., Wadley, V. G., Clay, O. J., & Howard, G. (2007). Race and gender differences in perceived caregiver availability for community-dwelling middle-aged and older adults. *The Gerontologist, 47,* 721–729.

Rozario, P. A., & DeRienzis, D. (2008). Familism beliefs and psychological distress among African American women caregivers. *The Gerontologist, 48,* 772–780.

Russell, D., & Taylor, J. (2009). Living alone and depressive symptoms: The influence of gender, physical disability, and social support among Hispanic and non-Hispanic older adults. *Journal of Gerontology: Social Sciences, 64B,* S95–S104.

Sarkisian, N., Gerena, M., & Gerstel, N. (2006). Extended family ties among Mexicans, Puerto Ricans, and whites: Superintegration or disintegration? *Family Relations, 55,* 331–344.

Shurgot, G. R., & Knight, B. G. (2005). Influence of neuroticism, ethnicity, familism, and social support on perceived burden in dementia caregivers: Pilot test of the transactional stress and social support model. *Journal of Gerontology: Psychological Sciences, 60B,* P331–P334.

Silverstein, M., & Chen, X. (1999). The impact of acculturation in Mexican-American families on the quality of adult grandchild-grandparent relationships. *Journal of Marriage and Family, 61,* 188–198.

Silverstein, M., Cong, Z., & Li, S. (2006). Intergenerational transfers and living arrangements of older people in rural China: Consequences for psychological well-being. *Journal of Gerontology: Social Sciences, 61,* S256–S266.

Silverstein, M., Gans, D., Lowenstein, A., Giarrusso, R., & Bengtson, V.L. (2010). Older parent-child relationships in six nations: The intersection of affection and conflict. *Journal of Marriage and Family, 72,* 1006–1021.

Silverstein, M., & Giarrusso, R. (2010). Aging and family life: A decade in review. *Journal of Marriage and Family, 72,* 1039–1058.

Silverstein, M., & Marenco, A. (2001). How Americans enact the grandparent role. *Journal of Family Issues 22,* 493–522.

Silverstein, M., & Parrott, T. (1997). Attitudes toward public support of the elderly: Does early involvement with grandparents moderate generational tensions? *Research on Aging, 19,* 108–132.

Simmons, T., & Lawler Dye, J. (2003). *Grandparents living with grandchildren: 2000* (Publication No. C2KBR-31). Washington, DC: U.S. Census Bureau. Retrieved from http://www.census.gov/prod/2003pubs/c2kbr-31.pdf

Strom, R. D., Buki, L. P., & Strom, S. K. (1997). Intergenerational perceptions of English speaking and Spanish speaking Mexican-American grandparents. *International Journal of Aging and Human Development, 45,* 1–21.

Sudha, S., & Mutran, E. J. (1999). Ethnicity and eldercare. *Research on Aging, 21,* 570–594.

Suitor, J. J., Sechrist, J., & Pillemer, K. (2007). Within-family differences in mother's support to adult children in black and white families. *Research on Aging, 29,* 410–435.

Szinovacz, M. E. (1997). Adult children taking parents into their homes: Effects of childhood living arrangements. *Journal of Marriage and Family, 59,* 700–717.

Szinovacz, M. E., DeViney, S., & Davey, A. (2001). Influences of family obligations and relationships on retirement: Variations by gender, race, and marital status. *Journal of Gerontology: Social Sciences, 56B,* S20–S27.

Taylor, R. J., Lincoln, K., & Chatters, L. (2005). Supportive relationships with church members among African Americans. *Family Relations, 54,* 501–511.

Telles, E. E., & Ortiz, V. O. (2008). *Generations of exclusion: Mexican Americans, assimilations, and race.* New York: Russell Sage Foundation.

Thomas, W. I., & Thomas, D. S. (1928). *The child in America: Behavior problems and programs.* New York: Knopf.

Timberlake, E. M., & Chipungu, S. S. (1992). Grandmotherhood: Contemporary meaning among African American middle-class grandmothers. *Social Work, 37,* 216–224.

Treas, J., & Chen, J. (2000). Living arrangements, income pooling, and the life course in urban Chinese families. *Research on Aging, 22,* 238–261.

Treas, J., & Mazumdar, S. (2002). Older people in America's immigrant families Dilemmas of dependence, integration, and isolation. *Journal of Aging Studies, 16,* 243–258.

Treas, J., & Mazumdar, S. (2004). Kinkeeping and caregiving: Contributions of older people in immigrant families. *Journal of Comparative Family Studies, 35,* 105–122.

Treas, J., & Torrecilha, R. (1995). The older population. In R. Farley (Ed.), *State of the Union: America in the 1990s* (pp. 47–92). New York: Russell Sage.

Uhlenberg, P., & Hammill, B. G. (1998). Frequency of grandparent contact with grandchild sets: Six factors that make a difference. *The Gerontologist, 38,* 276–285.

U.S. Bureau of the Census. (2002). *Race and Hispanic or Latino origin by age and sex for the United States: 2000* (Census 2000 PHC-T-8). Retrieved from http://www.census.gov/population/cen2000/phc-to8/phc-t-08.pdf

Waite, L.J., & Hughes, M.E. (1999). At risk on the cusp of old age: Living arrangements and functional status among black, white and Hispanic adults. *Journal of Gerontology: Social Sciences, 54B,* S136–S144.

Wallace, S.P., Levy-Storms, L., Kington, R.S., & Andersen, R.M. (1998). The persistence of race and ethnicity in the use of long-term care. *Journal of Gerontology: Social Sciences, 53B,* S104–S112.

White, T.M., Townsend, A.L., & Stephens, M.A.P. (2000). Comparisons of African American and white women in the parent care role. *The Gerontologist, 40,* 718–728.

Williams, S.W., & Dilworth-Anderson, P. (2002). Systems of social support in families who care for dependent African American elders. *The Gerontologist, 42,* 224–236.

Wilmoth, J. (2001). Living arrangements among older immigrants in the United States. *The Gerontologist, 41,* 228–238.

Wilmoth, J., & Chen, P-C. (2003). Immigrant status, living arrangements, and depressive symptoms among middle-aged and older adults. *Journal of Gerontology: Social Sciences, 53,* S303–S315.

Wong, R., Capoferro, C., & Soldo, B.J. (1999). Financial assistance from middle-aged couples to parents and children: Racial-ethnic differences. *Journal of Gerontology: Social Sciences, 54B,* S145–S153.

Young, H.M., McCormick, W.M., & Vitaliano, P.P. (2002). Attitudes toward community-based services among Japanese American families. *The Gerontologist, 42,* 814–825.

Zimmer, Z., & Dayton, J. (2005). Older adults in sub-Saharan Africa living with children and grandchildren. *Population Studies, 59,* 295–312.

13

Older Rural Adults and Their Families

Norah Keating and Stephanie Fletcher

WHY *RURAL* AGING FAMILIES?

For many years, the discourse on rural aging families in North America has been one of loss. There have been long-standing trends of outmigration of younger adults from farming areas (Bryant & Joseph, 2001; Johnson, 2006) and more recently from resource communities suffering from economic downturns (Hamilton, Hamilton, Duncan, & Colocousis, 2008). In combination, such trends have led to concern about older rural adults aging without local kin, in rural communities increasingly devoid of basic health and social services (Allan & Cloutier-Fisher, 2006). Despite these losses, there is evidence that on average, rural communities are tight knit and supportive to older adults (Keefe, Fancey, Keating, Frederick, Eales, & Dobbs, 2004), although there also are rising concerns that families at a distance and fragile local support systems cannot compensate for the erosion of services in rural places. There have been calls for special initiatives that would provide "rural proofing" of policy initiatives, and for service infrastructure that would adjust for additional costs associated with rurality toward enhancing the living situation of older rural adults (Asthana, Gibson, Moon, & Brigham, 2003).

The purpose of this chapter is to document the situation of rural aging families in North America and around the world. Population aging, household composition, and expectations of family support vary widely, providing insights into how regional contexts and rural settings can shape family relationships. The chapter is divided into the following sections, which together create a framework for understanding contemporary preoccupations and assumptions about rural aging families, while providing the basis for future knowledge creation across issues and places.

- Patterns of population aging in rural settings
- Rural aging families: Definitional challenges
- Families as compensating for vulnerable people in vulnerable places

• Family connections—living arrangements and family support
• Trends, gaps, and future directions

POPULATION AGING IN RURAL SETTINGS

Demographic trends in rural aging across world regions illustrate the contexts of family relationships of older rural adults. There are considerable national differences in age composition of rural populations. In many countries in sub-Saharan Africa, fewer than 5% of rural people are older adults (United Nations Statistics Division, 2002a, 2002b, 2002c). In contrast, in rural Japan almost 25% are over age 65 (United Nations Statistics Division, 2005a). The United States and Canada fall between these extremes with 12.8% and 13.4% of rural populations in these countries comprising people over age 65 (United Nations Statistics Division, 2000b, 2006).

These statistics suggest that rural aging is not a particularly important issue in developing countries. But despite their small proportions, the sheer number of rural older people is immense. Table 13.1 provides information on total numbers of older adults in rural areas. There are almost 59 million in China and 37 million in India (United Nations Statistics Division, 2000a, 2001). Both are far in excess of the 7.5 million living in the rural United States (United Nations Statistics Division, 2000b). Further, the vast majority of older adults in developing countries live in rural areas. Almost all older adults in Uganda (93.7%), Rwanda (87.3%) and Zimbabwe (83.1%) are rural (United Nations Statistics Division, 2002b, 2002a, 2002c).

In Asia, the majority of people of all ages reside in rural areas. In China and India, the two largest countries in this region, almost two-thirds (63%) of the Chinese and almost three-quarters (72%) of the Indian populations live in rural settlements (United Nations Statistics Division, 2000a, 2001). The largest concentration of adults over the age of 65 can also be found in the rural communities of these two countries: 67% of older adults in China and 75% of those living in India reside in rural areas (United Nations Statistics Division, 2000a, 2001). Paradoxically, India, Zimbabwe, Pakistan, Uganda, and Rwanda, which have the youngest populations in the world (United Nations Statistics Division, 2001, 2002c, 2003, 2002b, 2002a), have the greatest numbers of older rural adults and the largest proportions of older adults living in rural areas (Table 13.1).

In contrast, developed countries are typified by more aged populations. Rapid urbanization has resulted in lower proportions of the population living in rural areas compared to developing nations. But as illustrated in Table 13.1, in almost all of these countries, rural regions are more aged than urban areas. For example, in Finland, 35.1% of the total population is rural, whereas 41.7% of older adults are rural (United Nations Statistics Division, 2007). In the Republic of Korea (South Korea), differences are even more

TABLE 13.1 Percentage of Total Population and Total Population 65+ Living in Rural Areas

Country	Year	Source Year	Total Population	Total Rural Population	% of Total Population Living in Rural Areas	Total Population 65+	Total Rural Population 65+	% Total Population 65+ Living in Rural Areas
Uganda	2002	2004	24,442,084	21,442,697	87.73	737,274	690,820	93.70
Rwanda	2002	2004	8,128,553	6,755,949	83.11	235,566	205,561	87.26
India	2001	2003	1,028,610,328	742,490,639	72.18	49,105,542	36,792,745	74.93
Zimbabwe	2002	2006	11,631,657	7,601,950	65.36	419,188	348,395	83.11
Pakistan	2003	2005	138,979,270	89,339,166	64.28	4,708,561	3,106,170	65.97
China	2000	2002	1,242,612,226	783,841,243	63.08	88,274,022	58,808,800	66.62
Indonesia	2005	2007	213,375,287	121,370,218	56.88	9,925,983	6,215,460	62.62
Ghana	2000	2005	18,912,079	10,637,809	56.25	998,940	607,240	60.79
Finland	2007	2008	5,288,720	1,856,985	35.11	871,976	363,991	41.74
Netherlands	2008	2008	16,405,399	5,560,964	33.90	2,414,826	869,098	35.99
Ukraine	2008	2008	46,192,309	14,779,168	31.99	7,506,704	2,925,558	38.97
Russian Federation	2007	2008	142,008,838	38,235,803	26.92	19,588,954	5,872,143	29.98
Cuba	2007	2007	11,237,916	2,759,406	24.55	1,301,400	301,095	23.14
Peru	2007	2008	27,412,157	6,601,869	24.08	1,764,687	445,528	25.25
Mexico	2005	2007	103,263,388	24,276,536	23.51	5,716,359	1,600,846	28.00
United States	2000	2002	281,421,906	59,061,367	20.99	34,991,753	7,584,892	21.68
United Kingdom	2001	2006	58,789,194	11,781,767	20.04	9,340,999	2,061,345	22.07

(Continued)

TABLE 13.1 (Continued)

Country	Year	Source Year	Total Population	Total Rural Population	% of Total Population Living in Rural Areas	Total Population 65+	Total Rural Population 65+	% Total Population 65+ Living in Rural Areas
Canada	2006	2007	31,612,895	6,262,315	19.81	4,335,250	839,630	19.37
Brazil	2000	2001	169,799,170	31,845,211	18.75	9,935,100	1,821,484	18.33
Korea (Republic of)	2005	2007	47,041,434	8,703,735	18.50	4,365,218	1,618,385	37.07
Australia	2006	2006	19,855,288	3,469,839	17.48	2,644,389	528,313	19.98
New Zealand	2006	2006	4,143,282	580,150	14.00	515,556	59,540	11.55
Japan	2005	2007	127,767,994	17,503,670	13.70	25,672,005	4,208,971	16.40
Chile	2007	2007	16,598,074	2,176,688	13.11	1,390,812	215,635	15.50

Source: United Nations Statistics Division (2010). Population by age, sex, and urban/rural residence, http://data.un.org/Data.aspx?d=POP&f=tableCode%3A22

dramatic. In that country only 18.5% of the population live in rural areas compared to 37.1% of older adults, reflecting the rapid industrialization and migration of young people to cities at the end of the 20th century (United Nations Statistics Division, 2005b). In both the United States and Canada about 20% of older adults live in rural areas (United Nations Statistics Division, 2000b, 2006).

These population aging data provide a context for understanding the experiences of older rural adults and their families. Discussions about families and older adults in these regions differ considerably depending on their prevalence in rural areas, on cultural traditions, on values about family interdependence, and on regional economic status. Definitions of rural aging families also may differ in different contexts. These differences in definitions are addressed in the next section of the chapter.

RURAL AGING FAMILIES: DEFINITIONAL CHALLENGES

In order to review our state of knowledge about rural aging families, it is important to articulate what is meant by both rural and family. Each term is a contested construct, understood differently across time and place.

A Definition of *Rural*

There are two main approaches to defining *rural:* either as a distinctive type of locality, or as a set of beliefs or cultural practices (Atkin, 2003; Halfacree, 1993; Keating, 2008). *Locality* or place-based approaches distinguish rural places by their geographic characteristics such as population size, density, and distance from larger, urban centers (Hart, Larson, & Lishner, 2005). These criteria differ somewhat from country to country. In the United States, rural includes open country and small settlements of fewer than 2,500 persons in areas that have low population density (U.S. Department of Agriculture, Economic Research Service, 2003). In Canada the criterion for rural populations is fewer than 1,000 people (Statistics Canada, 2007, p. 231), with rural and small town definitions including settlements with fewer than 10,000 (Bollman & Clemenson, 2008). Similar to Canada, rural areas in the United Kingdom comprise villages, hamlets, isolated dwellings or remote small towns with fewer than 10,000 people (Barham & Begum, 2006).

Such structural definitions of rural are among the most commonly used and are the basis for census population statistics on rural populations. Locality approaches are useful because rural communities and their residents are physically situated. Issues such as the size and dispersion of rural populations are important when it comes to thinking about the ways in which rural residents stay connected to family members at a distance. They are important in understanding how distance from service centers can influence the ability of older adults to meet their needs for everyday services. Governments around the world use such approaches to understanding rural, although comparisons can be difficult given that definitions are not standard across countries. Despite their usefulness, such approaches also have been criticized because there are no clear assumptions about how these geographic features might structure rural life. Yet, in discussions of aging rural residents and their families, concerns about geographic isolation, bypassed economic areas, and lack of services are evident across world regions.

Cultural approaches define rural as a social construct—a reflection of a set of attitudes, behaviors, and beliefs that are a mix of personal experiences and handed-down beliefs that help people to order and organize complex reality. These beliefs are reflected in rural discourses: "people's everyday interpretations and constructions of the concept of rural and of the places they consider rural" (Haartsen, Groote, & Huigen, 2003, p. 246).

What are these cultural beliefs? In the literature from Europe and North America, rural people are typified as having similar characteristics. They are described as being family oriented; having a slower, less pressured way of life; strong community feeling, values of self-reliance and hard work; close connections to the land; and conservative, traditional values (Atkin, 2003; Blieszner, Roberto, & Singh, 2001). There is evidence that in Europe people living in the countryside believe that their lives differ in positive ways from those who live in the city (Cloke, Milbourne, & Thomas, 1997; Haartsen et al., 2003). From the developing world, rural places are viewed as much less benign, typified by harsh climates, poverty, and privation (Biao, 2007). Here, too, rural people are believed to be resilient and self-reliant, as well as both family oriented and family dependent (Cliggett, 2005).

A Definition of Families

The second key definitional issue is that of what is a *rural aging family*. Definitions of *families* are part of a long-standing tradition in family science. North American family scholars, including those at the Vanier Institute of the Family, increasingly favor definitions that include choice and are based on affectionate rather than obligatory relationships (Ross, Stein, Trabasso, Woody, & Ross, 2005; Walker, Allen, & Connidis, 2005), and that assume fluidity in family interaction and membership over time (Conger, Conger, Elder, Lorenz, Simons, & Whitbeck, 2008; Teachman, 2008; see also Blieszner & Bedford, chapter 1 in this volume). The small body of international research on family relationships in rural areas uses primarily a structural definition of families focusing on connections and exchanges between older adults and their close kin. Across regions, there are debates concerning the importance of household composition and geographic proximity of family members of older adults in providing them with material and other support (Bernard, Phillipson, Phillips, & Ogg, 2001; Bhat & Dhruvarajan, 2001; Bordone, 2009).

Given our focus, we draw on Johnson's (2000) call for family scholars to return to considering kinship relationships as part of understanding the family lives of older adults. She argued that lineal relationships formed both by intergenerational linkages and by collateral relationships with siblings and other same-generation kin determine resources of families. She also stated that this kinship perspective incorporates questions concerning how culture determines the norms that influence motivation to sustain kinship bonds. She noted that in the United States kinship networks are flexible in their expectations, lacking clear rules requiring supportiveness among kin, which allow for relationships that are "intimate at a distance or intimate and involved with each other" (p. 626). The intersection of kinship structure, proximity, and norms about supportiveness is at the heart of the debates about family relationships of older rural adults.

Based on the above discussion, the focus of the remainder of this chapter will be on older adults living in *locality rural* areas as defined within their countries. Social constructions of rural within these areas will be discussed where available. In all regions of the world, some older rural adults live in the same community as their family members; some have a mix of local and distant family members, and some have no proximate kin. Thus, we use the term *older rural adults and their families* rather than *older rural families* because only some members of the family network may live in rural areas.

RURAL CONTEXTS AND THE
FAMILY LIVES OF OLDER ADULTS

Around the world, beliefs about older rural adults and their families and rural places share some similarities. These are perhaps best captured in the phrase "vulnerable people in vulnerable places" (Joseph & Cloutier-Fisher, 2005, p. 133). Joseph and Cloutier-Fisher described rural communities as increasingly vulnerable because of declining infrastructure, regionalization of services, and reduced access to community care. In turn, older rural adults are vulnerable because of lack of access to basic and health care services and because of the increasingly complex *geography of the family* in which kin may be unavailable for assistance because of labor force engagement and distance. From this perspective, vulnerability arises from a combination of decreasing resources in both families and rural communities.

Although Joseph and Cloutier-Fisher are speaking of a particular set of rural communities in central Canada, there are discourses about vulnerability of older rural adults across regions of the world. Globalization, mobility patterns, poverty, and pandemics such as HIV/AIDS increase potential for vulnerability of older rural adults. Families are central to discussions concerning their support, often viewed as both essential to the well-being of their older family members and yet failing in their obligations to ensure adequate quality of life in the face of declining community and other resources. Discourses about older rural adults and their families differ considerably both across and within regions, illustrating variation in national views of advantages and disadvantages of rural aging.

Older Rural Adults and the Vulnerability Discourse in Asia

In many countries in south Asia, the vast majority of older adults live in rural areas. Rates of poverty among these older adults are high and national discussions are underway concerning how to support this aging population. A main argument is that older adults suffer as a result of young people becoming more independent and having weaker felt-obligations to support older family members. Bhat and Dhruvarajan (2001, p. 621) illustrated the concern in reference to India. They said that "urbanization, modernization, and globalization have led to changes in economic structure, erosion of societal values, and weakening of social institutions such as the joint family." They see evidence of the erosion of the traditional sense of duty and obligation of the younger generation to the old. Younger generations are searching for new identities encompassing economic independence, and changing economic structures have reduced the dependence of rural families on the land—a dependence that strengthened bonds between generations. The authors believe that significant erosion of the traditional Indian value of obligation of children to care for their parents has occurred, and they argued for a policy solution that is effective legislation for parents' right to be cared for by their children.

In eastern Asia, the majority of older adults also are rural. Here, too, there is concern about their marginalization. Biao (2007) spoke of older adults in China who may have no family members nearby as children migrate to cities to find work. Such older adults fare poorly in communities that have been bypassed socially and economically and can no longer provide support to those who are left behind. However, in contrast to India, land ownership acts as a buffer against privation. In rural China, (Jiangsu, Guangdon, Jilin, Hebie, and Gansu provinces), 93.9% of older persons are allocated land that can produce enough for their own consumption and sometimes a small surplus. In these areas, even a small contribution from children can increase monetary security and emotional satisfaction. Yet as in India, there is rising concern about whether families are willing and able to meet such support obligations to their older members.

Older Adults and the Vulnerability Discourse in Africa

Concerns about privation, subsistence, and pressures on older adults to support younger family members are evident in a region in which older adults are rural. HIV/AIDS has been a preoccupation in sub-Saharan Africa, and much of the discussion about older adults in the region has been embedded within the overall concern about the ability of families to cope with the devastation caused by the pandemic (Zaba, Whiteside, & Boerma, 2004; Ziehl, 2005). The following statement is representative of that concern: "AIDS is generating orphans so quickly that family structures can no longer cope. Typically, half of all people with HIV become infected before they are aged 25, developing AIDS and dying by the time they are 35, leaving behind a generation of children to be raised by their grandparents" (AVERT, 2010). Grandmothers often absorb responsibility for caring for their infected children and for their grandchildren who are orphaned by the disease. They assume large amounts of additional work but struggle to compensate for the loss of younger members' financial and labor contributions to the household (Bock & Johnson, 2008).

An additional theme evident in discussions about older adults in Africa is one of declining support of younger family members for their elders, a trend that has exposed older people to deprivation and poverty. Aboderin and Ferreira (2008) found competing beliefs about the source of this decline. The first is that traditional norms of filial obligation have weakened as a result of increasing individualism and a growing focus on the nuclear family. The second is that high levels of poverty throughout the region have led to growing resource constraints and the incapacity of the young to provide for older kin. In combination, increased family demands placed on older adults, especially women, combined with reduced support flowing from younger to older generations, have resulted in severe deprivation for many older adults. Despite such pressures on older adults, there are no comprehensive old age economic security policies for them (Aboderin & Ferreira, 2008).

Older Adults and the Vulnerability Discourse in Europe

Unlike discussions in Asia that resonate with alarm about aging rural populations and the inability or unwillingness of families to support their older members, in Europe interest is in the quality and solidarity of family relationships. Little research is specifically focused on older rural adults. However, scholars have raised questions about how social and demographic changes affecting the family and social networks of older people have influenced family solidarity and support for older people (Bernard et al., 2001). Yet, for the most part, discussions of kinship solidarities in Europe suggest that family relationships remain strong.

In Europe, family relationships are seen as based more on affection and choice than on obligation. Coresidence with adult children is not seen as an ideal living arrangement. In fact, research in western Europe has shown that coresidence may be costly to older adults. De Jong Gierveld, de Valk, and Blommesteijn (2002) found that issues such as crowding and poor social relationships among family members can lead to greater feelings of loneliness among older people living with adult children because the intense family household may result in older adults becoming isolated from their peers. The authors concluded that "as economic welfare increases in more and more countries in the Western world, there is less need for people to share their homes and become part of the same household" (p. 13).

Older Adults and the Vulnerability Discourse in North America

The vast rural regions of North America have resulted in discourses around migration patterns and distance from essential services and social connections. The discussions of older rural adults in Canada include themes of changing economic resources of rural communities, migration for employ-ment and for rural amenities, social isolation, and access to services. Migra-tion is viewed as an important mechanism for regional and local populations to adjust to changing economic and social circumstances (Bryant & Joseph, 2001). Patterns of outmigration from farming and remote communities, along with amenity driven in-migration of older adults to retirement destinations, result in high rates of population aging in many rural communities (Brown & Glasgow, 2008; Bryant & Joseph, 2001). Such patterns in turn are seen as evidence of increasing diversity among rural older adults and the communi-ties in which they live.

As a result of these macropatterns, some older adults are seen as vulnera-ble. In both the United States and Canada, there is concern that older people in some communities may be caught in a squeeze (Hanlon & Halseth, 2005; Joseph & Cloutier-Fisher, 2005). Reduction and centralization of services in rural communities and their own increasing age may render them less likely to be able to get access to services because of issues of driving, transportation, and affordability. Even retirement communities that attract relatively afflu-ent older adult in-migrants may disadvantage those who are no longer able to drive. Many of these communities are located in areas with attractive natural amenities such as lakes, mountains, and forests and are at a distance from some essential services (Brown & Glasgow, 2008; Keating, 2008).

Diversity in these communities makes it likely that older rural adults will have differential access to long-term family and other supportive relation-ships. In both the United States and Canada there is concern that outmigration of young people from rural communities will lead to rapid aging of rural communities and separation of older adults from their close kin (Brown & Glasgow, 2008; Joseph & Cloutier-Fisher, 2005). Distance from kin along with reduced services in many rural communities can increase vulnerability to social isolation and poorer health outcomes (Cloutier-Fisher & Kobayashi, 2009).

FAMILY CONNECTIONS OF OLDER RURAL ADULTS

Despite considerable differences in rural contexts and potential vulnerabilities of older adults, researchers in all regions emphasize links between rural contexts, living arrangements, and family support. The composition of the households in which older persons live and their familial embeddedness are important determinants of older adults' financial and social situation, the social support arrangements available to them, and their well-being. Around the world, living arrangements are viewed as being of central importance in the lives of older adults. Intergenerational distances and contacts are crucial because they reflect the role of families, determine the social and financial position of older adults, and influence their opportunities for care and assistance (Bordone, 2009; De Jong Gierveld et al., 2002).

In developing countries there is a special sense of urgency in understanding these connections. Family sociologists have traced decreases in the size and complexity of households as societies industrialize and urbanize (Bongaarts & Zimmer, 2002). In largely rural traditional societies, reflected in much of Africa and parts of Asia, residential families are more often extended than in industrialized societies where the independent nuclear family predominates. There are high levels of concern that, in the face of these changes, extended kinship ties will weaken, lineage patterns will dissolve, and a trend will occur toward the nuclear family becoming a more independent kinship unit. The expected result is "reduced social interaction and financial and physical support for the older generation, greater prevalence of separate living arrangements as countries develop" (Bongaarts & Zimmer, 2002, p. S146).

Living arrangements provide some evidence that this concern is warranted. One of the most comprehensive compilations of living arrangements of older adults in developing countries comes from Bongaarts and Zimmer (2002) who report on living arrangements of older adults across 43 countries in Africa, Asia, and Latin America.[1] They found that throughout the region, average household sizes are large in comparison to those in more developed countries. However, they also found that a substantially greater proportion of older adults live alone than do younger individuals; and that women are more likely to live alone than are men. They also found some broad differences within the regions. Coresidence with adult children is most common in Asia and least common in Africa; and coresidence is more frequent with sons than daughters in Asia and Africa but not in Latin America.

Despite these trends, there are indications that extended family living situations still predominate, suggesting that alarm about family demise may be overblown. Across the three regions, people age 65 and older have average household sizes of 5.8 (Africa), 5.5 (Asia), and 4.5 (Latin America). These households are smaller than the average for the whole population but still are relatively large compared to those in Europe and North America. Only a small proportion of people live alone (1.6% across all countries), although the percentage is higher for older adults (8.8%) and for women compared to men (11.1% vs. 6.5%). Living alone is especially uncommon among older men in Asia (3.6%). The strong patriarchal system in this region allows older men to retain control over their living situation. The assumption is that most choose to live with family members who can help meet their needs (Bongaarts & Zimmer, 2002).

As in other world regions, living arrangements are gendered. The majority of older men (76.7%) live with their spouse. Only 27.8% of older women live with a spouse because of men's higher age-specific mortality rates, although women are more likely than men to have coresident adult children (55.9%) or other extended kin (40%). Living with an adult child often is seen as a key indicator of potential for support. Across all countries, 53% of older men and 56% of older women live with children. The highest proportions are in Asia (66.3% of males and 68.3% of females). There are strong within-region variations. In Africa, the proportion of older men living with children ranges from 25% in Mozambique to 70% in Egypt.

In contrast, living with a young child is an indicator of support provided by older adults. Rates are highest in Africa where 69.8% of older women live with a young child. About 10% of older women in Africa live with young children with no other adults in the household. This proportion reflects high fertility during the past 18 years in this region and loss of adult children to diseases such as HIV/AIDS compared with the other two developing regions (Bongaarts & Zimmer, 2002, p. S149).

Overall, older adults in these regions appear to be embedded in household situations in which they may have access to shared resources. The relationship between household composition and resource sharing, discussed in the next section, illustrates strengths and weaknesses of these living arrangements.

Living Arrangements and Support in Africa and Asia

In comparison to European and North American families, African family systems are predominantly extended families. In this region adult children and extended kin often live in close physical proximity and older rural adults' experience of aging is shaped by their family relationships.

There is considerable overlap in terms for families and households in this region, illustrating the strong interconnections between kinship, household composition, and support. Nkosi and Daniels (2007, pp. 14–15) described families as a "collectivity of people who live together, whose relationship could be traced through kinship or marriage, and who considered themselves family." Households are distinguished by their productive contributions—" a common unit of social organization that combines those who reside together and who contribute to the income generation, consumption, and domestic activities as well as the extended family, who could live apart due to migration but do make contributions to household resources" (Nkosi & Daniels, 2007, p. 15).

These definitions suggest that there are normative obligations of family support and that these obligations are strongest for those living in close proximity. Contributions to domestic production and the rights to benefit from them are critically important to the survival of older rural adults. Cliggett (2005, p. 98) illustrated the survival benefit of having proximate kin. She stated that in rural Zambia, "the domestic setting also becomes the primary stage for elderly people to assert their identity and call upon obligations that are inherent to their position." In that area, the social composition of a household usually includes a married man, his wives and children, perhaps an elderly mother, unmarried sisters of the man, and matrilineal kin of the man such as a sister's son or daughter or mother's sister. Each adult has a separate house comprising as many as 20 buildings altogether. Nonetheless, she noted that support is not inevitable. Women and men share in and contribute to the subsistence economy. However, women without matrilineal kin such as a son or brother are vulnerable because others are not members of her proper family and thus not obliged to assist with food or other necessities.

In a region as large and diverse as Africa, one cannot assume homogeneity in living arrangements. However, research from Ghana on household composition of older adults shows striking similarities with other countries. Mba (2007) reported on the situation of older adults in Ghana based on the 2003 Ghana Demographic and Health Survey. Most (78.7%) live with others including children, grandchildren, sons-in-law, and daughters-in-law. Women are more likely to live in extended households after widowhood because they may need to move in with younger kin to receive support. Men have more options in living arrangements because they are more likely to control resources and can demand coresidence as a form of support. Evidence also shows that poor older people extensively share or are forced to share their pension benefits with their younger kin (Aboderin & Ferreira, 2008).

As in Africa, aging in Asia is likely to occur in a rural context and older adults' experience of aging is shaped by their family relationships. Living arrangements in rural China are evolving away from close-knit three-generation households (Whyte, 2004, p. 106). Public policy, market forces, and internal migration have lowered the prevalence of traditional living arrangements for rural older adults (Silverstein, Cong, & Li, 2006; Zhang, 2004) toward a normative family structure of nuclear family households comprising three to six persons (Cheng, Lee, Chan, Leung, & Lee, 2009; Xu, Xie, Liu, Xia, & Liu, 2007). Labor-related migration in the rural working age population has resulted in greater geographic separation between the generations, reducing opportunities for older people to live with their children in what traditionally has been viewed as a stable home environment (Silverstein et al., 2006).

In addition to nuclear households, nontraditional living arrangements for older adults also have increased. These include empty-nest households (older couples living alone), network households (children and older parents living separately but nearby), by-turns households (network families in which older parents rotate among sons' residences), and skipped-generation households (grandparents living with grandchildren without the middle generation present) (Silverstein et al., 2006). Acceptance of these network households is increasing, with parents living near several grown children who cooperate in providing support and assistance. Similar to Africa, older adults believe it is not necessary to coreside with a child to have old-age security (Whyte, 2004, p. 112). However, migration patterns of employment-aged adults can influence the prevalence of strong connections among households of kin in rural areas. In some areas, 90% of rural older adults have adult children living in the same village (Pei & Pillai, 1999). In contrast, Silverstein et al. (2006) found that only 36% of rural older adults had at least one proximate child in a region with a high level of outmigration of working age adults. Regardless, a general point of agreement is that traditional living arrangements in the form of multigenerational households are on the decline and nuclear family households are on the rise in rural China.

Rural India also shows a trend away from traditional multigeneration families in the mainly Hindu society. Joint families had as many as three generations including all brothers and sisters and their families living together under one roof and sharing common property and income. Within this tradition, family relationships were ritualized, and the family was a social as well as an economic unit, performing the tasks of guaranteed subsistence for all members. Marriage of the first son signified entry into old age in which mothers passed on household management to daughters-in-law and fathers gave up headship of their families (Bhat & Dhruvarajan, 2001). It is not clear whether such changes in families are supportive to older members who move into positions of having less work and responsibility, or are negative because they become powerless in their own households.

In both China and India, scholars come to different conclusions about the meaning of these changes in living arrangements. Based on the results from a national survey of children's support for older parents in rural and urban China, Lee and Xiao (1998) found that adult children are the most important source of old age security in rural areas: 70% of rural older parents receive financial support from their children. In their study of one Chinese village, Silverstein et al. (2006) found evidence of even higher levels of support. Economic assistance from children was almost universal, with 98% of parents having received financial transfers from at least one child in the preceding 12 months. Support often is reciprocal. About half of older parents received household help or personal care from their children, whereas one-third provided similar types of assistance to their children.

By implication then, regardless of changing household arrangements, rural Chinese elders continue to receive support from their children, but some important exceptions exist. Childless older adults in China have no clearly defined rights to receive family care (Zhang & Liu, 2007). The cultural norm is that extended family members will provide assistance, although help from extended family members is not automatic. Whereas childless older adults assume that they deserve such support, they believe that they must exchange resources in return (Zhang, 2007).

In contrast, in India there is great concern that older parents do not receive adequate levels of support. Bhat and Dhruvarajan (2001) described traditional Indian society as one in which parents were held in highest regard. Taking care of parents was a sacred duty with dire consequences in the afterlife should offspring fail to do so. Although this value persists, many young people are migrating from rural to urban areas for employment, disrupting family togetherness and family ties. The authors noted that contemporary preferences for nuclear households, characterized by individuality, independence, and desire for privacy, are gradually replacing a family model with strong emphasis on the family as a unit and deference to older members. Older people's status is being eroded because knowledge of agrarian traditions is not valued and older family members are not consulted. Bhat and Dhruvarajan (2001, p. 628) surmised that care by children can no longer be taken for granted and likely will continue to erode, concluding that "neither having authority in the family, nor being needed, they feel frustrated and depressed. If the older person is economically dependent on the children, the problem is likely to become even worse."

Living Arrangements and Support in Europe and North America

Household composition of older adults in Europe and North America stands in sharp contrast to that of other regions. Average household sizes are small in comparison to those of developing countries. Living together as a couple without others is the most common pattern in both Europe and North America. Beliefs about connections between household composition and family ties and support differ considerably from those in other regions as well. European and North American scholars believe that living with a spouse (and no other family members) is an ideal living situation because it "provides older men and women with the greatest possibilities to live independently and to realize reciprocal support on a daily basis, if needed" (De Jong Gierveld et al., 2002, p. 9).

Rates of living alone are similar across these regions and much higher than in other areas. In both North America and Europe, approximately 26% of older adults live alone. Gendered differences in living arrangements are even more pronounced than in other areas. Much higher proportions of women (34% in North America; 35% in Europe) than men (15% in North America; 13% in Europe) live alone (United Nations Department of Economic and Social Affairs/Population Division, 2005).

In North America, trends in living arrangements show continued movement toward two predominant patterns—living with a spouse and living alone. Living with a spouse is the most common type of household. In both the United States and Canada, older men are much more likely to live with a spouse (72% and 79%) than are older women (42% and 54%) (Statistics Canada, 2010; U.S. Census Bureau, Housing and Household Economics Statistics Division, Fertility and Family Statistics Branch, 2009).[2] Living alone is relatively common, although older women (35% in the United States and 37% in Canada) are more likely to live alone than are older men (13% in the United States and 17% in Canada) (Statistics Canada, 2010; U. S. Census Bureau, Population Division, 2009a, 2009b).[3] In stark contrast to developing countries, small proportions live with others. In both countries approximately 7% of older women and 2% of older men live with adult children or other relatives (Statistics Canada, 2010; U.S. Census Bureau, Population Division, 2009a).

Living arrangements of older adults in Europe show similar patterns to those in North America although there is more variation than in North America. Little explicit analysis by rural setting is available, although broad patterns across countries illustrate issues in availability of family connections. As in North America, living together as a couple is the most prevalent living situation (De Jong Gierveld et al., 2002). The proportion of older people living alone or with a spouse has grown and the proportion in households of more than one generation has declined (Bernard et al., 2001).

Within Europe, the greatest variation in living conditions lies in northern versus Mediterranean and eastern European countries. De Jong Gierveld et al. (2002) compared living arrangements of older women and men in Finland, United Kingdom, Italy, and Hungary. Overall the most common pattern for men was living with a spouse and without others, although higher proportions of widows lived alone in Finland and the United Kingdom. Living with children and grandchildren in addition to living with a spouse was more common in Italy and Hungary (De Jong Gierveld et al., 2002). The authors attributed these patterns to country-based differences in standard of living, income security, and health care systems that influence opportunities to retain independence and well-being in later life. From this perspective, living without coresident children is a positive choice reflecting relative economic security, desire for privacy, and a wish to avoid issues such as crowding, poor social relationships, and loneliness. For such older adults, pathways to coresidence are not normative. Living together occurs only in circumstances of particular family needs such as frailty of the older adult, caring for a child with disabilities or for grandchildren whose parents are in the labor market, or sheltering adult children with low income.

Northern European countries have traditionally reported lower levels of contact among generations in families than have Mediterranean countries. In a comparison of family interaction in Italy and Sweden, Bordone (2009) found evidence of these patterns in strong values about family connections, which were apparent in Italy. In that country, early home leaving by children was viewed as an indication of weak family ties and was a precursor to low levels of subsequent contact between parents and children. More affluent parents ensured ongoing contact through purchasing nearby apartments for their children. At every level of education, Italian parents were significantly more likely than Swedish to have higher frequency of contact and to live closer to children. The author argued that despite considerable differences in family contact and proximity in these two countries, the findings are not indicative of a crisis in generational relationships in either country. He also argued that greater intergenerational distance and lower contact in Sweden are indicative of modern societies in which independence of generations is valued and encouraged.

For the most part, the relatively solitary living situations of older rural adults in Europe and North America have not led to great alarm about their family connections or the potential for supportive exchanges with family members. Researchers from both Europe and North America have found that most older people are connected to social networks that may include close ties with friends as well as with kin (Bernard et al., 2001; Swindle, 2009). In both the United States and Canada, researchers have explored the location and membership of these networks. In research in rural United States, Beggs, Haines, and Hurlbert (1996) found that social networks primarily are kinship based though people draw on friends and neighbors as well as kin for support. Most networks are small, tightly knit, long-standing, and typified by frequent contact, although the authors also found evidence of diversity within rural communities on these elements of personal networks.

In Canada, Swindle (2009) furthered this research through developing a typology of social networks of older rural adults. Based on a national telephone survey, she found considerable diversity in social networks. A small proportion (2.8%) had networks comprising only themselves and their spouses. Others had large, diverse social networks with an average of 17 members that included relatives as well as friends and neighbors, and variety in age and proximity to the older adult. Not all members of social networks were actively engaged in providing support. On average, older adults received support from 3.3 people. Half received the majority of their support from spouses and children, whereas 40% had support networks that were predominantly friends and neighbors.

Swindle's research suggests that the vast majority of older rural adults have strong links with family and friends that have the potential to provide support. Yet there is evidence from both rural United States and Canada of loneliness and isolation of some older rural adults. Approximately 20% receive no support from family members or friends (Swindle, 2009), a potential indicator of lack of strong ties to kin and others. Isolation and loneliness are most prevalent among oldest rural residents who have lost a spouse (Dugan & Kivett, 1994), suggesting that the spouse-only living arrangement may be an indicator of vulnerability. Notably, visits with siblings reduced social isolation whereas visits with children did not (Dugan & Kivett, 1994), suggesting supportive connections to same-generation kin are particularly important.

One of the best illustrations of supportive relationships of older rural adults comes from Wenger's longitudinal research on the support networks of older adults in rural Wales (Wenger, 1989). She found five types of networks that reflected life course events such as widowhood, retirement migration, or whether their children had migrated out of the region to find work. Two groups of older adults had family-based networks that approximated some of the ideals in family support discussed earlier in the chapter. Family dependent networks had relatively small groups of close and extended kin, whereas those with locally integrated support networks also included friends and neighbors that fostered links to the community. A third group with wider community focused networks had no local kin but had friends nearby, a pattern that has been identified only in developed countries. In contrast, two other groups of older adults had more limited support networks, little or no involvement in their communities, and no close kin living nearby despite having lived in the area for long periods of time. These findings support Bernard and colleagues' (2001) contention that old age is now experienced within a variety of late-life kin and nonkin relationships that may be proximate or distant and which are more or less supportive to older adults.

Nonetheless, these diverse support networks did not endure into very late life. Over the 20 years of the Wenger study, the distribution of the support networks changed substantially as survivors reached very old age (Wenger &

Keating, 2008). Networks that had relatives as core members shifted toward even more family focus. Most were based on a wife, husband, coresident adult child (or children), or occasionally daughters, granddaughters, or sisters living nearby who provided all necessary support to enable the person to remain in the community, a pattern of close-kin support analogous to that found in parts of Asia and Africa. Compared to 20 years previously, only half as many very old adults had friendship-centered networks, another indication of the centrality of family members in difficult circumstances. Finally, among those who began with small restricted networks, only 20% received support from network members, illustrating vulnerability among those without close kin who had not established strong support networks earlier in life.

Enforcing Family Support

Throughout the world, older rural adults may be vulnerable if they have no family support. Many countries have addressed this family issue with public policy in the form of family responsibility legislation. Each has as its goal enforcement of normative obligations of family members to provide support to older adults. Laws differ in the strength of the imposed obligation, in which kin are responsible, and in the incorporation of legitimate reasons that might excuse responsibility for care and parental responsibility. In developing countries, legislation is couched in terms of the provision of basic necessities.

High levels of concern about the welfare of older adults are part of the vulnerability discourse in India. In that country, parents still prefer to live with their children even when relationships are poor (Bhat & Dhruvarajan, 2001). Although older rural adults often continue to work and may have some income, older people work in the informal sector and have no state benefits, leaving them heavily dependent on their children for support (Bhat & Dhruvarajan, 2001).

The Maintenance and Welfare of Parents and Senior Citizens Act (2007) formalized this obligation in India. Within this law, impoverished older adults have the right to be supported. It has an inclusive definition of family members who are legally obligated. Adult children including sons, daughters, grandsons, and granddaughters must provide support if needed. In addition, relatives who might inherit property of the older adult, such as legal heirs of a childless person, are obligated to maintain older persons so that such they may lead a normal life. The legislation reflects a strong belief that families must be responsible for taking care of aging parents. It is viewed as a vehicle to avoid erosion of desirable traditional family values that if lost might lead to a breakup of the institution of the family itself (Bhat & Dhruvarajan, 2001, p. 636).

In Mexico, the Law on the Rights of the Older Adult (Ley de los Derechos de las Personas Adultas Mayores, 2008) does not specify kin relationships of those obligated to support older adults, stating that the family of the older adult is obligated to provide basic support, although expectations of levels of support are modest. Adequate food is specified in Mexico. In other poor countries such as Mauritius, family obligation may extend to basic requirements such as shelter, clothing, and medical attention (Protection of Elderly Persons Act, 2005).

Chinese culture is known for its emphasis on family relationships and support and families have traditionally been crucial to the support of older adults in rural areas (Cheng et al., 2009; Silverstein et al., 2006; Xu et al., 2007; Zhang & Liu, 2007). The absence of universal public pension and long-term care programs in rural China has meant that adult children are likely to be the only sources of economic and social support to older parents (Silverstein et al., 2006). According to Pei and Pillai (1999), "The state spends a large proportion of its resources on protecting the interests of the urban elderly whereas the state expenditure on rural elderly is minimum. The elderly in China are now treated differently simply in accordance with where they live" (p. 198). Thus, having extended kin is especially crucial to older adults in rural China because the current social security policies do not cover most underdeveloped areas (Cheng et al., 2009; Xu et al., 2007; Zhang, 2004).

If children and extended kin are not available to provide assistance and support, the community and state are called upon to provide basic care (Zhang & Liu, 2007). State support for childless older adults consists of the *five guarantee* program, which guarantees food, clothing, medical care, housing, and burial expenses to those usually referred to as *five guarantee households* (Zhang, 2004, pp. 65–66; Zhang, 2007, p. 281; Zhang & Liu, 2007, p. 189). Eligibility for the five guarantee program is limited to those holding agricultural household registration status in rural areas, who are childless older adults, and who have no income, no capability to work, and no family. A large number of rural older adults are not eligible for this state support, with only 2.5 million covered by the end of 2003 (Zhang & Liu, 2007).

Parental obligation legislation in Europe and North America is more long-standing but somewhat more conditional. For example, all provinces in Canada have legislation requiring adult children to support their parents (see for example the Parents' Maintenance Act, Saskatchewan, 1978). In France, *l'obligation alimentaire* was enacted in 1804 and requires an individual to give support to his or her ascendants or descendants—that is parents, grandparents and, beyond, children and grandchildren. In these countries there is an expectation that support provided will be financial, based on parental need and enforced only after the individual's own children and spouse are taken care of (Oldham, 2001). Little information is available on the enforcement of this legislation, which may exceed the will of governments to impose public sanctions on private family matters. Nonetheless, the legislation illustrates strong normative beliefs about family responsibility for older adults.

TRENDS, GAPS, AND FUTURE DIRECTIONS

This discussion of older rural adults and their families has been set within the discourses of loss in rural communities and of vulnerability of older adults who live there. The international focus taken here was done advisedly. It provides context for our understanding in North America of the demography of rural aging, accenting the need to pay attention to young countries when it comes to aging in rural areas. It moves beyond the idealized notion that families outside of North America are more caring and supportive than those on this continent, by highlighting the immense challenges of living within contexts of poverty, pandemics, and large scale migration of young people away from rural areas. It illustrates how little we know about the family lives of older adults in rural North America.

The phrase "vulnerable people in vulnerable places" comes from scholars speaking of older people in rural communities in North America, but most of the research and commentary about vulnerability comes from Africa and Asia, where the focus on families as the core group of supporters is paramount. Apt (2002, p. 39) spoke to regional concerns about how social changes brought about by modernization are profoundly affecting the traditional systems of care for older people, especially in rural areas where "segregation of older people will become manifest." She wrote, "even though most older people requiring care are still looked after within the informal structures of the family, this can no longer be taken for granted as we move into the new century." There is much to learn about family connections of older adults in these regions, and about their decision-making in allocating scarce family resources.

Similar to other regions, there are no assumptions that family support can be taken for granted in more developed countries, but the sense of urgency about the welfare of older adults is absent. Scholars from North America and Europe have explored the strength of family connections and the types of support networks in which older adults are embedded. Only in this literature do they consider the importance of friends in the support networks of older adults and of solitary living as an asset that may enhance independence. Yet, one cannot conclude that older rural adults in these regions are living in a rural idyll. Evidence of social isolation and lack of family connections exists among a substantial minority of older rural adults, especially among those who are very old. Despite a great deal of research on families of older adults in these regions, scholars have much to learn about rural settings and how they influence the family lives of older adults.

Gaps in understanding the links among rural contexts, living arrangements, and family support are prevalent. Around the world, beliefs differ about what is the important set of family relationships of older rural adults and about how these relationships are important. Where living arrangements and access to support are tightly tied, the survival benefit of having coresident kin is a preoccupation. In these regions, research has been focused on documenting the relationship between proximity and the resources provided to older adults. In contrast, in areas in which households of individuals or couples are the norm, family researchers assume family relationships will be diverse and discretionary. In these areas, they have conducted less research on older rural adults and their families. Where studies exist, they encompass a wide range of questions about the nature of family relationships. Without asking similar questions about family relationships of older people across world regions, it is not possible to move forward with knowledge of both relationship obligations and choices afforded older rural adults and their families, nor of how living arrangements may be differentially important to the well-being of older rural adults.

Finally, questions remain about the ways in which rural context matters in the lives of older adults and their families. In this chapter we have chosen to focus on a geographic definition of rural in keeping with the national discussions about rural vulnerabilities. From this vantage point, we have explored discussions of vulnerability of older adults arising from a combination of decreasing resources in families and in rural communities. Much of the research on older rural adults and their families comes from regions in which economic migration of young people has resulted in separation of left-behind older persons from their adult children. But in Europe little research on rural families exists, whereas in North America current preoccupations are less on families than on the diversity of rural communities—from affluent retirement centers to those bypassed culturally and economically. Further comparative research will help tease out whether rural continues to be a useful explanatory construct in an era of increasing national and transnational mobility.

NOTES

1. Data from this article are not specific to rural areas. However, the authors stated that there are no significant differences between rural and urban statistics for older adults.

2. No national data on all living arrangements of older rural men and women in Canada or the United States exist. However, recent analyses of the Canadian census show that proportions of older men and women in rural Canada living with a spouse are similar to national statistics on living arrangements (79% of men vs. 50% of women) (Dobbs, Swindle, Keating, Eales, & Keefe, 2004).

3. The 2008 U.S. Census shows that 35% of women and 13% of men aged 65 and over live in "nonfamily households," meaning that they live alone or with nonrelatives. Also, 96.5% of these individuals live in *one person* nonfamily households. Based on this figure, we are assuming that the majority of women and men over the age of 65 who live in nonfamily households live alone.

REFERENCES

Aboderin, I., & Ferreira, M. (2008). Linking ageing to development agendas in sub-Saharan Africa: Challenges and approaches. *Journal of Population Ageing, 1,* 51–73.

Allan, D., & Cloutier-Fisher, D. (2006). Health service utilization among older adults in British Columbia: Making sense of geography. *Canadian Journal on Aging, 25,* 219–232.

Apt, N. A. (2002). Ageing and the changing role of the family and the community: An African perspective. *International Social Security Review, 55,* 39–47.

Asthana, S., Gibson, A., Moon, G., & Brigham, P. (2003). Allocating resources for health and social care: The significance of rurality. *Health and Social Care in the Community, 11,* 486–493.

Atkin, C. (2003). Rural communities: Human and symbolic capital development, fields apart. *Compare: A Journal of Comparative and International Education, 33,* 507–518.

AVERT. (2010). *AIDS orphans.* Retrieved from http://www.avert.org/aidsorphans.htm

Barham, C., & Begum, N. (2006). *The new urban/rural indicator in the Labour Force Survey.* London: Office for National Statistics, Labour Market Trends.

Beggs, J., Haines, V., & Hurlbert, J. (1996). Revisiting the rural-urban contrast: Personal networks in nonmetropolitan and metropolitan settings. *Rural Sociology, 61,* 306–325.

Bernard, M., Phillipson, C., Phillips, J., & Ogg, J. (2001). Continuity and change in the family and community life of older people. *Journal of Applied Gerontology, 20,* 259–278.

Bhat, A. K., & Dhruvarajan, R. (2001). Ageing in India: Drifting intergenerational relations, challenges and options. *Ageing & Society, 21,* 621–640.

Biao, X. (2007). How far are the left-behind left behind? A preliminary study in rural China. *Population, Space and Place, 13,* 179–191.

Blieszner, R., Roberto, K. A., & Singh, K. (2001). The helping networks of rural elders: Demographic and social psychological influences on service use. *Ageing International, 27,* 89–119.

Bock, J., & Johnson, S. E. (2008). Grandmothers productivity and the HIV/AIDS pandemic in sub-Saharan Africa. *Journal of Cross-Cultural Gerontology, 23,* 131–145.

Bollman, R., & Clemenson, H. (2008). Structure and change in Canada's rural demography: An update to 2006. *Rural and Small Town Canada Analysis Bulletin,* Catalogue no. 21-006-X, Vol. 7, No. 7.

Bongaarts, J., & Zimmer, Z. (2002). Living arrangements of older adults in the developing world: An analysis of demographic and health survey household surveys. *Journal of Gerontology: Social Sciences, 57B,* S145–S157.

Bordone, V. (2009). Contact and proximity of older people to their adult children: A comparison between Italy and Sweden. *Population, Space and Place, 15,* 359–380.

Brown, D. L., & Glasgow, N. (Eds.). (2008). *Rural retirement migration.* London: Springer.

Bryant, C., & Joseph, A.E. (2001). Canada's rural population: Trends in space and implications in place. *The Canadian Geographer, 45,* 123–137.

Cheng, S-T., Lee, C.K.L., Chan, A.C.M., Leung, E.M.F., & Lee, J-J. (2009). Social network types and subjective well-being in Chinese older adults. *Journal of Gerontology: Psychological Sciences, 64B,* P713–P722.

Cliggett, L. (2005). *Grains from grass: Aging, gender, and famine in rural Africa.* Ithaca, NY: Cornell University Press.

Cloke, P., Milbourne, P., & Thomas, C. (1997). Living lives in different ways? Deprivation, marginalization and changing lifestyles in rural England. *Transactions of the Institute of British Geographers, 22,* 210–230.

Cloutier-Fisher, D., & Kobayashi, K. (2009). Examining social isolation by gender and geography: Conceptual and operational challenges using public health data in Canada. *Gender, Place and Culture—A Journal of Feminist Geography, 16,* 181–199.

Conger, R.D., Conger, K.J., Elder, G.H., Jr., Lorenz, F.O., Simons, R.L., & Whitbeck, L.B. (2008). A family process model of economic hardship and adjustment of early adolescent boys. *Child Development, 63,* 526–541.

De Jong Gierveld, J., de Valk, H., & Blommesteijn, M. (2002). Living arrangements of older persons and family support in more developed countries, Nueva York. *Population Bulletin of the United Nations.*

Dobbs, B., Swindle, J., Keating, N., Eales, J., & Keefe, J. (2004). *Caring contexts of rural seniors: Phase 2 technical report* (submitted to Veterans Affairs Canada in partial fulfillment of PWGSC Contract #51019-017032/001/HAL). Edmonton, AB: Research on Aging, Policies and Practice.

Dugan, E., & Kivett, V.R. (1994). The importance of emotional social isolation to loneliness among very old rural adults. *The Gerontologist, 34,* 340–346.

Haartsen, T., Groote, P., & Huigen, P.P.P. (2003). Measuring age differentials in representations of rurality in the Netherlands. *Journal of Rural Studies, 19,* 245–252.

Halfacree, K. H. (1993). Locality and social representation: Space, discourse and alternative definitions of the rural. *Journal of Rural Studies, 9,* 23–37.

Hamilton, L.C., Hamilton, L.R., Duncan, C.M., & Colocousis, C.R. (2008). *Place matters: Challenges and opportunities in four rural Americas.* New Hampshire: Carsey Institute. Abstract. Retrieved from http://www.carseyinstitute.unh.edu/publications/Report_PlaceMatters.pdf

Hanlon, N., & Halseth, G. (2005). The greying of resource communities in northern British Columbia: Implications for health care delivery in already-underserviced communities. *The Canadian Geographer, 49,* 1–24.

Hart, L. G, Larson, E.H., & Lishner, D.M. (2005). Rural definitions for health policy and research. *American Journal of Public Health, 95,* 1149–1155.

Johnson, C. (2000). Perspectives on American kinship in the 1990s. *Journal of Marriage and Family, 62,* 623–639.

Johnson, K. (2006). *Demographic trends in rural and small town America.* New Hampshire: Carsey Institute. Retrieved from http://www.carseyinstitute.unh.edu/publications/Report_Demographics.pdf

Joseph, A.E., & Cloutier-Fisher, D. (2005). Ageing in rural communities: Vulnerable people in vulnerable places. In G.A. Andrews & D.R. Phillips (Eds.), *Ageing and place: Perspectives, policy, practice* (pp. 133–146). Oxon, UK: Routledge.

Keating, N. (Ed.) (2008). *Rural ageing: A good place to grow old?* Bristol, UK: Policy Press.

Keefe, J., Fancey, P., Keating, N., Frederick, J., Eales, J., & Dobbs, B. (2004). *Caring contexts of rural seniors: Phase 1 technical report.* (Submitted to Veterans Affairs Canada in partial fulfillment of PWGSC Contract #51019-017032/001/HAL). Edmonton, AB: Research on Aging, Policies and Practice.

Lee, Y-J., & Xiao, Z. (1998). Children's support for elderly parents in urban and rural China: Results from a national survey. *Journal of Cross-Cultural Gerontology, 13,* 39–62.

Ley de los Derechos de las Personas Adultas Mayores, 2008. Retrieved from http://www. ordenjuridico.gob.mx/Estatal/DISTRITO%20FEDERAL/Leyes/DFLEY30.pdf

Mba, C. J. (2007). Gender disparities in living arrangements of older people in Ghana: Evidence from the 2003 Ghana Demographic and Health Survey. *Journal of International Women's Studies, 9,* 153–166.

Nkosi, B., & Daniels, P. (2007). Family strengths: South Africa. *Marriage and Family Review, 41,* 11–26.

Oldham, M. (2001). Financial obligations within the family—Aspects of intergenerational maintenance and succession in England and France. *The Cambridge Law Journal, 60,* 128–177.

Pei, X., & Pillai, V. K. (1999). Old age support in China: The role of the state and the family. *International Journal of Aging and Human Development, 49,* 197–212.

Ross, H., Stein, N., Trabasso, T., Woody, E., & Ross, M. (2005). The quality of family relationships within and across generations: A social relations analysis. *International Journal of Behavioral Development, 29,* 110–119.

Silverstein, M., Cong, Z., & Li, S. (2006). Intergenerational transfers and living arrangements of older people in rural China: Consequences for psychological well-being. *Journal of Gerontology: Social Sciences, 61B,* S256–S266.

Statistics Canada. (2007). *2006 Census dictionary.* (Catalogue no 92-566-X). Retrieved from Statistics Canada, http://www12.statcan.gc.ca/census-recensement/2006/ref/dict/pdf/92-566-eng.pdf

Statistics Canada. (2010). *2006 Census of Canada topic based tabulations, families and households: Household Living Arrangements (11), Age Groups (20) and Sex (3) for the Population in Private Households of Canada, Provinces, Territories, Census Metropolitan Areas and Census Agglomerations, 2006 Census—20% Sample Data.* (Catalogue no. 97-553-XCB2006018). Retrieved from Statistics Canada, http://www12.statcan.gc.ca/census-recensement/2006/dp-pd/tbt/Rp-eng.cfm?LANG=E&APATH=3&DETAIL=0&DIM=0&FL=A&FREE=0&GC=0&GID=0&GK=0&GRP=1&PID=89028&PRID=0&PTYPE=88971,97154&S=0&SHOWALL=0&SUB=687&Temporal=2006&THEME=68&VID=0&VNAMEE=&VNAMEF

Swindle, J. (2009). *Social support resources of older adults in rural Canada.* Unpublished doctoral dissertation, the University of Alberta, Edmonton, AB, Canada.

Teachman, J. (2008). Complex life course patterns and the risk of divorce in second marriages. *Journal of Marriage and Family, 70,* 294–305.

United Nations Department of Economic and Social Affairs/Population Division. (2005). *Living arrangements of older persons around the world.* New York: United Nations.

United Nations Statistics Division. (2000a). *Population by age, sex, and urban/rural residence—China*. Retrieved from http://data.un.org/Data.aspx?d=POP&f=tableCode%3A22

United Nations Statistics Division. (2000b). *Population by age, sex, and urban/rural residence—United States*. Retrieved from http://data.un.org/Data.aspx?d=POP&f=tableCode%3A22

United Nations Statistics Division. (2001). *Population by age, sex, and urban/rural residence—India*. Retrieved from http://data.un.org/Data.aspx?d=POP&f=tableCode%3A22

United Nations Statistics Division. (2002a). *Population by age, sex, and urban/rural residence—Rwanda*. Retrieved from http://data.un.org/Data.aspx?d=POP&f=tableCode%3A22

United Nations Statistics Division. (2002b). *Population by age, sex, and urban/rural residence—Uganda*. Retrieved from http://data.un.org/Data.aspx?d=POP&f=tableCode%3A22

United Nations Statistics Division. (2002c). *Population by age, sex, and urban/rural residence—Zimbabwe*. Retrieved from http://data.un.org/Data.aspx?d=POP&f=tableCode%3A22

United Nations Statistics Division. (2003). *Population by age, sex, and urban/rural residence—Pakistan*. Retrieved from http://data.un.org/Data.aspx?d=POP&f=tableCode%3A22

United Nations Statistics Division. (2005a). *Population by age, sex, and urban/rural residence—Japan*. Retrieved from http://data.un.org/Data.aspx?d=POP&f=tableCode%3A22

United Nations Statistics Division. (2005b). *Population by age, sex, and urban/rural residence—Korea (Republic of)*. Retrieved from http://data.un.org/Data.aspx?d=POP&f=tableCode%3A22

United Nations Statistics Division. (2006). *Population by age, sex, and urban/rural residence—Canada*. Retrieved from http://data.un.org/Data.aspx?d=POP&f=tableCode%3A22

United Nations Statistics Division. (2007). *Population by age, sex, and urban/rural residence—Finland*. Retrieved from http://data.un.org/Data.aspx?d=POP&f=tableCode%3A22

United Nations Statistics Division. (2010). *Population by age, sex, and urban/rural residence*. Retrieved from http://data.un.org/Data.aspx?d=POP&f=tableCode%3A22

U.S. Department of Agriculture, Economic Research Service. (2003). *Measuring rurality: New definitions in 2003*. Retrieved from http://www.ers.usda.gov/briefing/rurality/NewDefinitions/

U.S. Census Bureau, Housing and Household Economics Statistics Division, Fertility and Family Statistics Branch. (2009). *America's families and living arrangements: 2008*. Table A.1 Marital Status of People 15 Years and Over, By Age, Sex, Personal Earnings, Race, and Hispanic Origin, 2008: All Races. Retrieved from http://www.census.gov/population/www/socdemo/hh-fam/cps2008.html

U.S. Census Bureau, Population Division. (2009a). *The older population in the United States: 2008*. Table 14. Households by Type and Age of Householder 55 Years and Over: 2008. Retrieved from http://www.census.gov/population/ www/socdemo/age/older_2008.html

U.S. Census Bureau, Population Division. (2009b). *The older population in the United States: 2008.* Table 15. Households by Type, Size, and Age of Householder 55 Years and Over: 2008. Retrieved from http://www.census.gov/population/www/socdemo/age/older_2008.html

Vanier Institute of the Family. (n.d.). *Definition of family.* Retrieved from http://www.vifamily.ca/about/definition.html

Walker, A. J., Allen, K. R., & Connidis, I. A. (2005). Theorizing and studying sibling ties in adulthood. In V. Bengtson, A. Acock, K. Allen, P. Dilworth-Anderson, & D. Klein (Eds.), *Sourcebook of family theory and research* (pp. 167–190). Thousand Oaks, CA: Sage.

Wenger, G. C. (1989). Support networks in old age: Constructing a typology. In M. Jefferys (Ed.), *Growing old in the 20th century* (pp. 166–185). London: Routledge.

Wenger, G. C., & Keating, N. (2008). The evolution of networks of rural older adults. In N. Keating (Ed.), *Rural Ageing: A good place to grow old?* (pp. 33–42). Bristol, UK: Policy Press.

Whyte, M. K. (2004). Filial obligations in Chinese families. Paradoxes of modernization. In C. Ikels (Ed.), *Filial piety: Practice and discourse in contemporary East Asia* (pp. 106–127). Stanford: Stanford University Press.

Xu, A., Xie, X., Liu, W., Xia, Y., & Liu, D. (2007). Chinese family strengths and resiliency. *Marriage and Family Review, 41*(1/2), 143–164.

Zaba, B., Whiteside, A., & Boerma, J. T. (2004). Demographic and socioeconomic impact of AIDS: Taking stock of the empirical evidence. *AIDS, 18*(Suppl. 2), S1–S7.

Zhang, H. (2004). "Living alone" and the rural elderly: Strategy and agency in post-Mao rural China. In C. Ikels (Ed.), *Filial piety: Practice and discourse in contemporary East Asia* (pp. 63–87). Stanford: Stanford University Press.

Zhang, W. (2007). Marginalization of childless elderly men and welfare provision: A study in a North China village. *Journal of Contemporary China, 16,* 275–293.

Zhang, W., & Liu, G. (2007). Childlessness, psychological well-being, and life satisfaction among the elderly in China. *Journal of Cross-Cultural Gerontology, 22,* 185–203.

Ziehl, S. C. (2005). Families in South Africa. In B. N. Adams & J. Trost (Eds.), *Handbook of world families* (pp. 47–63). Thousand Oaks, CA: Sage.

14

Aging Families and Immigration

Paula M. Usita and Holly B. Shakya

The study of aging families and immigration is a very important area of research in family gerontology. People from around the world continue to immigrate to and make the United States their new home. Some arrive when they are quite young and spend the rest of their lives in the United States. Others arrive as older adults. In either case, these immigrants adjust to living in a new land—they learn about its values, norms, and traditions. They also bring their rich traditions and values with them and enrich our cultural landscape.

The aim of our chapter is to examine six topics, which are germane to achieving a comprehensive understanding of older immigrants and their families: (1) demographics, (2) living arrangements, (3) conceptual perspectives, (4) intergenerational support, (5) elder care, and (6) health and access to care. As will be illustrated, through examination of these six topics, it is possible to more fully understand and appreciate immigrants' behavior and their family members' behaviors toward each other and their interactions with institutions in the United States. We consider an older immigrant to be a person who is 65 or more years of age, is foreign-born, and has lived in the United States. Sixty-five is a convenient number to use, as this is the age at which U.S. citizens have traditionally become eligible for elder services and benefits. So, for our review of the census literature, we use this age. However, in some studies mentioned in this chapter, people as young as their early 50s were included as older immigrants. Average life spans around the world vary owing to a variety of public health, safety, health care access, and care issues, so it makes intuitive sense to include those studies in this chapter.

AGING IMMIGRANT POPULATION DISTRIBUTIONS

The United States American Community Survey (2006–2008) estimated the foreign-born population of the United States to be approximately

37 million people. Whereas immigration to the United States has increased over the past few decades, the proportion of this population composed of older adults has steadily decreased from a high of 32% in 1960 to its current level of 12% (American Community Survey; He, 2002). While immigration in the earlier decades of the 20th century was dominated by Europeans, immigration policy shifts in the 1960s allowed greater numbers of immigrants from Latin America and Asia. By 1970, Mexican-born immigrants were the fourth most populous foreign-born group in the United States, and by 1980 they were the first. U.S. census information from 2000 listed Mexico, China, Philippines, India, and Cuba (in that order) as the countries of origin most represented within the foreign-born population.

Along with the easing of immigration restrictions against people originating from countries in Asia and Latin America, new rules have also prioritized entry for relatives of existing immigrants (Wilmoth, 2001). Because of these new rules, immigrant adults are able to apply for immigration visas for family members in their home countries, resulting in an increasing number of older parents coming into the country as new residents. Treas (1995) reported that over 60% of older adult immigrants to the United States arrived to join their previously settled immigrant children.

Census reports predict that because of these changes, within the next few decades the region-of-origin distribution among the foreign-born elderly population will shift, with increasing proportions of Asians and Latin Americans and decreasing proportions of Europeans (He, 2002). Figure 14.1 provides a breakdown of regions of origin of foreign-born people in the United States for those of all ages and those over 65. Figure 14.2 shows, within each region of origin, the proportion of the foreign-born population that is over the age of 65.

Since the mid-1990s welfare and immigration reforms, many immigrants became ineligible for federal and state benefits such as Supplemental Security Income (SSI), food stamps, and Medicaid, while others erroneously believed that they were ineligible (Estes, Goldberg, Wellin, Linkins, Shostak, & Beard, 2006). Family sponsors are responsible for the aging immigrants they bring to the United States (Treas, 2009). Once in the United States, aging immigrant parents are usually not in a financially or resource-rich situation, and they are usually not employable (Treas, 2009). This situation raises questions about the type of family lifestyle immigrant elders will experience once they arrive in the United States and its repercussions on their sense of well-being.

Naturalization statistics among elderly foreign-born persons vary according to place of origin, although foreign-born elderly adults have a much higher rate of naturalization (70%) than those in the foreign-born population overall (37%) (He, 2002). Possibly because European elderly persons have been residing in the United States for an average of 30 years or lon-

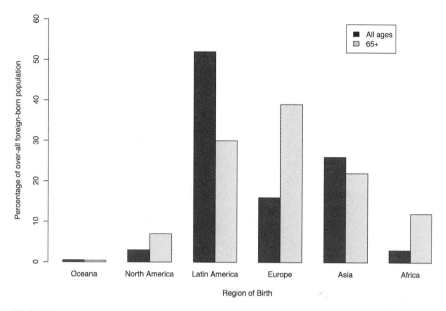

FIGURE 14.1 Proportion of overall foreign-born population by region of birth for older adults and all ages U.S. 2000 census.

Source: Adapted from He, W. (2002). *The older foreign-born population in the United States: 2000.* U.S. Census Bureau, Current Population Reports, Series P23,211. Washington, DC: Government Printing Office.

ger, many of them (80%) have been naturalized. In contrast, approximately 57% of Asian-born elders have been naturalized, probably because large numbers of Asians did not begin to immigrate to the United States until the 1970s and later. Among Latin Americans elders, the proportion that constituted U.S. citizens by 2000 was 65%. Very few illegal immigrants are over 65 years old and only approximately 11% are older than 40 (Passel, 2005).

Socioeconomic Indicators for the Aging Immigrant Population

Comparisons of foreign-born and native-born older adults show differences across education strata (He, 2002). While 18% of foreign-born older adults have a bachelor's degree or equivalent compared to 15% of the native-born population, 44.5% of the foreign-born older adult population did not complete high school compared to only 29% of the native-born population (He, 2002). Education levels of foreign-born adults vary greatly by country of origin and length of stay in the United States. Recent immigrants from Latin America have overall low education levels. In 1999, approximately 35% of immigrants from Latin America had less than a ninth grade education.

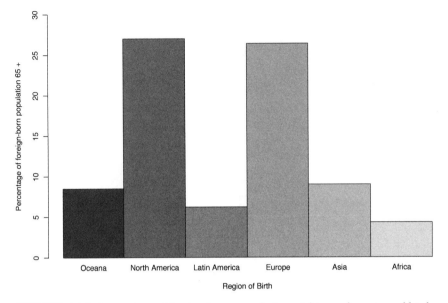

FIGURE 14.2 Proportion of foreign-born population within each region of birth that is 65+.

Source: Adapted from He, W. (2002). *The older foreign-born population in the United States: 2000.* U.S. Census Bureau, Current Population Reports, Series P23,211. Washington, DC: Government Printing Office.

Among immigrants from Asia, the percentage is much lower at 11% (American Community Survey).

Education levels also differ by length of time in the United States. Older immigrants who have been in the United States for many years are more likely to have a higher level of education, speak English more fluently, and be generally socioeconomically comparable to their native-born counterparts (Treas & Mazumdar, 2004). More recent immigrant elders tend to have come from developing countries in contrast to less recent immigrants who tend to have come from Europe. These more recent immigrant elders have lower levels of education and speak English with less proficiency.

Elderly immigrant socioeconomic dynamics become more complex when considering the overall socioeconomic status of the immigrant group to which an older adult belongs. For example, recent immigrants from India of working age typically have a bachelor's degree or higher (U.S. Census, 2000a), while immigrants from Mexico may have only a high school education or less (U.S. Census, 2000b). While the children of Indian immigrants may therefore be enjoying the benefits of a high socioeconomic status in the United States, these benefits may not fully translate to their elderly parents, who do not necessarily have the linguistic, educational, and social resources to navigate their new country with ease (Bhattacharya & Shibusawa, 2009).

The degree of education and income earning potential within groups can also be a determinant of how strongly clustered their communities are, because more highly educated immigrants are less likely to restrict their choice of location to tightly knit ethnic enclaves (Bauer, 2002; Ellis, 2005). This restriction of residence may in turn greatly influence older adults' access to important cultural resources. Bhattacharya and Shibusawa (2009) noted that while Indian immigrants are typically well educated, older Indian adults who have migrated to the United States to join their family members are often unable to speak English. Elders who are isolated within a nuclear family environment, and separated from the greater support networks of their ethnic communities, may experience poorer quality of life.

Considering the educational disparities between foreign-born older adults and native-born older adults, it is not surprising that a greater proportion of foreign-born elderly adults live in poverty (13.8%) than their native-born counterparts (9.3%) (He, 2002). A key difference, however, is that among foreign-born older adults, poverty levels are the same for men and women, but for native-born elderly adults, poverty levels are much higher for women. Poverty levels, and subsequent use of government assistance, are considerably higher for elderly immigrants who entered the United States at an older age versus those who have been living here since they were of working age (Hu, 1998). Factors contributing to this difference are lower education levels and language barriers, because immigrants who arrive in old age tend to have much lower English language proficiency than those who arrived earlier in their lives. Demographic changes in immigrant populations have contributed considerably to this trend, because the proportion of newly arriving immigrants who are elderly has increased substantially over the past few decades, from 3% in 1970 to 11% in 2006 (Leach, 2009). Immigration laws that encourage family unification have contributed to the increase in elderly immigrants arriving at an older age. These laws in combination with an increase in migration of immigrants from developing countries are factors suggesting that the trend of poverty among immigrant elders is likely to continue.

Poverty levels among immigrants differ depending upon the region of origin. Whereas Asian immigrants in general do experience poverty with 11% of Asian families living below the poverty level in 1999 (U.S. Census, 2000a), this number is approximately half the poverty rate experienced by those from Latin America, 20.7% (U.S. Census, 2000b). These differences translate into similar disparities among foreign-born elderly people as well. Figure 14.3 shows poverty levels among elderly adults by region of origin. Poverty levels also differ according to specific country of origin, even within similar world regions. For example, among South Asians living in New York City, the poverty rate among Indian elders, still substantial at 18.8%, is lower than among those from Bangladesh at 38.3% (Asian American Federation, 2008).

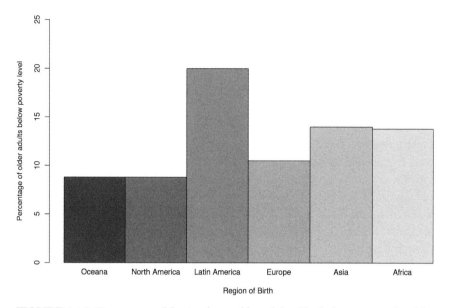

FIGURE 14.3 Percentage of foreign-born older adults 65+ below poverty level by region of origin.
Source: Adapted from He, W. (2002). *The older foreign-born population in the United States: 2000.* U.S. Census Bureau, Current Population Reports, Series P23,211. Washington, DC: Government Printing Office.

LIVING ARRANGEMENTS

Regional Settlement Characteristics

Region of residence for foreign-born older adults is strongly determined by existing enclaves of immigrant populations through which immigrant individuals are able to access networks, facilities, and other resources salient to their own social and cultural needs (Zavodny, 1999). Residing among similar others is particularly true for recent elderly immigrants from Asia and Latin America, who, as mentioned before, mainly resettle in the United States to join their children (Frey, 2000). This is in contrast to the European immigrants who have, for the most part, been living in this country for more than 30 years, having settled here as younger adults (He, 2002). Over the past several decades the immigration patterns of Latin Americans and Asians have concentrated the foreign-born populations in key locations around the country, shifting the distribution of foreign-born populations away from locations such as the east and Midwest, which were preferred by early 20th century immigrants from Europe who settled in those areas to farm and do industrial work (He, 2002; Rogers, 1999).

There are distinct differences in patterns of residence between native-born and foreign-born elders. Nearly 25% of all native-born older adults live in the Midwest compared to 10% of all foreign-born older adults (He, 2002). By comparison, 35% of foreign-born older adults live in the West versus only 17% of native-born elders. These figures represent dramatic shifts in the spatial distribution of foreign-born elderly persons because the ethnic characteristics of those who are foreign-born have changed since 1970 (Rogers, 1999). For example, in 1950 the Midwest was home to close to 30% of foreign-born elders, whereas the West was home to only 15%. Figure 14.4 provides a breakdown of region of residence in the United States for both foreign-born and native-born older adults.

Frey (2000) found that new immigrant elderly adults who came to the United States from 1985 to 1990 overwhelmingly chose to reside in classic immigrant gateway states such as California and New York, where they would join their children who had most likely sponsored their entry into the country. Metropolitan areas with the highest numbers of foreign-born individuals are Miami, Los Angeles, San Francisco, New York, and Chicago (Schmidley, 2001). However, in the last few years settlement choices for new immigrants in the United States have been changing. States such as Georgia, North

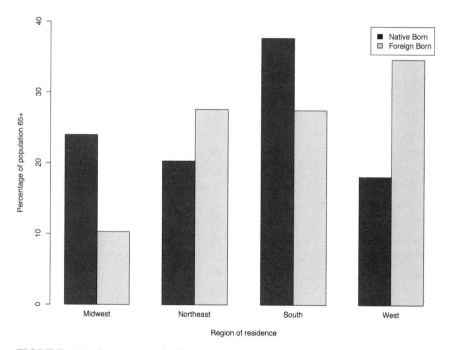

FIGURE 14.4 Proportion of older adults living in regions of the United States for foreign-born and native-born.
Source: Adapted from He, W. (2002). *The older foreign-born population in the United States: 2000.* U.S. Census Bureau, Current Population Reports, Series P23,211. Washington, DC: Government Printing Office.

Carolina, Nevada, and Arkansas are attracting increasing numbers of immigrants due to lower costs of living and higher wage opportunities (Leach, 2009). Furthermore, foreign-born elderly adults do move within the country, and to many of the same Sunbelt states that are magnets to native-born elderly adults: Florida and California (Frey, 2000). Given the high concentration of foreign-born people in New York, and the fact that Florida is the primary magnet state for elderly adult migrants from New York, this trend is not surprising. In contrast to their native-born counterparts, foreign-born elderly adults are also likely to move to snowbelt areas with large ethnic enclaves such as New York and New Jersey. Moves such as these could be motivated by efforts to seek out communities with higher proportions of coethnic persons and are so-called correction moves, being undertaken to improve over what was found in the first community in which elderly foreign-born adults happened to settle (Frey, 2000).

Residential Living Arrangements

Living arrangements for foreign-born older adults are dominated by a preference to live close to or with extended family. Living by or close to family members is particularly true for those elderly adults coming from more collectively oriented societies, in which family ties and obligations are strong and frequently dictate choices made by individuals (Treas, 2009; Wilmoth, 2001). Prioritizing family, culture, and community, and therefore making individual choices in line with those priorities, are cultural values shared by immigrants of diverse ethnic backgrounds. Filial piety, as it is known in China, shares a similar value of caring for the elders with what is known as familism amongst Latin Americans. The implementation of family unification laws has facilitated immigration to the United States of many elderly people who have come in order to join their younger working family members (Leach, 2009; Treas & Mazumdar, 2004). Family members who sponsor older parents not only have a cultural obligation to care for them, but are expected to sign an affidavit of economic support (although nonbinding) as part of the process by which the parent is sponsored for immigration (Wilmoth, De Jong, & Himes, 1997). Furthermore, coresidential living arrangements provide a cushion of support for a parent who at an older age may struggle with acculturation into a new environment and community (Treas, 2009; Wilmoth et al., 1997). Language difficulties, loss of traditional social support networks, and economic challenges are all obstacles to acculturation for new immigrant elders, and so the decision to coreside may in part be made in an effort to ameliorate these difficulties.

Consistent with these cultural determinants, numerous studies have shown that immigrant elders are more likely than nonimmigrant elders to be living with families. Wilmoth and colleagues' (1997) study found that immigrants who arrived past the age of 60, were less educated, and were less acculturated were more likely to be living in extended family situations, with those of Asian origin the most likely to coreside. Given that of all immigrant groups, those from Asia are the least likely to live in poverty and most likely to have elders with high educational attainment and strong health indicators, cultural preference seems to be a strong determinant of extended family living among Asian families and not economic need.

Wilmoth (2001) later published a more detailed study that demonstrated the difference in living arrangement preferences by immigrant groups in the United States with significant populations. Among Asians, elders from India are the most likely to prefer extended family living while those from Japan are the least. Indian elders are also the most likely to be living as dependents, defined as extended family coresidence in which the elder is not head of the household. As an example, only 27.4% of older unmarried men from India live independently, defined as living alone, compared to 56.4% of those from Japan. Consistent with findings from other research, Wilmoth's (2001) study found that more recently arrived and less acculturated immigrant elders were more likely to live with family members. Immigrants who have lived here for the longest periods of time are mostly European, and hold values more aligned with American views of individualism and independence than more recent arrivals of immigrant groups that value more family-oriented and therefore interdependent modes of living.

Conceptual Perspectives

Conceptual perspectives such as life course and social determinants of health offer a framework for understanding immigration patterns and immigrant lifestyles in the United States.

LIFE COURSE PERSPECTIVES

Life course perspectives are one of the most promising and effective conceptual lenses through which to understand aging families and immigration. Historical processes, social processes, and individual transitions and trajectories are considered by life course perspectives, as well as connections between individual and family transitions and trajectories (Clausen, 1986; Elder, 1998). Immigrants' age, gender, historical time of immigration, and location of settlement are just a few of the important types of individual factors that may have a bearing on the life course of both the offspring and the grandchildren of immigrants (Dilworth-Anderson, Burton, & Johnson, 1993).

Leaving a place for a new national destination is an event in the life course that has implications for many aspects of life, including family relationships. As a result of immigration, extended networks of family and friends are disassembled and new social networks are formed (Becker, Beyene, Newsom, & Mayen, 2003; Rogler, 1994), a distressful process of loss and gain (Rogler, 1994). Furthermore, immigrants' receiving communities can shape immediate and long-term patterns of social interaction and adjustment. People and cultural resources may assist immigrants with adjusting to life in a new country, but they may also act as impediments to acculturation, language acquisition, and educational attainment (Bauer, 2002). Alternatively, if new immigrants live in geographic regions where existing residents are not accustomed to welcoming newcomers from other countries, they may experience prejudice, discrimination, isolation, and a high level of immigrant stress.

Life course perspectives are also concerned about the accumulation of experiences over time and the impact of those experiences on health and well-being in old age (Dannefer, 2003). Immigrants who work in wage sector jobs, receive minimal pay, are exposed to toxins in the work environment, and have limited or no health care may experience an accumulation of disadvantages over their life course, and their old age may be a time of morbidity and disability (Angel, 2009).

Social Determinants of Health

The social determinants of the health conceptual framework consider health disparities to be the result of social inequities (Kelly, Morgan, Bonnefoy, Butt, & Bergman, 2007; Marmot, 2005). This ecologically oriented theoretical perspective acknowledges multiple layers of determinants affecting the health of any one individual, considering a network of factors from personal exposures within one's community to political decisions made by world governments, all of which may significantly affect health determinants such as psychosocial state of mind, access to health care, exposure to toxins or other disease-causing agents, social support, and opportunities for income and education (Kelly et al., 2007; Solar & Irwin, 2007). Immigrant older adults, who are exposed to a greater number of risks at any one or at several levels of the ecological model, may experience more health problems than older persons who are exposed to fewer risks. As a person's social standing in society improves and, concomitantly, access to social, economic, and educational resources improves, health also improves (Kelly et al., 2007). Family members may play a critical role in facilitating elder immigrants' improved social standing and subsequent positive health outcomes.

The social determinants framework is an appropriate complement to the life course perspective, because both consider the impact of a lifetime's accumulation of experiences. The healthy immigrant effect, discussed later in the chapter, can be seen as the accumulation of a lifetime of exposures to determinants that can influence the health of immigrants in comparison to that of native-born populations. Also, by considering the cumulative effect of many lifetime exposures on immigrants as they reach old age, social determinants scholars may question the most influential social determinants of well-being in later life, and investigate ways risk factors engendered as part of the immigrant experience can be ameliorated through the appropriate application of culturally and life course-sensitive interventions.

INTERGENERATIONAL SUPPORT

Families may take advantage of opportunities for assistance, influence, and interactions across family generations. There are two main types of interpersonal support: affective (emotional) and instrumental (material and practical). Affection is often described as close in aging parent–adult child relationships in the United States. Gendered relationships exist, with adult children usually feeling closer to aging mothers than to aging fathers (Lawton, Silverstein, & Bengtson, 1994; see an update on the intergenerational relationship literature in Sechrist et al., chapter 7 in this volume). Whereas grandparent-grandchild relationships are also close, older adults tend to perceive a closer relationship to their grandchildren than the level perceived by the grandchildren themselves (Giarrusso, Feng, Silverstein, & Bengtson, 2001; Giarrusso, Stallings, & Bengtson, 1995). Although connection and closeness between older adults and their offspring is common, these relationships are not completely free of strife (Usita & Blieszner, 2002). (See Hayslip & Page, chapter 8 in this volume, for a review of the current grandparent-grandchild literature.)

Of the major types of instrumental support, material support (e.g., money, gifts, and a place to live) is often unidirectional in exchange among families in the United States. Older parents provide money and gifts to adult children when they need it (Cooney & Uhlenberg 1992; Swartz, 2009) or until their health deteriorates (Eggebeen & Hogan 1990). Younger adult children who are still establishing themselves may continue to live with their parents (Swartz, 2009).

Many older immigrants are coming to the United States in order to reunite with their children. Given their limited resources and immigration rules, the type of instrumental support that they are usually able to offer their families differs from what is normative for the native-born older adult population in the United States. In immigrant families, elders typically provide practical support in the form of child care, housework, or other services (Treas, 2009; Treas & Mazumdar, 2004). The upside to this role for immigrant families is that grandparents who offer child care may serve as cultural conservators, teaching grandchildren about their culture and language. The downside to this role for elder immigrants is that they may experience feelings of social isolation, helplessness, and loss of autonomy. Immigrant aging parents who move to a new country and who immediately become full-time caregivers to their grandchildren face the risk of social isolation. These grandparents may be living in suburbs where there are limited cultural and linguistic resources available and they may be engaged in so much time-intensive child care that they have limited access to cultural resources. Another family arrangement is for grandparents to move from one adult child's household to another's to care for grandchildren while their adult children are at work or advancing their education (Treas, 2009). In this scenario, these grandparents leave behind the new friendships they have formed (Treas, 2009). Although cultural norms may dictate respect and submission to elders, research has shown that it is often the younger generations' lifestyle needs that are given top priority within multigenerational immigrant families. Though younger generation needs may be given priority in nonimmigrant families as well, two reasons have been forwarded for this altered living arrangement among immigrant families: immigrant aging parents often rely on their adult children for navigating and establishing themselves within a new cultural and linguistic environment, and the nuclear or immediate family has taken the central role in the United States (Treas, 2009; Wong, Yoo, & Stewart, 2006).

Some immigrant aging parents, as well as some native-born older adults, offer both affective and instrumental support on a full-time basis to their grandchildren. These aging immigrant grandparents are raising their grandchildren because their adult children have formally or informally relinquished their parental responsibilities due to factors such as drug and alcohol problems, incarceration, financial problems, and lack of parenting ability. Research with Latino immigrant families in San Diego County revealed that some immigrant Latino grandparents (primarily grandmothers) became primary caregivers of their grandchildren because their adult children were incapable of holding a stable job, had a string of unstable intimate relationships, had been deported from the country, or were using drugs or alcohol (Shakya, Usita, Eisenberg, Weston, & Liles, 2012). Whereas immigrant grandparents who are primary caretakers for their grandchildren clearly make sacrifices to their economic, psychological, and physical well-being when they assume responsibility for raising their grandchildren, the majority of these grandparents voluntarily accept this responsibility to avoid placement of the grandchild in foster care, and to ensure the best possible outcome for that grandchild. Many of these grandparent caregivers find their job rewarding and perceive it as an opportunity to rewrite their families' futures (Shakya et al., 2012).

Cultural belief systems drive emotional and instrumental aid expectations and patterns. In a study of patterns of mutual assistance across four ethnic groups, researchers investigated cultural expectations of family assistance among Latino Americans, African Americans, Filipino Americans, and Cambodian Americans (Becker et al., 2003). Based on multiple interviews with elders in each group, researchers found that group norms about the role of elders in the family were different. For example, African American elders were highly involved in the lives of their children, grandchildren, and other family members, yet they valued their personal autonomy. Latino elders valued emotionally interdependent relationships with their extended family. Filipino elders discussed the importance of economic support to the extended family. Cambodian elders valued multigenerational households and expected financial support from their adult children. Each group's position regarding the role of elders in the family was connected to their unique culture and history. These histories were varied and included surviving oppression, having family scattered throughout the United States and in other countries, immigration for better economic and health offerings, and escaping oppressive regimens to arrive in the United States with the remnants of their families (Becker et al., 2003). Moreover, culturally prescribed gender roles influenced patterns of mutual aid. Across the groups, family continuity was assured for women through their caregiving role. Men's social standing in the family and their sense of family continuity was assured when they exhibited role flexibility—men took on caregiving responsibilities rather than the traditional disciplinarian and sage responsibilities. Consistent with a life course perspective, people's pasts and their families' futures are interrelated.

Instrumental aid across the generations may also be affected by geographical context and the economic and social opportunities this context provides. When immigrant parents and adult children live in geographic regions where others are ethnically different from them, feelings of affection and tendencies to exchange support may diminish and strife may be high. According to one study, immigrant Japanese mothers and their adult daughters struggled to get along when they were ethnically or racially different from the majority of inhabitants in their geographic region. However, when they lived in multiethnic communities where other residents were more similar to them and where labor force success was dependent upon the ability to communicate in Japanese, their appreciation grew for each other, their relationship quality improved, and they were more likely to engage in intergenerational reciprocity (Usita & Blieszner, 2002).

Because of the historical tendency in the immigrant literature to problematize immigrants' experiences, it is also important to identify cases where immigrant families have shown great adaptability to their new country through cooperation and adaptation of their unique cultural norms to a new environment (Seller, 1994). Lewis (2009) studied Cambodian refugees living in the southeastern United States and found that they had recreated a village living environment commonly found in Cambodia. It began by an eldest child purchasing a house, followed by another family member purchasing an adjacent house. Over a few years, more extended family members bought houses behind the rest and a family compound had been created. This family planted fruits and vegetables that served as a visual reminder of the Cambodia landscape as well as a barrier around the family village for privacy.

CARING FOR ELDER FAMILY MEMBERS

Many immigrant families are collective in their orientation, and caring for elder family members is a part of their cultural norm (Phinney, Ong, & Madden, 2000). For example, young Korean American and Vietnamese American adults value independence and autonomy but also value reciprocal caregiving and respect for aging parents (Pyke, 2000). Among immigrant and minority groups, family members typically provide most if not all of the care needed by their family members. This tendency has been found among varied groups including Chinese, Filipinos, Hispanics, Indians, Koreans, Native Americans, Russians, Vietnamese, and African Americans (Bhattacharya & Shibusawa, 2009; Scharlarch, Kellam, Ong, Baskin, Goldstein, & Fox, 2006). Some research suggests that these strong normative expectations about filial responsibility are being felt or carried out by the grandchild generation. For instance, many Asian Indian grandchildren uphold filial piety beliefs toward their grandparents (Farver, Narang, & Bhada, 2002; Giles, Noels, Williams, Ota, Lim, Ng, Ryan, & Somera, 2003), even when grandchildren live in the United States and grandparents live overseas in India (Saxena & Sanders, 2009).

Researchers have looked at how immigrant families in the United States expect and deliver care to aging family members and have discovered that structural factors (see examples below), social need factors, and immigrant generation status are among the variables explaining cultural variations in caregiving. For example, in a study investigating filial duty of Japanese American, Chinese American, and Korean American families, researchers found that structural factors such as geographic proximity, financial standing, and parental need for assistance, along with social factors such as parental need for emotional support, were key to understanding when adult children were most likely to provide care to aging parents (Ishii-Kuntz, 1997). Group differences existed in the types and levels of care. Korean American adult children were more likely to provide various types of support to elderly parents compared with Chinese Americans and Japanese Americans. Being the most recent immigrant group, Korean American elderly adults may have needed more support to adapt to their new living situation (Ishii-Kuntz, 1997) than Chinese and Japanese Americans. Moreover, generational positioning and gender influence the strength of filial responsibility expectations of each generation. In Japanese families, immigrant parents claimed that they did not expect to live with their adult children or to receive care from them, whereas their adult children reported that their parents expected them to display filial duty (Yanagisako, 1985).

Immigrants may experience distress over matters such as negotiating preservation of their cultural tradition of care and assimilating to the new culture's ways of caring for elders. In one study, researchers examined the conditions under which filial care was being carried out among immigrant Filipino American and Chinese American female caregivers who were predominantly caring for their own aging parents (others were caring for parents-in-law) (Jones, Zhang, & Meleis, 2003). Results indicated that the caregivers experienced distress, but that they were also able to transform their vulnerability into strength and well-being, although this coping strategy varied to some extent, according to resources available. The process of transforming vulnerability into strength and well-being was accomplished by caregivers' gaining competence and finding meaning in their care work. The immigration process had helped some caregivers because the family had already bonded during the migration process, which facilitated family coherence and ability to endure the demands of care. This finding was true especially of those caregivers who had no other family support available (Jones et al., 2003). More educated and economically advantaged caregivers had more personal resources (e.g., connecting with one's own inner strength and faith) to draw upon to cope with the demands of caregiving than less educated and more economically disadvantaged caregivers, which helped with some aspects of caregiving. But despite differences in resources, some challenges could not be overcome and simply had to be endured, including aging parents' personality and persistence about insisting on cultural norms of care.

Immigrant families have a tendency in live in multigenerational households when they have an old family member in need of care (Moon, Lubben, & Villa, 1998; Wilmoth, 2001). However, it must be understood that decisions driving multigenerational living may be cultural in origin, or they may be driven by economic or other needs (Treas, 2009). It is also important to recognize that some immigrants do not have any family members available to care for them directly (Graham, Ivey, & Neuhauser, 2009).

Family Interaction and Care across International Borders

Prior to the advent of much of today's technological innovation such as telephones, accessible air travel, and, more recently, the Internet, parents of emigrant children may have seriously wondered when they would see, talk, or correspond with their emigrant child. With advanced technology available in many countries today, aging parents and adult children may have regular telephone, Internet, or in-person contact. Indeed, grandparent-grandchild communication is maintained via technological innovation (e.g., e-mail, phone) (Saxena & Sanders, 2009). However, aging parents with emigrant children who live in war-torn countries or countries with very minimal technology infrastructure may still worry about these kinds of communication matters and about whether they will ever see their emigrant child again.

The effect of child emigration on nonimmigrant aging parents' well-being is an important though grossly understudied topic. Whereas initially, middle-aged parents may feel very hopeful about their young adult children's educational and career prospects outside of their home country, as parents grow older they may wish their children were living closer to offer in-person assistance, affection, and cultural services such as proscribed life rituals. In a study of aging parents living in India with at least one adult offspring living in another country, researchers found that children often left India in young adulthood to pursue degrees at better educational institutions, careers in countries that offered more opportunities and better pay, and lifestyles in other countries that would offer more stability and happiness (Miltiades, 2002). Parents were happy for their children at the time they left India. However, as parents aged and began to lose a spouse or experience their own health problems, they often wished their children lived nearby to offer care and companionship. Moreover, aging parents reported feeling lonely, sad, and even depressed, and some believed there was some link between their mental suffering and having an emigrant child (Miltiades, 2002). How parents with an emigrant child cope with the problems of aging and how that differs according to personal as well as regional and national resources is a topic that deserves further research.

When adult children leave their native country, they leave behind siblings, parents, and extended family members. Leaving behind family members usually does not mean forgetting about them or about filial responsibilities, however. Indeed, young adult immigrants continue to feel connected to their family members back home and some seek to dutifully fulfill familial obligations. One aspect of immigrants' sense of filial responsibility for family members left behind is their connection to and fluidity of place, in this case, the immigrant's homeland (Becker, 2002; Usita, 2005). Characteristics of a place (e.g., immigrant homeland), such as its normative beliefs and practices, are embodied in those people who have lived there, who in turn take these beliefs and practices to new locations. Thus, although little research has investigated this topic, it is likely that immigrants' sense of filial responsibility to aging parents living overseas continues and that the logistical difficulties of living in one country while experiencing concern and feelings of obligation toward family in another country may be a source of considerable stress. Unfortunately, very little research has systematically examined the emotional toll on immigrant adults of leaving behind aging parents in their home country, how emigrant children provide long-distance care to aging parents in the homeland, and how siblings who remained in the home country and emigrant siblings negotiate parental care duties.

Since immigrant adults serve as gatekeepers of interaction between their aging parents and their offspring, the nature of long-distance cross-national three-generation relationships should be examined (Saxena & Sanders, 2009). Longitudinal studies of the life course of grandparent-grandchild relationships are needed (Mueller, Wilhelm, & Elder, 2002), including relationships that cross international borders. Some emigrant children may wish their elder parents to visit or move to their adopted country. Whether elder parents visit or move may be affected by the news they receive about the health benefits or challenges of life abroad.

Health and Access to Care

The health and well-being of elderly adult immigrants can be affected by many factors both prior to and after the act of immigrating. Because the need for health services increases with age, the ability to provide adequate health care for elderly adult immigrants is an important consideration within a national context. The increase in immigration to the United States over the past decade has also inspired much debate over its long-term impact. Immigration opponents frequently cite concerns regarding immigrant use of public services. There is a general concern that immigrants from developing countries, who now make up the large majority of the newly arriving immigrant population, will bring with them health problems such as infectious diseases that will take a toll on a health system that will soon be strained by the aging of the Baby Boomer generation. Immigrant elder health is not a straightforward area of research, because life exposures before immigration as well as conditions of life after arrival are important determinants of later-life health and well-being.

Healthy Immigrant Effect

Immigrants to the United States often have positive health indicators compared to native-born Americans and U.S.-born compatriots. For example, using 1992 to 1995 National Health Interview Survey data, researchers found recent immigrants from many groups (e.g., Chinese, Japanese, Filipino, Asian Indian, Korean, Vietnamese, Mexican, Cuban, Central American, and South American) reported better health than their U.S.-born counterparts (Singh & Miller, 2004). Mexican-origin persons show a favorable mortality profile compared with persons from other ethnic and racial groups for all ages (Elo, Turra, Kestenbaum, & Ferguson, 2004; Markides & Eschbach, 2005). Moreover, using data from 1990s Social Security Administration files, Lauderdale and Kestenbaum (2002) studied the death probabilities of the six largest Asian American subpopulations (Chinese, Japanese, Filipino,

Vietnamese, Indians, Koreans) and found that elderly Asian American adult mortality rates were lower than those of elderly white adults. This healthy immigrant effect is seen as a paradox, because it persists for immigrants such as those from Latin America, who in comparison to native-born whites experience the disadvantages of low socioeconomic status, yet enjoy a considerable health advantage over native-born whites (Wakabayashi, 2009). This healthy immigrant effect is generally considered to result from several different factors, although controversy reigns as to which is the most valid causal explanation and which possible explanations have been confounded by other less easily measurable factors (Kennedy, 2006).

An important possible explanation for the healthy immigrant phenomenon is that because the experience of immigrating and adapting to a foreign country is difficult, potential immigrants who are less fit, both mentally and physically, have been weeded out of the immigrant population by being unable or unwilling to make the journey. This hypothesis is supported by data from a four-country (of destination) study showing that immigrants are likely to have a higher educational level than those being left behind in their home country and are typically younger than native born residents of the same destination country (Kennedy, 2006). This selection effect could ensure that those immigrants who are now in the United States are more likely to live longer and healthier lives than their native-born counterparts (Swallen, 1997). Swallen (1997) found that adjusting for health behaviors, the superior health status of immigrants to the United States continues into old age, providing evidence for a selection effect. However, according to many other studies, the healthy immigrant effect tends to diminish over time. In other words, the longer that an immigrant has lived in the United States, the worse his or her health indicators and health behaviors are likely to be (Kennedy, 2006). This author concluded that whereas some selection effect is possible, a significant proportion of the risk is attributable to unobservable factors related to immigration to the United States, the effects of which increase with the length of time since immigration. Another explanation, which has received some statistical support, is the so-called salmon effect, which theorizes that immigrants experiencing ill-health are likely to return home to their native countries for medical care and social support, and therefore skew the distribution of existing elderly immigrant adults toward a healthier and more robust population (Kennedy, 2006).

Studies specifically investigating the health behaviors and outcomes of elderly immigrant adults have been few. Whereas some look at one particular ethnic group or country of origin, few studies of elderly immigrant adults have encompassed the wide diversity of backgrounds and social contexts that distinguish them. In general, studies have consistently shown that in comparison to native-born Americans, immigrant elders generally enjoy better health (Heron, Schoeni, & Morales, 2003). Singh and colleagues (2004) found that foreign-born blacks, Hispanics, and Asians all enjoyed a considerable mortality advantage (approximately 45% lower risk) over native-born whites given the same socioeconomic characteristics (Singh, 2002). When length of time in the United States increased, however, Singh found that prevalence of risk behaviors and chronic conditions increased as well. Immigrants who have lived in the United States for more than 15 years were significantly more likely than newly arrived immigrants to smoke, have hypertension, suffer from obesity, and report one or more chronic conditions, although for all of these indicators, levels were still below those reported by native-born Americans.

The results of Singh's analysis of health behaviors and health outcomes among immigrant groups suggest that the differences in health behaviors of elderly immigrant adults depends on how long they have lived in the United States and may be a direct reflection of how much exposure they have had to unhealthy American lifestyles. This acculturation argument suggests that because immigrants become more accustomed to life in a new culture, they are more likely to engage in unhealthy behaviors such as cigarette smoking, alcohol consumption, overeating, consumption of fattening foods, and sedentary behavior, than they would have in their home country (Kennedy, 2006; Singh, 2002).

Whereas this argument may have some validity when considering the health differences between younger immigrants and native-born whites, some doubt has been cast upon its validity when considering older adults (Gonzalez, 2009). Using cross-sectional data on Mexican American elders in five Southwest states, Gonzales (2009) discovered a nonlinear relationship between acculturation and negative health outcomes. Whereas years of time spent in the United States significantly increased the possibility of chronic disease diagnosis for Mexican-born versus U.S.-born elders, this relationship did not continue into older adulthood, suggesting that the positive gains from acculturation outweighed the negative after a certain length of time spent in the United States.

Another factor contributing to possible decreases in the immigrant health advantage over time is the fact that the very act of immigrating is stressful. Acculturative stress can negatively affect an immigrant, and this impact is potentially cumulative (Hovey, 2000; Thomas, 1995). Considering a social determinants of health perspective, whereas certain social advantages may have contributed to the ability of an immigrant to undergo the immigration process in the first place, the relative social disparity that an immigrant is likely to undergo as part of the immigration experience may negatively impact that immigrant's health outcomes over the long term. Struggles with language, cultural differences, lack of economic opportunities, inability to access service resources such as health care, and experience of racism are all significant challenges that can weaken the long-term cumulative resilience of an immigrant to a foreign country. Whereas health advantages that immigrants bring with them may be significant, the health disadvantages gained through the potentially interactive process of acculturative stress combined with the adaptation of Western health behaviors can be potential causal factors contributing to the loss of the immigrant health advantage over time. The level of acculturative stress, however, although cumulative, can itself decrease over time as an immigrant experiences increased comfort within and knowledge of the new cultural environment, as suggested by the Gonzales study. Given these considerations, immigrants who arrive at an older age as a result of family reunification laws potentially have the greatest level of vulnerability to health disparities. If a selection effect is at play, this effect could determine the health and long term well-being of the original immigrant, the younger adult who overcame the challenges necessary to immigrate to a new country, but it is not clear that this advantage would apply to that immigrant's elderly adult parents, who have arrived in the United States as beneficiaries of their child's persistence and motivation. These elderly immigrant adults are, furthermore, the ones at the greatest acculturative disadvantage, given their lower levels of education and English proficiency. And because adapting to new circumstances and learning new and complex skills become increasingly difficult as one ages, older immigrants who have arrived at a later stage of their lives may be particularly vulnerable to challenges to health and quality of life as a result of their immigrant status within a foreign land.

Health Care Access

Accessing health care could make a notable difference in the health of immigrants, but members of minority groups use fewer social welfare health services (as provided by the Administration on Aging) than members of the majority group (Wolinsky, 1994; Wolinsky & Johnson, 1991). A wide variety of cultural beliefs, values, and educational levels can strongly influence immigrant interactions with the medical profession.

Many South Asian elderly adults, for example, believe that good health is a reflection of inner harmony and prefer to take a natural, spiritually based approach to resolving health problems (Bhattacharya & Shibusawa, 2009). Such an outlook could come into conflict with the more biomedically focused treatment-based approach common in Western medical practice. Looking at complementary medicine usage, Wajm and colleagues (2003) found that Latino and Vietnamese elderly adults were both likely to use alternative medicine modalities, and that the specific modality used was determined by cultural traditions of usage (Wajm, Reinsch, Hoehler, & Tobis, 2003). Another study comparing the health behavior practices of Chinese American elders in Boston with a comparable population in Shanghai found that Chinese elders prefer a bicultural approach to health care and health behavior, integrating aspects of both Western and traditional Chinese medicine (Miltiades & Wu, 2008). They concluded that physician hostility to Chinese medicine could discourage Chinese elders from seeking health services, and a more integrated approach to medical care for Chinese elderly adults could be more effective and increase service utilization.

A lack of knowledge about disease conditions is another factor that may impede older immigrants from seeking health care. Qualitative and quantitative studies that have examined Asian immigrants' understanding of conditions such as Alzheimer's disease (AD), for example, consistently reveal that they lack knowledge about the causes, symptoms, and treatments for AD (Hinton, Franz, Yeo, & Levkoff, 2005; Jones, Chow, & Gatz, 2005). It is important to acknowledge and address such issues, because prevalence rates of AD among immigrants are expected to rise to levels similar to those of other groups in the United States (Chen, Borson, & Scanlan, 2000).

Literacy and linguistic proficiency are both important aspects of understanding the health-seeking behaviors of immigrant populations, because those with limited ability to speak or write English will face numerous barriers in utilization of health care services (Leclere, Jensen, & Biddlecom, 1994). One often overlooked dimension of the literacy aspect of health service usage is that in some immigrants' cultures, for example that of the Somali Bantu, there is no written version of language (Yoshida, Gordon, & Henkin, 2008). Problems such as these require a shift in the cultural paradigms of health care providers who need to adapt their services for the unique needs of these different populations.

Immigrants' general reluctance to use formal services is also related to factors associated with accessing them. Immigrants find eligibility and service information confusing or intimidating (Graham et al., 2009; Pang, Jordan-Marsh, Silverstein, & Cody, 2003), and they experience problems with transportation to services (Pang et al., 2003). Immigrants also prefer to use services provided by professionals they already know (Ruiz-Beltran & Kamau, 2001) and by individuals or organizations of the same ethnic background (Wong et al., 2006). Indeed, some immigrant families have subcontracted filial piety to ethnically matched service providers (Lan, 2002). Immigrants' reluctance to use services is also related to whom the services benefit. Services that benefit care recipients are more likely to be used than services that benefit caregivers (Scharlarch et al., 2006).

CONCLUSION

This chapter has illustrated that immigrant elders comprise and will continue to encompass a notable portion of the U.S. population, that key family issues such as contact and support across generations are culturally informed but negotiated post-immigration, and that health and access to care continue to be topics worthy of greater and deeper exploration. As new groups immigrate to the United States and enrich the cultural landscape, it will be important to continue to assess how immigrant elders and their families are adjusting, negotiating old with new traditions, and managing care from a distance. Life course and social determinants of health perspectives underscore the connections among individual biographies and family futures, as well as the piling up of vulnerabilities and strengths for immigrants. Finally, research is needed on life course and social determinants of health to reveal what it means for immigrants to have a lifetime of underutilization of preventive services and medical care.

REFERENCES

American Community Survey. (n.d.). Retrieved from http://factfinder.census.gov/servlet/DatasetMainPageServlet?_program=ACS&_submenuId=&_lang=en&_ts=

Angel, R. J. (2009). Structural and cultural factors in successful aging among older Hispanics. *Family Community Health, 32*, S46–S56.

Asian American Federation. (2008). *Working but poor: Asian American poverty in New York City.* New York: Asian American Federation.

Bauer, T. G. (2002). *Enclaves, Language and the Location Choice of Migrants.* Discussion paper No. 558, Institute for the Study of Labor. Retrieved from http://ftp.iza.org/dp558.pdf

Becker, G. (2002). Dying away from home: Quandaries of migration for elders in two ethnic groups. *Journal of Gerontology: Social Sciences, 57B*, S579–S595.

Becker, G., Beyene, Y., Newsom, E., & Mayen, N. (2003). Creating continuity through mutual assistance: Intergenerational reciprocity in four ethnic groups. *Journal of Gerontology: Social Sciences, 55B*, S151–S159.

Bhattacharya, G., & Shibusawa, T. (2009). Experience of aging among immigrants from India to the United States: Social work practice in global context. *Journal of Gerontological Social Work, 52*, 445–462.

Chen, J. C., Borson, S., & Scanlan, J. M. (2000). State-specific prevalence of behavioral symptoms in Alzheimer's disease in a multi-ethnic community sample. *American Journal of Geriatric Psychiatry 8*, 123–133.

Clausen, J. A. (1986). *The life course: A sociological perspective.* Englewood Cliffs, NJ: Prentice Hall.

Cooney, T. M., & Uhlenberg, P. (1992). Support from parents over the life course: The adult child's perspective. *Social Forces, 71*, 63–84.

Dannefer, D. (2003). Cumulative advantage/disadvantage and the life course: Cross-fertilizing age and social science theory. *Journal of Gerontology: Social Sciences, 58B*, S327–S337.

Dilworth-Anderson, P., Burton, L. M., & Johnson, L. B. (1993). Reframing theories for understanding race, ethnicity, and families. In P. G. Boss, W. J. Doherty, R. LaRossa, W. R. Schumm, & S. K. Steinmetz (Eds.), *Handbook of family theories and methods: A contextual approach* (pp. 627–646). New York: Plenum Press.

Eggebeen, D., & Hogan, D. (1990). Giving between generations in American families. *Human Nature, 1,* 211–232.

Elder, G. H., Jr. (1998). The life course and human development. In R. M. Lerner (Ed.), *Handbook of child psychology, Vol. 1: Theoretical models of human development* (5th ed., pp. 939–991). New York: Wiley.

Ellis, M. W. (2005). Assimilation and differences between the settlement patterns of individual immigrants and immigrant households. *Proceedings of the National Academy of Sciences, 102,* 15325–15330.

Elo, I. T., Turra, C. M., Kestenbaum, B., & Ferguson, R. F. (2004). Mortality among elderly Hispanics in the United States: Past evidence and new results. *Demography, 41,* 109–128.

Estes, C. L., Goldberg, S., Wellin, C., Linkins, K. W., Shostak, S., & Beard, R. L. (2006). Implications of welfare reform on the elderly: A case study of provider, advocate, and consumer perspectives. *Journal of Aging and Social Policy, 18,* 41–63.

Farver, J. A., Narang, S. K., & Bhadha, B. R. (2002). East meets west: Ethnic identity, acculturation and conflict in Asian Indian families. *Journal of Family Psychology, 16,* 338–350.

Frey, W. L. (2000). State magnets for different elderly migrant types in the United States. *International Journal of Population Geography, 6,* 21–44.

Giarrusso, R., Feng, D., Silverstein, M., & Bengtson, V. L. (2001). Grandparent-adult grandchild affection and consensus: Cross-generational and cross-ethnic comparisons. *Journal of Family Issues, 22,* 456–477.

Giarrusso, R., Stallings, M., & Bengtson, V. L. (1995). The intergenerational stake hypothesis revisited: Parent-child differences in perceptions of relationships 20 years later. In V. L. Bengtson, K. W. Schaie, & L. M. Burton (Eds.), *Adult intergenerational relations, effects of societal change* (pp. 227–263). New York: Springer.

Giles, H., Noels, K. A., Williams, A., Ota, H., Lim, T., Ng, S. H., Ryan, E. B., & Somera, L. (2003). Intergenerational communication across cultures: Young people's perceptions of conversations with family elders, non-family elders and same-age peers. *Journal of Cross-Cultural Gerontology, 18,* 1–32.

Gonzalez, H. (2009). The health of older Mexican Americans in the long run. *American Journal of Public Health, 99,* 1879–1885.

Graham, C. L., Ivey, S. L., & Neuhauser, L. (2009). From hospital to home: Assessing the transitional care needs of vulnerable seniors. *The Gerontologist, 49,* 23–33.

He, W. (2002). *The older foreign-born population in the United States: 2000.* U.S. Census Bureau, Current Population Reports, Series P23,211. Washington, DC: Government Printing Office.

Heron, M., Schoeni, R. F., & Morales, L. (2003). *Health status among older immigrants in the United States* (Report No. 03-548). Ann Arbor: University of Michigan, Institute for Social Research, Population Studies Center.

Hinton, L., Franz, C. E., Yeo, G., & Levkoff, S. (2005). Conceptions of dementia in a multiethnic sample of family caregivers. *Journal of American Geriatrics Society, 53,* 1405–1410.

Hovey, J. (2000). Acculturative stress, depression, and suicidal ideation in Mexican immigrants. *Cultural Diversity and Ethnic Minority Psychology, 6,* 134–152.

Hu, W. (1998). Elderly immigrants on welfare. *Journal of Human Resources, 33,* 711–741.

Ishii-Kuntz, M. (1997). Intergenerational relationships among Chinese, Japanese, and Korean Americans. *Family Relations, 46,* 23–32.

Jones, P. S., Chow, T. W., & Gatz. M. (2005). Asian Americans and Alzheimer's disease: Assimilation, culture, and beliefs. *Journal of Aging Studies, 20,* 11–25.

Jones, P. S., Zhang, X. E., & Meleis, A.I. (2003). Transforming vulnerability. *Western Journal of Nursing Research, 25,* 835–853.

Kelly, M. P., Morgan, A., Bonnefoy, J., Butt, J., & Bergman, V. (2007). *The social determinants of health: Developing an evidence base for political action.* Commission on the Social Determinants of Health. Geneva: World Health Organization.

Kennedy, S. M. (2006). *The healthy immigrant effect and immigrant selection: evidence from four countries.* Ontario: Program for Research on Social and Economic Dimensions of an Aging Population.

Lan, P. C. (2002). Subcontracting filial piety: Elder care in ethnic Chinese immigrant families in California. *Journal of Family Issues, 23,* 812–835.

Lauderdale, D. S., & Kestenbaum, B. (2002). Mortality rates of elderly Asian American populations based on Medicare and Social Security data. *Demography, 39,* 529–540.

Lawton, L., Silverstein, M., & Bengtson, V. L. (1994). Affection, social contact, and geographical distance between adult children and their parents. *Journal of Marriage and the Family, 56,* 57–68.

Leach, M. A. (2009). America's older immigrants: A profile. *Generations, 32,* 34–39.

Leclere, F., Jensen, L., & Biddlecom, A. (1994). Health care utilization, family context, and adaptation among immigrants to the United States. *Journal of Health and Social Behavior, 35,* 370–384.

Lewis, D. C. (2009). Aging out of place: Cambodian refugee elders in the United States. *Journal of Aging Studies, 37,* 376–393.

Markides, K. S., & Eschbach, K. (2005). Aging, migration, and mortality: Current status of research on the Hispanic paradox. *Journals of Gerontology: Social Sciences, 60,* S68–S75.

Marmot, M. (2005). Social determinants of health inequalities. *The Lancet, 365,* 1099–104.

Miltiades, H. B. (2002). The social and psychological effect of an adult child's emigration on non-immigrant Asian Indian elderly parents. *Journal of Cross-Cultural Gerontology, 17,* 33–55.

Miltiades, H. B., & Wu, B. (2008). Factors affecting physician visits in Chinese and Chinese immigrant samples. *Social Science & Medicine, 66,* 704–714.

Moon, A., Lubben, J. E., & Villa, V. (1998). Awareness and utilization of community long-term care services by elderly Korean and non-Hispanic white Americans. *The Gerontologist, 38,* 309–316.

Mueller, M. M., Wilheim, B., & Elder, G. H., Jr. (2002). Variations in grandparenting. *Research on Aging, 24,* 360–388.

Pang, E. C., Jordan-Marsh, M., Silverstein, M., & Cody, M. (2003). Health-seeking behaviors of elderly Chinese Americans: Shifts in expectations. *The Gerontologist, 43,* 864–874.

Passel, J. (2005). *Estimates of the size and characteristics of the undocumented population*. Pew Hispanic Center. Retrieved from http://pewhispanic.org/files/reports/44.pdf

Phinney, J.S., Ong, A., & Madden, T. (2000). Cultural values and intergenerational value discrepancies in immigrant and non-immigrant families. *Child Development, 71*, 528–539.

Pyke, K. (2000). The normal American family as an interpretive structure of family life among grown children of Korean and Vietnamese immigrants. *Journal of Marriage and Family, 62*, 240–255.

Rogers, A.R. (1999). The regional demographics of elderly foreign-born and native-born populations in the United States since 1950. *Research on Aging, 21*, 3–35.

Rogler, L.H. (1994). International migrations: A framework for directing research. *American Psychologist, 49*(8), 701–708.

Ruiz-Beltran, M., & Kamau, J.K. (2001). The socio-economic and cultural impediments to well-being along the U.S.-Mexico border. *Journal of Community Health, 26*, 123–133.

Saxena, D., & Sanders, G. F. (2009). Quality of grandparent-grandchild relationships in Asian-Indian immigrant families. *International Journal of Aging and Human Development, 68*, 321–337.

Scharlarch, A.E., Kellam, R., Ong, N., Baskin, A., Goldstein, C., & Fox, P.J. (2006). Cultural attitudes and caregiver service use. *Journal of Gerontological Social Work, 47*, 133–156.

Schmidley, D. (2001). *Profile of the foreign-born population in the United States: 2000*. U.S. Census Bureau, Current Population Reports, Series P23–206. Washington, DC : Government Printing Office.

Seller, M.S. (1994). *Immigrant women* (2nd ed.). New York: State University of New York Press.

Shakya, H.B., Usita, P. M., Eisenberg, C. M, Weston, J., & Liles, S. (2012). Family well-being concerns of grandparents in skipped generation families. *Journal of Gerontological Social Work, 55*, 39–54.

Singh, G.K. (2002). Ethnic-immigrant differentials in health behaviors, morbidity, and cause-specific mortality in the United States: An analysis of two national databases. *Human Biology, 74*, 83–109.

Singh, G.K., & Miller, B.A. (2004). Health, life expectancy, and mortality patterns among immigrant populations in the United States. *Canadian Journal of Public Health, 95*, 114–121.

Solar, O., & Irwin, A. (2007). *A conceptual framework for action on the social determinants of health*. Social Determinants of Health Discussion Paper 2 (Policy and Practice). Geneva: World Health Organization.

Swallen, K. (1997). Do health selection effects last? A comparison of morbidity rates for elderly adult immigrants and U.S. born elderly persons. *Journal of Cross-Cultural Gerontology, 12*, 317–339.

Swartz, T.T. (2009). Intergenerational family relations in adulthood: Patterns, variations, and implications in the contemporary United States. *Annual Review of Sociology, 35*, 191–212.

Thomas, T.N. (1995). Acculturative stress in the adjustment of immigrant families. *Journal of Social Distress and the Homeless, 4,* 131–142.

Treas, J. (1995). Older Americans in the 1990s and beyond. *Population Bulletin, 50,* 1–48.

Treas, J. (2009). Four myths about older adults in America's immigrant families. *Generations, 32,* 40–45.

Treas, J., & Mazumdar, S. (2004). Caregiving and kinkeeping: Contributions of older people to America's immigrant families. *Journal of Comparative Family Studies, 35,* 105–122.

U.S. Bureau of the Census. (2000a). *Foreign-Born Profiles.* Retrieved from http://www.census.gov/population/cen2000/stp-159/STP-159- india.pdf

U.S. Bureau of the Census. (2000b). *Foreign-Born Profiles.* Retrieved from http://www.census.gov/population/cen2000/stp-159/STP-159-Mexico.pdf

Usita, P. M. (2005). Social geography and continuity effects in immigrant women's narratives of negative social exchanges. *Journal of Aging Studies, 19,* 221–239.

Usita, P. M., & Blieszner, R. (2002). Communication challenges and intimacy strategies of immigrant mothers and adult daughters. *Journal of Family Issues, 23,* 266–286.

Wajm, W., Reinsch, S., Hoehler, F., & Tobis, J. (2003). Use of complementary and alternative medicine among the ethnic elderly. *Alternative Therapies, 9,* 50–57.

Wakabayashi, C. (2009). Effects of immigration and age on health of older people in the United States. *Journal of Applied Gerontology, 20,* 1–23.

Wilmoth, J.M. (2001). Living arrangements among older immigrants in the United States. *The Gerontologist, 41,* 228–238.

Wilmoth, J.M., De Jong, G., & Himes, C. (1997). Immigrant and non-immigrant living arrangements among America's white, Hispanic, and Asian elderly population. *International Journal of Sociology and Social Policy, 17,* 57–82.

Wolinsky, F.D. (1994). Health services utilization among older adults: Conceptual, measurement, and modeling issues in secondary analysis. *The Gerontologist, 34,* 470–475.

Wolinsky, F.D., & Johnson, R.J. (1991). The use of health services by older adults. *Journal of Gerontology: Social Sciences, 46B,* S345–S357.

Wong, S.T., Yoo, G.J., & Stewart, A.L. (2006). The changing meaning of family support among older Chinese and Korean immigrants. *Journal of Gerontology: Social Sciences, 61B,* S4–S9.

Yanagisako, S.J. (1985). *Transforming the past: Tradition and kinship among Japanese Americans.* Stanford, CA: Stanford University Press.

Yoshida, H., Gordon, D., & Henkin, N. (2008). *Community treasures: Recognizing the contributions of older immigrants and refugees.* Philadelphia: Temple University Center for Intergenerational Learning.

Zavodny, M. (1999). Determinants of recent immigrants' locational choices. *International Migration Review, 33,* 1014–1030.

15

U.S. Old Age Policy and Families

Madonna Harrington Meyer and Chantell Frazier

Families tend to provide a great deal of physical, emotional, and financial assistance to their frail older members, but just how much help they provide is shaped to a large extent by the amount of help offered through the old age welfare state. The U.S. old age welfare state affords a tremendous array of supports for older persons and their families, but that safety net is growing increasingly complex and controversial as employer-based benefits continue to shrink, and as some welfare programs prioritize market concerns over family concerns. In this chapter we examine social welfare for older people through income programs, including Social Security, Supplemental Security Income, and employer-based pensions, and through health programs, including Medicare, supplemental insurance, and Medicaid. Because the impact of public policy on older persons and their families is tightly linked to gender, race, class, and marital status, we pay careful attention to inequalities linked to these stratifying characteristics.

THE CHANGING OLD AGE WELFARE STATE

Historically, most societies relied on filial responsibility; each family was expected to care for its own older relatives. Over time, modern welfare states became increasingly involved in taking responsibility for the provision of at least some basic needs, particularly for older people. Most welfare states developed income, health, and family benefits. Older people were generally regarded as deserving poor and policymakers recognized that filial responsibility concentrated risk, privatized cost, and maximized inequality between families. Social welfare for older people became a priority through 1980, when the tides turned and policymakers noted that poverty rates among those age 65 and older had dropped sharply and the costs of old age provision had risen dramatically (Estes & Associates, 2001; Hacker, 2002; Harrington Meyer & Herd, 2007). Though some programs continued to expand over the next decades, cost cutting, privatization, and shifting risk and responsibility back to families became central foci. Social welfare for older people in the United States is growing increasingly complex and is now provided through four main streams: poverty-based welfare state programs; universal welfare state programs; tax subsidized employer-based programs; and tax subsidized private market-based programs.

Early programs for older people were *poverty-based* social assistance programs in which eligibility was based on income and assets. The United States has a long-standing preference for poverty-based, means-tested programs, such as Supplemental Security Income (SSI) and Medicaid. The intent of social assistance is to provide some relief to the most needy and deserving citizens. Proponents of targeted programs argue they are less expensive than universal programs because they target resources to very poor persons and discourage dependency on the welfare state by encouraging employment. Critics argue that these benefits are politically divisive because they pit tax-paying contributors against highly stigmatized welfare recipients (Harrington Meyer & Herd, 2007; Korpi, 2000; Korpi & Palme, 1998; Quadagno, 2005). Means-tested welfare programs are politically unpopular and, therefore, politically vulnerable. Moreover, they have limited efficacy and have generally not been effective at pulling people out of poverty.

Universal programs, by contrast, are based on an ideology of social insurance. Because all contribute and all receive benefits, these programs have historically been regarded as politically unifying and politically invincible. The United States has two universal programs, both for older and disabled citizens: Social Security and Medicare. Unlike targeted programs that emphasize selective acceptance, universal programs boast broad eligibility, redistributive benefit formulas, and widespread approval by voters (American Association of Retired Persons, 2005; Estes & Associates, 2001; Public Agenda, 2005; Quadagno, 2005). Universal programs are more effective than targeted programs at reducing poverty and inequality. Indeed, the combined value of Social Security and Medicare is credited with reducing poverty among older adults from more than 50% during the Great Depression, to 11% in 2005 (Engelhardt & Gruber, 2004; Korpi & Palme, 1998). But critics warn that with the aging of Baby Boomers the United States can no longer afford universal programs as there will be too many retirees for current workers to support.

Historically, *employer-based* private pensions and health insurance benefits have also been mainstays of U.S. social welfare provision. Subsidized through more than $100 billion in tax subsidies annually, employer-based benefits represent a substantial component of the U.S. old age welfare state (Employee Benefit Research Institute, 2005, 2009; Hacker, 2002). Benefits offered via employers are generally neither compulsory nor redistributive. In fact, private benefits tend to be maximally beneficial to those in higher income groups with the steadiest labor force participation. As a result, employer-based benefits have generally increased rather than decreased inequality among older people and their families (Harrington Meyer & Herd, 2007). In contrast to universal benefits, which tend to spread risk, share costs, and reduce gender, race, and class inequality, employer-based benefits tend to help only those with sufficiently strong links to the labor force to receive the benefits (Harrington Meyer & Pavalko, 1996; Korpi & Palme, 1998). Because they have weaker links to the labor force and lower average incomes, women, blacks and Hispanics, and part-time workers are significantly less likely to reap the rewards of employer-based benefits (Harrington Meyer & Herd, 2007; Korpi & Palme, 1998). The impact of employer-based benefits is dissipating, though, as both the coverage of workers and the size of benefits have dropped dramatically in recent decades (Employee Benefit Research Institute, 2005; Munnell & Sundén, 2004; Shuey & O'Rand, 2006).

Increasingly, the U.S. welfare state is relying on more *private market* provision of programs and services. Medicare Part C Advantage (MA) and Medicare Part D prescription drug coverage both represent the trend toward replacing government-run programs with publicly subsidized, private, for-profit, market-run programs that require older people to act as consumers in complex markets (Harrington Meyer & Herd, 2007). These programs are partially funded by the government but operate in the private market where they are less visible, accessible, and regulated. Weary of the price of public old age programs, opponents of big government have worked in recent years to downsize the federal government's provision of a social safety net. They aim to shift government spending on social welfare to private market programs that would ostensibly meet the needs of older people and their families at a profit (Becker, 2005; Estes & Associates, 2001; Friedman, 2002; Gilbert, 2002; Hacker, 2002; Quadagno, 2005; Yergin & Stanislaw, 1998). They argue that the United States needs to reduce government spending by getting the government out of the retirement business and privatizing both Social Security and Medicare. Critics point out that these efforts have thus far failed to contain costs, and have increased individual risk and responsibility, generating new sources of inequality and instability in old age (Harrington Meyer & Herd, 2007).

SOCIAL SECURITY

Social Security provides monthly benefits to millions of retirees, their spouses, and people who are permanently disabled. When it was enacted in 1935, older people were more likely than persons in other age groups to be poor. By the mid-1980s, however, primarily because of Social Security, poverty rates for those ages 65 and older dropped below poverty rates for those of other ages (Social Security Administration, 2009). Social Security initially excluded workers in many occupations, including agriculture and domestic service, as well as self-employed workers and those employed by religious, charitable, and educational organizations (Abramovitz, 1988; Quadagno, 1984). These exclusions eliminated from coverage nearly one-half of all workers and nearly all women and blacks. Over time, Social Security incorporated most of these workers, and by 2009, more than 94% of workers were covered and 91% of older people were receiving benefits (Social Security Administration, 2009).

Although initially designed as an income supplement, Social Security is the primary source of income for many older Americans. Social Security comprises about 40% of income for all older people, 60% of income for all older women, and 100% of income for one in five older women (Social Security Administration, 2009). Social Security is particularly important for women, blacks, and Hispanics. Because of reduced access to private pensions and private savings, one-half of older Hispanics and African Americans rely on Social Security for 90% or more of their income (Torres-Gil, Greenstein, & Kamin, 2005; Wu, 2005). Social Security comprises almost 80% of the income of black and Hispanic women. Social Security has transformed from a system that once excluded women and blacks, to one that provides a majority of their income in old age. The Social Security benefit structure is progressive, redistributing resources from higher to lower lifetime earners, and as a result has been credited with reducing poverty and inequality among older people (Engelhardt & Gruber 2004; Harrington Meyer & Herd, 2007).

Retired Worker Benefits

Social Security is a universal program with benefits based on worker contributions or family relationships rather than financial need. Retirees may be eligible for retired worker benefits, or spouse and widow benefits. To be eligible for worker benefits, workers must have worked in covered employment for a total of 10 years, or 40 quarters, over their life course (Social Security Administration, 2009). The quarters need not be consecutive, so eligibility is not compromised when workers disrupt waged labor to rear children or perform other unpaid care work. Such disruptions do, however affect benefit size. Maximum benefits, $2,346 a month in 2010, are available only to those with lengthy and continuous labor force participation in higher paying jobs. Those with interrupted participation and lower paying jobs receive much less. Blacks and Hispanics, who are more likely to struggle with higher unemployment and incarceration rates, lower education levels, and lower wages, receive smaller retired worker benefits than whites on average (Harrington Meyer & Herd, 2007). Women, who are more likely to be burdened by the conflicting demands of waged and unwaged labor and persistent gender segregation and discrimination in the labor force, receive significantly lower benefits than men (Social Security Administration, 2009). Even though the Social Security benefit formula is designed to redistribute from higher to lower paid workers, average retired worker Social Security benefits for black men are 83% of those for white men. Average retired worker benefits for white women are 76%, and average benefits for black women are just 69%, of those for white men (Social Security Administration, 2004).

Spouse and Widow Benefits

Eligibility for spouse and widow benefits is determined by marital rather than work history. Currently about 60% of older women receive spouse or widow, rather than retired worker, benefits. Despite advances in the labor force, the majority of women are expected to continue to rely on spouse and widow benefits for the next several cohorts as they reach old age (Levine, Mitchell, & Phillips, 2000; Social Security Administration, 2009). Spouse beneficiaries must be married at the time of eligibility, or, if divorced, have been married at least 10 years to a covered worker. Though the rules are gender neutral, nearly 97% of spousal beneficiaries are women (Social Security Administration, 2009). Women receiving spouse benefits receive an amount equal to 50% of their husbands' benefits, those receiving widow benefits receive an amount equal to 100% of their husbands' benefits. Even though the Social Security benefit formula is redistributive, race differences in men's wages translate into race differences in women's spouse and widow benefits. Black women's average spouse benefits are 82%, and their widow benefits just 78%, of white women's (Social Security Administration, 2004).

Many women are dually entitled, that is they are entitled as workers and as spouses or widows. The Social Security administration automatically gives them whatever is the largest benefit. The Social Security Administration (2009) describes dually entitled women who draw spouse or widow benefits as receiving a secondary benefit, but this implies that they are receiving two benefits, which is misleading. In fact they are receiving the amount they would have received if they had never contributed to the program because they are receiving an amount equal to 50% or 100% of their husbands' benefits.

Many scholars suggest that Social Security does not effectively compensate women for time spent out of the labor force caring for family members (Harrington Meyer & Herd, 2007; Quadagno, 1984). All workers are allowed to drop the five lowest years of earnings, but many women spend more than five years out of the labor force and in lower paying jobs while they are performing unpaid care work (Harrington Meyer & Herd, 2007; Social Security Administration, 2009). Historically, spouse and widow benefits have provided much-needed retirement income for women with low wages or interrupted labor. But access to these noncontributory benefits is linked to marital status, and currently there is both a retreat from marriage and a growing race gap in marriage. By the time women born in the 1960s reach old age, 80% of white and Hispanic women, compared to only 50% of black women, will be eligible to receive benefits based on marriage, widowhood, and divorce (Harrington Meyer, Wolf, & Himes, 2006). This means that older black women, who already have fewer economic resources and higher poverty rates, may be especially vulnerable in old age in future cohorts.

The United States has not seriously entertained policy changes that would help families juggle paid and unpaid work, such as care credits or a generous minimum benefit (Harrington Meyer & Herd, 2007; Social Security Administration, 2009). Nor has it acknowledged the growing legions of cohabitating couples, whether gay or straight. Attention to these adjustments would make Social Security more responsive to changing American families by broadening the program's capacity to shore up economic security in old age and by reducing inequalities linked to gender, race, class, and marital status.

Fiscal Considerations

Social Security benefits are funded through a regressive income tax system. In 2009, workers paid a flat tax of 6.2% on earnings up to the Social Security tax cap of $106,800 (Social Security Administration, 2009). Earnings above the ceiling are not subject to Social Security taxes, thus lower income earners contribute a higher proportion of their total earnings to Social Security than higher income earners. Because of race differences in annual family income, a higher percentage of blacks and Hispanics pay the tax on all of their income. In 2006, 27% of white and 27% of Asian, compare to 13% of black and 11% of Hispanic families had income above $100,000 that was, therefore, untaxed (U.S. Census Bureau, 2008a).

Social Security faces a fiscal shortfall in the next few decades. It is a pay-as-you-go system in which workers pay in through the FICA tax and the money is paid out to older beneficiaries. Aware that cohorts come in different sizes, and that aging Baby Boomers were going to draw out a great deal of benefits, the Social Security Administration purposely began accumulating a trust fund surplus decades ago. That surplus is now over $2.5 trillion and expected to be over $3.5 trillion by 2016 (Ruffing & Van de Water, 2009; Social Security Administration, 2009). As more Baby Boomers make claims, the surplus will begin to dwindle. In 2017, the predicted ratio of workers to those collecting Social Security benefits will be 2.7 to 1, down from 3.3 to 1 in 2007 (Board of Trustees, 2009). By 2037, it is estimated that the surplus will be gone and the amount coming in from workers each month will cover only 75% of the payouts. This shortfall can be readily addressed by raising the FICA tax 1%, raising the cap on taxable earnings to at least $140,000 and then indexing it to inflation, or broadening the eligibility base to include the 30% of state and local government employees who are currently not participating in Social

Security (American Association of Retired Persons, 2005; Harrington Meyer & Herd, 2007; Social Security Administration, 2009). The funds in the surplus have been borrowed by the U.S. government for expenditures unrelated to Social Security and those loans will need to be repaid with interest to the Social Security trust funds.

Concerns about the fiscal shortfall, coupled with the recognition that life expectancy has risen dramatically since the inception of the program, have led policymakers to implement changes aimed at encouraging people to delay taking benefits. Beginning in 2003, the age of eligibility for full retirement benefits has been gradually increasing from age 65 to age 67, where it will be in 2027. The age for early retirement remains age 62, but the penalty for taking early benefits, which most men and nearly all women take, has increased from 20% to 30% (Social Security Administration, 2009). Hardest hit are those who are unable to continue working due to poor health or unemployment. Women and blacks and Hispanics are more likely to be affected by both (Moon & Herd, 2002). Thus, many people, particularly those in jobs that are not physically demanding, are able to continue working until age 67, but those that are not able to do so find that their families have to make do with fewer economic resources.

Another policy that encourages people to delay taking Social Security benefits is that the Social Security earnings test penalizes wages among early retirees. Originally, the policy required retirees to be fully out of the labor force, and beneficiaries could not earn more than $15 a month without losing their entire benefit (Harrington Meyer & Herd, 2007). By 1994, the earnings test had been relaxed and those ages 65 to 69 could earn up to $11,000 a year, after which they forfeited $1 in benefits for every $3 earned. Those between 62 and 65 could earn up to $8,000 a year, after which they forfeited $1 in benefits for every $2 earned. Aware that many older persons need or want to continue working, policymakers have relaxed the earnings test further. Currently, there is no earnings test for those ages 65 and older, but those ages 62 to 65 lose $1 in benefits for every $2 in earnings after earning $14,000 for the year (Social Security Administration, 2009). The penalty on wages for early retirees tends to affect women more as they tend to take their Social Security benefits earlier than men, often timing their benefits to coincide with their slightly older husbands.

In its first half century, Social Security was expanded numerous times: Benefits were extended to wives and widows, formulas were made gender neutral, and strict earnings tests were relaxed. Supporters of the program have called for additional expansions that would help families juggle work and children and acknowledge the presence of unmarried couples (see Harrington Meyer & Herd, 2007). One solution would be a new minimum benefit. The United States had a minimum benefit previously, but it was terminated in the early 1980s. Today, Social Security has a special minimum benefit, but few qualify and the benefits are meager. Some policy analysts favor a plan that functions like the Earned Income Tax Credit (EITC), so that each year when older people with lower incomes file their tax returns, they receive additional Social Security benefits. Others prefer a plan in which the minimum benefit slides up with the number of years of contributing to the system, and in the European tradition, in which a care credit offsets time out of the labor market (Favrerault & Steurle, 2007). The simplest plan provides a minimum benefit to all who are eligible for Social Security (Harrington Meyer & Herd, 2007). If that minimum was set near the poverty line, it could eliminate poverty among older people. It would also reduce the need for spouse benefits or SSI, which would help pay for the benefit expansions. But critics have argued that with the aging of the Baby Boomers, the country can no longer afford such universal and redistributive polices and that the time has come to shift greater amounts of risk and responsibility away from the welfare state and markets and to older people and their families (Friedman, 2002; Yergin & Stanislaw, 1998).

SUPPLEMENTAL SECURITY INCOME

Supplemental Security Income (SSI) has provided monthly cash benefits to people who are age 65 and older, blind, and disabled poor people since it was created in 1972. Women live longer than men and are more likely to be poor, thus nearly two-thirds of older SSI recipients are women (Social Security Administration, 2009). SSI benefits have been indexed to cost of living increases since the implementation of the program and have risen slowly each year. These benefits do not raise many older people above the poverty line, however, because maximum federal benefits are equal to about 77% of the federal poverty line for single beneficiaries and 87% of the federal poverty line for older couples (Social Security Administration, 2009). Benefits for those who are not living independently, such as an older woman living with her adult daughter, are reduced by one-third under the assumption that other household members will provide in-kind benefits and that two can live almost as cheaply as one.

Like most poverty-based programs, SSI is underused. Only about one-third of poor older people, and only one-half of those who are SSI eligible, actually receive benefits. SSI use among those age 65 and older has dropped from 10% in 1975 to an all-time low of 3% in 2006 (Social Security Administration, 2009). Some of the decline is due to expansion of Social Security and the decrease in old age poverty over this period of time. But some of the decline is due to features of the SSI program itself (Harrington Meyer & Herd, 2007). Some older people who are eligible for SSI do not apply because they are unaware of the benefits, overwhelmed by the cumbersome eligibility forms, or discouraged by earnings and asset tests that have not been updated in decades. Unlike Social Security, which has been easing the earnings test for older people, SSI has maintained a strict earnings test that considers all earned and unearned income in calculating benefits. Under federal guidelines, the first $65 in earned income, along with an additional $20, is disregarded each month. Any additional earned income, beyond the first $65, decreases benefits by $1 for every $2 earned. Unearned income decreases benefits by $1 for every $1 received. Unearned income includes Social Security and gifts or payments from family and friends. Thus, a grandmother who is being paid to babysit her own grandchildren is likely to have her benefits reduced by $1 for every $1 she receives for her work. Assets, excluding a house, car, and burial funds under certain conditions, must be below $2,000 for individuals and $3,000 for couples. SSI's modest income disregards have been in place since 1981; the asset maximums mentioned above have been in place since 1989 (Social Security Administration, 2009). Neither has been linked to cost of living and neither can be raised except by congressional legislation. When poverty-based programs are left to languish in this way, older people who rely on these programs face even more difficult financial circumstances and have little choice but to turn to their families for additional assistance.

Though SSI is designed to be an income security program, recent research suggests that because the link between socioeconomic factors and health is so strong, SSI may actually help to reduce health inequality among older people. Herd, Schoeni, and House (2008) reported that an increase in monthly SSI benefits helped to reduce disability, particularly mobility limitations, significantly. Reducing mobility limitations among older people would assist in maximizing their independence and minimizing the caregiving burden on their family members. Thus, the underuse of SSI has far-reaching implications for the independence of older relatives and the care work performed by family members.

PRIVATE PENSIONS

Private pensions are the third largest income stream for older people, accounting for 18% of all old age income (He, Sangupta, Velkoff, & Debaros, 2005). Most Americans think of these pensions as an employer expense, but in fact, they are funded in part by forgone taxes that total more than $100 billion a year. Historically, the receipt of a private pension often reduced the likelihood of poverty for older families, but pensions have become less reliable and pension coverage has shrunk dramatically. Increasingly, the private pension income received by many older individuals and their families ranges from little to none (Selden & Gray, 2006).

The reliability of private pensions has changed dramatically with the shift from defined benefit to defined contribution plans. Historically, most employees received a pension based on a defined benefit plan that increased with hours, salaries, and years of service. Pension coverage changed significantly between 1979 and 2004, when the share of workers covered only by defined benefit plans dropped from 62% to 10% and the share covered only by defined contribution plans rose from 16% to 63% (Employee Benefit Research Institute, 2005). Now most covered workers receive a pension based on the defined contribution system, and the value of the benefit will be determined by subsequent contributions, investment decisions, and a fair amount of luck. Over time, employers are contributing less and less to these plans, making employees even more responsible for their own pension accumulations (Munnell & Sunden, 2004; Shuey & O'Rand, 2006). Defined contribution plans differ markedly from defined benefit plans because they shift the responsibility and risks, and often much of the costs, associated with private pension accumulation from employers to employees and their families. Because they are not as compulsory or as automatic as defined benefit plans, under defined contribution plans employees are more readily able to opt out, reduce their contributions, or withdraw money before retirement to cover education, health expenses, or family obligations. Lower income workers and their families are more likely to do all three and thus to be less economically secure in old age (Munnell & Sunden, 2004; Shuey & O'Rand, 2006).

Access to private pensions, which has long been unequal by gender, race, and income, is becoming more unequal as employers tighten the reins on this employee benefit. Today 70% of workers in the upper one-third of earnings work for an employer who offers a private pension, compared to only 30% of workers in the lowest one-third of earners (Karamcheva & Sanzenbacher, 2010). Take-up rates also vary by earnings bracket. Although defined benefit plans were compulsory and automatic, defined contribution plans are not. Nearly all high earners participate, but only 69% of lower earners did in 2008. Because they are more likely to be in the lower earnings brackets or have disruptions in employment, women, blacks, and Hispanics are both less likely to have pension coverage and, when they are covered, to have significantly smaller pension benefits (Munnell & Sunden, 2004; Shuey & O'Rand, 2006). The overall impact is that private pensions contribute little to the total income for lower earners and their families. In fact, households of individuals age 65 and older in the top one-third of the income distribution receive 31% of their nonearned income from private pensions, whereas households in the bottom one-third receive just 3% (Karamcheva & Sanzenbacher, 2010). Private pensions are an important source of old age income for older people and their families but fewer employees have access to them, and the benefits themselves have become much less secure with the shift to defined contributions.

MEDICARE

Since 1965, Medicare has provided universal health care benefits to people aged 65 and older, and to those who are permanently blind and disabled, and it has effectively increased access to many types of acute health care for older people. Before the program began, just 56% of those ages 65 and older had hospital insurance. By 2007, nearly 97% did (Harrington Meyer & Herd, 2007; Social Security Administration, 2009). Though Medicare provides broad coverage of acute care, other types of health care, most notably long-term care, remain uncovered. Medicare is particularly important for older women; 56% of the beneficiaries are women (Kaiser Family Foundation, 2010). Medicare is expensive both for the U.S. welfare state and for older people and their families. Some recent policy initiatives have shifted costs and responsibilities back to individuals and families.

Medicare has grown increasingly complex since the 1960s. Each of the four components is funded differently and each involves out-of-pocket expenses for older people including premiums, co-payments, deductibles, and amounts over the allowable rate. Medicare Part A, which is mandatory, pays for inpatient hospital stays, skilled nursing care, some home health visits, and hospice care (Kaiser Family Foundation, 2010). It is funded through the 1.45% Hospital Insurance tax paid by employees each month and matched by their employers. Part B, which is voluntary, covers out-patient physician visits and services, some preventative services, and some home health visits. By federal law, 25% of the cost of Part B is funded by beneficiary premiums, set at $96.40 a month in 2009, which are taken from Social Security checks before they are delivered. The remaining 75% of Part B is funded by general revenues. Part C refers to Medicare Advantage, through which beneficiaries forego traditional Medicare and instead enroll in a managed care or HMO program. Part C is funded through premiums and general revenues. Part D is the voluntary prescription drug plan. Beneficiaries pay an additional monthly premium, and the remaining costs are covered by general revenues and some state payments. Part D has come under fire because it requires beneficiaries to select and pay premiums to one private drug plan from a sea of complex and ever-changing private plan options (Hoadley, 2006). Beneficiaries then pay a monthly premium, an annual deductible, a co-payment, and then the full amount of any costs inside what has been dubbed "the donut hole" (Kaiser Family Foundation, 2009a). Out-of-pocket expenses may be as high as $3,600 a year for prescriptions alone for individuals enrolled in Medicare Part D.

Overall Medicare costs began rising dramatically from the moment Medicare was implemented. In 2010, Medicare expenditures are expected to top $504 billion, 15% of the federal budget, or nearly $11,000 per beneficiary

(Kaiser Family Foundation, 2010). Early efforts to control costs led policymakers to implement a prospective payment system aimed at reducing unnecessary medical treatment and thereby lowering costs. This 1984 legislation changed the way Medicare paid for services from a retrospective cost plus profit system to a prepaid, preset amount per person per primary diagnosis. Hospital stays shortened dramatically and the rate at which total costs were rising slowed measurably (Estes & Associates, 2001). But hospitals and clinics consequently shifted unprofitable care out of the hospital and back to families.

More recent efforts to control costs have prompted Congress to rely on the private market. For example, when creating and funding Medicare Part C, policymakers encouraged private, for-profit medical providers to enroll Medicare beneficiaries through managed care options. Legislation passed in 1982, 1997, and 2003 provided subsidies to the private market to lure HMOs and similar provider groups into developing managed care plans that would entice Medicare recipients to forfeit traditional Medicare and sign on to private plans. Now called Medicare Advantage, Medicare Part C covers 18% of all Medicare recipients (Kaiser Family Foundation, 2009a; MedPac, 2007; Social Security Administration, 2009). These efforts, however, have been ineffectual in reducing costs. In 2005, the government was paying an extra $546 per enrollee in private plans compared to those in traditional Medicare. Indeed, every Medicare Advantage plan pays more for every Medicare plan enrollee than the average of fee-for-service costs (Biles, Nicholas, & Guterman, 2006). The Congressional Budget Office estimated that Part C Medicare Advantage would add $14 billion in new Medicare costs over its first 10 years (Commonwealth Fund, 2005). Though policymakers argued that a shift from public to private provision of health insurance for those age 65 and older would reduce costs, it has not worked. Costs have risen even further. That change has, however, shifted millions of U.S. tax funds into the profitable managed care market.

Policymakers have also sought to reduce Medicare expenditures by shifting more and more of the costs onto older beneficiaries and their families. In addition to monthly premiums, Medicare recipients pay deductibles, coinsurance of 20%, any costs above the allowable rate, and uncovered goods and services such as long-term care, preventive care, dental care, vision care, and eyeglasses (Harrington Meyer, 2000; Social Security Administration, 2009). All of these out-of-pocket expenses have risen dramatically and are expected to continue rising at rates much higher than the cost of living. Some estimate that Medicare covers less than 50% of old age health care costs (Social Security Advisory Report, 2008). Four decades into the Medicare program, the costs of health care for older people are, in fact, a greater burden than before the program began both because of soaring health care costs and because Medicare coverage is spotty. Out-of-pocket expenses for older people rose from 15% of annual income in 1965 to 22% in 1998. By 2025, out-of-pocket health care expenses are expected to reach 30% (Moon & Herd, 2002).

Medicare costs have also been cut by shifting long-term care work back to families, particularly since the mid-1990s (Harrington Meyer & Herd, 2007; MedPac, 2008; Social Security Administration, 2009). The overall share of the Medicare budget devoted to home health care dropped from 8% in 1994 to just 4% in 2010 (Kaiser Family Foundation, 2010). There are now fewer licensed providers, fewer persons receiving home health care, fewer visits provided per person, and fewer types of care covered (Harrington Meyer & Herd, 2007; MedPac, 2008). Moreover, Medicare provides coverage of the first 100 days of nursing home care, but nursing home residents must meet several eligibility criteria and pay sizable deductibles, co-payments, and uncovered costs during those 100 days (Social Security Administration, 2009). Older people may purchase private long-term care insurance, but only about 10% do because of high premiums, denial of applicants with common conditions, and coverage exclusions (see Harrington Meyer & Herd, 2007). As a result of Medicare's spotty coverage of long-term care, many frail older people rely heavily on their families, more often the female members of their families, or do without needed care (Estes & Associates, 2001; Moon & Herd, 2002).

Care Work

Even though families have changed considerably in recent decades, scholars estimate that families continue to provide about 80% of all long-term care to their frail older relatives (Brody, 2004). Many family care providers are on call seven days a week for several hours a day (National Alliance for Caregiving & AARP, 2004; Navaie-Waliser, Spriggs, & Feldman, 2002). In addition to helping with medical care, care work includes cleaning, helping with finances, running errands, cooking, and assisting with eating, bathing, dressing, and mobility. The long-standing practice of women providing most of the care work has diminished somewhat, but women continue to perform almost twice as much as men. Seventy percent of spousal care workers are wives and 60% to 80% of children who care for their older parents are daughters (Kaiser Family Foundation, 2009b; National Alliance for Caregiving & AARP, 2004, 2009). Black and Hispanic women report higher levels of care work than do whites. Given that they have lower incomes and worse health, these additional duties add up to an even greater burden than those with more resources (National Alliance for Caregiving & AARP, 2009; Wolf, Freedman, & Soldo, 1997).

Some indicators show that family care work has intensified in recent years (Estes & Associates, 2001). Often, families, mainly wives and daughters, are expected to perform highly technical work including tubal feedings, dressing changes, chemotherapy and phototherapy administration, apnea monitoring, and oxygen tent management. Such work is particularly stressful for family members who have had little medical training. Estes (1989) calculated that in the first five years of the prospective payment system, more than 21 million days of care work had been transferred from hospitals to families. Stone (2000) estimated that there are 40 unpaid informal care workers for every paid formal care worker. The total value of annual care work is estimated to be over $50 billion (Holtz-Eakin, 2005; National Alliance for Caregiving & AARP, 2004).

Most care workers report that the work is rewarding, but many also report that they experience substantial burden and stress. Some care workers report high rates of sleeplessness, exhaustion, inadequate exercise, chronic conditions, anxiety, loneliness, family tension, and drug misuse (Brody, 2004; National Alliance for Caregiving & AARP, 2009; Pavalko & Woodbury, 2000; Stone, 2000). Care workers are at a significant risk for depression, with 50% of care workers reporting depressive symptoms (Clark & Diamond, 2010). Some studies suggest that long-term provision of care tends to weaken the immune systems, increase psychological distress, and accelerate aging (Epel et al., 2004; Pavalko & Woodbury, 2000). Care workers take on emotional and physical labor in addition to their own daily responsibilities, placing them in stressful situations where they require increased social, physical, and economic supports that they often do not receive.

Efforts to relieve the social, emotional, and economic burdens on care workers have been few and modest in their effectiveness. Some workers, especially women, add unpaid care work to their paid responsibilities, whereas others tend to reduce or eliminate paid work. Pavalko and Henderson (2006) found that women whose jobs provide flexible hours, unpaid family leave, and paid sick leave are likely to remain employed, improving financial security for their own old age. For care workers who would like to take time off from work to provide assistance to frail older relatives, the Family Leave Act provides up to 12 weeks of unpaid leave. But the leave is only mandated by law for large companies. In all, the act only covers about 60% of private sector workers and just under 50% are both covered and eligible (Waldfogel, 2001). Given that the leave is unpaid and covers only 12 weeks, taking it is not often a meaningful option for most long-term care workers. One policy proposal that would ease the financial and social burdens on women would be to expand Medicare to provide comprehensive coverage of long-term care. This would entail providing national, universal, compulsory coverage of long-term care in the community and in nursing homes (Harrington Meyer & Herd, 2007; Kaiser Family Foundation, 2009c). Such a plan would be particularly helpful to lower income families who often do not have sufficient resources to handle their own health care needs, let alone assist with the needs of their frail older relatives. (See Pruchno & Gitlin, chapter 21 in this volume, for a broad discussion of family caregiving in later life.)

RETIREE, MEDIGAP, AND LONG-TERM CARE INSURANCE

Because Medicare covers only about one-half of older people's health care expenses, many have supplemental forms of insurance designed to fill in some of the gaps. Historically, many retirees stayed on employment-based retiree insurance, using Medicare as a supplemental form of insurance. But retiree reliance on employment-based health insurance has dropped significantly in recent years. Even among large employers, the proportion offering retiree health benefits has dropped from 66% in 1988 to just 29% in 2009 (Kaiser Family Foundation, 2010). White, male, full-time, and high-paid workers are more likely than others to accrue these retiree health benefits, but even for those groups, coverage is on the decline. In 2006, only 37% of men and 33% of women ages 65 and older had an employer sponsored plan (Kaiser Family Foundation, 2009a). Moreover, employers who still offer retiree coverage are pushing more of the costs onto retirees by tightening eligibility requirements, capping benefits, and increasing cost-sharing (Employee Benefit Research Institute, 2005).

About 17% of older persons on Medicare pay private premiums for Medigap policies that cover costs that Medicare does not, notably Medicare premiums, co-pays, deductibles, and exclusions such as long-term care, eye exams, and hearing aids (Kaiser Family Foundation, 2010). Access to these private Medigap policies has become increasingly difficult because premiums have risen significantly (Moon & Herd, 2002). Moreover, navigating the market can be difficult because many private Medigap insurers deny, duplicate, or sever coverage (Moon & Herd, 2002). Those with fewer resources and poorer health, mainly older women, blacks, and Hispanics, are less likely to be able to obtain and retain private insurance, therefore they are more likely to have to rely on family members for assistance (Harrington Meyer & Herd, 2007).

Medicare coverage specifically excludes almost all long-term care, even though that is the type of care older people need most. One option for older people and their families is to purchase a private long-term care insurance plan by paying a monthly premium. Though about 40% of elders could reasonably afford a policy, only about 7% in fact have one (Commonwealth Fund, 2005; Holz-Eakin, 2005; Moon & Herd, 2002). The problems in the long-term care insurance market are numerous. Despite considerable government regulation, prices for policies are expensive and volatile, the market has experienced mismanagement and fraudulent behavior, and individuals with preexisting conditions are often denied policies or saddled with very high premiums (Harrington Meyer & Herd, 2007; Kaiser Family Foundation, 2009c).

MEDICAID

Since 1965, Medicaid has provided free and comprehensive coverage of health care for many poor and disabled individuals, including old ones. Thus, Medicaid is the primary source of long-term care funding for those aged 65 and older. Medicaid covers 43% of the nursing home bill (Kaiser Family Foundation, 2009b). Because they live longer, and have fewer resources and greater long-term care needs, over 70% of older Medicaid beneficiaries are women (Kaiser Family Foundation, 2009b; Social Security Administration, 2009). Blacks and Hispanics are also much more likely than whites to rely on Medicaid because they are more likely to have lower incomes and to need long-term care.

The proportion of older people relying on Medicaid has decreased from 16% in 1970 to 13% in 2006. Reliance on Medicaid is down because poverty among those age 65 and older is now below 10% and because Medicaid eligibility criteria are strict. The federal income maximum is set below 78% of the federal poverty line and the federal asset maximum has been frozen for decades at just $2,000 per individual and $3,000 per couple (Commonwealth Fund, 2005; Kaiser Family Foundation, 2009b; Social Security Administration, 2009). States can, and some do, make the income and asset limits more generous. Moreover, some states have set much higher income limits for those receiving Medicaid in nursing homes. Nonetheless, participation is low because the process of applying is arduous and stigmatizing, and the rules of participation are restrictive. In fact only one-third of poor older people, and only one-half of those who are Medicaid eligible, actually receive Medicaid (Kaiser Family Foundation, 2009b; Moon & Herd, 2002).

The majority of older Medicaid recipients is also covered by Medicare. In fact, among black and Hispanic Medicare beneficiaries, 30% and 25% respectively also rely on Medicaid (Kaiser Family Foundation, 2009b). For these dual-eligible beneficiaries, 70% of whom are women, Medicaid covers costs Medicare does not, including the Medicare Part B premiums, nursing home care, and all Medicare co-pays and deductibles (Harrington Meyer, 2000; Kaiser Family Foundation, 2009b; Social Security Administration, 2009). Because coverage is comprehensive for these dual enrollees and because health care providers are generally prohibited from charging costs above the allowable rates to Medicaid recipients, full Medicaid coverage with Medicare coverage reduces out-of-pocket expenses from 20% to about 5% of annual income, though out-of-pocket expenses are expected to continue rising (Kaiser Family Foundation, 2009b; Ku & Broaddhus, 2005). A subset of dual Medicare and Medicaid enrollees receive limited coverage under new rules that relax eligibility guidelines. For those in these special programs, out-of-pocket costs are reduced to 13% of total annual incomes (Kaiser Family Foundation, 2003). Unfortunately, the application procedures are complex and the rules restrictive, thus only a fraction of those who qualify under the relaxed guidelines actually participate (MedPac, 2008; Moon & Herd, 2002).

For those older Americans who rely on Medicaid for their health care, access to that care can be problematic. Medicaid reimbursement rates to providers are well below market rates, leading many doctors, clinics, labs, hospitals, and nursing homes to refuse to treat, or cap the number of, Medicaid patients (Commonwealth Fund, 2005; Harrington Meyer, 2000; MedPac, 2008). Thus, among primary care physicians in the United States in 2002, 85% were accepting new private payers, 83% were accepting new Medicare recipients, and only 66% were accepting new Medicaid patients (MedPac, 2008). In our interviews with nursing home administrators in Illinois, one told us that the reimbursement rates for Medicaid were so low that he would rather leave the nursing home bed empty than fill it with a Medicaid patient (Harrington Meyer & Kesterke-Storbakken, 2000). Another told us that as soon as she realized that the patient will be on Medicaid, she would conclude the application interview and file the application in her circular file (her trash can). Many providers discriminate on the basis of payer source and, because they are more likely to be on Medicaid, older women, blacks and Hispanics, and unmarried persons are more likely to face denial of or delays in treatment or admission.

Fiscal Considerations for Poverty-Based Eligibility

Reliance on Medicaid for any amount of health care can present financial hardships for the families of older recipients after their deaths. Because they are prompted to do so by the 1993 Omnibus Budget Reconciliation Act, nearly all states pursue estate recovery (Harrington Meyer & Herd, 2007). When applying for Medicaid coverage of nursing home care, applicants are permitted to except their home and car if they can demonstrate that they may be able to return to them. The estate recovery provision requires states to recover Medicaid expenses for nursing home, community-based, and hospital care for all older recipients (Centers for Medicare and Medicaid Services, 2005a, b). The recovery is made from Medicaid patient estates after they die, before the remainder is distributed to those cited in the will (Wood & Sabatino, 1996). Actual recovery efforts are uneven as states are more likely to pursue estate recovery when it appears that costs regained would outweigh the legal and administrative costs of the recovery itself. Supporters argue that estate recovery helps replenish the coffers for this financially strapped program whereas opponents argue that estate recovery discourages older people from seeking needed medical care and undermines the very meaning of the term *health insurance* (Schwartz & Sabatino, 1994). Katz Olson (2003) argued that estate recovery converts a public benefit into a loan that must be paid back by family members who forego items they would have received via the will. Family members who lived with the older person, many of whom may have provided intensive care work, may be impoverished and forced from their homes (Katz Olson, 2003). In any case, estate recovery does not generate large sums of money. In 2004, only eight states recovered enough money to offset 2% or more of state Medicaid nursing home expenditures; for the country as a whole, estate recovery collected an amount equal to 0.8% of Medicaid nursing home spending (Department of Health and Human Services, 2005).

For Medicaid recipients who live in nursing homes, relying on Medicaid can present difficult financial hardships. Unlike Medicaid recipients in the community, who keep their income and receive free health care through Medicaid, Medicaid recipients in nursing homes become wards of the state. In other words, all of their Social Security and any private monies go toward paying their nursing home costs; Medicaid is merely payer of last resort. Medicaid recipients in nursing homes are permitted to keep only a small monthly personal needs allowance, which ranges from $30 to $70 depending on the state, for basic necessities not covered by Medicaid, including clothing, haircuts, transportation, phone calls, cable, stamps, dentures, glasses, orthopedic shoes and devices, and dental work (Harrington Meyer & Kesterke-Storbakken, 2000). Nursing home Medicaid recipients report that it is very difficult even to send a wedding card to a granddaughter or replace their dentures, never mind buying a newspaper or seeing a movie, on a measly $1 a day. A few states have indexed the personal needs allowance to cost of living increases, but the federal monthly rate of $30 has remained steady for nearly two decades.

As with all welfare state programs, concerns over rising costs have caused policymakers to take several cost-cutting steps. Medicaid is a joint federal and state program in which both parties share the costs. Medicaid covers about 6 million older people paying over $11,000 per beneficiary per year (Kaiser Family Foundation, 2009b). In an effort to prevent Medicaid from completely usurping state budgets, many states have raised Medicaid co-payments for prescription drug coverage and some services. Other states have reduced the scope of coverage, eliminating dental and vision care, or limiting the number of prescriptions, physician visits, or pieces of medical equipment per year (Ku & Broaddus, 2005). The impact is higher out-of-pocket expenditures for older people and their families. Between 1997 and 2002, the average annual growth rate for out-of-pocket expenditures for poor Medicaid recipients was 9.4%, though their incomes rose just 4.6% per year in that time. Thus, out-of-pocket expenses rose at twice the rate of incomes; poor adults on Medicaid now spend 2.4% of annual income on out-of-pocket medical expenses (Ku & Broaddus, 2005). This increase in out-of-pocket expenses places more of a burden on the families of older people many of whom have few resources to spare.

DISCUSSION

Unlike other Western democracies, the United States restricts social insurance programs to older and permanently disabled persons. Social Security and Medicare boast near-universal participation rates and are widely praised for improving the social and economic status of older people. Yet these programs provide incomplete coverage. For those with tenuous relationships to the labor market, particularly women juggling work and family responsibilities, and for those with substantial long-term care needs, benefits are far from comprehensive. Those with lower incomes are the most vulnerable, and thus women, blacks, and Hispanics are particularly vulnerable under current guidelines, as they often fit into the category of having lower income and fewer opportunities.

Two poverty-based programs, SSI and Medicaid, provide safety nets of sorts. The poorest of the poor may be eligible for benefits through SSI but those benefits only bring their incomes up to about 77% of the federal poverty line, and the assets and earnings tests have not been updated in decades. Poor older adults may also be eligible for Medicaid; however, those who are eligible will still need to wrestle with gaps in coverage, discrimination by providers, and the stigma that accompanies reliance on welfare. Because of restrictive eligibility guidelines and stigmatized participation, many who are poor and eligible do not receive benefits through these poverty-based programs.

Older people and their families often rely on employment-based alternatives, but find that many, such as private pensions and retiree health insurance, are dissipating quickly. Yet another option is for older people to rely upon private market alternatives, such as Medicare Advantage, Medigap, prescription drug insurance, and long-term care insurance, but many of these programs are becoming too costly and too difficult to navigate without significant assistance. The United States has an increasingly costly and increasingly complex array of universal, poverty-based, private market, and employer-based programs, and yet many older people and their families remain vulnerable to economic and health insecurities. The fragmented old age welfare state places much of the burden for filling in the gaps on family members, often compromising their preparations for their own old age security. A reemphasis on universal old age programs that spread the risk across, rather than concentrating them amongst, families holds the greatest hope for relieving inequality linked to gender, race, class, and marital status in old age.

REFERENCES

Abramovitz, M. (1988). *Regulating the lives of women: Social welfare policy from colonial times to the present.* Boston, MA: South End Press.

American Association of Retired Persons. (2005). *Public attitudes toward Social Security and private accounts.* Washington, DC: AARP Knowledge Movement.

Becker, G. S. (2005, February 15). A political case for Social Security reform. *Wall Street Journal*, p. A18.

Biles, B., Nicholas, L.H., & Guterman, S. (2006). Medicare beneficiary out-of-pocket costs: Are Medicare Advantage plans a better deal? *Issue Brief 927.* New York: The Commonwealth Fund.

Board of Trustees. (2009). *Annual report of the board of trustees of the federal old age and survivors insurance and federal disability insurance trust funds.* Retrieved from http://www.ssa.gov/OACT/TR/2009/trTOC.html

Brody, E. M. (2004). *Women in the middle: Their parent care years* (2nd ed.). New York: Springer Publishing.

Centers for Medicare and Medicaid Services. (2005a). *Your Medicare coverage.* Retrieved from http://www.medicare.gov/Coverage/Home.asp

Centers for Medicare and Medicaid Services. (2005b). *Medicare aged and disabled enrollees by type of coverage all areas, as of July 1, 1966–2003.* Retrieved from http://www.cms.hhs.gov/statistics/enrollment/natltrends/hi_smi.asp

Clark, M. C., & Diamond, P. (2010). Depression in family caregivers of elders: A theoretical model of caregiver burden, sociotropy, and autonomy. *Research in Nursing and Health, 33*, 20–34.

Commonwealth Fund. (2005). *The long-term budget outlook.* Washington, DC: Congressional Budget Office.

Department of Health and Human Services (DHHS). (2005). *Medicaid estate recovery collections (Policy Brief #6).* Washington, DC: DHHS. Retrieved from http://aspe.hhs.gov/daltcp/reports/estreccol.pdfEmployee Benefit Research Institute. (2005). *EBRI databook on employee benefits, Chapter 4: Table 1. Participation in employee benefit programs.* Retrieved from http://www.ebri.org/publications/books/index.cfm?fa=databook

Employee Benefit Research Institute. (2009). *Sources of health insurance and characteristics of the uninsured (Issue Brief No. 334).* Retrieved from http://www.ebri.org/publications/ib/index.cfm?fa=ibDisp&content_id=4366

Engelhardt, G. V., & Gruber, J. (2004). *Social Security and the evolution of elderly poverty* (NBER Working Paper No. 10466). Cambridge, MA: National Bureau of Economic Research.

Epel, E. S., Blackburn, E. H., Lin, J,. Dhabhar, F. S., Adler, N. E., Morrow, J. D., & Cawthon, R. M. (2004). Accelerated telomere shortening in response to life stress. *Proceedings from the National Academy of Sciences of the United States of America, 101*, 17312–17315.

Estes, C. (1989). Aging, health and social policy. Crisis and crossroads. *Journal of Aging and Social Policy, 1*, 17–32.

Estes, C., & Associates. (2001). *Social policy and aging: A critical perspective.* Thousand Oaks, CA: Sage Publications.

Favrerault, M., & Steurle, E. (2007). *Social Security and spouse and survivor benefits for the modern family.* Retrieved from http://www.urban.org/UploadedPDF/311436_Social_Security.pdf

Friedman, M. (2002). *Capitalism and freedom* (40th Anniversary Ed.). Chicago: University of Chicago Press.

Gilbert, N. (2002). *Transformation of the welfare state: The silent surrender of public responsibility.* New York: Oxford University Press.

Hacker, J.S. (2002). *The divided welfare state: The battle over public and private social benefits in the United States.* New York: Cambridge University Press.

Harrington Meyer, M. (Ed.). (2000). *Care work: Gender, labor, and the welfare state.* New York: Routledge Press.

Harrington Meyer, M., & Herd, P. (2007). *Market friendly or family friendly? The state and gender inequality in old age.* New York: Russell Sage.

Harrington Meyer, M., & Kesterke-Storbakken, M. (2000). Shifting the burden back to families? How Medicaid cost-containment reshapes access to long term care in the US. In Harrington Meyer (Ed.), *Care work: Gender, labor and the welfare state* (pp. 217–228). New York: Routledge Press.

Harrington Meyer, M., & Pavalko, E. (1996). Family, work, and access to health insurance among mature women. *Journal of Health and Social Behavior, 37,* 311–325.

Harrington Meyer, M., Wolf, D., & Himes, C. (2006). Declining eligibility for Social Security spouse and widow benefits in the United States? *Research on Aging, 28,* 240–260.

He, W., Sangupta, M., Velkoff, V. A., & Debaros, K. A. (2005). 65+ in the United States. *Current Population Reports, Special Studies Series* 23 (209). Washington, DC: U.S. Census Bureau.

Herd, P., Schoeni, R. F., & House, J. (2008). Upstream solutions: Does the supplemental security income program reduce disability in the elderly? *The Milbank Quarterly, 86,* 5–45.

Hoadley, J. (2006). Medicare's new adventure: The Part D drug benefit. 911. New York: The Commonwealth Fund. Retrieved from http://www.cmwf.org/publications/publications_show.htm?doc_id=362249

Holtz-Eakin, D. (2005). The cost and financing of long-term care services. *Proceedings from the 2005 Subcommittee on Health Committee on Ways and Means U.S. House of Representatives.* Washington, DC: Congressional Budget Office.

Kaiser Family Foundation. (2009a). *Medicare's role for women fact sheet.* Washington, DC: Kaiser Family Foundation. Retrieved from http://www.kff.org/womenshealth/upload/7913.pdf

Kaiser Family Foundation. (2009b). *Medicaid and long-term care services and supports fact sheet.* Retrieved from http://www.kff.org/medicaid/upload/2186_06.pdf

Kaiser Family Foundation. (2009c). *Closing the long-term care funding gap: The challenge of private long-term care insurance.* Retrieved from http://www.kff.org/insurance/upload/Closing-the-Long-Term-Care-Funding-Gap-The-Challenge-of-Private-Long-Term-Care-Insurance-Report.pdf

Kaiser Family Foundation. (2010). *Medicare at a glance fact sheet.* Retrieved from http://www.kff.org/medicare/uploa d/1066–12.pdf

Karamcheva, N., & Sanzenbacher, G. (2010). *Is pension inequality growing? (Research Brief 10–1)*. Boston: Center for Retirement Research at Boston College. Retrieved from http://crr.bc.edu/images/stories/Briefs/ib_10-1.pdf

Katz Olson, L. (2003). *The not-so-golden years: Caregiving, the frail elderly, and the long-term care establishment*. Lanham, MD: Rowman & Littlefield.

Korpi, W. (2000). *Faces of inequality: Gender, class and patterns of inequalities in different types of welfare states*. Luxembourg Income Study Working Paper No. 224. Syracuse, NY: Syracuse University.

Korpi, W., & Palme, J. (1998). The paradox of redistribution and strategies of equality: Welfare state institutions, inequality, and poverty in the western countries. *American Sociological Review, 63*, 661–687.

Ku, L., & Broaddus, M. (2005). *Out-of-pocket medical expenses for Medicaid beneficiaries are substantial and growing*. Washington, DC: Center on Budget and Policy Priorities.

Levine, P. B., Mitchell, O. S., & Phillips, J.W.R. (2000). Benefit of one's own: Older women's entitlement to Social Security retirement. *Social Security Bulletin, 63*(2), 47–53.

MedPac. (2007). The Medicare Advantage Program and MedPac recommendations. *Proceedings from 2007 testimony before the Committee on Finance, U.S. Senate.* Washington, DC: Medicare Payment Advisory Committee.

MedPac. (2008). *A data book: Health care spending and the Medicare Program*. Washington, DC: Medicare Payment Advisory Commission.

Moon, M., & Herd, P. (2002). *A place at the table: Women's needs and Medicare reform*. New York: The Century Foundation.

Munnell, A. H., & Sundén, A. (2004). *Coming up short: The challenge of 401(k) plans*. Washington: Brookings Institution Press.

National Alliance for Caregiving & AARP. (2004). *Caregiving in the US*. Washington, DC: Author.

National Alliance for Caregiving & AARP. (2009). *Caregiving in the US 2009*. Washington, DC: Author.

Navaie-Waliser, M., Spriggs, A., & Feldman, P. H. (2002). Informal caregiving—Differential experiences by gender. *Medical Care, 40*, 1249–1259.

Pavalko, E. K., & Henderson, K. (2006). Combining care work and paid work: Do workplace policies make a difference? *Research on Aging, 28*, 359–374.

Pavalko, E.K., & Woodbury, S. (2000). Social roles as process: Caregiving careers and women's health. *Journal of Health and Social Behavior, 41*, 91–105.

Public Agenda. (2005). Medicare: Results of survey question re. federal budget. *Public Agenda.org Issue Guides*. New York: Public Agenda.

Quadagno, J.S. (1984). Welfare capitalism and the Social Security Act of 1935. *American Sociological Review, 49*, 632–647.

Quadagno, J.S. (2005). *One nation, uninsured: Why the U.S. has no national health insurance*. New York: Oxford University Press.

Ruffing, K., & Van de Water, P. N. (2009). *What the 2009 Trustees' Report shows about Social Security*. Washington, DC: Center on Budget and Policy Priorities. Retrieved from http://www.cbpp.org/files/5-18-09socsec.pdf

Schwartz, R. A., & Sabatino, C. P. (1994). *Medicaid estate recovery under OBRA '93: Picking the bones of the poor?* Washington, DC: American Bar Association, Commission on Legal Problems of the Elderly.

Selden, T., & Gray, B. (2006). Tax subsidies for employment based health insurance: Estimates for 2006. *Health Affairs, 25,* 1568–1579.

Shuey, K. M., & O'Rand, A. M. (2006). Changing demographics and new pension risks. *Research on Aging, 28,* 317–340.

Social Security Administration. (2004). Annual statistical supplement 2003. *Social Security Bulletin.* Washington, DC: Department of Health and Human Services.

Social Security Administration. (2009). Annual statistical supplement 2008. *Social Security Bulletin.* Washington, DC: Department of Health and Human Services.

Social Security Advisory Report. (2008). Annual Report. Washington DC: Social Security Advisory Board. http://www.ssab.gov/documents/AR_2008.pdf

Stone, R. I. (2000). *Long-term care for the elderly with disabilities: Current policy, emerging trends, and implications for the twenty-first century.* Washington, DC: Milbank Memorial Fund.

Torres-Gil, F., Greenstein, R., & Kamin, D. (2005). *Hispanics' large stake in the Social Security debate.* Washington, DC: Center on Budget and Policy Priorities.

U.S. Census Bureau. (2008a). *Current population reports, P60–235. Table 680. Money income of families—Percent distribution by income level in constant (2007) dollars: 1980 to 2007.* Retrieved from http://www.census.gov/prod/2008pubs/p60–235.pdf and http://www.census.gov/hhes/www/income

U.S. Census Bureau. (2008b). *Table MS-1. Marital status of the population 15 years old and over, by sex and race: 1950 to present* and *Table FM-1. Families by presence of own children under 18: 1950 to present.* Retrieved from http://www.census.gov/population/www/socdemo/hh-fam.html#ht

Waldfogel, J. (2001). Family and medical leave: Evidence from the 2000 surveys. *Monthly Labor Review, 124*(9), 17–23.

Wolf, D. A., Freedman, V., & Soldo, B. J. (1997). Division of family labor: Care for elderly parents. *Journals of Gerontology: Psychological and Social Sciences, 52B* (Special Issue), 102–109.

Wood, E. F., & Sabatino, C. P. (1996). Medicaid estate recovery and the poor: Restitution or retribution? *Generations, 20*(3), 84–87.

Wu, K. B. (2005). *African Americans age 65 and older: Their sources of income.* (Fact Sheet 100). Washington, DC: AARP Public Policy Institute.

Yergin, D., & Stanislaw, J. (1998). *The commanding heights: The battle between government and the marketplace that is remaking the modern world.* New York: Simon & Schuster.

16

Legal Issues in Aging Families

Marshall B. Kapp

With its pervasive emphasis on personal rights and obligations, American law generally treats citizens as isolated, atomistic individuals fending independently for themselves. According to traditional legal theory, people exist in an arms-length world of strangers, each person making and defending all of his or her own life choices in solitude. In terms of how people live, though, the reality may be quite different. Most people—including a substantial percentage of older persons—live their lives primarily embedded within various human relationships, among which the family is paramount for most of us.

Families as entities, separate and apart from the various rights and duties formally or informally assigned to their particular individual members, have legal significance (Foy, 2006). The specific legal issues arising within the family context are shaped by a multitude of changeable factors, including the aging of the family unit and its members. As Wassel and Cutler (2007) informed us, "Improvement in life expectancy has added more than years to life; it has added years to a person's responsibilities in a family role as son, daughter, (daughter-in-law, son-in-law), [sibling], parent, spouse, and grandparent" (p. 69). Moreover, they instructed, "To fully appreciate the intricacies of family aging, professionals and practitioners must be aware of how gerontological and demographic dynamics interact to reshape the financial and legal responsibilities of family members, as both (middle aged) children and (elderly) parents are living many more years than previously experienced" (p. 69).

The objective of this chapter is to assist those readers involved in planning, providing, monitoring, and studying services for older Americans to better deal with some of the legal intricacies of family aging. Following this brief introduction, I delve into a selective identification and analysis of roles and responsibilities involving the interaction of older persons and their families. In this endeavor, I concentrate mainly on the following contexts: families assisting older individuals to exercise their legal rights; families acting as surrogate decision makers for decisionally incapacitated older persons; families protecting and advocating for their older members; and families *qua* recipients of services from their aging relatives. The chapter concludes with some thoughts regarding directions for future research in this arena, focusing on the wisdom of examining relevant laws affecting older persons under the analytic lens of therapeutic jurisprudence, which asks about the actual good or bad impact of specific laws and forms of legal involvement on the intended beneficiaries of those laws and processes (Stolle, Wexler, & Winick, 2000).

The concept of family is used in this chapter in a consciously loose and imprecise fashion. It expansively includes individuals who function in what is generally considered to be a family role, as well as those who are related by blood or legal ties to another person. Policymakers should seriously consider amending current statutes and regulations, where necessary, to recognize the important familial roles often played by friends (especially of older persons who have no willing and available supportive family members related by blood or legal ties) and committed gay or lesbian partners, and to legally empower those persons to the same extent that blood or legally derived relatives are now empowered (Polikoff, 2009).

ROLES AND RELATIONSHIPS INVOLVING OLDER PERSONS AND THEIR FAMILIES

Older persons and their families may interrelate in a myriad of ways. Each category of interrelationship entails different legally relevant roles, rights, and responsibilities.

Families Assisting with and Sharing in Older Persons' Decisions

The legal system in the United States begins with a rebuttable presumption that each adult is an autonomous agent capable of making informed and voluntary choices regarding all aspects of his or her own life. An individual does not lose the benefit of that presumption merely because of advanced years, and the burden of overcoming the presumption and disproving decisional capacity in any particular case rests on the party challenging the presumption of capacity.

The spheres in which the large majority of older Americans may exercise personal direction and control run a broad gamut. They include, most importantly, such matters as: medical decision making (Frolik, 2006) and health care planning (Doukas, McCullough, & Hanson, 2009); participation in biomedical and behavioral research (Mody, Miller, McGloin, Freeman, Marcantonio, Magaziner, & Studenski, 2008); financial planning (American

Bar Association, 2006); residential choices and rights within specific kinds of residential settings (Pynoos, Nishita, Cicero et al., 2008; Frolik, 2008); long-term care services (Kunkel & Wellin, 2006); obtaining various public entitlements like Medicare and Medicaid (Cody & Scully-Hayes, 2007) and private contractual benefits from health, disability, and property insurers; and voting (Symposium, 2007).

The fact that an older individual may be cognitively and emotionally capable enough to autonomously decide about and otherwise control important facets of his or her own life in no way precludes the involvement of family members in supporting and assisting—physically, emotionally, and financially—the older person's exercise of that autonomy. In the strictest version of the law, only the atomistic, legally isolated older individual himself or herself owns and formally exercises the right to, for example, give or refuse informed permission to undergo a medical procedure, change a will, or enter an assisted living facility. In practice, however, the exercise of autonomy in such difficult and sensitive domains seldom occurs in such a theoretically pristine vacuum. Much more often, the older person's choice and control in matters like these are assisted (not supplanted, but rather buttressed) through the help and encouragement of concerned family members. Put differently, many decisions and directions regarding older persons' life issues are *de jure* individualistic and representative of pure personal autonomy on the part of the person directly affected, but *de facto* shared with—made with the consultation and support of—certain family members (e.g., when the older person says something to the effect, "Doctor, talk to my daughter and me together.")

Many older persons welcome the opportunity to share what they perceive as the burden, not just the right, of decision making. Contrary to the pure autonomy model, some individuals may not want to be empowered exclusively. Another reason an older person might be willing, even anxious, to share authority regarding important life decisions with family members is to minimize family burden. By accepting and even soliciting family assistance, the older person may intend to reduce feelings of tension or guilt that might bother a family who would otherwise be uneasy with the older person's own choices. The family's involvement may instill the individual's choices with special meaning, presenting an opportunity for the older person to act unselfishly by taking into account the impact of choices on the family as a whole.

In addition, otherwise decisionally capable older individuals may still have serious communication problems with divergent people upon whom their legal rights depend (for example, care providers), for reasons ranging from linguistic or ethnic differences to sensory impairments. In such circumstances, involving family members in the participatory loop facilitates the communication or translation of information requisite for the older person's effective exercise of autonomy. It may also contribute to greater patient satisfaction with the entire formal care process (Wolff & Roter, 2008).

When unassisted independence is not a realistic or desired alternative for an older person, interdependence between generations may help to stave off a stark choice between a total emasculation of legal power (see next section) on one hand, and an unassisted, neglectful, nihilistic facade of autonomy on the other. Partial control through a fluid relationship between dependency and interdependency is preferable to no control at all for the older person. Moreover, because the quality of the individual and family interaction may strongly influence, if not determine completely, the outcome of various activities (such as an aggressive course of medical treatment for a seriously ill person), having the family involved as thoroughly and early as possible in shared decision making usually is therapeutic for the older person.

The process of assisted autonomy (Ryan, 1996), which shares decision making authority through frank and concrete discussions between a still decisionally capable older person and that person's family, should lead to better, more accurate surrogate decision making if it subsequently becomes necessary as a result of the individual's mental deterioration. Assisted or shared decision making affords a chance for continuing dialogue that informs future substitute decision makers more fully about the individual's values and preferences concerning later decisions.

Families Acting as Surrogate Decision Makers

Autonomous decision making by older persons, whether done completely independently or with the assistance of supportive family members, is feasible only when the individual retains sufficient cognitive and emotional capacity to act autonomously. The topic of defining and assessing decisional capacity in the older population is enormous and complex (Herring, 2008), spawning a voluminous literature (American Bar Association/American Psychological Association, 2005, 2006, 2008; Drickamer & Lai, 2009; Spike, 2009); it suffices to note here that some older individuals—because of mental illness carried over from earlier life, developmental disability, organic brain disorders, paranoid disorders, mood disorders (depression, for instance), drug reactions, alcohol, or physical illness—lack the minimum level of capacity necessary to qualify as autonomous decision makers.

Incapacity does not obviate the need for decisions being made. The consequence of decisional incapacity is that someone else must stand in the shoes of the incapacitated person and act as a surrogate decision maker on that person's behalf. When a family member is willing and available, ordinarily he or she gets to act in the surrogate role.

Decision making surrogacy for incapacitated older persons may be divided into two broad categories. Formal surrogacy refers to explicit legal designation of a specific surrogate who is anointed with the official authority to engage in substitute decision making. Informal surrogacy, on the other hand, involves one or more people acting as the functional equivalent of surrogate decision maker for an incapacitated person, but without the formal, legal imprimatur to do so.

Formal Surrogacy

One mechanism for establishing a family member as the authorized decision making surrogate is the execution, in conformity with the statutory and regulatory requirements of one's particular jurisdiction, of a durable power of attorney (DPOA) instrument. A DPOA, which may empower the designated surrogate to make decisions regarding medical, financial, and other kinds of matters, is a form of proxy advance directive that permits a currently capable person (the principal or maker who creates the DPOA document) to delineate a particular person to act as the principal's surrogate decision maker (an attorney-in-fact or agent). A DPOA may be written to go into effect immediately upon its execution, although usually (especially when it confers medical decision making power) the DPOA is written to be springing and take legal effect only upon some specified occurrence such as a physician finding that the principal lacks present decisional capacity.

The DPOA has the virtue of permitting the older person, in anticipation of potential future incapacity, to exercise some degree of prospective autonomy. It also avoids the necessity for court involvement, operating privately based on the voluntarily written and executed DPOA document. Moreover, this legal mechanism assures that the surrogate will be the person—in most cases a family member—whom the older person would want exercising that function; importantly, a currently capable individual who wants to avoid having a relative act as the surrogate has an opportunity to preclude that contingency by naming someone else as agent.

Family members or others who are named as agents under a DPOA are required to function in a fiduciary or trust relationship. Historically, a fiduciary or trust agent was supposed to be dedicated to serving the best interests of the person who delegated away decisional authority. The best interests model is functionally equivalent to a parent-child relationship. The modern trend in surrogate or proxy decision making, however, has been toward expectation of a substituted judgment standard. Under this model, the fiduciary is obligated to make those decisions that the principal would make personally, according to the principal's own preferences and values to the extent those preferences and values can be accurately ascertained, if the patient were able presently to make and express his or her own autonomous decisions (Zikmund-Fisher, Sarr, Fagerlin et al., 2006).

A DPOA's advantages notwithstanding, once the principal has been found to lack sufficient decisional capacity and the transfer of decision making authority under the DPOA has sprung to the designated agent, there are several possible problems regardless of whether or not the agent is a family member. First, there is substantial evidence (derived from surveying both patients and their surrogates) that surrogate decision makers frequently make decisions that are not in close accord with the decisions that the principal would have made for himself or herself, and that family members serving as agents do as poor an overall job in applying the substituted judgment standard as do nonrelated agents (Carpenter, Kissel, & Lee, 2007; Shalowitz, Garrett-Mayer, & Wendler, 2006). Conflicts of interest (both financial and emotional) and deliberate bad faith on the part of a small percentage of surrogates cannot be ruled out (Moran, 2008; Shepherd, 2004–2005). However, a much larger part of the explanation for the apparent discordance between the principal's actual preferences and the preferences as surmised by the surrogate is that often little, if any, communication about relevant present values and future wishes takes place between the principal and the surrogate (even a family surrogate) while the principal still retains decisional capacity and therefore can express and explain autonomous and authentic choices. Such a conversation is not (although it should be) a legal prerequisite for the valid execution or acceptance of a DPOA.

A second, more serious problem is that some family members who have been placed in a position of trust by being named the agent in a DPOA misuse that position as an opportunity to take unfair advantage of the principal, most commonly by improperly diverting the available financial resources away from the principal's welfare and toward the agent's own enrichment. This form of elder abuse, facilitated by the very legal mechanism created to protect the vulnerable incapacitated elder, raises questions about the law's general presumption that families should be trusted to act in their loved ones' best interests and whether additional legal provisions are needed at the state level to protect vulnerable older persons from malevolent family members in whom they have mistakenly placed their trust (Black, 2008; Rhein, 2009).

When no DPOA (or advance instruction directive, such as a living will) has been executed in a timely manner (i.e., prior to the older person becoming decisionally incapacitated), surrogate decision making authority for an incapacitated older individual is, in the majority of states, delegated to another person by statute. Generically termed "default surrogate" or "family consent statutes," these legislative enactments transfer decision making authority from the incapacitated person to an available surrogate, with potential surrogates designated in a specific priority order. In a typical family consent statute, as the name implies, family members are listed at the top of the list of potential surrogates. When the default surrogate statute mechanism for formally identifying and empowering a family surrogate decision maker is utilized, there remains a danger that the same problems described above (namely, discordant choices not reflecting the older person's actual preferences and surrogates' outright abuse of trust) may materialize (Kohn & Blumenthal, 2008).

Another form of formal surrogacy is legal guardianship (termed conservatorship in certain jurisdictions) (Reynolds & Stiles, 2008). Under their inherent *parens patriae* power (the parental authority to protect those who cannot protect themselves from harm), each of the states has enacted statutory schemes that allow designated courts, based on petitions filed by "interested" parties, to adjudicate a person as being mentally incompetent and appoint a guardian for that incompetent ward. Guardianship petitions usually (although not necessarily) are filed by concerned family members, and ordinarily a relative of the ward is appointed the guardian when one is reasonably available and agreeable to the appointment.

When no family member is willing and able to accept court appointment, however, or when the court finds available family members to be unfit to carry out the surrogate decision making role in a trustworthy way, the court may appoint a financial or health care institution, a for-profit guardianship corporation, or a nonprofit volunteer (secular or religiously based) guardianship program. Most jurisdictions have statutes establishing public guardianship programs, under which government agencies provide the guardianship services, either directly or by contracting with a private sector entity for the services, as a last resort for "unbefriended" individuals who have no family or friends to fulfill the guardian role as surrogate decision maker.

A guardian is legally obligated to make decisions and take actions that represent the ward's substituted judgment, when that is feasible, or alternatively that are in the ward's best interests. Sometimes, though, even family guardians misuse this position of trust because of a conflict of interest. Under guardianship statutes, the appointing court maintains continuing jurisdiction to monitor the guardian's discharge of duties. However, local courts around the country vary considerably in their commitment, competence, and resources to carry out the ongoing oversight function. Some legal commentators, driven by an image of widespread inept, even unscrupulous conduct by untrustworthy guardians, support an aggressive policing-and-enforcement role for the courts regarding oversight of guardians and the fiduciary duties they owe to their wards. By contrast, other commentators favor a more collaborative, counseling role for ongoing post-appointment judicial involvement (especially when the guardian is a family member who should be presumed to be concerned with promoting the ward's well-being). This collaborative role would concentrate on the courts trying to help guardians perform their functions better, rather than catching and punishing fiduciary miscreants after the fact.

Informal Surrogates

As explained above, family members frequently act as formally authorized surrogate decision makers. However, situations arise in which an older person is *de facto* decisionally incapacitated but there is no valid DPOA, guardianship order, or pertinent default statute. Practically speaking, surrogate decision making authority may get transferred to a family member anyway, as a matter of custom and expediency without a formal legal stamp of approval, as when third parties such as health care providers look to family members to make crucial medical choices for a relative who cannot speak competently for himself or herself.

Many individuals in the gray zone of decisional capacity, and even a substantial percentage of those who are clearly factually incapacitated, never have the capacity issue formally raised. "Although incompetence denotes a legal status that in principle should be determined by a court, resorting to judicial review in every case of suspected impairment of capacity would probably bring both the medical and legal systems to a halt" (Appelbaum, 2007, p. 1834). Instead, in these circumstances the various parties generally bumble though outside of the legal system as best they can. This bumbling through can take place because of professionals' working, clinical judgments about capacity and the cooperation of willing, available family members, friends, and health care and human services providers. Families and friends tend to understand pragmatically that obtaining a court's imprimatur on every decision making arrangement that would have occurred informally anyway would rarely change the decisions made or provide additional protections to the incapacitated person. Because the current process of bumbling through ordinarily works well and without negative legal or other consequences, there is not much apparent benefit for anyone in altering everyday practice in a way that surely would create financial, emotional, and efficiency costs.

An exception to the foregoing observation may be advisable "when highly charged divisions appear between family members. . . . Throughout the process [of dealing with family discord], there must be cognizance of possible medical-legal issues to be confronted at a later date" (Serby, 2009, p. 28).

Families Protecting and Advocating for Older Persons

Consumer Protection

To ensure that older individuals' personal and financial choices are autonomous and authentic (i.e., representing the person's true wishes), American society has developed an extensive web of laws designed to protect consumers against the potential excesses of a completely unbridled, buyer beware marketplace. Fraud targeting older persons who reside in the community may take a number of forms: telemarketing fraud, pyramid schemes, and get-rich-quick enticements, among others. Older consumers may be scammed into bad investments, buying goods and services they do not need, or donating money to phony organizations.

Every state has unfair and deceptive acts and practices statutes that prohibit an array of activities, including common law fraud, taking unfair advantage of a consumer by using superior knowledge or bargaining position, and coercive or misleading sales practices. These laws may be enforced through criminal prosecutions brought by the state and private civil lawsuits brought by or on behalf of the victimized consumer.

Consumer protection laws often specifically identify older individuals as particularly at risk and hence needing special protection in the marketplace. For example, statutes may include enhanced criminal penalties for engaging in certain fraudulent activities if the victim is above a certain age (Carlson, 2006).

Families may play an important, albeit legally and emotionally delicate, role in protecting their older loved ones against consumer fraud and other forms of commercial exploitation. Unless the older person has become so decisionally incapacitated that legal authority has passed to another, through a previously executed proxy directive (DPOA) or a court-ordered guardianship, the family has no formal power to oversee the older person's finances. Nonetheless, family members should be vigilant in recognizing any irregularities in their loved one's habits, activities, or demeanor that might indicate out-of-the-ordinary financial circumstances, and should be prepared to intervene (e.g., by reporting the situation to law enforcement agencies) quickly if permitted to do so by the older person. In extreme cases, a family becoming aware of financial exploitation of their loved one may serve as the impetus for the initiation of a guardianship petition.

Elder Mistreatment

The types of financial fraud and exploitation just discussed, conducted by commercial entities or phony not-for-profit organizations, represent one sort of elder mistreatment. Families may be involved in protecting the older person against these and other categories of elder mistreatment that have been or might be perpetrated by others, either in the community or in institutional settings; arguably, families have an affirmative obligation to report elder mistreatment and attempt to prevent it from inflicting harm (Plaisance, 2008). Other categories of elder mistreatment include abuse (the infliction upon an older person of injury, unreasonable confinement, intimidation, or cruelty with resulting physical harm, pain, or mental anguish) and neglect (the failure to provide an older person with the goods or services necessary to avoid physical harm or mental anguish) (Paveza, 2008). The older person's welfare can also be threatened by self-neglect (Dong, Simon, Mendes de Leon et al., 2009), and families should be vigilant about checking for signs of this phenomenon.

Unfortunately, sometimes families themselves act as the perpetrators of elder mistreatment. This complex social problem (with many substantial legal implications) is discussed in more depth in Chapter 17 in this volume. Suffice it to recognize here that "[a] dysfunctional family is a dysfunctional family. The law may not remedy that, but the law can redress wrongs inflicted by one family member upon another" (Morgan, 2009, p. 149).

Every state has created a wide constellation of laws dealing with elder mistreatment committed by family members, other individuals or institutions, and the older person himself or herself (self-neglect). Some states rely on generic Adult Protective Services (APS) laws to address elder mistreatment, while other jurisdictions have enacted more targeted statutes on this matter. Additional relevant provisions are found in state criminal or penal codes, domestic violence laws, and probate statutes. Although mindful of the states' traditional *parens patriae* function, some commentators nevertheless caution the states to avoid the paradox of going so far in zealously overprotecting older persons thought to be at risk that elders' autonomy rights are jeopardized by excessive paternalism (Kohn, 2009).

Families Providing Services to Older Persons

A significant proportion of older individuals require various kinds of supportive services, often on a long-term basis, and the number of Americans in this category is likely to explode significantly in the next several decades (Polivka, 2008). As a consequence of acute or chronic medical conditions, older persons may need assistance in either activities of daily living (namely, bathing, dressing, moving in or out of bed or a chair, toileting, or eating) or instrumental activities of daily living (e.g., housecleaning, meal preparation, transportation, or financial management) (Buhler-Wilkerson, 2007; Graf, 2008; Lawton & Brody, 1969).

Families frequently are extensively involved in helping, indirectly (by paying, hiring, or coordinating paid service deliverers) or directly and hands-on, to provide long-term care services to their loved ones. Such family involvement ordinarily is undertaken on a voluntary basis, at least from a legal perspective (Wylie & Brank, 2009), although considerations of indebtedness or reciprocity, gratitude, intimacy, compassion, or guilt may act as compelling psychological, moral, and religious (Kaplan, 2007) pressures. "It is commonly observed that society cannot effectively legislate morality [or love. The key legal question is,] Can we mandate that families provide proper care for their elders?" (Morgan, 2009, p. 150).

Even if we cannot legally mandate that families care for their elders, there do exist legal mechanisms for economically encouraging or incentivizing such behavior. For example, a number of commentators have recommended that families be provided with tax credits in return for voluntarily taking on caregiving duties (Kaplan, 2005; Rickles-Jordan, 2007); such credits would likely be especially persuasive for family members who would need to discontinue paid employment outside the home (and thus suffer a diminution in their income) in order to undertake the care of their older relative. In some situations, the current dependent care tax credit may be available to assist with the costs of providing care to a disabled spouse or parent. Under Section 21 of the Internal Revenue Code, this tax credit is available for the care of an elderly relative only if applicant for the credit can sufficiently document that the person cared for was "physically or mentally incapable of caring for himself or herself" and had "the same principal place of abode as the taxpayer for more than one-half of such taxable year."

Filial Financial Responsibility

One arena in which society has attempted to legislate morality involves the enactment of legislation in approximately 30 states imposing a duty on adult children, if they are able, to provide financial assistance to indigent parents (Ross, 2008). For example, Ohio Revised Code § 2919.21 specifies that no person "shall abandon, or fail to provide adequate support to . . . [t]he person's aged or infirm parent . . . who from the lack of ability and means is unable to provide adequately for the parent's own support." However, if and when an adult child fails to satisfy that responsibility, it is a defense that the accused person "was unable to provide adequate support or the established support but did provide the support that was within the accused's ability and means." Comparable laws regarding the responsibilities of adult children exist in a number of other nations, including Italy, Israel, Japan, and Singapore (Rickles-Jordan, 2007).

The courts have tended to uphold the validity of state filial responsibility statutes against the objections (among others) that they violate the United States Constitution's Fourteenth Amendment mandate of equal protection of the law and the Constitution's Fifth Amendment prohibition against taking of private property without just compensation. As a practical matter, though, these laws are enforced only erratically; in a number of jurisdictions, the filial responsibility statute has never been invoked against any nonsupporting adult child.

Even putting aside the question of whether there is a relevant filial responsibility statute present in one's jurisdiction, the Baby Boom generation confronts a variety of pertinent considerations.

> Greater longevity for both the adult children and their parents increases the need for complex legal and financial planning. The combination of having more and older surviving parents means that, while they are legally and financially planning for their own retirement, many adult children will be helping their parents with . . . financial support. (Wassel & Cutler, 2007, p. 71)

An objection to greater expansion of filial responsibility as a matter of law is based on feminist gerontological theory. According to this view:

We know from existing data that women already assume a disproportionate share of responsibility for unpaid care; imposing financial responsibility on children does little more than shift additional responsibility to them, exacerbating these caregivers' long-term financial and personal vulnerability. . . . In short, expanding 'filial' responsibility for long term care of the elderly is not acceptable unless those women who take on the bulk of the legal obligation to provide care are, at a minimum, accommodated in the workplace. . . . (Dayton, 2009, p. 52)

The financial involvement of adult children regarding the formal care of disabled parents needs to be distinguished from the obligations of spouses of people receiving paid long-term care services. Under the traditional legal doctrine of "necessaries," each spouse has been held equally (jointly and severally, or individually) liable for debts incurred by the other spouse for "necessary" goods and services. A number of states have modified the apportionment of financial responsibility for necessaries between the two spouses by holding the spouse who incurred the necessary expense primarily liable for payment, with the other spouse becoming secondarily liable when the spouse who incurred the expense does not have sufficient assets or income to satisfy the debt. By contrast, the general common-law (judge-made) doctrine of necessaries does not apply to adult children; adult children are legally obligated to contribute financially to the support of an aging parent only if a jurisdiction's legislature has affirmatively enacted a specific family responsibility statute.

Families Qua Care Managers

"Older persons and their families often must make crucial decisions about long-term care (LTC) under very stressful and limiting circumstances; these decisions can affect the rest of their lives" (Kane, 2008, p. 55). Some or all of the LTC services needed by an older individual are provided by formal (i.e., paid professional) caregivers, through institutions (such as hospitals, nursing homes, and hospices), agencies (particularly home health agencies), or arrangements with individuals. In this regard, the family often functions as an indirect service provider by taking on the care management, or service broker, role responsible for hiring, directing, monitoring, and perhaps terminating the paid professionals (Bookman & Harrington, 2007). This care management function may be undertaken by the family in the form of assisting a competent loved one to make his or her own arrangements or, alternatively, as the surrogate decision maker and implementer for an incapacitated older person.

In either case, in the context of making choices about formal long-term care and monitoring its delivery, a variety of legal and ethical questions may arise regarding the relationship between family caregivers and their loved ones' health and human services professionals and organizational providers (Mitnick, Leffler, & Hood, 2010). For example, what about giving information about the patient's or client's problems and intervention needs to family members? Improper disclosure of patient- or client-specific information to a third-party—even a family member—without either prior authorization by the individual (i.e., a waiver of confidentiality rights), a guardianship or conservatorship order appointing the third party to act as decision maker for the incapacitated individual, or an applicable family consent statute empowering a family member to act as a surrogate violates professionals' or providers' common law confidentiality duties and codes of professional ethics.

When a family is thoroughly involved in managing care, there is no practical way to keep information regarding the patient or client away from the family. In that situation, the family ordinarily monitors and oversees the flow of information among the patient or client, professional care providers, and everyone else, as well as communication about the patient or client to third parties. Families justifiably need sufficient information to knowledgeably carry out their role in making and influencing important decisions.

The confidentiality issue is rendered more complicated by the medical privacy regulations implementing the Health Insurance Portability and Accountability Act (HIPAA), 45 Code of Federal Regulations Parts 160 and 164. These provisions impose restrictions and documentation requirements on health care providers (among others) concerning the release of identifiable medical information to people or entities other than the patient. HIPAA regulations permit limited exceptions when sharing personal health information (PHI) is needed for purposes of treatment coordination, payment, or health care operations. The effect of these regulations on the transmittal of medical information to family care managers, in the absence of explicit permission from the patient or a court order, is still unsettled.

When the family acting in its case manager role hires paid caregivers to come into the home to provide services to an older relative, several kinds of potential legal issues may arise (Knight, 2009a). This is generally true even when the caregiver is a private individual, such as a hired sitter, or an agency employee who emotionally (Piercy, 2001), but erroneously and naïvely, does not consider his or her relationship with the consumer to be a legal one.

If the caregiver is considered an independent contractor, then the rights and responsibilities of the respective parties are delineated in the family-caregiver contract. Conversely, when the family exercises substantial control and direction over the caregiver in terms of the when, what, and how aspects of the caregiver's work, the relationship may be one of employer and employee. The relationship is most likely to be characterized as one between an employer and an employee when the family supplies the necessary materials or equipment and the caregiver does not provide similar services to other clients.

When an employer (family)-employee (caregiver) relationship exists, related legal questions might include, for instance, whether the family is required to withhold (from the employee's paycheck) and pay the employer's portion of the employee's Social Security and Medicare taxes under the Federal Insurance Contributions Act (FICA). Additionally, federal and state unemployment and workers' compensation taxes may need to be paid. Other potential questions relating to the family *qua* employer of the caregiver concern verification and adequate documentation of the caregiver's eligibility to work in the United States, liability for injuries incurred by the caregiver on the job, and exposure to the risk of discrimination and harassment suits brought by caregivers.

Families employing caregivers need to purchase and keep up to date an adequate amount of homeowner's and general liability insurance coverage. Moreover, families may properly attempt to obviate or minimize most of these legal issues by purchasing elder care services only through an agency or organization (for example, the National Private Duty Association) that will function as the employer.

Direct Family Caregiving

"[F]or a society that wishes to respect the rights of its elderly, attending to their legal status is not enough. Attention to the social context or setting is also warranted, particularly to the immediate circle of people who actually care for the needs of the elderly" (Doron, 2009, pp. 64–65). In the United States, the most significant providers of care for elderly people are family members. The primary caregivers are most likely to be drawn from the immediate family (Parks & Winter, 2009). Particularly right after the older person is discharged from a hospital stay, the family's role in monitoring and medicating the patient, as well as meeting other needs, becomes even more paramount (Beck, 2009). The family caregiving dynamic is discussed thoroughly in chapter 21 in this volume.

An important question in this sphere is how formally structured the family caregiving arrangements ought to be. As observed earlier, most family caregiving occurs on a voluntary basis. However, in some circumstances, a more formal arrangement may be necessary or advisable, especially if the older person is paying the family member for caregiving services (Knight, 2009a). A useful tool may be "the personal service contract, sometimes known as a personal care agreement. This is a compact between parent and child that says the child agrees to provide certain services to the parent in exchange for a specified compensation" (Wainey, 2009, p. 30). One benefit of a caregiver contract, which could also involve relatives other than the care recipient's adult children, is that this arrangement can help reduce the size of a parent's estate and thereby improve their [*sic*] chances of becoming eligible for long-term care coverage under Medicaid. They [caregiver contracts] can also minimize battles between siblings and other family members. For many other families, the contracts simply help reward the significant amounts of time, effort and money that family members often spend watching over and taking care of an elderly relative. (Silverman, 2006, p. D1)

Whether or not they have a formal caregiving contract with their older relative, many family caregivers also are gainfully employed outside the home. This situation may raise labor law issues for the family member and his or her outside employer, most prominently regarding the family member-employee's right to take leave from work. The federal Family and Medical Leave Act (FMLA) of 1993, 29 U.S.C. §§ 2601–2654, requires businesses with 50 or more employees to provide employees with up to 12 weeks of unpaid leave for the birth or adoption of a child, to care for an ill family member, or for the worker's own health condition, without loss of their job. Workers are eligible for this benefit if they have worked for the particular employer for at least 12 months and have clocked at least 1,250 hours in the year prior to the leave (Lindsey, 2009). Individual employers, as well as each of the states in the American federal system (New York State Paid Family Leave Coalition, 2009), are allowed to adopt a more liberal policy for themselves. The Department of Labor, with jurisdiction over the FMLA, has proposed amending the federal regulations that implement the rights that eligible workers have to job protection for absences due to the birth or adoption of a child or for a serious health condition of the worker or a qualifying family member (73 Federal Register 7876–7993, Feb. 11, 2008).

Family caregivers also have legal protections for their family caregiving activities under the Americans with Disabilities Act (ADA). The ADA, 42 U.S.C. §12112(b)(4), prohibits associational discrimination, which would entail treating an employee differently (worse) than other employees because of the caregiver employee's association (i.e., caregiving relationship) with a disabled person. The ADA provides protection as long as the caregiver can—with or without reasonable accommodations—continue to perform essential work-related functions adequately (Bornstein & Rathmell, 2009).

Older Persons Providing Services and Resources to Their Families

The previous sections of this chapter discuss relationships in which family members provide various kinds of support to their older relatives needing assistance of some type. However, family–older person relationships can run in the other direction as well, with services and resources flowing from the older person to other members of the family.

One primary example of this dynamic is kinship care (Goelitz, 2007). In the United States (and internationally) growing numbers of children are being raised by their grandparents because the parents are not available to fulfill that role. In addition, there are many modern American families in which one (in single-family settings) or both parents of young children must, for financial reasons, work full-time or part-time outside of the home; in many of those families, grandparents assist—on a paid or unpaid basis—with the care and maintenance of their grandchildren or great-grandchildren while the parents are working at their paid employment (Shellenbarger, 2009). The range of issues pertaining to grandparent/grandchild/great-grandchild relationships is discussed comprehensively in chapter 8 of this volume.

There may be a flow of economic resources from the older person to specific family members after the older individual has died. This intergenerational transfer of wealth takes the form of inheritance. Inheritance of a deceased person's assets takes place according to a particular state's statutes and case law of intestate succession when no proper will was executed during the lifetime of the deceased person. However, when a valid will has been executed during the deceased's lifetime, it may dispose of property in the estate of the testator (i.e., the now-deceased will maker) to relatives either as a reward for their earlier providing care to the deceased person during his or her period of dependency (Tate, 2008) or as a gift specifically contemplated by the testator for any of a panoply of psychological reasons (Angel, 2008).

DIRECTIONS FOR FUTURE RESEARCH

"Family relationships evolve across time with changes and adjustments as individual members develop and as societal, cultural, and environmental factors change" (Dearborn, 2008, p. 354). So, too, the body of law pertaining to older persons and their family relationships must continue to evolve. As this evolutionary process unfolds, it must be continuously studied to assure that it fosters the goals intended by the legislatures, regulatory agencies, and the courts.

Only recently have scholars begun to use the analytic lens of therapeutic jurisprudence (Kapp, 2009) to explore the ways in which the law in practice (as contrasted with theory) can exert positive or negative physical, financial, psychological, and other effects on real older people in a variety of tangible family-related contexts, including those outlined in this chapter. For example, do legal contracts for family caregiving binding the older person and the related caregiver(s) improve the availability, affordability, and quality of needed services for the care receiver? Do laws that promote enhanced continuing judicial scrutiny of family guardians and their role performance provide valuable protection for vulnerable older people who are decisionally incapacitated, or do they discourage well-intentioned families from stepping forward to act as guardians even when needed?

Some legal scholars object to a therapeutic jurisprudence analysis as too dangerous to the right of older persons to be protected against state (and presumably family) interference, opting instead for stronger, stricter employment of due process requirements to shield older persons whose freedom and prerogatives might otherwise be in peril at the hands of lawmakers (and presumably overzealous relatives) (Schmidt, 2009). These critics vastly overstate their argument. Attention to due process protections, on one hand, and to the actual impact of our laws on real people, on the other, need not be antithetical at all. Indeed, only by identifying the therapeutic and antitherapeutic, productive and counterproductive, effects of particular laws and specific forms of legal system involvement can future law be better shaped in ways that diminish the antitherapeutic consequences and maximize the therapeutic potential for actual, identifiable (as opposed to abstract) older persons and their families.

Gerontological research in this arena can play an essential part in improving the impact of geriatric jurisprudence on the lives of older persons as members of families in the future. Opportunities for collaboration between family gerontologists and legal scholars abound. For example, some American legal commentators have advocated ongoing formal, external oversight (through the courts or other government agencies) of the actions of agents named under DPOAs, as a means of protecting older persons who execute DPOAs from exploitation by their chosen agents. Such a therapeutically motivated change in the legal system would raise a number of researchable questions, such as whether external oversight has the intended therapeutic effect for vulnerable elders or, conversely, whether greater formal, external oversight exerts the antitherapeutic effect of discouraging family members from serving as surrogate decision makers on behalf of decisionally incapacitated relatives absent the protection of an official, judicially issued, guardianship order—with all the time, expense, emotional turmoil, and deprivation of rights that an adversary guardianship proceeding ordinarily entails (Hope, 2010). Whatever the results of particular studies, a concerted interdisciplinary effort to address researchable questions at the intersection of family aging and the law will itself produce therapeutic results for individuals and society.

REFERENCES

American Bar Association. (2006). *Legal guide for Americans over 50*. Chicago: Author.

American Bar Association/American Psychological Association. (2005). *Assessment of older adults with diminished capacity: A handbook for lawyers*. Washington, DC: ABA/APA.

404 Handbook of Families and Aging

American Bar Association/American Psychological Association. (2006). *Judicial determination of capacity in older adults in guardianship proceedings.* Washington, DC: ABA/APA.

American Bar Association/American Psychological Association. (2008). *Assessment of older adults with diminished capacity: A handbook for psychologists.* Washington, DC: ABA/APA.

Angel, J. L. (2008). *Inheritance in contemporary America: The social dimensions of giving across generations.* Baltimore, MD: Johns Hopkins University Press.

Appelbaum, P. S. (2007). Assessment of patients' competence to consent to treatment. *New England Journal of Medicine, 357,* 1834–1840.

Beck, M. (2009, January 13). Home sick: When the burden of care falls on the family. *Wall Street Journal,* p. D1.

Black, J. A. (2008). The not-so-golden years: Power of attorney, elder abuse, and why our laws are failing a vulnerable population. *St. John's Law Review, 82,* 289–314.

Bookman, A., & Harrington, M. (2007). Family caregivers: A shadow workforce in the geriatric health care system? *Journal of Health Politics, Policy and Law, 32,* 1005–1041.

Bornstein S., & Rathmell, R. J. (2009). *Caregivers as a protected class?: The growth of state and local laws prohibiting family responsibilities discrimination.* San Francisco, CA: Center for Work Life Law, University of California, Hastings College of Law.

Buhler-Wilkerson, K. (2007). Care of the chronically ill at home: An unresolved dilemma in health policy for the United States. *Milbank Quarterly, 85,* 611–639.

Carlson, E. L. (2006). Phishing for elderly victims: As the elderly migrate to the internet fraudulent schemes targeting them follow. *Elder Law Journal, 14,* 423–452.

Carpenter, B. D., Kissel, E. C., & Lee, M. M. (2007). Preferences and life evaluations of older adults with and without dementia: Reliability, stability, and proxy knowledge. *Psychology and Aging, 22,* 650–655.

Cody, D. A., & Scully-Hayes, K. (2007). *A practical guide to Medicare appeals.* Chicago: American Bar Association.

Dayton, A. K. (2009). A feminist approach to elder law. In I. Doron (Ed.), *Theories on law and ageing: The jurisprudence of elder law* (pp. 45–57). Berlin: Springer-Verlag.

Dearborn, M. (2008). Family relationships. In S. Loue & M. Sajatovic (Eds.), *Encyclopedia of aging and public health* (pp. 352–354). New York: Springer Science+Business.

Dong, X., Simon, M., Mendes de Leon, C., Fulmer, T., Beck, T., Hebert, L., Dyer, C., Paveza, G., & Evans, D. (2009). Elder self-neglect and abuse and mortality risk in a community-dwelling population. *Journal of the American Medical Association, 302,* 517–526.

Doron, I. (2009). A multi-dimensional model of elder law. In I. Doron (Ed.), *Theories on law and ageing: The jurisprudence of elder law* (pp. 59–74). Berlin: Springer-Verlag.

Doukas, D. J., McCullough, L. B., & Hanson, S. S. (2009). Advance care planning: Values and families in end-of-life care. In C. Aronson, J. Busby-Whitehead, K. Brummel-Smith, J. G. O'Brien, M. H. Palmer, & W. Reichel (Eds.), *Reichel's care of the elderly: Clinical aspects of aging* (6th ed., pp. 596–607). New York: Cambridge University Press.

Drickamer, M. A., & Lai, J. M. (2009). Assessment of decisional capacity and competencies. In J. B. Halter, J. G. Ouslander, M. E. Tinetti, N. Woolard, S. Studenski, S. Asthana, & K. High (Eds.), *Hazzard's geriatric medicine and gerontology* (6th ed., pp. 171–176). New York: McGraw-Hill Medical.

Foy, A. C. (2006). Adult adoption and the elder population. *Marquette Elder's Advisor, 8,* 109–125.

Frolik, L. A. (2006). *The law of later-life health care and decision-making.* Chicago: American Bar Association.

Frolik, L. A. (2008). *Residence options for older and disabled clients.* Chicago: American Bar Association.

Goelitz, J. C. (2007). Answering the call to support elderly kinship caregivers. *Elder Law Journal, 15,* 233–263.

Graf, C. (2008). The Lawton instrumental activities of daily living scale. *American Journal of Nursing, 108,* 52–62.

Herring, J. (2008). Entering the fog: On the borderlines of mental capacity. *Indiana Law Journal, 83,* 1619–1649.

Hope, C. (2010, January 8). Relatives of elderly or disabled waiting for up to six months for lasting powers of attorney. *Telegraph.* Retrieved from www.telegraph.co.uk/news/newstopics/politics/lawandorder/6951412

Kane, R. L. (2008). Making better long-term care decisions. *Marquette Elder's Advisor, 10,* 55–73.

Kaplan, R. L. (2005). Federal tax policy and family provided care for older adults. *Virginia Tax Review, 25,* 509–562.

Kaplan, R. L. (2007). Honoring our parents: Applying the biblical imperative in the context of long-term care. *Notre Dame Journal of Law, Ethics and Public Policy, 21,* 493–515.

Kapp, M. B. (2009). A therapeutic approach. In I. Doron (Ed.), *Theories on law and ageing: The jurisprudence of elder law* (pp. 31–44). Berlin: Springer-Verlag.

Knight, V. E. (2009, January 15a). Relatives can be paid to look after elderly. *Wall Street Journal,* p. D2.

Knight, V. E. (2009, March 19b). What to do if you are the boss of a caregiver. *Wall Street Journal,* p. D2.

Kohn, N. A. (2009). Outliving constitutional rights: A rights-based critique of elder protectionism. *Washington University Law Review, 86,* 1053–1115.

Kohn, N. A., & Blumenthal, J. A. (2008). Designating health care decisionmakers for patients without advance directives: A psychological critique. *Georgia Law Review, 42,* 979–1018.

Kunkel, S. R., & Wellin, V. (Eds.). (2006). *Consumer voice and choice in long-term care.* New York: Springer Publishing Company.

Lawton, M. P., & Brody, E. M. (1969). Assessment of older people: Self maintaining and instrumental activities of daily living. *The Gerontologist, 9,* 179–186.

Lindsey, M. (2009). The Family and Medical Leave Act: Who really cares? *South Texas Law Review, 50*, 559–588.

Mitnick, S., Leffler, C., & Hood, V. L., for the American College of Physicians Ethics and Human Rights Committee. (2010). Family caregivers, patients and physicians: Ethical guidance to optimize relationships. *Journal of General Internal Medicine*, DOI 10.1007/s11606–009–1206–3.

Mody, L., Miller, D. K., McGloin, J. M., Freeman, M., Marcantonio, E. R., Magaziner, J., & Studenski, S. (2008). Recruitment and retention of older adults in aging research. *Journal of the American Geriatrics Society, 56*, 2340–2348.

Moran, J. D. (2008). Families, courts, and the end of life: Schiavo and its implications for the family justice system. *Family Court Review, 46*, 297–330.

Morgan, R. C. (2009). The future of elder law. In I. Doron (Ed.), *Theories on law and ageing: The jurisprudence of elder law* (pp. 145–153). Berlin: Springer-Verlag.

New York State Paid Family Leave Coalition. http://www.timetocareny.org/index.html

Parks, S. M., & Winter, L. (2009). The elderly, their families, and their caregivers. In C. Aronson, J. Busby-Whitehead, K. Brummel-Smith, J. G. O'Brien, M. H. Palmer, & W. Reichel (Eds.), *Reichel's care of the elderly: Clinical aspects of aging* (6th ed., pp. 572–576). New York: Cambridge University Press.

Paveza, G. J. (2008). Elder mistreatment: An overview. In E. A. Capezuit, E. L. Siegler, & M. D. Mezey (Eds.), *The encyclopedia of elder care* (pp. 259–261). New York: Springer Publishing Company.

Piercy, K. W. (2001). "We couldn't do without them!" The value of close relationships between older adults and their nonfamily caregivers. *Generations, 25*, 41–47.

Plaisance, L. Q. (2008). Will you still . . . when I'm sixty-four: Adult children's legal obligations to aging parents. *Journal of the American Academy of Matrimonial Lawyers, 21*, 245–270.

Polikoff, N. D. (2009). Equality and justice for lesbian and gay families and relationships. *Rutgers Law Review, 61*, 529–560.

Polivka, L. (2008). Closing the gap between knowledge and practice in the U.S. long-term care system. *Marquette Elder's Advisor, 10*, 75–118.

Pynoos, J., Nishita, C., Cicero, C., et al. (2008). Aging in place, housing, and the law. *Elder Law Journal, 16*, 77–105.

Reynolds, S. L., & Stiles, P. (2008). Guardianship and conservatorship. In E. A. Capezuti, E. L. Siegler, & M. D. Mezey (Eds.), *The encyclopedia of elder care* (2nd ed., pp. 377–380). New York: Springer.

Rhein, J. L. (2009). No one in charge: Durable powers of attorney and the failure to protect incapacitated principals. *Elder Law Journal, 17*, 165–199.

Rickles-Jordan, A. (2007). Filial responsibility: A survey across time and oceans. *Marquette Elder's Advisor, 9*, 183–204.

Ross, A. E. (2008). Taking care of our caretakers: Using filial responsibility laws to support the elderly beyond the government's assistance. *Elder Law Journal, 16*, 167–209.

Ryan, R. M. (1996). What is supportive about social support? On the psychological needs for autonomy and relatedness. In R. M. Ryan, J. A. Solky, & G. R. Pierce, (Eds.), *Handbook of social support and the elderly* (p. xv). New York: Plenum Press.

Schmidt, W. C. (2009). Law and aging: Mental health theory approach. In I. Doron (Ed.), *Theories on law and ageing: The jurisprudence of elder law* (pp. 121–143). Berlin: Springer-Verlag.

Serby, M. J. (2009). Dementia and the family: Intrapsychic and interpersonal issues. *Annals of Long Term Care, 17*(8), 27–28.

Shalowitz, D. I., Garrett-Mayer, E., & Wendler, D. (2006). The accuracy of surrogate decision-makers: A systematic review. *Archives of Internal Medicine, 166*, 493–497.

Shellenbarger, S. (2009 June 24). When granny is your nanny. *Wall Street Journal*, p. D1.

Shepherd, L. (2004–2005). Shattering the neutral surrogate myth in end-of-life decisionmaking: Terri Shiavo and her family. *Cumberland Law Review, 35*, 575–595.

Silverman, R. E. (2006, September 7). Who will mind mom? Check her contract. *Wall Street Journal*, p. D1.

Spike, J. P. (2009). Assessment of decision-making capacity. In C. Arenson, J. Busby-Whitehead, K. Brummel-Smith, J. G. O'Brien, M. H. Palmer, & W. Reichel (Eds.), *Reichel's care of the elderly: Clinical aspects of aging* (6th ed., pp. 487–493). New York: Cambridge University Press.

Stolle, D. P., Wexler, D. B., & Winck, B. J., (Eds.). (2000). *Practicing therapeutic jurisprudence: Law as a helping profession.* Durham, NC: Carolina Academic Press.

Symposium. (2007). Facilitating voting as people age: Implications of cognitive impairment. *McGeorge Law Review, 38*, 843–1137.

Tate, J. C. (2008). Caregiving and the case for testamentary freedom. *University of California Davis Law Review, 42*, 129–193.

Wainey, D. A. (2009). Preventing family feuds. *Trial, 45*, 30–33.

Wassel, J. I., & Cutler, N. E. (2007). Family aging and the practice of elder law: A financial gerontology perspective. *NAELA* (National Academy of Elder Law Attorneys) *Journal, 3*, 67–76.

Wolff, J. L., & Roter, D. L. (2008). Hidden in plain sight: Medical visit companions as a resource for vulnerable older adults. *Archives of Internal Medicine, 168*, 1409–1415.

Wylie, L. E., & Brank, E. M. (2009). Assuming elder care responsibility: Am I a caregiver? *Journal of Empirical Legal Studies, 6*, 899–924.

Zikmund-Fisher, B. J., Sarr, B., Fagerlin, A., et al. (2006). A matter of perspective: Choosing for others differs from choosing for yourself in making treatment decisions. *Journal of General Internal Medicine, 21*, 618–622.

17

Elder Abuse in Aging Families

Pamela B. Teaster, Tenzin Wangmo, and Frances B. Vorsky

Mrs. Harris is 75 years old and an active member of her community. She regularly attends church services and meetings. Mrs. Harris suffers from arthritis and was recently diagnosed with mild cognitive impairment. Her adult daughter, Samantha, who recently lost her job, returned home to live with Mrs. Harris. A few weeks after Samantha's arrival, Mrs. Harris stopped going to church, and now, she is rarely seen outside the house. Her friend, Dorothy, went to visit her but was turned away by Samantha stating that her mother was not in a condition to receive guests. The local pharmacist noted that Mrs. Harris had not picked up her monthly medications, which she always did regularly. Samantha has procured a legal power of attorney document and is solely responsible for managing the household budget. The bank clerk has noted that Samantha is making frequent and sizable withdrawals.

Unfortunately, Mrs. Harris is a victim of elder abuse, a growing problem for older adults and their families. This chapter aims to provide an understanding of this problem in the United States within the context of aging families. We present relevant demographic information, definitions of elder abuse and a theoretical framework appropriate for addressing the problem, followed by a review of salient research literature published on the topic. Our review comprises incidence and prevalence studies on elder abuse, victim and perpetrator characteristics, microlevel to macrolevel causes of elder abuse, and prevention and intervention efforts. The chapter ends with conclusions and recommendations for future research within the theoretical framework suggested.

DEMOGRAPHIC CONTEXT OF ELDER ABUSE

By 2030, there will be 72.1 million older adults living in the United States, representing approximately 20% of the total population (Administration on Aging, 2010). In 2002, the United Nations publication *World Population Aging* concluded that by 2050, 21% of the world population will be 60 years and older. These proportions reflect an international phenomenon, as the world's population of older adults continues to live to an advanced age because of better and greater access to health care, advances made in the area of public health, and reduced infant mortality (Albert, 2004; Lee & Estes, 2003; United Nations, 2002). Reflective of these advancements, in 1889 when Bismarck instituted social security for older adults in Germany, the system was predicated on the assumption that such benefits would be necessary for only a very few adults who lived to an old age in order to secure them from financial exigencies at the end of life. More than a century later, older adults in the United States can expect to live a decade or longer beyond their 65th birthday. For example, in 2007, on average, a 65-year-old female can expect to live for another 19.8 years, and a 65-year-old male can expect to live for an additional 17.1 years (Administration on Aging, 2010). Also, most older adults, at least in developed countries, enjoy far better health (i.e., physical, mental, and financial) and remain independent for a longer period of time than cohorts before them.

However, due to living to an advanced age, some older adults will be living longer with chronic illnesses, others will be living longer with encroaching dementia, and many may experience both maladies (Albert, 2004), situations that may create vulnerability to abuse by others. In addition, populations of individuals with mental retardation, developmental disabilities, and mental illnesses are also living longer than ever before and presenting new health and social support challenges (Ansello & O'Neill, 2010; Teaster, 2004). Elders with special needs will require services far longer and in a different manner than those received by previous cohorts, and this dependency may allow an opportunity for abuse to occur. In addition, care expectations (many will not need or have available the hands-on family care of earlier cohorts) of today's older adults are different from those of the past because of their experiencing better physical, mental, and financial health. For example, the availability of personal savings and social insurance such as Social Security, Medicare, and Medicaid enables older adults to seek formal caregiving from health care staff members or other service providers. Also, due to advances in the ability to communicate and to travel, many of today's elders live far from family members who might otherwise help them (Collins, Holt, Moore, & Bledsoe, 2003; Lewis, 2008).

At this point in U.S. history, compared to their younger counterparts, older adults control the largest portion of U.S. wealth (MetLife Mature Market Institute, 2009). This situation presents an opportunity for exploitation to occur. There are also implications for those less fortunate. Although some older adults remain quite powerful in social standing, the economic downturn that began in December 2007 has played havoc with investments of many adults, especially those older adults who placed life savings in the stock market. Although this financial situation is not unique to older adults, many of them lost far more than sheer economic value. Formerly retired older adults can and do return to the labor market, but they are less likely to do so than younger people. Also, they typically have a shorter period of life left to ride out an uncertain or lackluster economy. Consequently, unlike their younger counterparts, many older adults have fewer opportunities to recoup lost funds.

As with the complexities that accompany loss of economic ability, some older adults experience difficult health problems that require complex management strategies such as dealing with multiple chronic diseases, concomitant medications, and issues related to health insurance coverage (Hudson, 2003; Lee & Estes, 2003; Loeb, Penrod, Falkenstern, Gueldner, & Poon, 2003). Diminishing health increases older adults' vulnerability to abuse and neglect, particularly those aged 85 years and older. Changes in the population of elders, particularly those who may be compromised due to poor mental and physical health, create a rise in the number of elders experiencing abuse.

The fact of vulnerability can itself produce a vicious cycle of greater vulnerability. Older adults who experience abuse often do so at a huge price, including spiraling losses of autonomy, emotional well-being, and health (Dong, Simon, Odwazny, & Gorbien, 2008; Dyer, Pavlik, Murphy, & Hyman, 2001; Lachs, Willams, O'Brien, Pillemer, & Charlson, 1998).

DEFINITIONS AND DISTINCTIONS

Elder Abuse

Elder abuse is a global term referring to maltreatment perpetrated on an adult approximately 60 years of age and older. Elder abuse occurs in different forms, usually recognized as including physical abuse, emotional abuse, sexual abuse, caretaker neglect or abandonment, and financial exploitation, terms that will be explained in detail later in this chapter. Although the phenomenon is generally understood, elder abuse is defined differently by statutes, regulations, and institutions that vary by state. No national law exists to establish standard definitions (Payne, 2002). The lack of definitional consistency affects how abuse perpetrated on an older adult is addressed as well as how researchers use and combine data collected by and from different societal entities.

A Theoretical Underpinning

A number of frameworks and disciplines have been used to explain elder abuse. We contend that a particularly applicable and comprehensive one to consider is the ecological framework proposed by Uri Bronfenbrenner. Application of an ecological perspective (Bronfenbrenner, 1986; Moen, Elder, Lüscher, & Bronfenbrenner, 1995) to elder abuse allows a focus on individual characteristics of the victims through four relevant influencing and nested systems: (1) the microsystem (e.g., the victim, victim's home or care setting), (2) the mesosystem (e.g., family, neighbors, friends, care providers), (3) the exosystem (e.g., Adult Protective Services, law enforcement, health care providers), and (4) the macrosystem (e.g., global ethical principles of autonomy, beneficence, nonmaleficence, and justice) (Schiamberg & Gans, 2000). Understanding the influence of microsystems and mesosystems in victims' lives (such as in the case of Mrs. Harris above) permits an examination of personal histories, family relationships, and social and historical contexts in addition to understanding the influence of exosystems and macrosystems associated with the problem. This ecological model facilitates an understanding that elder abuse is a complex problem requiring systemic and coordinated responses from different levels of intervention.

OVERVIEW OF ELDER ABUSE

Elder abuse has been examined by dedicated researchers for approximately four decades, with some of the earliest work conducted on the efficacy of a government demonstration project involving a control group and a treatment group that provided enhanced social services to address the problem (Blenkner, Bloom, Nielson, & Weber, 1974). Ironically, the control group appeared to have better outcomes than the treatment group receiving the enriched services. Even upon re-analysis of the data, there were no significant between-group outcome differences (Berger & Piliavin, 1976), which was attributed to chance factors and randomization of the small sample. Although a system of Adult Protective Services (APS) was put into place in each state, from the outset of intellectual inquiry into services provided to abused older adults, research and practice approaches to this dilemma were controversial.

In addition to research findings that enriched social services did not necessarily improve the lives of abused elder adults, the very definitions of the phenomenon created a source of difficulty for determining the correct approach to addressing the problem. Definitional disagreements ranged from who constituted an elder adult or adult with a disability (i.e., all people 60 years of age and older versus those with developmental disabilities only), settings (i.e., elders living in domestic or facility settings), and types of abuse (i.e., abuse, neglect, and exploitation).

Exacerbating these problems was an overall lack of funding for meaningful research, particularly at the federal level. In 2003, Bonnie and Wallace noted that there were fewer than 15 projects on the topic funded by the

National Institute on Aging. Even those researchers fortunate enough to be funded sometimes labored under far too few dollars to conduct the research adequately. Other researchers simply conducted smaller scale, and, many times, unfunded studies. Because of funding limitations and ethical issues underlying research on elder abuse (e.g., confidentiality, mandated reporting, access to datasets, inaccurate administrative data), conducting credible and generalizable research was challenging. To the credit of research and practitioner communities, which often banded together, continuous improvements have been made in the quality of research produced. The review below highlights important recent attempts to understand the incidence and prevalence of elder abuse.

Attempts to Calculate Incidence and Prevalence of Elder Abuse

Studies on elder abuse reveal that it is more prevalent in community than facility settings (Laumann, Leitsch, & Waite, 2008; Pillemer & Moore, 1989). Using a random sample of 2,020 older adults (aged 65+) living in Massachusetts, Pillemer and Finkelhor (1988) found that 3.2% had been abused in one year. By inference, Pillemer and Finkelhor estimated that from 701,000 to 1,093,560 older adults were abused in the United States each year. Shortcomings of the study included that it concerned only one metropolitan area in the northeast (Boston) and did not measure exploitation.

Until 2008, few attempts were made to calculate elder abuse incidence and prevalence. In 1998, the first National Incidence Study was conducted by the National Center on Elder Abuse in collaboration with Westat, Inc. (Tatara, Kuzmeskas, Duckhorn, Bivens, & Thomas et al., 1998). Data came from APS reports of abuse and neglect made in 1996 in a sample of 20 counties from 15 states. In addition to the APS reports, sentinel reports were used to calculate incidence. Sentinels were trained individuals from community agencies who collected elder abuse and neglect data not reported to APS. From these two sources, findings revealed that about 450,000 older adults (60+) experienced abuse or neglect in domestic settings in 1996.

The study team concluded that this number represented the tip of the iceberg. The study team stated that abuse reaching more than five times the number of elder abuse reports made to APS goes unreported. Incidences of abuse may be unreported because many people do not recognize that abuse is occurring, some are unsure of what to do should they suspect it, and others do not want to become involved in the investigation or resolution of abuse. Although an improvement from the Massachusetts study conducted earlier, the National Incidence Study measured elder abuse in the community only, thereby excluding elders who lived in facility settings and who had infrequent contact with social services.

Over time, the U.S. Administration on Aging's National Center on Elder Abuse (NCEA, 2005) used administrative data from APS as a proxy measure of the prevalence of elder abuse at state and national levels. Tatara and Kuzmeskas (1997) reported that in one year APS received 293,000 reports of elder abuse. A decade later, another nationwide study of elder abuse estimated that in one year APS received a total of 381,430 reports of elder abuse (Teaster, Otto, Dugar, Mendiondo, Abner, & Cecil, 2006), amounting to a 20% increase in 10 years (Teaster, Lawrence, & Cecil, 2007). A major problem with the methodology in both studies was that they relied solely on administrative data. Many states were unable to provide even requested rudimentary information.

As reported in the APS results, along with the raw numbers from states' administrative data, the NCEA (2005) emphasized that the vast majority of elder abuse cases go unreported (i.e., for every one case of elder abuse that is reported, five such cases are unreported because of guilt, shame, and fear associated with reporting abuse). The number of unreported cases may mean that only the most severe cases are reported to authorities and that many victims of elder abuse never receive APS services.

Within the past four years, the National Institute on Aging and the National Institute of Justice have supported efforts to calculate incidence and prevalence, and two of these studies have recently been published. A study by Laumann, Leitch, and Waite (2008) explored the prevalence of elder abuse using a sample of 3,005 participants (57 to 85 years) recruited through a multistage area probability design for the National Social Life, Health, and Aging Project. An examination of three types of abuse revealed that 9% of the sample reported verbal abuse, 3.5% financial exploitation, and 0.2% reported physical abuse by a family member. The first study of its type to use a national database, its design was criticized for only examining family abuse in community-dwelling elders.

In 2010, Acierno, Hernandez, Amstadter, Resnick, Steve, Muzzy, and Kilpatrick conducted a study using random digit dialing of 5,777 community-dwelling adults over the age of 60. Results revealed that in the past year, 11.4% of respondents reported experiencing one or more of the mistreatment categories (i.e., neglect, sexual, emotional, and physical abuse). This study had two primary limitations. Prevalence rates were determined using self-reports of experiences typically unreported or underreported. Also, no assessments or measurements were in place to verify cognitive functioning. Findings were based on a "cognitively intact" sample, with no way to verify a respondents' claim to be cognitively intact. Without this verification, investigators were unable to use cognitive functioning as a risk factor or covariate.

From the studies presented above, it is clear that researchers use different age cutoffs for elder abuse. Not all studies investigate all types of elder abuse delineated in the following section. In addition, elder abuse data come from different sources: nonrandom APS sampling and random national sampling. What is clear is that elder abuse is a problem that U.S. society faces, and based on the most recent study, 1 in 10 older Americans have experienced at least one type of abuse in the preceding year.

Types of Elder Abuse

Related to how much abuse is occurring, the NCEA identified seven types of elder abuse. These include physical, sexual, and emotional abuse; exploitation, neglect by caregiver and self-neglect; and abandonment (NCEA, 2005). The definition of each type of abuse is presented in Table 17.1.

Studies have sought to understand these different types of elder abuse. For example, Jogerst et al. (2003) used secondary data of domestic elder abuse reports from all APS agencies in the nation for 1999. Results indicated that 242,430 investigations of domestic elder abuse took place in 47 states, representing a rate of 5.9 domestic elder abuse reports per 1,000 older adults. In the most recent national survey of APS, self-neglect was the most common category of investigated reports (29.4%), followed by caregiver neglect (26.1%), and financial exploitation (18.5%) (Teaster et al., 2006). Incidents of self-neglect and neglect by a caregiver are most common (Tatara et al., 1998), findings that have been verified by recent studies (Teaster et al., 2006; Teaster et al., 2010).

TABLE 17.1 Definitions of Elder Abuse

Term	Definition
Physical abuse	Use of force to threaten or physically injure a vulnerable elder
Sexual abuse	Contact that is forced, tricked, threatened, or otherwise coerced upon a vulnerable elder, including anyone unable to grant consent
Emotional abuse	Verbal attacks, threats, rejection, isolation, or belittling acts that cause or could cause mental anguish, pain, or distress to a senior
Neglect	A caregiver's failure or refusal to provide for a vulnerable elder's safety, physical, or emotional needs
Abandonment	Desertion of a frail or vulnerable elder by anyone with a duty of care
Self-neglect	An inability to understand the consequences of one's own actions or inaction, which leads to, or may lead to, harm or endangerment

Victims' Risk Factors for Abuse

As the incidence, prevalence, and frequency data show, the possibility of being abused in old age is a concern for many older adults. Certain risk factors appear to be indicators of the probability of being abused. Although past theoretical frameworks gave primacy to caregiver stress (Bergeron, 2001), other frameworks emphasize the dependence of the perpetrator on the victim (Lachs & Pillemer, 1995; Nerenberg, 2002; Pillemer & Finkelhor, 1989). Victim risk factors include frailty, cognitive impairment, age, gender, race, and poverty (Lachs & Pillemer, 1995, 2004; Lachs, Williams, O'Brien, Hurst, & Horowitz, 1997; Pillemer & Finkelhor, 1989). Laumann et al. (2008) found that older adults living alone are at risk for financial exploitation. Studies relying on APS case reports concluded that reports of abuse increased with age and that older women were at greater risk for abuse than older men (County Welfare Directors Association of California, 2004; Pavlik, Hyman, Festa, & Dyer, 2001). The National Survey of APS reported that the majority of elder abuse victims were female (65.7%) (Teaster et al., 2006). Of the total number of victims, approximately half (42.8%) of the victims were 80 years of age and older. Finally, the vast majority (89.3%) of elder abuse reports occurred in domestic settings, attributable to the fact that in all states APS has investigatory authority in domestic settings, although that is not the case for investigations in facility settings.

Perpetrators of Abuse

Perpetrators of elder abuse include spouses, children, grandchildren, and siblings (Pillemer & Finkelhor, 1988). That so many perpetrators are family members lends credence to the dependent perpetrator model, which posits that perpetrators need alcohol, money, support, housing, or drugs from the victim. The National APS study reported that 52.7% of alleged perpetrators of abuse were female. Over three-fourths (75.1%) of alleged perpetrators were under the age of 60. The most common relationship of victim to perpetrator was adult child (32.6%) (Teaster et al., 2006). Perpetrator risk factors included mental health and substance abuse problems, dependency, poor health, loneliness, and a history of violence (Kivela et al., 1992; Lachs & Pillemer, 1995; 2004).

Reporters and Settings of Abuse

Using models from child abuse and domestic violence, reporting of elder abuse is legally mandated by laws in most states, hence professionals who interact with older adults and who suspect abuse are legally obligated to report their suspicion to APS (Remick, 2009; Teaster, 2004). In some states, *any* person who suspects elder abuse is legally required to report it. The

Teaster (2006) study revealed that the most common sources of reports of elder abuse were from family members (17.0%), social service workers (10.6%), and friends and neighbors (8.0%). Reports by health care professionals were noticeably lacking.

A recent study using data from Kentucky APS revealed that abuse of older adults occurs more often in community settings than facility settings (in Kentucky, APS has investigatory authority in both community and facility settings). During the study period, 70% of alleged victims were residing in their own homes, 5.3% were in nursing homes, and 4.2% resided in an assisted living facility (Teaster et al., 2010).

The Effects of Abuse

Elder abuse studies have shown that previously abused elders are often more vulnerable than those who have never been abused. Using longitudinal data obtained from Connecticut's Long Term Care Ombudsman, Lachs et al. (1997) studied 2,812 community dwelling older adults statewide and found that 6.5% of participants from the initial cohort required elder protective services within nine years. Among those receiving protective services (6.5% of 2,812 adults), nursing home placement was highest for elder adults who were self-neglecting (69.2%), followed by elder adults who were mistreated (52.3%). It was lowest (31.8%) for those who had no contact with protective services (Lachs, Willams, O'Brien, & Pillemer 2002). Older adults who were abused had higher mortality rates than those with no history (Lachs et al., 1998).

CAUSES OF ABUSE

Although the studies above provide information as to what types of abuse are occurring, to whom, and how often, a critical issue to address is the question of why abuse occurs in the first place in order to intervene in situations in which it is currently occurring as well as to prevent it from happening. Drawing from the theoretical underpinnings section discussed above, the following section addresses causes, from micro and macro perspectives. First, we explore microlevel reasons. We do not know their frequency beyond anecdotal information.

Elder Abuse: Microsystem and Macrosystem Approaches

Caregiver Dependency Model

Research indicates that the vast majority of caregivers who abuse do so not because they are stressed in the provision of care, but because they are dependent on the care recipient (Nerenberg, 2002, 2008; Wolf, 1997). A frequently occurring scenario (as with the case of Mrs. Harris above) is one in which an adult child who has never learned to be independent from the parent or who suffers from mental illness or financial crises returns to the parent when life situations are beyond his or her ability to cope. Offspring may be unable to keep a job, sustain a marriage, raise their own children, or care for other dependents. The dependent adult child may be an alcohol or drug abuser or both, and so, when money runs out, he or she returns home to the parent. Situations may turn violent when the older adult declines or refuses to provide more money or other types of support, particularly when the dependent adult child becomes desperate. Often, health care, agency, or court intervention is required to break the cycle of dependency and provide safety for the older adult.

Some family members simply want to have money from an older relative. Some persons actually become family members in order to do so (Carlson, 2006; Metlife Mature Market Institute, 2009; Reed, 2005; Wilber & Reynolds, 1996). An example of this behavior is the "sweetheart scam." In this scenario, an older man who has amassed some money, property, or both loses his wife of many years to a fatal illness. Adult children may or may not live nearby. The adult children may be raising children of their own and may be involved in demands of employment, leaving little time to attend to the grieving older father. The father may be lonely and desire companionship that the children are unable or unwilling to provide. A younger woman steps in to befriend the lonely old man, only to demand greater and greater sums of money or possessions and then leave him when the funds are depleted or when family or friends realize that the relationship is based on extracting money rather than providing affection.

Caregiver Stress Model

Just as some people are easily able to care for children, others have an affinity for providing care for older adults. Some caregivers are naturally able to provide care, and, with more practice as well as information or training, they become even more adept. Alternately, others are impatient with the needs of old people who are ill or who have memory impairment (Post, 2000). Some individuals who are not equipped physically and psychologically to care for frail older persons may become abusive out of sheer frustration or inability to manage the situation (Quinn & Tomita, 1997; Wolf, 1997).

Closely related to persons who find providing care difficult are those who are poorly equipped to help. Care regimens for some frail adults may be extremely complex when multiple problems are present. A caregiver who could be struggling from chronic mental and physical fatigue may need to administer medications in a variety of ways and at a variety of times. It may be necessary for the care provider to monitor closely the care recipient's reactions to medications. Such care provision may be far too complicated or demanding for some care providers, particularly those who bear sole responsibility for care, have little or no preparation for it, and have no one to provide respite. Even caregivers who have the best intentions may simply be unable to carry such a heavy responsibility. For example, a caregiver who is frail himself or herself or who is cognitively compromised can find complex medication administration daunting and may unwittingly administer an incorrect dosage of medication. Alternately, he or she, through trying to assist an older adult with a hygiene regimen, could unintentionally cause severe bruising or even bone fracture. Intentional or unintentional, the effect on the care recipient will be the same (harm to the victim) and potentially life-threatening.

Mesolevel and Macrolevel Explanations of Elder Abuse

Explanations of elder abuse at the level of the individual or at the level of the individual in relationship with friends or family give an incomplete understanding of the issue and, consequently, intervention aimed only here is destined to fail. An understanding of systems and societal norms rounds out the explanation and provides a stronger basis for intervention.

Cumulative Inequality

At the level of the mesosystem, both young and old family members may grow up under multiple challenges, some for which control or escape is virtually impossible (Ferraro, Shippee, & Schafer, 2009; Shuey & Willson, 2008). Cumulative inequalities may include age, race, ethnicity, gender, and living in an environment that is unsafe, such as the inner city of some metropolitan areas or the isolation of rural areas. In many locations, opportunities to gain or sustain employment in order to sustain a living wage may be severely limited. Persons may grow up without opportunities for adequate nutrition and exercise. Some may not have the opportunity for an adequate education and may be hampered in their ability to make a living wage and exercise control over their own lives.

The Matthew effect is instructive and applicable in this situation (Merton, 1968). Based on the biblical passage in Matthew 25:29, "For unto every one that hath shall be given, and he shall have abundance: but from him that hath not shall be taken away even that which he hath." Simply put, the more resources available to an individual, the more the resources accrue. For older adults, the effect addresses access to medical care, educational opportunities, and a career trajectory. This effect can also be seen in resource allocation (Dannefer, 1987) and preparing for old age as well as living through the later years. Those who have the ability to prepare better for old age tend to fare better in old age.

Conversely, prenatal care may be poor, and although children mature to adulthood, they may continually experience compromised mental and physical health, the effects of which can increase as a person ages, thus increasing dependencies on others and decreasing the ability to care for oneself. As mentioned earlier, these problems lead to vulnerabilities, which create occasion for abuse to occur.

Ageism

Robert Butler (1975) coined this expression more than 30 years ago, and unfortunately, it is still very much alive today. As with any -ism, ageism has a significant and deleterious effect upon those it touches. At the macrosystem level, for elderly people, ageism has multiple implications, including but not limited to discrimination in the workplace; infantilization; disregard for human rights, devaluation, or diminution; too few or inadequate services; discounting of mental or physical health concerns; disrespect and dishonor; segregation from activities; and, of course, overt or covert abuse, neglect, or exploitation (Butler, 1975; Nelson, 2004; Palmore, 2001). In society, ageism contributes to a pervasive attitude by individuals and groups whereby the needs of older people are relegated as less important than those of younger adults or children. Evident in any number of spheres, ageism is starkly apparent in the allocation of funds that address the abuse of elders in contrast to those allocated for the prevention of child abuse. An example of attitudes toward the plight of abused elders, in 2002 the federal government allocated $6.7 billion for prevention of child abuse and $520 million for prevention of violence against women, but only $153.5 million to combat elder abuse (cited in Anonymous, 2002). Also, APS, the legal system, and the medical system may be inadequately prepared and funded to address elder abuse.

INTERVENTION AND PREVENTION EFFORTS

A variety of options are available for persons who are victims of abuse. In this section we describe typical responses to allegations of abuse and discuss efforts to prevent it from occurring.

Interventions for Elder Abuse

The first responding agency to cases of elder abuse is APS, which is typically the agency of first report when abuse, neglect, or exploitation occurs (Mathaisen, 1973; Quinn & Tomita, 1986; Regan, 1978). APS is located in each of the 50 states as well as Washington, DC, and Guam. Although terminology and responses vary by state statute and regulation, in general, APS receives a report from someone in a community or facility setting and then makes a determination of action regarding the report. APS staff members may refer the report to another entity or agency or may conduct an investigation, which, in some instances, may involve other entities such as the local long-term care ombudsman or the police. If an investigation is deemed appropriate, then an APS staff member, usually a social worker, attempts to make a home visit to the victim (a hallmark of how APS conducts its work).

Various actors involved in the alleged incident of abuse may also be interviewed. Services may be offered or arranged at some point; however, these services may not be accepted, because any competent adult has the right to refuse services (Duke, 1997; Schimer & Anetzberger, 1999). Finally, when enough information has been gathered to make an informed decision, the APS staff member makes a determination to substantiate (or not) a case. Substantiating a case means that, in the best opinion of the staff member, the alleged abuse (or parts of it) is determined to have occurred. It is quite possible that a case might not be substantiated even though abuse could have, in fact, occurred. This could happen if the evidence were insufficient to meet the agency's established criteria for substantiating a report. For example, the Kentucky APS study found that only 39 out of 132 investigations conducted during the study week were substantiated (Teaster et al., 2010).

Other entities may also be involved in intervention efforts, depending on the situations of each report. As mentioned earlier, although APS can investigate a report of abuse, neglect, or exploitation in all community settings, the same is not true for facility settings (Teaster et al., 2006). In these cases, other agencies or entities will take the report and determine a course of action. In some states, the local long-term care ombudsman would be involved in abuse, neglect, or exploitation occurring in long-term care facilities. In other states, the office of the attorney general could be involved. In instances where it seems very clear that a crime has been committed, the local police may conduct the investigation.

Beyond the investigation, many agencies and entities may assist the victim by providing different services or other intervention. Assistance provided to an older abuse victim can be quite varied, depending on the type and nature of the alleged abuse as well as available resources. The case study of Mrs. Harris presented at the beginning of this chapter suggests multiple possible interventions. APS could be involved to investigate. APS might suggest that the best course of action is to separate the mother and the daughter. If they are separated, intervention could be needed by an Area Agency on Aging to help locate appropriate housing, if Mrs. Harris prefers to move. If Samantha is threatening her mother, then the court may become involved in conducting a hearing before a judicial officer and issuing an order of protection so Samantha would not be legally permitted to contact her mother. Interventions could involve police, detectives, social workers, and medical professionals such as a physician, a counselor, or both (Teaster, Nerenberg, & Stansbury, 2003). Mrs. Harris's clergy may also be involved to help her cope with abuse that she has experienced or to help her reconnect to a social network (Rudnick, 2009). If Mrs. Harris's assets need protection, bank officials may also be involved so that the daughter is prevented from withdrawing any more money from Mrs. Harris's account (Metlife Mature Market Institute, 2009; Wilber & Reynolds, 1996). Finally, if crimes have been committed, then the perpetrator could be prosecuted (Heisler & Stiegel, 2004). Easily evident, a host of individuals and entities may be involved with intervention efforts, and intervention is guided by the unique instance of abuse.

Prevention Efforts for Abuse

Acute needs arising from abuse are critical to address, as some types of abuse are life-threatening or highly threatening to the quality of life of an older adult. The effect of the abuse on the elderly family member almost always extends to other family members who may be intimately involved in the abuse or involved in intervention efforts from a distance (Nerenberg, 2008; Quinn & Tomita, 1997). Such cases can be heartbreaking and result in irreparable fissures in the fabric of family life.

Prevention efforts are just as important as intervention efforts. Unfortunately, if there are too few resources for intervention efforts, there are even fewer directed toward prevention efforts. One reason that prevention efforts are so rare is that their impact is difficult to measure due to such challenges as lack of consensus about what constitutes abuse, what constitutes increased or reduced risk, and appropriate outcomes for reports (Teaster & Wangmo, 2010; Wiglesworth, Austin, Corona, Schneider, Liao, Gibbs, & Mosqueda, 2009). Oftentimes, the target of intervention is a shifting of prevention efforts best suited to one set of individuals that may be inappropriate for others. In the case of Mrs. Harris, prevention efforts could be addressed toward the daughter, who could be helped with her financial problems so that she might not be in a desperate situation that would prompt her to take money from her mother. Mrs. Harris's church members could be educated about warning signs related to the potential for abuse and establish a monitoring network. Bank officials could be trained to be alert to the potential for financial abuse and in what to do should they suspect it. Again, each entity would require a different approach.

A number of creative prevention efforts exist around the country. One example is the National Committee for the Prevention of Elder Abuse's Elder Justice Collaboration initiative. Partnering with the NCEA, the National Committee has nurtured more than 40 new elder justice initiatives around the country. These coalitions represent multidisciplinary teams who come together to address the issue of elder abuse. The teams identify service gaps, update members about new services, resources, and legislation on elder abuse, and advocate for needed change.

FUTURE DIRECTIONS FOR RESEARCH

Stressed earlier, the problem of elder abuse in a family setting presents challenges for prevention and intervention efforts. Also stated previously, elder abuse results in increased levels of chronic diseases, depression, and mortality (Dyer et al., 2001; Dong et al., 2008; Lachs et al., 1998). Elder abuse entails costs, not just to individuals and families, but also to health care, legal, and social services systems (Mouton, 2003; Spencer, 2000).

Refinements in research methodologies and research questions continue to develop, attributable in part to increases in funding from sources such as the Archstone Foundation in California, the Centers for Disease Control, the National Institute of Justice, and the National Institutes of Health. Recent funds were earmarked for studies calculating incidence and prevalence of abuse, forensic indicators of abuse, and linking existing datasets (e.g., APS and law enforcement, APS and the National Violent Death Reporting System). The most recent promising new source of support, still without dollars attached, is the passage of the Elder Justice Act in March 2010, which includes dollars earmarked for research. More research is needed on nearly every type of elder abuse. No research funding has so far been provided to measure the efficaciousness of prevention and intervention efforts. Bronfenbrenner's ecological model is extremely useful in guiding exploration of what types of abuse occur in what systems and what efforts are best suited to deal with them.

Research at the Microsystem Level

At the level of the victim and the victim's home emerge these questions: What do older adults regard as their greatest strengths to prevent elder abuse from occurring? Do older adults understand risks for elder abuse and how to prevent them? To what extent do victims of elder abuse trust professionals who might help them? Do family members of older adults trust professionals who might propose to intervene in abusive situations?

Research at the Mesosystem Level

At the level of the victim and the intersection of the family, how does abuse in family and home situations differ in physical and mental health consequences from abuse in facilities and by paid staff or a resident? When abuse has been identified in aging families, what are its long-term effects? How are social networks affected in the short and long term? If there could be repair for families, what are the best strategies to accomplish it? How are family perpetrators rehabilitated? What are the long-term effects of protection orders on family members who have been abused? What are the costs to families when there has been abuse? How is the abuse of older men in families different from and similar to abuse of older women? How are male family members who perpetrate abuse different from and similar to their female counterparts?

Research at the Exosystem Level

For the intersection of APS, law enforcement, health care, and the banking industry, questions concerning the intervention and prevention are critical. What is the most optimal way that these system actors can work together to prevent abuse? What is the most optimal way in which these systems can intervene in elder abuse? What are evidence-based indicators of the best intervention efforts by these systems working together? Is working together the most cost-effective intervention strategy? What formal mechanisms and entities appear to have the best success in intervention efforts? What outcomes for intervention are the most appropriate and do these outcomes differ across disciplines and entities? How can these entities assist in prevention efforts?

Research at the Macrosystem Level

It is critical to ascertain how societal norms can be better understood, and in some instances, altered. Some research questions for exploration at this level are these: How does poverty affect elder abuse, and how does ageism affect elder abuse? What are the appropriate balances between autonomy of capacitated individuals to engage in self-neglect and community interests in promoting public health standards? What is the appropriate role of government oversight in elder abuse, and where should the oversight be located or positioned most effectively (i.e., localities, states, federal entities)? What are the societal and economic costs of elder abuse?

CONCLUSION

From the discussion in this chapter, and on a variety of ecological systems levels, there is much to understand about elder abuse. With the impending wave of baby boomers poised to become older adults, the time to address elder abuse in families is upon us. Efforts have been made to address the problem in the past 40 years, but with older adults constituting approximately 20% of the population, the problem is likely to grow and it deeply affects not only older adults but also those who interface with them.

Abuse in families carries with it a potential severing of relationships, diffuse targets for intervention and prevention, and a lack of evidence-based strategies. An important task that lies ahead is to thoroughly examine the problem on microsystem, mesosystem, exosystem, and macrosystem levels, understanding that these systems are interlinked. It is incumbent on us all, researchers, theorists, and practitioners, to increase and improve efforts to prevent and best intervene in stopping the abuse of elders.

REFERENCES

Acierno, R., Hernandez, M. A., Amstadter, A. B., Resnick, H. S., Steve, K., Muzzy, W., & Kilpatrick, D. G. (2010). Prevalence and correlates of emotional, physical, sexual, and financial abuse and potential neglect in the United States: The national elder mistreatment study. *American Journal of Public Health, 100,* 292–297.

Administration on Aging. (2010). *Profile of Older Americans 2009.* Retrieved from http://www.aoa.gov/AoARoot/Aging_Statistics/Profile/2009/3.aspx

Albert, S. M. (2004). *Public health and aging: An introduction to maximizing function and well-being.* New York: Springer Publishing.

Anonymous. (2002). Protecting older Americans: A history of federal action on elder abuse, neglect, and exploitation. *Journal of Elder Abuse & Neglect, 14,* 9–31.

Ansello, E. F., & O'Neill, P. (2010). Abuse, neglect, and exploitation: Considerations in aging with lifelong disabilities. *Journal of Elder Abuse & Neglect, 21,* 105–130.

Berger, R., & Piliavin, I. (1976). The effect of casework: A research note. *Social Work, 21,* 205–208.

Bergeron, L.R. (2001). An elder abuse case study: Caregiver stress or domestic violence? You decide. *Journal of Gerontological Social Work, 34,* 47–63.

Blenkner, B., Bloom, M., Nielson, M., & Weber, R. (1974). *Final report: Protective services for older people: Findings from the Benjamin Rose Institute study.* Cleveland, OH: Benjamin Rose Institute.

Bonnie, R. J., & Wallace, R. B. (Eds.). (2003). *Elder mistreatment: Abuse, neglect, and exploitation in an aging America.* Washington, D.C.: National Academies Press.

Bronfenbrenner, U. (1986). Ecology of the family as a context for human development: Research perspectives. *Developmental Psychology, 22,* 723–742.

Butler, R. (1975). *Why survive?* New York: Harper Collins Publishers.

Carlson, E.L. (2006). Phishing for elderly victims: As the elderly migrate to the internet fraudulent schemes targeting them follow. *Elder Law Journal, 14,* 423–427.

Collins, W.L., Holt, T.A., Moore, S.E., & Bledsoe, L.K. (2003). Long-distance caregiving: A case study of an African-American family. *American Journal of Alzheimer's Disease and Other Dementias, 18,* 309–316.

County Welfare Directors Association of California. (2004). A day in the life of Adult Protective Services. Sacramento, CA: Protective Services Operations Committee.

Dannefer, D. (1987). Aging as intracohort differentiation: Accentuation, the Matthew effect, and the life course. *Sociological Forum, 2*(2), 211–236.

Dong, X., Simon, M. A., Odwazny, R., & Gorbien, M. (2008). Depression and elder abuse and neglect among a community-dwelling Chinese elderly population. *Journal of Elder Abuse Neglect, 20,* 25–41.

Duke, J. (1997). A national study of involuntary protective services to adult protective services clients. *Journal of Elder Abuse Neglect, 9,* 51–68.

Dyer, C. B., Pavlik, V. N., Murphy, K. P., & Hyman, D. J. (2001). The high prevalence of depression and dementia in elder abuse or neglect. *Journal of American Geriatric Society, 48,* 205–208.

Ferraro, K. F., Shippee, T. P., & Schafer, M. H. (2009). Cumulative inequality theory for research on aging and the life course. In V. L. Bengtson, D. Gans, N. M. Putney, & M. Silverstein (Eds.), *Handbook of theories of aging* (pp. 413–433). New York: Springer.

Heisler, C. J. & Steigel, L. A. (2004). Enhancing the justice system's response to elder abuse: Discussions and recommendations of the "improving prosecution" working group of the national policy summit on elder abuse. *Journal of Elder Abuse & Neglect, 14,* 31–54.

Hudson, R. B. (2003). Contemporary challenges to age-based public policy. In R. B. Hudson (Ed.), *The new politics of old-age policy* (pp. 1–19). Baltimore: Johns Hopkins Press.

Jogerst, G. J., Daly, J. M., Brinig, M. F., Dawson, J. D., Schmuch, G. A., & Ingram, J. G. (2003). Domestic elder abuse and the law. *American Journal of Public Health, 93,* 2131–2136.

Kivela, S. L., Kongas-Saviaro, P., , Kesti, E., Pahkala, K., & Ijas, M. L. (1992). Abuse in old age: Epidemiological data from Finland. *Journal of Elder Abuse and Neglect, 4,* 1–18.

Lachs, M. S., & Pillemer, K. (1995). Abuse and neglect of elderly persons. *New England Journal of Medicine, 332,* 437–443.

Lachs, M. S., & Pillemer, K. (2004). Elder abuse. *The Lancet, 364*(9441), 1263–1272.

Lachs, M. S., Willams, C., O'Brien, S., Hurst, L., & Horwitz, R. (1997). Risk factors for reported elder abuse and neglect: A nine-year observational cohort study. *The Gerontologist, 37,* 469–474.

Lachs, M. S., Willams, C., O'Brien, S., & Pillemer, K. (2002). Adult protective service use and nursing home placement. *The Gerontologist, 42,* 734–739.

Lachs, M. S., Willams, C., O'Brien, S., Pillemer, K., & Charlson, M. E. (1998). The mortality of elder mistreatment. *JAMA, 280,* 428–432.

Laumann, E. O., Leitsch, S. A., & Waite, L. J. (2008). Elder mistreatment in the United States: Prevalence estimates from a nationally representative study. *Journal of Gerontology: Social Sciences, 63B,* S248–S254.

Lee, P. R., & Estes, C.L. (Eds.). (2003). *The nation's health* (7th ed.). Boston: Jones & Bartlett Publishers.

Lewis, L. (2008). Long-distance caregiving. *American Journal of Nursing, 108,* 49–49.

Loeb, S. J., Penrod, J., Falkenstern, S., Gueldner, S. H., & Poon, L.W. (2003). Supporting older adults living with multiple chronic conditions. *Western Journal of Nursing Research, 25*, 8–29.

Mathiasen, G. (1973). *Guide to the development of protective services for older people.* Washington, DC: National Council on Aging.

Merton, R. (1968). The Matthew effect in science. *Science, 159*(3810), 56–63.

MetLife Mature Market Institute. (2009). *The 2009 Metlife market survey of nursing home, assisted living, adult day services, and home care costs.* Retrieved from: http://metlife.com/assets/cao/mmi/publications/studies/mmi-market-survey-nursing-home-assisted-living.pdf

Moen, P., Elder, G., Lüscher, K., & Bronfenbrenner, U. (1995). *Examining lives in context: Perspectives on the ecology of human development.* Washington, DC: American Psychological Association.

Mouton, C. P. (2003). Intimate partner violence and health status among older women. *Violence Against Women, 9*, 1465–1477.

National Center on Elder Abuse. (2005). *Fact Sheet, National Center on Elder Abuse.* Retrieved from http://www.ncea.aoa.gov/NCEAroot/Main_Site/pdf/publication/FinalStatistics050331.pdf

Nelson, T. D. (Ed.). (2004). *Ageism: Stereotyping and prejudice against older persons.* Cambridge, MA: MIT Press.

Nerenberg, L. (2002). *Preventing elder abuse by family caregivers.* Washington, DC: NCEA.

Nerenberg, L. (2008). *Elder abuse prevention: Emerging trends and promising strategies.* New York: Springer Publishing.

Palmore, E. (2001). The ageism survey: First findings. *The Gerontologist, 41*, 572–575.

Pavlik, V. N., Hyman, D. J., Festa, N. A., & Dyer, C. B. (2001). Quantifying the problem of abuse and neglect in adults—Analysis of a statewide database. *Journal of American Geriatrics Society, 49*, 45–48.

Payne, B. (2002). An integrated understanding of elder abuse and neglect. *Journal of Criminal Justice, 30*, 535–547.

Pillemer, K., & Finkelhor, D. (1988). The prevalence of elder abuse: A random sample survey. *The Gerontologist, 28*, 51–57.

Pillemer, K., & Finkelhor, D. (1989). Causes of elder abuse: Caregiver stress versus problem relatives. *American Journal of Orthopsychiatry, 59*, 179–187.

Pillemer, K., & Moore, D. W. (1989). Abuse of patients in nursing homes: Findings from a survey of staff. *The Gerontologist, 29*, 314–320.

Post, S. (2000). *The moral challenge of Alzheimer disease: Ethical issues from diagnosis to dying* (2nd ed.). Baltimore: Johns Hopkins University Press.

Quinn, M. J., & Tomita, S. K. (1986). *Elder abuse and neglect: Causes, diagnosis, and intervention strategies.* New York: Springer Publishing.

Quinn, M. J., & Tomita, S. K. (1997). *Elder abuse and neglect: Causes, diagnosis, and intervention strategies* (2nd ed.). New York: Springer Publishing.

Reed, K. (2005). When elders lose their cents: Financial abuse of the elderly. *Clinics in Geriatric Medicine, 21*, 365–382.

Regan, J. J. (1978). Intervention through adult protective services programs. *The Gerontologist, 18*, 250–254.

Remick, L. (2009). Failing to report and false reporting of elder abuse: Penalties under state adult protective services laws. *Bar Associations in Focus on Aging and the Law, 31,* 7–12.

Rudnick, J. (2009). Elder abuse and neglect: Staving off a 'social tsunami': Clergy and health care providers should be positioned to spot abuse. *Health Progress, 90,* 54–59.

Schiamberg, L., & Gans, D., (2000). Elder abuse by adult children: An applied ecological framework for understanding contextual risk factors and the intergenerational character of quality of life. *International Journal of Aging and Development, 50,* 329–359.

Schimer, M. R., & Anetzberger, G. J. (1999). Examining the gray zones in guardianship and involuntary protective services. *Journal of Elder Abuse & Neglect, 10,* 19–21.

Shuey, K. M., & Willson, A. E. (2008). Cumulative disadvantage and black-white disparities in life-course health trajectories. *Research in Aging, 30,* 200–225.

Spencer, C. (2000). Exploring the social and economic costs of abuse in later life. Retrieved from EconWPA: http://129.3.20.41/eps/le/papers/0004/0004006.pdf

Tatara, T., & Kuzmeskas, L. (1997). *Elder abuse in domestic settings.* Elder Abuse Information Series. Washington, DC: National Center on Elder Abuse.

Tatara, T., Kuzmeskas, L., Duckhorn, E., Bivens, L., Thomas, C., et al. (1998). *The National Elder Abuse Incidence Study.* Washington, DC: National Center on Elder Abuse and Westat Inc.

Teaster, P. B. (2004). What research teaches us about guardianship of last resort. In M. J. Quinn (Ed.), *Guardianships of adults: Achieving justice, autonomy, and safety.* New York: Springer.

Teaster, P. B., Lawrence, S., & Cecil, K. (2007). Elder abuse and neglect. *Aging Health, 3,* 115–128.

Teaster, P. B., Nerenberg, L., Stansbury, K. (2003). A national study of multidisciplinary teams. In E. Podnieks, J. I. Kosberg, & A. Lowenstein (Eds.), *Elder abuse: Selected papers from the Prague World Congress on Family Violence* (pp. 91–108). New York: Haworth Press.

Teaster, P. B., Otto, J. M., Dugar, T. D., Mendiondo, M. S., Abner, E. L., & Cecil, K. A. (2006). *The 2004 survey of state Adult Protective Services: Abuse of adults 60 years of age and older.* Report to the National Center on Elder Abuse, Administration on Aging, Washington, DC.

Teaster, P. B., & Wangmo, T. (2010). Kentucky's local elder abuse coordinating councils: A model for other states. *Journal of Elder Abuse of Neglect, 22,* 191–206.

Teaster, P. B., Wangmo, T., Mendiondo, M. S., Wong, W., Grace, J., & Blandford, C. (2010). *A week in the life of APS in the Commonwealth of Kentucky.* Unpublished manuscript.

United Nations. (2002). World population aging (Publication No. ST/ESA/SER.A/207). Retrieved from United Nations Population Division: http://www.un.org/esa/population/publications/worldageing19502050/index.htm

Wiglesworth, A., Austin, R., Corona, M., Schneider, D., Liao, S., Gibbs, L., & Mosqueda, M. (2009). Bruising as a marker of physical elder abuse. *Journal of the American Geriatrics Society, 57*, 1191–1196.

Wilber, K. H., & Reynolds, S. (1996). Introducing a framework for defining financial abuse of the elderly. *Journal of Elder Abuse & Neglect, 8*(2), 61–80.

Wolf, R. S. (1997). Elder abuse and neglect: Causes and consequences. *Journal of Geriatric Psychiatry, 30*, 155–159.

18

Family Gerontechnology: An Emergent Agenda for Research, Policy, and Practice

Jennifer M. Kinney and Cary S. Kart

The purpose of this chapter is to provide a conceptual framework for the emerging area of family gerontechnology. In the simplest terms, we define *family gerontechnology* as the theoretical and practical application of science and technology in service to later-life families. Although Lesnoff-Caravaglia (1988) associated advances in technology with population aging, Mollenkopf and Fozard (2004) traced the emergence of gerontechnology to the U.S. Office of Technology Assessment's (1984) report, *Technology and Aging in America*. The field took off in the subsequent decades, as evidenced by multiple edited volumes that explored a broad range of issues that merge aging with technology (e.g., Bouma & Graafmans, 1992; Burdick & Kwon, 2004; Charness & Schaie, 2003; Schaie, Wahl, Mollenkopf, & Oswald, 2003; Wahl, Scheidt, & Windley, 2004). The most widely cited definition of *gerontechnology* is "the study of technology and ageing for the benefit of a preferred living and working environment and of adapted medical care of the elderly" (Graafmans, Fozard, Rietsema, van Berlo, & Bouma, 1994, p 12). We conceptualize family gerontechnology as distinct from, but clearly grounded in, gerontechnology; its other foundations include social gerontology and family gerontology.

This chapter is organized into five sections. The first three sections summarize key concepts and ideas from each of the substantive areas that together provide the basis for the study of family gerontechnology: social gerontology, family gerontology, and gerontechnology. In each section we identify important building blocks in the development of family gerontechnology. In the fourth section we present a framework for conceptualizing family gerontechnology in which we integrate the three substantive areas and identify the gaps revealed by this effort. For example, within the broader family literature, relatively little is written about later-life families in recent comprehensive volumes (e.g., Coleman & Ganong, 2004). Similarly, much of the research in gerontechnology is motivated by practical efforts to overcome common age-related impairment or develop technologies to help older adults (and their families) manage their homes (e.g., Czaja, 1997; Gill, 2005; Sargent & Diaz, 2007). In the fifth section we propose recommendations for research, practice, and policy that derive from the family gerontechnology framework and conclude the chapter with a brief statement about the future development of family gerontechnology.

OVERARCHING CONCEPTS FROM SOCIAL GERONTOLOGY

Life Course and Life Span Developmental Psychology Approaches

The life course is arguably the most influential concept in social gerontology. Despite its widespread use, multiple definitions of the concept exist. Consistent with Elder (1996), we emphasize four paradigmatic themes of a life course approach: (a) human lives unfold in a specific historical time and geographic location, (b) development occurs in the context of both human agency and social constraints, (c) the timing of initiation and departure from social roles and events matters, and (d) lives are linked or interdependent. Settersten (2003) expanded these themes into emerging propositions that include, among others, the multidirectional and multidimensional lifelong nature of development; the salience of age in the life course; the fact that life course is not only embedded in historical time but it is also bound to cohort; and that the life course consists of a set of trajectories (i.e., events, transitions, turning points, timing, sequencing, spacing, density, duration) that are conditioned by demographic parameters, making it highly variable across individuals.

Settersten (2005, 2006, 2009) pointed to conceptual overlap between the life course and life span developmental psychology perspective (e.g., Baltes, 1987; Baltes, Lindenberger, & Staudinger, 1998). Consistent with the life course approach, the life span developmental psychology approach emphasizes the multidirectional, lifelong nature of development. Development consists of gains and losses and is characterized by plasticity; it is also influenced by historical-cultural conditions and can be understood as the outcome of the interactions of age-graded, history-graded, and nonnormative events (Baltes, 1987). Both approaches embrace a multidisciplinary and interdisciplinary view of lifelong development and Settersten (2006) outlined how application of these approaches could strengthen research on aging-related issues such as work and retirement, leisure, family ties, and health and illness. In one recent novel application, Kinney, Kart, and Reddecliff (2011) used both approaches to conceptualize the impact of early-onset dementia on the well-being of individuals with the disease and their relationships with their families.

Environmental Gerontology

Environmental gerontology has its foundation in Lewin's (1935, 1951) classic equation that behavior is a function of a person and the environment. Kleemeier (1959) applied this equation to the particular context of older adults, launching an area of inquiry the goal of which was to "provide environments that are congruent with the needs and capabilities of the older user, under the hypothesis that congruence will, in turn, be associated with a favorable outcome in terms of psychological well-being" (Lawton, 1988, p. 135). Lawton operationalized psychological well-being in terms of general indicators such as morale, life satisfaction and mental health.

The work of M. Powell Lawton and his colleagues (e.g., Lawton, 1970, 1982, 1983, 1998; Lawton & Nahemow, 1973; Lawton & Simon, 1968) has been most influential in the development of environmental gerontology. Lawton and Nahemow's (1973) press-competence model proposes that an older adult's behavior is a function of the interaction between the competence of the individual and demands (or press) in the environment. The model focuses on three basic functions of the environment: (a) maintenance (i.e., constancy and predictability), (b) stimulation (i.e., departures from the usual, typical environment to which an individual is accustomed), and (c) support (i.e., compensation for lost or diminished competencies) (Lawton, 1989).

Recent reviews of environmental gerontology document a substantial body of diverse research that identified interrelated, key challenges for the field (Wahl, 2001, 2003; Wahl & Weisman, 2003). Specifically, these challenges are to theoretically and empirically explore person-environment relations in later life, to comprehensively study older adults who vary widely in personal competencies across a range of living environments, and to maintain an appropriate balance between basic research and applied research so that findings can either directly or indirectly increase the quality of life for older adults by optimizing their living environments. As such, the fundamental principles of and hypotheses associated with the press-competence model can be used to support the proposed model of family gerontechnology.

Also, consistent with the life course and life span developmental perspectives, the environmental docility and environmental proactivity hypotheses are related to the concepts of social-structural constraints and agency, respectively. Application of the press-competence model to a proposed model of family gerontechnology will require an extension to include the impact of the environment on multiple members of the family at the same time as well as over time.

More than 20 years ago, Parmelee and Lawton (1990) lamented that environmental gerontology was languishing because, in part, recent research had been motivated by applied rather than theoretical concerns. Applying claims made about gerontology being "data rich but theory poor" (Bengtson & Schaie, 1999) to environmental gerontology, Wahl (2003) and Wahl and Weisman (2003) maintained that, with a renewed focus on theoretical advances, environmental gerontology has the potential to link descriptive and experimental research, microlevels and macrolevels of analysis, and diverse social policy perspectives. This view is consistent with Mollenkopf and Fozard's (2004) claim for the need to study technology along a continuum that ranges from micro (individual) to macro (policy) levels.

Empowerment

Haber (2009) maintained that large numbers of aging boomers will necessitate a new paradigm in gerontology, one of empowerment. He offered examples of six current trends or movements that could empower older adults (i.e., the shift from retirement to reengagement; from senior centers to community wellness centers, from aging in place to intentional housing, from nursing home institutions to supportive homes, from acute care medicine to chronic care management, from geriatric reminiscence to intergenerational life review). Early criticism of Haber's ideas included the question of whether the trends he identified are sufficient to represent the emergence of a new paradigm or the failure to embrace the heterogeneity of aging boomers and the irony of suggesting that gerontologists should empower older adults, as if power is a resource than can easily be distributed (Kane, 2009; Neufeld, 2009; Whittington, 2009). Despite these criticisms and the fact that Haber did not include families in the social institutions he provided as examples, we believe that empowerment is a core theme in the families of many aging Baby Boomers and is an important component in the development of family gerontechnology.

FAMILY GERONTOLOGY

Defining and Conceptualizing Later-Life Families

Early explorations defined the later-life family form as one that was beyond the child-rearing and child-launching years; as such, the later-life family was viewed as contracting rather than expanding in size and as returning the primary focus to the original marital dyad (Brubaker, 1990a, b). In retrospect, however, this definition was limited in several ways. First, it more accurately characterized midlife rather than later-life families. Second, two demographic processes, intragenerational contraction due to decreasing birth rate and intergenerational extension due to increasing life expectancy, necessitated a revised definition of a later-life family (Knipscheer, 1992). Third, the brevity of the definition prevented acknowledgement of the inherent diversity that characterizes families in general and later-life families in particular. Capitalizing on this diversity, Bedford and Blieszner (1997, 2000a, 2000b) defined a family as "a set of relationships determined by biology, adoption, marriage and in some societies, social designation and existing even in the absence of contact or affective involvement and, in some cases, even after the death of certain members" (1997, p. 526). This definition is inclusive of same-sex and common-law couples. According to Bedford and Blieszner (2000b), these relationships: (1) are not necessarily voluntary (i.e., they are ascribed), (2) endure from birth to death, (3) are sentimental and symbolic and do not necessarily involve face-to-face contact, (4) diminish with increased age, (5) are situated within a larger kinship network that includes multiple generations, and (6) consist of a range of family roles (e.g., spouse, child, sibling, parent, grandparent).

Several other factors contribute to the complexity of later-life families. First, aging happens not only to individuals; at the same time it happens to all family members—and the unit as a whole—as well (Hargrave & Anderson, 1992). As such, aging is not only an individual pursuit; it is also an interdependent one. Second, given the interdependencies between and among family members, it is important to recognize the distinction between the impacts of aging on families versus the impact of families on aging (Blieszner & Bedford, 1995).

Theorizing in Family Gerontology: Key Concepts That Can Help Us Move Forward

Roberto, Blieszner, and Allen (2006) recently claimed "family gerontology [the study of aging families], a branch of social gerontology, has come of age" (p. 513). They based this statement on five decade-based reviews of the field (Allen, Blieszner, & Roberto, 2000; Brubaker, 1990b; Strieb & Beck, 1980; Troll, 1971), including their own content and methodological analysis of 838 empirical articles published between 1990 and 1999.

Based on their analysis, Roberto et al. (2006) characterized research in family gerontology as increasingly making implicit use of multiple theoretical perspectives, especially those theories that acknowledge the importance of both personal agency and social structure. They proposed an agenda in which researchers and practitioners strive to make their reliance on theory more explicit, take advantage of increasingly sophisticated methodological and analytic techniques to grapple with family-level concerns rather than individual-level concerns, and embrace the challenge of informing practice and policy that promotes improved family life for all members.

There is no shortage of theoretical perspectives available to researchers and practitioners of family gerontology. Although an analysis of family gerontology research in the first decade of the 21st century has not yet appeared in print, the new century's edited volumes on families in general (e.g., Coleman & Ganong, 2004; Demo, Allen, & Fine, 2000; Harper, 2004; Milardo & Duck, 2000; Vangelisti, 2004) and later-life families in particular (e.g., Carter & McGoldrick, 2005; Sousa, 2009) suggest that family gerontologists are making good use of the plethora of perspectives available to them. Obviously, a comprehensive review of these perspectives is beyond the scope of this chapter. Rather, we identify and explain three key constructs from family gerontology that we believe are critical components in our proposed family gerontechnology framework.

Solidarity-Conflict

Originally introduced by Bengtson and colleagues as the solidarity perspective (Bengtson & Roberts, 1991), the renamed solidarity-conflict approach (Bengtson, Rosenthal, & Burton, 1996; Silverstein & Bengtson, 1997) identified six dimensions of solidarity (affectual, associational, structural, consensual, functional, normative) that can be used to characterize intergenerational family relationships. Rather than being a unidimensional conceptualization of family relationships, each of the dimensions of solidarity were conceptualized as orthogonal and as representing a dialectic; over time, Bengtson and colleagues specifically incorporated conflict (e.g., Bengtson, Rosenthal, & Burton, 1996) and negative aspects of solidarity into the model (Silverstein, Chen, & Heller, 1996). As such, the model allows for the classification of multiple family configurations and recognizes the synergistic relationships between and among the various dimensions of solidarity. A key contribution of the solidarity-conflict perspective has been to provide rich description of family relationships at a particular point in time and to assess outcomes of negotiating ambivalence (Connidis & McMullin, 2002a).

Ambivalence

Lüscher and Pillemer (1998) and Pillemer and Suitor (2004) conceptualized ambivalence as the result of incompatible role expectations that place contradictory demands on social actors. They identified two types of ambivalence: sociological or structural ambivalence and psychological or individual ambivalence. Connidis and McMullin (2002b) argued for a reconceptualization of ambivalence in which it is viewed as an aspect of structured sets of social relationships that emerge when individuals' efforts to exercise agency are constrained by social structural arrangements. Connidis and McMullin's elaboration highlights conflict, power, and variations in the resources that are available to individuals when negotiating social life. They maintained that the acknowledgment of ambivalence forces us to examine how role expectations are negotiated (e.g., prioritized or renegotiation of demands) and that ambivalence can be a catalyst for social action.

In what could be construed as an implicit attempt to integrate the solidarity-conflict and ambivalence perspectives, Bengtson, Giarrusso, Mabry, and Silverstein (2002) identified three ways that Connidis and McMullin's (2002b) construct of structured ambivalence can aid in the understanding of family relationships. First, exploration of ambivalence prevents a unidimensional examination of family relationships. Second, it normalizes conflict and opens the door to the study of how it is negotiated, managed, and resolved by family members whose resources vary as a function of social status. Third, to the extent that ambivalence is embedded in social structures, it is possible that policy change that restructures social relations could lessen structurally induced ambivalence.

We believe that the solidarity-conflict and ambivalence perspectives embrace several key features that have been called for in family gerontology (Cohler & Altergott, 1995; Marshall, Matthews, & Rosenthal, 1993). Specifically, both perspectives identify the importance of viewing conflict as a normative component of social (and thereby family) life, advocate for multilevel analyses that take into account social structure and culture, encourage a focus on family-level rather than individual-level data, and appreciate the importance of considering diversity between and within families. These features are characteristic of so-called bridging theories (i.e., they link individual agency with social structure; Marshall, 1996), thereby making important contributions to family gerontology and, by extension, to the emerging area of family gerontechnology.

Family Integrity

A third perspective that has great potential to inform the emerging area of gerontechnology is the family integrity perspective (King & Wynne, 2004). King and Wynne defined *family integrity* as the "ultimate, positive outcome of an older adult's developmental striving toward meaning, connection, and continuity within his or her multigenerational family" (p. 7). Family integrity is evidenced in three interrelated competencies of the family as a system. First, there is a transformation of a relationship over time in response to changing life cycle needs of the individual family members. Second, there is resolution or acceptance of past losses and conflicts with living and deceased relatives. Finally, there is a shared creation of meaning through legacies across the generations. The processes of family integrity occur at multiple levels of social organization. At the individual level, family integrity provides an older adult with a sense of completeness and satisfaction in her or his family relationships. At the family level, relational competencies and transactions provide older adults with an important sense of meaning, purpose, and connection with others. At the societal level, values and rituals influence the extent to which an older individual experiences meaning and purpose within her or his intergenerational family.

Although a relatively new perspective, the family integrity perspective has been used to examine the role of material inheritance in the construction of family integrity among later-life Portuguese families (Patrao & Sousa, 2009) and as an alternative to traditional conceptualizations of later life as a time of disconnection and alienation from the family (Sousa, Silva, Marques, & Santos, 2009).

GERONTECHNOLOGY

Defining and Conceptualizing Gerontechnology

In an effort to summarize the breadth of the field of gerontechnology, and based on the writings of Fozard and colleagues (Fozard, 2005; Van Bronswijk, Bouma, & Fozard, 2002), Table 18.1 presents five broad areas of application of gerontechnology: (1) daily living technology, which supports independence, convenience and safety; (2) mobility technology, which supports personal mobility and the use of personal and public transportation; (3) communication and information technology, which maintains and expands social contacts and allows self-, remote, or other monitoring of functioning; (4) work and leisure technology, which helps to continue work and enhance opportunities for educational, recreational, and creative activities; and (5) health technology, which supports physical, cognitive, and emotional functioning, as well as prevention, treatment, and monitoring of disease. Also based on Fozard (2005), the table shows a classification scheme for uses of gerontechnology: (a) prevention (i.e., technology used to prevent or delay physiological or behavioral changes that restrict functioning); (b) compensation and assistance (i.e., technology used by an older adult to compensate for age- and disease-related losses; (c) care support and organization (i.e., technology used by a family caregiver to compensate for an older adult's age-related and disease-related losses); and (d) engagement, enhancement, and satisfaction (i.e., technology used to expand the range and depth of activity).

Each cell in Table 18.1 contains a single example of a currently available technology, device, and even program or environment. These examples are not comprehensive nor are they meant to endorse the best or most representative technology in each cell. Further, some technologies or devices may have multiple uses across multiple areas of application. A thoughtful reader should easily be able to replace 1 or all 20 cells with a different array of examples.

TABLE 18.1 Areas of Application and Uses of Gerontechnology

Areas of Application of Gerontechnology	Uses of Gerontechnology			
	Prevention (Technology used to prevent or delay physiological/behavioral changes that restrict functioning)	Compensation and Assistance (Technology used by an older adult to compensate for age- and disease-related losses)	Care Support and Organization (Technology used by a family caregiver to compensate for an older adult's age- and disease-related losses)	Engagement, Enhancement, and Satisfaction (Technology used to expand the range and depth of activity)
Daily living technology (supports independence, convenience, and safety)	Walk-in bathtub	Roomba® (robot vacuum cleaner)	Chair lift	Adaptive footwear
Mobility technology (supports personal mobility, use of personal and public transport)	Adapted vehicle (hand controls)	Electronic wheelchair	Wheelchair lifting van	Public transportation services for disabled persons
Communication and information technology (maintains and expands social contacts, allows self-, remote, or other monitoring of health and function)	Memory phone	Keyboard communicator (text to speech)	On-line virtual support groups	Facebook

(Continued)

TABLE 18.1 (*Continued*)

Areas of Application of Gerontechnology	Uses of Gerontechnology		
Work and leisure technology (helps to continue work and enhance opportunities for educational, recreational, and creative activities)	On-line educational coursework	Home computer	Talking picture frame	MOAC (Museums and Online Archive of California)–web access to archives at 13 public and private museums in California
Health technology (supports physical, cognitive, and emotional functioning; treatment and prevention of disease; maintains independence)	Multi-alarm pill box	Talking prescription recorder	Remote monitoring system	Page magnifier

Source: Modified from Fozard (2005).

Although we applaud the breadth of Graafmans et al.'s (1994) definition of gerontechnology as "the study of technology and ageing for the benefit of a preferred living and working environment and of adapted medical care of the elderly" (p 12), it raises several important questions for the development of family gerontechnology. The definition implies a single, identifiable, optimal, preferred environment. Yet the entire field of environmental gerontology upon which gerontechnology is based is premised on the assumption of maximizing the fit between a particular individual and a particular environment (e.g., Fozard, 2005; Wahl, 2006).

Thus, there are two questions for the development of family gerontechnology: Who decides what is the preferred living or working environment? For whom should the environment be of benefit? An obvious (and easy) answer is that a particular older adult should determine whether and which technology is used, and that she or he should be the one who benefits from the technology. However, this answer fails to take into account the family systems in which older adults are embedded and the reality that oftentimes multiple family members, rather than individuals, are invested in the decisions surrounding the use of technology and are impacted by its use. A related aspect of the definition is that the inclusion of medical care, combined with the use of the word "elderly," suggests the possibility of a paternalistic rather than egalitarian partnership among the members of families who choose to use technology. Taken together, these issues raise the importance of incorporating key concepts from both social gerontology (e.g., interdependence of lives, empowerment) and family gerontology (ambivalence, solidarity-conflict, integrity) in the development of family gerontechnology.

Two issues in gerontechnology that are important considerations in the development of family gerontechnology are potential barriers and facilitators to the use of technology and the intended and unintended consequences of the use of technology. With respect to barriers and facilitators to the use of technology, a reasonable question is whether older adults actually use the technologies that fill the cells of Table 18.1. After all, some maintain that "new technologies are for the young" and, presumably, it remains as difficult today to teach old dogs new tricks as it ever was. Rogers, Mayhorn, and Fisk (2004) argued that such comments are part of a mythology that is inconsistent with reality (see also Demiris, Rantz, Aud, Marek, Tyrers, Skubic, & Hussam, 2004). Data on older adults in the United States, Canada, and Europe suggest that use of technology generally, and computer and Internet use specifically, is rising steadily (National Advisory Council on Aging, 2001).

Given the pervasiveness of technology in modern society, asking if there are barriers to technology use by older adults is like asking if there are barriers to their participation in daily life. From a sociological perspective, as Mollenkopf (2004) reminded us, "scarcely an area of human life, including the most intimate relations, is not permeated, regulated, controlled, or mediated by technology" (p. 54). In the modern world, is the organization of work or the personal domains of communication or mobility even possible without technology?

Although we lack a comprehensive understanding of the barriers and facilitators of technology use, borrowing from the life course perspective, it is useful to conceptualize the use of technology in the language of the classic age/period/cohort challenge. The advent of various technologies represents a series of period effects that, as evidenced by Mollenkopf's (2004) comments above, influence virtually all members of society. Although cohorts differ in the use of many of the technologies, the large within-cohort variability that occurs might be explained by examining life course factors among individuals and their families.

Whether the use of technology is preventative, proactive, compensatory, supportive, or enhancing (Fozard, 2005; Kahana & Kahana, 2009; Mollenkopf & Fozard, 2004; Morrow, 2003), it can result in overcompensation or undercompensation, neither of which is particularly helpful (Kemper, 2001). Fozard (2003) argued for the necessity of achieving a proper balance of preventive and compensatory technological interventions to assist older adults. This is consistent with Kahana and Kahana's (1996, 2003, 2009) application of their model of proactive use of technology by or for older adults. An important component of this model is the identification of two distinct functions of technology: empowerment-oriented (e.g., the Internet, online support groups, communication technology, and technology that facilitates memory and mobility) and control-oriented technology (e.g., health monitoring, safety monitoring, and telemedicine). Both empowerment- and control-oriented technology can be sources of empowerment as well as sources of threat (Kahana & Kahana, 2009). Much could be learned by examining these functions of technology in the context of family ambivalence, solidarity-conflict, and empowerment.

Whereas the increased use of technology can lead to new alternatives for personal action and result in positive consequences, it can also have negative, unintended consequences at the individual, familial, and societal level. At the individual level and familial levels, technology can promote independence, interdependence, and dependence, all of which can be positive or negative, depending on the particular context, and warrant consideration in the family gerontechnology framework. At the societal level, possible negative consequences include the creation of a great divide between those with access to the technology and the skill to use it and those, who by low socioeconomic status, race, gender, or homelessness, among other characteristics, have neither access to technology nor the skills to use it. For active, engaged, participating older adults, certain age-related physical and sensory impairment can threaten autonomy and make the everyday environment just that more demanding. For these individuals, depending on the parameters of impairment, technology (e.g., Bluetooth technology, voice activation) has the potential to preserve independence and maintain integration. However, superimpose age-related impairments on older adults with low socioeconomic status, who are nonwhite, female, and homeless, with little access to or experience with technology, for example, and any notion of independence or personal autonomy is likely seriously threatened or even lost. Of course, even with access to new technology, many of these individuals will not be able to reap the benefits the technology can offer. Thus, whereas advances in these technology domains have great potential for how some people will age across the life course, adapting to new technology may create barriers and dependencies that result in divisions among different cohorts or subgroups of older adults.

AN EMERGENT FRAMEWORK FOR FAMILY GERONTECHNOLOGY

Twenty years ago Knipscheer (1992) asked how gerontechnological innovations "can support older people in maintaining an independent life style as long as possible" (p. 39). We provide some broad answers to this question (at least in a family context) through our proposed family gerontechnology framework. Changes in population and family demographics have led to increased interest in later-life families (Cohler & Altergott, 1995), but most of this work has been focused on frail elders; as a result, most research has been on family caregiving (see Topo, 2009, for a review of research on technology to support individuals with dementia and their caregivers) rather than the more typical experiences of later-life families (Hughes & Waite, 2004). In contrast, Jaeger's (2005) edited volume on older adults and information and communication technologies is premised on the heterogeneity of the older population (i.e., not all older adults are frail) and, unlike so many volumes, the contributors focused on the use of these technologies by older adults themselves, rather than by professionals who are attempting to assist older adults. The proposed family gerontechnology framework is premised on the principles of fostering independence, promoting constructive interdependencies as appropriate, and nurturing healthy dependencies where necessary.

Fisher (1992) described two general perceptions of the effects of technology on social and, by extension, family life. One perception is that technology is a determinist, external force. The second perception is that technology reflects the cultural values that shape a society and its history. Fisher maintained that neither perception takes into account the reality that people can actively shape the use and influence of technology. Hughes and Hans (2004) indicated that at each technological development throughout history, social critics and technologists debated whether a particular development will empower or impoverish families. After reviewing empirical research on the effects of the Internet on family life, they concluded that it is not possible to understand the implications of new technologies in the short run. Rather, consistent with the life course and life span developmental perspectives, it is necessary to study families' longitudinal adaptation to technologies.

In an effort to synthesize and integrate key contributions from the fields of gerontology, family gerontology, and gerontechnology into the new area of family gerontechnology, we offer the conceptual framework presented in Figure 18.1. Before launching into a discussion of the framework, several caveats are in order. First, we view this framework as a starting point for discussion; we fully expect that it will raise more questions than it answers, both for ourselves and for others. Second, we did not even attempt to create a comprehensive framework. Rather, we present a heuristic that we hope will be useful in the development of the field of family gerontechnology.

A hallmark of the emergent framework for family gerontechnology is its dynamic, fluid, evolving nature. For this reason we chose to depict the framework as a system of ellipses representing three interrelated components that are in constant movement and interplay: family characteristics (i.e., the constructs borrowed from family gerontology); environmental characteristics (i.e., those borrowed from environmental gerontology); and the areas of application and uses of technology, which we borrow from gerontechnology. We purposefully avoid a more static presentation that consists of constructs within boxes that are linked by arrows (both recursive and nonrecursive) in an attempt to represent major relationships among the key components of the framework.

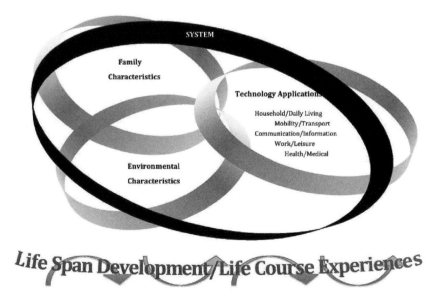

FIGURE 18.1 Emergent Framework for Family Gerontechnology

As seen in the figure, the substructure or foundation upon which the emergent framework is built are the life span development and life course perspectives, both of which emphasize continual development and interdependence among all later-life family members and the family itself. Lending support to this foundation, Silverstein (2004) explicitly proposed the use of the life course perspective to organize research on intergenerational family relationships, especially the principle of linked lives, and Settersten (2009) recently suggested that perhaps interdependence should be a more relevant hallmark of the life course in contemporary societies, identifying interdependence as "life's key hallmark" (p. 77).

Rather than discuss the interrelated components of the family gerontechnology framework in a traditional, piecemeal manner, Table 18.2 presents nine basic assumptions that underlie the family gerontechnology framework. These assumptions integrate concepts from family gerontology and environmental gerontology and apply them to areas of application of gerontechnology. Arguably, each assumption about a specific technological intervention could be written five different ways (i.e., one for each of the five areas of application). An example of how assumption number 7 could be elaborated is presented in Table 18.3. Just as we acknowledge that the family gerontechnology framework is emergent, we envision an exponential number of hypotheses that can be derived from the framework; thus, what is presented here is merely illustrative.

TABLE 18.2 Major Assumptions Underlying the Emergent Family Gerontechnology Framework

1. All elements of the framework for family gerontechnology are influenced by the life course experiences and life span development of all family members.
2. All later life families are characterized by varying degrees of solidarity and conflict.
3. All members of later-life families are characterized by varying degrees of ambivalence about the family.
4. The less competent an older adult is, the more demands will be placed on the later-life family to assume the success of a technological intervention.
5. The more competent an older adult is, the more likely that choice, autonomy, and independence within the later-life family will assure the success of a technological intervention.
6. Older adults in later-life families that are skilled at providing maintenance, support, and stimulation are more likely to experience a successful technological intervention.
7. Family integrity should be a goal of all successful technology interventions.
8. Empowerment of older adults within their families should be a goal of all successful technology interventions.
9. Empowerment of later-life families within the broader social structure should be a goal of all successful technology interventions.

TABLE 18.3 Elaboration of Assumption 7 Underlying the Emergent Family Gerontechnology Framework

7a.	Family integrity should be a goal of all successful health technology interventions.
7b.	Family integrity should be a goal of all successful daily living technology interventions.
7c.	Family integrity should be a goal of all successful mobility technology interventions.
7d.	Family integrity should be a goal of all successful communication and information technology interventions.
7e.	Family integrity should be a goal of all successful work and leisure technology interventions.

As important as it is to describe what is included in the figure, it is equally (or perhaps more) important to discuss certain elements that are not included in the figure. At this point, most readers have realized that the traditional endpoint in most models, outcomes, is not included in the model. This is not to suggest that outcomes are not important in the emergent framework of family gerontechnology. To the contrary, they are vitally important, and Lawton (1989) provided guidance in his claim that environments can provide maintenance, stimulation, and support, all of which contribute to well-being. But if we are to maximize the potential and promise of integrating key ideas from the areas of gerontology, family gerontology, and gerontechnology, identification of outcomes is but one of the challenges we face. In an effort to begin to identify these challenges, we turn our attention to proposing agendas for research, practice, and policy that will help transform the ideas contained in Figure 18.1 (and beyond) into a meaningful field of family gerontechnology.

FAMILY GERONTECHNOLOGY: WHERE DO WE GO FROM HERE?

Intuitively, our call to integrate gerontology, family gerontology, and gerontechnology into a field of family gerontechnology should be an obvious and relatively easy undertaking. After all, each of these three areas of study emerged out of a desire to document and understand the processes and consequences of aging in later-life families and larger social systems including U.S. society and beyond, and use this understanding to develop interventions for individuals, families, and larger social units. Thus, it is not surprising that these three areas of study share so many fundamental concepts. Because of this overlap and interdependence, we were forced to make somewhat arbitrary decisions about where to include certain concepts in the review that began this chapter. So, for example, to identify the importance of historical and current context, the principle of linked lives, or the importance of fit as the purview of only one of the three fields of study does a disservice to the other two.

Notwithstanding this high degree of conceptual overlap, we were surprised to find relatively little integration of these areas of study in the literature. Some might be quick to lament that this omission reflects a larger problem within gerontology in particular and the social sciences in general; an overspecialization to the detriment of the greater good (i.e., a comprehensive understanding of particular phenomena in a larger context). And the argument could be made that encouraging the development of a field of family gerontechnology could serve to further fragment the three contributing areas of study. But we see so much potential for the proposed integration that we prefer to focus our attention on an agenda to move family gerontechnology forward. To the extent that we are successful, a future challenge will be to keep the parameters that define family gerontechnology fluid enough that the area of study is one of inclusion rather than exclusion. Using the major assumptions that underlie the family gerontechnology framework as a starting point (see Table 18.2), we present preliminary recommendations for research, policy, and practice that both derive from and will advance family gerontechnology. Then, in the context of this framework, we briefly critique an ongoing program of research.

Recommendations for Research

Family gerontechnology will benefit from longitudinal investigations that take into account the historical and current contexts of older adults and the members of their later-life families, including family characteristics such as solidarity, conflict, ambivalence, and the changing interdependencies among family members across the life course. Comprehensive longitudinal analysis will allow for assessment over time and, more important, identification of mechanisms and processes by which documented change occurs.

All too often, research on gerontechnology focuses on the family caregiver to the exclusion of the older adult; we ourselves have been guilty of this (e.g., Kinney & Kart, 2006; Kinney, Kart, Murdoch, & Conley, 2004; Kinney, Kart, Murdoch, & Ziemba, 2003). The issue of who is the intended target of the technological intervention is important. Research in which the goals are caregiver-related (e.g., reduce burden, distress, and depression; increase social support and satisfaction) has a very different orientation than research that is based on the premise that well-designed technology can play an integral role in promoting independence and quality of life among older people. What is important for the development of family gerontechnology is that funding be devoted to research efforts that focus on later-life families (including the individuals that comprise them) as the units of analysis and have the potential to empower and promote family integrity among older adults and their family members.

It is important to begin to understand how older adults' levels of personal competence and current and past family characteristics influence the selection, implementation, use, and success of a technological intervention.

What defines the success of a technological intervention is not at all evident. Based on the family gerontechnology framework, at the individual level, goals might include restoration or maintenance of competence and functioning, stimulation, or support for the older adult and possibly other members of the later life family. But it is also important to consider outcomes at the family level. To merely suggest the goal of increasing solidarity and decreasing conflict and ambivalence is unrealistic and naive. But it is possible, perhaps even likely, to expect that a particular intervention might have some consequence for these family characteristics, and it is especially important to begin to understand how technological interventions might empower later-life families and promote family integrity.

Family gerontechnology will benefit from researchers' efforts to adopt a broad approach to the exploration of various applications of technology and their impacts across domains and across members of later life families.

Recommendations for Policy and Practice

The degree of solidarity, conflict, and ambivalence within a later-life family at a particular point in time results in a unique profile of family functioning that can be used to identify strengths and weaknesses that should influence the design of appropriate technological interventions. We need to avoid dichotomizing families as either good or bad or successful or not, and embrace ambivalence among members of later-life families as an important and informative individual or family characteristic. The astute practitioner will integrate these elements of family functioning with traditional assessments of an older adult's strengths and weaknesses (i.e., levels of personal competence) when designing and evaluating the success of a particular technological intervention.

Despite the documented success of technological interventions, there are barriers to the use of technology. Because of the demand characteristics associated with participation in research, practitioners more so than researchers are well-positioned to begin to identify the individual- and family-level factors that impede the use of technological interventions by later-life families.

It is easy enough to embrace the abstract values of family empowerment and integrity as the goals of technological interventions in later-life families. But once researchers and practitioners agree on the operationalization, measurement, and integration of these values into tangible interventions, policies must support the availability of these interventions for all later-life families who have the potential to benefit from them.

Reflections on the Recommendations for Research, Practice, and Policy

In reviewing the recommendations stated above, we cannot help but think about our own program of research on the impact of monitoring technology on family members who care for a relative with dementia. We have completed two studies of the use of remote monitoring technology for community-dwelling older adults with dementia. First, with funding from two Ohio state Area Agencies on Aging, we conducted focus groups with caregivers to determine how electronic technology might be used to assist family members who care for a relative with dementia at home (Kinney, Kart, Murdoch, & Ziemba, 2003). Based on these findings, we installed an Internet-based monitoring system in the homes of 19 such caregivers and monitored the use of the system for six months. Results indicated that community dwelling family caregivers were able to master the technology, and the technology was associated with increased safety and security for the person with dementia, but the use of the technology was not a panacea and actually required increased vigilance by the caregivers (Kinney & Kart, 2006; Kinney, Kart, Murdoch, & Conley, 2004).

Second, with funding from the National Institute on Aging, we have been exploring some of the fundamental issues introduced by remote monitoring technologies: the potential conflict or contradiction among individual values of privacy, safety, and personal control, and family caregivers' trust in the technology. Using a quasi-experimental design, 28 family caregivers who care for a relative with dementia at home were enrolled—14 in an intervention group with an Internet-based monitoring system and 14 in a comparison group who did not receive the monitoring system. Families in the intervention group were assessed at baseline and 10 and 20 weeks after the installation of the technology. Families in the comparison group were assessed at baseline and 20 weeks later. Key outcomes included major components of the caregiving process (e.g., caregiving hassles, caregiver burden, depressive symptomatology, quality of life), changes in caregivers' values over time, and, for families in the intervention group, caregivers' expectations for and experiences with the monitoring technology, and change in their trust in the technology over time. Analysis of these data are ongoing; preliminary findings have been presented at national meetings (e.g., Kinney, Kart, & Reddecliff, 2012).

When examining our research in the context of family gerontechnology, the challenge of fully embracing the recommendations is evident. Our program of research was first initiated in response to a request from an Area

Agency on Aging about how technology could be used to support and extend the length of time that family caregivers could keep their relative with dementia at home in the community. Although one could argue that the family (or at least the persons with dementia and their primary caregivers) was the focus of the research, by virtue of the level of impairment of the individuals with dementia, they did not have a voice in the research.

Because the individuals with dementia were not able to share their preferences with us, we relied on caregivers to represent their own interests, as well as those of their relatives. But it is possible, even likely, that the caregivers and the relatives for whom they cared had disparate or even conflicting goals. As such, decisions made by caregivers about the technology that was installed might simultaneously empower the caregivers and restrict the ability of the persons with dementia to wander throughout the home due to safety concerns, resulting in different outcomes for the two family members. We did not include other coresident (or noncoresident) family members in the research; obviously the inclusion of each additional family member would add complexity to the research but, more importantly, to the richness and veracity of the data.

Although we were sensitive to caregiving as a process in our research, the 20 week and 6 month monitoring periods are mere snapshots in the context of the life course or life span development perspectives. Further, our research did not capitalize on the potential afforded by inclusion of key concepts from the life course perspective and family gerontology. We asked caregivers in our research about their experience with various technologies (e.g., cell phones, computers, the Internet), but important information on family values, solidarity and conflict, and ambivalence only emerged in conversations with our participants; they were not a part of our formal interview protocol. Consistent with our independent variables, which were caregiver-focused, our dependent variables emphasized caregiver well-being. Had we incorporated empowerment of each family member and family integrity as important components of the research, we would be better positioned to make recommendations about future interventions and their impact.

As we have described above, in our recently concluded NIH-funded project, we enrolled 14 households into the intervention group; in each, we installed an Internet-based monitoring system tailored to the specific needs of the caregiving situation. At the conclusion of the 20-week intervention protocol, seven of the caregivers wanted to continue to use the technology. We strategized with a local Area Agency on Aging in concert with a chapter of the Alzheimer's Association to help develop a service program, and we are optimistic about the transition. In most circumstances, one or both of these agencies has history with the caregiver and the older adult, either through caregiver support or respite and adult day care programs. As a result, in many cases agency staff have been in the home, are familiar with the physical layout, and know the strengths and weaknesses of the household members; these families also know that the agencies are committed to meeting their needs for the long term. We have learned that service providers (especially nonprofits and nongovernmental agencies) need to be acutely concerned with budget integrity and public relations, but they are not constrained by the need to define success in common terms that fit all enrolled households. Rather, the success of assuring a caregiver's nightly rest in one household can be equated with reducing wandering outside the home in another household. Perhaps the true potential of family gerontechnology will be realized when research begins with a partnership between experienced researchers and knowledgeable service providers to conduct evidence-based, translational research that can inform policy that strengthens families in later life.

CONCLUDING COMMENTS

In this chapter we have presented an emerging conceptual framework for family gerontechnology, along with a first attempt to operationalize the framework via suggestions for research, policy, and practice initiatives. We defined family gerontechnology as the theoretical and practical application of science and technology in service to later-life families. From our vantage point, the family gerontechnology framework derives from identification and integration of some of the most important concepts from the fields of gerontology, family gerontology, and gerontechnology. Gerontology contributes the life span development and life course perspectives as a solid foundation for the framework; it also provides fundamental principles from environmental gerontology and the heretofore unrealized potential of the empowerment framework. In recent decades, family gerontology has developed a comprehensive and inclusive definition of later-life families, and has amply documented the complexity of these diverse families. Family gerontology contributes a realistic characterization of later-life families that includes various dimensions of both solidarity and conflict and does not shy away from the ambivalence experienced by individual family members. Finally, gerontechnology offers many potential areas of application and impact of various technological interventions—for individual older adults and their families. These three fields of study have provided us with the tools we need to advance the emerging field of gerontechnology. We invite interested readers to join us in this endeavor.

ACKNOWLEDGMENTS

The preparation of this chapter was supported in part by a grant from the National Institute on Aging (R21 AG029224). The authors would like to thank Luann Reddecliff, doctoral student in social gerontology at Miami

University, for her helpful comments and technical assistance in the development of the chapter.

REFERENCES

Allen, K.R., Blieszner, R., & Roberto, K.A. (2000). Families in the middle and later years: A review and critique of research in the 1990s. *Journal of Marriage and Family, 62*, 911–926.

Baltes, P.B. (1987). Theoretical propositions of life-span developmental psychology: On the dynamics between growth and decline. *Developmental Psychology, 23*, 611–626.

Baltes, P.B., Lindenberger, U., & Staudinger, U.M. (1998). Life-span theory in developmental psychology. In R. M, Lerner (Ed.), *Handbook of child psychology, Vol. 1: Theoretical Models of human development* (5th ed., pp. 1029–1143). New York: Wiley.

Bedford, V.H., & Blieszner, R. (1997). Personal relationships in later-life families. In S. Duck (Ed.), *Handbook of personal relationships* (2nd ed., pp. 523–539). Chichester, England: John Wiley.

Bedford, V.H., & Blieszner, R. (2000a). Older adults and their families. In D.H. Demo, K.R. Allen, & M.A. Fine (Eds.), *Handbook of family diversity* (pp. 216–231). West Oxford, UK: Oxford University Press.

Bedford, V.H., & Blieszner, R. (2000b). Personal relationships in later life families. In R.M. Milardo & S. Duck (Eds.), *Families as relationships* (pp. 157–174). West Sussex, UK: John Wiley & Sons.

Bengtson, V.L., Giarrusso, R., Mabry, J.B., & Silverstein, M. (2002). Solidarity, conflict, and ambivalence: Complementary or competing perspectives on intergenerational relationships? *Journal of Marriage and Family, 64*, 568–576.

Bengtson, V.L., & Roberts, R.E.L. (1991). Intergenerational solidarity in aging families: an example of formal theory construction. *Journal of Marriage and Family, 53*, 856–870.

Bengtson, V.L., Rosenthal, C.J., & Burton, L.M. (1996). Paradoxes of families and aging. In R.H. Binstock & L.K. George (Eds.), *Handbook of aging and the social sciences* (4th ed., pp. 253–282). San Diego, CA: Academic Press.

Bengtson, V.L., & Schaie, K.W. (1999). Preface. In V.L. Bengtson & K.W. Schaie (Eds.), *Handbook of theories of aging* (pp. ix–xii). New York: Springer Publishing Company.

Blieszner, R., & Bedford, V.H. (1995). *Handbook of aging and the family*. Westport, CT: Greenwood Press.

Bouma, H., & Graafmans, J.A.M. (Eds.). (1992). *Gerontechnology*. Amsterdam, The Netherlands: IOS Press.

Brubaker, T. H. (1990a). An overview of family relationships in later life. In T.H. Brubaker (Ed.), *Family relationships in later life* (2nd ed., pp. 13–26). Newbury Park: Sage Publications.

Brubaker, T.H. (1990b). Families in later life: A burgeoning research area. *Journal of Marriage and Family, 52*, 959–981.

Burdick, D. C., & Kwon, S. (2004). *Gerontechnology: Research and practice in technology and aging.* New York: Springer Publishing Company.

Carter, E., & McGoldrick, M. (Eds.). (2005). *The expanded family life cycle: Individual, family, and social perspectives* (3rd ed.). Boston: Allyn & Bacon.

Charness, N., & Schaie, K. W. (Eds.). (2003). *Impact of technology on successful aging.* New York: Springer Publishing Company.

Cohler, B. J., & Altergott, K. (1995). The family of the second half of life: Connecting theories and findings. In R. Blieszner & V. H. Bedford (Eds.), *Handbook of aging and the family* (pp. 59–94). Westport, CT: Greenwood Press.

Coleman, M. & Ganong, L. H. (Eds.). (2004). *Handbook of contemporary families: Considering the past, contemplating the future.* Thousand Oaks, CA: Sage Publications.

Connidis, I. A., & McMullin, J. A. (2002a). Ambivalence, family ties, and doing sociology. *Journal of Marriage and Family, 64,* 594–601.

Connidis, I. A., & McMullin, J. A. (2002b). Sociological ambivalence and family ties: A critical perspective. *Journal of Marriage and Family, 64,* 558–567.

Czaja, S. J. (1997). Using technologies to aid the performance of home tasks. In A. D. Fisk & W. A. Rogers (Eds.), *Handbook of human factors and the older adult* (pp. 311–334). San Diego: Academic Press.

Demiris, G., Rantz, M. J., Aud, M. A., Marek, K. D., Tyrers, H. W., Skubic, M., & Hussam, A. A. (2004). Older adults' attitudes towards and perceptions of 'smart home' technologies: A pilot study. *Medical Informatics, 29,* 87–94.

Demo, D. H., Allen, K. R., & Fine, M. A. (Eds.). (2000). *Handbook of family diversity.* New York: Oxford University Press.

Elder, G. H., Jr. (1996). Human lives in changing societies: Life course and developmental insights. In R. B. Cairns, G. H. Elder Jr., & J. E. Costello (Eds.), *Developmental science* (pp. 31–62). New York: Cambridge University Press.

Fisher, C. S. (1992). *America calling.* Berkeley: University of California Press.

Fozard, J. L. (2003). Enabling environments for physical aging: A balance of preventive and compensatory interventions. In K. W. Schaie, H.-W. Wahl, H. Mollenkopf, & F. Oswald (Eds.), *Aging independently: Living arrangements and mobility* (pp. 31–45). New York: Springer Publishing Company.

Fozard, J. L. (2005). Gerontechnology: Optimising relationships between ageing people and changing technology. In V. Minichiello & I. Coulson (Eds.), *Contemporary issues in gerontology: Promoting positive aging* (pp. 241–268). London: Routledge Taylor and Francis Group.

Gill, J. (2005). Priorities for technological research for visually impaired people. *Visual Impairment Research, 7,* 59–61.

Graafmans, J., Fozard, J. L., Rietsema, J., van Berlo, A., & Bouma, H. (1994). Gerontechnology: A sustainable development in society. In C. Wild & A. Kirschner (Eds.), *Safety-alarm systems, technology aids and smart homes* (pp. 9–23). Knegsel, Netherlands: Akontes Publishing.

Haber, D. (2009). Gerontology: Adding an empowerment paradigm. *Journal of Applied Gerontology, 28,* 283–297.

Hargrave, T. K., & Anderson, W. T. (1992). *Finishing well: Aging and reparation in the intergenerational family.* New York: Brunner/Mazel.

Harper, S. (Ed.). (2004). *Families in ageing societies: A multi-disciplinary approach*. Oxford, UK: Oxford University Press.

Hughes, M.E., & Waite, L.J. (2004). The American family as a context for healthy ageing. In S. Harper (Ed.), *Families in ageing societies: A multi-disciplinary approach* (pp. 176–189). Oxford, UK: Oxford University Press.

Hughes, R., Jr., & Hans, J.D. (2004). Understanding the effects of the Internet on family life. In M. Coleman & L.H. Ganong (Eds.), *Handbook of contemporary families: Considering the past, contemplating the future* (pp. 506–520). Thousand Oaks, CA: Sage Publications.

Jaeger, B. (Ed.). (2005). *Young technologies in old hands: An international view on senior citizen's utilization of ICT*. Copenhagen, Denmark: DJOF Publishing.

Kahana, E., & Kahana, B. (1996). Conceptual and empirical advances in understanding aging well through proactive adaptation. In V. Bengtson (Ed.), *Adulthood and aging: Research on continuities and discontinuities* (pp. 18–41). New York: Springer Publishing Company.

Kahana, E., & Kahana, B. (2003). Contextualizing successful aging: New directions in age-old search. In R. Settersten Jr. (Ed.), *Invitation to the life course: A new look at old age* (pp. 225–255). Amityville, NY: Baywood Publishing.

Kahana, E., & Kahana, B. (2009, May). *Ethics of technology for monitoring and managing frail elders*. Presented at the University of Washington's Forum on Technology and Design for Health Aging: What You Can Do NOW, Seattle, WA.

Kane, R.A. (2009). Empowerment of seniors and paradigm change: A commentary on Haber's empowerment paradigm. *Journal of Applied Gerontology, 28*, 298–303.

Kemper, S. (2001). Over-accommodations and under-accommodations to aging. In N. Charness, D.C. Parks, & B.A Sabel (Eds.), *Communication, technology and aging* (pp. 30–46). New York: Springer Publishing Company.

King, D.A., & Wynne, L.C. (2004). The emergence of "family integrity" in later life. *Family Process, 43*, 7–21.

Kinney, J.M., & Kart, C.S. (2006). Somewhere between panacea and impossibility: Assessing the place of technology in facilitating caregiving to a relative with dementia. *Generations, 30*, 64–66.

Kinney, J.M., Kart, C.S., Murdoch, L.D., & Conley, C.J. (2004). Striving to provide safety assistance for families of elders: The SAFE House Project. *Dementia: The International Journal of Social Research and Practice, 3*, 351–370.

Kinney, J.M., Kart, C.S., Murdoch, L.D., & Ziemba, T.F. (2003). Challenges in caregiving and creative solutions using technology to facilitate caring for a relative with dementia. *Ageing International, 28*, 295–314.

Kinney, J.M., Kart, C.S., & Reddecliff, L. (2011). "That's me, the Goother": Evaluation of a program for individuals with early-onset dementia. *Dementia: The International Journal of Social Research and Practice, 10*, 361–377.

Kinney, J.M., Kart, C.S., & Reddecliff, L. (2012). Assessing the impact of an Internet-based monitoring system on caregiver values and quality of life. *Journal of Applied Gerontology*. Manuscript submitted for publication.

Kleemeier, R.W. (1959). Behavior and the organization of the bodily and external environment. In J.E. Birren (Ed.), *Handbook of aging and the individual* (pp. 400–451). Chicago: University of Chicago Press.

Knipscheer, C.P.M. (1992). Interdependency among the generations within the family: A sociological approach. In H. Bouma & J.A.M. Graafmans (Eds.), *Gerontechnology* (pp. 39–49). Amsterdam, The Netherlands: IOS Press.

Lawton, M.P. (1970). Ecology and aging. In L.A. Pastalan & D.H. Carson (Eds.), *Spatial behavior of older people* (pp. 40–67). Ann Arbor, MI: Institute of Gerontology, University of Michigan.

Lawton, M.P. (1982). Competence, environmental press, and the adaptation of older people. In M.P. Lawton, P.G. Windley, & T.O. Byerts (Eds.), *Aging and the environment: Theoretical approaches* (pp. 33–59). New York: Springer Publishing Company.

Lawton, M.P. (1983). Environment and other determinants of well-being in older people. *The Gerontologist, 23,* 349–357.

Lawton, M.P. (1988). Environmental proactivity and affect in older people. In S. Spacapan & S. Oskamp (Eds.), *The social psychology of aging* (pp. 135–163). Newbury Park, CA: Sage Publications.

Lawton, M.P. (1989). Three functions of the residential environment. *Journal of Housing for the Elderly, 5,* 25–50.

Lawton, M.P. (1998). Future society and technology. In J.A.M. Graafmans, V. Taipele, & N. Charness (Eds.), *Gerontechnology: A sustainable investment in the future* (pp. 12–22). Amsterdam, The Netherlands: IOS Press.

Lawton, M.P., & Nahemow, L. (1973). Ecology and the aging process. In C. Eisdorfer & M.P. Lawton (Eds.), *The psychology of adult development and aging* (pp. 619–674). Washington, DC: American Psychological Association.

Lawton, M.P., & Simon, B.B. (1968). The ecology of social relationships in housing for the elderly. *The Gerontologist, 8,* 108–115.

Lesnoff-Caravaglia, G. (1988). *Aging in a technological society.* New York: Human Sciences Press.

Lewin, K. (1935). *A dynamic theory of personality.* New York: McGraw Hill.

Lewin, K. (1951). *Field theory in social science.* New York: Harper.

Lüscher, K., & Pillemer, K. (1998). Intergenerational ambivalence: A new approach to the study of parent-child relations in later life. *Journal of Marriage and Family, 60,* 413–425.

Marshall, V. (1996). The state of theory in aging and the social sciences. In R.H. Binstock & L.K. George (Eds.), *Handbook of aging and the social sciences* (4th ed., pp. 12–30). San Diego: Academic Press.

Marshall, V., Matthews, S.H., & Rosenthal, C.J. (1993). Elusiveness of family life: A challenge for the sociology of aging. In G.L. Maddox & M.P. Lawton (Eds.), *Annual review of gerontology and geriatrics* (vol. 13, pp. 39–72). New York: Springer Publishing Company.

Milardo, R.M., & Duck, S. (Eds.). (2000). *Families as relationships.* New York: John Wiley & Sons.

Mollenkopf, H. (2004). Aging and technology: Social science approaches. In D.C. Burdick, & S. Kwon (Eds.), *Gerontechnology: Research and practice in technology and aging* (pp. 54–67). New York: Springer Publishing Company.

Mollenkopf, H., & Fozard, J.L. (2004). Technology and the good life: Challenges for current and future generations of aging people. In H.-W. Wahl, R.J. Scheidt,

P. G. Windley, & K. W. Schaie (Eds.), *Annual review of gerontology and geriatrics: Aging in context: Socio-physical environments* (vol. 23, pp. 250–279). New York: Springer Publishing Company.

Morrow, D. (2003). Technology as environmental support for older adults' daily activities. In N. Charness, & K. W. Schaie, (Eds.), *Impact of technology on successful aging* (pp. 290–305). New York: Springer Publishing Company.

National Advisory Council on Aging. (2001). *Seniors and technology.* Ottawa: Canadian Public Works Printing Office.

Neufeld, S. (2009). Empowerment? For boomers? A commentary on Haber's empowerment paradigm. *Journal of Applied Gerontology, 28,* 304–307.

Parmelee, P. A., & Lawton, M. P. (1990). The design of special environments for the aged. In J. E. Birren & K. W. Schaie (Eds.), *Handbook of the psychology of aging* (3rd ed., pp. 465–489). New York: Academic Press.

Patrao, M., & Sousa, L. (2009). Material inheritance: Constructing family integrity in later life. In L. Sousa (Ed.), *Families in later life: Emerging themes and challenges* (pp. 49–74). Fargo, ND: Nova Science Publishers.

Pillemer, K., & Suitor, J. J. (2004). Ambivalence and the study of intergenerational relations. In M. Silverstein & K. Schaie (Eds.), *Annual review of gerontology and geriatrics: Intergenerational relations across time and place* (vol. 24, pp. 3–28). New York: Springer Publishing Company.

Roberto, K. A., Blieszner, R., & Allen, K. R. (2006). Theorizing in family gerontology: New opportunities for research and practice. *Family Relations, 55,* 513–525.

Rogers, W. A., Mayhorn, C. B., & Fisk, A. D. (2004). Technology in everyday life for older adults. In D. C. Burdick & S. Kwon (Eds.), *Gerontechnology: Research and practice in technology and aging* (pp. 3–17). New York: Springer Publishing Company.

Sargent, E. W., & Diaz, R. (2007). Gerontechnology and hearing. In G. Lesnoff-Caravaglia (Ed.), *Gerontechnology: Growing old in a technological society* (pp. 128–150). Springfield, IL: Charles C. Thomas.

Schaie, K. W., Wahl, H.-W., Mollenkopf, H., & Oswald, F. (Eds.). (2003). *Aging independently: Living arrangements and mobility.* New York: Springer Publishing Company.

Settersten, R. A., Jr. (2003). Propositions and controversies in life-course scholarship. In R. A. Settersten Jr. (Ed.), *Invitation to the life course: Toward new understandings of later life* (pp. 15–48). Amityville, NY: Baywood Publishing Company.

Settersten, R. A., Jr., (2005). Toward a stronger partnership between life-course sociology and life-span psychology. *Research in Human Development, 2,* 25–41.

Settersten, R. A., Jr. (2006). Aging and the life course. In R. H. Binstock & L. K. George (Eds.), *Handbook of aging and the social sciences* (6th ed., pp. 3–19). San Diego: Academic Press.

Settersten, R. A., Jr. (2009). It takes two to tango: The (un)easy dance between life-course sociology and life-span psychology. *Advances in Life Course Research, 14,* 74–81.

Silverstein, M. (2004). Introduction. In M. Silverstein & K. W. Schaie (Eds.), *Annual review of gerontology and geriatrics: Intergenerational relations across time and place* (vol. 24, pp. xiii–xix). New York: Springer Publishing Company.

Silverstein, M., & Bengtson, V. L. (1997). Intergenerational solidarity and the structure of adult child-parent relationships in American families. *American Journal of Sociology, 103*, 429–460.

Silverstein, M., Chen, X., & Heller, K. (1996). Too much of a good thing? Intergenerational social support and the psychological well-being of aging parents. *Journal of Marriage and Family, 58*, 970–982.

Sousa, L. (2009). (Ed.). *Families in later life: Emerging themes and challenges*. Fargo, ND: Nova Science Publishers.

Sousa, L., Silva, A. R., Marques, F., & Santos, L. (2009). Constructing family integrity in later life. In L. Sousa (Ed.), *Families in later life: Emerging themes and challenges* (pp. 163–184). Fargo, ND: Nova Science Publishers.

Strieb, G. F., & Beck, W. R. (1980). Older families: A decade review. *Journal of Marriage and Family, 42*, 937–956.

Topo, P. (2009). Technology studies to meet the needs of people with dementia and their caregivers: A literature review. *Journal of Applied Gerontology, 28*, 5–37.

Troll, L. E. (1971). The family of later life: A decade review. *Journal of Marriage and Family, 33*, 263–290.

U.S. Office of Technology Assessment (1984). *Technology and aging in America* (vol. OTA-BA-265). Washington, DC: U.S. Congress, Office of Technology Assessment.

Van Bronswijk, J.E.M.H., Bouma, H., & Fozard, J. L. (2002). Technology for quality of life: An enriched taxonomy. *Gerontechnology, 2*, 169–172.

Vangelisti, A. L. (2004) Introduction. In A. L. Vangelisti (Ed.), *Handbook of family communication* (pp. xiii–xx). Mahwah, NJ: Lawrence Erlbaum Associates.

Wahl, H.-W. (2001). Environmental influences on aging and behavior. In J. E. Birren & K. W. Schaie (Eds.), *Handbook of the psychology of aging* (5th ed., pp. 215–237). San Diego: Academic Press.

Wahl, H.-W. (2003). Research on living arrangements in old age for what? In K. W. Schaie, H.-W. Wahl, H. Mollenkopf, & F. Oswald (Eds.), *Aging independently: Living arrangements and mobility* (pp. 3–17). New York: Springer Publishing Company.

Wahl, H.-W. (2006). Introduction: The person-environment perspective in ageing research. In H.-W. Wahl, H. Brenner, H. Mollenkopf, D. Rothenbacher, & C.Rott (Eds.), *The many faces of health, competence and well-being in old age* (pp. 3–6). Dordrecht, The Netherlands: Springer Publishing Company.

Wahl, H.-W., Scheidt, R. J., & Windley, P. G. (Eds.). (2004). *Annual review of gerontology and geriatrics: Aging in context: Socio-physical environments* (vol. 23). New York: Springer Publishing Company.

Wahl, H.-W., & Weisman, G. D. (2003). Environmental gerontology at the beginning of the new millennium: Reflections on its historical, empirical, and theoretical development. *The Gerontologist 43*, 616–627.

Whittington, F. J. (2009). Boomer rumors: A commentary on Haber's empowerment paradigm. *Journal of Applied Gerontology, 28*, 308–313.

Part IV

Turning Points in Family Life

19

Families and Retirement

Maximiliane E. Szinovacz, David J. Ekerdt, Abigail Butt, Kelli Barton, and Corina R. Oala

During the past decades there have been fundamental changes in the institutions of family, work, and retirement. These changes manifest themselves not only in the separate structures of each institution but also in their interlinkages. Women's increased labor force participation has implications for couples' retirement decisions, the rise in divorce has repercussions for women's postretirement financial security, and care responsibilities for older parents and grandchildren impinge on retirement decisions.

Although researchers have paid increasing attention to retirement-family linkages, most of their endeavors focused on a handful of such connections, especially the impact of past and present family responsibilities on retirement timing decisions and retirement benefits, as well as the effects of retirement on marital relations and household roles. What continue to be lacking are systematic explorations of intertwined family, work, and retirement trajectories.

In this chapter we first present a life course perspective for understanding linkages between family and work and retirement trajectories. We then present relevant demographic trends, followed by a summary of research showing family-retirement connections. Next we address retirement policies and their implications for families. We conclude with a brief assessment of future research needs. As much as possible, the chapter focuses on recent contributions to the literature. For summaries of earlier work see Szinovacz (2006) and Szinovacz and Ekerdt (1995).

FAMILY RELATIONSHIPS AND RETIREMENT: A LIFE COURSE PERSPECTIVE

From a life course perspective, family-retirement linkages are best understood through exploration of intertwining family–work and retirement trajectories (Settersten, 2003, 2006). *Trajectories* or pathways reflect the sequence of states, events, and transitions in each life sphere over the life course (Settersten, 2003). The term *state* refers to stable statuses and roles during a specified life period, such as marital status, grandparenthood, or employment (Settersten, 2003). These states not only define individuals' resources (financial, time, social) but also constitute important bases for the relative importance of each life realm. For example, childless individuals may attach more importance to their work life than individuals with many children. Although the individual's status may be stable, there can be changes within these roles. For example, an individual may remain married during a life period but the quality of the marriage may fluctuate within this time frame.

Events are specific, abrupt occurrences that signify changes in individuals' trajectories, whereas *transitions* imply more gradual changes (Settersten, 2003). Events can imply changes in states, for example, from married to not married, but they can also reflect changes within given states such as the addition of a new grandchild. Individuals' family–work and retirement trajectories are also interlinked with those of significant others, especially spouses, partners, and other kin (Settersten, 2003). Events and transitions in one person's trajectory may trigger events or transitions in the partner's trajectory, such as when one spouse's retirement prompts the retirement of the other.

The life course perspective further speaks to the importance of past experiences in each life sphere and the timing of events and transitions in relation to each other (Settersten, 2003, 2006). Family-related work interruptions and past changes in family life (e.g., parenthood, divorce) shape occupational careers and, with them, the eventual decision to retire, the level of pension income, and retiree's lifestyle. For example, midlife divorce can reduce a woman's income and the prospects of sharing in a spouse's pension, and these reductions may force postponement of retirement in the later years (Yabiku, 2000). In addition, timing of events and transitions matters.

Events and transitions may be on time or off time with respect to societal standards or individuals' expectations, and off-time transitions can hinder adaptation to the transition. Furthermore, sequencing and timing of transitions influence future trajectories as well as adjustment to specific events or transitions. For example, widowhood following shortly after retirement precludes the implementation of couple-oriented retirement plans.

The life course perspective further emphasizes the embeddedness of individuals' lives in societal contexts (Settersten, 2003). Societal structures such as gender discrimination in the workplace can hinder or further movement along specific trajectories (Settersten, 2003) and may constrain access to resources that are essential to individuals' well-being, for example, when policies favoring heterosexual over homosexual unions undermine gay individuals' access to pensions and Social Security benefits.

The life span perspective helps to conceptualize long-term interlinkages among individuals' and their family members' life realms, but offer few concrete assumptions about how such trajectories mutually influence each other and how specific events and transitions within these trajectories affect individuals' and their family members' well-being. Reliance on other theoretical perspectives is necessary to develop such hypotheses. Because the relevance of specific theories varies according to the research question, we will pursue these theoretical frameworks as we discuss findings from past research.

DEMOGRAPHIC TRENDS

In this section we explore some implications of demographic changes for the retirement experience of individuals and their families. Since the inception of Social Security, there has been a nationally accepted and expected retirement age of approximately 65. Because the retirement age has not increased at the same rate as life expectancy, improved life expectancy has changed the sequencing of retirement and widowhood. This is particularly true for women. For example, whereas 20.3% of women and 4.0% of men aged 55 to 64 years were widowed in 1975, these proportions dropped to 8.1% and 2.5%, respectively, by 2010. Among men aged 65 and over, 13.6% were widowed in 1975, compared to 12.7% in 2010, whereas 52.5% of women in this age range were widowed in 1975, compared to 39.9% in 2010 (U.S. Bureau of the Census, 1985, 2010). However, increased survivorship is partially offset by family structural changes, especially by increases in the divorce rate. In 1975, 4.5% of men and 5.3% of women aged 55 to 64 were currently divorced. By 2010 these numbers more than doubled to 14.5% for men and 17.8% for women. For those aged 65 and over, 2.5% of men and 2.6% of women were divorced in 1975, compared to 8.7% and 11.1%, respectively, in 2010 (U.S. Bureau of the Census, 1985, 2010). However, these differences in family structure have not led to drastic changes in living arrangements. In 1983, 30.5% of individuals aged 65 and over lived alone, 54.2% with a spouse, and 15.2% with other partners and kin, compared to 30.1%, 54.8%, and 15.1%, respectively, in 2009.

The potential impact of such changes in longevity, family structure, and diverse living arrangements on the retirement experience is as yet little understood. A potential consequence of the increases in life expectancy is that many individuals in the pre- and postretirement years still have living parents who may require care and economic support. Another family structural change likely to bear on future generations of retirees is the trend toward delayed marriage and delayed parenthood among young and middle-aged adults. As the age gap between generations increases, more retirees will have dependent children on the eve of retirement, and more will have either very young or no grandchildren at all by the time they retire. A second possible

outcome related to the structural changes seen in recent decades relates to
the economic well-being of individuals during their retirement years. The
precarious financial situation of many divorced people (especially women)
and their lack of spousal supports may render this group particularly vulnerable during later life.

Two truly profound changes for the retirement experience are the increases
in labor force participation among married women and the beginning trend
away from early retirement. As shown in Figure 19.1, labor force participation rates for women aged 45 to 64 years have begun to converge over
the past six decades. Most notably, married and ever-married (i.e., "other")
women in this category show a dramatically increased participation rate
(from 21.8% to 68.5% for married women and from 50.2% to 69.7% for
"other" women). By 2010, about three-quarters of all women aged 45 to 54
and more than two-thirds of women aged 55 to 59 were in the labor force
(U.S. Department of Labor, Bureau of Labor Statistics, 2011). At the same
time, among persons aged 65 and older (lower panels of Figure 19.1), a pronounced trend toward nonparticipation for all groups has begun to reverse
in the past decade. These patterns hold across racial groups (U.S. Bureau of
the Census, 1976, 1996, 2011; U.S. Department of Labor, Bureau of Labor
Statistics, 1988).

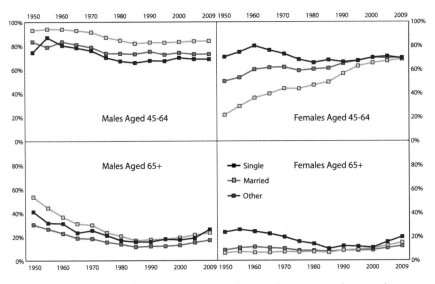

FIGURE 19.1 Labor force participation by gender, age, and marital status,
1950–2009.
Source: Based on U.S. Census data from the Current Population Surveys.
*The data in the figure are based on 5-year intervals from 1950 through 2009. Population bases for 1950
and 1955 are the total civilian population.*

Older workers have also augmented the hours they spend working. In 1994, 54.9% of employed men and 39.4% of employed women aged 65 to 69 worked full time, compared to 70.1% of men and 53.3% of women in 2007 (Gendell, 2008). Overall, these demographic trends portend significant changes in the retirement process. For those who are married, retirement will become more of a couple experience, requiring decisions on spouses' retirement timing and mutual adaptation to each other's retirement. Increased numbers of divorcees will bring about greater diversity in the living arrangements, household structure, and family obligations of retirees. Changes in family structure as well as in the age gap between generations may also alter intergenerational supports and obligations among future retirees.

FAMILY EFFECTS ON RETIREMENT TRANSITIONS AND THE POSTRETIREMENT EXPERIENCE

Family Effects on Retirement Timing

One of the focal issues in retirement research is the decision when to retire. Studies have looked at this issue by exploring factors impinging on planned and actual retirement age, as well as the probability of retiring within a given time frame. There is also variation in regard to the conceptualization of retirement itself. Some investigations focus on exit from the labor force or one's career job, whereas others use self-reported retirement status or pension and Social Security receipt as retirement indicators (Cahill, Giandrea, & Quinn, 2006; Ekerdt & DeViney, 1990; Szinovacz & DeViney, 1999). In summarizing the literature, we use a broad definition that encompasses these diverse operationalizations.

Economists' explanations of retirement decisions are typically founded in rational choice theory although the life cycle model of saving that focuses on lifetime income versus consumption needs has been used as well (Hatcher, 2003). According to the rational choice model, retirement decisions reflect the relative utility (cost to benefit ratio) of using one's time for paid work or leisure (Hatcher, 2003). Utility is typically determined on the basis of economic factors such as income or retirement benefits (Ekerdt, 2010; Gruber & Wise, 1999), although sociologists and psychologists prefer a broader conceptualization of utility that includes subjective noneconomic factors. This perspective essentially casts utility as workers' motivation to retire (Barnes-Farrell, 2003; Szinovacz, 2003).

Several family circumstances influence workers' motivation to retire. Numerous studies attest to the effect of marital status on individuals' retirement decisions. Generally, married individuals tend to plan for earlier retirement and actually retire earlier than their nonmarried counterparts (Brown & Warner, 2008; Cahill, Giandrea, & Quinn, 2008; Mermin, Johnson, &

Murphy, 2007). However, this finding may not hold cross-nationally. For example, Schils (2008) found a delay of retirement only for German but not for British and Dutch single individuals. The influence of marital status may also vary by occupational contexts. Married Finnish farmers are more prone than their unmarried counterparts to delay farm transfers and closures (Väre, 2006). One of the reasons for these inconsistencies is that mere inclusion of marriage as a status ignores considerable variability within the group of married individuals. Married persons' retirement decisions are often contingent on marital contexts such as spouses' employment status or the age difference between spouses (Szinovacz, 2002). Similarly, preretirement marriages and remarriages as well as marital disruptions impinge on retirement behaviors (Williamson & McNamara, 2003).

As more women participate in the labor force during middle age, retirement timing has increasingly become a decision faced by both spouses (Szinovacz, 1989a). The importance of this demographic trend for retirement decisions is evident from research attesting to couples' synchronization of retirement, that is, spouses' retirement decisions are interdependent (Curl & Townsend, 2008; Gustman & Steinmeier, 2002; Johnson, 2004), and one spouse's retirement hastens the retirement of the other spouse (Brown & Warner, 2008; Lee, 2005; Pienta, 2003; Schils, 2008). These investigations confirm that spouses time their retirement in relation to each other and tend to opt for joint retirement unless adverse circumstances preclude or render the joint retirement option too costly.

What explains this tendency toward joint retirement? One explanation pertains to gender norms. Husbands' retirement prior to their wives' is off-time from a normative perspective because it undermines the husband's status as main provider. Retired husbands may then seek to alter this situation by pressuring their employed wives into retirement (Cahill et al., 2008; Szinovacz, 1989a; Szinovacz & DeViney, 2000). However, gender norms can only account for wives' retirement close to their husbands' retirement but not vice versa. Other explanations refer to shared restrictions such as regional unemployment rates, spouse selection in regard to such characteristics as age or education, and mutual influencing, that is, selected characteristics of one spouse directly influence retirement decisions of the other spouse (Henkens, Kraaykamp, & Siegert, 1993). Although studies confirm spouses' tendency to retire jointly, findings are inconsistent in regard to which spouse's employment or retirement has a stronger effect on the employment or retirement of the other spouse, perhaps because these effects are quite sensitive to model specifications (Gustman & Steinmeier, 2009). For example, Gustman and Steinmeier's (2009) most recent model indicates that wives' employment status is more important for husbands' retirement than vice versa, but other studies showed opposite results (Szinovacz & DeViney, 2000) or at least suggest that husbands' employment status influences their wives' retirement decisions (Brown & Warner, 2008). Studies that included direct questions about spousal influence in retirement decisions confirm such influence but again differ in regard to whether husbands or wives have more influence (Henkens & van Solinge, 2002; Smith & Moen, 1998).

Nonetheless, many couples do not retire jointly. Separate retirement has been tied to adverse circumstances that render the joint retirement transition too costly. Such circumstances include both early family experiences such as work interruptions during the child-rearing years or divorce as well as current family conditions such as presence of dependent children, health limitations of the spouse, spouses' health insurance, spouses' work commitment, or large age differences between spouses and their implications for pension and Social Security eligibility (Kapur & Rogowski, 2006; O'Rand & Farkas, 2002; Szinovacz, 2002). Findings from these studies often yield contradictory results. For example, some studies indicate that one spouse's illness hastens the retirement of the other spouse, whereas others demonstrate the opposite (Berger & Messer-Pelkowski, 2004; Cahill et al., 2008; Dentinger & Clarkberg, 2002; Gustman & Steinmeier, 2004; Szinovacz & DeViney, 2000). One reason for these inconsistencies is that time demands of caregiving may conflict with job demands promoting earlier labor force exits, whereas costs associated with the spouse's illness (health care bills, the spouse's lost income) may require continued labor force participation (Coile, 2003a).

Financial incentives (eligibility for and amount of Social Security and pension benefits) play an important role in retirement decisions (Coile, 2003b; Gruber & Wise, 1999). Less well documented is whether a spouse's financial incentives impinge on retirement timing. One of the most recent U.S. studies addressing this topic indicated that husbands are responsive to their wives' financial incentives to keep working, but wives are not responsive to husbands' incentives (Coile, 2003b), whereas data from Norway suggest that a spouse's benefit receipt contributes more to labor force exit of wives than husbands (Dahl, Nilsen, & Vaage, 2003), and yet other research shows no effect of spouses' pensions on retirement timing (Szinovacz & DeViney, 2000).

The prospect of spending much time with one's spouse after retirement likely appeals to couples who enjoy a satisfying relationship. Studies examining this issue confirm that couples who share leisure activities and look forward to more time together in retirement are inclined to retire earlier, whereas couples in conflictual relationships or in which husbands anticipate losing power after retirement expect to retire later and postpone the retirement transition (Gustman & Steinmeier, 2004; Henkens, 1999; Szinovacz & DeViney, 2000). Expectations of earlier retirement also abound among couples in which spouses discussed their retirement with each other (Pienta & Hayward, 2002).

Although most research has focused on spouse characteristics as predictors of retirement timing decisions, some studies included other family variables.

Perhaps most interesting from a life course perspective is the influence of childbearing trajectories on women's retirement decisions. Most U.S. studies indicate that childless women or those with fewer children tend to retire sooner (Choi, 2002; Chung, 2010; Hank, 2004; Pienta, 1999; Szinovacz & DeViney, 2000), although this is not the case in Hong Kong where having more children hastens retirement as children are still seen as a support system for aged parents. Findings on Finnish farmers further demonstrate the importance of cultural context for the relationship between childbearing and retirement timing (Lee, 2005). Farmers with many children tend to hasten farm transfers but postpone farm closures, most likely in an effort to retain the farm in the family (Väre, 2006).

Studies addressing effects of childbearing timing on retirement decisions yield conflicting results. Recent analyses of Health and Retirement Study data showed that early childbearing is associated with postponement of retirement (Chung, 2010), whereas other studies indicated that delayed childbearing and employment during the childbearing years led to postponement of retirement among women (Hank, 2004; Pienta, 1999), possibly due to greater work commitment. The financial obligations associated with raising children tend to delay retirement, whereas care obligations for dependent children hasten retirement. These counteracting influences have led to conflicting results about the relationship between presence of dependent children in the household and timing of retirement. Furthermore, results seem contingent on contextual factors such as gender, race, or cohort (Brown & Warner, 2008; Choi, 2002; Hank, 2004; Pienta, 2003; Schils, 2008; Szinovacz & DeViney, 2000; Szinovacz, DeViney, & Davey, 2001). There is also some evidence that frequency of contacts with adult children influences retirement decisions although these effects vary by gender and marital status (Szinovacz et al., 2001), reflecting perhaps gender and marital status variations in child-rearing involvement and closeness to children.

Evidence also links some retirement decisions of individuals and couples to caregiving responsibilities. Studies demonstrate consistently that the caregiving needs of relatives lead at least some women to quit the labor force, to retire early, and to retire jointly with their spouses rather than to continue working after the husband's retirement (Dentinger & Clarkberg, 2002; Evandrou & Glaser, 2003), although caregiving men tend to postpone retirement (Dentinger & Clarkberg, 2002). Nevertheless, time spent to help parents reduces work hours for both men and women (Johnson & Lo Sasso, 2000), and perceived conflict between work and family obligations increases preference for future part-time work or retirement (Raymo & Sweeney, 2006).

These findings provide a basis for expanding the conceptualization of how family experiences and trajectories influence retirement decisions. We suggest that family life course trajectories, selected family states (married, caregiver), and selected family experiences (marital quality, spouses' gender role attitudes, timing of grandparenthood or widowhood in relation to retirement) raise or lower the costs of retiring at a given point in time. Disruptions in career trajectories due to childbearing or caregiving undermine career development and financial preparedness for retirement through their impact on pension eligibility and Social Security benefits (Budig & England, 2001). In addition, the financial pressures experienced by single mothers may prohibit saving for retirement (Johnson, Favreault, & Goldwyn, 2003). These work interruptions thus increase the costs of retiring early unless current marital status and spouse's income, savings, or retirement benefits override the economic penalties of motherhood and caregiving. Costs of retiring may also be higher for individuals whose family trajectories (e.g., conflictual relationships with children, having no grandchildren) reduce leisure opportunities with kin as an outlet for postretirement activities or who have financial obligations for kin. In contrast, benefits of retiring derive from reduced conflict between family and work obligations such as child or parent care, as well as freeing time for family endeavors.

One limitation of the rational choice model is that it cannot account for involuntary retirement. When the retirement transition is involuntary, it is no longer subject to choice and thus to cost-benefit calculations (Szinovacz & Davey, 2004, 2005a). Involuntary retirement is usually attributed to illness or job loss (Beehr, 1986). Even though family situations rarely render retirement objectively involuntary, they can contribute to perceptions of no choice or what Szinovacz and Davey (2005a) called restricted choice. Pressure by the partner to retire or to stay employed, caregiving obligations, and marital disruptions have all been linked to perceptions of involuntary retirement (Szinovacz & Davey, 2005a; Szinovacz & DeViney, 2000; Van Solinge & Henkens, 2007). Consequently, to the extent that family scenarios subjectively restrict choice, they will influence retirement transitions regardless of utility.

Family Effects on the Postretirement Experience

Research illustrating family effects on postretirement adaptation and activities shows that the retirement experience depends on the sort of kin convoy that accompanies individuals over the retirement process—whether people are married, have children and grandchildren, or have surviving parents and siblings. Recent investigations relied on role, control, and stress theories as well as on the life course perspective to address postretirement adjustment. Role theoretical applications refer foremost to the importance of identities in retirement as well as to role conflict or strain versus role enhancement associated with continued employment (Reid & Hardy, 1999; Reitzes & Mutran, 2006). Based on these theories, retirement is most beneficial for individuals' well-being if it enables them to pursue activities in line with their identities, if it reduces role strain and stress associated with conflicting work and other obligations, and if work fails to provide important resources or outlets for tensions. Control theory emphasizes the importance of control over life experiences as a basis for well-being (Szinovacz & Davey, 2004). Thus, involuntary retirement tends to undermine postretirement well-being (Szinovacz & Davey, 2004).

There is ample evidence that family relations are important for retirement adjustment. Studies show with relative consistency that being married yields more positive retirement attitudes, higher retirement satisfaction, and better postretirement adaptation than being unmarried (Reitzes & Mutran, 2004; Szinovacz, 2006). Furthermore, high importance of the spouse identity, improved spouse relations, and shared interests and activities of spouses contribute to retirement adjustment (Austrom, Perkins, Damush, & Hendrie, 2003; Reitzes & Mutran, 2006) as well as to spouses' adjustment to their partners' retirement (Austrom et al., 2003; van Solinge & Henkens, 2005). Men tend to rely foremost on their partners for social and emotional support and are thus more prone to lack such support in retirement if they are unmarried or if spousal support is disrupted by the partner's illness or death (Calvo, Haverstick, & Sass, 2009; Szinovacz, 1992b).

Relationships with other family members such as adult children or grandchildren can matter as well. For example, retired men expressed need for family support (Nuttman-Shwartz, 2007), and a strong parent identity seemed to enhance short-term (6 months) and longer-term (2 years) retirement adjustment among men (Reitzes & Mutran, 2004, 2006).

Family life events surrounding the retirement transition also affect postretirement adaptation and activities. Retirement that is motivated by family events (e.g., caregiving needs caused by illness of spouse or parents) might be viewed as untimely (Szinovacz & Davey, 2005a) and result in adaptation problems (Barnes & Parry, 2004; Szinovacz, 1989; Szinovacz & Davey, 2004). Family needs such as extensive parent or grandchild care obligations can spoil the retirement experience, keeping individuals from enjoying the activities they had planned (Szinovacz & Davey, 2006; Szinovacz & Washo, 1992; Vinick & Ekerdt, 1991b). The retirement experience is an outcome of enduring marital and family relationships (Nuttman-Shwartz, 2007). For example, conflictual marriages are less likely to produce joint retirements and, later, are more likely to experience difficulties when both partners eventually find themselves at home together (van Solinge & Henkens, 2005). Similarly, preretirement relationships with adult children or other family members can influence plans for, and engagement in, postretirement activities. However, such activities are also contingent on the wishes of kin. Children may avoid frequent contacts with retired parents to counteract too much parental dependence on them (Remnet, 1987).

RETIREMENT EFFECTS ON MARITAL AND FAMILY RELATIONSHIPS

Research addressing retirement effects on marriage peaked in the 1990s but seems to have faded subsequently, perhaps because one of the major data sources for current retirement research, the Health and Retirement Study, offers few opportunities for studying retirement effects on marital relations longitudinally. Fewer efforts have been made to study retirement's implications for kin relationships and this trend continues to this day.

Division of Household Work

Some conclusions about retirement and housework have been fairly well established. Retirement does not seriously alter the preretirement division of household work along traditional gender lines once both partners have retired (Szinovacz & DeViney, 2000). Nevertheless, spouses do adjust the distribution of housework to their relative work obligations (Szinovacz, 2000; Szinovacz & Harpster, 1994). Some retired husbands participate more in household work and female tasks—"helping" their wives—and for these couples the division of labor becomes more egalitarian after retirement (Szinovacz, 2000). Retired husbands also help more when wives are in poor health (Szinovacz, 2000). But the total effort expended on household tasks, even if shared more evenly, might actually increase for women because retired wives as well as husbands devote more time to homemaking and maintenance (Szinovacz, 1989b).

Although an egalitarian division of labor is gratifying to couples in retirement (Hill & Dorfman, 1982), both too much and too little involvement of the husband can induce marital tensions. The husband's presence in the wife's domain as well as his increased scrutiny of her housework performance can increase perceptions of conflict and disenchantment between both partners, a problem often referred to as the "husband underfoot issue" (Barnes & Parry, 2004; Vinick & Ekerdt, 1991b). Other research shows that husbands and wives attach different meanings to their postretirement household activities. Whereas women seem to gain some satisfaction from instrumental aspects of housework (creative cooking), men seem to profit more from household work if they see it as a contribution to their spouse or if they lack opportunities for other involvements (Szinovacz, 1992a).

Marital Quality

Popular myths that retirement disrupts marriages (Harbert, Vinick, & Ekerdt, 1992) are not supported by research. If anything, retirement seems to reinforce the type of relationship that existed before retirement—happy couples tend to become happier, and unhappy couples even more unhappy, most likely because marriage becomes a more focal life realm after retirement and spouses spend more time together (Davey & Szinovacz, 2004; Myers & Booth, 1996). Studies also showed that spouses' retirement adjustment impinges on marital quality (van Solinge & Henkens, 2005), but it is not clear whether husbands' or wives' retirement is more influential for the marital relationship (Davey & Szinovacz, 2004; Szinovacz & DeViney, 2000; Szinovacz, 1996). Perhaps the sequence of transitions (who retires first), time since retirement, and how couples organize postretirement life determine whose retirement matters more.

That the sequence of spouses' retirement matters is evident from research demonstrating that the coordination of retirement timing among dual-earner couples influences their postretirement experience. Generally, the dual-retired pattern seems most gratifying to couples (Barnes & Parry, 2004; O'Rand, Henretta, & Krecker, 1992), whereas marital strain has been linked to husbands' retiring prior to their wives (Davey & Szinovacz, 2004; Kim & Moen, 2002; Myers & Booth, 1996; Szinovacz, 1996; Szinovacz & DeViney, 2000; Szinovacz, 1989a). The overall trend reported in these studies is hardly surprising, considering that the husband-retired, wife-employed pattern runs counter to the traditional gender roles held by the cohorts under study.

Although retirement effects on marital quality tend to be modest and usually short-term, they are not inconsequential. Qualitative analyses demonstrate both positive and negative retirement effects on marital relationships. Positive changes brought about by retirement include increased freedom to develop joint endeavors, increased companionship, fewer time pressures, and a more relaxed atmosphere at home. Spouses engaging in joint decision-making and shared activities are especially likely to benefit from retirement. In addition, support from the spouse, confirmation of the retiree's self-concept, and adjustment to the retired spouse's needs seem important prerequisites for marital adjustment after retirement (Barnes & Parry, 2004; Rogers & May, 2003; van Solinge & Henkens, 2005; Vinick & Ekerdt, 1991a, 1991b).

Among negative changes the dominant theme is wives' complaints about husbands being underfoot, lack of privacy, and too much togetherness (Vinick & Ekerdt, 1991b). Impingement problems seem to abound when spouses are highly dependent on each other and lack other social relationships (Kulik & Bareli, 1997; Myers & Booth, 1996). Husbands further reported dismay over their wives' monotonous routines and narrow interests (Vinick & Ekerdt, 1991b).

Retirement can also bring about actual or perceived shifts in the marital power structure (Barnes & Parry, 2004). Such shifts can undermine retirement adaptation if they lead to more dominance on the part of the partner (Szinovacz & Davey, 2005b). Marital problems have further been tied to unexpected retirement as well as caregiving for the spouse (Barnes & Parry,

2004; Dentinger & Clarkberg, 2002). Thus, most couples seem to adjust well to retirement after some initial adjustments. However, retirement is not likely to cure already troubled marriages.

Relationships with Extended Kin

Although family relationships are often the primary life sphere for retirees, research on this topic remains meager (Szinovacz, 2006). Retirement can free individuals to devote themselves to family relationships. For retired men, in particular, increased contacts with adult children and grandchildren may compensate for inattention to family relations during their working years (Nuttman-Shwartz, 2007; Szinovacz & Davey, 2001). However, kin can also claim retirees' time (e.g., for daily care of grandchildren or to take over caregiving responsibilities from still-employed siblings) to the point of perhaps spoiling the retirement experience (Dentinger & Clarkberg, 2002; Vinick & Ekerdt, 1991b).

What can these diverse findings tell us about retirement effects on families? They suggest that normative life transitions such as retirement tend to reinforce rather than alter established life patterns in marital and kin relationships unless the life transition is particularly stressful or changes in another life realm require direct adjustments to the transition. To the extent that change does occur, it seems to have a compensatory function. That is, life transitions that open up available time provide chances to compensate for missed opportunities in other life realms, as is the case when fathers revisit previously neglected relationships with children and grandchildren. Retirement seems to have negative consequences if it occurs under adverse circumstances or runs counter to metarules such as spouses' gender role attitudes. Such negative consequences may then spill over into other life realms, including family relationships. Easing potentially negative retirement effects on marital and family relationships can likely be achieved by preparing couples and families for the potential impact of retirement on relationships and by interventions offered early in the retirement process.

RETIREMENT POLICY AND THE FAMILY

People are able to retire if they can access a stream of income that replaces the wages or salary obtained from employment. The present societal arrangements that support retirement income have far-reaching implications for work and family careers. As Szinovacz (2006, p. 179) noted: "Old age security programs are linked to family concerns in three main ways: they shift provision for old family members from the family to the state; they offer albeit partial relief to families with disabled workers and provide for workers' survivors; and they incorporate regulations that favor specific family arrangements and life course trajectories." (See also Harrington Meyer & Frazier, chapter 15 in this volume.)

The Institutionalization of Social Security and Its Effects on Families

Historically, for individuals fortunate to live long enough, retirement income was arranged privately, either through lifelong family strategies designed to secure financial resources for the later years or through direct economic dependence on the younger generation (Haber & Gratton, 1994; Moen & Gratton, 2000). Family-based economic support for older persons in the past involved considerable sacrifices on the part of the younger generation (especially in terms of reduced education due to early labor force activity, marital opportunities forgone, or the delay of economic independence due to late land transfers) and constituted a source of intergenerational conflict, as is still the case in some Asian and nondeveloped countries. Even if attempted, family-based strategies for old-age support were vulnerable to sudden shifts in fortune and lacked long-term reliability, necessitating community and public relief.

With the emergence of the modern welfare state, the responsibility for economic support of older people has shifted, in part, from the family onto the state and onto employers, who supply Social Security and other pensions, leading to the institutionalization of retirement as we now know it (Myles, 1989). Social Security and pensions free parents to invest in the support and education of their children and tend to promote intergenerational relationships that are based on affection rather than obligation (Cai, Giles, & Meng, 2006; Costa, 1998). These programs also reduce the need for high fertility as insurance for old age security (Boldrin, De Nardi, & Jones, 2005).

Social Security and pensions not only shift financial responsibility for elderly relatives from the family to the state, they also serve as social control mechanisms by tying benefit eligibility and amounts to age, marital status, and, in most countries, to work history. These requirements can contribute to cumulative disadvantage (O'Rand, 2006) in the later years by favoring already advantaged groups. For example, work interruptions and early retirements that are family-related (and largely socially approved) exact a homemaking and child-care penalty on retirement benefits (Budig & England, 2001). Because women characteristically carry the main responsibility for child rearing and care of ill relatives, they are most affected by these regulations.

In the United States, the spouse allowance supports a traditional division of labor where couples' retirement income is tied to the assumption of husbands' continuous employment and the wife's reliance on his Social Security and pension income. This strategy can earn good Social Security and pension prospects for the household if the marriage remains intact, but eroded prospects for the wife if the marriage dissolves (McNamara, O'Grady-LeShane, & Williamson, 2003). Although wives are increasingly relying on their own earnings records when claiming Social Security, more than one-quarter still rely solely on spousal benefits. In 2008, 28% of females received Social Security benefits based solely on their husbands' earning records (Social Security Administration, 2009a). For single parents, the duty to compile a continuous work career is not relaxed, even when family responsibilities are pressing. Thus, current Social Security and pension programs, on the one hand, reinforce traditional gender roles but, on the other hand, penalize wives for work disruptions devoted to family care and negate their own work accomplishments and Social Security tax contributions (Pampel, 1998; Sainsbury, 1996). Furthermore, the spouse allowance clearly favors traditional marriage through its emphasis on the male provider role and its inapplicability to those who are not married (except for divorcees with lengthy marriages) or in same-sex unions. Inequalities based on gender, marital status, or sexual orientation thus extend into the retirement years (Johnson et al., 2003; Johnson, Sambomoorthi, & Crystal, 2003).

In contrast to the U.S. Social Security system, which addresses the income and benefit loss of parents and caregivers through a spouse allowance (that is, however, not contingent on such care responsibilities), many other countries have resorted to care credit policies or direct care benefits. The care credit policies vary greatly by country, depending on who is receiving care and how the beneficiary is compensated. For example, in Germany, the care credit policy compensates certain caregivers for their time with pension contribution credits, as one would earn if employed (Social Security Administration, 2008). The United Kingdom acknowledges child care responsibilities with a policy that allows dropout years: In calculating the flat benefit, caregivers' years without earnings are ignored. The dropout-years policy in the United Kingdom is also applicable for periods of time spent providing care to sick or disabled persons (Favreault, Sammartino, & Steuerle, 2002). In contrast, both Austria and Ireland provide care benefits in the form of direct monetary compensation to the pensioner and caregiver, respectively. Germany's long-term care insurance combines cash transfers to the insured older person (which can be used to pay family caregivers) with Social Security credits for the caregivers (Gibson & Redfoot, 2007).

Social Security also entails numerous direct benefits for family members, including spouse and survivor benefits. As noted above, spouses are provided with half of the retired worker's full benefits or their own, whichever is higher. A divorced unmarried spouse may receive spouse benefits as well, provided that the marriage lasted for at least 10 years (Social Security Administration, 2010a; see also Harrington Meyer & Frazier, chapter 15 in this volume). The provision for survivor benefits—monetary allotments for the beneficiary's survivors upon his or her death—is another social insurance policy linked to Social Security that supports beneficiaries' families. This life insurance function of public pension systems is common throughout the world, and these benefits are often critical in maintaining a level of financial stability for dependent survivors of employed or retired workers. Allowances for widowed spouses are usually contingent on age and subsequent marital status. Such contingencies, along with gender, also govern benefits to dependent children. Survivor benefits in some nations can also include dependent parents as well as stepchildren (Social Security Administration, 2008, 2010b).

Changing cultural norms and increasing acceptance of same-sex couples have led to the inclusion of same-sex partners in some social insurance programs. In the United States, although several states have legalized same-sex marriages (Human Rights Campaign, 2010a), the federal Social Security program does not recognize same-sex partners or their families. Thus, although older gay and lesbian Americans contribute to Social Security throughout their lives, they are not able to receive benefits equal to those of heterosexual married couples (Human Rights Campaign, 2010b). Based on Social Security Administration calculations from 2002 (Human Rights Campaign, 2010b), the estimated loss of survivor benefits is $9,780 per year for a surviving same-sex partner 60 years old. In contrast, Denmark and Canada have extended federal-level survivor provisions to same-sex couples (Social Security Administration, 2008, 2009b).

Although welfare states generally have collectivized responsibility for later-life familial security, adult children often remain responsible for the well-being of parents in old age. According to the U.S. National Center for Policy Analysis, 30 states have some form of filial responsibility laws (Pakula, 2005), although these laws are rarely enforced. In regions of the world where filial piety traditionally has provided the cornerstone for support in old age, poverty is increasing among older adults. According to Oppong (2006), in sub-Saharan Africa, respect for older adults by younger generations has declined, as has younger people's willingness to provide support to their older relatives. Thus, many older individuals have to sustain themselves. Women are specifically affected by this cultural change because they often marry older partners, are less likely to remarry after the loss of a spouse, and live on average longer than men (Oppong, 2006).

China is another example of a country with traditionally strong filial piety norms. Although old age insurance has been available in a number of rural regions since 1991 (Zhang & Goza, 2006), many older individuals residing in rural China are unfamiliar with old age insurance programs or cannot afford them. To complicate matters, young adults are outmigrating from rural China in search of better work opportunities, leaving older adults without family support. Hardships of the older population are further exacerbated by China's one-child policy, which limits the available number of family members who can support older individuals (Zhang & Goza, 2006). These examples highlight the significance of social insurance policies not only for older adults themselves but for their families as well.

In recent years, discussion about privatizing Social Security has increased, largely due to projections of a financial shortfall. Privatizing Social Security would mean that individuals' retirement contributions would accrue in personal saving accounts, leaving future benefits subject to market performance and thus considerably higher investment risk than traditional Social Security benefits. More important, such personal accounts would not include many of the family benefits associated with traditional Social Security. Because the personal account would belong to retired individuals, they would have discretion over how they use the funds and who would receive any remaining funds upon their death. This discretion could be problematic as there is no guarantee that all dependent survivors would be named beneficiaries or that they would be left with adequate means of support.

Employers' Pensions

Over the past three decades, a profound change has been under way in the nature of pension and retirement saving, and this change has implications for marital and family life both pre- and postretirement.

In the U.S. pension mix, defined contribution (DC) plans—the 401(k) is a prominent version—have progressively replaced traditional, defined benefit (DB) pensions. Between 1980 and 2008, the proportion of workers in the private sector participating in DB plans fell from 38% to 20%, while the proportion only in DC plans rose from 8% to 31% (Butrica, Iams, Smith, & Toder, 2009). Some workers have both kinds of plans and a minority of the workforce is also covered by hybrid plans that combine features of the two models.

What this pension environment means for various segments of the population, especially women, has been discussed extensively (Holden & Fontes, 2009; O'Rand & Shuey, 2007; Schulz & Binstock, 2006). The major implication is that the responsibility for ensuring a stream of retirement income passes from the employer to the individual. Instead of spreading both investment risk and longevity risk across a group of workers, these risks are individualized or "familized." With DB pensions, the twin challenges of accruing wealth while working and managing it well throughout retirement are a corporate, collective responsibility; with DC plans, this responsibility resides in the household.

Given the increased need for retirement financial planning within this pension environment, it is important to assess how partners influence each other in retirement preparation. Research suggests that husbands' and wives' planning is related, although spouses' relative influence on each other seems to depend on age cohort and the presence of children in the home (Moen,

Huang, Plassmann, & Dentinger, 2006). Sexual orientation also matters: Lesbian couples tend to plan less but are more interdependent in their financial planning than heterosexual couples (Mock & Cornelius, 2007).

The household management of DC pensions involves repeated decision-making about a number of issues, including whether to join a plan if one is offered, at what level to contribute, what funds to select, or how to diversify. Research suggests that spouses influence each other in regard to DC investment decisions and that dual-earner spouses coordinate their behaviors in regard to DC plans. For example, when both spouses are offered such plans, having one spouse participate raises the chances that the other will enroll (Shuey, 2004). Similarly, spouses affect each other's investment decisions. One study indicated that husbands whose wives are inclined to take at least average investment risks tend toward more risky investments, whereas wives whose husbands are inclined to take at least average investments risks tend toward less risky investments (Bernasek & Shwiff, 2001). Another investigation showed that wives who hold more financial power than their husbands or are married to older men tend toward low-risk investments, whereas wives' characteristics have little effect on husbands' investment decisions (Lyons & Yilmazer, 2004; Yilmazer & Lyons, 2010). By all accounts, however, American couples have managed their DC plans less than optimally (Ghilarducci, 2008). According to Uccello (2000), dual-earner couples do not sufficiently diversify their pension plans to share risks.

Household responsibility for the sound management of DC funds continues into the postretirement stage, at which point a further risk, longevity, replaces uncertainty about employment. Hitherto the question had been how much savings are needed for retirement; the next question is how to make the savings last. With increased life expectancy, there is more retirement to provision with a stream of income—even more so among women. The signal feature of DB pensions and Social Security is a guaranteed monthly payout for life that is sex-neutral as to life expectancy. In Social Security, but less commonly in private plans, these amounts are indexed to inflation. Upon the death of the primary beneficiary, the surviving spouse can continue to receive benefits. Whereas DB plans annuitize benefits on behalf of retirees and surviving spouses, DC households are on their own. Pension wealth is individually owned, and spouses do not have an automatic claim as with DB plans or Social Security. One family advantage of DC funds, if they are not annuitized, is that they can be passed to heirs. However, pension wealth can be passed on to nonfamily and thus undermine the financial well-being of surviving widow(er)s and dependent children. In addition, exhausting pension wealth early in retirement increases the risk of later financial dependence on adult children.

Household members face many challenges in understanding and managing pension benefits. These are matters that bear on the comfort and economic security of the immediate household and are also relevant to the wider circle of family members. Couples need to discuss such further planning matters as health insurance, life insurance, long-term care options, wills and estates, and the management of assets.

FUTURE RESEARCH NEEDS

During the past decades, research on family-retirement linkages made considerable progress. Much of this progress centers on the influence of family relationships on the timing of and adjustment to retirement, whereas studies addressing retirement effects on family relationships remain scarce. Despite this progress, much needs to be done.

Theoretical advances, especially the development of the life course perspective and its integration with other pertinent theories, open opportunities for theory-based research on the linkages among marital, family, and work trajectories. To date most studies have focused on how specific characteristics (marital status, parenthood, spouse's characteristics) influence retirement transitions and thus lack the long-term view necessary to assess linkages among family, work, and retirement pathways. The life course perspective also suggests the need for more emphasis on cohort and intergenerational influences and comparisons. At least one study suggests, for example, that children's pension participation mirrors their fathers' pension participation even when controlling for socioeconomic status (Gouskova, Chiteji, & Stafford, 2010).

As the Baby Boomer cohorts enter retirement, it will become necessary to reevaluate family-retirement linkages. These cohorts not only face a very different economic and demographic reality than their parents did, they also bring to retirement different family- and work-related attitudes (e.g., about gender roles) as well as different work and family histories than earlier cohorts.

Similarly, the life course perspective's emphasis on context deserves more attention in family-retirement research. Although studies increasingly pay tribute to gender differences, much less is known about variations in family-retirement linkages by race, ethnicity, or socioeconomic status. Even more interesting from a policy perspective are macro contexts such as variations across welfare states in family and retirement policies. Are linkages between family-work trajectories different in countries that offer opportunities for mothers' employment through state-subsidized child care, that provide extended parental leave, or that offer Social Security credits to caregivers of elderly relatives? With the advent of comparable large-scale longitudinal surveys such as the Health and Retirement Study (HRS) in the United States and the Survey of Health, Ageing, and Retirement in Europe (see http://hrsonline.isr.umich.edu/ and http://www.share-project.org/ for details), such research questions are feasible. Of course, large surveys rarely allow insights into the intricacies of work and family life. Thus, smaller, qualitative studies will remain important to fill the gaps left by large survey research and to advance theory development. Although retrospective accounts are always suspect, techniques such as event history calendars can reduce bias inherent in retrospective data (Belli, Stafford, & Alwin, 2009).

As for content, several topics should be added to the current agenda of family-retirement research. The field needs additional research about family-retirement linkages that extend beyond the marital unit. These include relationships with children, grandchildren, siblings, and parents. Such research should not be restricted to studies of retirement effects on the frequency of kin contacts. Rather, it seems essential to explore whether extended family members' expectations for kin contacts and supports change upon retirement (i.e., can relatives claim retirees' time?), whether and how retirement-related increases or decreases in kin contacts affect the quality of kin relationships, and to what extent interactions with adult children and other kin substitute for the social commerce of the workplace (Francis, 1990). In addition, we need to know more about influences of family obligations on retirement decisions. More exploration of caregiving is warranted, not only to parents and spouses, but also to other relatives such as disabled adult children, siblings, or custodial grandchildren.

Given current changes in family structure, more attention should also be directed at retirees involved in alternative family lifestyles. As yet, we know practically nothing about the retirement experiences of gay and lesbian, cohabiting, or living apart together (LAT) couples, and very little about those of never-married and divorced couples (Connidis, 2010; Mock & Cornelius, 2007). Particularly important will be the assessment of family-related inequities in retirement benefits and policies. Current policies favor individuals involved in traditional family arrangements and especially penalize women for their involvement in family work. We need more research, however, on how such policies will affect future cohorts of retirees who are even more likely than today's retirees to approach and enter retirement as members of nontraditional family arrangements. Can we foresee which of the many current proposals to reduce inequities in Social Security and pension coverage are most likely to succeed and what implications they will have for retired couples, retirees in alternative living arrangements, and their families?

Current research evidence confirms the rich interplay between family and retirement experiences and renders future research on this topic essential. We will learn much more about families and retirement if we follow individuals' family and career trajectories over the life course, explore contextual influences, and acknowledge the diversity of family structures.

NOTE

Preparation of this chapter was funded in part by a grant from the National Institute of Aging (R01AG013180), Maximiliane E. Szinovacz, PI. It is a considerably revised and updated version of the chapter that appeared in the first edition of *Handbook of Aging and the Family* (1995).

REFERENCES

Austrom, M.G., Perkins, A.J., Damush, T.M., & Hendrie, H.C. (2003). Predictors of life satisfaction in retired physicians and spouses. *Social Psychiatry and Psychiatric Epidemiology, 38,* 131–141.

Barnes, H., & Parry, J. (2004). Renegotiating identity and relationships: Men and women's adjustment to retirement. *Ageing and Society, 24,* 213–233.

Barnes-Farrell, J.L. (2003). Beyond health and wealth: Attitudinal and other influences on retirement decision-making. In G.A. Adams & T.A. Beehr (Eds.), *Retirement: Reasons, processes, and results.* New York: Springer.

Beehr, T.A. (1986). The process of retirement: A review and recommendations for future investigation. *Personnel Psychology, 39,* 31–55.

Belli, R.F., Stafford, F.P., & Alwin, D.F. (Eds.). (2009). *Calendar and time diary methods in life course research.* Thousand Oaks, CA: Sage.

Berger, M.C., & Messer-Pelkowski, J. (2004). Health and family labor force transitions. *Quarterly Journal of Business and Economics, 43*(3/4), 113–138.

Bernasek, A., & Shwiff, S. (2001). Gender, risk, and retirement. *Journal of Economic Issues, 35*(2), 345–356.

Boldrin, M., De Nardi, M., & Jones, L.E. (2005). *Fertility and Social Security.* Cambridge, MA: National Bureau of Economic Research.

Brown, T.H., & Warner, D.F. (2008). Divergent pathways? Racial/ethnic differences in older women's labor force withdrawal. *The Journals of Gerontology: Social Sciences, 63B,* S122–S134.

Budig, M.J., & England, P. (2001). The wage penalty for motherhood. *American Sociological Review, 66,* 204–225.

Butrica, B.A., Iams, H.M., Smith, K.E., & Toder, E.J. (2009). *The disappearing defined benefit pension and its potential impact on the retirement incomes of Boomers.* Chestnut Hill, MA: Center for Retirement Research at Boston College.

Cahill, K.E., Giandrea, M.D., & Quinn, J.F. (2006). Retirement patterns from career employment. *The Gerontologist, 46,* 514–523.

Cahill, K.E., Giandrea, M.D., & Quinn, J. (2008). *A micro-level analysis of recent increases in labor force participation among older workers* (Working Paper 2008-8). Chestnut Hill, MA: Center for Retirement Research at Boston College.

Cai, F., Giles, J., & Meng, X. (2006). How well do children insure parents against low retirement income? An analysis using survey data from urban China. *Journal of Public Economics, 90,* 2229–2255.

Calvo, E., Haverstick, K., & Sass, S.A. (2009). Gradual retirement, sense of control, and retirees' happiness. *Research on Aging, 31*(1), 112.

Choi, N. (2002). Self-defined retirement status and engagement in paid work among older working-age women: Comparison between childless women and mothers. *Sociological Inquiry, 72*(1), 43–71.

Chung, H. (2010). *The effects of childbearing patterns on the timing of retirement.* Unpublished dissertation, University of Massachusetts, Boston, MA.

Coile, C. (2003a). *Health shocks and couples' labor supply decisions.* Chestnut Hill, MA: Center for Retirement Research at Boston College.

Coile, C. (2003b). Retirement incentives and couples' retirement decisions (2003). Retrieved from http://www.nber.org/papers/w9496

Connidis, I. A. (2010). *Family ties and aging.* Los Angeles, CA: Pine Forge Press.

Costa, D. L. (1998). *The evolution of retirement: An American economic history, 1880–1990.* Chicago: University of Chicago Press.

Curl, A. L., & Townsend, A. L. (2008). Retirement transitions among married couples. *Journal of Workplace Behavioral Health, 23*(1–2), 89–107.

Dahl, S., Nilsen, O. A., & Vaage, K. (2003). Gender differences in early retirement behaviour. *European Sociological Review, 19*(2), 179–198.

Davey, A., & Szinovacz, M. E. (2004). Dimensions of marital quality and retirement. *Journal of Family Issues, 25*(4), 431–464.

Dentinger, E., & Clarkberg, M. (2002). Informal caregiving and retirement timing among men and women: Gender and caregiving relationships in late midlife. *Journal of Family Issues, 23*(7), 857–879.

Ekerdt, D. J. (2010). Frontiers of research on work and retirement. *Journal of Gerontology: Social Sciences, 65B*, S68–S80.

Ekerdt, D. J., & DeViney, S. (1990). On defining persons as retired. *Journal of Aging Studies, 4*, 211–229.

Evandrou, M., & Glaser, K. (2003). Combining work and family life: the pension penalty of caring. *Ageing and Society, 23*, 583–601.

Favreault, M., Sammartino, F. J., & Steuerle, C. E. (Eds.). (2002). *Social Security and the family: Addressing unmet needs in an underfunded system.* Washington, DC: The Urban Institute Press.

Francis, D. (1990). The significance of work friends in later life. *Journal of Aging Studies, 4*, 405–424.

Gendell, M. (2008). Older workers: Increasing their labor force participation and hours of work. *Monthly Labor Review, 131*(1), 41–54.

Ghilarducci, T. (2008). *When I'm sixty-four: The plot against pensions and the plan to save them.* Princeton, NJ: Princeton University Press.

Gibson, M. J., & Redfoot, D. L. (2007). Comparing long-term care in Germany and the United States: What can we learn from each other? Retrieved from http://assets.aarp.org/rgcenter/il/2007_19_usgerman_ltc.pdf

Gouskova, E., Chiteji, N., & Stafford, F. (2010). Pension participation: Do parents transmit time preference? *Journal of Family Economic Issues, 31*, 138–150.

Gruber, J., & Wise, D. (1999). *Social Security programs and retirement around the world.* Chicago: University of Chicago Press.

Gustman, A. L., & Steinmeier, T. (2002). *Social Security, pensions, and retirement behavior within the family.* Cambridge, MA: National Bureau of Economic Research.

Gustman, A.L., & Steinmeier, T. (2004). *Personal accounts and family retirement* (Working Paper 10305). Cambridge, MA: National Bureau of Economic Research.

Gustman, A.L., & Steinmeier, T. (2009). *Integrating retirement models.* Cambridge, MA: National Bureau of Economic Research.

Haber, C., & Gratton, B. (1994). *Old age and the search for security: An American social history.* Bloomington: Indiana University Press.

Hank, K. (2004). Effects of early family life events on women's late life labour market behaviour. *European Sociological Review, 20*(3), 189–198.

Harbert, E., Vinick, B.H., & Ekerdt, D.J. (1992). Marriage and retirement: Advice to couples in popular literature. In J.F. Gilgun, K. Daly, & G. Handel (Eds.), *Qualitative methods in family research* (pp. 263–278). Newbury Park, CA: Sage.

Hatcher, C.B. (2003). The economics of the retirement decision. In G.A. Adams & T.A. Beehr (Eds.), *Retirement: Reasons, processes, and results* (pp. 136–156). New York: Springer.

Henkens, K. (1999). Retirement intentions and spousal support: A multi-actor approach. *Journal of Gerontology: Social Sciences, 54B*, S63–S74.

Henkens, K., Kraaykamp, G., & Siegert, J. (1993). Married couples and their labour market status. *European Sociological Review, 9*, 67–78.

Henkens, K., & van Solinge, H. (2002). Spousal influences on the decision to retire. *International Journal of Sociology, 32*(2), 55–74.

Hill, E.A., & Dorfman, L.T. (1982). Reactions of housewives to the retirement of their husbands. *Family Relations, 31*, 195–200.

Holden, K.C., & Fontes, A. (2009). Economic security in retirement: How changes in employment and marriage have altered retirement-related economic risks for women. *Journal of Women, Politics, & Policy, 30*, 173–197.

Human Rights Campaign. (2010a). Marriage and relationship recognition. Retrieved from http://www.hrc.org/issues/marriage.asp

Human Rights Campaign. (2010b). Social Security survival benefits. Retrieved from http://www.hrc.org/issues/aging/2688.htm

Johnson, R.W. (2004). Do spouses coordinate their retirement decisions? *Issues in Brief* (pp. 1–7). Chestnut Hill, MA: Center for Retirement Research at Boston College.

Johnson, R.W., Favreault, M.M., & Goldwyn, J.H. (2003). *Employment, Social Security, and future retirement outcomes for single mothers* (Working Paper 2003–14). Chestnut Hill, MA: Center for Retirement Research at Boston College.

Johnson, R.W., & Lo Sasso, A.T. (2000). *The trade-off between hours of paid employment and time assistance to elderly parents at midlife* (Research Report). Washington, DC: The Urban Institute Press.

Johnson, R.W., Sambomoorthi, U., & Crystal, S. (2003). Gender differences in pension wealth and their impact on late-life inequality. *Annual Review of Gerontology and Geriatrics, 22*, 116–137.

Kapur, K., & Rogowski, J. (2006). *Love or money? Health insurance and retirement among married couples.* Cambridge, MA: National Bureau of Economics Research.

Kim, J.E., & Moen, P. (2002). Retirement transitions, gender, and psychological well-being: A life-course, ecological model. *Journals of Gerontology: Psychological Sciences, 57*(3), P212–222.

Kulik, L., & Bareli, H. Z. (1997). Continuity and discontinuity in attitudes toward marital power relations: Pre-retired vs. retired husbands. *Ageing and Society, 17*, 571–595.

Lee, W.K.M. (2005). Gender differences in retirement decision in Hong Kong. *Journal of Women and Aging, 17*(4), 59–76.

Lyons, A. C., & Yilmazer, T. (2004). *How does marriage affect the allocation of assets in women's defined contribution plans?* (Working Paper 2004–28). Chestnut Hill, MA: Center for Retirement Research at Boston College.

McNamara, T. K., O'Grady-LeShane, R., & Williamson, J. B. (2003). The role of marital history, early retirement benefits, and the economic status of women (Working Paper 2003-01). Chestnut Hill, MA: Center for Retirement Research at Boston College.

Mermin, G.B.T., Johnson, R. W., & Murphy, D. (2007). Why do boomers plan to work longer? *Journal of Gerontology: Social Sciences, 62B*(5), S286–S294.

Mock, S. E., & Cornelius, S. W. (2007). Profiles of independence: The retirement planning of married, cohabiting, and lesbian couples. *Sex Roles, 56,* 793–800.

Moen, P., & Gratton, B. (2000). Tracking the majority: households, older workers, and retirement during the Great Depression. *Journal of Gerontology: Social Sciences, 55*(1), S28–S32.

Moen, P., Huang, Q., Plassmann, V., & Dentinger, E. (2006). Deciding the future. Do dual-earner couples plan together for retirement? *American Behavioral Scientist, 49*(10), 1422–1443.

Myers, S. M., & Booth, A. (1996). Men's retirement and marital quality. *Journal of Family Issues, 17,* 336–358.

Myles, J. (1989). *Old age in the welfare state.* Lawrence: University of Kansas Press.

Nuttman-Shwartz, O. (2007). Men's perceptions of family during the retirement transition. *Families in Society: The Journal of Contemporary Social Services, 88*(2), 192–202.

Oppong, C. (2006). Familial roles and social transformations: Older men and women in sub-Saharan Africa. *Research on Aging, 28*(6), 654–688.

O'Rand, A. M. (2006). Stratification and the life course: Life course capital, life course risks, and social inequality. In R. H. Binstock & L. K. George (Eds.), *Handbook of aging and the social sciences* (6th ed., pp. 145–162). Amsterdam: Elsevier.

O'Rand, A. M., & Farkas, J. I. (2002). Couples' retirement timing in the United States in the 1990's. *International Journal of Sociology, 32*(2), 11–29.

O'Rand, A. M., Henretta, J. C., & Krecker, M. L. (1992). Family pathways to retirement. In M. E. Szinovacz, D. J. Ekerdt, & B. H. Vinick (Eds.), *Families and retirement* (pp. 81–98). Newbury Park, CA: Sage.

O'Rand, A. M., & Shuey, K. M. (2007). Gender and the devolution of pension risks in the U.S. *Current Sociology, 55,* 287–304.

Pakula, M. (2005). *The legal responsibility of adult children to care for indigent parents* (pp. 1–2): Dallas, TX: National Center for Policy Analysis.

Pampel, F. C. (1998). *Aging, social inequality, and public policy.* Thousand Oaks, CA: Pine Forge Press.

Pienta, A. M. (1999). Early childbearing patterns and women's labor force behavior in later life. *Journal of Women & Aging, 11*, 69–83.

Pienta, A. M. (2003). Partners in marriage: An analysis of husbands' and wives' retirement behavior. *Journal of Applied Gerontology, 22*(3), 340–358.

Pienta, A. M., & Hayward, M. D. (2002). Who expects to continue working after age 62? The retirement plans of couples. *Journal of Gerontology: Social Sciences, 57*(4), S199–S208.

Raymo, J. M., & Sweeney, M. M. (2006). Work-family conflict and retirement preferences. *Journal of Gerontology: Social Sciences, 61B*(3), S161–S169.

Reid, J., & Hardy, M. (1999). Multiple roles and well-being among midlife women: Testing role strain and role enhancement theories. *Journal of Gerontology: Social Sciences, 54*(6), S329–S338.

Reitzes, D. C., & Mutran, E. J. (2004). The transition to retirement: Stages and factors that influence retirement adjustment. *International Journal of Aging and Human Development, 59*(1), 63–84.

Reitzes, D. C., & Mutran, E. J. (2006). Lingering identities in retirement. *The Sociological Quarterly, 47*, 333–359.

Remnet, V. L. (1987). How adult children respond to role transitions in the lives of their aging parents. *Educational Gerontology, 13*, 341–355.

Rogers, S. J., & May, D. C. (2003). Spillover between marital quality and job satisfaction: Long-term patterns and gender differences. *Journal of Marriage and Family, 65*(2), 482–495.

Sainsbury, D. (1996). *Gender equality and welfare states*. Cambridge: Cambridge University Press.

Schils, T. (2008). Early retirement in Germany, the Netherlands, and the United Kingdom: A longitudinal analysis of individual factors and institutional regimes. *European Sociological Review, 24*(3), 315–329.

Schulz, J. H., & Binstock, J. H. (2006). *Aging nation: The economics and politics of growing older in America*. Westport, CT: Praeger.

Settersten, R. A. (2003). Propositions and controversies in life-course scholarship. In R. A. Settersten (Ed.), *Invitation to the life course* (pp. 15–48). Amityville, NY: Baywood Publishing Company.

Settersten, R. A. (2006). Aging and the life course. In R. H. Binstock & L. K. George (Eds.), *Handbook of aging and the social sciences* (6th ed., pp. 3–19). Amsterdam: Elsevier.

Shuey, K. M. (2004). Worker preferences, spousal coordination, and participation in an employer-sponsored pension plan. *Research on Aging, 26*(3), 287–316.

Smith, D. B., & Moen, P. (1998). Spousal influence on retirement: His, her, and their perceptions. *Journal of Marriage and Family, 60*, 734–744.

Social Security Administration. (2008). Social Security programs throughout the World: Europe. Retrieved from http://www.socialsecurity.gov/policy/docs/progdesc/ssptw/2008–2009/europe/ssptw08euro.pdf

Social Security Administration. (2009a). *Facts and Figures about Social Security, 2009*.

Social Security Administration. (2009b). Social Security programs throughout the world: The Americas. Retrieved from http://www.socialsecurity.gov/policy/docs/progdesc/ssptw/2008–2009/americas/ssptw09americas.pdf

Social Security Administration. (2010a, January). Retirement benefits. Retrieved from http://www.socialsecurity.gov/pubs/10035.pdf

Social Security Administration. (2010b). Widows, widowers, & other survivors. Retrieved from http://www.ssa.gov/ww&os2.htm

Szinovacz, M. E. (1989a). Decision-making on retirement timing. In D. Brinberg & J. Jaccard (Eds.), *Dyadic decision making* (pp. 286–310). New York: Springer.

Szinovacz, M. E. (1989b). Retirement, couples, and household work. In S. J. Bahr & E. T. Peterson (Eds.), *Aging and the family* (pp. 33–58). Lexington: Lexington Books.

Szinovacz, M. E. (1992a). Is housework good for retirees? *Family Relations, 41,* 230–238.

Szinovacz, M. E. (1992b). Social activities and retirement adaptation: Gender and family variations. In M. Szinovacz, D. J. Ekerdt, & B. H. Vinick (Eds.), *Families and retirement* (pp. 236–253). Newbury Park, CA: Sage.

Szinovacz, M. E. (1996). Couple's employment/retirement patterns and marital quality. *Research on Aging, 18,* 243–268.

Szinovacz, M. E. (2000). Changes in housework after retirement: A panel analysis. *Journal of Marriage and Family, 62,* 78–92.

Szinovacz, M. E. (2002). Couple retirement patterns and retirement age. *International Journal of Sociology, 32*(2), 30–54.

Szinovacz, M. E. (2003). Contexts and pathways: Retirement as institution, process, and experience. In G. E. Adams & T. A. Beehr (Eds.), *Retirement: Reasons, processes, and outcomes* (pp. 6–52). New York: Springer.

Szinovacz, M. E. (2006). Families and retirement. In L. O. Stone (Ed.), *New frontiers of research on retirement* (pp. 165–198). Ottawa: Statistics Canada.

Szinovacz, M. E., & Davey, A. (2001). Retirement effects on parent-adult child contacts. *The Gerontologist, 41*(2), 191–200.

Szinovacz, M. E., & Davey, A. (2004). Retirement transitions and spouse disability: Effects on depressive symptoms. *Journal of Gerontology: Social Sciences, 59B*(6), S333–S342.

Szinovacz, M. E., & Davey, A. (2005a). Predictors of perceptions of involuntary retirement. *The Gerontologist, 45*(1), 36–47.

Szinovacz, M. E., & Davey, A. (2005b). Retirement and marital decision-making: Effects on retirement satisfaction. *Journal of Marriage and Family, 67*(2), 387–398.

Szinovacz, M. E., & Davey, A. (2006). Effects of retirement and grandchild care on depressive symptoms. *International Journal of Aging and Human Development, 62*(1), 1–20.

Szinovacz, M. E., & DeViney, S. (1999). The retiree identity: Gender and race differences. *Journal of Gerontology: Social Sciences, 54B,* S207–S218.

Szinovacz, M. E., & DeViney, S. (2000). Marital characteristics and retirement decisions. *Research on Aging, 22,* 470–489.

Szinovacz, M. E., DeViney, S., & Davey, A. (2001). Influences of family obligations and relationships on retirement: Variations by gender, race, and marital status. *Journal of Gerontology: Social Sciences, 56B,* S20–S27.

Szinovacz, M.E., & Ekerdt, D.J. (1995). Families and retirement. In R. Blieszner & V.H. Bedford (Eds.), *Handbook on aging and the family* (pp. 375–400). Westport, CT: Greenwood Press.

Szinovacz, M.E., & Harpster, P. (1994). Couple's employment/retirement status and the division of household work. *Journal of Gerontology: Social Sciences, 49,* S125–S136.

Szinovacz, M. E., & Washo, C. (1992). Gender differences in exposure to life events and adaptation to retirement. *Journal of Gerontology: Social Sciences, 47,* S191–S196.

Uccello, C.E. (2000). *Do spouses coordinate their investment decisions in order to share risks?* (Working Paper 2000–09). Chestnut Hill, MA: Center for Retirement Research at Boston College.

U.S. Bureau of the Census. (1976). *Statistical abstract of the United States.* Retrieved from http://www.census.gov/prod/www/abs/statab1951–1994.htm

U.S. Bureau of the Census. (1985). *Statistical abstract of the United States.* Retrieved from http://www.census.gov/prod/www/abs/statab1951–1994.htm

U.S. Bureau of the Census. (1996). *Statistical abstract of the United States.* Retrieved from http://www.census.gov/prod/2/gen/96statab/labor.pdf

U.S. Bureau of the Census. (2010). Table 57: Marital status of the population by sex and age: 2008. Retrieved from http://www.census.gov/prod/2009pubs/10statab/pop.pdf

U.S. Bureau of the Census. (2011). *Statistical abstract of the United States.* Retrieved from http://www.census.gov/prod/2011pubs/11statab/labor.pdf

U.S. Department of Labor Bureau of Labor Statistics. (1988). *Labor force statistics derived from the Current Population Survey, 1948–1987.* Washington, DC: Government Printing Office.

U.S. Department of Labor Bureau of Labor Statistics. (2011). Household data: Annual averages. Retrieved from http://www.bls.gov/cps/cpsaat3.pdf

Van Solinge, H., & Henkens, K. (2005). Couples' adjustment to retirement: A multiactor panel study. *Journal of Gerontology: Social Sciences, 60B*(1), S11–S20.

Van Solinge, H., & Henkens, K. (2007). Involuntary retirement: The role of restrictive circumstances, timing, and social embeddedness. *Journal of Gerontology: Social Sciences, 62B*(5), S295–S303.

Väre, M. (2006). Spousal effect and timing of retirement. *Journal of Agricultural Economics, 57*(1), 65–80.

Vinick, B.H., & Ekerdt, D.J. (1991a). Retirement: What happens to husband-wife relationships? *Journal of Geriatric Psychiatry, 24,* 23–40.

Vinick, B.H., & Ekerdt, D.J. (1991b). The transition to retirement: Responses of husbands and wives. In B.B. Hess & E.W. Markson (Eds.), *Growing old in America* (4th ed., pp. 305–317). New Brunswick, NJ: Transaction Books.

Williamson, J.B., & McNamara, T.K. (2003). Interrupted trajectories and labor force participation. *Research on Aging, 25*(2), 87–121.

Yabiku, S.T. (2000). Family history and pensions: The relationships between marriage, divorce, children, and private pension coverage. *Journal of Aging Studies, 14,* 293–312.

Yilmazer, T., & Lyons, A. C. (2010). Marriage and the allocation of assets in women's defined contribution plans. *Journal of Family and Economic Issues, 31,* 121–137.

Zhang, Y., & Goza, F. W. (2006). Who will care for the elderly in China?: A review of the problems caused by China's one-child policy and their potential solutions. *Journal of Aging Studies, 20*(2), 151–164.

20

Divorce and Widowhood
in Later Life

Deborah Carr and Tetyana Pudrovska

Marital dissolution, whether through divorce or widowhood, has been described as among the most stressful of all life events (Holmes & Rahe, 1967). One of the most influential research discoveries of the past two decades, however, is the recognition that marital dissolution is not universally distressing; rather, the nature and consequences of dissolution vary widely based on characteristics of both spouses, the marriage, the sociohistorical context, and the context of the marital transition. In this chapter, we review recent research on the experiences of widowhood and divorce in later life, with particular attention to the implications of marital dissolution for older adults' psychological, physical, economic, and social well-being.

We begin by describing patterns of later-life divorce and widowhood in the contemporary United States. We then discuss conceptual issues that guide research on the consequences of late-life marital dissolution, and highlight the importance of considering both social selection and social causation perspectives. The next section provides a detailed summary of recent and cutting-edge research documenting the impact of divorce and widowhood on older adults' psychological, physical, economic, and social well-being. We pay close attention to sources of heterogeneity, including gender, characteristics of the marriage, and characteristics of the marital transition. The final two sections set forth a series of recommendations for researchers, policymakers, and practitioners. An important challenge over the coming decades is to understand how marital dissolutions and their consequences may vary across birth cohorts; much of what scholars know about late-life divorce and widowhood is based on current cohorts of older adults, who may differ starkly from the large cohort of 75 million Baby Boomers who will be transitioning to later life in the next decade.

DIVORCE AND WIDOWHOOD TRENDS AMONG OLDER ADULTS

Divorce Trends and Patterns

Divorce refers to the legal termination of marriage, whereas separation refers to the point in a relationship when spouses stop living together due to difficulties in their marriage. Divorce rates have increased among older adults throughout the past three decades, yet divorces are still rare among persons aged 65 and older. Just 7% of men and 9% of women aged 65 and older are currently divorced and not remarried. (Although some may be in committed romantic or cohabiting relationships, these statuses would not be captured in most federal statistics). As Figure 20.1 reveals, the proportion that is currently divorced declines steadily with age. The percentages currently divorced are 9.6 and 13.0 for men and women aged 65 to 74 years, respectively, 5.5 and 7.0 at ages 75 to 84, and 2.4 and 4.2 at ages 85 and older. Older adults who are now divorced typically ended their marriages much earlier in the life course. According to the National Center for Health Statistics, only 2 out of every 1,000 persons aged 65 and older will divorce in a given year.

Demographers continue to debate whether the low divorce rates observed among older adults today reflect the influence of *age* versus *cohort member-*

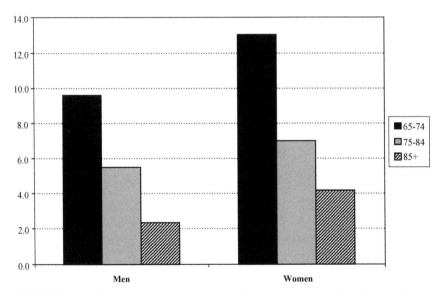

FIGURE 20.1 Proportion currently divorced, by age and gender: United States, 2007

Source: Federal Interagency Forum on Aging Related Statistics. (2007). *Older Americans 2008: Key Indicators of Well-Being.* Table 3: Marital Status of the Population Age 65 and Over, by Age Group and Sex.

ship; the resolution of this debate will have important implications for understanding patterns of divorce among future cohorts of older adults. An *age* effect would mean that the likelihood of any married couple divorcing decreases over the life course, due to the stabilizing effect of being in a long-term marriage, improvements in marital quality as one ages, inertia, or aspects of physical, emotional, and cognitive maturation that reduce one's likelihood of divorcing later in life. Demographers have documented that the risk of divorce is greatest during the first seven years of marriage, and declines over the duration of the marriage (e.g., Cherlin, 1992). Some researchers have speculated that long-term marriages are resilient; if a married couple has managed to survive the stressors of the early and middle years of marriage—such as childbearing, childrearing, financial strains, and the empty nest and retirement transitions—then that couple will be well-equipped to weather the ups and downs of later-life marriage (e.g., Teachman, 2002).

A *cohort*-based explanation, by contrast, holds that current cohorts of older men and women who were born in the early decades of the 20th century and who married in the 1940s, 1950s, and 1960s, were socialized to view marriage as a permanent relationship that could end only by death of one partner (Bumpass, 1990). Those who wanted to divorce often were reluctant to do so because of stigma, religious prohibitions, or concerns that marital dissolution would be harmful to their children. Women who lacked work experience and the earnings necessary to support themselves would be particularly reluctant to exit a problematic marriage (Holden & Smock, 1991). Although divorce rates in the United States rose steeply during the 1970s and 1980s, older couples did not necessarily adopt the "new" cultural view that the pursuit of individual happiness is more important than family stability (Bumpass, 1990).

Current cross-sectional data reveal that Baby Boomers, born in the mid-1940s through mid-1960s, are more likely to divorce than their predecessors. They are less likely than prior cohorts to believe that couples should stay together for the "sake of the children," and instead endorse divorce if the marriage does not meet their personal needs (Bumpass, 1990). Increases in women's educational attainment, occupational status, and earnings over the past four decades also have enabled women to leave troubled or unsatisfying marriages (Holden & Smock, 1991). As Figure 20.2 reveals, the proportion of Americans who has ever divorced by age 50 increased steadily across recent cohorts, providing some evidence that future cohorts of older adults will be more likely than their predecessors to have divorced.

A full assessment of these competing perspectives will not be possible until the large cohort of Baby Boomers enters late life. However, some scholars have speculated that divorce in later life will become an increasingly common life event as life expectancy continues to increase. Older adults anticipating a long and relatively healthy future may be motivated to dissolve unfulfilling,

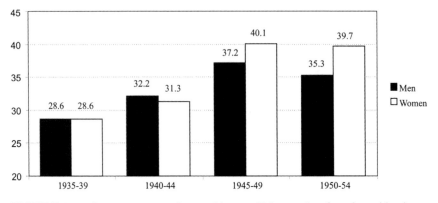

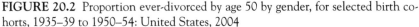

FIGURE 20.2 Proportion ever-divorced by age 50 by gender, for selected birth cohorts, 1935–39 to 1950–54: United States, 2004

Source: U.S. Census Bureau. (2004). *Survey of Income and Program Participation (SIPP), 2004 Panel, Wave 2 Topical Module.* Table 1: Marital History by Sex for Selected Birth Cohorts, 1935–39 to 1980–84.

troubled, or stale marriages (Wu & Schimmele, 2007). Despite media images of older husbands trading in their wives for "newer models," evidence suggests that older women are more likely than their male peers to initiate divorce, as they seek out new opportunities for themselves after their children have grown and left the family home (Montenegro, 2004).

Widowhood Trends and Patterns

Widowhood in the United States today is largely an experience of older women. Although public images of distraught widows and widowers often feature young adults—the youthful brides of fallen soldiers in the Iraq war or the junior executives who lost their wives during the September 11 attacks—widowhood today is a transition overwhelmingly experienced by persons aged 65 and older. Of the 900,000 persons who become widowed annually in the United States today, nearly three-quarters are aged 65 or older (Federal Interagency Forum on Aging-Related Statistics, 2008). Widowhood patterns mirror mortality patterns. The death rate, or the number of all persons who die in a given year per 100,000 persons in the population, increases sharply beyond age 65 (see Figure 20.3). Life expectancy at birth today is 76 for men and 80 for women, so women are much more likely than men to become widowed.

Among persons aged 65 to 74 years, 26.3% of women but just 7.3% of men are widowed. These proportions jump to 58.2% of women and 20.5% of men aged 75 and older (see Figure 20.4). The stark gender gap in the proportion currently widowed also reflects the fact that widowers are far more likely than widows to remarry, and thus exit the widowed category. Widows are less

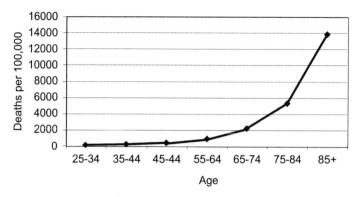

FIGURE 20.3 Death rates by age (all causes): United States, 2004
Source: National Vital Statistics Reports. (2007, August 21). *Deaths: Final Data for 2004.* Vol. 55, No. 10.

likely than widowers to remarry because of the dearth of potential partners. Among persons ages 65 and older in the United States, the sex ratio is 1.5 women per every 1 man. By age 85, this ratio is more than 3 women per every man. As a result, few widows have the opportunity to remarry even if they would like to do so. In addition, cultural norms encourage men to marry women younger than themselves, so widowed men may opt to remarry a younger woman, whereas older widows do not typically have access to a similarly expanded pool of potential spouses.

Mounting research suggests that older widowed persons who have committed romantic relationships may choose not to remarry or coreside, and instead prefer to maintain an arrangement called living apart together (LAT).

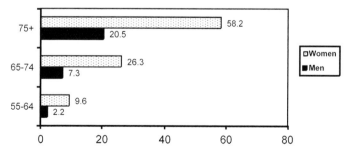

FIGURE 20.4 Proportion currently widowed, by age and gender, United States 2006
Source: U.S. Census Bureau. (2007, March 27). *America's Families and Living Arrangements: 2006.* Table A1. Marital Status of People 15 Years and Over, by Age, Sex, Personal Earnings, Race, and Hispanic Origin, 2006. Current Population Reports, P20–547.

In the United States, an estimated 7% of women and 6% of men report that they live apart together (Strohm, Seltzer, Cochran, & Mays, 2008). Older adults who choose this arrangement tend to own their own homes, and neither partner wants to move and combine possessions nor create inheritance complications for their children. Older women also may not want to take on the homemaking and caregiving responsibilities that often accompany marriage or coresidence; this concern is articulated most frequently by widows who had intensive caregiving responsibilities in their late marriage (van den Hoonard, 2002).

Although widowhood historically has been characterized as an event that occurs upon the death of one's spouse, contemporary late-life widowhood is best conceptualized as a process. Most deaths among older adults today occur due to chronic disease or long-term illnesses for which there is no cure (Federal Interagency Forum on Aging-Related Statistics, 2008). The four leading causes of death to older adults today—heart disease, cancer, cerebrovascular disease, and chronic obstructive pulmonary disorder (COPD)—account for nearly two-thirds of all deaths to older adults. Thus, most older adults become widowed after at least one spell of caregiving for an ailing spouse. As we will discuss later in this chapter, the context surrounding a spouse's death shapes bereavement experiences among current cohorts of older adults.

THE IMPACT OF MARITAL DISSOLUTION ON LATE-LIFE HEALTH AND WELL-BEING: CONCEPTUAL ISSUES

An immense body of research over the past two decades has documented that divorce and spousal death are associated with decrements in one's mental and physical health, and an increased mortality risk (Hughes & Waite, 2009; Lamb, Lee, & DeMaris, 2003; Manzoli, Villari, Pirone, & Boccia, 2007; Simon, 2002), as well as declines in one's economic well-being (Holden & Smock, 1991). Although divorce compromises the quality of older adults' (especially men's) relationships with their adult children (Ganong & Coleman, 1998; Kalmijn, 2007), older widowed persons often grow closer with their children and other relatives (Ha, 2008).

Early research, based on classic models of stress, presumed that all major changes in one's living conditions or social contexts posed a health threat (e.g., Holmes & Rahe, 1967; Selye, 1936). However, research conducted in the past two decades documents that marital dissolution does not have universally detrimental effects on health and well-being. Rather, the magnitude, duration, and direction of these effects vary based on characteristics of the individual, the former marital relationship, the transition, and the specific health outcome considered (Carr, House, Kessler, Nesse, Sonnega, & Wortman, 2000; Hawkins & Booth, 2005; Kalmijn & Monden, 2006; Sweeney & Horwitz, 2001).

Social Causation versus Social Selection Perspectives

Two conceptual models typically are proposed to explain linkages among marital transitions and health: social causation and social selection. The social causation perspective comprises two distinctive yet complementary arguments. The marriage benefit model holds that the economic, socioemotional, and health-enhancing resources of being married enhance health (Waite & Gallagher, 2001). Consequently, divorced and widowed persons are deprived of such resources, and their quality of life suffers accordingly. The crisis model proposes that the strains associated with the process of exiting marriage compromise one's well-being (Williams & Umberson, 2004). Exiting marriage may affect well-being directly, due to the stress of the transition, or indirectly via secondary stressors resulting from the transition, such as a drop in household income, or managing domestic responsibilities on one's own (Johnson & Wu, 2002). These perspectives offer different predictions with respect to the time course of marital dissolution effects. The crisis perspective suggests that the harmful effects of marital dissolution are temporary; well-being declines immediately after a marital transition, but then returns to the predissolution level as one adjusts to the stressor. The marital benefit model counters that the disadvantages of being divorced or widowed persist indefinitely, or until one remarries.

The social selection hypothesis states that the association between marital dissolution and well-being reflects the fact that persons with the fewest resources are most likely to divorce or lose a spouse, to remain unmarried following dissolution, and also have poorer health due in part to their disadvantaged status (Johnson & Wu, 2002). Most researchers concur that the physical and mental health disadvantages documented among formerly married persons reflect both social selection and causation processes (Wade & Pevalin, 2004). Three primary mechanisms are offered for the poorer well-being of formerly married persons: diminished economic resources, social control, and psychosocial support and strain.

Economic Resources

Formerly married persons have fewer socioeconomic resources than their married peers, and these resources are well documented predictors of multiple health conditions and mortality risk (Rogers, Hummer, & Nam, 2000). This association reflects selection processes where healthier and wealthier persons are more likely to marry, and social causation, where marriage provides economic stability (Goldman, 2001). Formerly married persons (especially women) also are less likely than married persons to have private health insurance, retain coverage upon job loss, and draw on a spouse's benefits. Private health insurance coverage, in turn, is associated with timely access to high quality care (Hadley, 2003). Although Social Security and Medicare provide income security and health insurance coverage to older adults, these later-life benefits cannot undo the earlier harmful effects of intermittent access to care and compromised economic resources.

Social Control

Spouses monitor each other's behaviors, and this protection disappears when a marriage dissolves. Evidence generally shows that formerly married men and (to a lesser extent) women engage in more unhealthy practices including substance use, smoking, unhealthy diet, and poorer compliance with medication regimens (DiMatteo, 2004). Effects are stronger for men because women are more vigilant monitors and they engage in fewer unhealthy practices that require monitoring (Duncan, Wilkerson, & England, 2006).

Psychosocial Support and Strain

Formerly married persons are presumed to have fewer sources of socio-emotional support than their married peers. Social support, such as having a close confidante and persons who provide instrumental help, is a powerful influence on health and well-being (House, Landis, & Umberson, 1988). However, recent empirical studies find that the marital advantage in social support is observed only when persons in happy marriages are used as the reference group (Kiecolt-Glaser & Newton, 2001). Formerly married older adults often have a broad network of persons they can turn to, including siblings, adult children, and friends (Ha, 2008). These persons provide support that may have direct effect on older adults' well-being, but this support does not necessarily buffer the distressing effects of dissolution, at least during the earliest stages of the transition (Stroebe, Zech, Stroebe, & Abakoumkin, 2005).

DIVORCE AND LATE-LIFE WELL-BEING

Over the past two decades, researchers have sought to document why and how marital dissolution affects older adults' well-being. Because divorce typically occurs during the first decade of marriage, studies of the consequences of divorce focus overwhelmingly on younger adults, particularly those who have children under the age of 18 (Amato, 2000). Most currently divorced older adults dissolved their marriages in young or middle adulthood, and many subsequently remarried. In the following sections, we review highlights of recent studies that document the consequences of divorce for older adults; the vast majority of these studies focus on the long-term consequences of divorces that occurred earlier in life, given that few married persons divorce their spouses in later life. Taken together, studies conducted over the past two decades have moved away from the question, does divorce affect well-being? Rather, studies now explore the questions, for which outcomes, for which individuals, and under which conditions does divorce compromise well-being?

Psychological and Physical Health Consequences

There is broad consensus that divorce takes a toll on the mental health of both men and women, where mental health is typically operationalized as depressive symptoms. Early research and theory proposed that men fare worse than women because men benefit more from marriage, and thus have more to lose when their relationship ends (Bernard, 1972; Gove & Tudor, 1973). However, researchers now point out that prior studies failed to consider that the time course of men's and women's symptoms differ, and studies that focus on long time horizons (or variable time horizons) fail to capture short-term reactions. Strohschein and colleagues (Strohschein, McDonough, Monette, & Shao, 2005) recently showed that when growth curve models are used and divorced persons are tracked across three two-year periods, both men and women evidence similar levels of psychological distress. The effects on depressive symptoms also are relatively short-lived for both genders (Blekesaune, 2008; Lorenz, Wickrama, Conger, & Elder, 2006). Other studies found neither gender fares systematically worse, but that reactions differ, where women are more likely to evidence depressive symptoms and men increase their alcohol consumption (Simon, 2002).

Research on mortality rates shows clear-cut trends, but these studies cannot disentangle the effects due to selection versus causation. A meta-analysis of studies of marital status and mortality rates found that divorced persons had an elevated risk of mortality compared to married persons in 12 out of 14 studies (Manzoli et al., 2007). However, the studies included in the meta-analysis were based largely on European administrative records, and thus could not control for selection into divorce, or pathways that potentially explain the differential. Similarly, an analysis of National Longitudinal Mortality Study (NLMS) data found that divorced persons (both men and women, black and white) had an elevated risk of all-cause mortality, cardiovascular disease, and cancer relative to married persons (see also Zhang & Hayward, 2006). Analyses of mortality data also reveal that divorced persons have higher suicide rates than their married counterparts (Stack, 2000). However, the data sources used do not include health or marital status trajectory data, and thus cannot shed insights into the processes linking divorce to mortality.

Heterogeneity in the Divorce Experience

Researchers now recognize that divorce is not a monolithic experience; as such, adjustment to the transition may be contingent upon the nature of the former marriage and the context of the divorce. This line of inquiry builds upon the contemporary classic article by Wheaton (1990), which proposes that the consequences of stressful role transitions are contingent upon one's "role history," or the rewards, costs, and strains experienced prior to the transition. Wheaton (1990) argued that the effects of role loss are far less detrimental when individuals are exiting roles that were unrewarding or distressing. Recent empirical studies provide mixed empirical support for this observation.

Williams and Umberson (2004) found that persons who dissolved highly strained marriages evidenced gains in self-rated health over an eight-year observation period. Similarly, Hawkins and Booth (2005) tracked married couples over a 12-year period and found that persons who remained in unhappy marriages later reported poorer self-rated health and greater depressive symptoms than those who exited equally problematic marriages. The authors concluded that dissolving an unhappy marriage may be more protective to one's well-being than remaining in an unhappy marriage.

However, other studies find that exiting an unhappy marriage does not enhance one's mental health, and, in fact, may be worse than staying married. Kalmijn and Monden (2006) found that persons who exited marriages marked by verbal and physical aggression showed an increase in depressive symptoms, and this increase was more pronounced than for persons exiting less problematic marriages. The authors do not argue that individuals should remain in problematic marriages; rather, they observe that many of the strains of a problematic marriage may persist, at least during the first five to seven years after the dissolution, particularly in cases where hostile ex-spouses must negotiate difficult custody or financial arrangements.

Other studies explore whether the nature of the marital transition affects well-being. An emerging literature on the moral nature of stressful events suggests that psychological reactions will be strongest for events viewed as unfair or unjust. Such studies have considered factors such as whether one forgives the ex-spouse for the dissolution (Rye, Folck, Heim, Olszewski, & Traina, 2005), and whether the divorce was triggered by infidelity (Sweeney & Horwitz, 2001). Further, life events characterized as anticipated or desired are believed to be less distressing; as such, recent studies have explored whether divorce initiation (that is, whether one requests the divorce) moderates the effect of the transition (Sweeney & Horwitz, 2001).

Empirical studies offer limited support for the provocative hypothesis that divorce is less distressing for those who anticipate the transition, or view it as morally just and fair. Sweeney and Horwitz (2001) found that the effects of divorce on depressive symptoms did not vary based on whether one initiated the divorce, or whether infidelity precipitated the dissolution. However, they found that persons who both initiated divorce and who reported that their ex-spouse was unfaithful showed significantly fewer depressive symptoms than their counterparts.

Taken together, prior studies reveal that divorce has a strong effect on older adults' emotional well-being in the short-term following divorce, that these effects are comparable for men and women, and are contingent upon the outcome considered, the nature of the marriage, and characteristics of the transition. Divorce also is strongly related to mortality risk, although the causal pathways have not yet been adequately specified. Two important questions remain unresolved, however. First, we do not know how the stress of divorce affects physical health of older adults. Laboratory-based research offers promising new insights. Divorce-related stressors may affect blood pressure reactivity, which, if persistent, could impede health (Sbarra, Law, Lee, & Mason, 2009). Second, studies fail to consider that divorce occurs within a larger family context, and its consequences could vary based on other concurrent family roles and obligations such as caring for ailing parents or negotiating relationships with stepchildren (see Ganong & Coleman, chapter 9 in this volume).

Economic Consequences

Divorce takes a significant toll on economic well-being, and these effects are significantly larger for women than men. Divorce has direct financial consequences, including the direct costs of the dissolution process (e.g., lawyer fees), and indirect costs, such as the loss of the financial advantage of sharing household expenses between two people. The financial strains of divorce, in turn, contribute to emotional strain. Women experience a much more drastic decline in their material well-being than men, and this decline is steeper for women in older birth cohorts, given the limited work, educational, and financial opportunities afforded to them (Smock, 1993). For many older divorced women, the loss of husband's income also requires a residential relocation—typically to a poorer quality neighborhood or home (Astone & McLanahan, 1994).

Even though divorced women over age 65 are provided some income security by Social Security, they are still disadvantaged relative to their married peers. According to some estimates, a divorced woman loses one-third of the benefits she and her husband would have received as a couple. Under Social Security rules, a divorcee is eligible for a share of her ex-spouse's benefits if she is at least 60 years old, not remarried, and had been married at least 10 years. Women who dissolved short-term marriages are at a high risk of poverty (Quadagno, 2011). By contrast, men typically do not experience the same drops in economic status and may even gain economically following divorce. McManus and DiPrete (2001) suggested that this trend may change for future cohorts; most of the men in their nationally representative sample did lose economic status due to the loss of their partner's income and an increase in support payments.

Consequences for Social Relationships

Divorce may hurt older adults' relationships with their adult children, particularly for divorced parents who were not custodial parents or who had sporadic contact with their children. Ganong and Coleman (1998) found that people believe adult children of divorce should help their aging parents, yet the level of support should be contingent upon the amount of contact the child had with that parent in earlier years. Silverstein and Bengtson (1997) also found that adult children whose parents divorced report a weaker sense of obligation to provide instrumental and expressive support than do children from intact families. These weakened ties are evident even when parents divorce later in life, after their children are grown (Kalmijn, 2007).

Given rigid allocation of men's and women's social roles among current cohorts of older adults, men are far less likely than women to have maintained close ties with their children after divorce. One study of divorced older men found that 10% maintained no contact with their adult children. Roughly half reported that they had weekly contact, yet this proportion is significantly lower than the 90% of married fathers who had equally frequent contact with their adult children (Cooney & Uhlenberg, 1990). Similarly, Webster and Herzog (1995) found that adult children of divorce reported poorer quality relationships with their aging parents than children from intact families. This toll was particularly severe for father-child relationships; children of divorce are less likely to report that they felt loved and listened to by their fathers compared to their mothers. Divorced fathers who subsequently remarry and have new biological or stepchildren have even more tenuous ties to their children from their prior marriage(s) (Kalmijn, 2007). However, among future cohorts of older adults, for whom "his" and "her" family roles have become increasingly blurred, the social ties between divorced fathers and their children may be closer and stronger.

WIDOWHOOD AND LATE-LIFE WELL-BEING

Psychological and Physical Health Consequences

Widowhood is associated with elevated risk of mortality (Manzoli et al., 2007), disability and functional limitations (Schoenborn, 2004), and depressive symptoms (Lee & DeMaris, 2007) during the first two years after loss;

effects are consistently larger for men than women. Whereas popular lore suggests that emotionally devastated widowers may "die of a broken heart" shortly after their wives die, research shows that the loss of a helpmate and caretaker is really the culprit. Wives monitor their husbands' diets, remind them to take their daily medications, and urge them to give up vices like smoking and drinking (Umberson, Wortman, & Kessler, 1992). Widowers are more likely than married men to die of accidents, alcohol-related deaths, lung cancer, and chronic ischemic heart disease during the first six months after their loss, but not from causes that are less closely linked to health behaviors (Martikainen & Valkonen, 1996).

In the past two decades, bereavement researchers have moved away from comparing the health of widowed persons with their married counterparts, and instead focus on sources of heterogeneity among widowed persons—especially with respect to their psychological health. This shift in focus is driven, in part, by three forces. First, a minority (just 15% to 30%) of older bereaved spouses experience long-term clinically significant depressive symptoms; thus, practitioners are particularly interested in identifying bereaved persons at greatest risk (Hansson & Stroebe, 2006). Second, researchers have debunked the notion that bereaved persons go through a universal set of stages or symptoms (Zisook & Shear, 2009), thus encouraging researchers to focus on variations in symptom trajectories. Finally, data sources that focus specifically on bereaved individuals are available to researchers. One such study, the Changing Lives of Older Couples (CLOC), was designed to study prospectively the distinctive experiences of widow(er)s (Carr, Nesse, & Wortman, 2006). This resource enables researchers to pinpoint factors that contribute to variations in well-being among the bereaved in the four years after loss.

Heterogeneity among Widow(er)s

Recently widowed older adults' well-being varies based on the context of the death and the late marriage. Researchers have documented that adjustment is affected by the timing and quality of the late spouse's death. In general, anticipated deaths tend to be less distressing than unanticipated ones. However, for older persons, anticipated deaths often are accompanied by painful images of a loved one's suffering, intensive caregiving for one's terminally ill spouse, and neglect of one's own health concerns, thus taking a toll on one's health that may persist post-loss (Carr, House, Wortman, Nesse, & Kessler, 2001). Older adults who believe that their loved one was in pain or received problematic medical care at the end of life reported greater anxiety and anger than persons whose loved one had a "good death" (Carr, 2003). Use of hospice or palliative care services at the end of life is associated with better bereavement outcomes (Christakis & Iwashyna, 2003).

The consequences of widowhood, like divorce, also vary based on the nature of the late marriage. Early writings, based on the psychoanalytic tradition, proposed that bereaved persons with the most troubled marriages would suffer heightened and pathological grief (Parkes & Weiss, 1983). This perspective held that persons who had conflicted marriages would find it hard to let go of their spouses, yet also feel angry at the deceased for abandoning them. However, longitudinal studies that track married persons over time through the widowhood transition find that older persons whose late marriages were marked by high levels of warmth and dependence and low levels of conflict experience elevated grief symptoms after loss (Carr et al., 2000).

Economic Consequences

Widows are more likely than widowers to experience economic hardship; financial strains, in turn, compromise psychological well-being (Umberson et al., 1992). Although age-based income assistance programs such as Social Security provide economic support for older widowed persons, widow(er)s remain significantly worse off than their married peers. Within three years of the death of her husband, a widow's income drops by 44% on average (Holden & Kuo, 1996). Widowed persons are more likely to live below the poverty line than their married counterparts, and they tend to cyclically re-enter poverty after losing their partner. More than half of elderly widows in poverty were not poor prior to the death of their husbands (Bound, Duncan, Laren, & Oleinik, 1991). Costs associated with the funeral, long-term and medical care, or estate-related legal proceedings can devastate the fixed income of older adults (Fan & Zick, 2004). For younger women, remarriage may be a pathway out of poverty, yet a highly imbalanced sex ratio in later life makes this option difficult for older women.

Widows' economic disadvantage reflects lifelong patterns of gendered inequality. In traditional marriages, wives tended to childrearing and family responsibilities, whereas husbands were responsible for supporting the family financially (Bernard, 1972). As a result, older women have had fewer years of paid work experience than their male peers. Moreover, because women typically earn less than men even when they perform the same job, women's accumulated pension and Social Security benefits based on their own earnings are typically much lower than those based on their husband's lifetime earnings (Harrington Meyer & Herd, 2007). Older widows who try to reenter the labor force also may lack the experience to secure a good job, or may face age discrimination. This disadvantage is even more pronounced for women of color, reflecting the lower average incomes of blacks and Hispanics over the life course. Whereas 11% of all persons aged 65 and older (and just 3% of married white men) live below the federal poverty line, comparable proportions are 37.5% and 40.5% for Hispanic and black women who live alone (Federal Interagency Forum on Aging-Related Statistics, 2008).

Consequences for Social Relationships

Women's emotionally intimate social relations over the life course are an important resource as they adjust to spousal loss. Older widows typically receive more instrumental and emotional support from their children than do widowers, given mothers' closer relationships with their children throughout the life course. Women also are more likely to have larger and more varied friendship networks than men, and these friendships provide an important source of support as women cope with their loss (Ha, 2008). Men, by contrast, often seek social support in new romantic relationships, whether dating or remarriage (Carr, 2004a). Social scientists expect that among future cohorts of older adults, the gender gap in widowed persons' well-being will diminish, as current cohorts of older women have more education, more continuous work histories, and higher earnings than their predecessors (Padavic & Reskin, 2002), and men maintain closer and more emotionally intimate ties with their children, other family, and friends.

DIRECTIONS FOR FUTURE RESEARCH

Over the past two decades, scholars have made major advances in conceptualizing and measuring the prevalence and meaning of marital dissolution in later life and documenting the implications of these transitions for late-life well-being. We anticipate that five topics are ripe for further exploration in the coming decades: sexuality and sexual health, racial and ethnic differences, the dissolution of same-sex relationships, relationship transitions of Baby Boomers, and the use of research methods that incorporate multiple sources of health and relationship data.

Sexuality and Sexual Health in Later Life

Even at the turn of the 21st century, most studies of marital dissolution focus on the loss or decline in instrumental and emotional support. However, research fails to consider another important component of well-being that may be lacking in the lives of formerly married persons, sexual relations. Waite and colleagues (Waite, Laumann, Das, & Schumm, 2009) suggested that older adults with high-quality sexual relations will have better trajectories of physical and mental health than those whose relationships function less well (or who lack such relationships). Consistent with this hypothesis, Carr (2008) found that the significantly higher levels of psychological distress and lower levels of self-acceptance among formerly married women in the Midlife in the United States (MIDUS) study were fully accounted for when sexual satisfaction was controlled.

The recently collected National Social Life, Health, and Aging Project (NSHAP), a nationally representative sample of community-dwelling individuals aged 57 to 85, provides in-depth measures of sexual behavior, practices, and health. The NSHAP may be an invaluable resource as social gerontologists further investigate the nature of sexual relationships maintained by formerly married versus currently married older adults, and the implications of these relationships for their physical, social, and emotional well-being.

Racial and Ethnic Differences in Late-Life Divorce and Widowhood

Most research on late-life widowhood and divorce focuses on white Americans. This pattern partly reflects the fact that older blacks and Latinos are underrepresented in large-scale sample surveys, given their elevated rates of mortality and morbidity. However, documenting the nature and consequences of relationship dissolution for ethnic minorities is an important inquiry. In 2006, whites, blacks, Latinos, and Asians accounted for 81%, 9%, 6%, and 3% of the U.S. population aged 65 and older, respectively. By 2050, these proportions will be 61%, 12%, 18%, and 8%, respectively (Federal Interagency Forum on Aging-Related Statistics, 2008).

Studies reveal that blacks report poorer marital quality and more marital conflict than whites, and that the economic gains of marriage are less for blacks than whites given black men's disadvantaged economic prospects (Broman, 1993). Given these patterns, marriage may be less protective (and dissolution less distressing) for blacks compared to whites. It is plausible that the effects of dissolution also are weaker for Asians and Latinos than for whites, given high levels of intergenerational integration and support in these communities. Consistent with these speculations, there is limited evidence that blacks fare better than whites upon spousal death, because their marriages are poorer quality on average, and they have a broader base of social support outside of marriage, especially support from their religious communities (Carr, 2004b).

A question for future exploration is how nonmarital relations and their dissolution affect later-life well-being. Demographers have documented a retreat from marriage among black women, due in part to the lack of marriageable men (Lichter, McLaughlin, Kephart, & Landry, 1992). High rates of imprisonment, unemployment, and murder among young black men have created an imbalanced sex ratio, and thus a limited pool of potential husbands (Wilson, 1987). Future cohorts of blacks will be much more likely than whites never to marry, and thus will never experience legal divorce or widow-hood. Goldstein and Kenney (2001) projected that among late Baby Boomer women, born between 1960 and 1964, 7% of whites but 36% of blacks will never marry. Future studies should explore the implications of both nonmarital breakups as well as lifelong singlehood for older adults, especially racial differences in these patterns.

Dissolution of Same-Sex Relationships

Researchers know very little about how older gays and lesbians adjust to the loss of their long-term life partners, whether through death or a breakup. This lack of research reflects the fact that no official statistics are widely available for same-sex unions. Older homosexuals may have distinctive challenges and resources as they cope with relationship loss. Bereaved gays and lesbians may encounter conflict with their deceased partner's family, particularly with respect to the dispersion of personal possessions following death. Legal rights extended to heterosexual married couples are not typically available for same-sex couples, including the opportunity to make health care and end-of-life decisions for ill partners. Gay men and lesbian women may not receive sufficient emotional support when their relationships dissolve, because their relationships might not have been recognized or acknowledged in the wider community (Friend, 1990).

However, gay men and lesbian women have some resources that may enable better coping with relationship dissolution. They may create their own support networks of friends and selected family members. They also may be more likely than their heterosexual peers to enact flexible gender roles throughout the life course. Because they are not bound to traditional gender-typed family roles, they may be better prepared to manage the daily challenges and responsibilities faced by newly bereaved persons (Friend, 1990). As more states legalize gay marriage, however, researchers in the coming decades will be better able to investigate whether the effects of dissolution vary based on the legal status of the union (King & Bartlett, 2006). Of particular interest is the extent to which the impact of such dissolutions varies by gender, race, and social class.

Social Relationships of Baby Boomers

Much of what scholars know about late-life widowhood and divorce is based on the experiences of current cohorts of older adults; those men and women born in the early 20th century who were socialized into rigid gender-typed social roles during their formative years and who often maintained a traditional division of labor in their marriages—where men were primary breadwinners, and women were primary caretakers for their husbands and children. It is not surprising, then, that the studies reported in this chapter reveal that women have closer ties to friends and children than men, that women are an important source of health control to their husbands, that men typically fare worse emotionally and physically than women upon widowhood, and that women fare worse financially following relationship dissolution.

For members of the Baby Boomer cohorts, the 75 million persons born between 1946 and 1964, late-life relationships may be reinvented. Future cohorts of older women are more likely than their predecessors to have received college degrees, held professional occupations, and shared childrearing tasks with their husbands. Future cohorts of men, by contrast, may have more emotionally intimate friendships than prior cohorts of men who were socialized to be self-reliant and independent. They also may be more involved parents, maintaining close ties to their children even following divorce. Thus, we might expect future cohorts to fare better in the face of spousal loss and divorce—given that women may have the economic resources and men the interpersonal resources to cope with the multiple challenges that arise post-transition.

However, there is reason to suspect that the emotional toll of relationship dissolution may be more intense for future cohorts of older adults. Baby Boomers faced fewer social obstacles to divorce during their young and midlife years, and thus we might expect that marriages that survive until late life will be of higher quality than for current elderly cohorts and the emotional sting will be more severe when a partner dies. Moreover, Baby Boomers and succeeding cohorts have postponed childbearing, often to their 30s and even 40s. As a result, persons who divorce (or are widowed) at midlife and later may still coreside with dependent children, creating a source of possible stress and role overload. Reflecting these and other major shifts in family structure and gender role socialization over the past 30 years, we expect that scholars' understanding of late-life marital dissolution may be transformed in coming decades.

Methodological Innovations

Social scientists overwhelmingly rely on large-scale sample survey data to document the nature and consequences of older adults' relationship transitions. However, survey-based studies of relationship trajectories and health historically have relied on self-reports of symptoms and conditions, rather than physiological indicators that may capture short-term responses to relationship dissolution. As such, scholars still do not fully understand how older adults' social relationships and the dissolution thereof "get under the skin" to affect physical and emotional health. Laboratory research, conducted primarily by psychologists, has made important advances by measuring the physiological responses of persons experiencing dissolution-related stressors (e.g., Sbarra, Law, Lee, & Mason, 2009).

In the past decade, a number of large representative sample surveys of older adults including the Health and Retirement Study (HRS), MIDUS, National Health and Nutrition Examination Survey (NHANES), NSHAP, and Wisconsin Longitudinal Study (WLS), have supplemented their self-reported health data with extensive genetic and biological indicators, such as immune response measures. We are optimistic about the scientific discoveries that may develop in the coming decades, as interdisciplinary teams of researchers continue to investigate the complex ways that demographic, socioeconomic, biological, psychosocial, and genetic factors link relationship dissolution to health and well-being among older adults.

IMPLICATIONS FOR POLICY AND PRACTICE

The research reviewed in this chapter underscores an important message for policymakers and practitioners: The effects of marital dissolution vary widely based on one's gender, the nature of the loss, the quality of one's former marriage, and one's other social and emotional resources. By identifying precisely what is lost upon marital dissolution, clinicians can provide individually tailored interventions that address at least one of the following areas: psychological, social, instrumental, or economic support.

Women, in particular, may experience declines in their economic well-being and subsequent anxiety about their financial security. Men, by contrast, may require assistance with homemaking and healthy meal preparation. The development of support groups and peer support programs, where newly single persons gain mastery over those tasks for which they lack skills, training, or experience, may be particularly useful (Silverman, 1986). For example, the Pathfinders program was designed to provide a supportive environment where widowed persons can discuss their frustrations with daily tasks and learn practical skills related to household management (Caserta, Lund, & Obray, 2004).

Federal policy initiatives could help to reduce economic-related distress among formerly married persons, especially women and members of ethnic and racial minority groups. Financial aid through more equitable and generous Social Security survivor benefits that recognize the economic value of women's unpaid labor may help to offset the decline in income often experienced upon marital dissolution. Moreover, recognition of the ways that women's contributions to the home (e.g., child and elder care) impede their pension earnings may be used to guide future policy decisions.

At the community or senior center level, the provision of social activities and social support also may be effective interventions for helping older adults to cope with the stress and loneliness that accompany widowhood.

However, we caution against the development of informal community programs that are based on a simple keep-busy philosophy. Rather than creating new recreational or social opportunities for bereaved persons, intervention efforts should instead enable older adults' maintenance of their predissolution social activities, interpersonal relationships, and hobbies—provided these activities are still enjoyable and meaningful.

Clinicians should recognize that whereas bereaved and divorced persons may experience grief or anxiety related to the end of their marriages, some may also have underlying depression symptoms—especially women, given that women are twice as likely as men to evidence depression over the life course (Rieker & Bird, 2005). Clinicians and medical professionals should identify older bereaved or divorced persons with past histories of major depression. Both short and longer-term treatment goals should take into account that depression may be a chronic and recurring condition that the patient has dealt with prior to (and likely in the years beyond) the marital transition. For such persons, treatments focused on the grief only may do little to enhance the patient's overall well-being (Bonanno & Lilienfeld, 2008).

More generally, adjustment to marital loss is a process that many begin far earlier than the actual moment of death or when the divorce papers were signed. Interventions targeted toward the stressors preceding the transition, such as assistance for persons caring for their ailing partners, witnessing their partner die of a long and painful illness, or persons trapped in stressful or abusive marriages, may be as important for alleviating distress as interventions offered after the transition. Improved medical care, increased availability of pain management programs, and access to affordable nursing home, long-term, or hospice care may not only benefit the dying person but also may enable a smoother transition for the bereaved survivor.

REFERENCES

Amato, P. R. (2000). The consequences of divorce for adults and children. *Journal of Marriage and Family, 62,* 1269–1287.

Astone, N., & McLanahan, S. (1994). Family structure, residential mobility, and school dropout: A research note. *Demography, 31,* 575–584.

Bernard, J. (1972). *The future of marriage.* New York: Bantam.

Blekesaune, M. (2008). Partnership transitions and mental distress: Investigating temporal order. *Journal of Marriage and Family, 70,* 879–890.

Bonanno, G. A., & Lilienfeld, S. O. (2008). Let's be realistic: When grief counseling is effective and when it's not. *Professional Psychology: Research and Practice, 39,* 377–380.

Bound, J., Duncan, G. J., Laren, D. S., & Olneinick, L. (1991). Poverty dynamics in widowhood. *Journal of Gerontology: Social Sciences, 46,* S115–S124.

Broman, C. L. (1993). Race differences in marital well-being. *Journal of Marriage and Family, 55,* 724–732.

Bumpass, L. (1990). What's happening to the family? Interactions between demographic and institutional change. *Demography, 27*, 483–498.

Carr, D. (2003). A good death for whom? Quality of spouse's death and psychological distress among older widowed persons. *Journal of Health & Social Behavior, 44*, 215–232.

Carr, D. (2004a). The desire to date and remarry among older widows and widowers. *Journal of Marriage and Family, 66*, 1051–1068.

Carr, D. (2004b). Black/white differences in psychological adjustment to spousal loss among older adults. *Research on Aging, 26*, 591–622.

Carr, D. (2008). Social and emotional well-being of single women in contemporary America. In R. M. Bell & V. Yans (Eds.), *Women on their own: Interdisciplinary perspectives on being single* (pp. 58–81). New Brunswick, NJ: Rutgers University Press.

Carr, D., House, J. S., Kessler, R. C., Nesse, R. M., Sonnega, J., & Wortman, C. (2000). Marital quality and psychological adjustment to widowhood among older adults: A longitudinal analysis. *Journals of Gerontology: Social Sciences, 55B*, S197–S207.

Carr, D., House, J. S., Wortman, C. B., Nesse, R. M., & Kessler, R. C. (2001). Psychological adjustment to sudden and anticipated spousal death among the older widowed. *Journal of Gerontology Series B: Psychological Sciences and Social Sciences, 56*, S237–S248.

Carr, D., Nesse, R. M., & Wortman, C. B. (Eds.). (2006). *Spousal bereavement in late life*. New York: Springer Publishing.

Caserta, M. S., Lund, D. A., & Obray, S. J. (2004). Promoting self-care and daily living skills among older widows and widowers: Evidence from the Pathfinders demonstration project. *Omega: Journal of Death & Dying, 49*, 217–236.

Cherlin, A. (1992). *Marriage, divorce, remarriage* (Rev. and enl. ed.). Cambridge, MA: Harvard University Press.

Christakis, N. A., & Iwashyna, T. J. (2003). The health impact on families of health care: A matched cohort study of hospice use by decedents and mortality outcomes in surviving, widowed spouses. *Social Science and Medicine, 57*, 465–475.

Cooney, T., & Uhlenberg, P. (1990). The role of divorce in men's relations with their adult children after midlife. *Journal of Marriage and Family, 52*, 677–88.

DiMatteo, M. (2004). Social support and patient adherence to medical treatment: A meta-analysis. *Health Psychology, 23*, 207–218.

Duncan, G., Wilkerson, B., & England, P. (2006). Cleaning up their act: The effects of marriage and cohabitation on licit and illicit drug use. *Demography, 43*, 691–710.

Fan, J. X., & Zick, C. D. (2004). An examination of the burden imposed by health care, funeral, and burial expenses at the end of life. *Journal of Consumer Affairs, 38*, 35–55.

Federal Interagency Forum on Aging-Related Statistics. (2008). *Older Americans 2008: Key indicators of well-being*. Washington, DC: Government Printing Office.

Friend, R. A. (1990). Older lesbian and gay people: A theory of successful aging. *Journal of Homosexuality, 23*, 99–118.

Ganong, L.H., & Coleman, M. (1998). Attitudes regarding filial responsibilities to help elderly divorced parents and stepparents. *Journal of Aging Studies, 12*, 271–290.

Goldman, N. (2001). Social inequalities in health: Disentangling the underlying mechanisms. *Annals of the New York Academy of Sciences, 954*, 118–139.

Goldstein, J., & Kenney, C.T. (2001). Marriage delayed or marriage forgone? New cohort forecasts of first marriage for U.S. women. *American Sociological Review, 66*, 506–519.

Gove, W.R., & Tudor, J.E (1973). Adult sex roles and mental illness. *American Journal of Sociology, 98*, 812–835.

Ha, J. (2008). Changes in support from confidantes, children, and friends following widowhood. *Journal of Marriage and Family, 70*, 306–318.

Hadley, J. (2003). Sicker and poorer—the consequences of being uninsured: A review of the research on the relationship between health insurance, medical care use, health, work, and income. *Medical Care Research and Review, 60*, 3S–75S.

Hansson, R.O., & Stroebe, M.S. (2006). *Bereavement in late life: Coping, adaptation and developmental influences*. Washington, DC: American Psychological Association.

Harrington Meyer, M., & Herd, P. (2007). *Market friendly or family friendly? The state and gender inequality in old age*. New York: Russell Sage.

Hawkins, D., & Booth, A. (2005). Unhappily ever after: Effects of long-term, low-quality marriages on well-being. *Social Forces, 84*, 445–465.

Holden, K.C., & Kuo, D.H. (1996). Complex marital histories and economic well-being: The continuing legacy of divorce and widowhood as the HRS cohort approaches retirement. *The Gerontologist, 35*, 383–390.

Holden, K.C., & Smock, P.J. (1991). The economic costs of marital dissolution: Why do women bear a disproportionate cost? *Annual Review of Sociology, 17*, 51–78.

Holmes, T., & Rahe, R. (1967). The social readjustment scale. *Journal of Psychosomatic Research, 11*, 213–218.

House, J.S., Landis, K.R., & Umberson, D. (1988). Social relationships and health. *Science, 241*, 540–545.

Hughes, M.E., & Waite, L.J. (2009). Marital biography and health at midlife. *Journal of Health and Social Behavior, 50*, 344–358.

Johnson, D.R., & Wu, J. (2002). An empirical test of crisis, social selection, and role explanations of the relationship between marital disruption and psychological distress: A pooled time-series analysis of four-wave panel data. *Journal of Marriage and Family, 64*, 211–224.

Kalmijn, M. (2007). Gender differences in the effects of divorce, widowhood, and remarriage on intergenerational support: Does marriage protect fathers? *Social Forces, 85*, 1079–1104.

Kalmijn, M., & Monden, C.W. (2006). Are the negative effects of divorce on well-being dependent on marital quality? *Journal of Marriage and Family, 68*, 1197–1213.

Kiecolt-Glaser, J.K., & Newton, T.L. (2001). Marriage and health: His and hers. *Psychological Bulletin, 127*, 472–503.

King, M., & Bartlett, A. (2006). What same-sex civil partnerships may mean for health. *Journal of Epidemiology and Community Health, 60,* 553–568.

Lamb, K. A., Lee, G. R., & DeMaris, A. (2003). Union formation and depression: Selection and relationship effects. *Journal of Marriage and Family, 65,* 953–962.

Lee, G. R., & DeMaris, A. (2007). Widowhood, gender, and depression: A longitudinal analysis. *Research on Aging, 29,* 56–72.

Lichter, D. T., McLaughlin, D. K., Kephart, G., & Landry, D. J. (1992) Race and the retreat from marriage: A shortage of marriageable men?. *American Sociological Review, 57,* 781–799.

Lorenz, F., Wickrama, K. A., Conger, R., & Elder, G. (2006). The short-term and decade-long effects of divorce on women's midlife health. *Journal of Health and Social Behavior, 47,* 111–125.

Manzoli, L., Villari, P., Pirone, G. M., & Boccia, A. (2007). Marital status and mortality in the elderly: A systematic review and meta-analysis. *Social Science and Medicine, 64,* 77–94.

Martikainen, P., & Valkonen, T. (1996). Mortality after the death of a spouse: Rates and causes of death in a large Finnish cohort. *American Journal of Public Health, 86,* 1087–1093.

McManus, P. A., & DiPrete, T. A. (2001). Losers and winners: The financial consequences of separation and divorce for men. *American Sociological Review, 66,* 246–268.

Montenegro, X. P. (2004). *The divorce experience: A study of divorce at midlife and beyond.* Washington, DC: AARP.

Padavic, I., & Reskin, B. F. (2002). *Women and men at work* (2nd ed.). Thousand Oaks, CA: Pine Forge Press.

Parkes, C. M., & Weiss, R. S. (1983). *Recovery from bereavement.* New York: Basic.

Quadagno, J. (2011). *Aging and the life course: An introduction to social gerontology* (5th ed.). New York: McGraw-Hill.

Rieker, P. P., & Bird, C. E. (2005). Rethinking gender differences in health: Why we need to integrate social and biological perspectives. *Journal of Gerontology: Social Sciences, 60* (Special Issue 2), S40–S47.

Rogers, R. G., Hummer, R. A., & Nam, C. B. (2000). *Living and dying in the USA: Behavioral, health, and social differentials of adult mortality.* San Diego, CA: Academic Press.

Rye, M. S., Folck, C. D., Heim, T. A., Olszewski, B. T., & Traina, E. (2005). Forgiveness of an ex-spouse: How does it relate to mental health following a divorce? *Journal of Divorce and Remarriage, 73,* 880–892.

Sbarra, D. A., Law, R. W., Lee, L. A., & Mason, A. E. (2009). Marital dissolution and blood pressure reactivity: Evidence for the specificity of emotional intrusion-hyperarousal and task-rated emotional difficulty. *Psychosomatic Medicine, 71,* 532–540.

Schoenborn, C. (2004). Marital status and health: United States, 1999–2002. *U.S. National Center for Health Statistics: Advance Data from Vital and Health Statistics,* 1–32.

Selye, H. (1936). Syndrome produced by diverse nocuous agents. *Nature, 138,* 32.

Silverman, P. R. (1986). *Widow-to widow.* New York: Springer Publishing.

Silverstein, M., & Bengtson, V. (1997). Intergenerational solidarity and the structure of adult child-parent relationships in America families. *American Journal of Sociology 103,* 429–460.

Simon, R. (2002). Revisiting the relationship among gender, marital status, and mental health. *American Journal of Sociology, 107,* 1065–1096.

Smock, P. J. (1993). The economic costs of marital disruption for young women over the past two decades. *Demography, 30,* 353–371.

Stack, S. (2000). Suicide: A 15-year review of the sociological literature. *Suicide & Life Threatening Behavior, 30,* 163–176.

Stroebe, W., Zech, E., Stroebe, M. S., & Abakoumkin, G. (2005). Does social support help in bereavement? *Journal of Social and Clinical Psychology, 24,* 1030–1050.

Strohm, C., Seltzer, J. A., Cochran, S. D., & Mays, V. (2008). *Living apart together relationships in the United States* (Working Paper No. 042-08), Los Angeles: California Center for Population Research, University of California.

Strohschein, L., McDonough, P., Monette, G., & Shao, Q. (2005). Marital transitions and mental health: Are there gender differences in the short-term effects of marital status change? *Social Science and Medicine, 61,* 2293–2303.

Sweeney, M. M., & Horwitz, A. V. (2001). Infidelity, initiation, and the emotional climate of divorce: Are there implications for mental health? *Journal of Health and Social Behavior, 42,* 295–310.

Teachman, J. D. (2002). Stability across cohorts in divorce risk factors. *Demography, 39,* 331–51.

Umberson, D., Wortman, C. B., & Kessler, R. C. (1992). Widowhood and depression: Explaining long-term gender differences in vulnerability. *Journal of Health and Social Behavior, 33,* 10–24.

van den Hoonard, D. K. (2002). Attitudes of older widows and widowers in New Brunswick, Canada toward new partnerships. *Ageing International, 27,* 79–92.

Wade, T. J., & Pevalin, D. J. (2004). Marital transitions and mental health. *Journal of Health and Social Behavior, 45,* 155–170.

Waite, L. J., & Gallagher, M. (2001). *The case for marriage: Why married people are happier, healthier, and better off financially.* New York: Doubleday.

Waite, L., Laumann, E. O., Das, A., & Schumm, L. P. (2009). Sexuality: Measures of partnerships, practices, attitudes, and problems in the National Social Life, Health, and Aging Study. *Journal of Gerontology: Social Sciences, 61B,* 71–79.

Webster, P., & Herzog, A. R. (1995). Effects of parental divorce and memories of family problems on relationships between adult children and their parents. *Journal of Gerontology: Social Sciences, 50B,* S24–S34.

Wheaton, B. (1990). Life transitions, role histories, and mental health. *American Sociological Review, 55,* 209–223.

Williams, K., & Umberson, D. (2004). Marital status, marital transitions, and health: A gendered life course perspective. *Journal of Health and Social Behavior, 45,* 81–98.

Wilson, W.J. (1987). *The truly disadvantaged: The inner city, the underclass, and public policy*. Chicago: University of Chicago Press.

Wu, Z., & Schimmele, C.M. (2007). Uncoupling in late life. *Generations, 31*, 41–46.

Zhang, Z., & Hayward, M.D. (2006). Gender, the marital life course, and cardiovascular disease in late midlife. *Journal of Marriage and Family, 68*, 639–657.

Zisook, S., & Shear, K. (2009). Grief and bereavement: What psychiatrists need to know. *World Psychiatry, 8*, 67–74.

21

Family Caregiving in Later Life: Shifting Paradigms

Rachel Pruchno and Laura N. Gitlin

Family members from all socioeconomic statuses, races, and ethnic groups provide the lion's share of requisite care to one another throughout the life course. Although caring for another person is the sine qua non of primary relationships, in this chapter we use the term caregiving to refer to the extraordinary care provided in the face of serious health conditions to a person in a close relationship. In later life, caregiving relationships assume a variety of forms, including adult children caring for aging parents, spouses and adult siblings caring for one another, grandparents caring for grandchildren, and parents caring for adult children with physical or emotional disabilities.

This chapter focuses on the experiences of family caregivers in later life in the United States when either the provider of care (the caregiver) or the person receiving care (the care recipient) is middle-aged or older. We use the classic definitions of the care recipient as a person with at least one activity of daily living limitation that leads to physical dependence on others, and the primary caregiver as the person with the main responsibility for providing care to that individual (Stone, Cafferata, & Sangl, 1987). We provide a comprehensive historical overview of research on family caregiving beginning with descriptive studies initiated in the 1960s, followed by explanatory or correlational studies conducted throughout the 1980s, ending with recent predictive and intervention studies. A historical lens affords an understanding of how our incremental knowledge base has been shaped by demographic and societal trends, shifting theoretical assumptions, and increasingly more sophisticated methodological approaches. We then provide a contemporary understanding of family caregiving, highlighting the wide varieties of caregiving situations, and reviewing the public health response. Finally, although evidence-based data exist about caregiving, we suggest that interventions and policies have been developed from a foundation that suffers from serious methodological design flaws and reliance on theoretical perspectives that limit the nature of questions addressed. We conclude by suggesting that the next generation of research requires paradigm shifts in the theories used to understand caregiving, the methodological designs employed, and the interventions developed to improve the lives of caregiving families.

DEBUNKING THE MYTH

Initial fascination with family caregiving in the United States was stimulated in part by a myth prevalent in the 1960s, suggesting that parents and their young children were the mainstay of family structures and that older people were isolated from and even abandoned by their families (Brody, 1985). Thus, the first significant wave of caregiver scholarship examined the veracity of this belief. A decade of research found that older people had family members who were significantly involved in their lives and daily care. This research consistently showed that ties between the generations were strong and viable; families assumed responsibility for 80–90% of medically related and personal care, household tasks, transportation, and shopping; families responded in emergencies and provided intermittent acute care; families shared their homes with severely impaired older people; most older people lived proximate to at least one adult child; intergenerational exchanges were the rule rather than the exception; and institutionalization of older people was a last resort (Shanas & Streib, 1965; Shanas, Townsend, Wedderburn, Friis, Milhoj, & Stehouwer, 1968).

These studies revealed a hierarchical pattern by which a family member became the dominant caregiver when help was needed. According to the "principle of substitution" (Shanas et al., 1968), the first person typically tapped for the role was a wife, and in her absence, an adult daughter. In the absence of wives and daughters, another relative, usually female, assumed the caregiving role. When family members were not available, older people relied on neighbors or friends for assistance. Formal care was a last resort, used only after resources of family and ancillary helpers were exhausted.

Data from the 1982 National Long-Term Care Survey and Informal Caregivers Survey revealed that approximately 2.2 million caregivers provided unpaid assistance to 1.6 million noninstitutionalized disabled elderly persons, and that only a minority of care recipients used formal services (Stone et al., 1987). Many informal caregivers, who were predominantly female and over age 65, had competing demands, with 21% having child care responsibilities and 31% working for pay.

While it established caregiving as a field of inquiry and provided the groundwork for future endeavors, this first wave of studies was primarily descriptive. After two decades of research aimed at debunking the myth of abandonment, this "hydra-headed monster," as Shanas (1979) referred to it, still would not die. The studies taken as a whole were hindered by significant methodological limitations including samples that were small, focused on the primary caregiver only, volunteer-based, not representative, geographically constricted, and lacking in racial and ethnic variability. Cross-sectional study designs were the norm, and most of the research was not based in theory.

CAREGIVING TAKES A TOLL

By 1985, after almost 20 years of descriptive research, family caregiving became fully recognized as a normative experience (Brody, 1985), and a second wave of studies emerged. These studies were explanatory in scope and sought to discover the physical and emotional health correlates of caregiving, compare the health and well-being of caregivers to noncaregivers, and identify specific physiological effects of caregiving.

Driven by Theory

A particular strength of this second wave of studies was that they were theory-driven. Recognizing that the demands associated with providing care to a family member were stressful, family caregiving became a model for scientists studying chronic stress. Within this context, the underlying premises were that caregiving demands created physical and psychological strain over extended periods of time, were accompanied by high levels of unpredictability and uncontrollability, had the capacity to create secondary stress in multiple life domains, and frequently required high levels of vigilance.

The initial conceptual schema of the stress process model developed by Pearlin, Mullan, Semple, and Skaff (1990) still dominates caregiving research, as illustrated by an ISI Web of Knowledge search revealing 919 citations referencing this model. The model has four multidimensional domains: background and context, stressors, mediators of stress, and outcomes. It suggests that background characteristics of the caregiver (age, gender, ethnicity, educational achievement, occupation, and economic attainment) influence the way the stress process is experienced. Other contextual variables are the structural relationship of the caregiver to the care recipient (e.g., spouse, daughter, or son), quality of the previous relationship, duration of caregiving relationship, and access to informal and formal resources. Stressors, the heart of the stress process model, are the conditions, experiences, and activities that are challenging to caregivers. The model distinguishes between primary stressors (those stemming directly from the needs of the care recipient) and secondary stressors (those stemming from the primary stressors, including role strain, interpersonal conflict, and intrapsychic strain). Mediators of stress, such as coping strategies and social support, explain why people exposed to seemingly similar stressors are affected by them in dissimilar ways. Iterations of this basic model have evolved to incorporate additional objective conditions such as the environment in which care is provided and the characteristics of the care recipient.

Negative Outcomes of Family Caregiving

The caregiving literature flourished as scientists sought to test hypotheses derived from the stress process model. While outcomes predicted by the stress process model included well-being, physical and mental health, and ability to sustain social roles, the primary outcome of interest was depressive symptoms.

A series of meta-analyses of this vast body of research conducted by Pinquart and Sörensen (2003a; 2003b; 2004; 2005; 2006; 2007) identified the following important findings: (1) care recipients' behavior problems had stronger associations with caregiver outcomes than did other stressors (Pinquart & Sörensen, 2003a); (2) amount of care provided and care receivers' physical impairments were less strongly related to burden and depression for dementia caregivers than for caregivers of nondemented older adults (Pinquart & Sörensen, 2003a); (3) physical impairments and care recipients' behavior problems had a stronger relationship to burden experienced by spouses than by adult children (Pinquart & Sörensen, 2003a); (4) caregiving uplifts were associated with subjective well-being and caregiving stressors were associated with depression (Pinquart & Sörensen, 2004); (5) ethnic minority caregivers received more informal support and provided more care than did white caregivers (Pinquart & Sörensen, 2005); (6) although African American caregivers had lower levels of caregiver burden and depression than white caregivers, Hispanic and Asian American caregivers were more depressed than their white non-Hispanic peers (Pinquart & Sörensen, 2005); (7) gender differences in the caregiving experience, which ranged from small to very small, were seen in terms of women having higher levels of burden and depression and lower levels of subjective well-being and physical health than men; studies consistently showed that women reported more behavioral symptomatology in care recipients, provided more hours of care, helped with more caregiving tasks, and assisted with more personal care (Pinquart & Sörensen, 2006); and (8) caregivers fared more poorly than noncaregivers in terms of depression, stress, self-efficacy, and general subjective well-being; in levels of physical health, small differences favored noncaregivers (Pinquart & Sörensen, 2003b; Pinquart & Sörensen, 2007; Vitaliano, Zhang, & Scanlan, 2003).

In other research addressing physical health, results from immunology studies revealed that caregivers had poorer immune responses to influenza virus and pneumococcal pneumonia vaccines (Kiecolt-Glaser, Glaser, Gravenstein, Malarkey, & Sheridan, 1996), their wounds healed more slowly (Kiecolt-Glaser, Marucha, Malarkey, Mercado, & Glaser, 1995), and levels of IL-6 were higher than those of noncaregivers (Kiecolt-Glaser et al., 2003; Von Kanel et al., 2006).

One of the few studies to examine the relationship between caregiving demands and four-year all-cause mortality showed that after adjusting for sociodemographic factors, prevalent disease, and subclinical cardiovascular disease, people who were providing care to a spouse and experiencing caregiver strain had mortality risks that were 63% higher than those experienced by noncaregiving controls (Schulz & Beach, 1999). People who were providing care but not experiencing strain, and those with disabled spouses who were not providing care did not have elevated adjusted mortality rates relative to the noncaregiving controls. Others similarly found that spouse caregivers had elevated rates of all-cause mortality and fatal and nonfatal coronary heart disease (Christakis & Allison, 2006; Lee, Colditz, Berkman, & Kawachi, 2003). These mortality effects, however, were limited to spouse caregivers who provided extraordinary levels of help.

With the growing number of middle-aged and older women who were caregivers as well as active participants in the labor force, research attention turned to examining how these dual roles were shouldered. Pavalko and Artis (1997) found that employment status did not predict whether or not women began a caregiving role. Once women started providing care to a dependent older person, however, caregiving responsibilities affected the work role. Caregivers frequently arrive late to work, leave early, miss work, and experience frequent interruptions (Barnett, 2005; Wakabayashi & Donato, 2005). Some employed caregivers quit their jobs to accommodate caregiving responsibilities; although the extent to which this occurs is unclear (Masuy, 2009). Caregiving takes an economic toll on women, with evidence suggesting that caregiving in midlife raised women's poverty risks in later life by intensifying the negative effects of both stopping work and declining health (Wakabayashi & Donato, 2006). Employers bear significant costs that are directly attributable to having employees with caregiving responsibilities, including absenteeism, partial absenteeism, and late arrivals to and early departures from work. According to the MetLife Mature Market Institute study (2006), these costs are estimated at $2,110 per year per full-time, employed caregiver, for a total cost of $33.6 billion a year.

The Positive Side of Caregiving

Given the dominance of the stress process model, it is not surprising that studies of negative outcomes far outnumbered those focusing on positive outcomes. Nevertheless, Lawton, Moss, Kleban, Glicksman, and Rovine

(1991) initiated a small but consistent thread of research examining positive aspects of caregiving. Their two-factor model of well-being posited that caregiving was an activity of mixed valence for caregivers. They suggested that because caregivers were committed to their role, they found it positively affirming. But because the caregiver role also competed with other roles and could exceed resources, it could be burdensome. As such, they argued that caregiving activities could both enhance caregiving satisfaction and increase caregiving burden. They posited that caregiving satisfaction should be associated with positive affect, but it would be less effective in mitigating depression, and that caregiving burden should increase depressive symptoms. Empirical work has supported this model and revealed that uplifts or benefits associated with the caregiving role, which include feeling needed, making it possible to give back to a loved one, having pleasant interactions with the care recipient, and finding enhanced meaning of life, were associated with subjective well-being (Pinquart & Sörensen, 2004).

Taken as a whole, the second wave of research advanced this field of inquiry by adding theory to an empirically driven knowledge base. However, the dominance of the stress model limited understanding because it restricted the questions addressed and outcomes examined to psychological processes and psychological outcomes. Also, despite increased theoretical sophistication, methodological limitations prevailed, as studies continued to rely on nonrepresentative samples that were not racially or ethnically diverse, and most were limited to cross-sectional designs. The few studies that did incorporate longitudinal designs followed people for a relatively brief period of time and did not typically include a meaningful baseline.

INTERVENTIONS TO EASE CAREGIVER BURDEN

The empirical knowledge base generated by these two waves of research laid the foundation for developing and testing a wide range of interventions designed to improve the lives of caregivers. This third major wave of caregiver research, which has spanned the past 20 years, tested a wide range of interventions, most focused on dementia caregivers.

Initial intervention studies based on the stress process model sought to change caregiver appraisals of their situation through support groups, individual counseling, and education. A meta-analysis of these intervention studies by Knight, Lutzky, and Macofsky-Urban (1993) revealed inconsistent findings and only modest therapeutic benefits. The studies had significant limitations, including the lack of well-controlled randomized trials, small sample sizes, an inability to contrast the effects of multiple interventions, and poorly documented interventions that frequently lacked manuals and hence replication potential. Studies were geographically confined and characterized by inadequate inclusion of caregiver samples that were racially and ethnically diverse.

In view of these limitations, the National Institute on Aging and the National Institute for Nursing Research funded the first of two multisite trials aimed at increasing knowledge about interventions that could improve the well-being of diverse caregivers of persons with dementia. The initial trial, Resources for Enhancing Alzheimer's Caregiver Health (REACH I), compared the effectiveness of six different multicomponent social, behavioral, and environmental interventions, each conducted at one of six sites, using randomized clinical methods (Schulz, Belle, Gitlin, Czaja, Wisniewski, & Ory, 2003; Wisniewski et al., 2003). Results examining pooled treatment effects indicated that active treatments were superior to control conditions in reducing caregiver burden over a six-month period (Gitlin, Belle, et al., 2003). Subsequent analyses found that interventions using active techniques (e.g., role-playing and interactive practice) were more effective at relieving depressive symptoms than those using passive methods (e.g., providing information; Belle et al., 2003). Each intervention was also shown to improve different domains of well-being for family caregivers. REACH I advanced caregiver intervention research by its use of rigorous randomized trial designs, development of manualized interventions, monitoring of interviewers' and interventionists' performance for treatment fidelity, documentation and examination of treatment processes, and advancement of data safety and monitoring procedures for behavioral-type interventions.

Based on the outcomes of REACH I, the National Institutes of Health supported a second phase, REACH II. REACH II developed an intervention that incorporated the most promising components of the REACH I site-specific studies and tested it across five sites using a research design that included adequate numbers of African American, white, and Hispanic caregivers. The multicomponent intervention, consisting of 12 sessions over six months, included education, social support, problem-solving to address behavioral symptoms, and training in home safety, stress reduction, and how to take care of oneself as a caregiver. One of its novel features was tailoring dose and intensity of exposure to intervention components based on a caregiver's risk profile. That is, whereas all caregivers were exposed to each intervention component, the amount of time and depth of exposure depended upon need and risk level. Caregivers were recruited and randomly assigned to either an intervention or attention control group. Results indicated that white and Hispanic caregivers who participated in the intervention experienced significant improvements in their quality of life compared with their counterparts in an attention control group. Among African American caregivers, however, only spouses in the intervention group improved compared to spouses in the attention control group. It is unclear why the pattern of findings differed for African American caregivers. The rate of clinical depression among caregivers in the intervention group was significantly lower than that of the control group. While there were no statistically significant differences in the rate of institutionalization, rates were somewhat higher in the control group (Belle et al., 2006).

REACH II advanced caregiver intervention research considerably by developing and demonstrating the value of using a risk profile for tailoring intervention strategies, comparing active treatment to an attention control group, applying strict adherence to operation manuals and treatment fidelity, including participants from multiple geographic regions and racial ethnic groups, and blinding assessors to group assignment.

Another successful intervention developed by Mittelman and her colleagues (1995, 1996, 2004) found impressive short- and long-term effects of an intensive, long-term intervention that included an acute phase of individual and family counseling, a maintenance program focused on participation in support groups, and ongoing opportunities to consult with counselors during the course of the caregiving experience.

While important progress has been demonstrated, caregiver interventions have yielded only modest benefits for caregivers and key methodological challenges remain. In a review of recent intervention studies, Zarit, Femia, Kim, and Whitlatch (2010) suggested that future caregiving interventions could be improved by adopting a strategy of assessing a wide array of risk factors and outcomes, determining a caregiver's individual need for intervention, providing a multicomponent treatment program that addresses the caregiver's specific risks, and then modifying the treatment plan as a function of the caregiver's changing risk profile (extending the REACH II model).

A relatively new direction in intervention research involves including the care recipient as part of the treatment program. Recent studies, including a meta-analysis, demonstrated a wide range of positive outcomes for caregivers and care recipients when a dyadic-focused approach was implemented (Martire, Lustig, Schulz, Miller, & Helgeson, 2004). Interventions that instructed caregivers in problem-solving, tailored activities to the care recipient's capacities, involved pleasant events or exercise, and modified the home environment to enhance care recipient functioning were the most promising, revealing reduced behavioral symptoms, increased functional ability, and decreased depression in the care recipients as well as improved well-being in the caregivers (Gitlin, Reever, Dennis, Mathieu, & Hauck, 2006; Gitlin, Winter, et al., 2003; Gitlin, Winter, Dennis, Hodgson, & Hauck, 2010a, Gitlin, Winter, Dennis, Hodgson, & Hauck, 2010b; McCurry, Gibbons, Logsdon, Vitiello, & Teri, 2005; Teri, Logsdon, Uomoto, & McCurry, 1997).

CONTEMPORARY CAREGIVING

Who Are Today's Caregivers?

One of the most important surveys on the prevalence and characteristics of caregivers was recently conducted by the National Alliance for Caregiving, in collaboration with AARP and the MetLife Foundation. Their 2009 survey found that 65.7 million people in the United States (28.5% of the population) served as unpaid family caregivers to an adult or child within the past year. The majority of these caregivers (48.9 million) provided assistance to a person over the age of 18; 3.9 million people provided care to a child under the age of 18 who had a medical or behavioral condition or other disability; and 12.9 million people provided care to both an adult and a child with a disability. Caregivers are predominantly female (66%) and have an average age of 48 years. Most caregivers (70%) take care of someone who is 50 years of age or older, whereas 14% take care of an adult age 18 to 49, and 14% take care of a child with a disability under the age of 18. Caregivers report serving in that role for an average of 4.6 years; 31% provided care to their loved one for 5 years or more.

The typical care recipient is female (62%) and has an average age of 61 years. On average, care recipients receive 20.4 hours of help per week from their caregivers. Care recipients typically receive help with at least one activity of daily living, the most common being getting in and out of a bed or chair. Help with other personal care tasks is also common. Care recipients also receive help with an average of 4.4 instrumental activities of daily living, including transportation, housework, grocery shopping, meal preparation, managing finances, and arranging for outside services. Half of all care recipients live in their own home (51%), whereas 29% live with their caregiver. Coresidence is associated with lower incomes, suggesting that it arises out of necessity. Among care recipients who do not live with the caregiver, 76% see them at least once a week.

Some interesting trends have characterized the caregiving experience over the past several years. Since 2004, both caregivers of adults and their care recipients are older than their counterparts were five years ago. The mean age of caregivers of adults increased from 46.4 to 49.2 and the average care recipient's age rose from 66.5 to 69.3 years, with the most substantial increases being in those care recipients age 75 and older. The proportion of caregivers who reported that at least one other unpaid person helped their care recipient increased (from 59% in 2004 to 68% in 2009), but the use of paid help decreased (from 41% in 2004 to 35% in 2009). The increased involvement of other unpaid caregivers is most likely due to an increase in the number of intensive caregiving situations. The decrease in those who receive paid help may be a function of the 2008 recession, as its financial aftermath has had a significant impact on families providing care

Variation in Caregiving Situations

Family caregiving takes a variety of forms. It can be intermittent, temporary, or long-term. Caregiving affects people differentially depending in large part on the type of care needed, resources available, and point in the life course when caregiving occurs.

Dementia Care

Approximately 10 million families provide care to persons with dementia (Alzheimer's Association, 2010). Dementia caregiving is the most frequently studied caregiving situation (Schulz & Martire, 2004). The cognitive impairment characterizing dementia increases dependency on others for fulfillment of the most basic needs, totally altering family relationships. Whereas assistance, communication, and affection between family members were once characterized by bidirectional reciprocity, with dementia caregiving, relationships become unidirectional, leading Pearlin et al. (1990) to conclude "it is difficult to imagine many situations that equal—let alone surpass—the stressfulness of caregiving to relatives and friends with severe chronic impairments" (p. 584).

Older adults with dementia primarily receive assistance from their spouse. When the spouse is no longer alive or able to provide assistance, care is provided by adult children. Adult daughters and daughters-in-law are more likely than sons and sons-in-law to provide routine assistance with household chores and personal care over long periods of time. Whereas in some families caregiving tasks are shared, most of the time care is provided by one individual. Research contrasting the experiences of providing care to a person with dementia with that of providing care to a person with a physical impairment has found that dementia caregivers provide more assistance, report feeling more stressed, experience more work-related difficulties, and give up more of their free time (Bertrand, Fredman, & Saczynski, 2006; Ory, Hoffman, Yee, Tennstedt, & Schulz, 1999).

Developmental Disabilities

Families are the lifelong mainstay of care for persons with developmental disabilities. Changing demographic trends, including increased life expectancies and lower fertility rates, have resulted in both an extended period of caregiving for adults with developmental disabilities and fewer family members who are available to help (Heller, Caldwell, & Factor, 2007).

Mothers of adults with developmental disabilities have lower rates of employment than mothers whose children do not have a developmental disability (Parish, Seltzer, Greenberg, & Floyd, 2004; Seltzer, Greenberg, Floyd,

Pettee, & Hong, 2001). Although there is good evidence that mothers of young children with developmental disabilities experience higher levels of depression than mothers whose children do not have these disabilities (Singer, 2006), studies that have examined the well-being of parents of adults with developmental disabilities reported that their physical and mental health is similar to that of the general population (Chen, Ryan-Henry, Heller, & Chen 2001; Seltzer et al., 2001). In addition, Hill-Smith and Hollins (2002) found that having a child with intellectual disabilities had no significant impact on caregiver mortality. Explanations for these differences include that (a) the additional caregiving challenges faced by these parents may have prolonged their motivation to stay healthy (Hill-Smith & Hollins, 2002); (b) because of increasing stability in routines, a reduction in behavioral problems, greater acceptance of the family member, and greater reciprocity on the part of the person with disability, caregivers adapt to their role over time (Heller et al., 2007); and (c) children with developmental disabilities living at home pro-vide companionship and support to their aging parents and help with house-hold chores, activities that become particularly valued as parents age (Heller, Hsieh, & Rowitz, 1997; Heller, Miller, & Factor, 1997).

In one of the few studies contrasting the experiences of mothers and fa-thers of persons with developmental disabilities, Heller, Hsieh, and Rowitz (1997) found that fathers spent less time performing caregiving tasks, offered fewer types of supports to their children, experienced less burden, and were less affected by the behavioral challenges of their child than were mothers. Essex, Seltzer, and Krauss (1999) found that mothers and fathers used differ-ent coping strategies, and that these coping strategies had different effects on the psychological well-being of mothers and fathers. Although the caregiv-ing roles of fathers intensify after their wives become incapacitated or upon her death (Gordon, Seltzer, & Krauss, 1996), investigation of fathers of adults with developmental disabilities remains relatively neglected by researchers.

Sibling relationships in the context of developmental disabilities are strong and viable. Adult siblings maintain high levels of involvement with one another across the life course (Seltzer, Begun, Seltzer, & Krauss, 1991; Zetlin, 1986). Nondisabled siblings often assume responsibility for those with disability, and sometimes siblings coreside when parents die or are no longer able to provide care (Freedman, Wyngaarden Krauss, & Seltzer, 1997; Green-berg, Seltzer, Orsmond, & Krauss, 1999; Heller & Kramer, 2006; Krauss, Seltzer, Gordon, & Friedman, 1996; Pruchno, Patrick, & Burant, 1996). However, most nondisabled siblings say that they were not included in family discussions about future planning for their siblings with disabilities (Heller & Kramer, 2006; Krauss et al., 1996), and no research has examined the per-spectives of adults with disabilities toward their siblings (Heller et al., 2007). (See Bedford & Avioli, chapter 6 in this volume, for a discussion of sibling caregiving more generally.)

Mental Illness

When a family member has a mental health problem, the lives of their parents, siblings, and children are deeply affected. A significant literature documents the burdens experienced by relatives of adults with mental illness (Lefley, 1996, 2004; Lefley & Johnson, 2002; Marsh & Lefley, 2009). Despite an array of community services, family members, especially parents, often fill gaps in the service system (Smith, Greenberg, & Seltzer, 2007). As parents age and their ability to provide support diminishes, it is generally assumed that siblings will become the next generation of caregivers for adults with mental illness (Hatfield & Lefley, 2005), yet whether this will occur is not clear. Smith et al. (2007) found that early socialization experiences, the quality of the sibling relationship, and personal caregiver gains propel siblings toward future caregiving roles, but that geographic distance and beliefs about the controllability of psychiatric symptoms may reduce expectations for future involvement.

People with Physical Health Problems

More than 11 million people in the United States are living with cancer, close to 24 million have diabetes, and more than 500,000 are on dialysis. Not only do these chronic diseases affect patients as well as families, but the role of family caregiving in the context of these conditions has become more demanding in the past decades as care has shifted to outpatient facilities, patients return home from hospitalizations sooner, and patients survive longer with active disease and disabilities (Northouse & McCorkle, 2010). Spouses, typically the primary caregivers for these people, receive little or no preparation for their role, yet the level of technical, psychological, and physical support demanded of them is unprecedented (Hagedoorn, Sanderman, Bolks, Tuinstra, & Coyne, 2008). Needs of persons caring for a patient with chronic physical health conditions include information, support, effective communication with the patient, and help developing effective coping strategies (Northouse & McCorkle, 2010). It is not uncommon for the health of spouses to be as compromised, or even more so, as that of the patients for whom they provide care (Given, Wyatt, & Given, 2004; Mellon, Northouse, & Weiss, 2006), suggesting that in these situations, definitions of patients and caregivers are fluid (Pruchno, Wilson-Genderson, & Cartwright, 2009).

Given the combination of extensive caregiving demands and dependence on older spouses as caregivers, it is particularly surprising that cancer caregiving has received relatively little attention from researchers (Kim & Schulz, 2008). Studies that do exist have documented the detrimental impact of cancer on caregivers' physical health (Kurtz, Kurtz, Given, & Given, 2004), emotional well-being (Hodges, Humphris, & Macfarlane, 2005), and economic resources (Longo, Fitch, Deber, & Williams, 2006). However, few studies are theory-driven and gaps remain regarding how some of the unique aspects of cancer, including its sudden onset, life-threatening nature, and sporadic need for care, affect caregiving families. In one of the few studies to contrast the experiences of caregivers of persons with cancer, dementia, diabetes, and general frailty, Kim and Schulz (2008) found that both cancer and dementia caregivers reported greater levels of physical burden and psychological distress than other caregivers, highlighting the importance of further research in this area.

Stroke is another condition typically requiring sudden and ongoing caregiver assistance but for which little is known about caregiver well-being and needs. As a stroke occurs suddenly and deficits may be far ranging, families usually are thrown into this caregiving situation with little training, support, or knowledge. A recent study by Haley, Roth, Howard, and Safford (2010) of caregivers of individuals with stroke using a national probability sample from the REasons for Geographic And Racial Differences in Stroke (REGARDS) study, found that high caregiving strain was associated with greater stroke risk and that this association was stronger in men, particularly African Americans. A systematic review by Gaugler (2010) highlights the importance of longitudinal research regarding stroke caregiving.

Grandparent Caregivers

Grandparents comprise an emerging category of caregivers that deserves special attention. In 2000, 5.7 million grandparents lived with their grandchildren (Bryson & Casper, 1999), and approximately 2.4 million such individuals were raising their grandchildren. These figures represent a 30% increase in the number of children living in households maintained by grandparents since 1990 (Fuller-Thomson & Minkler, 2001). Grandparent caregivers are a heterogeneous group of people. Although most are Caucasian (51%), significant numbers are African American (38%) and Hispanic (13%; Fuller-Thomson & Minkler, 2001). Proportionally, African Americans (4.3%) and Hispanics (2.9%) are more likely to be caring for grandchildren than are Caucasians (1%). Although grandparent caregiving cuts across all levels of socioeconomic status, the number of grandparents raising grandchildren living below the poverty line far exceeds that for other types of families (Hayslip & Kaminski, 2005; Minkler & Fuller-Thomson, 2005). Grandparents assume custodial roles vis-à-vis their grandchildren for a number of reasons, but divorce, parent drug abuse, and child abuse are the most common (Fuller-Thomson & Minkler, 2001). Teen pregnancy, incarceration of the parent generation, and death of an adult child can also thrust grandparents into the custodial role.

Custodial grandparents, especially grandmothers, experience significant threats to their physical, mental, and economic well-being. Rates of depression, diabetes, hypertension, heart disease, and insomnia are higher for these people than for their age peers who are not raising grandchildren (Lee et al., 2003; Minkler & Fuller-Thomson, 1999). Many grandparents, especially grandmothers, give up working outside the home to raise a grandchild, losing current as well as future income and employment benefits (Musil, Schrader, & Mutikani, 2000). (See Hayslip & Page, chapter 8 in this volume, for a more extensive discussion of grandparent caregiving.)

Long-Distance Caregivers

Although we know very little about families providing long-distance care, this trend is growing as families are more mobile and geographically dispersed than ever before. Approximately 15% of caregivers to older adults live at least an hour away from their relatives. Caring at a distance includes checking in frequently, accompanying care recipients to medical appointments, coordinating care, and monitoring well-being (Schulz & Tomkins, 2010; National Alliance for Caregiving & AARP, 2004). A profile of long-distance caregivers suggests that these people tend to be highly educated and affluent, and are more likely to play a secondary helper role when compared to in-home caregivers (National Alliance for Caregiving & AARP, 2004).

THE SOCIETAL VALUE OF FAMILY CAREGIVING AND PUBLIC HEALTH RESPONSE

Although the national economic value of unpaid family caregiving is difficult to discern, annual estimates range between $350 billion (Gibson & Houser, 2007) and $375 billion (Evercare & National Alliance for Caregiving, 2009). These figures are comparable to 2005 Medicare expenditures and exceed those for Medicaid. They dwarf the value of paid home health care, and nearly match the total national spending on home health care and nursing home care combined. A recent analysis concluded that if the informal care provided by families in the last year of life were replaced with a home aide, the total economic cost to the United States would be approximately $1.4 billion (Rhee, Degenholtz, LoSasso, & Emanuel, 2009).

Over the past decade, several federal policy initiatives have sought to reduce the burdens experienced by caregiving families (Elmore & Talley, 2009). These initiatives include direct services such as in-home support and respite care (supported by the National Family Caregiver Support Program, the Aging and Disability Resource Centers, and the Lifespan Respite Care Act), consumer-directed approaches (e.g., cash & counseling model; Foster, Brown,

Phillips, & Carlson, 2005; Foster, Dale, & Brown, 2007), employment-based mechanisms, and financial incentives and compensation.

Perhaps the most well-known federal policy directed at improving the lives of family caregivers is the Family and Medical Leave Act (FMLA), signed into law in 1993. This policy allows 12 weeks of unpaid leave annually for full-time employees to care for a family member with an illness or for a new child. The initiative enables many family caregivers to care for their loved one and maintain their employment. Unfortunately FMLA does not provide coverage for all workers (e.g., employers with fewer than 50 employees are exempt) and does not assist those who cannot afford to take unpaid leave. A new initiative recently made California the first state to implement paid family leave. Covered by the state's employment disability program, it provides for people caring for a newborn or adopted child or a seriously ill family member. Despite these public policy attempts to better the lives of family caregivers, many families continue to struggle as they attempt to balance caregiving, work, and other family responsibilities.

SHIFTING PARADIGMS

Providing care to family members is not a new phenomenon, yet today's caregivers are qualitatively different than their predecessors. This difference is due to a combination of increased life expectancy, the shift from acute to chronic diseases being more often experienced by older people, cutbacks in health care reimbursement, and advances in medical technology. As a result, the number of caregivers has increased, the length of time that people spend as caregivers has expanded, and the complexities of tasks completed by caregivers has intensified to levels on par with those once performed exclusively by professional health care providers. A confluence of demographic and societal structural factors guarantees that the roles and responsibilities of family caregivers will not only continue, but will expand in the future; hence, understanding the variations of family caregiving and its outcomes remains a public health imperative.

As family structures change, and rates of divorce, remarriage, blended families, and same-sex relationships increase, questions arise to challenge long-held views about who should assume care responsibilities. Moreover, with newly emerging familial structures, legal rights of people in relationships without the sanction of marriage are unclear and confusing, particularly as they concern health care decision-making and caregiving.

The caregiving challenges for families are great, and they look to become even greater as life-supporting technologies such as ventilators and dialysis move from the intensive care unit to the family home. Although the technology to support these changes exists, important questions regarding what families should do in this regard remain unanswered. Is it the responsibility of family members, for example, to become educated so that they can use these technologies? Who should pay for this education? How can a family member provide this labor-intensive care and still fulfill other family and work responsibilities? How do family members decide when they have reached their caregiving limit? No longer should we question whether families are doing enough; we now must wonder whether we are expecting too much from family members.

Just as some technologies require caregivers to provide more care, other technological advances can support family caregiving. Newly emerging health information technologies, smart home concepts, and modular "parent pads" that are outfitted with sensors can provide important information to caregivers that enable them to be more efficient in their caregiving roles. The Internet is another form of technology that has become an important resource, as many caregivers use it to obtain information and communicate with other family caregivers. As technological advances continue, studies examining how technology affects the caregiving role will become critical. These trends demand paradigm shifts in the methodologies used to study caregivers, the theories about caregiving, and the intervention strategies most likely to benefit caregivers.

Methodological Considerations

Most of what we know about caregiving has been based on small, non-representative samples of people restricted to a particular geographic region or socioeconomic status, with studies often relying on recruitment strategies that target individuals using formal service programs. As such, there is good cause to be concerned about the generalizability of findings. A recent analysis contrasting data derived from respondents recruited using convenience strategies and those recruited using random digit dial (RDD) procedures found significant mean differences in demographic characteristics of caregivers, care recipient characteristics, and outcome variables (Pruchno et al., 2008). Respondents identified using convenience methods had higher levels of education and income, were more likely to be married to and living with the care recipient, were more likely to be caring for a recipient diagnosed with Alzheimer's disease, had higher levels of caregiver burden and depressive symptomatology, reported more negative relationships with the care recipient, provided more hours of help to the care recipient, and were more likely to be the sole provider of care than those recruited using RDD methods. Moreover, correlations among stressors and outcomes were significantly stronger for the convenience sample, suggesting that the effects of caregiving are experienced more intensely by these people than among caregivers in the population at large, and that reliance on results from convenience samples may result in programs and policies that do not adequately address the circumstances of the broader population of caregivers.

Recent studies using representative sampling strategies yield conclusions that are strikingly different than those developed using convenience samples. They reveal that most caregivers do not experience psychological problems and that adverse effects are experienced only by those people providing the most intensive levels of care (Hirst, 2005). Three recent epidemiological studies found that caregivers had lower mortality risks than noncaregivers when adjusted for sociodemographic, care recipient demands, and health variables (Brown et al., 2009; Fredman, Cauley, Hochberg, Ensrud, & Doros, 2010; O'Reilly, Connolly, Rosato, & Patterson, 2008). These studies help explain some of the inconsistencies in findings of previous studies that did not use representative samples and suggest that many of their conclusions about the effects of caregiving may not be generalizable.

In addition to limitations imposed by nonrepresentative samples, most caregiving studies have used cross-sectional designs; hence, conclusions regarding causality are not possible. Even studies using longitudinal designs have typically enrolled people who were already providing care at baseline. As such, they were unable to distinguish between health status before caregiving began and changes in health that resulted from caregiving. In the few studies to include information about health before caregiving began, Burton, Zdaniuk, Schulz, Jackson, and Hirsch (2003) found no difference in baseline measures of depression or self-rated health between spouses who remained noncaregivers and those who began caregiving. McCann, Hebert, Bienias, Morris, and Evans (2004) found that physically healthier individuals were significantly more likely to become caregivers and to continue caregiving. Moreover, although McCann et al. (2004) found that mental health had little influence on initiating the caregiving role, those whose mental health deteriorated over time were more likely to cease being a caregiver.

A related methodological limitation is that little is known about the way families experience trajectories of caregiving. Most of the knowledge base was developed using cross-sectional research designs that focused on people providing care, yet the typical care recipient requires assistance for many years. Little is known about the experiences of either becoming a caregiver or relinquishing the role of caregiver. We do not know, for example, the extent to which there are changes in the person assuming the role of primary caregiver over time or how families negotiate these changes. The ability to address these issues will require sophisticated longitudinal designs that combine both short- and long-term follow-up assessments.

Another important methodological limitation is the tendency to study caregiving individuals rather than caregiving families. Although some studies examine caregiving dyads (Pruchno et al., 2009; Wilson-Genderson, Pruchno, & Cartwright, 2009), we need more research that broadens our understanding of how multiple lives are affected by caregiving demands and how families, rather than only primary caregivers, provide care. This goal will require collecting data from multiple family members and using sophisticated multilevel modeling analyses that control for nesting (Lyons & Sayer, 2005). It will also be critical to better incorporate the care receiver's voice in both basic and intervention research.

Theoretical Considerations

The almost exclusive reliance on the stress process model has limited the types of questions asked and constrained the development of measures and interventions to those addressing psychological outcomes. Thus, there continues to be a strong emphasis on psychological stress and the use of measures of caregiver burden and depression, to the exclusion of other important factors such as knowledge, skills, self-efficacy, and quality of relationships. It seems likely that the use of a stress process model to frame intervention research may not adequately explain the experiences of all caregivers. For example, male caregivers typically do not evaluate their caregiving experience in emotional terms; thus, measures of caregiver burden consistently show that they report less distress and burden than women. As most interventions target the concerns of female caregivers and seek to reduce distress and burden, it is not surprising that studies show that women tend to have better outcomes than men. Use of the stress process model involves selection of measures that are bound to outcomes representing aspects of the stress process and intervention processes that favor the experience of women. As the number of men who are providing care grows, new models for understanding gender differences in caregiving experiences will become necessary.

It will be imperative to continue to develop new theories and models for understanding caregiving. An exemplar is the healthy caregiver hypothesis used to explain emerging findings that not all caregivers experience decline in health (Fredman, Doros, Ensrud, Hochberg, & Cauley, 2009). This hypothesis suggests that because caregiving demands are significant, individuals who become caregivers may have exceptional health. Using data from the Caregiver Study of Osteoporotic Fractures, Fredman and colleagues (2009) found that at baseline, high-intensity caregivers reported the most stress but had the best physical functioning, whereas noncaregivers had the poorest physical functioning. Low-intensity caregivers experienced greater declines in performance-based functioning than did noncaregivers over a two-year period, but high-intensity caregivers did not. These data suggest that caregiving tasks may have kept respondents physically active, caregivers may have had stronger feelings of purpose than noncaregivers, and satisfaction from caregiving experiences, especially among low-stress caregivers, may have benefited their health. Furthermore, as caregiving families continue to become more culturally diverse, it will be important to develop and test conceptual models across ethnic and racial groups (Knight & Sayegh, 2010). Finally, although living in a rural setting is associated with reduced availability of and access to formal health services, little is known about the effects of rural residence on informal care provision (Goins, Spencer, & Byrd, 2009); hence this focus should have a higher priority in future research.

The Future of Intervention Research

A great deal of progress has been made in caregiver intervention research, but more needs to be achieved. Future work should be targeted at enhancing treatment effects; evaluating the need for, timing of, and outcomes of booster interventions; identifying and supporting those caregivers at greatest risk; and evaluating the cost and cost-effectiveness of different supportive approaches. The few economic evaluations conducted to date suggest that caregiver interventions are highly cost-effective when considering outcomes such as quality-adjusted life years and time spent caregiving (Gitlin, Hodgson, Jutkowitz, & Pizzi, 2010; Graff, Adang, & Vernooij-Dassen, 2008; Nichols, Chang, & Lummus, 2007). However, with few exceptions, interventions have not been evaluated for their cost-effectiveness or for the willingness of caregivers to pay for them (Jutkowitz, Gitlin, & Pizzi, 2010). Economic evaluations are critical in order to effectively translate proven interventions for delivery from theory into practice

Of greatest importance is the need to translate existing proven interventions for families into service delivery settings, as caregivers continue to be underserved or to receive services that are not evidence-based. With few exceptions, proven interventions remain out of the mainstream of service offerings (Burgio, Collins, Schmid, Wharton, McCallum, & DeCoster, 2009; Gitlin, Jacobs, & Vause-Earland, 2010). Recent efforts at translation have successfully demonstrated the potential of sustaining programs delivered through the Veteran's Administration (Nichols, Martindale-Adams, Burns, Graney, & Zuber, 2011), Medicare Part B (Gitlin, Jacobs, et al., 2010), and Area Agencies on Aging (Burgio et al., 2009). Targeted interventions require adequate risk assessment tools (e.g., see Czaja et al., 2009), and staff who are able to determine how to allocate scarce resources. To support these efforts, advancements need to be made in training programs that will enhance the competencies of health and human service professionals in working effectively with caregiving families.

Finally, efforts at the federal and state levels to modify policies in order to meet growing demands from caregiving families, and to close the gap between research, policy, and practice, need to continue. Caregiver well-being is a critical public health issue in its own right, given the number of persons engaged in this role and the potential health risks caregivers face. Because caregivers are the linchpin of the informal support system, when their health is jeopardized, so too are the lives of the people for whom they provide care (Gitlin & Schulz, 2012). The question originally posed as to whether family members care for one another in late life has been clearly and un-equivocally answered in the affirmative. Moreover, the costs to family members in terms of their physical health, emotional well-being, and economic livelihood have also been consistently documented. Failure to support families in their caregiving efforts bodes poorly for older people, their family members, and society at large. Caregiving is, and will continue to be in the future, a public health issue that warrants our careful attention.

To conclude, changing demographic and societal trends as well as the movement toward providing health care at home have placed unprecedented pressures on families to perform increasingly complex care tasks for extended periods of time. Research based on representative samples will ensure that findings are generalizable and that the magnitude of effects and characteristics associated with risks are understood. Such research will in turn drive innovations in both the types and targets of interventions. Greater effort needs to be focused on translating tested and proven programs for delivery in service settings, and on determining supportive structures necessary for their sustainability, in current and changing reimbursement structures. Also needed are development and testing of new interventions that address an increasingly diverse caregiver population, as well as those who provide care long-distance and intermittently. As unparalleled expectations are placed on families to carry out complex medical, social, and emotional supportive tasks, a public health response to bolster their efforts must be put into place and strengthened.

REFERENCES

Alzheimer's Association. (2010). *2010 Alzheimer's disease facts and figures.* Retrieved from http://www.alz.org/documents_custom/report_alzfactsfigures2010.pdf

Barnett, R.C. (2005). Ageism and sexism in the workplace. *Generations, 20,* 25–30.

Belle, S.H., Burgio, L., Burns, R., Coon, D., Czaja, S., Gallagher-Thompson, D., et al. (2006). Enhancing the quality of life of dementia caregivers from different ethnic or racial groups. *Annals of Internal Medicine, 145,* 727–738.

Belle, S.H., Czaja, S.J., Schulz, R., Zhang, S., Burgio, L.D., Gitlin, L.N., et al. (2003). Using a new taxonomy to combine the uncombinable: Integrating results across diverse interventions. *Psychology and Aging, 18,* 396–405.

Bertrand, R.J., Fredman, L., & Saczynski, J. (2006). Are all caregivers created equal? Stress in caregivers to adults with and without dementia. *Journal of Aging and Health, 18,* 534–551.

Brody, E.M. (1985). Parent care as a normative family stress. *The Gerontologist, 25,* 19–29.

Brown, S.L., Smith, D.M., Schulz, R., Kabeto, M.U., Ubel, P.A., Poulin, M., et al. (2009). Caregiving behavior is associated with decreased mortality risk. *Psychological Science, 20,* 488–494.

Bryson, K.R., & Casper, L.M. (1999). *Coresident grandparents and grandchildren.* Washington, DC: U.S. Bureau of the Census.

Burgio, L., Collins, C., Schmid, B., Wharton, T., McCallum, D., & DeCoster, J. (2009). Translating the REACH caregiver intervention for use by Area Agency on Aging personnel: The REACH OUT program. *The Gerontologist, 49*, 103–116.

Burton, L. C., Zdaniuk, B., Schulz, R., Jackson, S., & Hirsch, C. (2003). Transitions in spousal caregiving. *The Gerontologist, 43*, 230–241.

Chen, S. C., Ryan-Henry, S., Heller, T., & Chen, E. H. (2001). Health status of mothers of adults with intellectual disability. *Journal of Intellectual Disability Research, 45*, 439–449.

Christakis, N. A., & Allison, P. D. (2006). Mortality after the hospitalization of a spouse. *New England Journal of Medicine, 354*, 719–730.

Czaja, S. J., Gitlin, L. N., Schulz, R., Zhang, S., Burgio, L. D., Stevens, A. B., et al. (2009). Development of the risk appraisal measure: A brief screen to identify risk areas and guide interventions for dementia caregivers. *Journal of the American Geriatrics Society, 57*, 1064–1072.

Elmore, D. L., & Talley, R. C. (2009). Family caregiving and U.S. federal policy. In S. H. Qualls & S. H. Zarit (Eds.), *Aging families and caregiving* (pp. 209–231). Hoboken, NJ: John Wiley & Sons.

Essex, E. L., Seltzer, M. M., & Krauss, M. W. (1999). Differences in coping effectiveness and well-being among aging mothers and fathers of adults with mental retardation. *American Journal on Mental Retardation, 104*, 545–563.

Evercare & National Alliance for Caregiving. (2009). *The Evercare survey of the economic downturn and its impact on family caregiving.* Retrieved from http://www.caregiving.org/data/EVC_Caregivers_Economy_Report%20FINAL_4-28-09.pdf

Foster, L., Brown, R., Phillips, B., & Carlson, B. L. (2005). Easing the burden of caregiving: The impact of consumer direction on primary informal caregivers in Arkansas. *The Gerontologist, 45*, 474–485.

Foster, L., Dale, S. B., & Brown, R. (2007). How cash & counseling affects informal caregivers: Findings from Arkansas, Florida, and New Jersey. *Health Services Research, 42*, 510–532.

Fredman, L., Cauley, J. A., Hochberg, M., Ensrud, K. E., & Doros, G. (2010). Mortality associated with caregiving, general stress, and caregiving-related stress in elderly women: Results of Caregiver Study of Osteoporotic Fractures. *Journal of the American Geriatrics Society, 58*, 937–943.

Fredman, L., Doros, G., Ensrud, K. E., Hochberg, M. C., & Cauley, J. A. (2009). Caregiving intensity and change in physical functioning over a 2-year period: Results of the Caregiver-Study of Osteoporotic Fractures. *American Journal of Epidemiology, 170*, 2203–2210.

Freedman, R., Wyngaarden Krauss, M., & Seltzer, M. M. (1997). Aging parents' residential plans for adult children with mental retardation. *Mental Retardation, 35*, 114–123.

Fuller-Thomson, E., & Minkler, M. (2001). American grandparents providing extensive childcare to their grandchildren: Prevalence and profile. *The Gerontologist, 41*, 201–209.

Gaugler, J. E. (2010). The longitudinal ramifications of stroke caregiving: A systematic review. *Rehabilitation Psychology, 55*, 108–125.

Gibson, M.J., & Houser, A. (2007). *Valuing the invaluable: A new look at the economic value of family caregiving.* AARP Issue Brief IB-82, June.

Gitlin, L.N., Belle, S.H., Burgio, L.D., Czaja, S.J., Mahoney, D., Gallagher-Thompson, D., et al. (2003). Effect of multicomponent interventions on caregiver burden and depression: The REACH multisite initiative at a 6-month follow-up. *Psychology and Aging, 18,* 361–374.

Gitlin, L., Hodgson, N., Jutkowitz, E., & Pizzi, L. (2010). The cost-effectiveness of a nonpharmacologic intervention for individuals with dementia and family caregivers: The Tailored Activity Program. *American Journal of Geriatric Psychiatry, 18,* 510–519.

Gitlin, L., Jacobs, M., & Vause-Earland, T. (2010). Translation of a dementia caregiver intervention for delivery in home care as a reimbursable Medicare service: Outcomes and lessons learned. *The Gerontologist,50 (6),847–854.*

Gitlin, L., Reever, K.E., Dennis, M.P., Mathieu, E., & Hauck, W.W. (2006). Enhancing quality of life of families who use adult day services: Short and long-term effects of the "Adult Day Services Plus" program. *The Gerontologist, 46,* 630–639.

Gitlin, L.N., & Schulz, R. (2012). Family caregiving of older adults. In T. Prohaska, L. Anderson, & R. Binstock (Eds.), *Public health for an aging society* (pp. 181–204). Baltimore, MD: Johns Hopkins University Press.

Gitlin, L.N., Winter, L., Corcoran, M., Dennis, M., Schinfeld, S., & Hauck, W.H. (2003). Effects of the home environmental skill-building program on the caregiver-care recipient dyad: 6-month outcomes from the Philadelphia REACH initiative. *The Gerontologist, 43,* 532–546.

Gitlin, L., Winter, L., Dennis, M.P., Hodgson, N., & Hauck, W.W. (2010a). Effects of a nonpharmacologic, biobehavioral home-based intervention on functional status and quality of life of patients with dementia and well-being of their caregivers: A randomized trial. *JAMA, 304(9),* 983–991.

Gitlin, L., Winter, L., Dennis, M.P., Hodgson, N., & Hauck, W.W. (2010b). Targeting and managing behavioral symptoms in individuals with dementia: A randomized trial of a nonpharmacologic intervention. *Journal of the American Geriatric Society, 58,* 1465–1474.

Given, B., Wyatt, G., & Given, C. (2004). Burden and depression among caregivers of patients with cancer at the end of life. *Oncology Nursing Forum, 31,* 1105–1115.

Goins, R.T., Spencer, M., & Byrd, J.C. (2009). Research on rural caregiving: A literature review. *Journal of Applied Gerontology, 28,* 139–170.

Gordon, R.M., Seltzer, M.M., & Kraus, M.W. (1996). The aftermath of parental death: Changes in the context and quality of life. In R.L. Schalock (Ed.), *Quality of life: Its applications to persons with disabilities* (pp. 23–40). Washington, DC: American Association on Mental Retardation.

Graff, M.J., Adang, E.M., & Vernooij-Dassen, M.J. (2008). Community occupational therapy for older patients with dementia and their caregivers: Cost effectiveness study. *British Medical Journal, 336,* 134–138.

Greenberg, J.S., Seltzer, M.M., Orsmond, G.I., & Krauss, M.W. (1999). Siblings of adults with mental illness or mental retardation: Current involvement and expectation of future caregiving. *Psychiatric Services, 50,* 1214–1219.

Hagedoorn, M., Sanderman, R., Bolks, H.N., Tuinstra, J., & Coyne, J.C. (2008). Distress in couples coping with cancer: A meta-analysis and critical review of role and gender effects. *Psychological Bulletin, 134,* 1–30.

Haley, W.E., Roth, D.L., Howard, G., & Safford, M.M. (2010). Caregiving strain and estimated risk for stroke and coronary heart disease among spouse caregivers: Differential effects of race and sex. *Stroke, 41,* 331–336.

Hatfield, A., & Lefley, H.P. (2005). Future involvement of siblings in the lives of persons with mental illness. *Community Mental Health Journal, 41,* 327–338.

Hayslip, B., & Kaminski, P.L. (2005). Grandparents raising their grandchildren: A review of the literature and suggestions for practice. *The Gerontologist, 45,* 262–269.

Heller, T., Caldwell, J., & Factor, A. (2007). Aging family caregivers: Policies and practices. *Mental Retardation and Developmental Disabilities Research Reviews, 13,* 136–142.

Heller, T., Hsieh, K., & Rowitz, L. (1997). Maternal and paternal caregiving of persons with mental retardation across the life span. *Family Relations, 46,* 407–415.

Heller, T., & Kramer, J. (2006). *Involvement of adult siblings of people with disabilities in future planning.* Chicago: University of Illinois at Chicago.

Heller, T., Miller, A.B., & Factor, A. (1997). Adults with mental retardation as supports to their parents: Effects on parental caregiving appraisal. *Mental Retardation, 35,* 338–346.

Hill-Smith, A.J., & Hollins, S.C. (2002). Mortality of parents of people with intellectual disabilities. *Journal of Applied Research in Intellectual Disabilities, 15,* 18–27.

Hirst, M. (2005). Carer distress: A prospective, population-based study. *Social Science & Medicine, 61,* 697–708.

Hodges, L.J., Humphris, G.M., & Macfarlane, G. (2005). A meta-analytic investigation of the relationship between the psychological distress of cancer patients and their careers. *Social Science & Medicine, 60,* 1–12.

Jutkowitz, E., Gitlin, L., & Pizzi, L. (2010). Evaluating willingness to pay thresholds for dementia caregiving interventions: Application to the Tailored Activity Program. *Value in Health, 13,* 720–725.

Kiecolt-Glaser, J.K., Glaser, R., Gravenstein, S., Malarkey, W.B., & Sheridan, J.T. (1996). Chronic stress alters the immune response to influenza virus vaccine in older adults. *Proceedings of the National Academy of Sciences USA, 93,* 3043–3047.

Kiecolt-Glaser, J.K., Marucha, P.T., Malarkey, W.B., & Glaser, R. (1995). Slowing of wound healing by psychological stress. *Lancet, 346,* 1194–1196.

Kiecolt-Glaser, J.K., Preacher, K.J., MacCallum, R.C., Atkinson, C., Malarkey, W.B., et al. (2003). Chronic stress and age-related increases in the proinflammatory cytokine IL-6. *Proceedings of the National Academy of Sciences USA, 100,* 9090–9095.

Kim, Y., & Schulz, R. (2008). Family caregivers' strains: Comparative analysis of cancer caregiving with dementia, diabetes, and frail elderly caregiving. *Journal of Aging and Health, 20,* 483–503.

Knight, B. G., Lutzky, S. M., & Macofsky-Urban, F. (1993). A meta-analytic review of interventions for caregiver distress: Recommendations for future research. *The Gerontologist, 33,* 240–248.

Knight, B. G., & Sayegh, P. (2010). Cultural values and caregiving: The updated sociocultural stress and coping model. *Journal of Gerontology: Psychological Sciences, 65B,* 5–13.

Krauss, M. W., Seltzer, M. M., Gordon, R., & Friedman, D. H. (1996). Binding ties: The roles of adult siblings of persons with mental retardation. *Mental Retardation, 34,* 83–93.

Kurtz, M. E., Kurtz, J. C., Given, C. W., & Given, B. A. (2004). Depression and physical health among family caregivers of geriatric patients with cancer: A longitudinal view. *Medical Science Monitor, 10,* CR447–CR456.

Lawton, M. P., Moss, M., Kleban, M. H., Glicksman, A., & Rovine, M. (1991). A two-factor model of caregiving appraisal and psychological well-being. *Journal of Gerontology: Psychological Sciences, 46,* P181–P189.

Lee, S., Colditz, G. A., Berkman, L., & Kawachi, I. (2003). Caregiving and risk of coronary heart disease in U.S. women. *American Journal of Preventive Medicine, 24,* 113–119.

Lefley, H. P. (1996). *Family caregiving in mental illness.* Thousand Oaks, CA: Sage.

Lefley, H. P. (2004). Intercultural similarities and differences in family caregiving and family interventions in schizophrenia. *Psychiatric Times, 20,* 70–82.

Lefley, H. P., & Johnson, D. L. (2002). *Family interventions in mental illness: International perspectives.* Westport, CT: Praeger.

Longo, C. J., Fitch, M., Deber, R. B., & Williams, A. P. (2006). Financial and family burden associated with cancer treatment in Ontario, Canada. *Supportive Care in Cancer, 14,* 1077–1085.

Lyons, K. S., & Sayer, A. G. (2005). Longitudinal dyad models in family research. *Journal of Marriage and Family, 67,* 1048–1060.

Marsh, D. T., & Lefley, H. (2009). Serious mental illness: Family experiences, needs, and interventions. In J. H. Bray & M. Stanton (Eds.), *The Wiley-Blackwell handbook of family psychology* (pp. 742–754). Hoboken, NJ: Wiley-Blackwell.

Martire, L. M., Lustig, A. P., Schulz, R., Miller, G. E., & Helgeson, V. S. (2004). Is it beneficial to involve a family member?: A meta-analysis of psychosocial interventions for chronic illness. *Health Psychology, 23,* 599–611.

Masuy, A. J. (2009). Effect of caring for an older person on women's lifetime participation in work. *Aging & Society, 29,* 745–763.

McCann, J. J., Hebert, L. E., Bienias, J. L., Morris, M. C., & Evans, D. A. (2004). Predictors of beginning and ending caregiving during a 3-year period in a biracial community population of older adults. *American Journal of Public Health, 94,* 1800–1806.

McCurry, S. M., Gibbons, L. E., Logsdon, R. G., Vitiello, M. V., & Teri, L. (2005). Nighttime insomnia treatment and education for Alzheimer's disease: A randomized, controlled trial. *Journal of the American Geriatrics Society, 53,* 793–802.

Mellon, S., Northouse, L. L., & Weiss, L. K. (2006). A population-based study of the quality of life of cancer survivors and their family caregivers. *Cancer Nursing, 29,* 120–131.

Metlife Mature Market Institute and National Alliance for Caregiving (2006). *The MetLife caregiving cost study: Productivity losses to U.S. business.* Westport, CT: MetLife Market Institute. Retrieved from http://www.caregiving.org/data/ Caregiver%20Cost%20Study.pdf

Minkler, M., & Fuller-Thomson, E. (1999). The health of grandparents raising grandchildren: Results of a national study. *American Journal of Public Health, 89,* 1–6.

Minkler, M., & Fuller-Thomson, E. (2005). African American grandparents raising grandchildren: A national study using the Census 2000 American Community Survey. *Journal of Gerontology: Social Sciences, 60B,* S82–S92.

Mittelman, M.S., Ferris, S.H., Shulman, E., Steinberg, G., Ambinder, A., Mackell, J.A., et al. (1995). A comprehensive support program: Effect on depression in spouse-caregivers of AD patients. *The Gerontologist, 35,* 792–802.

Mittleman, M.S., Ferris, S.H., Shulman, E., Steinberg, E., Steinberg, G., & Levin, B. (1996). A family intervention to delay nursing home placement of patients with Alzheimer's disease. *JAMA, 276,* 1725–1731.

Mittelman, M.S., Roth, D.L., Coon, D.W., & Haley, W.E. (2004). Sustained benefit of supportive intervention for depressive symptoms in caregivers of patients with Alzheimer's disease. *American Journal of Psychiatry, 161,* 850–856.

Musil, C., Schrader, S., & Mutikani, J. (2000). Social support stress and the special coping tasks of grandmother caregivers. In C. Cox (Ed.), *To grandmother's house we go and stay: Perspective on custodial grandparents* (pp. 56–70). New York: Springer.

National Alliance for Caregiving & AARP. (2004). *Caregiving in the U.S.* Washington, DC: Authors. National Alliance for Caregiving & AARP. (2009). *Caregiving in the U.S.: A focused look at those caring for someone age 50 or older.* Washington, DC: Authors.

Nichols, L.O., Chang, C., & Lummus, A. (2007). The cost-effectiveness of a behavior intervention for caregivers of patients with Alzheimer's disease. *Journal of the American Geriatrics Society, 56,* 413–420.

Nichols, L.O., Martindale-Adams, J., Burns, R., Graney, M.J., & Zuber, J. (2011). Translation of a dementia caregiver support program in a health care system: REACH VA. *Archives of Internal Medicine, 171 (4),* 353–359.

Northouse, L.L., & McCorkle, R. (2010). Spouse caregivers of cancer patients. In J. Holland, W.S. Breitbart, P.B. Jacobson, M.S. Lederberg, M.J. Loscalzo, & R. McCorkle (Eds.), *Psycho-oncology.* New York: Oxford University Press.

O'Reilly, D., Connolly, S., Rosato, M., & Patterson, C. (2008). Is caring associated with an increased risk of mortality? A longitudinal study. *Social Science & Medicine, 67,* 1282–1290.

Ory, M., Hoffman, R.R., Yee, J.L., Tennstedt, S., & Schulz, R. (1999). Prevalence and impact of caregiving: A detailed comparison between dementia and non-dementia caregivers. *The Gerontologist, 39,* 177–186.

Parish, S.L., Seltzer, M.M., Greenberg, J.S., & Floyd, F. (2004). Economic implications of caregiving at midlife: Comparing parents with and without children who have developmental disabilities. *Mental Retardation, 42,* 413–426.

Pavalko, E., & Artis, J.E. (1997). Women's caregiving and paid work: Casual relationships in late midlife. *Journal of Gerontology: Social Sciences, 52B,* S170–S179.

Pearlin, L. I., Mullan, J. T., Semple, S. J., & Skaff, M. M. (1990). Caregiving and the stress process: An overview of concepts and their measures. *The Gerontologist, 30*, 583–591.

Pinquart, M., & Sörensen, S. (2003a). Associations of stressors and uplifts of caregiving with caregiver burden and depressive mood: A meta-analysis. *Journal of Gerontology: Psychological Sciences, 58B*, P112–P128.

Pinquart, M., & Sörensen, S. (2003b). Differences between caregivers and noncaregivers in psychological health and physical health: A meta-analysis. *Psychology and Aging, 18*, 250–267.

Pinquart, M., & Sörensen, S. (2004). Associations of caregiver stressors and uplifts with subjective well-being and depressive mood: A meta-analytic comparison. *Aging and Mental Health, 8*, 438–449.

Pinquart, M., & Sörensen, S. (2005). Ethnic differences in stressors, resources, and psychological outcomes of family caregiving: A meta-analysis. *The Gerontologist, 45*, 90–106.

Pinquart, M., & Sörensen, S. (2006). Helping caregivers of persons with dementia: Which interventions work and how large are their effects? *International Psychogeriatrics, 18*, 577–595.

Pinquart, M., & Sörensen, S. (2007). Correlates of physical health of informal caregivers: A meta-analysis. *Journals of Gerontology, Series B: Psychological Sciences and Social Sciences, 62*, P126–P137.

Pruchno, R. A., Brill, J. E., Shands, Y., Gordon, J. R., Genderson, M. W., Rose, M., et al. (2008). Convenience samples and caregiving research: How generalizable are the findings? *The Gerontologist, 48*, 820–827.

Pruchno, R. A., Patrick, J. H., & Burant, C. J. (1996). Aging women and their children with chronic disabilities: Perceptions of sibling involvement and effects on well-being. *Family Relations, 45*, 318–326.

Pruchno, R. A., Wilson-Genderson, M., & Cartwright, F. P. (2009). Self-rated health and depressive symptoms in patients with end stage renal disease and their spouses: A longitudinal dyadic analysis of late-life marriages. *Journal of Gerontology: Psychological Sciences, 64B*, 212–221.

Rhee, Y., Degenholtz, H. B., LoSasso, A. T., & Emanuel, L. L. (2009). Estimating the quantity and economic value of family caregiving for community-dwelling older persons in the last year of life. *Journal of the American Geriatrics Society, 57*, 1654–1659.

Schulz, R., & Beach, S. R. (1999). Caregiving as a risk factor for mortality: The caregiver health effects study. *JAMA, 282*, 2215–2219.

Schulz, R., Belle, S. H., Gitlin, L. N., Czaja, S. J., Wisniewski, S. R., & Ory, M. G. (2003). Introduction to the Special Section on Resources for Enhancing Alzheimer's Caregiver Health (REACH). *Psychology and Aging, 18*, 357–360.

Schulz, R., & Martire, L. M. (2004). Family caregiving of persons with dementia: Prevalence, health effects, and support strategies. *American Journal of Geriatric Psychiatry, 12*, 240–249.

Schulz, R., & Tompkins, C. A. (2010). *Informal caregivers in the United States: Prevalence, characteristics, and ability to provide care. Human factors in home health care.* Washington, DC: National Academies of Sciences Press.

Seltzer, G. B., Begun, A., Seltzer, M. M., & Krauss, M. W. (1991). Adults with mental retardation and their aging mothers: Impacts of siblings. *Family Relations, 40,* 310–317.

Seltzer, M. M., Greenberg, J., Floyd, F. J., Pettee, Y., & Hong, J. (2001). Life course impacts of parenting a child with a disability. *American Journal on Mental Retardation, 106,* 265–286.

Shanas, E. (1979). Social myth as hypothesis: The case of the family relations of old people. *The Gerontologist, 19,* 3–9.

Shanas, E., & Streib, G. E. (1965). *Social structure and the family.* Englewood Cliffs, NJ: Prentice-Hall.

Shanas, E., Townsend, P., Wedderburn, H., Friis, H., Milhoj, P., & Stehouwer, J. (1968). *Old people in three industrial societies.* New York: Atherton Press.

Singer, G.H.S. (2006). Meta-analysis of comparative studies of depression in mothers of children with and without developmental disabilities. *American Journal on Mental Retardation, 11,* 155–169.

Smith, M. J., Greenberg, J. S., & Seltzer, M. M. (2007). Siblings of adults with schizophrenia: Expectations about future caregiving roles. *American Journal of Orthopsychiatry, 77,* 29–37.

Stone, R., Cafferata, G. L., & Sangl, J. (1987). Caregivers of the frail elderly: A national profile. *The Gerontologist, 27,* 616–626.

Teri, L., Logsdon, R., Uomoto, J., & McCurry, S. M. (1997). Behavioral treatment of depression in dementia patients: A controlled clinical trial. *Journal of Gerontology: Psychological Sciences, 52B,* P159–P166.

Vitaliano, P. P., Zhang, J., & Scanlan, J. M. (2003). Is caregiving hazardous to one's physical health? A meta-analysis. *Psychological Bulletin, 129,* 946–972.

Von Kanel, R., Dimsdale, J. E., Mills, P. J., Ancoli-Israel, S., Patterson, T. L., Mausbach, B. T., et al. (2006). Effect of Alzheimer caregiving stress and age on frailty markers Interleukin-6, C-Reactive Protein, and D-Dimer. *Journal of Gerontology: Medical Sciences, 61A,* 963–969.

Wakabayashi, C., & Donato, K. M. (2005). The consequences of caregiving: Effects on women's employment and earnings. *Population Research and Policy Review, 24,* 467–488.

Wakabayashi, C., & Donato, K. M. (2006). Does caregiving increase poverty among women in later life? Evidence from the Health and Retirement Survey. *Journal of Health and Social Behavior, 47,* 258–274.

Wilson-Genderson, M., Pruchno, R. A., & Cartwright, F. P. (2009). Effects of caregiver burden and satisfaction on affect of older end-stage-renal disease patients and their spouses. *Psychology & Aging, 24,* 955–967.

Wisniewski, S. R., Belle, S. H., Coon, D., Marcus, S. M., Ory, M., Burgio, L., et al. (2003). The resources for Enhancing Alzheimer's Care Health (REACH): Project design and baseline characteristics. *Psychology and Aging, 18,* 375–384.

Zarit, S. H., Femia, E. E., Kim, K., & Whitlatch, C. J. (2010). The structure of risk factors and outcomes for family caregivers: Implications for assessment and treatment. *Aging & Mental Health, 14,* 220–231.

Zetlin, A. G. (1986). Mentally retarded adults and their siblings. *American Journal of Mental Deficiency, 91,* 217–225.

22

Turning Points in Later Life: Grief and Bereavement

Brian de Vries

Families come in many shapes and sizes. There is a growing recognition of the diversity of family forms, challenging norms and practices in North American society and making more complex the experience of family membership. Age, of course, adds yet another dimension to this complexity; grief adds many more.

The study of later-life families has achieved a relatively mature status in social science research, as evidenced by this *Handbook;* the study of the diversity of their forms is also gaining ground and currency exploring the expressions and experiences of intimacy in connection with those we identify as family. The study of loss and grief in later life has similarly advanced. These two areas, however—the study of later-life families and the study of later-life losses—remain relatively independent, rendering our knowledge of both incomplete. That is, the parallel proliferation of these literatures obscures the perspective that grief is the reflection of intimacy (de Vries, 2001). As Deck and Folta (1989) observed, grief "is the study of people and their most intimate relationships" (p. 80). The complete understanding of an individual's grief is only possible through an appreciation of the specific and particular relationships forever changed by the death; the complete understanding of an individual's relationship to another is given surprising clarity and focus by an appreciation of why and what individuals grieve and how death organizes our relationships to one another.

Through this lens and with this intention, this chapter examines the loss experiences of older family members, more specifically the deaths of a spouse in later life (only introduced here, explored more fully in Carr & Pudrovska, chapter 20 in this volume), an elderly parent, an adult child, a grandchild, a sibling, and a close friend (a member of one's chosen family with recognition of the diversity of family forms). I conclude this chapter with reference to

future directions for research, theory, and practice, including potential interventions for working with bereaved family members in later life.

BRACKETS AROUND THAT WHICH FOLLOWS

This chapter is necessarily bracketed by parameters that limit its breadth;
some of these brackets are inherent in the bereavement literature, some are
inherent in the later-life family literature, and some are of my own doing. For
example, the literature on a family death in later life, with the possible exception of widowhood, is relatively modest in size and scope compared with the
research on family deaths earlier in life. Most research papers in the areas of
particular family losses (perhaps excepting, again, widowhood and to a lesser
extent the death of a child) include a comment describing how understudied
the topic is and how more research is needed. There seems to have been a
peak in the literature contributions in the 1990s, and, surprisingly, contributions to these many areas appear to have comparatively diminished in more
recent years.

Within this general area, grief and bereavement (the distinction between
them are elucidated below) are primarily studied as individual, intrapersonal
processes. This approach is certainly understandable and reasonable; our responses to the death of a loved one are very personal, self-defining, and self-
illuminating experiences. But, except in very rare cases, the death of a loved
one is experienced by multiple individuals, many of whom know and relate
to each other, as is the case of families and social networks more broadly
(Vachon & Stylianos, 1988). Little is known about the proliferation of stress
and grief among connected individuals; hence, little is reported herein. Furthermore, as d'Epinay, Cavalli, and Guillet (2010) noted, whereas most research on bereavement dwells on its disruptive effects, especially on health,
Dutton and Zisook underlined people's ability to cope with it: "Accumulating
evidence suggests that resilience to grief in the face of bereavement is the
norm, rather than an exception" (2005, p. 877). There are references to the
growth enabled by grief, but these are certainly minority contributions.

Anything said about grief simplifies and obscures its pervasive complexity (Rosenblatt & Barner, 2006); our narrative understandings of the experience are but snapshots of an endless reel of personal, interpersonal, and
social turning points. Similarly, there have been recent discussions about the
feminization of bereavement. Williams, Baker, Allman, and Roseman (2006)
analyzed 30 months of observations from the University of Alabama longitudinal study of aging and found significant differences between women and
men for all types of loss (spousal, nonspousal family, nonfamily), as well as
differences in the sociodemographic predictors of loss between and within
gender categories. This study revealed the extent to which older women disproportionately bear the burden of loss and points to the need for greater at-

tention to bereavement as a women's issue, something infrequently formally considered in bereavement research. An interesting contrast, however, is the experience of older men as widowers (Moore & Stratton, 2002) whose voices are seldom heard.

The family literature has adopted a fairly consistent heteronormative stance (i.e., privileging heterosexuality and heterosexual relationships), focusing on the more traditional stages and experiences of fairly traditional families. The diversity of family forms referenced in the opening of this chapter is lesser represented both in the literature describing later-life family losses and in this review. Persons and families of color are similarly underrepresented in the research literature, also echoed in this review.

Each of the sections that follow could easily be expanded well beyond what is presented here. I have taken the liberty to selectively review materials to highlight the grief reactions and expressions noted in later-life families; omissions are inevitable and unintentional and for that I accept responsibility.

BACKGROUND AND THEORY

Thanatologists distinguish grief, mourning, and bereavement, and the former of these is the focus of this chapter and represents the personal psychological experiences of those who have lost a loved one through death. Grief is most typically assessed by measures by the same name (e.g., the Texas Revised Inventory of Grief; Faschingbauer, Zisook, & De Vaul, 1987) and often misinterpreted as depression, which is related to grief but grief comprises a great deal more. Mourning conveys the cultural scripts that govern grief behaviors (e.g., mourning rituals) and bereavement refers to the objective experience of loss (e.g., bereft persons; Stroebe, Stroebe, & Hanssen, 1993).

The early, traditional (and still active) theories of bereavement focus on the emotional work of grief. Freud (1917/1958) believed that bereaved persons had to withdraw energy from their attachment to the lost loved object and work through their grief in order to recover from their narcissistic wound. Bowlby (1980) saw this movement to recovery as comprising cognitive, emotional, and identity changes and as evolving through stages including numbness, yearning, and depressive withdrawal, leading to reorganization and recovery; Parkes (1993) described the process in similar terms of transition. Worden (1982) elaborated on these changes and stages, proposing that bereft individuals have to experience the reality of their loss, experience the pain, and adjust to the new environment without the deceased prior to withdrawing emotional energy from the lost relationship and investing anew. Working through the emotional pain of detachment (Lindeman, 1944) often was thought to require an extended period of time en route to what is commonly referred to recovery (Parkes & Weiss, 1983; Weiss, 1993).

Recent efforts to reconsider the work involved in coping with loss have led Stroebe and Schut (1999) to consider a couple of embedded processes as presented in their theoretical model of coping, the dual process model (DPM). They proposed two concurrent types of stressors and coping processes that characterize the grief response: loss-orientation and restoration-orientation. Loss orientation involves the coping processes directly related to the stress that is attributable to the death itself. In other words, loss-orientation is the emotion-focused, grief-related feelings that dominate early in the process and reemerge throughout the course of bereavement. Restoration-orientation comprises processes used to address the secondary stressors that accompany the transition into the new status of widow or widower, such as mastering new tasks, making decisions, and other domains of self-care. The DPM asserts that bereaved persons will oscillate between these two processes (loss-orientation and restoration-orientation) throughout the course of bereavement, as demands and circumstances dictate. Significant recent work addresses this model and supports its multidimensionality (e.g., Caserta & Lund, 2007).

Questions about the nature and meaning of recovery in bereavement and mounting findings that a continuing bond with the deceased loved one is not necessarily an indicator of pathology have also led to a recent theoretical perspective entitled continuing bonds (Klass, Silverman, & Nickman, 1996). Contemporary theorists in this emerging tradition have emphasized how, in opposition to a relinquishing of the bond, its constructive reorganization can be achieved by the consideration of the lost loved one as an extension of the self and maintaining psychological rather than physical proximity to the attachment figure (Neimeyer, Baldwin, & Gillies, 2006). In such contexts, relations with the deceased person may take the form of considering that person a role model, appreciating that individual's unique legacy, or cultivating a sense of the figure's comforting presence at times of stress (Field, Gao, & Paderna, 2005). Such ongoing connection makes intuitive sense and is now supported by an emerging increasingly complex body of literature, including the recognition of how maladaptive bonds may persist (or be formed) even after death and the need to situate continuing bonds within a broader conceptual framework addressing the major psychosocial tasks entailed in coming to terms with the death of a loved one (Field, 2006).

A significant part of this broader conceptual context includes the others with whom the bereft individual has a relationship and the others grieving the death. It is worth mentioning in this context that the death of an older man may be the death of a spouse for his now-widow, the death of a father for his children (each of whom may grieve the different and particular relationship they had with their father), the death of a child for his surviving older parent, and the death of a good friend, among the many other roles he played. Nadeau (1998) used a mobile to represent this extended family, demonstrating the unbalancing and instability that occurs in a family-network when a member dies. With the removal of one member-component of this mobile, the entire fixture becomes unstable and out of balance. Achieving a new balance involves taking on new positions and roles, which might be occasioned by the huddling together of some member-components and the wider dispersion of others. This broader, network-collective view is sometimes engaged in discussions of loss, but rarely employed in analyses.

RELATIONSHIP LOSSES

Death of a Spouse

The death of a spouse in later life, often after many years of marriage, is identified as one of the most stressful of all life events or transitions (Holmes & Rahe, 1967; Lund, Caserta, de Vries & Wright, 2004). The consequences of this loss have now been well documented and include, with considerable variability, profound sadness, loneliness, depression, identity reevaluation, and negative health outcomes (Lund, Caserta, Utz, & de Vries, 2010). In addition to these personal and psychological changes, considerable stress accompanies the role changes associated with widowhood involving disruptions in daily routines, taking on new and unfamiliar tasks, and changes in social activities and networks (Utz, Reidy, Carr, Neese, & Wortman, 2004). It is worth noting that the changes associated with and responses to loss are not exclusively negative; an emerging body of literature identifies the resiliency and personal growth of those recently bereft of their spouses (e.g., Calhoun & Tedeschi, 2006; Caserta, Lund, Utz, & de Vries, 2009). The literature on stress-related growth in bereavement suggests a transformation on the part of widowed persons, a newfound sense of strength, appreciation for relationships with others, and revised priorities (Caserta et al., 2009). The dual process model, referenced earlier, has particular implications for understanding and working with bereaved older spouses and has been the focus of our recent work (e.g., Caserta et al., 2009; Lund et al., 2004; 2008; 2010).

Death of a Parent

The death of a parent is a poignantly common loss experienced by adults (adult children) in their middle years (de Vries, 2001) and often the first death experience of young children (grandchildren). Owing to increased longevity and the frequency of multiple generations of older adults within families, the death of a parent is an increasingly common experience of older adults. Notwithstanding this frequency, only modest research exists on the experiences of parent-loss among later-life individuals and families (Umberson, 2003).

The tie between parents and children spans the offspring's total life course and assumes multidimensional forms throughout; death does not sever this tie (Moss, Resch, & Moss, 1997). Moss and Moss (1989b) claimed that the essential qualities of the relationship continue: "The child continues to hear echoes of the parent's voice, which may be carried over a lifetime" (p. 101). The pattern of grieving appears to be associated differently with the death of the first or the second parent (and crossed by gender), one of the unique characteristics of parental death. The death of the first parent is typically the death of the father (owing to gender differences in life expectancy and the tendency for women to marry men older than themselves). There is some suggestion that recently bereft adult children experience some disenfranchisement or exclusion from the grieving process, or both, as condolences are offered the widow and less so the children (de Vries, 2001). An adult child may assume more of a caregiving role in relation to the surviving parent.

The death of the second parent, typically the mother, may usher in a vivid reexperience of the impact of the first death (Moss & Moss, 1989b). When both parents have died, bereft children experience changes in perceptions of the self and the meaning of time, particularly when a second parental loss has left the middle-aged child psychologically orphaned and next in line to die (Pope, 2005). The now-orphaned child moves into the *omega* role (the oldest living member of the family; Hagestad, 1982), a role replete with new roles and responsibilities such as having others rely on them for family histories. Such role promotions often come with a recognition of personal limitations; in addition to being a source of growth, doubts, and acknowledgment of inabilities to meet the demands of these new roles.

In the paradox of grief, adult children gain access to their parent's perspective and experience in a way that was unavailable (or not accessed) during the parent's life. Bereaved adult children comment on the loss of their past with the death of their parent; they express their lost "repository of love" and source of emotional support (Pope, 2005, p. 113). They become attuned to the friendship dimension they had shared with the parent and the concomitant loss of companionship.

Institutionalization and dementia are circumstances that have been studied as mediators of the effects of death on the grief of former caregivers, mostly spouses and adult children. Pruchno, Moss, Burant, and Schinfeld (1995) examined the experiences of adult children before and after the death of a parent in a long-term care facility. They found that predeath indicators of caregiving strain predicted the extent to which adult children reported feeling sad, experiencing persistent thoughts about the parent, feeling a sense of comfort in memories, and having a sense of relief. Relief was the predominant emotion expressed by the majority of caregivers (not limited to but inclusive of adult children; Schulz et al., 2003) following the death of the dementia patient for whom care was provided; an even larger proportion reported that they believed the death was a relief to the patient. Both of these areas await further empirical attention.

Research has uncovered gender differences in this area, interestingly, more attributable to the gender of the children than the gender of the deceased parent. Sons and daughters responded in ways anticipated by traditional gender roles; sons are somewhat more stoic and less expressive, and daughters more connected to the deceased parent and more likely to report depressive symptoms. Interestingly, the daughters of deceased fathers, unlike other dyads, reported a better quality of relationships with their parent and were less accepting of the death, suggesting that the quality of the relationship between daughters and their fathers may be unique and hence uniquely manifested in the bereavement process (Moss, Resch, & Moss, 1997). As indicated previously (and is acknowledged throughout this chapter), more research on gender differences is needed.

As noted previously, the focus of research into responses to loss has been at the individual level, as if the death would not affect other relationships and as if other relationships would not affect responses to the death. Rosenblatt and Barner (2006) proffered that some of the reactions and fundamental changes of a bereaved adult child have the potential to affect the couple relationship and the partner. For example, grieving may lead one at times to want more of certain kinds of closeness with a partner and at times to want more of certain kinds of distance, illustrating part of the closeness-distance dance, as described by Rosenblatt and Barner (2006). They reported through their in-depth qualitative interviews with couples, an exemplary study in an area of great paucity of research, that couples experienced a sense of liberation in many forms (ranging from freedom from criticism to freedom from responsibility). They also reported greater intimacy (appreciating the finitude of life—and each other—in a new way) or greater distance (as one member addressed the needs of estate settlement or even continued the now-deceased parent's manipulative hostility) and responded in ways that complemented each other or created additional conflicts and barriers to intimacy (e.g., not meeting each other's needs for support).

Few other studies have explored this proliferation of grief and stress. Pope (2005), in his qualitative study of older bereaved adult children, found that the death of the second parent had a significant impact on sibling relationships—an impact brought about by the changing life circumstances introduced by the parent's death and by the participants' perceptions of how their parents had wished them to get along. Parental death may serve to intensify or distance sibling relationships (Connidis, 1992). For example, in Scharlach and Fredriksen's (1993) retrospective study, one-quarter of the respondents noted that following the death of their mother greater conflict had developed with their siblings; Connidis (1992) reported similar findings. In one of the few large-scale, quantitative examinations, Fuller-Thomson (1999) found that respondents who had experienced the death of at least one parent were more likely to report that they do not get along well with at least one of their siblings. Older respondents, African Americans, Hispanics, and respondents in good or excellent health are less likely to have conflict with a sibling— independent of parent death (see Bedford & Avioli, chapter 6 in this volume, for a more extensive discussion of sibling affect and its predictors).

Death of an Adult Child

Although of small comfort to bereft people, the death of an elderly parent is a normative, on-time loss; it is expected, timely, and natural. Perhaps this fact serves as a reason for the reported reduced support based on a misguided belief of there being less to grieve (given the death's predictability, in a life course context). The death of a child is the counterpoint—a nonnormative, off-time loss compromising our assumptive worlds (Janoff-Bulman, 1992). Rando (1993) noted that a child's death "shatters the very laws of nature in which the young grow up to replace the old" (p. 618). Parents, and especially older parents, ask: How is it my child could be taken when I am old and still here? (de Vries, Dalla Lana, & Falck, 1994).

Children represent the hopes and dreams of their parents, and the selves the parents could not or did not achieve (de Vries, Blieszner, & Blando, 2002). Yalom (1989) described children as the immortality projects of their parents, expressing the generativity inherent in parenting. In this same context, a child's death has often been described by parents in the terms of amputation; a part of the self is now missing (Rando, 1986). Klass and Marwitt (1989) proposed that this theme of amputation remains "in the form of an empty historical track" (p. 41) found lifelong in many bereaved parents—speaking further to the continuing bonds perspective introduced before. Bereaved parents follow what would have been their child's normative developmental progress and comment, for example, that their now deceased child would have been married and have children of his or her own by now. The deceased child continues to occupy a part of the parents' inner world (Klass & Marwitt, 1989).

Although some have commented that the death of an adult child is a more difficult loss for parents than the death of a younger child (Sanders, 1979–1980), a more measured statement would address the parent, child, and family developmental stages and the various issues represented therein. de Vries and colleagues (1994) reviewed the literature with a focus on family stage describing the course and consequence of a child's death; the age of a child at the time of death can lead to qualitatively different experiences of loss (Rando, 1986). For older parents, for example, and as evidenced in the quote about off-time death above, the death of an adult child represents life's dyssynchrony and the concomitant stress such incongruity heralds. Guilt related to surviving is a common feeling associated with such an experience, varying with cause of death; that is, bereft parents of a child who died from suicide express greater guilt and are more likely to report that their guilt was the most distressing aspect of their grief than do bereft parents whose children died in accidents or from chronic disease (Miles & Demi, 1992).

Fingerman (2001) described the older parent-adult child relationship as the paradox of distant closeness (similar to the closeness-distance dance; Rosenblatt & Barner, 2006); the role the deceased played in the lives of the bereft parents has an effect on the grief experience. For example, de Vries and colleagues (1994) reported that a bereft older father questioned why he should continue his hobby of carving wooden figurines, at which he evidenced considerable skill, following the death of his only child; he said he had no one to whom to leave this work upon his death. More immediate and tangible concerns are also noted. Moore and Stratton (2002) reported that losing an adult child who provided material and financial assistance to parents, particularly among low income families and families where norms of filial obligations were strong, proved disastrous, with implications for financial and social security as well as the receipt and the provision of care (e.g., being cared for by the adult child; caring for grandchildren). Moss, Lesher, and Moss (1986) had previously noted a similarly striking effect; over one-third of those in the long-term care facility they surveyed had experienced the death of a child. Although the relationship between the child's death and institutionalization cannot be affirmed definitively, the association is dramatic and suggests the strength of the effect of loss or the precariousness of caregiving receipt, or both.

The nature of the death of the child has an effect on the grief of parents. Older parents have reported grief exacerbated by their perceived reduced involvement; their adult children's family have often played a more immediate and significant role in the decisions and experiences prior to and even leading up to the death of the adult child (de Vries et al., 1994). Dean, McClement, Bond, Daeninck, and Nelson (2005) reported that parents experienced a tension between their strong desire to parent their child, and their recognition that their child was an autonomous adult, sometimes with a spouse and children who took precedence over them. Poignantly, just as the adult children report a sense of exclusion from the condolences expressed following the death of an elderly parent with a surviving spouse, so, too, do elderly parents feel somewhat excluded from the grief and related rituals following the death of a married, adult child.

The particular causes of death also have an impact on the grief trajectories of older parents. For example, among bereaved late midlife parents whose deceased (mostly male) children were adolescents or early young adults, Matthews and Marwit (2003–2004) found that parents bereft by homicide saw the world as a more malevolent place than did parents bereft by accident;

homicide survivors also reported less self-worth (both of which the authors attribute to self-blame). Murphy, Das Gupta, Cain, Clark Johnson, Lohan, Wu, and Mekwa, (1999) found, in their comparison of bereaved parents whose child had died from homicide, suicide, or accident, that cause of children's death significantly affected the prevalence of post-traumatic stress disorder (PTSD) symptoms. Twice as many mothers and fathers whose children were murdered met PTSD criteria compared with parents whose children died by accident and suicide.

Research suggests that mothers and fathers grieve differently and on different trajectories. For example, Murphy, Braun, Tillery, Cain, Clark Johnson and Beaton (1999) found that fathers reported higher repressive coping (e.g., "I act as though it didn't really happen") than did mothers; relatedly, the grief symptoms of fathers did not significantly decrease (and some increased) during the two-year period these 261 bereaved parents were studied, whereas the grief symptoms of mothers significantly decreased. Arbuckle and de Vries (1995) found similar results in their longer-term investigation. These different manifestations and patterns of grief challenge relationship quality and even relationship longevity; research shows the stress experienced by these bereaved couples can lead to greater marital discord and distress following the death (Schwab, 1999), although there is contrasting evidence for older couples for whom somewhat greater marital satisfaction and sources of support were found (de Vries, Davis, Wortman, & Lehman, 1997).

The loss of a child restructures a family. Surviving siblings may experience feelings similar to those of parents, including guilt and sadness; parents may be less available to their surviving children, and older children, in particular, may become supporters of their grieving parents. Ponzetti (1992), for example, noted that the majority of bereaved parents in his study reported feeling or acting differently toward their surviving children as a consequence of the loss. As suggested before by the evocative model of the mobile, families reorganize following a loss (e.g., roles, responsibilities, rituals), and a new equilibrium is sought, although not always found.

Death of a Grandchild

Research into the experiences of grief following the death of a grandchild is itself a rare recognition of the proliferation of stress and grief—considerations missing in so much of the extant bereavement literature. Rando (1986), for example, noted the duality of grandparents' grief: "They not only lose their grandchild, but they 'lose' their child as well, as they cannot rescue their child from bereaved-parent status" (p. 37). Similar themes were echoed in the work of Reed (2000), among others. These comments and observations neatly articulate the family interconnections as well as the shared, complementary, and sometimes conflicting grief experiences of those remaining.

As Reed (2003) noted, this interesting observation stands out in a literature disproportionately and sadly small. Reed posited that such relative professional and societal neglect derives from the misperception of reduced grief and pain on the part of grandparents, given that generations separate grandparents from their grandchildren, and perhaps a further misguided belief that owing to the advanced age of the grandparents, they have had more experience with grief and are ostensively better able to deal with it. Of course, the experience of grandparents is vastly different than either of these suppositions assumes.

Fry (1997), for example, studied 152 grandparents whose grandchild had died within the previous three years. Through open-ended questionnaires followed by content and factor analyses, she identified two central factors of grandparent grief, emotional rupturing and survivor guilt, describing the immense emotional upheaval and dyssynchrony of the loss, respectively. Like bereaved parents, bereaved grandparents commented on shattered belief systems, the unfairness of life, and the need to restructure relationships with other family members and with living grandchildren, also noted by Ponzetti (1992). The hopes and dreams of the grandparent (sometimes even a namesake) are invested in a grandchild. Losing that child leaves grandparents struggling through a grieving process for what feels like a loss of part of them.

Galinsky's (1999) small qualitative study of grandmothers offers further support for these findings, while introducing evocative observations worthy of further empirical pursuit. No grandfathers, for example, agreed to be interviewed for the study, suggesting interesting gender differences in the reporting of such grief experiences; further, not all of the grandmothers were able to receive support from their spouses. Most of the grandmothers in the study did not talk to their families about their grief, perhaps attempting to protect their child from further emotional distress. As further evidence of this protection (and survivor guilt), Galinsky noted (p. 7) that many said to her, "I've lived a long life. Why couldn't it have been me who was taken?"

As Reed (2003) commented, a grandchild's death sends shock waves through the entire family. Rando (1986) mentioned potential family relationship problems, the important role of grandparents, and the difficulty in enacting this role in this distressed and disrupted context. That is, grandparents often are the ones a family looks to for strength, inspiration, understanding, and care. Being the source of strength for the entire family is a difficult expectation for grandparents to handle as they are challenged to carry on with grace and dignity in their dual mourning while receiving little support from either society or bereavement professionals (Reed, 2003).

Death of a Sibling

I highlight with monotonous frequency the paucity of research into the responses to the death of a particular family member in later life; as true as this statement is of bereaved adult children and grandparents, it is even truer of bereaved siblings. This lack of research is a surprising state of affairs given the frequency with which older adults experience this loss; as Rando (1991) has noted, while we have only one mother, one father, and one spouse (at least at any given point in time), it is not uncommon to have several siblings. Therefore, we are more exposed to sibling deaths than to other family losses; almost three out of four deaths among close relatives of older adults are of siblings (d'Epinay et al., 2010–2011). Still, society fails to recognize the potential enormity of this loss. Godfrey (2006, p. 6) described her experience as follows: "How many times did I hear, 'Oh, your brother died; how are your *parents* doing? How awful for them!' Yes, it was awful for them. But it was awful for me as well and very few people seemed to notice this."

Differing from the losses discussed thus far, with the exception of widowhood, the death of a sibling represents the death of an intimate (to varying degrees, as reviewed by Bedford and Avioli, chapter 6 in this volume) with probable shared generation and history (de Vries, 2001). The death of a sibling is the death of one's cobiographer, having been a part of each other's life stories and lifetimes (Connidis, 2010). Moss and Moss (1989a) provided evidence of this theme in qualitative explorations with bereaved older siblings, one of whom reported that with the death of her brother, "there was a part of my childhood that went. There were things I couldn't verify. . . . Suddenly I was alone with my memories" (p. 104). Siblings, in large proportion, also share genetic legacy and these factors combine in ways that may lead bereaved siblings to feel that his or her own mortality is threatened by the death. Hays, Gold, and Pieper (1997) reported that older surviving siblings "weigh the death of kin very highly when calculating their overall health status" (p. 37).

Such interpretations of the loss are likely associated with findings such as those reported by Hays and colleagues (1997), who found that bereaved siblings exhibited high cognitive and functional impairment following the death and rated their overall health as worse than either bereaved spouses or bereaved friends. Interestingly, d'Epinay and colleagues (2009–2010) found no effect for depression on bereaved siblings; a possible explanation, based on the observation that the intensity of grief is a function of the quality of the relationship between the survivor and the deceased (Moss & Moss, 1989a), is that perhaps relationship quality varies more among siblings than among spouses and parents, for example. Along such lines, Cicirelli (2009) found that depressive symptomatology in old age was influenced by death fear, itself influenced by sibling death, as well as by poor relationships with siblings. These findings demonstrate a broad and related situational context within which sibling relationships, including sibling death, must be understood.

Rando (1991) wrote that guilt may well be a common component of the response to the death of a sibling. The guilt may have many facets from survival guilt (as noted in the loss experiences of parents and grandparents, manifested by concern that one is alive when another is not), to guilt for having not sustained a relationship in the ways that one would have preferred (or thought to be ideal), to guilt from the relational parameters of interactions when both siblings were young, to guilt from other manners and forms of interaction. These forms of guilt remain largely conjectures as research has not fully examined these issues.

So, too, may bereaved siblings grow through their experience of loss. Godfrey (2006) reminded us that bereaved siblings may also emerge from their experiences with a deeper appreciation for life and for relationships. Thus, they may honor their deceased sibling through their health-promoting and life-affirming activities.

There is little research addressing any particular role of gender in the few analyses of sibling death. Hays and colleagues (1997) reported the evocative finding that the bereaved brothers and sisters of a deceased brother reported, respectively, excessive economic hardship and mood impairment. The former of these findings (economic hardship) may suggest the financial ties that bind siblings (as in shared business ventures, for example); the latter (mood impairment) suggests the unique relationship between brothers and sisters, echoing the evocative role of gender, and daughters in particular, following the death of a father. The death of a sibling will change the position the surviving sibling holds in a family, a clear example of role and position realignment following the death (as suggested by the mobile analogy). The surviving sibling may now be the only remaining child or may now become the caregiver (of the parent or another family member); the surviving sibling may now be called upon to perform the kinkeeping functions, something that was typically performed by the deceased. As such, contact among surviving siblings may change following the death of one (Bedford & Avioli, 2001), drawing individuals together in grief or dissipating the connections. Moss and Moss (1989a, p. 105) suggested that most connections persist, as evidenced by the following quote from a participant in their research: "There are so few of us left, we like each other more." Such connections, of course, are mediated by the different reactions of surviving siblings, made even more complex by the experience of a surviving parent who has lost a child and may either call upon or be less available to other children in their grief. This proliferation of stress and grief has a ready path in this example, rarely examined.

Death of a Friend—A Loss in the Chosen Family

The only later-life death more frequent than that of a sibling is that of a friend (de Vries & Blando, 2000), a normative yet rarely studied loss of the later years. d'Epinay and colleagues (2009–2010) found that almost half of their sample had lost at least one friend over the 10-year interval of their research on oldest-old adults. Friends have a natural, if not universally accepted, place in the understanding and study of families. The organization of black families serves as a relevant example in their capacity to enlarge the extended family beyond lineal ties and enlarge its potential supportive resources (Johnson, 1999). Furthermore, as kinship networks expand with remarriage, decisions and personal choices commonly determine whether relationships continue or cease—and many continue. Such chosen kin or constructed kin also may be seen among older people who are without traditional family (Barker, 2002; Rubinstein, Alexander, Goodman, & Luborsky, 1991) and even more frequently in gay and lesbian communities (Allen & Demo, 1995; de Vries & Hoctel, 2007; de Vries & Megathlin, 2009; Weston, 1991). In fact, a recent report on a national sample of lesbian, gay, bisexual, and transgender (LGBT) boomers (Met Life Mature Market Institute, 2010) found that over 60% reported that they had a chosen family, what Maupin (2007) cleverly called *logical kin*, in contrast to biological kin.

Among the very few studies to have explored the experience of *friend-grievers* (Deck & Folta, 1989) or *survivor friends* (Sklar, 1991–1992; Sklar & Hartley, 1990) in later life, de Vries & Johnson (2002) found significant evidence of both the effects of friendship loss and the friend-family link; many respondents spoke of the emotional toll exacted by such a loss often in the context of the fluid boundaries between friends and kin ("she was like a sister"); respondents spoke of friendships of durations as long as or longer than those of their sibling ties. Roberto and Stanis (1994) found that even following an extended period of time, older women bereft of their friends reported feelings of deep loss and a sense of aloneness. D'Epinay and colleagues (2009–2010) found sharp increases in depressive symptoms amongst those bereft of a friend and that those who had lost a friend did not receive any special support from their social network and hence remained alone with their grief.

Overall, those who are peer bereaved tend to be ignored, an experience regularly reproduced by family, doctors, and the legal system (Deck & Folta, 1989). Close friends are not conventionally recognized as grievers and not identified by norms, expectations, or rights; all of this may contribute to increased levels of distress and grief.

The study of friendship loss also serves as an introduction into the vastly understudied arena of multiple losses. It is probably unreasonable to assume, although it is the convention to do so, that any one loss we study or experience is understood uniquely in that singular context. D'Epinay and colleagues (2009–2010) are among the few, outside of the domain of AIDS bereavement, to have picked up on this issue and note that over the 10-year period of the time frame of their research, one elder lost two children, about 50 lost more than one sibling, and 100 lost several friends (10 elders mentioned the loss of between five and eight friends). Kastenbaum, years ago (1969), offered insight into this area by suggesting that it is likely that older persons will experience multiple losses and will show some cumulative effect, which he termed *bereavement overload*. Along similar lines, Moss and Moss (1989b) suggested that the experiences of death over a lifetime form a pool of grief that persists and intensifies with subsequent losses.

RESEARCH AND THEORY

The field of bereavement in later life is undergoing an exciting transformation; recent theoretical activities such as Klass's (2006) work with continuing bonds and Stroebe and Schut's (2010) work with the dual process model are stimulating exciting research (e.g., Field & Filanosky, 2010; Lund et al., 2010). This focus is encouraging and follows a period of relatively slower growth in the field, perhaps as it engaged in a critical self-reflection, akin to the paradigm shifts made famous by Thomas Kuhn (1970). Theorists and researchers are questioning and testing long-held assumptions about the course and consequence of grief, including its endpoints, paths to recovery, and the constituents of normal and abnormal grief. These are important questions; examining them will help better shape the field and our understanding of loss and its pivotal role in lives of bereft persons.

Ample opportunities for field advancement remain, of course. For example, notwithstanding the invaluable contributions of Doka (e.g., 1989) and our related awareness of *disenfranchised grief* and the entitlements of the grief and bereavement systems in North America, relatively little work has been done on those whose relationships fall outside of sanctioned, conventional, and traditionally defined families. As the definition and experience of family continues to evolve, despite political maneuvers to prevent this inclusive evolution, our awareness of the depth and breadth of connections to others will also continue to expand, including our responses to their death. Little work, for example, has been conducted on the death of a same-sex spouse, with Shernoff (1997) standing as one of the few notable exceptions. *Chosen* (or *logical*) kin has also been an area of infrequent exploration, yet, as noted previously, a domain well-populated in gay and lesbian lives as well as in the experiences of African American families, and likely far more generally.

Even within the more traditional family ties, more research is sorely needed. Sibling connections are almost ignored in the literature (with a few exceptions as noted earlier); the response of older adult children to the death of a parent is similarly vastly understudied, as are the responses of grandparents to the death of a grandchild. In general, with the possible exception of widowhood (which increasingly may be seen as the prototype of loss in later life), older persons are infrequently identified as grievers. This neglect, itself, is an interesting observation and speaks to our limited understanding and framing of later life experiences. The normative nature of death in later life does not diminish its impact.

There is an increasing awareness of the specificity of loss; that is, the nature of the grief is probably most clearly articulated by the nature of the relationship to and with the deceased (de Vries, 1997). This self-obvious statement has not been so obvious in the field; the notion of one size not fitting all is surprisingly revelatory. As noted previously, the relatively closed nature of fields of study, that is, the tendency to look within fields rather than across them, as has been the case between relationship researchers and bereavement researchers, has hampered our awareness of the particular domains that exist within relationships and are manifest in our responses to the loss of such relationships that give meaning to both the relationship and the loss.

At the same time, few studies have adopted an examination of loss in the context of the other experienced life losses, as advanced by Kastenbaum and Moss and Moss several years ago. As mentioned previously, the AIDS literature is an interesting exception to this statement. Nonetheless, it is probably unreasonable to assume that an individual arrives at his or her later years (or even middle years) without having experienced several and perhaps multiple losses; we have little understanding of how these multiple losses present themselves anew (if at all) with each subsequent grief. Is grief part of a pattern of response? These questions may appear to contradict previous statements about relationship specificity, but both may be and probably are true. Our relationships are unique and patterned; our grief may be the same.

Just as we search for support from those in our networks, so, too, do our network members experience grief with the death of one of their own. This network response is becoming better understood in families, as the mobile analogy suggested, but as families change and expand, so must our conceptualization of this mobile. Research has infrequently adopted this perspective, which is probably not surprising given the complexity and complication it introduces for our framing of issues and our analysis of variables. It is a challenge to which we must rise, however, if we are to fully understand the nature of ties and grief in the lives of older adults and of persons of all ages.

APPLICATIONS

Bereavement intervention efforts have typically assumed the form of mutual-support (self-help) groups as a means to bolster informal support and counter loneliness and social isolation (Lieberman, 1993). Research into the efficacy of these efforts, however (e.g., Schut, Stroebe, Van Den Bout, & Terheggen, 2001), reveals inconsistent and sometimes minimal impact on outcomes. Often absent from or implicit in these efforts to strengthen social support is a focus on the skills needed to master the daily tasks of single life in the new and uncharted personal territory (Arbuckle & de Vries, 1995).

Previous research has revealed the somewhat unanticipated finding of a strong association between competence in tasks of daily living and positive grief responses (Lund, Caserta, Dimond, & Shaffer, 1989). That is, by addressing both the emotion-focused and skill-focused needs, the resulting mastery of and efficacy in performing household tasks may strengthen and bolster bereft persons, promoting confidence, personal growth, and progress through grief.

The emotion-focused and skill-focused efforts are identified as loss-orientation and restoration-orientation, respectively, in the dual process model previously introduced (Stroebe & Schut, 1999). Traditional mutual-support intervention programs primarily target loss-orientation; restoration may be achieved through practical instruction and the availability of information and resources about self-care and other skills necessary to accomplish the tasks of daily living. Our research with recently bereaved older spouses (based on the dual process model and called the living after loss (LAL) program; Lund, Caserta, de Vries, & Wright, 2004) was designed to facilitate both loss-orientation and restoration-orientation, thus incorporating grief work and practical skills training in the intervention.

The LAL program consists of a 14-week group-based intervention that integrates grief work and emotion-focused support based on previous experience with a self-care, skill-based health education program (Caserta, Lund, & Rice, 1999; Caserta, Lund, & Obray, 2004). Each of the weekly sessions emphasizes either loss-orientation or restoration-orientation; loss-orientation is more prominent in earlier sessions with restoration-orientation emphasized in later sessions. Topics included in the restoration-oriented presentations include nutrition, health maintenance, and health care access, legal and financial management, household and automobile maintenance, and strategies for remaining socially active (Lund et al., 2004). To optimize the synergistic effect of these two theoretically different but necessary coping styles, each session encourages oscillation between loss-orientation and restoration-orientation as complementary aspects of bereavement adaptation.

This sort of synthesis between theoretical models, research, and interventions and those at the helm of each will lead to further theoretical discussions as well as practical interventions that ultimately benefit all, most of all (ideally) the bereaved persons, but also the theory and theorists, the researchers, the practitioners, and those in the social environment of loss. These recipients represent all of us, as we navigate life and loss and as we seek, consider, and reconsider our place in families, networks, and the world.

REFERENCES

Allen, K., & Demo, D. H. (1995). The families of lesbians and gay men: A new frontier of family research. *Journal of Marriage and Family, 57*, 111–127.

Arbuckle, N., & de Vries, B. (1995). The long-term effects of later life spousal and parental bereavement on personal functioning. *The Gerontologist, 35,* 637–647.

Barker, J. (2002). Neighbors, friends, and other nonkin caregivers of community living dependent elders. *Journal of Gerontology, 57,* 158–167.

Bedford, V.H., & Avioli, P.S. (2001). Variations on sibling intimacy in old age. *Generations, 25,* 34–40.

Bowlby, J. (1980). *Loss: Sadness and depression: Vol. 3. Attachment and loss.* New York: Basic Books.

Calhoun, I. G., & Tedeschi, R. G. (2006). The foundations of posttraumatic growth: An expanded framework. In I. G. Calhoun & R. G. Tedeschi (Eds.), *Handbook of posttraumatic growth: Research and practice.* Mahwah, NJ: Lawrence Erlbaum and Associates.

Caserta, M.S., & Lund, D.A. (2007). Toward the development of an Inventory of Daily Widowed Life (IDWL): Guided by the dual process model of coping with bereavement. *Death Studies, 31,* 505–535.

Caserta, M.S., Lund, D.A., & Obray, S.J. (2004). Promoting self-care and daily living skills among older widows and widowers: Evidence from the Pathfinders demonstration project. *Omega, 49,* 217–236.

Caserta, M. S., Lund, D. A., & Rice, S. J. (1999). Pathfinders: A self-care and health education program for older widows and widowers. *The Gerontologist, 33,* 619–629.

Caserta, M. S., Lund, D., Utz, R., & de Vries, B. (2009). Stress-related growth among the recently bereaved. *Aging and Mental Health, 13,* 463–467.

Cicirelli, V.G. (2009). Sibling loss and death fear in relation to depressive symptomatology in older adults. *Journal of Gerontology: Psychological Sciences. 64,* 24–32.

Connidis, I.A. (1992). Life transitions and the adult sibling tie: A qualitative study. *Journal of Marriage and Family, 54,* 972–982.

Connidis, I. A. (2010). *Family ties and aging* (2nd ed.). Los Angeles: Pine Forge Press/Sage.

Dean, M., McClement, S., Bond, J., Daeninck, P., & Nelson, F. (2005). Parental experiences of adult child death from cancer. *Journal of Palliative Medicine. 8,* 751–765.

Deck, E. S., & Folta, J. R. (1989). The friend-griever. In J. K. Doka (Ed.), *Disenfranchised grief: Recognizing hidden sorrow* (pp. 77–89). Lexington, MA: Lexington Books.

d'Epinay, C., Cavalli, S., & Guillet, L. (2009–2010). Bereavement in very old age: Impact on health and relationships of the loss of a spouse, a child, a sibling, or a close friend. *Omega, 60,* 301–325.

de Vries, B. (1997). Kinship bereavement in later life: Understanding variations in cause, course, and consequence. *Omega, 35,* 141–157.

de Vries, B. (2001). Grief: Intimacy's reflection. *Generations, 25,* 75–80.

de Vries, B., & Blando, J.A. (2000). Friendship at the end of life. In M. P. Lawton (Ed.), *Annual Review of Gerontology and Geriatrics* (pp. 144–162). New York: Springer.

de Vries, B., Blieszner, R., & Blando, J. A. (2002). Faces of grief and intimacy in later life. In K. Doka (Ed.), *Living with grief: Loss in later life* (pp. 225–241). Washington, DC: Hospice Foundation of America.

de Vries, B., Dalla-Lana, R., & Falck, V. (1994). Parental bereavement over the life course: A theoretical integration and empirical review. *Omega, 29,* 47–69.

de Vries, B., Davis, C., Wortman, C., & Lehman, D. (1997). The long term psychological and somatic consequences of later life parental bereavement. *Omega, 35,* 97–118.

de Vries, B., & Hoctel, P. (2007). The family friends of older gay men and lesbians. In N. Teunis & G. Herdt (Eds.), *Sexual inequalities and social justice* (pp. 213–232). Berkeley: University of California Press.

de Vries, B., & Johnson, C. L. (2002). The death of friends in later life. *Advances in life-course research: New frontiers in socialization* (Vol. 7, pp. 299–324). New York: JAI Press.

de Vries, B., & Megathlin, D. (2009). The meaning of friends for gay men and lesbians in the second half of life. *Journal of GLBT Family Studies, 5,* 82–98.

Doka, J. K. (Ed.). (1989). *Disenfranchised grief: Recognizing hidden sorrow.* Lexington, MA: Lexington Books.

Dutton, Y., & Zisook, S. (2005). Adaptation to bereavement. *Death Studies, 29,* 877–903.

Faschingbauer, T.R., Zisook, S., & De Vaul, R. (1987). The Texas Revised Inventory of Grief. In S. Zisook (Ed.), *Biopsychosocial aspects of bereavement* (pp. 111–124). Washington, DC: American Psychiatric press.

Field, N. P. (2006). Continuing bonds in adaptation to bereavement: Introduction. *Death Studies, 30,* 709–714.

Field, N. P., & Filanosky, C. (2010). Continuing bonds, risk factors for complicated grief, and adjustment to bereavement. *Death Studies, 34,* 1–29.

Field, N. P., Gao, B., & Paderna, L. (2005). Continuing bonds in bereavement: An attachment theory based perspective. *Death Studies, 29,* 277–299.

Fingerman, K. (2001). A distant closeness: Intimacy between parents and their children in later life. *Generations, 25,* 26–33.

Freud, S. (1917/1957). Mourning and melancholia. In J. Strachey (Ed. and trans.), *The standard edition of the complete psychological works of Sigmund Freud* (Vol. 16, pp. 237–259). London: Hogarth Press.

Fry, P. (1997). Grandparents' reactions to the death of a grandchild: An exploratory factor analytic study. *Omega, 35,* 119–140.

Fuller-Thomson, E. (1999). Loss of the kin-keeper? Sibling conflict following parental death. *Omega, 40,* 547–559.

Galinsky, N. (1999). *When a grandchild dies: What to do, what to say, how to cope.* Houston, TX: Gal in Sky Publishing.

Godfrey, A. (2006). Losing a sibling in adulthood. *The Forum, 3*(1), 6–7.

Hagestad, G.O. (1982). Parent and child: Generations in the family. In T.M. Field et al. (Eds.), *Review of human development* (pp. 485–499). New York: Wiley.

Hays, J. C., Gold, D. T., & Pieper, C. F. (1997). Sibling bereavement in late life. *Omega, 35,* 25–42.

Holmes, T. H., & Rahe, R. H. (1967). The social readjustments rating scales. *Journal of Psychosomatic Research, 11,* 213–218.

Janoff-Bulman, R. (1992). *Shattered assumptions: Towards a new psychology of trauma.* New York: The Free Press.

Johnson, C. L. (1999). Fictive kin among oldest old African Americans in the San Francisco Bay Area. *Journal of Gerontology, 54*, 368–375.

Kastenbaum, R. (1969). Death and bereavement in later life. In A. J. Kutscher (Ed.), *Death and bereavement* (pp. 28–54). Boston: Allyn & Bacon.

Klass, D. (2006). Continuing conversations about continuing bonds. *Death Studies, 30*, 843–858.

Klass, D., & Marwitt, S. (1989). Toward a model of parental grief. *Omega, 19*, 31–50.

Klass, D., Silverman, P., & Nickman, S.L. (Eds.). (1996). *Continuing bonds: New understandings of grief.* Washington, DC: Taylor & Francis.

Kuhn, T. (1970). *The structure of scientific revolutions.* Chicago: University of Chicago Press.

Lieberman, M. A. (1993). Bereavement self-help groups: A review of conceptual and methodological issues. In M. S. Stroebe, W. Stroebe, & R. O. Hansson (Eds.), *Handbook of bereavement: Theory, research, and intervention* (pp. 411–426). New York: Cambridge University Press.

Lindeman, E. (1944). Symptomatology and management of acute grief. *American Journal of Psychiatry, 101*, 141–148.

Lund, D., Caserta, M., de Vries, B., & Wright, S. (2004). Restoration after bereavement. *Generations Review, 14*(4), 9–15.

Lund, D., Caserta, M., Dimond, M. F., & Shaffer, S. K. (1989). Competencies: Tasks of daily living and adjustments to spousal bereavement in later life. In D. A. Lund (Ed.), *Older bereaved spouses: Research with practical applications* (pp. 135–156). Washington, DC: Taylor-Francis/Hemisphere Press.

Lund, D., Caserta, M., Utz, R., & de Vries, B. (2010). Experiences and early coping of bereaved spouses/partners in an intervention based on the Dual Process Model (DPM). *Omega, 61*, 293–315.

Lund, D., Utz, R., Caserta, M., & de Vries, B. (2008). Humor, laughter and happiness in the daily lives of recently bereaved spouses. *Omega, 58*, 87–105.

Matthews, L., & Marwit, S. (2003–2004). Examining the assumptive world view of parents bereaved by accident, murder, and illness. *Omega, 48*, 115–136.

Maupin, A. (2007). *Michael Tolliver lives.* San Francisco, CA: HarperCollins.

MetLife Mature Market Institute. (2010). *Still out, still ging: The MetLife study of lesbian, gay, bisexual and transgender Baby Boomers.* New York: The Mature Market Institute.

Miles, M., & Demi, A. (1992). A comparison of guilt in bereaved parents whose children died by suicide, accident, or chronic disease. *Omega, 24*, 205–215.

Moore, A., & Stratton, D. (2002). *Resilient widowers: Older men speak for themselves.* New York: Springer.

Moss, M. S., Lesher, E., & Moss, S. Z. (1986). Impact of the death of an adult child on elderly parents: Some observations. *Omega, 17*, 209–218.

Moss, M. S., & Moss, S. Z. (1989a). The impact of the death of an elderly sibling: Some considerations of a normative loss. *American Behavioral Scientist, 33*, 94–106.

Moss, M. S., & Moss, S. Z. (1989b). The death of a parent. In R. Kalish (Ed.), *Midlife loss: Coping strategies* (pp. 89–114). Newbury Park: Sage.

Moss, M. S., Resch, N., & Moss, S. Z. (1997). The role of gender in middle-aged children's responses to parent death. *Omega, 35*, 43–65.

Murphy, S., Braun, T., Tillery, L., Cain, K., Clark Johnson, L., & Beaton, R. (1999). PTSD among bereaved parents following the violent deaths of their 12- to 28-year-old children: A longitudinal prospective analysis. *Journal of Traumatic Stress, 12,* 273–291.

Murphy, S., Das Gupta, A., Cain, K., Clark Johnson, L., Lohan, J., Wu, L. & Mekwa, J. (1999). Changes in parent's mental distress after the violent death of an adolescent or young adult child: A longitudinal prospective analysis. *Death Studies, 23,* 129–159.

Nadeau, J. W. (1998). *Families making sense of death.* Thousand Oaks, CA: Sage.

Neimeyer, R. A., Baldwin, S. A., & Gillies, J. (2006). Continuing bonds and reconstructing meaning: Mitigating complications in bereavement. *Death Studies, 30,* 715–738.

Parkes, C. M. (1993). Bereavement as a psychosocial transition: Processes of adaptation to change. In M. S. Stroebe, W. Stroebe, & R. O. Hansson (Eds.), *Handbook of bereavement: Theory, research, and intervention* (pp. 91–101). Cambridge, UK: Cambridge University Press.

Parkes, C. M., & Weiss, R. S. (1983). *Recovery from bereavement.* New York: Basic Books.

Ponzetti, J. (1992). Bereaved families: A comparison of parents' and grandparents' reactions to the death of a child. *Omega, 25,* 63–71.

Pope, A. (2005). Personal transformation in midlife orphanhood: An empirical phenomenological study. *Omega, 51,* 107–123.

Pruchno, R., Moss, M., Burant, C., & Schinfeld, S. (1995). Death of an institutionalized parent: Predictors of bereavement. *Omega, 31,* 99–119.

Rando, T. (1986). *Parental loss of a child.* Champaign, IL: Research Press.

Rando, T. (1991). *How to go on living when someone you love dies.* New York: Bantam.

Rando, T. (1993). *Treatment of complicated mourning.* Champaign, IL: Research Press.

Reed, M. L. (2000). *Grandparents cry twice: Help for bereaved grandparents.* Amityville, NY: Baywood.

Reed, M. L. (2003). Grandparent's grief: Who is listening? *The Forum, 29*(1), 1–3.

Roberto, K. A., & Stanis, P. (1994). Reactions of older women to the death of their close friends. *Omega, 29,* 17–27.

Rosenblatt, P., & Barner, J. (2006). The dance of closeness-distance in couple relationships after the death of a parent. *Omega, 53,* 277–293.

Rubinstein, R. B., Alexander, B., Goodman, M., & Luborsky, M. (1991). Key relationships of never-married, childless, white women: A cultural analysis. *Journal of Gerontology: Social Sciences, 46,* S270–S277.

Sanders, C. M. (1979–1980). A comparison of adult bereavement in the death of a spouse, child and parent. *Omega, 10,* 303–322.

Schut, H., Stroebe, M. S., Van Den Bout, J., & Terheggen, M. (2001). The efficacy of bereavement interventions: Determining who benefits. In M. S. Stroebe, R. O. Hansson, W. Stroebe, & H. Schut (Eds.), *Handbook of bereavement research: Consequences, coping, and care* (pp. 705–737). Washington, DC: American Psychological Association.

Scharlach, A. E., & Fredriksen, K. I. (1993). Reactions to the death of a parent during midlife. *Omega, 27,* 307–319.

Schulz, R., Mendelsohn, A. B., Haley, W. E., Mahoney, D., Allen, R., Zhang, S., . . . Bell, S. H. (2003). End-of-life care and the effects of bereavement on family caregivers of persons with dementia. *New England Journal of Medicine, 349,* 1936–1942.

Schwab, R. (1999). A child's death and divorce: Dispelling the myth. *Death Studies, 22,* 445–468.

Shernoff, M. (1997). *Gay widowers: Life after the death of a partner.* Binghamton, NY: Haworth Press.

Sklar, F. (1991–1992). Grief as a family affair: Property rights, grief rights, and the exclusion of close friends as survivors. *Omega, 24,* 109–121.

Sklar, F., & Hartley, S. F. (1990). Close friends as survivors: Bereavement patterns in a "hidden" population. *Omega, 21,* 103–112.

Stroebe, M., & Schut, H. (1999). The dual process model of coping with bereavement: Rationale and description. *Death Studies, 23,* 197–224.

Stroebe, M., & Schut, H. (2010). The Dual Process Model of coping with bereavement: A decade on. *Omega, 61,* 273–289.

Stroebe, M., Stroebe, W., & Hansson, R. (1993). Bereavement research and theory: An introduction to the Handbook. In M. S. Stroebe, W. Stroebe, & R. O. Hansson (Eds.), *Handbook of bereavement: Theory, research, and intervention* (pp. 3–21). Cambridge, UK: Cambridge University Press.

Umberson, D. (2003). *Death of a parent: Transition to a new adult identity.* Cambridge, UK: Cambridge University Press.

Utz, R., Reidy, E., Carr, D., Neese, R., & Wortman, D. (2004). The daily consequences of widowhood: The role of gender and intergenerational transfers on subsequent household performance. *Journal of Family Issues, 25,* 683–712.

Vachon, M.L.S., & Stylianos, S. K. (1988). The role of social support in bereavement. *Journal of Social Issues, 44,* 175–190.

Weiss, R. S. (1993). Loss and recovery. In M. S. Stroebe, W. Stroebe, & R. O. Hansson (Eds.), *Handbook of bereavement: Theory, research, and intervention* (pp. 271–284). Cambridge, UK: Cambridge University Press.

Weston, K. (1991). *Families we choose: Lesbians, gays and kinship.* New York: Columbia University Press.

Williams, B., Baker, P., Allman, R., & Roseman, J. (2006). The feminization of bereavement among community-dwelling older adults. *Journal of Women and Aging, 18,* 3–18.

Worden, W. (1982). *Grief counseling and grief therapy.* New York: Springer Publishing Company.

Yalom, I. (1989). *Love's executioner and other tales of psychotherapy.* New York: Basic Books.

Part V

Future Research

23

New Directions for Family Gerontology: Where Do We Go from Here?

Victoria Hilkevitch Bedford
and Rosemary Blieszner

Aging families are of central importance to individuals of all ages, given old relatives' contributions to intergenerational and intragenerational family members whether as caregivers, sources of social support and aid, keepers of family history, and, indirectly, as workers and volunteers in the larger community. Old relatives may also impact their families when they are in need, such as for care, aid, and emotional support when experiencing life transitions; to ward off loneliness; and when requiring financial assistance. As the population of old adults increases due to reduced infant mortality, improved health care, and expanding life expectancy, the number of vulnerable old adults grows. At the same time, the birthrate has declined and traditional family forms are decreasing due to marriage dissolution and new forms of family unions. The impact of these changes on the care of the growing population of old adults, many of whom are frail and vulnerable, is likely to be significant (Agree & Hughes, chapter 2 in this volume). The influx of new immigrants adds the complexity of ethnic diversity to the growing challenges families may face (Usita & Shakya, chapter 14 in this volume). Increased life expectancy has also resulted in more generations of surviving adults (Silverstein & Giarrusso, 2010) and more surviving horizontal kin (siblings, cousins), both of which are potential sources as well as recipients of support. In order for social policy to keep up with these changes (Harrington Meyer & Frazier, chapter 15 in this volume), the designers are dependent on family gerontologists to provide state-of-the-art information. As yet, little is known about how late-life families will be affected by these changes, which are, in fact, global. Therefore, we depend on scholars in subdisciplines of family gerontology to apply their expertise to help direct future research that will attempt to address these issues.

PURPOSE

The chapter authors of this *Handbook* have each given careful thought to recommending future research within the content area of their respective chapters, based on their review of current research and intervention needs. For this final chapter we have extracted eight themes derived from the authors' recommendations in an effort to conclude the volume with a synthesis of new directions for the field of family gerontology. Although there is overlap among the themes, each represents an amalgam of focused ideas drawn from the various content areas covered in this volume, a few outside sources, and our own knowledge base.

The first seven themes were addressed in some way by many of the authors either implicitly or explicitly. The eighth theme was only addressed by one author but is included because of the promise it holds for research across many content areas. We now turn to a description of each of the themes: (a) the dimension of time—personal, family, and historical—in the study of aging families, (b) ethnic cultural diversity in aging families, (c) structurally diverse and nontraditional family forms in relation to later-life families, (d) complexity in the quality of relationships in families of old adults, (e) interconnections among family relationships, (f) using multiple within-family respondents in research on families in later life, (g) the advantages of transdisciplinary research, and (h) flexibility in paradigm selection for family gerontology research.

THEMES FOR FUTURE RESEARCH IN FAMILY GERONTOLOGY

Multiple Dimensions of Time

Unlike in the first edition, no single chapter of this volume focused exclusively on time with respect to the individual within the context of older families, but many chapters addressed continuity and change over historical time at least indirectly by recommending the use of longitudinal research designs, taking a life course perspective, and examining the history that eventuated in demographic changes, such as population shifts in age distribution and the increasing prevalence of nontraditional family forms. Each of these time-related suggestions addresses the importance of studying trajectories of phenomena over time in order to better understand (a) causality, namely, what may account for the slice of time under consideration, (b) future predictions, or where the phenomenon under consideration may be headed (such as how nontraditional families might address the needs of impaired old relatives), and (c) complexity of change over time with respect to any one phenomenon, that is, the change represented by multiple parallel trajectories and their interactions, as they occur in the microlayer, mesolayer, and macrolayer of the environments individuals inhabit. Especially germane to aging families are changes in personal resources of old adults and their family members that are likely to impact families of old adults in essential ways, such as disrupting previous interaction patterns or promoting resilience. We suggest future research should not neglect individual development in the context of family life, because clarifying it is key to understanding the micromechanisms of family dynamics as they unfold in response to individual-level changes. Studies of individual developmental processes over time can benefit from relatively new research designs and statistical tools that are able to address complex contexts assessed repeatedly.

The study of family-level development over time is also important given the potential insights it offers on the functioning of aging families as they address caregiving needs, social isolation, and the use of formal services and entitlements, for example. A content area for which this approach would be appropriate is the study of how old immigrants and their family members' behaviors toward each other and their interactions with institutions in the United States have evolved (Usita & Shakya, chapter 14 in this volume). The more general question is how individual, societal, and cultural changes over time have an impact on the family relationships of old adults. Such research is essential to assuring that laws pertaining to aging families remain relevant and that appropriate changes are made for them to continue meeting the purposes for which they were enacted (Kapp, chapter 16 in this volume).

Historical time should be incorporated into future research as well. One significant content area that illustrates the importance of this idea is changing aspects of work and retirement in aging families. In order to understand these changes and their implications, the effects of various historical movements should be recognized. For example, in addition to the very different economic and demographic realities that Baby Boomers experienced compared to previous cohorts, they also were exposed to (and many embraced) different attitudes toward gender roles, resulting in different work histories (Szinovacz, Ekerdt, Butt, Barton, & Oala, chapter 19 in this volume). Another content area for which a focus on historical context is recommended is marital or partner dissolution. Historical analysis can be used to predict changes in the consequences of divorce and widowhood for old adults and their families. Because of greater equality between men and women in education, careers, and parenting, research will need to determine whether postmarriage families in later life will be more resilient than current ones. In addition, other historical changes, such as later marriage and childbearing, bear investigation to determine whether late-life marriage dissolution is easier or harder than when marriage and childbearing occurred at earlier ages (Carr & Pudrovska, chapter 20 in this volume).

Ethnic Cultural Diversity in Aging Families

Another important theme for future research to address is ethnic cultural differences in the nature and structure of family relationships both within the United States and abroad. The need for this research is increasingly pressing within the United States because of the rapid growth of immigrant populations, especially those of Hispanic and Asian origin, which signals a change from earlier cohorts of immigrants. This is a global issue, too, as immigration into other countries also increases the complexity of families and potentially challenges policy and social service arrangements.

Diversity issues have been framed often in terms of individualism and communalism, which has been linked to familism in aging families. Whereas communalism puts family obligations above the needs of the individual, individualism functions in service of fulfilling American dreams related to rising out of poverty, achieving an education, and moving up the social-economic ladder. In a zero-sum scenario, the gain of the group (family) is the loss for the individual and vice versa. Research is needed to examine other scenarios for these social orientations, including an option wherein familial and individual gains are both possible. For example, which kinds of interdependencies in the family contribute to individual success and which kinds thwart it? Further, what processes (societal, ethnic, personal) may account for the development of one type of interdependency over the other? Finally, what kind of interventions can help family members achieve both personal and familial goals? Some family therapy practices have incorporated these goals (e.g., Qualls & Noecker, 2009). Through the use of transdisciplinary research, perhaps these practices would prove useful when applied to immigrant families.

Ethnic cultural diversity should also be pursued through more international research (Silverstein, Lendon, & Giarrusso, chapter 12 in this volume). Such studies would help us understand and prepare for future influxes of families who emigrate from various countries. They would be useful for discerning the role old people expect to play in their families, caregiving norms and behaviors, and the effects of social welfare structures and their absence on families with older members. Whereas families may be more participatory in caregiving in the absence of governmental support, scholars should investigate other outcomes of government support besides concern about family neglect of old members. Perhaps with sufficient public support programs, family interactions are freed up for attention to other needs, similar to the gendered responses of offspring to the caregiving needs of their parents: Daughters tend to personal care that frees sons to engage parents in recreational activities.

International studies that focus on countries with high proportions of old adults would serve another purpose as well. By evaluating the effectiveness of their social policies, family gerontologists would be better prepared to advise U.S. policymakers when the United States faces similar population structures and the consequences for aging families.

Finally, many immigrant families maintain relationships with relatives abroad, creating transnational families (Calasanti & Kiecolt, chapter 11 in this volume). Although aging research has begun to investigate such topics, such as long-distance caregiving when adult children live out of easy reach of their frail parents, how families manage their relationships across national borders is a topic in need of more intense research. Such research could reveal how these relationships are maintained and what contributes to their quality and effectiveness in meeting relatives' needs.

Several unexplored aspects of ethnic cultural diversity are recommended. One such topic addresses the potential homogenization of families, whether due to similar media exposure, international currency structure, or other forces. How this potential process aids and interferes with family functioning across nations would be important to assess and understand dynamically. Another unexplored area addresses the growth of multiethnic families. How do such families age over time compared to other families (Silverstein et al., chapter 12 in this volume)? Authors differ on the importance they attribute to pursuing research on rural families. Given the increasing rate of national and transnational mobility, one author questioned whether *rural* continues to be a useful explanatory construct (Keating & Fletcher, chapter 13 in this volume). In another content area (informal caregiving), other authors pled for making rural aging families a top research priority (Pruchno & Gitlin, chapter 21 in this volume). Finally, investigating how aging families are differentially affected by retirement due to ethnic cultural influences, socioeconomic status, and macrocontexts such as welfare states that vary in their retirement policies would be fruitful (Szinovacz et al., chapter 19 in this volume).

Ethnic cultural diversity intersects with other kinds of diversity. An important aspect of these intersections is inequality of resources, an area of research greatly needed in family gerontology because of its potentially devastating effects on the well-being of old adults and their families (Calasanti & Kiecolt, chapter 11 in this volume). Intersectionality concerns inequalities based on gender, race and ethnicity, class, sexuality, and age as well as the intersections among them. It is the theoretical lens recommended for understanding these inequalities. Systems of inequality refer to differences in the chance to exceed in life due to power differentials, which are allocated exclusively on the basis of ascribed group membership. Whereas research on this topic has taken hold in the social sciences in general, it has yet to address old adults and their families extensively. Given the dire consequences of inequalities across groups, the pursuit of research that addresses intersectionality in family gerontology is extremely important. An example is the effects of divorce of late-life couples which vary widely based on one's gender, the nature of the dissolution, the quality of one's former marriage, available economic resources, and one's other social and emotional resources.

Structurally Diverse and Nontraditional Family Forms

Most authors recommended more research that targets new family forms and reconstituted families, and their effects on family relationships in old age given their growing prevalence in recent years. The membership of such families depends on how family is defined. As mentioned in the first chapter of this handbook, the definition used by many of the authors is particularly inclusive: "a set of relationships determined by biology, adoption, marriage, and, in some societies, social designation and existing even in the absence of contact or affective involvement, and, in some cases, even after the death of certain members" (Bedford & Blieszner, 1997, p. 526). Accordingly, some families include couples, whether traditional or nontraditional; the latter may be cohabiting or in living apart together (LAT) unions and couples may consist of heterosexual or same-sex pairs. Other families are composed of single adults, whether partnered before (divorced, widowed, separated) or never partnered. Still another distinction focuses on families that include parents (and stepparents) versus those who are childfree. Repartnered families include both persons in a repartnered relationship for the first time and those who have been repartnered more than once. Finally, some families include or consist entirely of socially designated ties, or fictive kin (Voorpostel, chapter 10 in this volume). It remains to be seen what the long-term trajectories will look like for increasingly diverse forms of repartnerships, whether the repartnered persons are old adults or family members of old adults. The legal status of chosen and fictive kin, particularly in making key legal decisions with or on behalf of old family members, is another topic for future research and advocacy.

At the time the Bedford and Blieszner definition was formulated, many old adults were excluded from family-level research because the definition of family typically was based on household composition. Today, nontraditional family forms have proliferated, but few studies have addressed them in sufficient detail, particularly with respect to old family members, who both have relatives and are relatives of other people (Blieszner & Bedford, 1995), and their well-being. New research on the myriad forms of families that include old members, particularly when based on large representative samples and when investigating change over time, could provide deeper insight into benefits and challenges associated with being an old family member of relatives in nontraditional unions and having old relatives who are in such unions themselves.

Complexity in Relationship Quality

Relationship quality has been an ongoing topic of family gerontology research. The quality itself, its causes, and its outcomes are clearly of central importance. Several chapter authors recommended a focus on relationship quality in order to further an understanding of its complexity, as a mediating influence on various outcomes, and in terms of its predictors. Each of these research foci holds much promise for better understanding of family dynamics in later life. In stark contrast to this need, in a recent editorial in the *Journal of Gerontology, Psychological Sciences*, Blieszner and Sanford (2010) reviewed manuscript submission topics from 2000 to 2008 and found that only 6.7% of the total number of submissions to that journal addressed relationships, nearly 94% were exclusively focused on individuals, and about two-thirds included only old adults, no respondents of other ages (Blieszner & Sanford, 2010). These numbers point to an absence of research reports on aging in broader context, suggesting that within the psychological study of old age, there appears to be a dearth of relationship research, implying a lack of family research as well. It is hard to imagine how the experiences of aging adults can be well understood independent of considering their location in relationships. We encourage interdisciplinary collaborations to help psychologists fill this gap and to help advance a more holistic approach to the study of old adults that includes their family context.

Investigators have made great strides recently in identifying theory for the study of relationship quality. This effort has been enriched by a greater appreciation of the complexity of influences on family relationship quality and an awareness of former biases concerning normative expectations about family bonds; both advances are encapsulated in the theoretical development of the concept of ambivalence, and many chapter authors embraced it. The concept of emotional ambivalence has begun to take root in empirical research on families in middle and late life, but sociological ambivalence remains an abstract construct. Because it refers to contradictions and conflicts that are created by social structure and negotiated in interactions among family members (Connidis, chapter 3 in this volume), sociological ambivalence has enormous potential for providing insights into family functioning and the well-being of its members. As such, sociological ambivalence also deserves attention by researchers in the future. This concept will be useful in framing caregiving research, especially for understanding the conflicts and their resolutions resulting from the intersection between gender and the well-being of caregivers. It may also prove similarly useful for understanding dynamics in other areas of family life, such as the emotional and behavioral struggle of old adults when role norms, loyalties, and affection conflict in relationships with former relatives and steprelatives.

Application of the ambivalence concept to later-life families will help future research to redefine family outcomes. Kinney and Kart (chapter 18 in this volume) noted that outcomes that dichotomize families as either good or bad, or successful or not, fail to recognize the prevalence of ambivalence among family members. Taking ambivalence into account can be used to delineate family characteristics in more detail and determine whether relationships become more ambivalent with age, whether determinants of ambivalence change with age, and whether well-being outcomes related to ambivalence change with age. Another important question is whether family outcomes differ if old adults are ambivalent toward their relatives or other relatives are ambivalent toward the old members of the family.

One important focus of the quality of a particular family relationship is its function as a critical mediator between stressors and well-being outcomes. For example, Sechrist, Suitor, Pillemer, Gilligan, Howard, and Keeton (chapter 7 in this volume) pointed out that researchers frequently investigate the effects of status transitions, such as marriage, divorce, widowhood, and grandparenthood, on physical and psychological well-being in the later years without considering the possible mediating effects of intergenerational relationship quality. They urged researchers to include relationship quality with the study of such transitions. One promising example is to study the contribution of relationship quality to dependency as an outcome of transitions such as divorce and widowhood in parent–adult child relations.

It is also important for researchers to evaluate the determinants as well as the consequences of relationship quality, given its importance to the well-being of family members and to family dynamics. Bookwala (chapter 5 in this volume) recommended the use of longitudinal studies to pursue these goals. Societal attitudes and biases as well as historical change are important to consider for understanding how family roles are enacted, which, in turn, affects the quality of the relationships, according to Hayslip and Page (chapter 8 in this volume). Various authors listed many potential contributors to relationship quality outcomes that should be pursued, such as, in the case of stepfamily relationships, the death of a parent and gender expectations (Ganong & Coleman, chapter 9 in this volume).

Interconnections among Family Relationships

Although several chapters in the *Handbook* focus on a specific role in the family (maritallike partner, sibling, grandparent, great-grandparent), some authors questioned whether specific relationships should remain a focus in the future (e.g., Silverstein et al., chapter 12 in this volume). Clearly family relationships do not function in isolation from one another, influences are likely to be reciprocal, and future research should address the intersecting influences on relationships. At the same time, it is still valuable to focus on individual relationships in order to identify their unique roles in the lives of individuals as well as in the larger family context. In fact, more, not fewer, aspects of specific relationships probably need additional research attention. Among the most neglected relationships are the lateral bonds at each generational level: nephews and nieces, great nieces and great nephews, siblings, cousins, uncles and aunts, great uncles and aunts (but see Milardo, 2010). The effect of retirement on family relationships in later life is an excellent example for which we recommend such research. The focus has mostly been on the marital bond and its quality after retirement. Szinovacz et al. (chapter 19 in this volume) explained that the field needs additional research about family-retirement linkages that extend beyond the marital unit to other relationships. They advocated for research on the effects of retirement on children, grandchildren, siblings, and parents in terms of contact frequency, expectations for different relationships, and the quality of those relationships.

Another related issue is whether future research should target shared commonalities among extended family relationships and whether any such commonalities justify grouping those relationships into one category such as "other kin." This grouping has often been employed in past comparisons of the more distal family network with the proximal, high profile parent-child and spousal relationships. Perhaps the issue of commonalities among some or all kin should be researched in new ways, such as to determine the role such groupings may play in the lives of old adults. In his chapter on bereavement, de Vries (chapter 22 in this volume) illustrated the importance of focusing on specific relationships in the case of grief, but also acknowledged the value of general, nonspecific relationships. That is, his research indicated that the nature of loss is highly relationship-specific, but at the same time, losses of the past have a cumulative effect on subsequent losses, indicating some degree of universality across relationships. It is important that similar investigations probe other general and specific dimensions of family relationships to help advance theory development and empirical studies in family gerontology.

Multiple Within-Family Respondents in Family Gerontology Research

Any understanding of the complexity of family relationships and family functioning would be shortchanged if data were obtained from only one member. Collection of multiple informants' perceptions and observations of multiple family members' behavior can move the field forward in many ways. Therefore, authors in this volume encouraged researchers to include dyads, triads, and larger family groups in the designs of future studies, unless a study deliberately targets the perceptions of one family member. The actual number of multiple within-family informants may be limited by practical considerations as well as the purpose of the study, but chapter authors recommended that, at the very least, relationship dyads should be represented by data from both partners.

The most obvious function of using multiple within-family informants is descriptive. Obtaining multiple perspectives on the same phenomenon can provide deep, rich details illustrating the complexity of families, encapsulating both commonalities and discrepancies among their perceptions.

Another recommended use of multiple informants is triangulation, which is typically used to get at the truthfulness of reports. Hayslip and Page (chapter 8 in this volume) pointed out that when designing intervention strategies for families with grandparents rearing grandchildren, accuracy of information may be particularly important. In this case, not only are family members good sources of data, but also inclusion of other relevant informants may hold promise, such as the grandchild's teacher or coach. As indicated by Townsend (chapter 4 in this volume), it is now possible to analyze complex designs due to advances in statistical techniques suitable for large samples. Also, new developments in software to aid in analysis of narrative and other nonnumerical data enhance options for qualitative and mixed-methods designs.

Other reasons for using multiple family informants to study old adults and their families also exist. Pruchno and Gitlin (chapter 21 in this volume) stressed the importance of multiinformant designs for understanding family-wide effects of caregiving. Hayslip and Page (chapter 8 in this volume) recommended incorporating more family members into studies on grandparenting to better understand interdependence among multiple family members, for example, in exploring how adult offspring influence the grandparent-grandchild relationship in which their parents and children participate.

Crossing Disciplinary Boundaries

Transdisciplinary refers to theory and methods that cross several disciplinary boundaries, used to create holistic approaches to research designs that have the potential of yielding more comprehensive knowledge about complex family processes. As alluded to earlier, without a transdisciplinary mindset, investigators run the risk of being unaware of relevant discoveries in disciplines other than their own, which may truncate the knowledge base or result in unproductive replication rather than expanding available findings. One example is the isolation of most twin research in behavioral genetics, with little penetration of research on aging twins into family gerontology (a notable exception is Neyer, 2002). Informing family gerontology about the wealth of sibling knowledge behavioral geneticists are uncovering holds promise for advancing sibling research as well as research on family relationships more generally (Bedford & Avioli, chapter 6 in this volume). One possibility is to apply insights gained from behavioral genetic research on twins to investigating the role that various degrees and kinds of similarity play in relationship dynamics and quality. This research could have important implications for understanding the effects of various degrees of genetic relatedness on relationships in older families, as in the case of steprelatives and half-relatives.

Interdisciplinary and multidisciplinary collaborations among sociologists and economists are now enhancing understanding of family caregiving issues. Sechrist et al. (chapter 7 in this volume) indicated that such collaborations are likely to advance intergenerational research as well. They highlighted the interplay of complex social, economic, and demographic trends with psychological factors in parent-child relationships. Important findings can result from exchanges between sociologists and their understanding of social structural influences on family relationships (such as gender and family roles) and psychologists' individual-level and relationship-level expertise (Sechrist et al., chapter 7 in this volume).

Carr and Pudrovska (chapter 20 in this volume) expressed great optimism regarding future research using data from the many available surveys of large representative samples of older adults. These data sets contain extensive genetic and biological indicators as well as self-reported health data. By enlisting interdisciplinary teams of researchers who can collectively address data on demographic, socioeconomic, biological, psychosocial, and genetic factors, it is possible to find links between marriage dissolution and health and well-being in the lives of older adults that reveal highly complex mechanisms at play. Research on other relationships and other family transitions in later-life families are also likely to benefit from examination of these data sets using interdisciplinary teams.

Flexible Paradigms for Family Gerontology Research

Pruchno and Gitlin (chapter 21 in this volume) identified an important need for future research on caregiving that no doubt applies to other content areas as well. The stress process model has dominated caregiving research. Although this model has been extremely valuable, it is one that targets individuals, whereas some families share primary caregiving. The authors pointed out another problem with the model: It is missing important factors that contribute to the experience and outcomes of family caregiving. These factors include caregiver knowledge, skills, and sense of self-efficacy. No doubt other content areas are wed to particular paradigms and models that restrict the lens through which the issues are studied. We recommend that researchers in family gerontology consider whether available theories are applicable to a broad spectrum of families and whether theories not typically applied to common family gerontology research topics might be useful for uncovering new dimensions of the situation being investigated. Likewise, it is important to consider the utility of various research approaches. Whereas large-scale surveys and interview studies are needed for establishing prevalence of phenomena across subgroups of families, in-depth questioning employed in qualitative studies allows unanticipated factors to emerge. Collaborative research across relevant disciplines and transdisciplinary research also expand the boundaries of knowledge, as described previously, and have the added benefit of enabling researchers to acquire expertise in additional relevant disciplines.

CONCLUSION

This revision of the earlier edition of the *Handbook* presents new family gerontology topics for consideration and points to new directions that the original topics are taking. As we have illustrated in this chapter, the volume offers many potential avenues for future research on aging families. The emphasis on future research should serve the purpose of sustaining momentum in family gerontology. The complexity of families can make studying them seem daunting, but the chapter authors have provided useful guidance for fruitful directions to pursue. Because of the fundamental importance of family members and others to the lives of old adults and vice versa, continuing to strengthen research in family gerontology is essential. Our aim for this chapter was to facilitate new research in this challenging field by delineating the broad issues to consider when choosing a purpose and focus for a study, planning the methods, and interpreting the results. The highlighted themes were syntheses of the recommendations made by authors in 21 content areas, with some input from other writings and our own expertise. The resulting integration of ideas and suggestions make abundantly clear the benefits of transdisciplinary research and interdisciplinary collaborations, whether across subdisciplines within family gerontology, across the social and behavioral sciences, or across biological and other life sciences. The next steps involve translating research findings into applications that are accessible to laypersons, professionals, and policymakers. Given the rapid rates of social change, identification of applied implications based on new findings is imperative for sustaining the quality of family experiences for old people and their relatives.

REFERENCES

Bedford, V. H., & Blieszner, R. (1997). Personal relationships in later life families. In S. Duck (Ed.), *Handbook of personal relationships* (2nd ed., pp. 523–539). New York: Wiley.

Blieszner, R., & Bedford, V. H. (1995). The family context of aging: Trends and challenges. In R. Blieszner & V. H. Bedford (Eds.), *Handbook of aging and the family* (pp. 3–12). Westport, CT: Greenwood Press.

Blieszner, R., & Sanford, N. (2010). Editorial: Looking back and looking ahead as *Journal of Gerontology: Psychological Sciences* turns 65. *Journal of Gerontology: Psychological Sciences, 65B*, 3–4.

Milardo, R. M. (2010). *The forgotten kin: Aunts and uncles*. New York: Cambridge University Press.

Neyer, F. J. (2002). Twin relationships in old age: A developmental perspective. *Journal of Social and Personal Relationships, 19*, 155–177.

Qualls, S. H., & Noecker, T. L. (2009). Caregiver family therapy for conflicted families. In S. H. Qualls & S. H. Zarit (Eds.), *Aging families and caregiving* (pp. 155–188). Hoboken, NJ: Wiley.

Silverstein, M., & Giarrusso, R. (2010). Aging and family life: A decade review. *Journal of Marriage and Family, 10*, 1039–1058.

About the Editors and Contributors

THE EDITORS

ROSEMARY BLIESZNER is alumni distinguished professor of human development, associate dean of the Graduate School, and associate director of the Center for Gerontology at Virginia Polytechnic Institute and State University (Virginia Tech), Blacksburg. She received her PhD from Pennsylvania State University in human development–family studies with an emphasis in adult development and aging. Her research focuses on family and friend relationships, life events, and psychological well-being in adulthood and old age. She has studied the contributions of spirituality to resiliency and how families cope with a diagnosis of mild cognitive impairment in an old relative. Blieszner is coeditor of *Older Adult Friendship: Structure and Process* (Sage, 1989) and *Handbook of Aging and the Family* (Greenwood, 1995), coauthor of *Adult Friendship* (Sage, 1992), *Spiritual Resiliency in Older Women: Models of Strength for Challenges through the Life Span* (Sage, 1999), and *Spiritual Resiliency and Aging: Hope, Relationality, and the Creative Self* (Baywood, 2012). She is author of numerous articles published in gerontology, family studies, and personal relationships journals. Blieszner is a fellow of the American Psychological Association (Division 20), Association for Gerontology in Higher Education, Gerontological Society of America, and National Council on Family Relations. In 1997–1998 she received the university's Alumni Award for Teaching Excellence, and in 2002 she was named alumni distinguished professor, a position held by 10 faculty members at the university.

VICTORIA HILKEVITCH BEDFORD is professor emerita of psychology at the University of Indianapolis. She attended Brandeis University (BA), Boston University (EdM), and Rutgers University (PhD in life span developmental psychology). She completed a postdoctoral fellowship in social gerontology with the Midwest Council for Social Research on Aging at Purdue University's Department of Child Development and Family Studies. Dr. Bedford's specialty is family gerontology and its intersection with sibling relationships, family caregiving, intergenerational relationships, personal networks, social support, well-being, and, most recently, twinships. It is not by accident that Dr. Bedford developed a passion for sibling research; she is a monozygotic twin and middle sibling. Among Dr. Bedford's contributions to the field of family gerontology are early explorations into the topics of parental favoritism, relationship troubles, and the use of multiple within-family informants to understand family caregiving. She has given nearly 100 conference and guest presentations, published 37 journal articles, book chapters, and encyclopedia entries, plus coedited five special journal issues and books, including *Handbook of Aging and the Family* (Greenwood, 1995) and *Men in Relationships: A New Look from a Life Course Perspective* (Springer, 2006). Bedford is a fellow of the Gerontological Society of America and the American Psychological Association (Division 20). In 2008 she received the University of Indianapolis School of Psychological Sciences Undergraduate Teaching Award.

THE CONTRIBUTORS

EMILY M. AGREE is associate professor of population at Johns Hopkins University. She is director of the Hopkins Center for Population Aging and Health and associate director of the Hopkins Population Center. She has degrees in Sociology (PhD, Duke University) and Demography (MA, Georgetown University). Agree's research examines the ways that population aging affects the health of the older population, as well as the adaptation of families to the longevity of older parents and relatives. Her research focuses on the use of assistive technology in community-based long-term care arrangements, and age differences in use of the Internet to seek health information. Agree also studies gender differences in health and intergenerational support among families in Asia, Latin America, and the Middle East.

PAULA SMITH AVIOLI is professor of psychology at Kean University, where she also serves as the executive director of the School of Psychology. She attended Cornell University (BS), Harvard University (EdM), and Rutgers University (PhD). She did postdoctoral work in sociocultural gerontology at University of California, San Francisco. Her areas of expertise are life span developmental psychology and aging. She was named a Kean University presidential teaching scholar and received the Alpha Sigma Lambda Distinguished Teacher Award. She has published in such journals as *Generations*, *The International Journal of Aging and Human Development*, *Sex Roles*, *American Behavioral Scientist*, and *Journal of Marriage and Family*. Her current research focus on twin relationships stems in no small measure from her experience of parenting twin sons.

KELLI BARTON earned a BA in psychology from St. Louis University and a MS in gerontology from University of Massachusetts, Boston, where she is currently a research assistant and doctoral candidate. Her research interests include older driver behavior and policy, alternative transportation options, social insurance, and health care policy. She has published in the *Transportation Research Record* and has presented research at the Gerontological Society of America and the Transportation Research Board annual conferences.

JAMILA BOOKWALA, PhD, is professor of psychology at Lafayette College in Easton, PA. Her research focuses broadly on couple relationships, stress, and psychological and physical well-being over the adult life span. Most recently, she has examined the direct role of marital quality in midlife and late-life well-being; the extent to which marital characteristics moderate the link between stress and well-being in the context of such stressors as informal caregiving, physical disability, and visual function; and the role of psychosocial resources in promoting well-being in never-married adults. She also studies gender-related issues in adult well-being. She has published her recent research in *Journal of Gerontology: Psychological Sciences; Journal of Gerontology: Social Sciences; The Gerontologist;* and *Journal of Aging and Health.*

ABIGAIL BUTT, MSc, received her master's degree in gerontology from the University of Massachusetts, Boston, where she is currently a PhD candidate in gerontology. Her research interests include social demography, place attachment, migration, and geographic mobility as they relate to aging and policy. She has published in *What's Hot,* a publication of the Gerontological Society of America, and is a member of Sigma Phi Omega, the national gerontological honor society.

TONI CALASANTI, PhD, is professor of sociology at Virginia Tech, where she is also a faculty affiliate of both the Center for Gerontology and Women's and Gender Studies. She is coauthor of *Gender, Social Inequalities, and Aging* and co-editor of *Age Matters: Re-Aligning Feminist Thinking* (both with Kathleen Slevin), coeditor of *Nobody's Burden: Lessons from the Great Depression on the Struggle for Old-Age Security* (with Ruth Ray), and has published in such journals as *Journal of Gerontology: Social Sciences, The Gerontologist, Social Forces, Journal of Aging Studies,* and *Men and Masculinities.* Her recent work has focused on gender, age, and care work; on age and gender in relation to aging bodies and the anti-aging industry; and gender and health in later life.

DEBORAH CARR is professor of sociology at Rutgers University and codirector of the National Institute of Mental Health postdoctoral training program at Rutgers's Institute for Health, Health Care Policy, and Aging Research. She is a life course sociologist whose work focuses on family relationships and transitions over the life course and their implications for physical and mental health. Her current work focuses on death, dying, and end-of-life planning. She has published more than 75 journal articles and book chapters, and is author or editor of five books including *Spousal Bereavement in Later Life* (Springer, 2006) and the *Encyclopedia of the Life Course and Human Development* (Cengage, 2009). Carr is a fellow of the Gerontological Society of America and Academy of Behavioral Medicine.

MARILYN COLEMAN is curators' professor of human development and family studies at the University of Missouri. She is an affiliate faculty member with Women's and Gender Studies and a fellow in the Missouri University Center for Excellence on Aging and the Center for Family Policy and Research. Coleman has conducted research on stepfamilies for more than 30 years. Her recent work with Ganong has focused on intergenerational family responsibilities following divorce and remarriage and the development of stepparent-stepchild relationships. Together they have coauthored more than 150 articles and book chapters as well as 7 books. Coleman is a past editor of the *Journal of Marriage and Family*.

INGRID ARNET CONNIDIS is professor of sociology at the University of Western Ontario. Her work on family ties and aging, adult siblings, the family lives of gay and lesbian adults, intergenerational relations, and conceptual and policy issues appears in a variety of books and journals including *Journal of Family Theory & Review, Journal of Gerontology, Journal of Marriage and Family, Canadian Journal on Aging*, and *The Gerontologist* (www.ingridconnidis.com). She is corecipient of the GSA 2004 Richard Kalish Innovative Publication Award (Sociological ambivalence and family ties: A critical perspective, JMF, 2002, with Julie McMullin). The second edition of her book *Family Ties & Aging* was published in 2010 (Pine Forge Press). She tries to practice balance in her life by painting whenever she can.

BRIAN DE VRIES, PhD, is professor of gerontology at San Francisco State University. He received his doctorate in life-span social psychology from the University of British Columbia. He is a fellow of the Gerontological Society of America, member of the leadership council of the American Society on Aging, and cochair of the LGBT Aging Issues Network constituent group. He has edited four books, written more than 80 journal articles and book chapters, and has given more than 100 presentations to professional audiences on a variety of topics such as the social and psychological well-being of midlife and older LGBT persons, friendships and social relationships across the adult life course, as well as end-of-life issues and bereavement.

DAVID J. EKERDT is professor of sociology and director of the Gerontology Center at the University of Kansas. His funded studies of work and retirement have examined the retirement process and its effects on health, well-being, and the marital relationship, as well as behavioral expectations on later life. He is presently conducting research on the ways that people manage and dispose of their possessions in later life. Ekerdt is editor-in-chief of the four-volume Macmillan *Encyclopedia of Aging*, a million-word publication. He has served as editor of the *Journal of Gerontology: Social Sciences*, chair of the Aging and Life Course Section of the American Sociological Association, and chair of the Behavioral and Social Sciences Section of the Gerontological Society of America.

STEPHANIE FLETCHER is a PhD student in the Department of Human Ecology, University of Alberta. She holds a master's degree in women's studies from Mount Saint Vincent University, and a bachelor's degree in women's studies from Queen's University. Stephanie has assisted on research projects for the Research on Aging, Policies, and Practice Group and the Maritime Data Centre for Aging Research and Policy Analysis. Her research focuses on family gerontology; beliefs about responsibility for meeting the needs of older adults; and beliefs about the connection between older adults' contributions and their entitlement to societal benefits.

CHANTELL FRAZIER is a PhD candidate at Syracuse University's Maxwell School of Citizenship and Public Affairs. She holds a master's degree in sociology, received her bachelor's degrees in sociology and biology from DePaul University in Chicago, and is a member of the American Sociological Association and the Sociology Honor Society, Alpha Kappa Delta. Her research interests include quantitative methodology, medical sociology, women's health inequalities, and reproductive health in the United States and globally. Frazier has presented research on women's health issues including the medicinal use of oral contraceptives, reproductive health as a human right, and the prevalence and consequences of dysmenorrhea. She is currently working on her dissertation, an analysis of health care access and other socioeconomic factors that influence women's reproductive health outcomes in the United States.

LAWRENCE GANONG, PhD, is professor and cochair of human development and family studies and professor in the Sinclair School of Nursing at the University of Missouri. He has coauthored more than 200 articles and book chapters as well as 7 books, including *Stepfamily Relationships* (2004) and *Handbook of Contemporary Families* (2004) with Marilyn Coleman and *Family Life in 20th Century America* (2007) with Coleman and Kelly Warzinik. His primary research program has focused on postdivorce families, especially stepfamilies and what stepfamily members do to develop satisfying and effective relationships. He is a fellow in the Missouri University Center for Excellence on Aging and the Center for Family Policy and Research.

ROSEANN GIARRUSSO, PhD, is associate professor of sociology at California State University, Los Angeles. Giarrusso received her doctorate in sociology from the University of California, Los Angeles. She has more than 50 publications, most of which apply a social psychological perspective to the study of intergenerational family relationships and aging. She was formerly coinvestigator and project director of the Longitudinal Study of Generations.

MEGAN GILLIGAN, MS, is a PhD candidate in the Department of Sociology and a member of the Center on Aging and the Life Course at Purdue University. Her research interests focus on later-life families, with particular emphasis on parent–adult child relationships.

LAURA N. GITLIN, an applied sociologist, is professor in the Department of Health Systems and Outcomes, School of Nursing, with joint appointments in the Department of Psychiatry and Division of Geriatrics and Gerontology, School of Medicine at Johns Hopkins University. She also is the director of a new interdivisional and interprofessional initiative, the Center for Innovative Care in Aging at Johns Hopkins School of Nursing. Her areas of expertise include developing and testing home and community-based interventions to improve quality of life of family caregivers and persons with dementia and older adults with other chronic illnesses. Her current research focus is also on translating caregiver evidence-based programs into systems of care. Gitlin has more than 25 years of NIH-funded randomized trials and has received numerous awards for her research and community partnerships.

BERT HAYSLIP JR. (PhD, University of Akron, 1975) is regents professor of psychology at the University of North Texas. He is a fellow of the American Psychological Association, the Gerontological Society of America, and the Association for Gerontology in Higher Education. He is associate editor of *Experimental Aging Research*, editor of *The International Journal of Aging and Human Development*, and associate editor of *Developmental Psychology*. His coauthored books include *Emerging Perspectives on Resilience in Adulthood and Later Life* (Springer, 2012), *Resilient Grandparent Caregivers: A Strengths-based Perspective* (Routledge, 2012), *Adult Development and Aging* (Krieger, 2011), and *Parenting the Custodial Grandchild* (Springer, 2008). He is coPI on a NINR-funded project dealing with interventions to improve the functioning of grandparent caregivers and their grandchildren.

ABIGAIL R. HOWARD, MS, is a graduate student in the Department of Sociology and a member of the Center on Aging and the Life Course at Purdue University. Her research focuses on the relationship between early life adversity and health over the life course.

MARY ELIZABETH HUGHES is assistant professor in the Department of Population, Family, and Reproductive Health at the Johns Hopkins Bloomberg School of Public Health. She is a social demographer whose research examines the influence of families on individuals' health across the life course. In past work, she studied the relationship between household supports and demands and health among people in midlife, the impact of caring for grandchildren on grandparents' health, and the relationship between men's and women's marital biographies and their health. Current projects consider the impact of family life on the intergenerational transmission of low birth weight, the link between childhood family characteristics and adult chronic disease, and the implications of U.S. family change for older people.

MARSHALL B. KAPP was educated at Johns Hopkins University (BA), George Washington University Law School (JD with honors), and Harvard University School of Public Health (MPH). He is the director of the Florida State University Center for Innovative Collaboration in Medicine and Law with a primary faculty appointment as professor, Department of Geriatrics, FSU College of Medicine and a courtesy faculty appointment in the FSU College of Law. He also is affiliated with the FSU Pepper Institute on Aging and Public Policy. He is editor emeritus of the *Journal of Legal Medicine*, a fellow of the Gerontological Society of America and the American College of Legal Medicine, and a recipient of GSA's Kent Award.

CARY S. KART is senior researcher at the Scripps Gerontology Center, Miami University, Ohio. He spent 26 years at the University of Toledo, retiring in 2000.

He received his PhD in sociology in 1974 from the University of Virginia, and was a National Institute of Aging postdoctoral fellow in aging at the University of Michigan during 1988–1989. Professor Kart is author, coauthor, or editor of several textbooks in gerontology and numerous scholarly publications. His research has appeared in *Social Forces, Journal of Gerontology, The Gerontologist,* and *Journal of Aging and Health,* among others, as well as in many edited volumes. Dr. Kart served for many years on several different NIH study sections. He is a fellow of the Gerontological Society of America.

NORAH KEATING is professor of family studies and codirector of Research on Aging, Policies, and Practice in the Department of Human Ecology at the University of Alberta. She also is director of the Global Social Initiative on Ageing, which addresses the intersections of population aging and globalization and their impact on families, livability, and care of older adults. Her research interests are in normative and nonnormative issues faced by families as they grow older and in the physical and social contexts that can include or exclude them. She has a long-standing interest in aging in rural contexts and has published in related topics including the transfer of rural family businesses, connectivities of older rural persons, age-friendly rural communities, and social exclusion of older rural adults.

SHIRLEY A. KEETON received her doctorate from the Department of Sociology of Louisiana State University. Her research focuses on the intersections of identity theory, social networks, and status transitions. Her research has appeared in *Social Forces, Social Networks, Current Research in Social Psychology,* and *The American Sociologist.*

K. JILL KIECOLT, PhD, is associate professor of sociology at Virginia Tech and a faculty affiliate of both the Center for Gerontology and the Virginia Institute for Psychiatric and Behavioral Genetics at Virginia Commonwealth University. Her current research focuses on intergenerational ambivalence and well-being; race, self-concept, and mental health; and genetic and environmental influences on alcohol-related outcomes and well-being. Her work has appeared in such journals as *Journal of Marriage and Family, Personal Relationships,* the *Journal of Health and Social Behavior,* and *Generations.*

JENNIFER M. KINNEY is professor of gerontology in the Department of Sociology and Gerontology and a research fellow at the Scripps Gerontology Center at Miami University, Ohio. She obtained her PhD in psychology from Kent State University and completed an NIA postdoctoral fellowship in social aspects of mental health and aging at Case Western Reserve University. The majority of her research focuses on later life families. She has published in such journals as *Dementia, Journal of Applied Gerontology,* and *The Gerontologist.* Her recent research includes the use and impact of Internet-based in-home monitoring systems by family members who care for a relative with dementia and the evaluation of interventions designed to improve quality of life and well-being among individuals with dementia and their families.

JESSICA LENDON, PhD., recently graduated from the Leonard Davis School of Gerontology at the University of Southern California. She also holds an MA in sociology from Middle Tennessee State University and a BS in psychology from Berry College. Lendon has worked for the Longitudinal Study of Generations and researched ideology changes across the life course, the intergenerational transmission of religiosity, and the concept of intergenerational ambivalence. Her dissertation research investigated the mixed positive and negative aspects inherent in the relationships between older parents and their adult child over the life course. Her long-term research interests are in investigating the mutual interplay between intergenerational support and physical and mental health, with a particular emphasis on policy solutions to improve family caregiving support.

MADONNA HARRINGTON MEYER is professor of sociology and senior research associate at the Center for Policy Research at Syracuse University. Her book with Pamela Herd, *Market Friendly or Family Friendly? The State and Gender Inequality in Old Age* (Russell Sage, 2007), was awarded the Gerontological Society of America's Kalish Publication Award. She is editor of *Care Work: Gender, Labor, and the Welfare State* (Routledge Press, 2000). She is a member by the National Academy of Social Insurance and a fellow of the Gerontological Society of America. She is coeditor, with Christine Himes, of Baywood Publishing's Society and Aging Series. She is currently writing *Grandmas at Work: Juggling Work and Family across the Life Course*, under contract with NYU Press.

CORINA R. OALA is a PhD student in gerontology at the University of Massachusetts, Boston, where she also received her MS degree. Her primary areas of interest include religiosity and spirituality in older adults, particularly in relation to health disparities, end-of-life care, and volunteering. Corina currently has two articles under peer review and has been independently contracted by both the Alzheimer's Association and Easter Seals national headquarters to write several reports. She was also independently contracted and primarily responsible for the development of a lifespan respite manual for Access to Respite Care and Health (ARCH) National Respite Network and Resource Center, made available online in February 2012, a project originally commissioned by the U.S. Administration on Aging.

KYLE S. PAGE, M.S., is a doctoral candidate in counseling psychology at the University of North Texas. His research and clinical interests include working with older adults, fear of dementia, custodial grandparents, and caregiving. He is a member of the American Psychological Association, the Gerontological Society of America, and Psychologists in Long-Term Care.

KARL PILLEMER, PhD, is professor of human development at Cornell University and professor of gerontology in medicine at the Weill Cornell Medical College. His major interests center on human development over the life course, with a special emphasis on family and social relationships in middle age and beyond.

RACHEL PRUCHNO earned a BA from Michigan State University, an MA from Oakland University, and a PhD from Pennsylvania State University. She has maintained an uninterrupted stream of grant funding support for research projects focused on a variety of topics related to geriatrics and gerontology, such as caregiving for sick and demented family members and differences in the effects of alternative forms of long-term care. She has published nearly 100 journal articles that have appeared in *Psychology and Aging, Journals of Gerontology, The Gerontologist, Family Relations, Journal of Applied Social Psychology, Journal of Aging & Health, Research on Aging, Medical Decision Making, American Journal of Mental Retardation, Journal of Marriage and Family, Environment and Behavior,* and *Journal of Mental Health and Aging.*

TETYANA PUDROVSKA received her PhD in sociology from the University of Wisconsin–Madison. She is currently assistant professor of sociology and a research associate at the Population Research Institute at Pennsylvania State University. She is a demographer of health and aging. Her current research projects include the influence of life-course marital trajectories on health, mortality, and health behaviors of older adults; the consequences of childhood disadvantage for health and mortality in later life; the social etiology of cancer over the life course; and psychological adjustment to chronic illness among older adults.

JORI SECHRIST, PhD, is assistant professor of sociology at the University of Texas–Pan American. Her research focuses on relationship quality and exchange between older parents and their adult children, with an emphasis on variations by race and ethnicity.

HOLLY B. SHAKYA is a doctoral candidate in the University of California, San Diego–San Diego State University joint doctoral program in global public health. She holds a BA in philosophy from Pomona College. Her current areas of research interest are in the social determinants of health with a focus on social networks, social norms, family processes, and culture. Her previous research has included using mixed methods to investigate the challenges of skipped generation grandparent-headed families. She is currently finishing her dissertation, focusing on the relation between networks and health in diverse settings and the utilization of different name generators in the context of a developing country.

MERRIL SILVERSTEIN, PhD, is the Marjorie Cantor Professor of Aging in the Department of Sociology and School of Social Work at Syracuse University. Professor Silverstein received his doctorate in sociology from Columbia University. He has more than 130 scholarly publications on topics related to social gerontology, most of which focus on intergenerational relationships over the life course and international perspectives on aging families. He was formerly principal investigator of the Longitudinal Study of Generations and currently has projects in China, Sweden, the Netherlands, and Israel. He is a fellow of the Gerontological Society of America, the Brookdale National Fellowship Program, and the Fulbright International Senior Scholars Program. He currently serves as editor-in-chief of the *Journal of Gerontology: Social Sciences.*

J. JILL SUITOR, PhD, is professor of sociology and a member of the Center on Aging and the Life Course at Purdue University. Her research focuses on the relationship between parents and adult children, with particular interest in the predictors and consequences of parental favoritism in the middle and later years.

MAXIMILIANE E. SZINOVACZ is professor in the Gerontology Department at the University of Massachusetts, Boston. She received her doctorate from the University of Vienna, Austria. She has coauthored or edited five books, most recently *Caregiving Contexts* (Springer, 2008), and published more than 70 articles and book chapters. She is a fellow of the Gerontological Society of America and of the National Council on Family Relations. Her research interests focus on retirement, intergenerational relationships, caregiving, and grandparenthood.

PAMELA B. TEASTER is professor in the Department of Health Behavior, director of doctoral studies, and associate dean for research in the College of Public Health at the University of Kentucky. She directs the Kentucky Justice Center for Elders and Vulnerable Adults. She serves on the editorial boards of the *Journal of Applied Gerontology* and the *Journal of Elder Abuse and Neglect*. Teaster is a fellow of the Gerontological Society of America and the Association for Gerontology in Higher Education, a recipient of the Rosalie Wolf Award for Research on Elder Abuse, the Outstanding Affiliate Member Award from the Kentucky Guardianship Association, and the Distinguished Educator Award from the Kentucky Association for Gerontology. She is the author of more than 75 peer-reviewed articles, reports, books, and book chapters.

ALOEN L. TOWNSEND is professor of social work and chair of the doctoral program in the Mandel School of Applied Social Sciences at Case Western Reserve University, faculty associate in the University Center on Aging and Health, and associate member of the Cancer and Aging Research Program of the Case Comprehensive Cancer Center. She received her PhD in social psychology from the University of Michigan, Ann Arbor. Her research focuses on adult development and aging, family relationships, mental and physical health, and the interface between families and formal service systems. Her methodological interests include survey research, longitudinal and dyadic analyses, structural equation modeling, and multilevel modeling. Dr. Townsend is a fellow of the Behavioral and Social Sciences Section of the Gerontological Society of America.

PAULA M. USITA is associate professor of health promotion and behavioral sciences in the Graduate School of Public Health, San Diego State University. She attended the University of Puget Sound (BA), Western Washington University (MS), and Virginia Polytechnic Institute and State University (PhD). She was on the family studies faculty at Purdue University. Her research has explored the role of individual, social, and cultural factors on quality of life among minority and immigrant populations, midlife and late-life adults and families, family caregivers, and persons with Alzheimer's disease. Recently, she studied predictors of interpersonal violence among immigrant Korean women in

California and well-being concerns of families in which grandparents raise their grandchildren.

MARIEKE VOORPOSTEL currently works as a senior researcher with the Swiss Household Panel at FORS (the Swiss Centre of Expertise in the Social Sciences) in Lausanne, Switzerland. She holds a PhD in sociology from Utrecht University, the Netherlands. Her research interests lie in the field of family sociology, and she has published on various topics in that domain, such as sibling relationships and social support, couple relationships, and political and civic participation in the context of the family. She also has an interest in less explored aspects of the family, such as fictive kin relationships and black sheep in the family.

FRANCES B. VORSKY earned her bachelor's degree in psychology with a minor in gerontology from Chestnut Hill College. She earned her master of science degree in the administration of human services with a focus on elder care management, also from Chestnut Hill College. Vorsky earned a graduate certificate in college teaching and learning from the University of Kentucky while attending the university's Graduate Center for Gerontology. Her research interests include elder volunteerism, elder protection, and media representations of older adults and their effects.

TENZIN WANGMO is a researcher at the Institute for Biomedical Ethics, University of Basel, Switzerland. She completed her BA at Berea College and PhD in Gerontology at the University of Kentucky. Under the mentorship of Dr. Pamela Teaster, she finished a year of postdoctoral experience in Kentucky during which she worked on exploring elder mistreatment in nursing homes. Her research experience in the field of elder abuse includes collaborative work with experts on several research projects including APS response to elder abuse, local elder abuse coordinating councils, and international study on elder abuse. From these collaborations, several peer-reviewed manuscripts were published. Her research interests include elder mistreatment, ethical care of older adults and other vulnerable groups, human rights, and public policy.

Index